SELECTED
POETRY OF
LORD BYRON

SELECTED POETRY OF LORD BYRON

Edited by Leslie A. Marchand

Introduction by Thomas M. Disch

Notes by Jeffery Vail

THE MODERN LIBRARY

NEW YORK

2001 Modern Library Paperback Edition

Mr. Disch's Introduction first appeared in *The Hudson Review,*
Volume LIV, No. 4 (Winter 2002).

LIBRARY OF CONGRESS CATALOGING-IN-PUBLICATION DATA
Byron, George Gordon Byron, Baron, 1788–1824.
[Poems. Selections]
Selected poetry of Lord Byron ; introduction by Thomas Disch / edited by
Leslie A. Marchand ; notes by Jeffery Vail.
p.   cm.
ISBN 0-375-75814-3
I. Marchand, Leslie Alexis, 1900– II. Title.
PR4353 .M34 2001
821'.7—dc21   2001042771

Modern Library website address: www.modernlibrary.com

Printed in the United States of America

2   4   6   8   9   7   5   3   1

LORD BYRON

George Gordon, sixth Lord Byron, was born in London on January 22, 1788. His early years were spent in Aberdeen, where he was brought up in narrowed circumstances by his widowed mother, the last of the Gordons of Gight, whose wastrel husband had spent her considerable fortune before he died in 1791. Lame from birth, Byron early developed a sharp sensitivity to his deformity which stayed with him through life. In 1798, when he inherited the title and the ancient Byron estate at Newstead Abbey, his mother took him to England. He was enrolled at Harrow in 1801 and at Trinity College, Cambridge, in 1805. His first book of poems, *Hours of Idleness,* was published in 1807. After his next work, *English Bards, and Scotch Reviewers,* a rejoinder to a harsh review of his early poems, was published in 1809, he embarked on a tour of Europe and the Levant which took him through Portugal, Spain and Albania to Greece, Asia Minor and Constantinople. When he returned in 1811 he carried with him the manuscript of the first two cantos of *Childe Harold's Pilgrimage.* On its publication the following year he became famous overnight and was lionized in the drawing rooms of a high society of which he had known very little before he went abroad. Handsome, with a Greek beauty of profile, he was much sought after by women of that society and became involved in several intrigues before he was married on January 2, 1815, to Anne Isabella Milbanke, who bore him a daughter (Augusta Ada) in December of that year. In

January, 1816, Lady Byron left him and returned to her parents. The reasons for the separation never having been made public, the darkest crimes were hinted, including incest with his half sister Augusta Leigh. (Later evidence rather conclusively indicates that Byron was involved in a liaison with Augusta before his marriage, but since Lady Byron was not convinced of it until after the separation, it could not have been the cause.) To escape the éclat of the scandal, Byron left England in April, never to return. After a summer on Lake Geneva, where he first met Shelley, he proceeded to Italy, which was his home for more than six years. Settling first in Venice, he entered into the dissipations of the place, and had nearly ruined his health (though at the same time he had written some of his best poetry in that environment, including *Beppo* and the first cantos of *Don Juan*) when he met and fell in love with the Countess Teresa Guiccioli. Following her to Ravenna (1819–1821), he became involved through her family in the Italian revolutionary movement. After her separation from her husband, he continued the liaison, which was generally beneficial to his health and spirits. They lived for a time at Pisa (1821–1822), where he was again associated with Shelley until the latter was drowned in July of 1822 (Byron was present at the cremation ceremony on the beach at Viareggio). After a year at Genoa, Byron left in July, 1823, to aid the Greeks in their struggle for independence from Turkish rule. He died of a fever at Missolonghi, in Western Greece, on April 19, 1824, and his body was returned to England. Refused burial in Westminster Abbey, the remains were deposited in the ancestral vault at Hucknall Torkard near Newstead Abbey.

CONTENTS

Domestic Pieces

Jeux d'Esprit and Ephemeral Verses

INTRODUCTION

Thomas M. Disch

In my youth's summer I did sing of One,
The wandering outlaw of his own dark mind;...
CHILDE HAROLD'S PILGRIMAGE, Canto the Third

It would have pleased Lord Byron to know that, having been the most renowned, imitated, and execrated of the major romantic poets, he is now, almost two centuries later, the least honored and the most ignored and deplored of that select few. For he thrived on giving offense. He was a sexy, swaggering contrarian whose wisecrack answer to the earnest inquiry of Concerned Virtue, "What are you rebelling *against?*" would have been the same as Marlon Brando's: "What have ya got?"

As with Brando, behind the mask of the rebel shaking his fist at prim respectability was the furrowed brow of a sensitive guy not afraid to cry, a misunderstood teenage werewolf or, better yet, a vampire—a possibility he darkly hinted at in his letters.* Byron pictured himself (under the alias of Childe Harold) wandering about the Alps at midnight alternately exulting in thunderstorms and crying tears of secret melancholy. Generations of readers have thrilled with a sympathetic vibration to that particular passage ("Childe Harold," Canto 3, stanzas xcii–xcvii). But the storm passes and the poet moves to other scenes, other feelings, other roles. He roars at the ocean—a splendid roar (Canto 4, stanza clxxix); he luxuriates among the odalisques of his

---

* Recently that hint has been taken up by the novelist Tom Holland, who has portrayed Byron as a vampire in his three horror novels, *Lord of the Dead, Slave of My Thirst,* and *Deliver Us from Evil.*

harem or runs off with someone else's, then addresses songs to her—such songs! lyrics of irresistible seductiveness—following which he joins his gentlemen friends for brandy and cigars and brags to them of his exploits on the tilting grounds of love, a perfect cad.

Those who prize sincerity in poets and would hold them to their word, as to a marriage vow, cannot but take exception to such will-o'-the-wisp fickleness of purpose. That was the Prosecution's chief charge against Lord Byron back when; that is its charge now. And now it is a graver charge, for the one sin a poet cannot be forgiven in our age is lying in the confessional of his poetry. Read any of his poems titled "Stanzas for Music"; for instance, the one that begins:

> I speak not, I trace not, I breathe not thy name,
> There is grief in the sound, there is guilt in the fame:
> But the tear which now burns on my cheek may impart
> The deep thoughts that dwell in that silence of heart.

The sound is so smooth that the comma-spliced phrases glide by almost without making sense. Indeed, some of his best-loved lyrics don't bear thinking about at all. "She walks in Beauty, like the night / Of cloudless climes and starry skies." What or who is being likened to the night, she or beauty?

To ask such a question is to be deaf to the poem. As well ask the meaning of the viola's recurring theme in Berlioz's *Harold in Italy,* or of a kiss. Byron's love lyrics are pure blarney, part of the apparatus of seduction of the nineteenth century's most accomplished make-out artist. One doesn't ask for good sense from such entertainers but rather intoxication, which together with love is one of the favorite themes of their songs. "Oh, Believe Me If All Those Endearing Young Charms," an internationally popular song of Byron's time, was written by Thomas Moore, his best friend, professional rival, biographer, and literary executor, and it was the beau ideal and bull's-eye of poetic aspiration: a "parlor song" of lilting melody, elegant diction, sweet sentimentality, and unexceptionable good taste. Moore, who was also an accomplished performer, was the most successful purveyor of such goods in the early Romantic era, but Byron wrote a couple of dozen almost as endearing and enduring, including one addressed to Moore himself, which he wrote, drunk, on a Carnival night in Venice:

So we'll go no more a-roving
   So late into the night,
Though the heart be still as loving,
   And the moon be still as bright.

For the sword outwears its sheath,
   And the soul wears out the breast,
And the heart must pause to breathe,
   And Love itself have rest.

Though the night was made for loving,
   And the day returns too soon,
Yet we'll go no more a-roving
   By the light of the moon.

"Ode to a Nightingale" it's not. Indeed, it comes close to the doggerel of greeting card verse, and an academic critic isn't given much of substance to "interrogate," but the three stanzas approach the platonic condition of lyric utterance and engrave themselves on memory at a first reading.

It was Byron's knack to speak in marble, as it was for only a few other poets—Shakespeare, Ben Jonson, Pope, Keats, Tennyson, Yeats. Auden was the last, since when, though there have been a few poets who've earned two or three citations in Bartlett's, there are none who have been so unfailing a source of plums and one-liners as Byron.

———

If this selection of Byron's poetry were limited to his various "Stanzas for Music" and poems of love, loss, and ineffable self-pity, it would need no more by way of an introduction than *Enjoy!* But that would leave the main continent unexplored. For Byron was much more than another crooner of old sweet songs. He had ambitions that could only be satisfied on the scale of the big players—Shakespeare, Dante, Tasso, Goethe; accordingly he wrote a goodly number of long narrative poems, sustained meditations, and verse dramas. However, in none of these ventures—except the picaresque verse-novel, *Don Juan*—has Byron won friends among today's critics. Indeed, a major vein of his work, the many Oriental tales, such as "The Bride of Abydos" or "The Giaour," have become the bêtes noirs of an entire school of criticism, postcolonial theory, as exemplified in the work of Edward Said, author of *Orientalism*. These critics are concerned to show that the machinery of such romances—the harems and their doe-eyed odalisques, the sighs, the pirates, the derring-do—are all not simply beneath the notice of mature readers but bad for us, because they trivialize foreign cultures and fail to do justice to their diversity. In short, Byron is politically incorrect, and not only with respect to his Orientalism but in the way his art embodies the Male Gaze. Breathes there a sophomore who would not bring a charge of harassment against the professor who required her to read such verses as these?

> Her eye's dark charm 'twere vain to tell,
> But gaze on that of the Gazelle,
> It will assist thy fancy well;
> As large, as languishingly dark,
> But Soul beamed forth in every spark
> That darted from beneath the lid,
> Bright as the jewel of Giamschid.
> Yea, *Soul,* and should our prophet say
> That form was nought but breathing clay,
> By Alla! I would answer nay; . . .
> "The Giaour," 1. 473–482

This is the territory not of Apollo and his Muses but of *Xena, Warrior Princess.* Indeed, if poets have left off catering to such needs, it is only because movies and television do the job so much better. Byron's Oriental tales must be read in the same spirit as one watches Valentino as the sheik or Hedy Lamarr as DeMille's Delilah—a spirit not of camp in the snickering, Sontagean sense but rather of a happy surrender to one's own inner twelve-year-old and sheer bad taste.

Byron can be thought of as one of the inventors of Hollywood, but so too can Sir Walter Scott—and such composers as Verdi and Berlioz, such painters as Delacroix and J.M.W. Turner. I mention these four in particular because each found inspiration for major work in Byron's verse tales and dramas. As have myriad others. There have been six operas based on "The Bride of Abydos," another six taken from "The Corsair," and eight from "Sardanapalus" (not to mention the songs set to his lyrics: seventy-three just for "She Walks in Beauty"). Such posthumous creativity is a surer testimony to the merit of a poet's work than any amount of critical "interrogation." The poet who inflamed the imaginations of Verdi, Mascagni, Schoenberg, Gounod, Hindemith, and Busoni certainly had to have been doing something right.

And still we have not touched on Byron's greatest works, the four cantos of "Childe Harold's Pilgrimage," and the unending epic impromptu, *Don Juan.* The latter is a book-length work and would need an introduction all its own. The Byron who wrote it was another poet than the one who wrote any of the other poems in this volume, with the exception of "Beppo," a short-story told in ninety-nine stanzas of ottava rima, the same verse form employed in *Don Juan,* in which Byron found, for perhaps the first time in all poetry, the cadences of his own voice. Not the voice of The Poet, in its bardic or lyric vein, but the voice of the funny, flirty, snobbish, bawdy, brawling celebrity, rock superstar, and aristocrat that was George Gordon, aka Lord Byron.

Of course, it may simply be a mask, a persona, but the illusion that one is meeting a real person who has been transformed into ottava rima is still compelling two centuries later, and once your ear is tuned to that voice the entire oeuvre begins to resonate.

For that reason Byron may be the most living of all the Dead White Males who wrote poetry. Keats will shiver your soul to a deeper depth, and Wordsworth elevate it to a higher altitude, but if you simply want to spend the night with your best friend, Byron's the man.

Begin with "Childe Harold." That's how his own world got to know him first, and it's still the best entrée. Here is the Byron who became the first matinee idol poet. He sets his wit aside and fixes his gaze on you and pours his heart out in a nonstop monologue about Napoleon and all the brave soldiers who died at Waterloo; about the most spine-tingling of Alpine thunderstorms and the sheer genius of Jean-Jacques Rousseau; and, oh yes, his half sister Augusta, whom he too dearly loved, and the daughter separated from him by an ocean. He will open the door to his soul, and to yours, too—though with Byron it is sometimes hard to get a word in edgewise, but that's the problem of having a genius for a friend. "Childe Harold" is the ultimate all-night bull session, and to read it is to be twenty-four again and know you'll live forever.

THOMAS DISCH, winner of the 1999 Hugo award for nonfiction, is the author of ten books of poetry and more than fifteen novels, including, most recently, *Camp Concentration*. He lives in upstate New York.

CHILDE HAROLD'S PILGRIMAGE

A Romaunt

[*The first two cantos of* Childe Harold *were written during Byron's travels in the Eastern Mediterranean countries. Canto I was begun at Janina, Albania (now Greece), October 31, 1809, and Canto II was finished at Smyrna, March 28, 1810. It was published in March 1812, and brought Byron immediate fame, surpassing that of any young poet, perhaps of any poet during his lifetime. Canto III was mostly written while Byron was living at the Villa Diodati near Geneva. It was begun early in May and finished at Ouchy, near Lausanne, on June 27, 1816, and was published the same year. The fourth canto, inspired by Byron's trip to Rome in the spring of 1817, was begun on June 26 and a first draft was finished on July 20, but he added many more stanzas before the poem was published in 1818.*]

"L'univers est une espèce de livre, dont on n'a lu que la première page quand on n'a vu que son pays. J'en ai feuilleté un assez grand nombre, que j'ai trouvé également mauvaises. Cet examen ne m'a point été infructueux. Je haïssais ma patrie. Toutes les impertinences des peuples divers, parmi lesquels j'ai vécu, m'ont réconcilié avec elle. Quand je n'aurais tiré d'autre bénéfice de mes voyages que celui-là, je n'en regretterais ni les frais ni les fatigues."

—Fougeret de Monbron,
Le Cosmopolite, ou,
Le Citoyen du Monde
Londres, 1753.

PREFACE

(TO THE FIRST AND SECOND CANTOS)

The following poem was written, for the most part, amidst the scenes which it attempts to describe. It was begun in Albania; and the parts relative to Spain and Portugal were composed from the author's observations in those countries. Thus much it may be necessary to state for the correctness of the descriptions. The scenes attempted to be sketched are in Spain, Portugal, Epirus, Acarnania and Greece. There, for the present, the poem stops: its reception will determine whether the author may venture to conduct his readers to the capital of the East, through Ionia and Phrygia: these two cantos are merely experimental.

A fictitious character is introduced for the sake of giving some connection to the piece; which, however, makes no pretension to regularity. It has been suggested to me by friends, on whose opinions I set a high value, that in this fictitious character, "Childe Harold," I may incur the suspicion of having intended some real personage: this I beg leave, once for all, to disclaim—Harold is the child of imagination, for the purpose I have stated.

In some very trivial particulars, and those merely local, there might be grounds for such a notion; but in the main points, I should hope, none whatever.

It is almost superfluous to mention that the appellation "Childe," as "Childe Waters," "Childe Childers," etc., is used as more consonant with the old structure of versification which I have adopted. The "Good Night" in the beginning of the first Canto, was suggested by Lord Maxwell's "Good Night" in the *Border Minstrelsy*, edited by Mr. Scott.

With the different poems which have been published on Spanish subjects, there may be found some slight coincidence in the first part, which treats of the Peninsula, but it can only be casual; as, with the exception of a few concluding stanzas, the whole of the poem was written in the Levant.

The stanza of Spenser, according to one of our most successful poets, admits of every variety. Dr. Beattie makes the following observation:—

"Not long ago I began a poem in the style and stanza of Spenser, in which I propose to give full scope to my inclination, and be either droll or pathetic, descriptive or sentimental, tender or satirical, as the humour strikes me; for, if I mistake not, the measure which I have adopted admits equally of all these kinds of composition." Strengthened in my opinion by such authority, and by the example of some in the highest order of Italian poets, I shall make no apology for attempts at similar variations in the following composition; satisfied that, if they are unsuccessful, their failure must be in the execution, rather than in the design sanctioned by the practice of Ariosto, Thomson, and Beattie.

London, February, 1812.

ADDITION TO THE PREFACE

I have now waited till almost all our periodical journals have distributed their usual portion of criticism. To the justice of the generality of their criticisms I have nothing to object; it would ill become me to quarrel with their slight degree of censure, when, perhaps, if they had been less kind they had been more candid. Returning, therefore, to all and each my best thanks for their liberality, on one point alone I shall venture an observation. Amongst the many objections justly urged to the very indifferent character of the "vagrant Childe" (whom, notwithstanding many hints to the contrary, I still maintain to be a fictitious personage), it has been stated, that, besides the anachronism, he is very *unknightly*, as the times of the Knights were times of Love, Honour, and so forth. Now it so happens that the good old times, when "l'amour du bon vieux temps, l'amour antique," flourished, were the most profligate of all possible centuries. Those who have any doubts on this subject may consult Sainte-Palaye, *passim,* and more particularly vol. ii. p. 69. The vows of chivalry were no better kept than any other vows whatsoever; and the songs of the Troubadours were no more decent, and certainly were much less refined, than those of Ovid. The "Cours d'Amour, parlemens d'amour, ou de courtoisie et de gentilesse" had much more of love than of courtesy or gentleness. See Rolland on the same subject with Sainte-Palaye.

Whatever other objection may be urged to that most unamiable personage Childe Harold, he was so far perfectly knightly in his attributes—"No waiter, but a knight templar." By the by, I fear that Sir Tristrem and Sir Lancelot were no better than they should be, although very poetical personages and true knights, "sans peur," though not "sans reproche." If the story of the institution of the "Garter" be not a fable, the knights of that order have for several centuries borne the badge of a Countess of Salisbury, of indifferent memory. So much for chivalry. Burke need not have regretted that its days are over, though Marie-Antoinette was quite as chaste as most of those in whose honour lances were shivered, and knights unhorsed.

Before the days of Bayard, and down to those of Sir Joseph Banks (the most chaste and celebrated of ancient and modern times) few exceptions will be found to this statement; and I fear a little investigation will teach us not to regret these monstrous mummeries of the middle ages.

I now leave "Childe Harold" to live his day such as he is; it had been more agreeable, and certainly more easy, to have drawn an amiable character. It had been easy to varnish over his faults, to make him do more and express less, but he never was intended as an example, further than to show, that early perversion of mind and morals leads to satiety of past pleasures and disappointment in new ones, and that even the beauties of nature and the stimulus of travel (except ambition, the most powerful of all excitements) are lost on a soul so constituted, or rather misdirected. Had I proceeded with the Poem, this character would have deepened as he drew to the close; for the outline which I once meant to fill up for him was, with some exceptions, the sketch of a modern Timon, perhaps a poetical Zeluco.

To Ianthe

Not in those climes where I have late been straying,
Though Beauty long hath there been matchless deemed,
Not in those visions to the heart displaying
Forms which it sighs but to have only dreamed,
Hath aught like thee in Truth or Fancy seemed:
Nor, having seen thee, shall I vainly seek
To paint those charms which varied as they beamed—
To such as see thee not my words were weak;
To those who gaze on thee what language could they speak?

Ah! may'st thou ever be what now thou art,   10
Nor unbeseem the promise of thy Spring—
As fair in form, as warm yet pure in heart,
Love's image upon earth without his wing,
And guileless beyond Hope's imagining!
And surely she who now so fondly rears
Thy youth, in thee, thus hourly brightening,
Beholds the Rainbow of her future years,
Before whose heavenly hues all Sorrow disappears.

Young Peri of the West!—'tis well for me
My years already doubly number thine;   20
My loveless eyes unmoved may gaze on thee,
And safely view thy ripening beauties shine;
Happy, I ne'er shall see them in decline;
Happier, that, while all younger hearts shall bleed,
Mine shall escape the doom thine eyes assign
To those whose admiration shall succeed,
But mixed with pangs to Love's even loveliest hours decreed.

Oh! let that eye, which, wild as the Gazelle's,
Now brightly bold or beautifully shy,
Wins as it wanders, dazzles where it dwells,   30
Glance o'er this page, nor to my verse deny
That smile for which my breast might vainly sigh
Could I to thee be ever more than friend:

This much, dear Maid, accord; nor question why
To one so young my strain I would commend,
But bid me with my wreath one matchless Lily blend.

Such is thy name with this my verse entwined;
And long as kinder eyes a look shall cast
On Harold's page, Ianthe's here enshrined
Shall thus be *first* beheld, forgotten *last:*   **40**
My days once numbered—should this homage past
Attract thy fairy fingers near the Lyre
Of him who hailed thee loveliest, as thou wast—
Such is the most my Memory may desire;
Though more than Hope can claim, could Friendship less require?

Canto the First

I

Oh, thou! in Hellas deemed of Heavenly birth,
Muse! formed or fabled at the Minstrel's will!
Since shamed full oft by later lyres on earth,
Mine dares not call thee from thy sacred Hill:
Yet there I've wandered by thy vaunted rill;
Yes! sighed o'er Delphi's long deserted shrine,
Where, save that feeble fountain, all is still;
Nor mote my shell awake the weary Nine
To grace so plain a tale—this lowly lay of mine.

II

Whilome in Albion's isle there dwelt a youth,
Who ne in Virtue's ways did take delight;
But spent his days in riot most uncouth,
And vexed with mirth the drowsy ear of Night.
Ah me! in sooth he was a shameless wight,
Sore given to revel, and ungodly glee;
Few earthly things found favour in his sight
Save concubines and carnal companie,
And flaunting wassailers of high and low degree.

10

III

Childe Harold was he hight:—but whence his name
And lineage long, it suits me not to say;   20
Suffice it, that perchance they were of fame,
And had been glorious in another day:
But one sad losel soils a name for ay,
However mighty in the olden time;
Nor all that heralds rake from coffined clay,
Nor florid prose, nor honied lies of rhyme,
Can blazon evil deeds, or consecrate a crime.

IV

Childe Harold basked him in the Noontide sun,
Disporting there like any other fly;
Nor deemed before his little day was done   30
One blast might chill him into misery.
But long ere scarce a third of his passed by,
Worse than Adversity the Childe befell;
He felt the fulness of Satiety:
Then loathed he in his native land to dwell,
Which seemed to him more lone than Eremite's sad cell.

V

For he through Sin's long labyrinth had run,
Nor made atonement when he did amiss,
Had sighed to many though he loved but one,
And that loved one, alas! could ne'er be his.   40
Ah, happy she! to 'scape from him whose kiss
Had been pollution unto aught so chaste;
Who soon had left her charms for vulgar bliss,
And spoiled her goodly lands to gild his waste,
Nor calm domestic peace had ever deigned to taste.

VI

And now Childe Harold was sore sick at heart,
And from his fellow Bacchanals would flee;
'Tis said, at times the sullen tear would start,
But Pride congealed the drop within his ee:

Apart he stalked in joyless reverie,   50
And from his native land resolved to go,
And visit scorching climes beyond the sea;
With pleasure drugged, he almost longed for woe,
And e'en for change of scene would seek the shades below.

VII

The Childe departed from his father's hall:
It was a vast and venerable pile;
So old, it seeméd only not to fall,
Yet strength was pillared in each massy aisle.
Monastic dome! condemned to uses vile!
Where Superstition once had made her den   60
Now Paphian girls were known to sing and smile;
And monks might deem their time was come agen,
If ancient tales say true, nor wrong these holy men.

VIII

Yet oft-times in his maddest mirthful mood
Strange pangs would flash along Childe Harold's brow,
As if the Memory of some deadly feud
Or disappointed passion lurked below:
But this none knew, nor haply cared to know;
For his was not that open, artless soul
That feels relief by bidding sorrow flow,   70
Nor sought he friend to counsel or condole,
Whate'er this grief mote be, which he could not control.

IX

And none did love him!—though to hall and bower
He gathered revellers from far and near,
He knew them flatterers of the festal hour,
The heartless Parasites of present cheer.
Yea! none did love him—not his lemans dear—
But pomp and power alone are Woman's care,
And where these are light Eros finds a feere;
Maidens, like moths, are ever caught by glare,   80
And Mammon wins his way where Seraphs might despair.

X

Childe Harold had a mother—not forgot,
Though parting from that mother he did shun;
A sister whom he loved, but saw her not
Before his weary pilgrimage begun:
If friends he had, he bade adieu to none.
Yet deem not thence his breast a breast of steel:
Ye, who have known what 'tis to dote upon
A few dear objects, will in sadness feel
Such partings break the heart they fondly hope to heal.   90

XI

His house, his home, his heritage, his lands,
The laughing dames in whom did delight,
Whose large blue eyes, fair locks, and snowy hands,
Might shake the Saintship of an Anchorite,
And long had fed his youthful appetite;
His goblets brimmed with every costly wine,
And all that mote to luxury invite,
Without a sigh he left, to cross the brine,
And traverse Paynim shores, and pass Earth's central line.

XII

The sails were filled, and fair the light winds blew,   100
As glad to waft him from his native home;
And fast the white rocks faded from his view,
And soon were lost in circumambient foam:
And then, it may be, of his wish to roam
Repented he, but in his bosom slept
The silent thought, nor from his lips did come
One word of wail, whilst others sate and wept,
And to the reckless gales unmanly moaning kept.

XIII

But when the Sun was sinking in the sea
He seized his harp, which he at times could string,   110
And strike, albeit with untaught melody,
When deemed he no strange ear was listening:

And now his fingers o'er it he did fling,
And tuned his farewell in the dim twilight;
While flew the vessel on her snowy wing,
And fleeting shores receded from his sight,
Thus to the elements he poured his last "Good Night."

CHILDE HAROLD'S GOOD NIGHT

1

"Adieu, adieu! my native shore
    Fades o'er the waters blue;
The night-winds sigh, the breakers roar,   120
    And shrieks the wild sea-mew.
Yon Sun that sets upon the sea
    We follow in his flight;
Farewell awhile to him and thee,
    My native Land—Good Night!

2

"A few short hours and He will rise
    To give the Morrow birth;
And I shall hail the main and skies,
    But not my mother Earth.
Deserted is my own good Hall,   130
    Its hearth is desolate;
Wild weeds are gathering on the wall;
    My Dog howls at the gate.

3

"Come hither, hither, my little page!
    Why dost thou weep and wail?
Or dost thou dread the billows rage,
    Or tremble at the gale?
But dash the tear-drop from thine eye;
    Our ship is swift and strong:
Our fleetest falcon scarce can fly   140
    More merrily along."

4

"Let winds be shrill, let waves roll high,
    I fear not wave nor wind:
Yet marvel not, Sir Childe, that I
    Am sorrowful in mind;
For I have from my father gone,
    A mother whom I love,
And have no friends, save these alone,
    But thee—and One above.

5

"My father blessed me fervently,   150
    Yet did not much complain;
But sorely will my mother sigh
    Till I come back again."—
"Enough, enough, my little lad!
    Such tears become thine eye;
If I thy guileless bosom had,
    Mine own would not be dry.

6

"Come hither, hither, my staunch yeoman,
    Why dost thou look so pale?
Or dost thou dread a French foeman?   160
    Or shiver at the gale?"—
"Deem'st thou I tremble for my life?
    Sir Childe, I'm not so weak;
But thinking on an absent wife
    Will blanch a faithful cheek.

7

"My spouse and boys dwell near thy hall,
    Along the bordering Lake,
And when they on their father call,
    What answer shall she make?"—
"Enough, enough, my yeoman good,   170
    Thy grief let none gainsay;
But I, who am of lighter mood,
    Will laugh to flee away.

8

"For who would trust the seeming sighs
  Of wife or paramour?
Fresh feeres will dry the bright blue eyes
  We late saw streaming o'er.
For pleasures past I do not grieve,
  Nor perils gathering near;
My greatest grief is that I leave   180
  No thing that claims a tear.

9

"And now I'm in the world alone,
  Upon the wide, wide sea:
But why should I for others groan,
  When none will sigh for me?
Perchance my Dog will whine in vain,
  Till fed by stranger hands;
But long ere I come back again,
  He'd tear me where he stands.

1 0

"With thee, my bark, I'll swiftly go   190
  Athwart the foaming brine;
Nor care what land thou bear'st me to,
  So not again to mine.
Welcome, welcome, ye dark-blue waves!
  And when you fail my sight,
Welcome, ye deserts, and ye caves!
  My native Land—Good Night!"

X I V

On, on the vessel flies, the land is gone,
And winds are rude in Biscay's sleepless bay.
Four days are sped, but with the fifth, anon,   200
New shores descried make every bosom gay:
And Cintra's mountain greets them on their way,
And Tagus dashing onward to the Deep,
His fabled golden tribute bent to pay;

And soon on board the Lusian pilots leap,
And steer 'twixt fertile shores where yet few rustics reap.

XV

Oh, Christ! it is a goodly sight to see
What Heaven hath done for this delicious land!
What fruits of fragrance blush on every tree!
What goodly prospects o'er the hills expand!   210
But man would mar them with an impious hand:
And when the Almighty lifts his fiercest scourge
'Gainst those who most transgress his high command,
With treble vengeance will his hot shafts urge
Gaul's locust host, and earth from fellest foeman purge.

XVI

What beauties doth Lisboa first unfold!
Her image floating on that noble tide,
Which poets vainly pave with sands of gold,
But now whereon a thousand keels did ride
Of mighty strength, since Albion was allied,   220
And to the Lusians did her aid afford:—
A nation swoln with ignorance and pride,
Who lick yet loathe the hand that waves the sword
To save them from the wrath of Gaul's unsparing Lord.

XVII

But whoso entereth within this town,
That, sheening far, celestial seems to be,
Disconsolate will wander up and down,
'Mid many things unsightly to strange ee;
For hut and palace show like filthily:
The dingy denizens are reared in dirt;   230
Ne personage of high or mean degree
Doth care for cleanness of surtout or shirt,
Though shent with Egypt's plague, unkempt, unwashed, unhurt.

XVIII

Poor, paltry slaves! yet born 'midst noblest scenes—
Why, Nature, waste thy wonders on such men?

Lo! Cintra's glorious Eden intervenes
In variegated maze of mount and glen.
Ah, me! what hand can pencil guide, or pen,
To follow half on which the eye dilates
Through views more dazzling unto mortal ken   240
Than those whereof such things the Bard relates,
Who to the awe-struck world unlocked Elysium's gates!

XIX

The horrid crags, by toppling convent crowned,
The cork-trees hoar that clothe the shaggy steep,
The mountain-moss by scorching skies imbrowned,
The sunken glen, whose sunless shrubs must weep,
The tender azure of the unruffled deep,
The orange tints that gild the greenest bough,
The torrents that from cliff to valley leap,
The vine on high, the willow branch below,   250
Mixed in one mighty scene, with varied beauty glow.

XX

Then slowly climb the many-winding way,
And frequent turn to linger as you go,
From loftier rocks new loveliness survey,
And rest ye at "Our Lady's house of Woe;"
Where frugal monks their little relics show,
And sundry legends to the stranger tell:
Here impious men have punished been, and lo!
Deep in yon cave Honorius long did dwell,
In hope to merit Heaven by making earth a Hell.   260

XXI

And here and there, as up the crags you spring,
Mark many rude-carved crosses near the path:
Yet deem not these Devotion's offering—
These are memorials frail of murderous wrath:
For wheresoe'er the shrieking victim hath
Poured forth his blood beneath the assassin's knife,
Some hand erects a cross of mouldering lath;

And grove and glen with thousand such are rife
Throughout this purple land, where Law secures not life.

XXII

On sloping mounds, or in the vale beneath 270
Are domes where whilome kings did make repair;
But now the wild flowers round them only breathe:
Yet ruined Splendour still is lingering there.
And yonder towers the Prince's palace fair:
There thou too, Vathek! England's wealthiest son,
Once formed thy Paradise, as not aware
When wanton Wealth her mightiest deeds hath done,
Meek Peace voluptuous lures was ever wont to shun.

XXIII

Here didst thou dwell, here schemes of pleasure plan,
Beneath yon mountain's ever beauteous brow: 280
But now, as if a thing unblest by Man,
Thy fairy dwelling is as lone as Thou!
Here giant weeds a passage scarce allow
To Halls deserted, portals gaping wide:
Fresh lessons to the thinking bosom, how
Vain are the pleasaunces on earth supplied,
Swept into wrecks anon by Time's ungentle tide!

XXIV

Behold the hall where chiefs were late convened!
Oh! dome displeasing unto British eye!
With diadem hight Foolscap, lo! a Fiend, 290
A little Fiend that scoffs incessantly,
There sits in parchment robe arrayed, and by
His side is hung a seal and sable scroll,
Where blazoned glare names known to chivalry,
And sundry signatures adorn the roll,
Whereat the Urchin points and laughs with all his soul.

XXV

Convention is the dwarfish demon styled
That foiled the knights in Marialva's dome:

Of brains (if brains they had) he them beguiled,
And turned a nation's shallow joy to gloom.   300
Here Folly dashed to earth the victor's plume,
And Policy regained what arms had lost:
For chiefs like ours in vain may laurels bloom!
Woe to the conquering, not the conquered host,
Since baffled Triumph droops on Lusitania's coast!

XXVI

And ever since that martial Synod met,
Britannia sickens, Cintra! at thy name;
And folks in office at the mention fret,
And fain would blush, if blush they could, for shame.
How will Posterity the deed proclaim!   310
Will not our own and fellow-nations sneer,
To view these champions cheated of their fame,
By foes in fight o'erthrown, yet victors here,
Where Scorn her finger points through many a coming year?

XXVII

So deemed the Childe, as o'er the mountains he
Did take his way in solitary guise:
Sweet was the scene, yet soon he thought to flee,
More restless than the swallow in the skies:
Though here awhile he learned to moralise,
For Meditation fixed at times on him;   320
And conscious Reason whispered to despise
His early youth, misspent in maddest whim;
But as he gazed on truth his aching eyes grew dim.

XXVIII

To horse! to horse! he quits, for ever quits
A scene of peace, though soothing to his soul:
Again he rouses from his moping fits,
But seeks not now the harlot and the bowl.
Onward he flies, nor fixed as yet the goal
Where he shall rest him on his pilgrimage;
And o'er him many changing scenes must roll   330

Ere toil his thirst for travel can assuage.
Or he shall calm his breast, or learn experience sage.

X X I X

Yet Mafra shall one moment claim delay,
Where dwelt of yore the Lusians' luckless queen;
And Church and Court did mingle their array,
And Mass and revel were alternate seen;
Lordlings and freres—ill-sorted fry I ween!
But here the Babylonian Whore hath built
A dome, where flaunts she in such glorious sheen,
That men forget the blood which she hath spilt,   340
And bow the knee to Pomp that loves to varnish guilt.

X X X

O'er vales that teem with fruits, romantic hills,
(Oh, that such hills upheld a freeborn race!)
Whereon to gaze the eye with joyaunce fills,
Childe Harold wends through many a pleasant place.
Though sluggards deem it but a foolish chase,
And marvel men should quit their easy chair,
The toilsome way, and long, long league to trace,
Oh! there is sweetness in the mountain air,
And Life, that bloated Ease can never hope to share.   350

X X X I

More bleak to view the hills at length recede,
And, less luxuriant, smoother vales extend:
Immense horizon-bounded plains succeed!
Far as the eye discerns, withouten end,
Spain's realms appear whereon her shepherds tend
Flocks, whose rich fleece right well the trader knows—
Now must the Pastor's arm his *lambs* defend:
For Spain is compassed by unyielding foes,
And *all* must shield their *all,* or share Subjection's woes.

X X X I I

Where Lusitania and her Sister meet,   360
Deem ye what bounds the rival realms divide?

Or ere the jealous Queens of Nations greet,
Doth Tayo interpose his mighty tide?
Or dark Sierras rise in craggy pride?
Or fence of art, like China's vasty wall?
Ne barrier wall, ne river deep and wide,
Ne horrid crags, nor mountains dark and tall,
Rise like the rocks that part Hispania's land from Gaul:

XXXIII

But these between a silver streamlet glides,
And scarce a name distinguisheth the brook,   370
Though rival kingdoms press its verdant sides,
Here leans the idle shepherd on his crook,
And vacant on the rippling waves doth look,
That peaceful still 'twixt bitterest foemen flow;
For proud each peasant as the noblest duke:
Well doth the Spanish hind the difference know
'Twixt him and Lusian slave, the lowest of the low.

XXXIV

But ere the mingling bounds have far been passed,
Dark Guadiana rolls his power along
In sullen billows, murmuring and vast,   380
So noted ancient roundelays among.
Whilome upon his banks did legions throng
Of Moor and Knight, in mailéd splendour drest:
Here ceased the swift their race, here sunk the strong;
The Paynim turban and the Christian crest
Mixed on the bleeding stream, by floating hosts oppressed.

XXXV

Oh, lovely Spain! renowned, romantic Land!
Where is that Standard which Pelagio bore,
When Cava's traitor-sire first called the band
That dyed thy mountain streams with Gothic gore?   390
Where are those bloody Banners which of yore
Waved o'er thy sons, victorious to the gale,
And drove at last the spoilers to their shore?
Red gleamed the Cross, and waned the Crescent pale,
While Afric's echoes thrilled with Moorish matrons' wail.

XXXVI

Teems not each ditty with the glorious tale?
Ah! such, alas! the hero's amplest fate!
When granite moulders and when records fail,
A peasant's plaint prolongs his dubious date.
Pride! bend thine eye from Heaven to thine estate,   400
See how the Mighty shrink into a song!
Can Volume, Pillar, Pile preserve thee great?
Or must thou trust Tradition's simple tongue,
When Flattery sleeps with thee, and History does thee wrong?

XXXVII

Awake, ye Sons of Spain! awake! advance!
Lo! Chivalry, your ancient Goddess, cries,
But wields not, as of old, her thirsty lance,
Nor shakes her crimson plumage in the skies:
Now on the smoke of blazing bolts she flies,
And speaks in thunder through yon engine's roar: 410
In every peal she calls—"Awake! arise!"
Say, is her voice more feeble than of yore,
When her war-song was heard on Andalusia's shore?

XXXVIII

Hark!—heard you not those hoofs of dreadful note?
Sounds not the clang of conflict on the heath?
Saw ye not whom the reeking sabre smote,
Nor saved your brethren ere they sank beneath
Tyrants and Tyrants' slaves?—the fires of Death,
The Bale-fires flash on high:—from rock to rock
Each volley tells that thousands cease to breathe;   420
Death rides upon the sulphury Siroc,
Red Battle stamps his foot, and Nations feel the shock.

XXXIX

Lo! where the Giant on the mountain stands,
His blood-red tresses deepening in the Sun,
With death-shot glowing in his fiery hands,
And eye that scorcheth all it glares upon;
Restless it rolls, now fixed, and now anon

Flashing afar,—and at his iron feet
Destruction cowers, to mark what deeds are done;
For on this morn three potent Nations meet,   430
To shed before his Shrine the blood he deems most sweet.

XL

By Heaven! it is a splendid sight to see
(For one who hath no friend, no brother there)
Their rival scarfs of mixed embroidery,
Their various arms that glitter in the air!
What gallant War-hounds rouse them from their lair,
And gnash their fangs, loud yelling for the prey!
All join the chase, but few the triumph share;
The Grave shall bear the chiefest prize away,
And Havoc scarce for joy can number their array.   440

XLI

Three hosts combine to offer sacrifice;
Three tongues prefer strange orisons on high;
Three gaudy standards flout the pale blue skies;
The shouts are France, Spain, Albion, Victory!
The Foe, the Victim, and the fond Ally
That fights for all, but ever fights in vain,
Are met—as if at home they could not die—
To feed the crow on Talavera's plain,
And fertilise the field that each pretends to gain.

XLII

There shall they rot—Ambition's honoured fools!   450
Yes, Honour decks the turf that wraps their clay!
Vain Sophistry! in these behold the tools,
The broken tools, that Tyrants cast away
By myriads, when they dare to pave their way
With human hearts—to what?—a dream alone.
Can Despots compass aught that hails their sway?
Or call with truth one span of earth their own,
Save that wherein at last they crumble bone by bone?

XLIII

Oh, Albuera! glorious field of grief!
As o'er thy plain the Pilgrim pricked his steed,   460
Who could foresee thee, in a space so brief,
A scene where mingling foes should boast and bleed!
Peace to the perished! may the warrior's meed
And tears of triumph their reward prolong!
Till others fall where other chieftains lead,
Thy name shall circle round the gaping throng,
And shine in worthless lays, the theme of transient song.

XLIV

Enough of Battle's minions! let them play
Their game of lives, and barter breath for fame:
Fame that will scarce reanimate their clay,   470
Though thousands fall to deck some single name.
In sooth 'twere sad to thwart their noble aim
Who strike, blest hirelings! for their country's good,
And die, that living might have proved her shame;
Perished, perchance, in some domestic feud,
Or in a narrower sphere wild Rapine's path pursued.

XLV

Full swiftly Harold wends his lonely way
Where proud Sevilla triumphs unsubdued:
Yet is she free? the Spoiler's wished-for prey!
Soon, soon shall Conquest's fiery foot intrude,   480
Blackening her lovely domes with traces rude.
Inevitable hour! 'Gainst fate to strive
Where Desolation plants her famished brood
Is vain, or Ilion, Tyre might yet survive,
And Virtue vanquish all, and Murder cease to thrive.

XLVI

But all unconscious of the coming doom,
The feast, the song, the revel here abounds;
Strange modes of merriment the hours consume,
Nor bleed these patriots with their country's wounds:
Nor here War's clarion, but Love's rebeck sounds;   490

Here Folly still his votaries inthralls;
And young-eyed Lewdness walks her midnight rounds:
Girt with the silent crimes of Capitals,
Still to the last kind Vice clings to the tott'ring walls.

XLVII

Not so the rustic—with his trembling mate
He lurks, nor casts his heavy eye afar,
Lest he should view his vineyard desolate,
Blasted below the dun hot breath of War.
No more beneath soft eve's consenting star
Fandango twirls his jocund castanet: 500
Ah, Monarchs! could ye taste the mirth ye mar,
Not in the toils of Glory would ye fret;
The hoarse dull drum would sleep, and Man be happy yet!

XLVIII

How carols now the lusty muleteer?
Of Love, Romance, Devotion is his lay,
As whilome he was wont the leagues to cheer,
His quick bells wildly jingling on the way?
No! as he speeds, he chants "Vivá el Rey!"
And checks his song to execrate Godoy,
The royal wittol Charles, and curse the day   510
When first Spain's queen beheld the black-eyed boy,
And gore-faced Treason sprung from her adulterate joy.

XLIX

On yon long level plain, at distance crowned
With crags, whereon those Moorish turrets rest,
Wide-scattered hoof-marks dint the wounded ground;
And, scathed by fire, the greensward's darkened vest
Tells that the foe was Andalusia's guest:
Here was the camp, the watch-flame, and the host,
Here the bold peasant stormed the Dragon's nest;
Still does he mark it with triumphant boast,   520
And points to yonder cliffs, which oft were won and lost.

L

And whomsoe'er along the path you meet
Bears in his cap the badge of crimson hue,
Which tells you whom to shun and whom to greet:
Woe to the man that walks in public view
Without of loyalty this token true:
Sharp is the knife, and sudden is the stroke;
And sorely would the Gallic foeman rue,
If subtle poniards, wrapt beneath the cloke,
Could blunt the sabre's edge, or clear the cannon's smoke.   530

L I

At every turn Morena's dusky height
Sustains aloft the battery's iron load;
And, far as mortal eye can compass sight,
The mountain-howitzer, the broken road,
The bristling palisade, the fosse o'erflowed,
The stationed bands, the never-vacant watch,
The magazine in rocky durance stowed,
The holstered steed beneath the shed of thatch,
The ball-piled pyramid, the ever-blazing match,

L I I

Portend the deeds to come:—but he whose nod   540
Has tumbled feebler despots from their sway,
A moment pauseth ere he lifts the rod;
A little moment deigneth to delay:
Soon will his legions sweep through these their way;
The West must own the Scourger of the world.
Ah! Spain! how sad will be thy reckoning-day,
When soars Gaul's Vulture, with his wings unfurled,
And thou shalt view thy sons in crowds to Hades hurled.

L I I I

And must they fall? the young, the proud, the brave,
To swell one bloated Chief's unwholesome reign?   550
No step between submission and a grave?
The rise of Rapine and the fall of Spain?
And doth the Power that man adores ordain

Their doom, nor heed the suppliant's appeal?
Is all that desperate Valour acts in vain?
And Counsel sage, and patriotic Zeal—
The Veteran's skill—Youth's fire—and Manhood's heart of steel?

LIV

Is it for this the Spanish maid, aroused,
Hangs on the willow her unstrung guitar,
And, all unsexed, the Anlace hath espoused,   560
Sung the loud song, and dared the deed of war?
And she, whom once the semblance of a scar
Appalled, an owlet's 'larum chilled with dread,
Now views the column-scattering bay'net jar,
The falchion flash, and o'er the yet warm dead
Stalks with Minerva's step where Mars might quake to tread.

LV

Ye who shall marvel when you hear her tale,
Oh! had you known her in her softer hour,
Marked her black eye that mocks her coal-black veil,
Heard her light, lively tones in Lady's bower,   570
Seen her long locks that foil the painter's power,
Her fairy form, with more than female grace,
Scarce would you deem that Saragoza's tower
Beheld her smile in Danger's Gorgon face,
Thin the closed ranks, and lead in Glory's fearful chase.

LVI

Her lover sinks—she sheds no ill-timed tear;
Her Chief is slain—she fills his fatal post;
Her fellows flee—she checks their base career;
The Foe retires—she heads the sallying host;
Who can appease like her a lover's ghost?   580
Who can avenge so well a leader's fall?
What maid retrieve when man's flushed hope is lost?
Who hang so fiercely on the flying Gaul,
Foiled by a woman's hand, before a battered wall?

LVII

Yet are Spain's maids no race of Amazons,
But formed for all the witching arts of love:
Though thus in arms they emulate her sons,
And in the horrid phalanx dare to move,
'Tis but the tender fierceness of the dove,
Pecking the hand that hovers o'er her mate: 590
In softness as in firmness far above
Remoter females, famed for sickening prate;
Her mind is nobler sure, her charms perchance as great.

LVIII

The seal Love's dimpling finger hath impressed
Denotes how soft that chin which bears his touch:
Her lips, whose kisses pout to leave their nest
Bid man be valiant ere he merit such:
Her glance how wildly beautiful! how much
Hath Phœbus wooed in vain to spoil her cheek
Which glows yet smoother from his amorous clutch!   600
Who round the North for paler dames would seek?
How poor their forms appear! how languid, wan, and weak!

LIX

Match me, ye climes! which poets love to laud;
Match me, ye harems of the land! where now
I strike my strain, far distant, to applaud
Beauties that ev'n a cynic must avow;
Match me those Houries, whom ye scarce allow
To taste the gale lest Love should ride the wind,
With Spain's dark-glancing daughters—deign to know,
There your wise Prophet's Paradise we find,   610
His black-eyed maids of Heaven, angelically kind.

LX

Oh, thou Parnassus! whom I now survey,
Not in the phrensy of a dreamer's eye,
Not in the fabled landscape of a lay,
But soaring snow-clad through thy native sky,
In the wild pomp of mountain-majesty!

What marvel if I thus essay to sing?
The humblest of thy pilgrims passing by
Would gladly woo thine Echoes with his string,
Though from thy heights no more one Muse will wave her
    wing.   620

LXI

Oft have I dreamed of Thee! whose glorious name
Who knows not, knows not man's divinest lore:
And now I view thee—'tis, alas! with shame
That I in feeblest accents must adore.
When I recount thy worshippers of yore
I tremble, and can only bend the knee;
Nor raise my voice, nor vainly dare to soar,
But gaze beneath thy cloudy canopy
In silent joy to think at last I look on Thee!

LXII

Happier in this than mightiest Bards have been,   630
Whose Fate to distant homes confined their lot,
Shall I unmoved behold the hallowed scene,
Which others rave of, though they know it not?
Though here no more Apollo haunts his Grot,
And thou, the Muses' seat, art now their grave,
Some gentle Spirit still pervades the spot,
Sighs in the gale, keeps silence in the Cave,
And glides with glassy foot o'er yon melodious wave.

LXIII

Of thee hereafter. Ev'n amidst my strain
I turned aside to pay my homage here;   640
Forgot the land, the sons, the maids of Spain;
Her fate, to every freeborn bosom dear;
And hailed thee, not perchance without a tear.
Now to my theme—but from thy holy haunt
Let me some remnant, some memorial bear;
Yield me one leaf of Daphne's deathless plant,
Nor let thy votary's hope be deemed an idle vaunt.

LXIV

But ne'er didst thou, fair Mount! when Greece was young,
See round thy giant base a brighter choir,
Nor e'er did Delphi, when her Priestess sung   650
The Pythian hymn with more than mortal fire,
Behold a train more fitting to inspire
The song of love, than Andalusia's maids
Nurst in the glowing lap of soft Desire:
Ah! that to these were given such peaceful shades
As Greece can still bestow, though Glory fly her glades.

LXV

Fair is proud Seville; let her country boast
Her strength, her wealth, her site of ancient days;
But Cadiz, rising on the distant coast
Calls forth a sweeter, though ignoble praise.   660
Ah, Vice! how soft are thy voluptuous ways!
While boyish blood is mantling, who can 'scape
The fascination of thy magic gaze?
A Cherub-Hydra round us dost thou gape,
And mould to every taste thy dear delusive shape.

LXVI

When Paphos fell by Time—accurséd Time!
The Queen who conquers all must yield to thee—
The Pleasures fled, but sought as warm a clime;
And Venus, constant to her native Sea,
To nought else constant, hither deigned to flee,   670
And fixed her shrine within these walls of white:
Though not to one dome circumscribeth She
Her worship, but, devoted to her rite,
A thousand Altars rise, for ever blazing bright.

LXVII

From morn till night, from night till startled Morn
Peeps blushing on the Revel's laughing crew,
The Song is heard, the rosy Garland worn;
Devices quaint, and Frolics ever new,

Tread on each other's kibes. A long adieu
He bids to sober joy that here sojourns: 680
Nought interrupts the riot, though in lieu
Of true devotion monkish incense burns,
And Love and Prayer unite, or rule the hour by turns.

LXVIII

The Sabbath comes, a day of blesséd rest:
What hallows it upon this Christian shore?
Lo! it is sacred to a solemn Feast:
Hark! heard you not the forest-monarch's roar?
Crashing the lance, he snuffs the spouting gore
Of man and steed, o'erthrown beneath his horn;
The thronged arena shakes with shouts for more;   690
Yells the mad crowd o'er entrails freshly torn,
Nor shrinks the female eye, nor ev'n affects to mourn.

LXIX

The seventh day this—the Jubilee of man!
London! right well thou know'st the day of prayer:
Then thy spruce citizen, washed artisan,
And smug apprentice gulp their weekly air:
Thy coach of hackney, whiskey, one-horse chair,
And humblest gig through sundry suburbs whirl,
To Hampstead, Brentford, Harrow make repair;
Till the tired jade the wheel forgets to hurl,   700
Provoking envious gibe from each pedestrian churl.

LXX

Some o'er thy Thamis row the ribboned fair,
Others along the safer turnpike fly;
Some Richmond-hill ascend, some scud to Ware,
And many to the steep of Highgate hie.
Ask ye, Bœotian Shades! the reason why?
'Tis to the worship of the solemn Horn,
Grasped in the holy hand of Mystery,
In whose dread name both men and maids are sworn,
And consecrate the oath with draught, and dance till morn.   710

LXXI

All have their fooleries—not alike are thine,
Fair Cadiz, rising o'er the dark blue sea!
Soon as the Matin bell proclaimeth nine,
Thy Saint-adorers count the Rosary:
Much is the VIRGIN teased to shrive them free
(Well do I ween the only virgin there)
From crimes as numerous as her beadsmen be;
Then to the crowded circus forth they fare:
Young, old, high, low, at once the same diversion share.

LXXII

The lists are oped, the spacious area cleared,   720
Thousands on thousands piled are seated round;
Long ere the first loud trumpet's note is heard,
Ne vacant space for lated wight is found:
Here Dons, Grandees, but chiefly Dames abound,
Skilled in the ogle of a roguish eye,
Yet ever well inclined to heal the wound;
None through their cold disdain are doomed to die,
As moon-struck bards complain, by Love's sad archery.

LXXIII

Hushed is the din of tongues—on gallant steeds,
With milk-white crest, gold spur, and light-poised lance,   730
Four cavaliers prepare for venturous deeds
And lowly-bending to the lists advance;
Rich are their scarfs, their chargers featly prance:
If in the dangerous game they shine to-day,
The crowd's loud shout and ladies' lovely glance,
Best prize of better acts! they bear away;
And all that kings or chiefs e'er gain their toils repay.

LXXIV

In costly sheen and gaudy cloak arrayed,
But all afoot, the light-limbed Matadore
Stands in the centre, eager to invade   740
The lord of lowing herds; but not before

The ground, with cautious tread, is traversed o'er,
Lest aught unseen should lurk to thwart his speed:
His arms a dart, he fights aloof, nor more
Can Man achieve without the friendly steed—
Alas! too oft condemned for him to bear and bleed.

LXXV

Thrice sounds the Clarion; lo! the signal falls,
The den expands, and Expectation mute
Gapes round the silent circle's peopled walls:
Bounds with one lashing spring the mighty brute,   750
And, wildly staring, spurns, with sounding foot,
The sand, nor blindly rushes on his foe:
Here, there, he points his threatening front, to suit
His first attack, wide-waving to and fro
His angry tail; red rolls his eye's dilated glow.

LXXVI

Sudden he stops—his eye is fixed—away—
Away, thou heedless boy! prepare the spear;
Now is thy time, to perish, or display
The skill that yet may check his mad career!
With well-timed croupe the nimble coursers veer;   760
On foams the Bull, but not unscathed he goes;
Streams from his flank the crimson torrent clear:
He flies, he wheels, distracted with his throes;
Dart follows dart—lance, lance—loud bellowings speak his woes.

LXXVII

Again he comes; nor dart nor lance avail,
Nor the wild plunging of the tortured horse;
Though Man and Man's avenging arms assail,
Vain are his weapons, vainer is his force.
One gallant steed is stretched a mangled corse;
Another, hideous sight! unseamed appears,   770
His gory chest unveils life's panting source;
Though death-struck, still his feeble frame he rears;
Staggering, but stemming all, his Lord unharmed he bears.

LXXVIII

Foiled, bleeding, breathless, furious to the last,
Full in the centre stands the Bull at bay,
'Mid wounds, and clinging darts, and lances brast,
And foes disabled in the brutal fray:
And now the Matadores around him play,
Shake the red cloak, and poise the ready brand:
Once more through all he bursts his thundering way—   780
Vain rage! the mantle quits the conynge hand,
Wraps his fierce eye—'tis past—he sinks upon the sand!

LXXIX

Where his vast neck just mingles with the spine,
Sheathed in his form the deadly weapon lies.
He stops—he starts—disdaining to decline:
Slowly he falls, amidst triumphant cries,
Without a groan, without a struggle dies.
The decorated car appears—on high
The corse is piled—sweet sight for vulgar eyes—
Four steeds that spurn the rein, as swift as shy,   790
Hurl the dark bulk along, scarce seen in dashing by.

LXXX

Such the ungentle sport that oft invites
The Spanish maid, and cheers the Spanish swain.
Nurtured in blood betimes, his heart delights
In vengeance, gloating on another's pain.
What private feuds the troubled village stain!
Though now one phalanxed host should meet the foe,
Enough, alas! in humble homes remain,
To mediate 'gainst friend the secret blow,
For some slight cause of wrath, whence Life's warm stream
          must flow.   800

LXXXI

But Jealousy has fled: his bars, his bolts,
His withered Centinel, Duenna sage!
And all whereat the generous soul revolts,

Which the stern dotard deemed he could encage,
Have passed to darkness with the vanished age.
Who late so free as Spanish girls were seen,
(Ere War uprose in his volcanic rage,)
With braided tresses bounding o'er the green,
While on the gay dance shone Night's lover-loving Queen?

LXXXII

Oh! many a time and oft, had Harold loved,   810
Or dreamed he loved, since Rapture is a dream;
But now his wayward bosom was unmoved,
For not yet had he drunk of Lethe's stream;
And lately had he learned with truth to deem
Love has no gift so grateful as his wings:
How fair, how young, how soft soe'er he seem,
Full from the fount of Joy's delicious springs
Some bitter o'er the flowers its bubbling venom flings.

LXXXIII

Yet to the beauteous form he was not blind,
Though now it moved him as it moves the wise;   820
Not that Philosophy on such a mind
E'er deigned to bend her chastely-awful eyes:
But Passion raves herself to rest, or flies;
And Vice, that digs her own voluptuous tomb,
Had buried long his hopes, no more to rise:
Pleasure's palled Victim! life-abhorring Gloom
Wrote on his faded brow curst Cain's unresting doom.

LXXXIV

Still he beheld, nor mingled with the throng;
But viewed them not with misanthropic hate:
Fain would he now have joined the dance, the song;   830
But who may smile that sinks beneath his fate?
Nought that he saw his sadness could abate:
Yet once he struggled 'gainst the Demon's sway,
And as in Beauty's bower he pensive sate,
Poured forth his unpremeditated lay,
To charms as fair as those that soothed his happier day.

To Inez

1

Nay, smile not at my sullen brow;
    Alas! I cannot smile again:
Yet Heaven avert that ever thou
    Shouldst weep, and haply weep in vain.   840

2

And dost thou ask what secret woe
    I bear, corroding Joy and Youth?
And wilt thou vainly seek to know
    A pang, ev'n thou must fail to soothe?

3

It is not love, it is not hate,
    Nor low Ambition's honours lost,
That bids me loathe my present state,
    And fly from all I prized the most:

4

It is that weariness which springs
    From all I meet, or hear, or see: 850
To me no pleasure Beauty brings;
    Thine eyes have scarce a charm for me.

5

It is that settled, ceaseless gloom
    The fabled Hebrew Wanderer bore;
That will not look beyond the tomb,
    But cannot hope for rest before.

6

What Exile from himself can flee?
    To zones though more and more remote,
Still, still pursues, where'er I be,
    The blight of Life—the Demon Thought.   860

7

Yet others rapt in pleasure seem,
    And taste of all that I forsake;

Oh! may they still of transport dream,
   And ne'er—at least like me—awake!

8

Through many a clime 'tis mine to go,
   With many a retrospection curst;
And all my solace is to know,
   Whate'er betides, I've known the worst.

9

What is that worst? Nay do not ask—
   In pity from the search forbear: 870
Smile on—nor venture to unmask
   Man's heart, and view the Hell that's there.
                                    January 25, 1810.

L X X X V

Adieu, fair Cadiz! yea, a long adieu!
Who may forget how well thy walls have stood?
When all were changing thou alone wert true,
First to be free and last to be subdued:
And if amidst a scene, a shock so rude,
Some native blood was seen thy streets to dye,
A traitor only fell beneath the feud:
Here all were noble, save Nobility;   880
None hugged a Conqueror's chain, save fallen Chivalry!

L X X X V I

Such be the sons of Spain, and strange her Fate!
They fight for Freedom who were never free,
A Kingless people for a nerveless state;
Her vassals combat when their Chieftains flee,
True to the veriest slaves of Treachery:
Fond of a land which gave them nought but life,
Pride points the path that leads to Liberty;
Back to the struggle, baffled in the strife,
War, war is still the cry, "War even to the knife!"   890

LXXXVII

Ye, who would more of Spain and Spaniards know,
Go, read whate'er is writ of bloodiest strife:
Whate'er keen Vengeance urged on foreign foe
Can act, is acting there against man's life:
From flashing scimitar to secret knife,
War mouldeth there each weapon to his need—
So may he guard the sister and the wife,
So may he make each curst oppressor bleed—
So may such foes deserve the most remorseless deed!

LXXXVIII

Flows there a tear of Pity for the dead?   900
Look o'er the ravage of the reeking plain;
Look on the hands with female slaughter red;
Then to the dogs resign the unburied slain,
Then to the vulture let each corse remain,
Albeit unworthy of the prey-bird's maw;
Let their bleached bones, and blood's unbleaching stain,
Long mark the battle-field with hideous awe:
Thus only may our sons conceive the scenes we saw!

LXXXIX

Nor yet, alas! the dreadful work is done;
Fresh legions pour adown the Pyrenees: 910
It deepens still, the work is scarce begun,
Nor mortal eye the distant end foresees.
Fall'n nations gaze on Spain; if freed, she frees
More than her fell Pizarros once enchained:
Strange retribution! now Columbia's ease.
Repairs the wrongs that Quito's sons sustained,
While o'er the parent clime prowls Murder unrestrained.

XC

Not all the blood at Talavera shed,
Not all the marvels of Barossa's fight,
Not Albuera lavish of the dead,   920
Have won for Spain her well asserted right.
When shall her Olive-Branch be free from blight?

When shall she breathe her from the blushing toil?
How many a doubtful day shall sink in night,
Ere the Frank robber turn him from his spoil,
And Freedom's stranger-tree grow native of the soil!

XCI

And thou, my friend!—since unavailing woe
Bursts from my heart, and mingles with the strain—
Had the sword laid thee with the mighty low,
Pride might forbid e'en Friendship to complain: 930
But thus unlaurelled to descend in vain,
By all forgotten, save the lonely breast,
And mix unbleeding with the boasted slain,
While Glory crowns so many a meaner crest!
What hadst thou done to sink so peacefully to rest?

XCII

Oh, known the earliest, and esteemed the most!
Dear to a heart where nought was left so dear!
Though to my hopeless days for ever lost,
In dreams deny me not to see thee here!
And Morn in secret shall renew the tear   940
Of Consciousness awaking to her woes,
And Fancy hover o'er thy bloodless bier,
Till my frail frame return to whence it rose,
And mourned and mourner lie united in repose.

XCIII

Here is one fytte of Harold's pilgrimage:
Ye who of him may further seek to know,
Shall find some tidings in a future page,
If he that rhymeth now may scribble moe.
Is this too much? stern Critic! say not so:
Patience! and ye shall hear what he beheld   950
In other lands, where he was doomed to go:
Lands that contain the monuments of Eld,
Ere Greece and Grecian arts by barbarous hands were quelled.

CANTO THE SECOND

I

Come, blue-eyed maid of Heaven!—but thou, alas!
Didst never yet one mortal song inspire—
Goddess of Wisdom! here thy temple was,
And is, despite of War and wasting fire,
And years, that bade thy worship to expire:
But worse than steel, and flame, and ages slow,
Is the dread sceptre and dominion dire
Of men who never felt the sacred glow
That thoughts of thee and thine on polished breasts bestow.

II

Ancient of days! august Athena! where,
Where are thy men of might? thy grand in soul?
Gone—glimmering through the dream of things that were:
First in the race that led to Glory's goal,
They won, and passed away—is this the whole?
A schoolboy's tale, the wonder of an hour!
The Warrior's weapon and the Sophist's stole
Are sought in vain, and o'er each mouldering tower,
Dim with the mist of years, gray flits the shade of power.

10

III

Son of the Morning, rise! approach you here!
Come—but molest not yon defenceless Urn: 20
Look on this spot—a Nation's sepulchre!
Abode of Gods, whose shrines no longer burn.
Even Gods must yield—Religions take their turn:
'Twas Jove's—'tis Mahomet's—and other Creeds
Will rise with other years, till Man shall learn
Vainly his incense soars, his victim bleeds;
Poor child of Doubt and Death, whose hope is built on reeds.

IV

Bound to the Earth, he lifts his eye to Heaven—
Is't not enough, Unhappy Thing! to know
Thou art? Is this a boon so kindly given,   30
That being, thou would'st be again, and go,
Thou know'st not, reck'st not to what region, so
On Earth no more, but mingled with the skies?
Still wilt thou dream on future Joy and Woe?
Regard and weigh yon dust before it flies:
That little urn saith more than thousand Homilies.

V

Or burst the vanished Hero's lofty mound;
Far on the solitary shore he sleeps:
He fell, and falling nations mourned around;
But now not one of saddening thousands weeps,   40
Nor warlike worshipper his vigil keeps
Where demi-gods appeared, as records tell.
Remove yon skull from out the scattered heaps:
Is that a Temple where a God may dwell?
Why ev'n the Worm at last disdains her shattered cell!

VI

Look on its broken arch, its ruined wall,
Its chambers desolate, and portals foul:
Yes, this was once Ambition's airy hall,
The Dome of Thought, the Palace of the Soul:
Behold through each lack-lustre, eyeless hole,   50

The gay recess of Wisdom and of Wit
And Passion's host, that never brooked control:
Can all Saint, Sage, or Sophist ever writ,
People this lonely tower, this tenement refit?

VII

Well didst thou speak, Athena's wisest son!
"All that we know is, nothing can be known."
Why should we shrink from what we cannot shun?
Each hath its pang, but feeble sufferers groan
With brain-born dreams of Evil all their own.
Pursue what Chance or Fate proclaimeth best—   60
Peace waits us on the shores of Acheron:
There no forced banquet claims the sated guest,
But Silence spreads the couch of ever welcome Rest.

VIII

Yet if, as holiest men have deemed, there be
A land of Souls beyond that sable shore,
To shame the Doctrine of the Sadducee
And Sophists, madly vain of dubious lore;
How sweet it were in concert to adore
With those who made our mortal labours light!
To hear each voice we feared to hear no more!   70
Behold each mighty shade revealed to sight,
The Bactrian, Samian sage, and all who taught the Right!

IX

There, Thou!—whose Love and Life together fled,
Have left me here to love and live in vain—
Twined with my heart, and can I deem thee dead
When busy Memory flashes on my brain?
Well—I will dream that we may meet again,
And woo the vision to my vacant breast:
If aught of young Remembrance then remain,
Be as it may Futurity's behest,   80
For me 'twere bliss enough to know thy spirit blest!

X

Here let me sit upon this massy stone,
The marble column's yet unshaken base;
Here, son of Saturn! was thy favourite throne:
Mightiest of many such! Hence let me trace
The latent grandeur of thy dwelling-place.
It may not be: nor ev'n can Fancy's eye
Restore what Time hath laboured to deface:
Yet these proud Pillars claim no passing sigh;
Unmoved the Moslem sits, the light Greek carols by.   90

XI

But who, of all the plunderers of yon Fane
On high—where Pallas lingered, loth to flee
The latest relic of her ancient reign—
The last, the worst, dull spoiler, who was he?
Blush, Caledonia! such thy son could be!
England! I joy no child he was of thine:
Thy free-born men should spare what once was free;
Yet they could violate each saddening shrine,
And bear these altars o'er the long-reluctant brine.

XII

But most the modern Pict's ignoble boast,   100
To rive what Goth, and Turk, and Time hath spared:
Cold as the crags upon his native coast,
His mind as barren and his heart as hard,
Is he whose head conceived, whose hand prepared,
Aught to displace Athena's poor remains:
Her Sons too weak the sacred shrine to guard,
Yet felt some portion of their Mother's pains,
And never knew, till then, the weight of Despot's chains.

XIII

What! shall it e'er be said by British tongue,
Albion was happy in Athena's tears?   110
Though in thy name the slaves her bosom wrung,
Tell not the deed to blushing Europe's ears;
The Ocean Queen, the free Britannia, bears

The last poor plunder from a bleeding land:
Yes, she whose generous aid her name endears,
Tore down those remnants with a Harpy's hand,
Which envious Eld forbore, and tyrants left to stand.

XIV

Where was thine Ægis, Pallas! that appalled
Stern Alaric and Havoc on their way?
Where Peleus' son? whom Hell in vain enthralled,   120
His shade from Hades upon that dread day
Bursting to light in terrible array!
What! could not Pluto spare the Chief once more,
To scare a second robber from his prey?
Idly he wandered on the Stygian shore,
Nor now preserved the walls he loved to shield before.

XV

Cold is the heart, fair Greece! that looks on Thee,
Nor feels as Lovers o'er the dust they loved;
Dull is the eye that will not weep to see
Thy walls defaced, thy mouldering shrine removed   130
By British hands, which it had best behoved
To guard those relics ne'er to be restored:—
Curst be the hour when from their isle they roved,
And once again thy hapless bosom gored,
And snatched thy shrinking Gods to Northern climes abhorred!

XVI

But where is Harold? shall I then forget
To urge the gloomy Wanderer o'er the wave?
Little recked he of all that Men regret;
No loved-one now in feigned lament could rave;
No friend the parting hand extended gave,   140
Ere the cold Stranger passed to other climes:
Hard is his heart whom charms may not enslave;
But Harold felt not as in other times,
And left without a sigh the land of War and Crimes.

XVII

He that has sailed upon the dark blue sea
Has viewed at times, I ween, a full fair sight,
When the fresh breeze is fair as breeze may be,
The white sail set, the gallant Frigate tight—
Masts, spires, and strand retiring to the right,
The glorious Main expanding o'er the bow,   150
The Convoy spread like wild swans in their flight,
The dullest sailer wearing bravely now—
So gaily curl the waves before each dashing prow.

XVIII

And oh, the little warlike world within!
The well-reeved guns, the netted canopy,
The hoarse command, the busy humming din,
When, at a word, the tops are manned on high:
Hark, to the Boatswain's call, the cheering cry!
While through the seaman's hand the tackle glides;
Or schoolboy Midshipman that, standing by,   160
Strains his shrill pipe as good or ill betides,
And well the docile crew that skilful Urchin guides.

XIX

White is the glassy deck, without a stain,
Where on the watch the staid Lieutenant walks:
Look on that part which sacred doth remain
For the lone Chieftain, who majestic stalks,
Silent and feared by all—not oft he talks
With aught beneath him, if he would preserve
That strict restraint, which broken, ever balks
Conquest and Fame: but Britons rarely swerve   170
From law, however stern, which tends their strength to nerve.

XX

Blow! swiftly blow, thou keel-compelling gale!
Till the broad Sun withdraws his lessening ray;
Then must the Pennant-bearer slacken sail,
That lagging barks may make their lazy way.
Ah! grievance sore, and listless dull delay,
To waste on sluggish hulks the sweetest breeze!

What leagues are lost, before the dawn of day,
Thus loitering pensive on the willing seas,
The flapping sail hauled down to halt for logs like these!   180

XXI

The Moon is up; by Heaven, a lovely eve!
Long streams of light o'er dancing waves expand;
Now lads on shore may sigh, and maids believe:
Such be our fate when we return to land!
Meantime some rude Arion's restless hand
Wakes the brisk harmony that sailors love;
A circle there of merry listeners stand
Or to some well-known measure featly move,
Thoughtless, as if on shore they still were free to rove.

XXII

Through Calpe's straits survey the steepy shore;   190
Europe and Afric on each other gaze!
Lands of the dark-eyed Maid and dusky Moor
Alike beheld beneath pale Hecate's blaze:
How softly on the Spanish shore she plays!
Disclosing rock, and slope, and forest brown,
Distinct, though darkening with her waning phase;
But Mauritania's giant-shadows frown,
From mountain-cliff to coast descending sombre down.

XXIII

'Tis night, when Meditation bid us feel
We once have loved, though Love is at an end: 200
The Heart, lone mourner of its baffled zeal,
Though friendless now, will dream it had a friend.
Who with the weight of years would wish to bend,
When Youth itself survives young Love and Joy?
Alas! when mingling souls forget to blend,
Death hath but little left him to destroy!
Ah! happy years! once more who would not be a boy?

XXIV

Thus bending o'er the vessel's laving side,
To gaze on Dian's wave-reflected sphere,

The Soul forgets her schemes of Hope and Pride,   210
And flies unconscious o'er each backward year;
None are so desolate but something dear,
Dearer than self, possesses or possessed
A thought, and claims the homage of a tear;
A flashing pang! of which the weary breast
Would still, albeit in vain, the heavy heart divest.

XXV

To sit on rocks—to muse o'er flood and fell—
To slowly trace the forest's shady scene,
Where things that own not Man's dominion dwell,
And mortal foot hath ne'er or rarely been;   220
To climb the trackless mountain all unseen,
With the wild flock that never needs a fold;
Alone o'er steeps and foaming falls to lean;
This is not Solitude—'tis but to hold
Converse with Nature's charms, and view her stores unrolled.

XXVI

But midst the crowd, the hum, the shock of men,
To hear, to see, to feel, and to possess,
And roam along, the World's tired denizen,
With none who bless us, none whom we can bless;
Minions of Splendour shrinking from distress!   230
None that, with kindred consciousness endued,
If we were not, would seem to smile the less,
Of all that flattered—followed—sought, and sued;
This is to be alone—This, This is Solitude!

XXVII

More blest the life of godly Eremite,
Such as on lonely Athos may be seen,
Watching at eve upon the Giant Height,
Which looks o'er waves so blue, skies so serene,
That he who there at such an hour hath been
Will wistful linger on that hallowed spot;   240
Then slowly tear him from the 'witching scene,

Sigh forth one wish that such had been his lot,
Then turn to hate a world he had almost forgot.

XXVIII

Pass we the long unvarying course, the track
Oft trod, that never leaves a trace behind;
Pass we the calm—the gale—the change—the tack,
And each well known caprice of wave and wind;
Pass we the joys and sorrows sailors find,
Cooped in their wingéd sea-girt citadel;
The foul—the fair—the contrary—the kind—   250
As breezes rise and fall and billows swell,
Till on some jocund morn—lo, Land! and All is well!

XXIX

But not in silence pass Calypso's isles,
The sister tenants of the middle deep;
There for the weary still a Haven smiles,
Though the fair Goddess long hath ceased to weep,
And o'er her cliffs a fruitless watch to keep
For him who dared prefer a mortal bride:
Here, too, his boy essayed the dreadful leap
Stern Mentor urged from high to yonder tide;   260
While thus of both bereft, the Nymph-Queen doubly sighed.

XXX

Her reign is past, her gentle glories gone:
But trust not this; too easy Youth, beware!
A mortal Sovereign holds her dangerous throne,
And thou may'st find a new Calypso there.
Sweet Florence! could another ever share
This wayward, loveless heart, it would be thine:
But checked by every tie, I may not dare
To cast a worthless offering at thy shrine,
Nor ask so dear a breast to feel one pang for *mine*.   270

XXXI

Thus Harold deemed, as on that Lady's eye
He looked, and met its beam without a thought,

Save Admiration glancing harmless by:
Love kept aloof, albeit not far remote,
Who knew his Votary often lost and caught,
But knew him as his Worshipper no more,
And ne'er again the Boy his bosom sought:
Since now he vainly urged him to adore,
Well deemed the little God his ancient sway was o'er.

XXXII

Fair Florence found, in sooth with some amaze,   280
One who, 'twas said, still sighed to all he saw,
Withstand, unmoved, the lustre of her gaze,
Which others hailed with real or mimic awe,
Their hope, their doom, their punishment, their law;
All that gay Beauty from her bondsmen claims:
And much she marvelled that a youth so raw
Nor felt, nor feigned at least, the oft-told flames,
Which, though sometimes they frown, yet rarely anger dames.

XXXIII

Little knew she that seeming marble heart,
Now masked in silence or withheld by Pride,   290
Was not unskilful in the spoiler's art,
And spread its snares licentious far and wide;
Nor from the base pursuit had turned aside,
As long as aught was worthy to pursue:
But Harold on such arts no more relied;
And had he doted on those eyes so blue,
Yet never would he join the lover's whining crew.

XXXIV

Not much he kens, I ween, of Woman's breast,
Who thinks that wanton thing is won by sighs;
What careth she for hearts when once possessed?   300
Do proper homage to thine Idol's eyes,
But not too humbly—or she will despise
Thee and thy suit, though told in moving tropes:
Disguise ev'n tenderness, if thou art wise;

Brisk Confidence still best with woman copes:
Pique her and soothe in turn—soon Passion crowns thy hopes.

XXXV

'Tis an old lesson—Time approves it true,
And those who know it best, deplore it most;
When all is won that all desire to woo,
The paltry prize is hardly worth the cost: 310
Youth wasted—Minds degraded—Honour lost—
These are thy fruits, successful Passion! these!
If, kindly cruel, early Hope is crost,
Still to the last it rankles, a disease,
Not to be cured when Love itself forgets to please.

XXXVI

Away! nor let me loiter in my song,
For we have many a mountain-path to tread,
And many a varied shore to sail along,
By pensive Sadness, not by Fiction, led—
Climes, fair withal as ever mortal head   320
Imagined in its little schemes of thought,
Or e'er in new Utopias were ared,
To teach Man what he might be, or he ought—
If that corrupted thing could ever such be taught.

XXXVII

Dear Nature is the kindest mother still!
Though always changing, in her aspect mild;
From her bare bosom let me take my fill,
Her never-weaned, though not her favoured child.
Oh! she is fairest in her features wild,
Where nothing polished dares pollute her path: 330
To me by day or night she ever smiled,
Though I have marked her when none other hath,
And sought her more and more, and loved her best in wrath.

XXXVIII

Land of Albania! where Iskander rose,
Theme of the young, and beacon of the wise,

And he his namesake, whose oft-baffled foes
Shrunk from his deeds of chivalrous emprize:
Land of Albania! let me bend mine eyes
On thee, thou rugged Nurse of savage men!
The Cross descends, thy Minarets arise,   340
And the pale Crescent sparkles in the glen,
Through many a cypress-grove within each city's ken.

XXXIX

Childe Harold sailed, and passed the barren spot,
Where sad Penelope o'erlooked the wave;
And onward viewed the mount, not yet forgot,
The Lover's refuge, and the Lesbian's grave.
Dark Sappho! could not Verse immortal save
That breast imbued with such immortal fire?
Could she not live who life eternal gave?
If life eternal may await the lyre,   350
That only Heaven to which Earth's children may aspire.

XL

'Twas on a Grecian autumn's gentle eve
Childe Harold hailed Leucadia's cape afar;
A spot he longed to see, nor cared to leave:
Oft did he mark the scenes of vanished war,
Actium—Lepanto—fatal Trafalgar;
Mark them unmoved, for he would not delight
(Born beneath some remote inglorious star)
In themes of bloody fray, or gallant fight,
But loathed the bravo's trade, and laughed at martial wight.   360

XLI

But when he saw the Evening star above
Leucadia's far-projecting rock of woe,
And hailed the last resort of fruitless love,
He felt, or deemed he felt, no common glow:
And as the stately vessel glided slow
Beneath the shadow of that ancient mount,
He watched the billows' melancholy flow,
And, sunk albeit in thought as he was wont,
More placid seemed his eye, and smooth his pallid front.

XLII

Morn dawns; and with it stern Albania's hills,   370
Dark Suli's rocks, and Pindus' inland peak,
Robed half in mist, bedewed with snowy rills,
Arrayed in many a dun and purple streak,
Arise; and, as the clouds along them break,
Disclose the dwelling of the mountaineer:
Here roams the wolf—the eagle whets his beak—
Birds—beasts of prey—and wilder men appear,
And gathering storms around convulse the closing year.

XLIII

Now Harold felt himself at length alone,
And bade to Christian tongues a long adieu;   380
Now he adventured on a shore unknown,
Which all admire, but many dread to view:
His breast was armed 'gainst fate, his wants were few;
Peril he sought not, but ne'er shrank to meet:
The scene was savage, but the scene was new;
This made the ceaseless toil of travel sweet,
Beat back keen Winter's blast, and welcomed Summer's heat.

XLIV

Here the red Cross, for still the Cross is here,
Though sadly scoffed at by the circumcised,
Forgets that Pride to pampered priesthood dear,—   390
Churchman and Votary alike despised.
Foul Superstition! howsoe'er disguised,
Idol—Saint—Virgin—Prophet—Crescent—Cross—
For whatsoever symbol thou art prized,
Thou sacerdotal gain, but general loss!
Who from true Worship's gold can separate thy dross?

XLV

Ambracia's gulf behold, where once was lost
A world for Woman, lovely, harmless thing!
In yonder rippling bay, their naval host
Did many a Roman chief and Asian King   400
To doubtful conflict, certain slaughter bring:

Look where the second Cæsar's trophies rose!
Now, like the hands that reared them, withering:
Imperial Anarchs, doubling human woes!
GOD! was thy globe ordained for such to win and lose?

XLVI

From the dark barriers of that rugged clime,
Ev'n to the centre of Illyria's vales,
Childe Harold passed o'er many a mount sublime,
Through lands scarce noticed in historic tales:
Yet in famed Attica such lovely dales   410
Are rarely seen; nor can fair Tempe boast
A charm they know not; loved Parnassus fails,
Though classic ground and consecrated most,
To match some spots that lurk within this lowering coast.

XLVII

He passed bleak Pindus, Acherusia's lake,
And left the primal city of the land,
And onwards did his further journey take
To greet Albania's Chief, whose dread command
Is lawless law; for with a bloody hand
He sways a nation, turbulent and bold: 420
Yet here and there some daring mountain-band
Disdain his power, and from their rocky hold
Hurl their defiance far, nor yield, unless to gold.

XLVIII

Monastic Zitza! from thy shady brow,
Thou small, but favoured spot of holy ground!
Where'er we gaze—around—above—below,—
What rainbow tints, what magic charms are found!
Rock, river, forest, mountain, all abound,
And bluest skies that harmonise the whole:
Beneath, the distant Torrent's rushing sound   430
Tells where the volumed Cataract doth roll
Between those hanging rocks, that shock yet please the soul.

XLIX

Amidst the grove that crowns yon tufted hill,
Which, were it not for many a mountain nigh
Rising in lofty ranks and loftier still,
Might well itself be deemed of dignity,
The Convent's white walls glisten fair on high:
Here dwells the caloyer, nor rude is he,
Nor niggard of his cheer; the passer by
Is welcome still; nor heedless will he flee   440
From hence, if he delight kind Nature's sheen to see.

L

Here in the sultriest season let him rest,
Fresh is the green beneath those agéd trees;
Here winds of gentlest wing will fan his breast,
From Heaven itself he may inhale the breeze:
The plain is far beneath—oh! let him seize
Pure pleasure while he can; the scorching ray
Here pierceth not, impregnate with disease:
Then let his length the loitering pilgrim lay,
And gaze, untired, the Morn—the Noon—the Eve away.   450

L I

Dusky and huge, enlarging on the sight,
Nature's volcanic Amphitheatre,
Chimæra's Alps extend from left to right:
Beneath, a living valley seems to stir;
Flocks play, trees wave, streams flow—the mountain-fir
Nodding above; behold black Acheron!
Once consecrated to the sepulchre.
Pluto! if this be Hell I look upon,
Close shamed Elysium's gate—my shade shall seek for none.

L I I

Ne city's towers pollute the lovely view;   460
Unseen is Yanina, though not remote,
Veiled by the screen of hills: here men are few,
Scanty the hamlet, rare the lonely cot:
But, peering down each precipice, the goat

Browseth; and, pensive o'er his scattered flock,
The little shepherd in his white capote
Doth lean his boyish form along the rock,
Or in his cave awaits the Tempest's short-lived shock.

LIII

Oh! where, Dodona! is thine agéd Grove,
Prophetic Fount, and Oracle divine?   470
What valley echoed the response of Jove?
What trace remaineth of the Thunderer's shrine?
All, all forgotten—and shall Man repine
That his frail bonds to fleeting life are broke?
Cease, Fool! the fate of Gods may well be thine:
Wouldst thou survive the marble or the oak?
When nations, tongues, and worlds must sink beneath the stroke!

LIV

Epirus' bounds recede, and mountains fail;
Tired of up-gazing still, the wearied eye
Reposes gladly on as smooth a vale   480
As ever Spring yclad in glassy dye:
Ev'n on a plain no humble beauties lie,
Where some bold river breaks the long expanse,
And woods along the banks are waving high,
Whose shadows in the glassy waters dance,
Or with the moonbeam sleep in Midnight's solemn trance.

LV

The Sun had sunk behind vast Tomerit,
And Laos wide and fierce came roaring by;
The shades of wonted night were gathering yet,
When, down the steep banks winding warily,   490
Childe Harold saw, like meteors in the sky,
The glittering minarets of Tepalen,
Whose walls o'erlook the stream; and drawing nigh,
He heard the busy hum of warrior-men
Swelling the breeze that sighed along the lengthening glen.

LVI

He passed the sacred Haram's silent tower,
And underneath the wide o'erarching gate
Surveyed the dwelling of this Chief of power,
Where all around proclaimed his high estate.
Amidst no common pomp the Despot sate,   500
While busy preparation shook the court,
Slaves, eunuchs, soldiers, guests, and santons wait:—
Within, a palace, and without, a fort—
Here men of every clime appear to make resort.

LVII

Richly caparisoned, a ready row
Of arméd horse, and many a warlike store,
Circled the wide-extending court below;
Above, strange groups adorned the corridore;
And oft-times through the area's echoing door
Some high-capped Tartar spurred his steed away: 510
The Turk—the Greek—the Albanian—and the Moor,
Here mingled in their many-hued array,
While the deep war-drum's sound announced the close of day.

LVIII

The wild Albanian kirtled to his knee,
With shawl-girt head and ornamented gun,
And gold-embroidered garments, fair to see;
The crimson-scarféd men of Macedon;
The Delhi with his cap of terror on,
And crooked glaive—the lively, supple Greek,
And swarthy Nubia's mutilated son;   520
The bearded Turk that rarely deigns to speak,
Master of all around, too potent to be meek,

LIX

Are mixed conspicuous: some recline in groups,
Scanning the motley scene that varies round;
There some grave Moslem to devotion stoops,
And some that smoke, and some that play, are found;
Here the Albanian proudly treads the ground;

Half-whispering there the Greek is heard to prate;
Hark! from the Mosque the nightly solemn sound,
The Muezzin's call doth shake the minaret,   530
"There is no god but God!—to prayer—lo! God is great!"

L X

Just at this season Ramazani's fast
Through the long day its penance did maintain:
But when the lingering twilight hour was past,
Revel and feats assumed the rule again:
Now all was bustle, and the menial train
Prepared and spread the plenteous board within;
The vacant Gallery now seemed made in vain,
But from the chambers came the mingling din,
As page and slave anon were passing out and in.   540

L X I

Here woman's voice is never heard; apart,
And scarce permitted—guarded, veiled—to move,
She yields to one her person and her heart,
Tamed to her cage, nor feels a wish to rove:
For, not unhappy in her Master's love,
And joyful in a mother's gentlest cares,
Blest cares! all other feelings far above!
Herself more sweetly rears the babe she bears,
Who never quits the breast—no meaner passion shares.

L X I I

In marble-paved pavilion, where a spring   550
Of living water from the centre rose,
Whose bubbling did a genial freshness fling,
And soft voluptuous couches breathed repose,
ALI reclined, a man of war and woes:
Yet in his lineaments ye cannot trace,
While Gentleness her milder radiance throws
Along that agéd venerable face,
The deeds that lurk beneath, and stain him with disgrace.

LXIII

It is not that yon hoary lengthening beard
Ill suits the passions which belong to Youth;   560
Love conquers Age—so Hafiz hath averred,
So sings the Teian, and he sings in sooth—
But crimes that scorn the tender voice of ruth,
Beseeming all men ill, but most the man
In years, have marked him with a tiger's tooth;
Blood follows blood, and, through their mortal span,
In bloodier acts conclude those who with blood began.

LXIV

'Mid many things most new to ear and eye
The Pilgrim rested here his weary feet,
And gazed around on Moslem luxury,   570
Till quickly wearied with that spacious seat
Of Wealth and Wantonness, the choice retreat
Of sated Grandeur from the city's noise:
And were it humbler it in sooth were sweet;
But Peace abhorreth artificial joys,
And Pleasure, leagued with Pomp, the zest of both destroys.

LXV

Fierce are Albania's children, yet they lack
Not virtues, were those virtues more mature.
Where is the foe that ever saw their back?
Who can so well the toil of War endure?   580
Their native fastnesses not more secure
Than they in doubtful time of troublous need:
Their wrath how deadly! but their friendship sure,
When Gratitude or Valour bids them bleed—
Unshaken rushing on where'er their Chief may lead.

LXVI

Childe Harold saw them in their Chieftain's tower
Thronging to War in splendour and success;
And after viewed them, when, within their power,
Himself awhile the victim of distress;
That saddening hour when bad men hotlier press: 590

But these did shelter him beneath their roof,
When less barbarians would have cheered him less,
And fellow-countrymen have stood aloof—
In aught that tries the heart, how few withstand the proof!

LXVII

It chanced that adverse winds once drove his bark
Full on the coast of Suli's shaggy shore,
When all around was desolate and dark;
To land was perilous, to sojourn more;
Yet for awhile the mariners forbore,
Dubious to trust where Treachery might lurk: 600
At length they ventured forth, though doubting sore
That those who loathe alike the Frank and Turk
Might once again renew their ancient butcher work.

LXVIII

Vain fear! the Suliotes stretched the welcome hand,
Led them o'er rocks and past the dangerous swamp,
Kinder than polished slaves though not so bland,
And piled the hearth, and wrung their garments damp,
And filled the bowl, and trimmed the cheerful lamp,
And spread their fare—though homely, all they had:
Such conduct bears Philanthropy's rare stamp: 610
To rest the weary and to soothe the sad,
Doth lesson happier men, and shames at least the bad.

LXIX

It came to pass, that when he did address
Himself to quit at length this mountain-land,
Combined marauders half-way barred egress,
And wasted far and near with glaive and brand;
And therefore did he take a trusty band
To traverse Acarnania's forest wide,
In war well-seasoned, and with labours tanned,
Till he did greet white Achelous' tide,   620
And from his further bank Ætolia's wolds espied.

LXX

Where lone Utraikey forms its circling cove,
And weary waves retire to gleam at rest,
How brown the foliage of the green hill's grove,
Nodding at midnight o'er the calm bay's breast,
As winds come lightly whispering from the West,
Kissing, not ruffling, the blue deep's serene:—
Here Harold was received a welcome guest;
Nor did he pass unmoved the gentle scene,
For many a joy could he from Night's soft presence glean.   630

LXXI

On the smooth shore the night-fires brightly blazed,
The feast was done, the red wine circling fast,
And he that unawares had there ygazed
With gaping wonderment had stared aghast;
For ere night's midmost, stillest hour was past,
The native revels of the troop began;
Each Palikar his sabre from him cast,
And bounding hand in hand, man linked to man,
Yelling their uncouth dirge, long daunced the kirtled clan.

LXXII

Childe Harold at a little distance stood   640
And viewed, but not displeased, the revelrie
Nor hated harmless mirth, however rude:
In sooth, it was no vulgar sight to see
Their barbarous, yet their not indecent, glee;
And, as the flames along their faces gleamed,
Their gestures nimble, dark eyes flashing free,
The long wild locks that to their girdles streamed,
While thus in concert they this lay half sang, half screamed:—

1

Tambourgi! Tambourgi! thy 'larum afar
Gives hope to the valiant, and promise of war;   650
All the Sons of the mountains arise at the note,
Chimariot, Illyrian, and dark Suliote!

2

Oh! who is more brave than a dark Suliote,
In his snowy camese and his shaggy capote?
To the wolf and the vulture he leaves his wild flock,
And descends to the plain like the stream from the rock.

3

Shall the sons of Chimari, who never forgive
The fault of a friend, bid an enemy live?
Let those guns so unerring such vengeance forgo?
What mark is so fair as the breast of a foe?   660

4

Macedonia sends forth her invincible race;
For a time they abandon the cave and the chase;
But those scarfs of blood-red shall be redder, before
The sabre is sheathed and the battle is o'er.

5

Then the Pirates of Parga that dwell by the waves,
And teach the pale Franks what it is to be slaves,
Shall leave on the beach the long galley and oar,
And track to his covert the captive on shore.

6

I ask not the pleasures that riches supply,
My sabre shall win what the feeble must buy;   670
Shall win the young bride with her long flowing hair,
And many a maid from her mother shall tear.

7

I love the fair face of the maid in her youth,
Her caresses shall lull me, her music shall soothe;
Let her bring from the chamber her many-toned lyre,
And sing us a song on the fall of her Sire.

8

Remember the moment when Previsa fell,
The shrieks of the conquered, the conquerors' yell;
The roofs that we fired, and the plunder we shared,
The wealthy we slaughtered, the lovely we spared.   680

9

I talk not of mercy, I talk not of fear;
He neither must know who would serve the Vizier:
Since the days of our Prophet the Crescent ne'er saw
A chief ever glorious like Ali Pashaw.

1 0

Dark Muchtar his son to the Danube is sped,
Let the yellow-haired Giaours view his horse-tail with dread;
When his Delhis come dashing in blood o'er the banks,
How few shall escape from the Muscovite ranks!

1 1

Selictar! unsheathe then our chief's Scimitār;
Tambourgi! thy 'larum gives promise of War.   690
Ye Mountains, that see us descend to the shore,
Shall view us as Victors, or view us no more!

LXXIII

Fair Greece! sad relic of departed Worth!
Immortal, though no more; though fallen, great!
Who now shall lead thy scattered children forth,
And long accustomed bondage uncreate?
Not such thy sons who whilome did await,
The hopeless warriors of a willing doom,
In bleak Thermopylæ's sepulchral strait—
Oh! who that gallant spirit shall resume,   700
Leap from Eurotas' banks, and call thee from the tomb?

LXXIV

Spirit of Freedom! when on Phyle's brow
Thou sat'st with Thrasybulus and his train,
Couldst thou forebode the dismal hour which now
Dims the green beauties of thine Attic plain?
Not thirty tyrants now enforce the chain,
But every carle can lord it o'er thy land;
Nor rise thy sons, but idly rail in vain,
Trembling beneath the scourge of Turkish hand,
From birth till death enslaved—in word, in deed, unmanned.   710

LXXV

In all save form alone, how changed! and who
That marks the fire still sparkling in each eye,
Who but would deem their bosoms burned anew
With thy unquenchéd beam, lost Liberty!
And many dream withal the hour is nigh
That gives them back their fathers' heritage:
For foreign arms and aid they fondly sigh,
Nor solely dare encounter hostile rage,
Or tear their name defiled from Slavery's mournful page.

LXXVI

Hereditary Bondsmen! know ye not   720
Who would be free *themselves* must strike the blow?
By their right arms the conquest must be wrought?
Will Gaul or Muscovite redress ye? No!
True—they may lay your proud despoilers low,
But not for you will Freedom's Altars flame.
Shades of the Helots! triumph o'er your foe!
Greece! change thy lords, thy state is still the same;
Thy glorious day is o'er, but not thine years of shame.

LXXVII

The city won for Allah from the Giaour
The Giaour from Othman's race again may wrest;   730
And the Serai's impenetrable tower
Receive the fiery Frank, her former guest;
Or Wahab's rebel brood who dared divest
The Prophet's tomb of all its pious spoil,
May wind their path of blood along the West;
But ne'er will Freedom seek this fated soil,
But slave succeed to slave through years of endless toil.

LXXVIII

Yet mark their mirth—ere Lenten days begin,
That penance which their holy rites prepare
To shrive from Man his weight of mortal sin,   740
By daily abstinence and nightly prayer;

But ere his sackcloth garb Repentance wear,
Some days of joyaunce are decreed to all,
To take of pleasaunce each his secret share,
In motley robe to dance at masking ball,
And join the mimic train of merry Carnival.

LXXIX

And whose more rife with merriment than thine,
Oh Stamboul! once the Empress of their reign?
Though turbans now pollute Sophia's shrine,
And Greece her very altars eyes in vain: 750
(Alas! her woes will still pervade my strain!)
Gay were her minstrels once, for free her throng,
All felt the common joy they now must feign,
Nor oft I've seen such sight, nor heard such song,
As wooed the eye, and thrilled the Bosphorus along.

LXXX

Loud was the lightsome tumult on the shore;
Oft Music changed, but never ceased her tone,
And timely echoed back the measured oar,
And rippling waters made a pleasant moan:
The Queen of tides on high consenting shone,   760
And when a transient breeze swept o'er the wave,
'Twas, as if darting from her heavenly throne,
A brighter glance her form reflected gave,
Till sparkling billows seemed to light the banks they lave.

LXXXI

Glanced many a light Caique along the foam,
Danced on the shore the daughters of the land,
No thought had man or maid of rest or home,
While many a languid eye and thrilling hand
Exchanged the look few bosoms may withstand,
Or gently prest, returned the pressure still: 770
Oh Love! young Love! bound in thy rosy band,
Let sage or cynic prattle as he will,
These hours, and only these, redeem Life's years of ill!

LXXXII

But, midst the throng in merry masquerade,
Lurk there no hearts that throb with secret pain,
Even through the closest searment half betrayed?
To such the gentle murmurs of the main
Seem to re-echo all they mourn in vain;
To such the gladness of the gamesome crowd
Is source of wayward thought and stern disdain: 780
How do they loathe the laughter idly loud,
And long to change the robe of revel for the shroud!

LXXXIII

This must he feel, the true-born son of Greece,
If Greece one true-born patriot still can boast:
Not such as prate of War, but skulk in Peace,
The bondsman's peace, who sighs for all he lost,
Yet with smooth smile his Tyrant can accost,
And wield the slavish sickle, not the sword:
Ah! Greece! they love thee least who owe thee most—
Their birth, their blood, and that sublime record   790
Of hero Sires, who shame thy now degenerate horde!

LXXXIV

When riseth Lacedemon's Hardihood,
When Thebes Epaminondas rears again,
When Athens' children are with hearts endued,
When Grecian mothers shall give birth to men,
Then may'st thou be restored; but not till then.
A thousand years scarce serve to form a state;
An hour may lay it in the dust: and when
Can Man its shattered splendour renovate,
Recall its virtues back, and vanquish Time and Fate?   800

LXXXV

And yet how lovely in thine age of woe,
Land of lost Gods and godlike men, art thou!
Thy vales of evergreen, thy hills of snow,
Proclaim thee Nature's varied favourite now:

Thy fanes, thy temples to thy surface bow,
Commingling slowly with heroic earth,
Broke by the share of every rustic plough:
So perish monuments of mortal birth,
So perish all in turn, save well-recorded *Worth:*

LXXXVI

Save where some solitary column mourns   810
Above its prostrate brethren of the cave;
Save where Tritonia's airy shrine adorns
Colonna's cliff, and gleams along the wave;
Save o'er some warrior's half-forgotten grave,
Where the gray stones and unmolested grass
Ages, but not Oblivion, feebly brave;
While strangers, only, not regardless pass,
Lingering like me, perchance, to gaze, and sigh "Alas!"

LXXXVII

Yet are thy skies as blue, thy crags as wild;
Sweet are thy groves, and verdant are thy fields,   820
Thine olive ripe as when Minerva smiled,
And still his honied wealth Hymettus yields;
There the blithe Bee his fragrant fortress builds,
The free-born wanderer of thy mountain-air;
Apollo still thy long, long summer gilds,
Still in his beam Mendeli's marbles glare:
Art, Glory, Freedom fail—but Nature still is fair.

LXXXVIII

Where'er we tread 'tis haunted, holy ground;
No earth of thine is lost in vulgar mould,
But one vast realm of Wonder spreads around,   830
And all the Muse's tales seem truly told,
Till the sense aches with gazing to behold
The scenes our earliest dreams have dwelt upon;
Each hill and dale, each deepening glen and wold
Defies the power which crushed thy temples gone:
Age shakes Athena's tower, but spares gray Marathon.

LXXXIX

The Sun, the soil—but not the slave, the same;
Unchanged in all except its foreign Lord—
Preserves alike its bounds and boundless fame
The Battle-field, where Persia's victim horde   840
First bowed beneath the brunt of Hellas' sword,
As on the morn to distant Glory dear,
When Marathon became a magic word;
Which uttered, to the hearer's eye appear
The camp, the host, the fight, the Conqueror's career,

XC

The flying Mede, his shaftless broken bow—
The fiery Greek, his red pursuing spear;
Mountains above—Earth's, Ocean's plain below—
Death in the front, Destruction in the rear!
Such was the scene—what now remaineth here?   850
What sacred Trophy marks the hallowed ground,
Recording Freedom's smile and Asia's tear?
The rifled urn, the violated mound,
The dust thy courser's hoof, rude stranger! spurns around.

XCI

Yet to the remnants of thy Splendour past
Shall pilgrims, pensive, but unwearied, throng;
Long shall the voyager, with th' Ionian blast,
Hail the bright clime of Battle and of Song:
Long shall thine annals and immortal tongue
Fill with thy fame the youth of many a shore;   860
Boast of the agéd! lesson of the young!
Which Sages venerate and Bards adore,
As Pallas and the Muse unveil their awful lore.

XCII

The parted bosom clings to wonted home,
If aught that's kindred cheer the welcome hearth;
He that is lonely—hither let him roam,
And gaze complacent on congenial earth.

Greece is no lightsome land of social mirth:
But he whom Sadness sootheth may abide,
And scarce regret the region of his birth,   870
When wandering slow by Delphi's sacred side,
Or gazing o'er the plains where Greek and Persian died.

XCIII

Let such approach this consecrated Land,
And pass in peace along the magic waste;
But spare its relics—let no busy hand
Deface the scenes, already how defaced!
Not for such purpose were these altars placed:
Revere the remnants Nations once revered:
So may our Country's name be undisgraced,
So may'st thou prosper where thy youth was reared,   880
By every honest joy of Love and Life endeared!

XCIV

For thee, who thus in too protracted song
Hath soothed thine Idlesse with inglorious lays,
Soon shall thy voice be lost amid the throng
Of louder Minstrels in these later days:
To such resign the strife for fading Bays—
Ill may such contest now the spirit move
Which heeds nor keen Reproach nor partial Praise,
Since cold each kinder heart that might approve—
And none are left to please when none are left to love.   890

XCV

Thou too art gone, thou loved and lovely one!
Whom Youth and Youth's affections bound to me;
Who did for me what none beside have done,
Nor shrank from one albeit unworthy thee.
What is my Being! thou hast ceased to be!
Nor staid to welcome here thy wanderer home,
Who mourns o'er hours which we no more shall see—
Would they had never been, or were to come!
Would he had ne'er returned to find fresh cause to roam!

XCVI

Oh! ever loving, lovely, and beloved!   900
How selfish Sorrow ponders on the past,
And clings to thoughts now better far removed!
But Time shall tear thy shadow from me last.
All thou couldst have of mine, stern Death! thou hast;
The Parent, Friend, and now the more than friend:
Ne'er yet for one thine arrows flew so fast,
And grief with grief continuing still to blend,
Hath snatched the little joy that Life had yet to lend.

XCVII

Then must I plunge again into the crowd,
And follow all that Peace disdains to seek?   910
Where Revel calls, and Laughter, vainly loud,
False to the heart, distorts the hollow cheek,
To leave the flagging spirit doubly weak;
Still o'er the features, which perforce they cheer,
To feign the pleasure or conceal the pique:
Smiles form the channel of a future tear,
Or raise the writhing lip with ill-dissembled sneer.

XCVIII

What is the worst of woes that wait on Age?
What stamps the wrinkle deeper on the brow?
To view each loved one blotted from Life's page,   920
And be alone on earth, as I am now:
Before the Chastener humbly let me bow,
O'er Hearts divided and o'er Hopes destroyed:
Roll on, vain days! full reckless may ye flow,
Since Time hath reft whate'er my soul enjoyed,
And with the ills of Eld mine earlier years alloyed.

CANTO THE THIRD

"Afin que cette application vous forçât à penser à autre chose. Il n'y a en vérité de remède que celui-là et le temps."
—*Lettres du Roi de Prusse et de M. D'Alembert.* [*September 7, 1776.*]

I

Is thy face like thy mother's, my fair child!
Ada! sole daughter of my house and heart?
When last I saw thy young blue eyes they smiled,
And then we parted,—not as now we part,
But with a hope.—
                              Awaking with a start,
The waters heave around me; and on high
The winds lift up their voices: I depart,
Whither I know not; but the hour's gone by,
When Albion's lessening shores could grieve or glad mine eye.

II

Once more upon the waters! yet once more!   10
And the waves bound beneath me as a steed
That knows his rider. Welcome to their roar!
Swift be their guidance, wheresoe'er it lead!
Though the strained mast should quiver as a reed,
And the rent canvass fluttering strew the gale,
Still must I on; for I am as a weed,
Flung from the rock, on Ocean's foam, to sail
Where'er the surge may sweep, the tempest's breath prevail.

III

In my youth's summer I did sing of One,
The wandering outlaw of his own dark mind;   20
Again I seize the theme, then but begun,
And bear it with me, as the rushing wind
Bears the cloud onwards: in that Tale I find
The furrows of long thought, and dried-up tears,
Which, ebbing, leave a sterile track behind,
O'er which all heavily the journeying years
Plod the last sands of life,—where not a flower appears.

IV

Since my young days of passion—joy or pain—
Perchance my heart and harp have lost a string—
And both may jar: it may be that in vain   30
I would essay, as I have sung, to sing:
Yet, though a dreary strain, to this I cling;
So that it wean me from the weary dream
Of selfish grief or gladness—so it fling
Forgetfulness around me—it shall seem
To me, though to none else, a not ungrateful theme.

V

He, who grown agéd in this world of woe,
In deeds, not years, piercing the depths of life,
So that no wonder waits him—nor below
Can Love or Sorrow, Fame, Ambition, Strife,   40
Cut to his heart again with the keen knife
Of silent, sharp endurance—he can tell
Why Thought seeks refuge in lone caves, yet rife
With airy images, and shapes which dwell
Still unimpaired, though old, in the Soul's haunted cell.

VI

'Tis to create, and in creating live
A being more intense, that we endow
With form our fancy, gaining as we give
The life we image, even as I do now—
What am I? Nothing: but not so art thou,   50
Soul of my thought! with whom I traverse earth,

Invisible but gazing, as I glow
Mixed with thy spirit, blended with thy birth,
And feeling still with thee in my crushed feelings' dearth.

VII

Yet must I think less wildly:—I *have* thought
Too long and darkly, till my brain became,
In its own eddy boiling and o'erwrought,
A whirling gulf of phantasy and flame:
And thus, untaught in youth my heart to tame,
My springs of life were poisoned. 'Tis too late!   60
Yet am I changed; though still enough the same
In strength to bear what Time can not abate,
And feed on bitter fruits without accusing Fate.

VIII

Something too much of this:—but now 'tis past,
And the spell closes with its silent seal:
Long absent HAROLD re-appears at last—
He of the breast which fain no more would feel,
Wrung with the wounds which kill not, but ne'er heal;
Yet Time, who changes all, had altered him
In soul and aspect as in age: years steal   70
Fire from the mind as vigour from the limb;
And Life's enchanted cup but sparkles near the brim.

IX

His had been quaffed too quickly, and he found
The dregs were wormwood; but he filled again,
And from a purer fount, on holier ground,
And deemed its spring perpetual—but in vain!
Still round him clung invisibly a chain
Which galled for ever, fettering though unseen,
And heavy though it clanked not; worn with pain,
Which pined although it spoke not, and grew keen,   80
Entering with every step he took through many a scene.

X

Secure in guarded coldness, he had mixed
Again in fancied safety with his kind,

And deemed his spirit now so firmly fixed
And sheathed with an invulnerable mind,
That, if no joy, no sorrow lurked behind;
And he, as one, might 'midst the many stand
Unheeded, searching through the crowd to find
Fit speculation—such as in strange land
He found in wonder-works of God and Nature's hand.   90

XI

But who can view the ripened rose, nor seek
To wear it? who can curiously behold
The smoothness and the sheen of Beauty's cheek,
Nor feel the heart can never all grow old?
Who can contemplate Fame through clouds unfold
The star which rises o'er her steep, nor climb?
Harold, once more within the vortex, rolled
On with the giddy circle, chasing Time,
Yet with a nobler aim than in his Youth's fond prime.

XII

But soon he knew himself the most unfit   100
Of men to herd with Man, with whom he held
Little in common; untaught to submit
His thoughts to others, though his soul was quelled
In youth by his own thoughts; still uncompelled,
He would not yield dominion of his mind
To Spirits against whom his own rebelled,
Proud though in desolation—which could find
A life within itself, to breathe without mankind.

XIII

Where rose the mountains, there to him were friends;
Where roll'd the ocean, thereon was his home;   110
Where a blue sky, and glowing clime, extends,
He had the passion and the power to roam;
The desert, forest, cavern, breaker's foam,
Were unto him companionship; they spake
A mutual language, clearer than the tome
Of his land's tongue, which he would oft forsake
For Nature's pages glassed by sunbeams on the lake.

XIV

Like the Chaldean, he could watch the stars,
Till he had peopled them with beings bright
As their own beams; and earth, and earthborn jars,   120
And human frailties, were forgotten quite:
Could he have kept his spirit to that flight
He had been happy; but this clay will sink
Its spark immortal, envying it the light
To which it mounts, as if to break the link
That keeps us from yon heaven which woos us to its brink.

XV

But in Man's dwellings he became a thing
Restless and worn, and stern and wearisome,
Drooped as a wild-born falcon with clipt wing,
To whom the boundless air alone were home: 130
Then came his fit again, which to o'ercome,
As eagerly the barred-up bird will beat
His breast and beak against his wiry dome
Till the blood tinge his plumage—so the heat
Of his impeded Soul would through his bosom eat.

XVI

Self-exiled Harold wanders forth again,
With nought of Hope left—but with less of gloom;
The very knowledge that he lived in vain,
That all was over on this side the tomb,
Had made Despair a smilingness assume,   140
Which, though 'twere wild,—as on the plundered wreck
When mariners would madly meet their doom
With draughts intemperate on the sinking deck,—
Did yet inspire a cheer, which he forbore to check.

XVII

Stop!—for thy tread is on an Empire's dust!
An Earthquake's spoil is sepulchred below!
Is the spot marked with no colossal bust?
Nor column trophied for triumphal show?
None; but *the moral's truth* tells simpler so.

As the ground was before, thus let it be;— 150
How that red rain hath made the harvest grow!
And is this all the world has gained by thee,
Thou first and last of Fields! king-making Victory?

XVIII

And Harold stands upon this place of skulls,
The grave of France, the deadly Waterloo!
How in an hour the Power which gave annuls
Its gifts, transferring fame as fleeting too!—
In "pride of place" here last the Eagle flew,
Then tore with bloody talon the rent plain,
Pierced by the shaft of banded nations through; 160
Ambition's life and labours all were vain—
He wears the shattered links of the World's broken chain.

XIX

Fit retribution! Gaul may champ the bit
And foam in fetters;—but is Earth more free?
Did nations combat to make *One* submit?
Or league to teach all Kings true Sovereignty?
What! shall reviving Thraldom again be
The patched-up Idol of enlightened days?
Shall we, who struck the Lion down, shall we
Pay the Wolf homage? proffering lowly gaze 170
And servile knees to Thrones? No! *prove* before ye praise!

XX

If not, o'er one fallen Despot boast no more!
In vain fair cheeks were furrowed with hot tears
For Europe's flowers long rooted up before
The trampler of her vineyards; in vain, years
Of death, depopulation, bondage, fears,
Have all been borne, and broken by the accord
Of roused-up millions: all that most endears
Glory, is when the myrtle wreathes a Sword—
Such as Harmodius drew on Athens' tyrant Lord. 180

XXI

There was a sound of revelry by night,
And Belgium's Capital had gathered then
Her Beauty and her Chivalry—and bright
The lamps shone o'er fair women and brave men;
A thousand hearts beat happily; and when
Music arose with its voluptuous swell,
Soft eyes looked love to eyes which spake again,
And all went merry as a marriage bell;
But hush! hark! a deep sound strikes like a rising knell!

XXII

Did ye not hear it?—No—'twas but the Wind,   190
Or the car rattling o'er the stony street;
On with the dance! let joy be unconfined;
No sleep till morn, when Youth and Pleasure meet
To chase the glowing Hours with flying feet—
But hark!—that heavy sound breaks in once more,
As if the clouds its echo would repeat;
And nearer—clearer—deadlier than before!
Arm! Arm! it is—it is—the cannon's opening roar!

XXIII

Within a windowed niche of that high hall
Sate Brunswick's fated Chieftain; he did hear   200
That sound the first amidst the festival,
And caught its tone with Death's prophetic ear;
And when they smiled because he deemed it near,
His heart more truly knew that peal too well
Which stretched his father on a bloody bier,
And roused the vengeance blood alone could quell;
He rushed into the field, and, foremost fighting, fell.

XXIV

Ah! then and there was hurrying to and fro—
And gathering tears, and tremblings of distress,
And cheeks all pale, which but an hour ago   210
Blushed at the praise of their own loveliness—
And there were sudden partings, such as press

The life from out young hearts, and choking sighs
Which ne'er might be repeated; who could guess
If ever more should meet those mutual eyes,
Since upon night so sweet such awful morn could rise!

XXV

And there was mounting in hot haste—the steed,
The mustering squadron, and the clattering car,
Went pouring forward with impetuous speed,
And swiftly forming in the ranks of war—   220
And the deep thunder peal on peal afar;
And near, the beat of the alarming drum
Roused up the soldier ere the Morning Star;
While thronged the citizens with terror dumb,
Or whispering, with white lips—"The foe! They come! they come!"

XXVI

And wild and high the "Cameron's Gathering" rose!
The war-note of Lochiel, which Albyn's hills
Have heard, and heard, too, have her Saxon foes:—
How in the noon of night that pibroch thrills,
Savage and shrill! But with the breath which fills   230
Their mountain pipe, so fill the mountaineers
With the fierce native daring which instils
The stirring memory of a thousand years,
And Evan's—Donald's—fame rings in each clansman's ears!

XXVII

And Ardennes waves above them her green leaves,
Dewy with Nature's tear-drops, as they pass—
Grieving, if aught inanimate e'er grieves,
Over the unreturning brave,—alas!
Ere evening to be trodden like the grass
Which *now* beneath them, but *above* shall grow   240
In its next verdure, when this fiery mass
Of living Valour, rolling on the foe
And burning with high Hope, shall moulder cold and low.

XXVIII

Last noon beheld them full of lusty life:—
Last eve in Beauty's circle proudly gay;
The Midnight brought the signal-sound of strife,
The Morn the marshalling in arms,—the Day
Battle's magnificently-stern array!
The thunder-clouds close o'er it, which when rent
The earth is covered thick with other clay   250
Which her own clay shall cover, heaped and pent,
Rider and horse,—friend,—foe—in one red burial blent!

XXIX

Their praise is hymned by loftier harps than mine;
Yet one I would select from that proud throng,
Partly because they blend me with his line,
And partly that I did his Sire some wrong,
And partly that bright names will hallow song;
And his was of the bravest, and when showered
The death-bolts deadliest the thinned files along,   260
Even where the thickest of War's tempest lowered,
They reached no nobler breast than thine, young, gallant Howard!

XXX

There have been tears and breaking hearts for thee,
And mine were nothing, had I such to give;
But when I stood beneath the fresh green tree,
Which living waves where thou didst cease to live,
And saw around me the wide field revive
With fruits and fertile promise, and the Spring
Come forth her work of gladness to contrive,
With all her reckless birds upon the wing,
I turned from all she brought to those she could not bring.   270

XXXI

I turned to thee, to thousands, of whom each
And one as all a ghastly gap did make
In his own kind and kindred, whom to teach
Forgetfulness were mercy for their sake;
The Archangel's trump, not Glory's, must awake

Those whom they thirst for; though the sound of Fame
May for a moment soothe, it cannot slake
The fever of vain longing, and the name
So honoured but assumes a stronger, bitterer claim.

XXXII

They mourn, but smile at length—and, smiling, mourn: 280
The tree will wither long before it fall;
The hull drives on, though mast and sail be torn;
The roof-tree sinks, but moulders on the hall
In massy hoariness; the ruined wall
Stands when its wind-born battlements are gone;
The bars survive the captive they enthral;
The day drags through though storms keep out the sun;
And thus the heart will break, yet brokenly live on:

XXXIII

Even as a broken Mirror, which the glass
In every fragment multiplies—and makes   290
A thousand images of one that was
The same—and still the more, the more it breaks;
And thus the heart will do which not forsakes,
Living in shattered guise; and still, and cold,
And bloodless, with its sleepless sorrow aches,
Yet withers on till all without is old,
Showing no visible sign, for such things are untold.

XXXIV

There is a very life in our despair,
Vitality of poison,—a quick root
Which feeds these deadly branches; for it were   300
As nothing did we die; but Life will suit
Itself to Sorrow's most detested fruit,
Like to the apples on the Dead Sea's shore,
All ashes to the taste: Did man compute
Existence by enjoyment, and count o'er
Such hours 'gainst years of life,—say, would he name three-score?

xxxv

The Psalmist numbered out the years of man:
They are enough; and if thy tale be *true,*
Thou, who didst grudge him even that fleeting span,
More than enough, thou fatal Waterloo!   310
Millions of tongues record thee, and anew
Their children's lips shall echo them, and say—
"Here, where the sword united nations drew,
Our countrymen were warring on that day!"
And this is much—and all—which will not pass away.

xxxvi

There sunk the greatest, nor the worst of men,
Whose Spirit, antithetically mixed,
One moment of the mightiest, and again
On little objects with like firmness fixed;
Extreme in all things! hadst thou been betwixt,   320
Thy throne had still been thine, or never been;
For Daring made thy rise as fall: thou seek'st
Even now to re-assume the imperial mien,
And shake again the world, the Thunderer of the scene!

xxxvii

Conqueror and Captive of the Earth art thou!
She trembles at thee still, and thy wild name
Was ne'er more bruited in men's minds than now
That thou art nothing, save the jest of Fame,
Who wooed thee once, thy Vassal, and became
The flatterer of thy fierceness—till thou wert   330
A God unto thyself; nor less the same
To the astounded kingdoms all inert,
Who deemed thee for a time whate'er thou didst assert.

xxxviii

Oh, more or less than man—in high or low—
Battling with nations, flying from the field;
Now making monarchs' necks thy footstool, now
More than thy meanest soldier taught to yield;
An Empire thou couldst crush, command, rebuild,

But govern not thy pettiest passion, nor,
However deeply in men's spirits skilled,   340
Look through thine own, nor curb the lust of War,
Nor learn that tempted Fate will leave the loftiest Star.

XXXIX

Yet well thy soul hath brooked the turning tide
With that untaught innate philosophy,
Which, be it Wisdom, Coldness, or deep Pride,
Is gall and wormwood to an enemy.
When the whole host of hatred stood hard by,
To watch and mock thee shrinking, thou hast smiled
With a sedate and all-enduring eye;—
When Fortune fled her spoiled and favourite child,   350
He stood unbowed beneath the ills upon him piled.

XL

Sager than in thy fortunes; for in them
Ambition steeled thee on too far to show
That just habitual scorn, which could contemn
Men and their thoughts; 'twas wise to feel, not so
To wear it ever on thy lip and brow,
And spurn the instruments thou wert to use
Till they were turned unto thine overthrow:
'Tis but a worthless world to win or lose;
So hath it proved to thee, and all such lot who choose.   360

XLI

If, like a tower upon a headlong rock,
Thou hadst been made to stand or fall alone,
Such scorn of man had helped to brave the shock;
But men's thoughts were the steps which paved thy throne,
Their admiration thy best weapon shone;
The part of Philip's son was thine—not then
(Unless aside thy Purple had been thrown)
Like stern Diogenes to mock at men:
For sceptred Cynics Earth were far too wide a den.

XLII

But Quiet to quick bosoms is a Hell,   370
And *there* hath been thy bane; there is a fire
And motion of the Soul which will not dwell
In its own narrow being, but aspire
Beyond the fitting medium of desire;
And, but once kindled, quenchless evermore,
Preys upon high adventure, nor can tire
Of aught but rest; a fever at the core,
Fatal to him who bears, to all who ever bore.

XLIII

This makes the madmen who have made men mad
By their contagion; Conquerors and Kings,   380
Founders of sects and systems, to whom add
Sophists, Bards, Statesmen, all unquiet things
Which stir too strongly the soul's secret springs,
And are themselves the fools to those they fool;
Envied, yet how unenviable! what stings
Are theirs! One breast laid open were a school
Which would unteach Mankind the lust to shine or rule:

XLIV

Their breath is agitation, and their life
A storm wherein they ride, to sink at last,
And yet so nursed and bigoted to strife,   390
That should their days, surviving perils past,
Melt to calm twilight, they feel overcast
With sorrow and supineness, and so die;
Even as a flame unfed, which runs to waste
With its own flickering, or a sword laid by,
Which eats into itself, and rusts ingloriously.

XLV

He who ascends to mountain tops, shall find
The loftiest peaks most wrapt in clouds and snow;
He who surpasses or subdues mankind,
Must look down on the hate of those below.   400
Though high *above* the Sun of Glory glow,

And far *beneath* the Earth and Ocean spread,
Round him are icy rocks, and loudly blow
Contending tempests on his naked head,
And thus reward the toils which to those summits led.

XLVI

Away with these! true Wisdom's world will be
Within its own creation, or in thine,
Maternal Nature! for who teems like thee,
Thus on the banks of thy majestic Rhine?
There Harold gazes on a work divine,   410
A blending of all beauties; streams and dells,
Fruit, foliage, crag, wood, cornfield, mountain, vine,
And chiefless castles breathing stern farewells
From gray but leafy walls, where Ruin greenly dwells.

XLVII

And there they stand, as stands a lofty mind,
Worn, but unstooping to the baser crowd,
All tenantless, save to the crannying Wind,
Or holding dark communion with the Cloud.
There was a day when they were young and proud;
Banners on high, and battles passed below;   420
But they who fought are in a bloody shroud,
And those which waved are shredless dust ere now,
And the bleak battlements shall bear no future blow.

XLVIII

Beneath these battlements, within those walls,
Power dwelt amidst her passions; in proud state
Each robber chief upheld his arméd halls,
Doing his evil will, nor less elate
Than mightier heroes of a longer date.
What want these outlaws conquerors should have,
But History's purchased page to call them great?   430
A wider space—an ornamented grave?
Their hopes were not less warm, their souls were full as brave.

XLIX

In their baronial feuds and single fields,
What deeds of prowess unrecorded died!
And Love, which lent a blazon to their shields,
With emblems well devised by amorous pride,
Through all the mail of iron hearts would glide;
But still their flame was fierceness, and drew on
Keen contest and destruction near allied,
And many a tower for some fair mischief won,   440
Saw the discoloured Rhine beneath its ruin run.

L

But Thou, exulting and abounding river!
Making thy waves a blessing as they flow
Through banks whose beauty would endure for ever
Could man but leave thy bright creation so,
Nor its fair promise from the surface mow
With the sharp scythe of conflict,—then to see
Thy valley of sweet waters, were to know
Earth paved like Heaven—and to seem such to me,
Even now what wants thy stream?—that it should Lethe be.   450

LI

A thousand battles have assailed thy banks
But these and half their fame have passed away,
And Slaughter heaped on high his weltering ranks:
Their very graves are gone, and what are they?
Thy tide washed down the blood of yesterday,
And all was stainless, and on thy clear stream
Glassed, with its dancing light, the sunny ray;
But o'er the blackened Memory's blighting dream
Thy waves would vainly roll, all sweeping as they seem.

LII

Thus Harold inly said, and passed along,   460
Yet not insensible to all which here
Awoke the jocund birds to early song
In glens which might have made even exile dear:
Though on his brow were graven lines austere,

And tranquil sternness, which had ta'en the place
Of feelings fierier far but less severe—
Joy was not always absent from his face,
But o'er it in such scenes would steal with transient trace.

LIII

Nor was all Love shut from him, though his days
Of passion had consumed themselves to dust.   470
It is in vain that we would coldly gaze
On such as smile upon us; the heart must
Leap kindly back to kindness, though Disgust
Hath weaned it from all worldlings: thus he felt,
For there was soft Remembrance, and sweet Trust
In one fond breast, to which his own would melt,
And in its tenderer hour on that his bosom dwelt.

LIV

And he had learned to love,—I know not why,
For this in such as him seems strange of mood,—
The helpless looks of blooming Infancy,   480
Even in its earliest nurture; what subdued,
To change like this, a mind so far imbued
With scorn of man, it little boots to know;
But thus it was; and though in solitude
Small power the nipped affections have to grow,
In him this glowed when all beside had ceased to glow.

LV

And there was one soft breast, as hath been said,
Which unto his was bound by stronger ties
Than the church links withal; and,—though unwed,
That love was pure—and, far above disguise,   490
Had stood the test of mortal enmities,
Still undivided, and cemented more
By peril, dreaded most in female eyes;
But this was firm, and from a foreign shore
Well to that heart might his these absent greetings pour!

1

The castled Crag of Drachenfels
Frowns o'er the wide and winding Rhine,
Whose breast of waters broadly swells
Between the banks which bear the vine;
And hills all rich with blossomed trees,   500
And fields which promise corn and wine,
And scattered cities crowning these,
Whose far white walls along them shine,
Have strewed a scene, which I should see
With double joy wert *thou* with me.

2

And peasant girls, with deep blue eyes,
And hands which offer early flowers,
Walk smiling o'er this Paradise;
Above, the frequent feudal towers
Through green leaves lift their walls of gray;   510
And many a rock which steeply lowers,
And noble arch in proud decay,
Look o'er this vale of vintage-bowers;
But one thing want these banks of Rhine,—
Thy gentle hand to clasp in mine!

3

I send the lilies given to me—
Though long before thy hand they touch,
I know that they must withered be,
But yet reject them not as such;
For I have cherished them as dear,   520
Because they yet may meet thine eye,
And guide thy soul to mine even here,—
When thou behold'st them drooping nigh,
And know'st them gathered by the Rhine,
And offered from my heart to thine!

4

The river nobly foams and flows—
The charm of this enchanted ground,

And all its thousand turns disclose
Some fresher beauty's varying round:
The haughtiest breast its wish might bound   530
Through life to dwell delighted here;
Nor could on earth a spot be found
To Nature and to me so dear—
Could thy dear eyes in following mine
Still sweeten more these banks of Rhine!

LVI

By Coblentz, on a rise of gentle ground,
There is a small and simple Pyramid,
Crowning the summit of the verdant mound;
Beneath its base are Heroes' ashes hid—
Our enemy's—but let not that forbid   540
Honour to Marceau! o'er whose early tomb
Tears, big tears, gushed from the rough soldier's lid,
Lamenting and yet envying such a doom,
Falling for France, whose rights he battled to resume.

LVII

Brief, brave, and glorious was his young career,—
His mourners were two hosts, his friends and foes;
And fitly may the stranger lingering here
Pray for his gallant Spirit's bright repose;—
For he was Freedom's Champion, one of those,
The few in number, who had not o'erstept   550
The charter to chastise which she bestows
On such as wield her weapons; he had kept
The whiteness of his soul—and thus men o'er him wept.

LVIII

Here Ehrenbreitstein, with her shattered wall
Black with the miner's blast, upon her height
Yet shows of what she was, when shell and ball
Rebounding idly on her strength did light:—
A Tower of Victory! from whence the flight
Of baffled foes was watched along the plain:
But Peace destroyed what War could never blight,   560

And laid those proud roofs bare to Summer's rain—
On which the iron shower for years had poured in vain.

LIX

Adieu to thee, fair Rhine! How long delighted
The stranger fain would linger on his way!
Thine is a scene alike where souls united,
Or lonely Contemplation thus might stray;
And could the ceaseless vultures cease to prey
On self-condemning bosoms, it were here,
Where Nature, nor too sombre nor too gay,
Wild but not rude, awful yet not austere,   570
Is to the mellow Earth as Autumn to the year.

LX

Adieu to thee again! a vain adieu!
There can be no farewell to scene like thine;
The mind is coloured by thy every hue;
And if reluctantly the eyes resign
Their cherished gaze upon thee, lovely Rhine!
'Tis with the thankful glance of parting praise;
More mighty spots may rise—more glaring shine,
But none unite, in one attaching maze,
The brilliant, fair, and soft,—the glories of old days.   580

LXI

The negligently grand, the fruitful bloom
Of coming ripeness, the white city's sheen,
The rolling stream, the precipice's gloom,
The forest's growth, and Gothic walls between,—
The wild rocks shaped, as they had turrets been,
In mockery of man's art; and these withal
A race of faces happy as the scene,
Whose fertile bounties here extend to all,
Still springing o'er thy banks, though Empires near them fall.

LXII

But these recede. Above me are the Alps,   590
The Palaces of Nature, whose vast walls

Have pinnacled in clouds their snowy scalps,
And throned Eternity in icy halls
Of cold Sublimity, where forms and falls
The Avalanche—the thunderbolt of snow!
All that expands the spirit, yet appals,
Gather around these summits, as to show
How Earth may pierce to Heaven, yet leave vain man below.

LXIII

But ere these matchless heights I dare to scan,
There is a spot should not be passed in vain,—   600
Morat! the proud, the patriot field! where man
May gaze on ghastly trophies of the slain,
Nor blush for those who conquered on that plain;
Here Burgundy bequeathed his tombless host,
A bony heap, through ages to remain,
Themselves their monument;—the Stygian coast
Unsepulchred they roamed, and shrieked each wandering ghost.

LXIV

While Waterloo with Cannæ's carnage vies,
Morat and Marathon twin names shall stand;
They were true Glory's stainless victories,   610
Won by the unambitious heart and hand
Of a proud, brotherly, and civic band,
All unbought champions in no princely cause
Of vice-entailed Corruption; they no land
Doomed to bewail the blasphemy of laws
Making Kings' rights divine, by some Draconic clause.

LXV

By a lone wall a lonelier column rears
A gray and grief-worn aspect of old days;
'Tis the last remnant of the wreck of years,
And looks as with the wild-bewildered gaze   620
Of one to stone converted by amaze,
Yet still with consciousness; and there it stands
Making a marvel that it not decays,

When the coeval pride of human hands,
Levelled Aventicum, hath strewed her subject lands.

L X V I

And there—oh! sweet and sacred be the name!
Julia—the daughter—the devoted—gave
Her youth to Heaven; her heart, beneath a claim
Nearest to Heaven's, broke o'er a father's grave.
Justice is sworn 'gainst tears, and hers would crave 630
The life she lived in—but the Judge was just—
And then she died on him she could not save.
Their tomb was simple, and without a bust,
And held within their urn one mind—one heart—one dust.

L X V I I

But these are deeds which should not pass away,
And names that must not wither, though the Earth
Forgets her empires with a just decay,
The enslavers and the enslaved—their death and birth;
The high, the mountain-majesty of Worth
Should be—and shall, survivor of its woe, 640
And from its immortality, look forth
In the Sun's face, like yonder Alpine snow,
Imperishably pure beyond all things below.

L X V I I I

Lake Leman woos me with its crystal face,
The mirror where the stars and mountains view
The stillness of their aspect in each trace
Its clear depth yields of their far height and hue:
There is too much of Man here, to look through
With a fit mind the might which I behold;
But soon in me shall Loneliness renew 650
Thoughts hid, but not less cherished than of old,
Ere mingling with the herd had penned me in their fold.

L X I X

To fly from, need not be to hate, mankind:
All are not fit with them to stir and toil,

Nor is it discontent to keep the mind
Deep in its fountain, lest it overboil
In the hot throng, where we become the spoil
Of our infection, till, too late and long,
We may deplore and struggle with the coil,
In wretched interchange of wrong for wrong   660
Midst a contentious world, striving where none are strong.

LXX

There, in a moment, we may plunge our years
In fatal penitence, and in the blight
Of our own Soul turn all our blood to tears,
And colour things to come with hues of Night;
The race of life becomes a hopeless flight
To those that walk in darkness: on the sea
The boldest steer but where their ports invite—
But there are wanderers o'er Eternity,
Whose bark drives on and on, and anchored ne'er shall be.   670

LXXI

Is it not better, then, to be alone,
And love Earth only for its earthly sake?
By the blue rushing of the arrowy Rhone,
Or the pure bosom of its nursing Lake,
Which feeds it as a mother who doth make
A fair but froward infant her own care,
Kissing its cries away as they awake;—
Is it not better thus our lives to wear,
Than join the crushing crowd, doomed to inflict or bear?

LXXII

I live not in myself, but I become   680
Portion of that around me; and to me
High mountains are a feeling, but the hum
Of human cities torture: I can see
Nothing to loathe in Nature, save to be
A link reluctant in a fleshly chain,
Classed among creatures, when the soul can flee,

And with the sky—the peak—the heaving plain
Of ocean, or the stars, mingle—and not in vain.

LXXIII

And thus I am absorbed, and this is life:—
I look upon the peopled desert past,   690
As on a place of agony and strife,
Where, for some sin, to Sorrow I was cast,
To act and suffer, but remount at last
With a fresh pinion; which I feel to spring,
Though young, yet waxing vigorous as the Blast
Which it would cope with, on delighted wing,
Spurning the clay-cold bonds which round our being cling.

LXXIV

And when, at length, the mind shall be all free
From what it hates in this degraded form,
Reft of its canal life, save what shall be   700
Existent happier in the fly and worm,—
When Elements to Elements conform,
And dust is as it should be, shall I not
Feel all I see less dazzling but more warm?
The bodiless thought? the Spirit of each spot?
Of which, even now, I share at times the immortal lot?

LXXV

Are not the mountains, waves, and skies, a part
Of me and of my Soul, as I of them?
Is not the love of these deep in my heart
With a pure passion? should I not contemn   710
All objects, if compared with these? and stem
A tide of suffering, rather than forgo
Such feelings for the hard and worldly phlegm
Of those whose eyes are only turned below,
Gazing upon the ground, with thoughts which dare not glow?

LXXVI

But this is not my theme; and I return
To that which is immediate, and require

Those who find contemplation in the urn,
To look on One, whose dust was once all fire,—
A native of the land where I respire   720
The clear air for a while—a passing guest,
Where he became a being,—whose desire
Was to be glorious; 'twas a foolish quest,
The which to gain and keep, he sacrificed all rest.

LXXVII

Here the self-torturing sophist, wild Rousseau,
The apostle of Affliction, he who threw
Enchantment over Passion, and from Woe
Wrung overwhelming eloquence, first drew
The breath which made him wretched; yet he knew
How to make Madness beautiful, and cast   730
O'er erring deeds and thoughts, a heavenly hue
Of words, like sunbeams, dazzling as they past
The eyes, which o'er them shed tears feelingly and fast.

LXXVIII

His love was Passion's essence—as a tree
On fire by lightning; with ethereal flame
Kindled he was, and blasted; for to be
Thus and enamoured, were in him the same.
But his was not the love of living dame,
Nor of the dead who rise upon our dreams,
But of ideal Beauty, which became   740
In him existence, and o'erflowing teems
Along his burning page, distempered though it seems.

LXXIX

This breathed itself to life in Julie, *this*
Invested her with all that's wild and sweet;
This hallowed, too, the memorable kiss
Which every morn his fevered lip would greet,
From hers, who but with friendship his would meet;
But to that gentle touch, through brain and breast
Flashed the thrilled Spirit's love-devouring heat;
In that absorbing sigh perchance more blest   750
Than vulgar minds may be with all they seek possest.

LXXX

His life was one long war with self-sought foes,
Or friends by him self-banished; for his mind
Had grown Suspicion's sanctuary, and chose,
For its own cruel sacrifice, the kind,
'Gainst whom he raged with fury strange and blind.
But he was phrensied,—wherefore, who may know?
Since cause might be which Skill could never find;
But he was phrensied by disease or woe,
To that worst pitch of all, which wears a reasoning show.   760

LXXXI

For then he was inspired, and from him came,
As from the Pythian's mystic cave of yore,
Those oracles which set the world in flame,
Nor ceased to burn till kingdoms were no more:
Did he not this for France? which lay, before,
Bowed to the inborn tyranny of years,
Broken and trembling to the yoke she bore,
Till by the voice of him and his compeers,
Roused up to too much wrath which follows o'ergrown fears?

LXXXII

They made themselves a fearful monument!   770
The wreck of old opinions—things which grew,
Breathed from the birth of Time: the veil they rent,
And what behind it lay, all earth shall view;
But good with ill they also overthrew,
Leaving but ruins, wherewith to rebuild
Upon the same foundation, and renew
Dungeons and thrones, which the same hour refilled,
As heretofore, because Ambition was self-willed.

LXXXIII

But this will not endure, nor be endured!
Mankind have felt their strength, and made it felt.   780
They might have used it better, but, allured
By their new vigour, sternly have they dealt
On one another; Pity ceased to melt

With her once natural charities. But they,
Who in Oppression's darkness caved had dwelt,
They were not eagles, nourished with the day;
What marvel then, at times, if they mistook their prey?

LXXXIV

What deep wounds ever closed without a scar?
The heart's bleed longest, and but heal to wear
That which disfigures it; and they who war   790
With their own hopes, and have been vanquished, bear
Silence, but not submission: in his lair
Fixed Passion holds his breath, until the hour
Which shall atone for years; none need despair:
It came—it cometh—and will come,—the power
To punish or forgive—in *one* we shall be slower.

LXXXV

Clear, placid Leman! thy contrasted lake,
With the wild world I dwelt in, is a thing
Which warns me, with its stillness, to forsake
Earth's troubled waters for a purer spring.   800
This quiet sail is as a noiseless wing
To waft me from distraction; once I loved
Torn Ocean's roar, but thy soft murmuring
Sounds sweet as if a Sister's voice reproved,
That I with stern delights should e'er have been so moved.

LXXXVI

It is the hush of night, and all between
Thy margin and the mountains, dusk, yet clear,
Mellowed and mingling, yet distinctly seen,
Save darkened Jura, whose capt heights appear
Precipitously steep; and drawing near,   810
There breathes a living fragrance from the shore,
Of flowers yet fresh with childhood; on the ear
Drops the light drip of the suspended oar,
Or chirps the grasshopper one good-night carol more.

He is an evening reveller, who makes
His life an infancy, and sings his fill;
At intervals, some bird from out the brakes
Starts into voice a moment, then is still.
There seems a floating whisper on the hill,
But that is fancy—for the Starlight dews   820
All silently their tears of Love instil,
Weeping themselves away, till they infuse
Deep into Nature's breast the spirit of her hues.

LXXXVIII
Ye Stars! which are the poetry of Heaven!
If in your bright leaves we would read the fate
Of men and empires,—'tis to be forgiven,
That in our aspirations to be great,
Our destinies o'erleap their mortal state,
And claim a kindred with you; for ye are
A Beauty and a Mystery, and create   830
In us such love and reverence from afar,
That Fortune,—Fame,—Power,—Life, have named themselves a
    Star.

LXXXIX
All Heaven and Earth are still—though not in sleep,
But breathless, as we grow when feeling most;
And silent, as we stand in thoughts too deep:—
All Heaven and Earth are still: From the high host
Of stars, to the lulled lake and mountain-coast,
All is concentrated in a life intense,
Where not a beam, nor air, nor leaf is lost,
But hath a part of Being, and a sense   840
Of that which is of all Creator and Defence.

XC
Then stirs the feeling infinite, so felt
In solitude, where we are *least* alone;
A truth, which through our being then doth melt,
And purifies from self: it is a tone,

The soul and source of Music, which makes known
Eternal harmony, and sheds a charm
Like to the fabled Cytherea's zone,
Binding all things with beauty;—'twould disarm
The spectre Death, had he substantial power to harm.   850

XCI

Not vainly did the early Persian make
His altar the high places, and the peak
Of earth-o'ergazing mountains, and thus take
A fit and unwalled temple, there to seek
The Spirit, in whose honour shrines are weak,
Upreared of human hands. Come, and compare
Columns and idol-dwellings—Goth or Greek—
With Nature's realms of worship, earth and air—
Nor fix on fond abodes to circumscribe thy prayer!

XCII

The sky is changed!—and such a change! Oh Night,   860
And Storm, and Darkness, ye are wondrous strong,
Yet lovely in your strength, as is the light
Of a dark eye in Woman! Far along,
From peak to peak, the rattling crags among
Leaps the live thunder! Not from one lone cloud,
But every mountain now hath found a tongue,
And Jura answers, through her misty shroud,
Back to the joyous Alps, who call to her aloud!

XCIII

And this is in the Night:—Most glorious Night!
Thou wert not sent for slumber! let me be   870
A sharer in thy fierce and far delight,—
A portion of the tempest and of thee!
How the lit lake shines, a phosphoric sea,
And the big rain comes dancing to the earth!
And now again 'tis black,—and now, the glee
Of the loud hills shakes with its mountain-mirth,
As if they did rejoice o'er a young Earthquake's birth.

XCIV

Now, where the swift Rhone cleaves his way between
Heights which appear as lovers who have parted
In hate, whose mining depths so intervene, 880
That they can meet no more, though brokenhearted:
Though in their souls, which thus each other thwarted,
Love was the very root of the fond rage
Which blighted their life's bloom, and then departed:—
Itself expired, but leaving them an age
Of years all winters,—war within themselves to wage:

XCV

Now, where the quick Rhone thus hath cleft his way,
The mightiest of the storms hath ta'en his stand:
For here, not one, but many, make their play
And fling their thunder-bolts from hand to hand, 890
Flashing and cast around: of all the band,
The brightest through these parted hills hath forked
His lightnings,—as if he did understand,
That in such gaps as Desolation worked,
There the hot shaft should blast whatever therein lurked.

XCVI

Sky—Mountains—River—Winds—Lake—Lightnings! ye!
With night, and clouds, and thunder—and a Soul
To make these felt and feeling, well may be
Things that have made me watchful; the far roll
Of your departing voices, is the knoll 900
Of what in me is sleepless,—if I rest.
But where of ye, O Tempests! is the goal?
Are ye like those within the human breast?
Or do ye find, at length, like eagles, some high nest?

XCVII

Could I embody and unbosom now
That which is most within me,—could I wreak
My thoughts upon expression, and thus throw
Soul—heart—mind—passions—feelings—strong or weak—
All that I would have sought, and all I seek,

Bear, know, feel—and yet breathe—into *one* word,   910
And that one word were Lightning, I would speak;
But as it is, I live and die unheard,
With a most voiceless thought, sheathing it as a sword.

XCVIII

The Morn is up again, the dewy Morn,
With breath all incense, and with cheek all bloom—
Laughing the clouds away with playful scorn,
And living as if earth contained no tomb,—
And glowing into day: we may resume
The march of our existence: and thus I,
Still on thy shores, fair Leman! may find room   920
And food for meditation, nor pass by
Much, that may give us pause, if pondered fittingly.

XCIX

Clarens! sweet Clarens, birthplace of deep Love!
Thine air is the young breath of passionate Thought;
Thy trees take root in Love; the snows above,
The very Glaciers have his colours caught,
And Sun-set into rose-hues sees them wrought
By rays which sleep there lovingly: the rocks,
The permanent crags, tell here of Love, who sought
In them a refuge from the worldly shocks,   930
Which stir and sting the Soul with Hope that woos, then mocks.

C

Clarens! by heavenly feet thy paths are trod,—
Undying Love's, who here ascends a throne
To which the steps are mountains; where the God
Is a pervading Life and Light,—so shown
Not on those summits solely, nor alone
In the still cave and forest; o'er the flower
His eye is sparkling, and his breath hath blown,
His soft and summer breath, whose tender power
Passes the strength of storms in their most desolate hour.   940

CI

All things are here of *Him;* from the black pines,
Which are his shade on high, and the loud roar
Of torrents, where he listeneth, to the vines
Which slope his green path downward to the shore,
Where the bowed Waters meet him, and adore,
Kissing his feet with murmurs; and the Wood,
The covert of old trees, with trunks all hoar,
But light leaves, young as joy, stands where it stood,
Offering to him, and his, a populous solitude.

CII

A populous solitude of bees and birds,   950
And fairy-formed and many-coloured things,
Who worship him with notes more sweet than words,
And innocently open their glad wings,
Fearless and full of life: the gush of springs,
And fall of lofty fountains, and the bend
Of stirring branches, and the bud which brings
The swiftest thought of Beauty, here extend
Mingling—and made by Love—unto one mighty end.

CIII

He who hath loved not, here would learn that lore,
And make his heart a spirit; he who knows   960
That tender mystery, will love the more;
For this is Love's recess, where vain men's woes,
And the world's waste, have driven him far from those,
For 'tis his nature to advance or die;
He stands not still, but or decays, or grows
Into a boundless blessing, which may vie
With the immortal lights, in its eternity!

CIV

'Twas not for fiction chose Rousseau the spot,
Peopling it with affections; but he found
It was the scene which Passion must allot   970
To the Mind's purified beings; 'twas the ground
Where early Love his Psyche's zone unbound,

And hallowed it with loveliness: 'tis lone,
And wonderful, and deep, and hath a sound,
And sense, and sight of sweetness; here the Rhone
Hath spread himself a couch, the Alps have reared a throne.

C V

Lausanne! and Ferney! ye have been the abodes
Of Names which unto you bequeathed a name;
Mortals, who sought and found, by dangerous roads,
A path to perpetuity of Fame: 980
They were gigantic minds, and their steep aim
Was, Titan-like, on daring doubts to pile
Thoughts which should call down thunder, and the flame
Of Heaven again assailed—if Heaven, the while,
On man and man's research could deign do more than smile.

C V I

The one was fire and fickleness, a child
Most mutable in wishes, but in mind
A wit as various,—gay, grave, sage, or wild,—
Historian, bard, philosopher, combined;
He multiplied himself among mankind,   990
The Proteus of their talents: But his own
Breathed most in ridicule,—which, as the wind,
Blew where it listed, laying all things prone,—
Now to o'erthrow a fool, and now to shake a throne.

C V I I

The other, deep and slow, exhausting thought,
And hiving wisdom with each studious year,
In meditation dwelt—with learning wrought,
And shaped his weapon with an edge severe,
Sapping a solemn creed with solemn sneer;
The lord of irony,—that master spell,   1000
Which stung his foes to wrath, which grew from fear,
And doomed him to the zealot's ready Hell,
Which answers to all doubts so eloquently well.

CVIII

Yet, peace be with their ashes,—for by them
If merited, the penalty is paid;
It is not ours to judge,—far less condemn;
The hour must come when such things shall be made
Known unto all,—or hope and dread allayed
By slumber, on one pillow, in the dust,
Which, thus much we are sure, must lie decayed;   1010
And when it shall revive, as is our trust,
'Twill be to be forgiven—or suffer what is just.

CIX

But let me quit Man's works, again to read
His Maker's, spread around me, and suspend
This page, which from my reveries I feed,
Until it seems prolonging without end.
The clouds above me to the white Alps tend,
And I must pierce them, and survey whate'er
May be permitted, as my steps I bend
To their most great and growing region, where   1020
The earth to her embrace compels the powers of air.

CX

Italia, too! Italia! looking on thee,
Full flashes on the Soul the light of ages,
Since the fierce Carthaginian almost won thee,
To the last halo of the Chiefs and Sages
Who glorify thy consecrated pages;
Thou wert the throne and grave of empires—still,
The fount at which the panting Mind assuages
Her thirst of knowledge, quaffing there her fill,
Flows from the eternal source of Rome's imperial hill.   1030

CXI

Thus far have I proceeded in a theme
Renewed with no kind auspices:—to feel
We are not what we have been, and to deem
We are not what we should be,—and to steel
The heart against itself; and to conceal,

With a proud caution, love, or hate, or aught,—
Passion or feeling, purpose, grief, or zeal,
Which is the tyrant Spirit of our thought,—
Is a stern task of soul:—No matter,—it is taught.

CXII

And for these words, thus woven into song,   1040
It may be that they are a harmless wile,—
The colouring of the scenes which fleet along,
Which I would seize, in passing, to beguile
My breast, or that of others, for a while.
Fame is the thirst of youth,—but I am not
So young as to regard men's frown or smile,
As loss or guerdon of a glorious lot;—
I stood and stand alone,—remembered or forgot.

CXIII

I have not loved the World, nor the World me;
I have not flattered its rank breath, nor bowed   1050
To its idolatries a patient knee,
Nor coined my cheek to smiles,—nor cried aloud
In worship of an echo: in the crowd
They could not deem me one of such—I stood
Among them, but not of them—in a shroud
Of thoughts which were not their thoughts, and still could,
Had I not filed my mind, which thus itself subdued.

CXIV

I have not loved the World, nor the World me,—
But let us part fair foes; I do believe,
Though I have found them not, that there may be   1060
Words which are things,—Hopes which will not deceive,
And Virtues which are merciful, nor weave
Snares for the failing: I would also deem
O'er others' grief that some sincerely grieve—
That two, or one, are almost what they seem,—
That Goodness is no name—and Happiness no dream.

CXV

My daughter! with thy name this song begun!
My daughter! with thy name thus much shall end!—
I see thee not—I hear thee not—but none
Can be so wrapt in thee; Thou art the Friend
To whom the shadows of far years extend:
Albeit my brow thou never should'st behold,
My voice shall with thy future visions blend,
And reach into thy heart,—when mine is cold,—
A token and a tone, even from thy father's mould.

CXVI

To aid thy mind's development,—to watch
Thy dawn of little joys,—to sit and see
Almost thy very growth,—to view thee catch
Knowledge of objects,—wonders yet to thee!
To hold thee lightly on a gentle knee,
And print on thy soft cheek a parent's kiss,—
This, it should seem, was not reserved for me—
Yet this was in my nature:—as it is,
I know not what is there, yet something like to this.

CXVII

Yet, though dull Hate as duty should be taught,
I know that thou wilt love me,—though my name
Should be shut from thee, as a spell still fraught
With desolation, and a broken claim:
Though the grave closed between us,—'twere the same—
I know that thou wilt love me—though to drain
My blood from out thy being were an aim,
And an attainment,—all would be in vain,—
Still thou would'st love me, still that more than life retain.

CXVIII

The child of Love! though born in bitterness,
And nurtured in Convulsion! Of thy sire
These were the elements,—and thine no less.
As yet such are around thee,—but thy fire

1070

1080

1090

Shall be more tempered, and thy hope far higher.
Sweet be thy cradled slumbers! O'er the sea
And from the mountains where I now respire,   1100
Fain would I waft such blessing upon thee,
As—with a sigh—I deem thou might'st have been to me!

CANTO THE FOURTH

"Visto ho Toscana, Lombardia, Romagna,
Quel monte che divide, e quel che serra
Italia, e un mare e l' altro, che la bagna."

Ariosto, *Satira* iv. lines 59–61.

TO

JOHN HOBHOUSE, ESQ., A.M.,
F.R.S., &C., &C., &C.

VENICE, *January* 2, 1818.

My dear Hobhouse,

    After an interval of eight years between the composition of the first and last cantos of *Childe Harold,* the conclusion of the poem is about to be submitted to the public. In parting with so old a friend, it is not extraordinary that I should recur to one still older and better,—to one who has beheld the birth and death of the other, and to whom I am far more indebted for the social advantages of an enlightened friendship, than—though not ungrateful—I can, or could be, to *Childe Harold,* for any public favour reflected through the poem on the poet,—to one, whom I have known long, and accompanied far, whom I have found wakeful over my sickness and kind in my sorrow, glad in my prosperity and firm in my adversity, true in counsel and trusty in peril,—to a friend often tried and never found wanting;—to yourself.

    In so doing, I recur from fiction to truth; and in dedicating to you in its complete, or at least concluded state, a poetical work which is the longest, the most thoughtful and comprehensive of my compositions, I wish to do honour to myself by the record of many years' intimacy with a man of learning, of talent, of steadiness, and of honour. It is not for minds like ours to give or to receive flattery; yet the praises of sincerity have ever been permitted to the voice of friendship; and it is not for you, nor even for others, but to relieve a heart which has not elsewhere, or lately, been so much accustomed to the encounter of good-will as to withstand the shock firmly, that I thus attempt to commemorate your good qualities, or rather the advantages which I have derived from their exertion. Even the recurrence of the date of this letter, the anniversary of the most unfortunate day of my past existence, but which cannot poison my future while I retain the resource of your friendship, and of my own faculties, will henceforth have a more agreeable recollection for both, inasmuch as it will remind us of this my attempt to thank you for an indefatigable regard, such as few men have experienced, and no one could experience without thinking better of his species and of himself.

It has been our fortune to traverse together, at various periods, the countries of chivalry, history, and fable—Spain, Greece, Asia Minor, and Italy; and what Athens and Constantinople were to us a few years ago, Venice and Rome have been more recently. The poem also, or the pilgrim, or both, have accompanied me from first to last; and perhaps it may be a pardonable vanity which induces me to reflect with complacency on a composition which in some degree connects me with the spot where it was produced, and the objects it would fain describe; and however unworthy it may be deemed of those magical and memorable abodes, however short it may fall of our distant conceptions and immediate impressions, yet as a mark of respect for what is venerable, and of feeling for what is glorious, it has been to me a source of pleasure in the production, and I part with it with a kind of regret, which I hardly suspected that events could have left me for imaginary objects.

With regard to the conduct of the last canto, there will be found less of the pilgrim than in any of the preceding, and that little slightly, if at all, separated from the author speaking in his own person. The fact is, that I had become weary of drawing a line which every one seemed determined not to perceive: like the Chinese in Goldsmith's *Citizen of the World,* whom nobody would believe to be a Chinese, it was in vain that I asserted, and imagined that I had drawn, a distinction between the author and the pilgrim; and the very anxiety to preserve this difference, and disappointment at finding it unavailing, so far crushed my efforts in the composition, that I determined to abandon it altogether— and have done so. The opinions which have been, or may be, formed on that subject are *now* a matter of indifference: the work is to depend on itself, and not on the writer; and the author, who has no resources in his own mind beyond the reputation, transient or permanent, which is to arise from his literary efforts, deserves the fate of authors.

In the course of the following canto it was my intention, either in the text or in the notes, to have touched upon the present state of Italian literature, and perhaps of manners. But the text, within the limits I proposed, I soon found hardly sufficient for the labyrinth of external objects, and the consequent reflections: and for the whole of the notes, excepting a few of the shortest, I am indebted to yourself, and these were necessarily limited to the elucidation of the text.

It is also a delicate, and no very grateful task, to dissert upon the literature and manners of a nation so dissimilar; and requires an attention and impartiality which would induce us,—though perhaps no inattentive observers, nor ignorant of the language or customs of the people amongst whom we have recently abode—to distrust, or at least defer our judgment, and more narrowly examine our information. The state of literary, as well as political party, appears to run, or to *have* run, so high, that for a stranger to steer impartially between them, is next to impossible. It may be enough, then, at least for my purpose, to quote from their own beautiful language—"Mi pare che in un paese tutto poetico, che vanta la lingua la più nobile ed insieme la più dolce, tutte tutte le vie diverse si possono tentare, e che sinche la patria di Alfieri e di Monti non ha perduto l'antico valore, in tutte essa dovrebbe essere la prima." Italy has great names still—Canova, Monti, Ugo Foscolo, Pindemonte, Visconti, Morelli, Cicognara, Albrizzi, Mezzofanti, Mai, Mustoxidi, Aglietti, and Vacca, will secure to the present generation an honourable place in most of the departments of Art, Science, and Belles Lettres; and in some the very highest—Europe—the World— has but one Canova.

It has been somewhere said by Alfieri, that "La pianta uomo nasce più robusta in Italia che in qualunque altra terra—e che gli stessi atroci delitti che vi si commettono ne sono una prova." Without subscribing to the latter part of his proposition, a dangerous doctrine, the truth of which may be disputed on better grounds, namely, that the

Italians are in no respect more ferocious than their neighbours, that man must be wilfully blind, or ignorantly heedless, who is not struck with the extraordinary capacity of this people, or, if such a word be admissible, their *capabilities,* the facility of their acquisitions, the rapidity of their conceptions, the fire of their genius, their sense of beauty, and, amidst all the disadvantages of repeated revolutions, the desolation of battles, and the despair of ages, their still unquenched "longing after immortality,"—the immortality of independence. And when we ourselves, in riding round the walls of Rome, heard the simple lament of the labourers' chorus, "Roma! Roma! Roma! Roma non è più come era prima!" it was difficult not to contrast this melancholy dirge with the bacchanal roar of the songs of exultation still yelled from the London taverns, over the carnage of Mont St. Jean, and the betrayal of Genoa, of Italy, of France, and of the world, by men whose conduct you yourself have exposed in a work worthy of the better days of our history. For me,—

> "Non movero mai corda
> Ove la turba di sue ciance assorda."

What Italy has gained by the late transfer of nations, it were useless for Englishmen to enquire, till it becomes ascertained that England has acquired something more than a permanent army and a suspended Habeas Corpus; it is enough for them to look at home. For what they have done abroad, and especially in the South, "Verily they *will have* their reward," and at no very distant period.

Wishing you, my dear Hobhouse, a safe and agreeable return to that country whose real welfare can be dearer to none than to yourself, I dedicate to you this poem in its completed state; and repeat once more how truly I am ever

Your obliged
And affectionate friend,
BYRON.

I

I stood in Venice, on the "Bridge of Sighs";
A Palace and a prison on each hand:
I saw from out the wave her structures rise

As from the stroke of the Enchanter's wand:
A thousand Years their cloudy wings expand
Around me, and a dying Glory smiles
O'er the far times, when many a subject land
Looked to the wingéd Lion's marble piles,
Where Venice sate in state, throned on her hundred isles!

II

She looks a sea Cybele, fresh from Ocean,   10
Rising with her tiara of proud towers
At airy distance, with majestic motion,
A Ruler of the waters and their powers:
And such she was;—her daughters had their dowers
From spoils of nations, and the exhaustless East
Poured in her lap all gems in sparkling showers:
In purple was she robed, and of her feast
Monarchs partook, and deemed their dignity increased.

III

In Venice Tasso's echoes are no more,
And silent rows the songless Gondolier;   20
Her palaces are crumbling to the shore,
And Music meets not always now the ear:
Those days are gone—but Beauty still is here.
States fall—Arts fade—but Nature doth not die,
Nor yet forget how Venice once was dear,
The pleasant place of all festivity,
The Revel of the earth—the Masque of Italy!

IV

But unto us she hath a spell beyond
Her name in story, and her long array
Of mighty shadows, whose dim forms despond   30
Above the Dogeless city's vanished sway;
Ours is a trophy which will not decay
With the Rialto; Shylock and the Moor,
And Pierre, can not be swept or worn away—
The keystones of the Arch! though all were o'er,
For us repeopled were the solitary shore.

V

The Beings of the Mind are not of clay:
Essentially immortal, they create
And multiply in us a brighter ray
And more beloved existence: that which Fate   40
Prohibits to dull life in this our state
Of mortal bondage, by these Spirits supplied,
First exiles, then replaces what we hate;
Watering the heart whose early flowers have died,
And with a fresher growth replenishing the void.

VI

Such is the refuge of our youth and age—
The first from Hope, the last from Vacancy;
And this wan feeling peoples many a page—
And, may be, that which grows beneath mine eye:
Yet there are things whose strong reality   50
Outshines our fairy-land; in shape and hues
More beautiful than our fantastic sky,
And the strange constellations which the Muse
O'er her wild universe is skilful to diffuse:

VII

I saw or dreamed of such,—but let them go,—
They came like Truth—and disappeared like dreams;
And whatsoe'er they were—are now but so:
I could replace them if I would; still teems
My mind with many a form which aptly seems
Such as I sought for, and at moments found;   60
Let these too go—for waking Reason deems
Such over-weening phantasies unsound,
And other voices speak, and other sights surround.

VIII

I've taught me other tongues—and in strange eyes
Have made me not a stranger; to the mind
Which is itself, no changes bring surprise;
Nor is it harsh to make, nor hard to find
A country with—aye, or without mankind;

Yet was I born where men are proud to be,—
Not without cause; and should I leave behind   70
The inviolate Island of the sage and free,
And seek me out a home by a remoter sea,

I X

Perhaps I loved it well; and should I lay
My ashes in a soil which is not mine,
My Spirit shall resume it—if we may
Unbodied choose a sanctuary. I twine
My hopes of being remembered in my line
With my land's language: if too fond and far
These aspirations in their scope incline,—
If my Fame should be, as my fortunes are,   80
Of hasty growth and blight, and dull Oblivion bar

X

My name from out the temple where the dead
Are honoured by the Nations—let it be—
And light the Laurels on a loftier head
And be the Spartan's epitaph on me—
"Sparta hath many a worthier son than he."
Meantime I seek no sympathies, nor need—
The thorns which I have reaped are of the tree
I planted,—they have torn me,—and I bleed:
I should have known what fruit would spring from such a seed.   90

X I

The spouseless Adriatic mourns her Lord,
And annual marriage now no more renewed—
The Bucentaur lies rotting unrestored,
Neglected garment of her widowhood!
St. Mark yet sees his Lion where he stood
Stand, but in mockery of his withered power,
Over the proud Place where an Emperor sued,
And monarchs gazed and envied in the hour
When Venice was a Queen with an unequalled dower.

XII

The Suabian sued, and now the Austrian reigns—   100
An Emperor tramples where an Emperor knelt;
Kingdoms are shrunk to provinces, and chains
Clank over sceptred cities; Nations melt
From Power's high pinnacle, when they have felt
The sunshine for a while, and downward go
Like Lauwine loosened from the mountain's belt;
Oh for one hour of blind old Dandolo!
Th' octogenarian chief, Byzantium's conquering foe.

XIII

Before St. Mark still glow his Steeds of brass,
Their gilded collars glittering in the sun;   110
But is not Doria's menace come to pass?
Are they not bridled?—Venice, lost and won,
Her thirteen hundred years of freedom done,
Sinks, like a sea-weed, unto whence she rose!
Better be whelmed beneath the waves, and shun,
Even in Destruction's depth, her foreign foes,
From whom Submission wrings an infamous repose.

XIV

In youth She was all glory,—a new Tyre,—
Her very by-word sprung from Victory,
The "Planter of the Lion," which through fire   120
And blood she bore o'er subject Earth and Sea;
Though making many slaves, Herself still free,
And Europe's bulwark 'gainst the Ottomite;
Witness Troy's rival, Candia! Vouch it, ye
Immortal waves that saw Lepanto's fight!
For ye are names no Time nor Tyranny can blight.

XV

Statues of glass—all shivered—the long file
Of her dead Doges are declined to dust;
But where they dwelt, the vast and sumptuous pile
Bespeaks the pageant of their splendid trust;   130
Their sceptre broken, and their sword in rust,

Have yielded to the stranger: empty halls,
Thin streets, and foreign aspects, such as must
Too oft remind her who and what enthrals,
Have flung a desolate cloud o'er Venice' lovely walls.

XVI

When Athens' armies fell at Syracuse,
And fettered thousands bore the yoke of war,
Redemption rose up in the Attic Muse,
Her voice their only ransom from afar:
See! as they chant the tragic hymn, the car   140
Of the o'ermastered Victor stops—the reins
Fall from his hands—his idle scimitar
Starts from its belt—he rends his captive's chains,
And bids him thank the Bard for Freedom and his strains.

XVII

Thus, Venice! if no stronger claim were thine,
Were all thy proud historic deeds forgot—
Thy choral memory of the Bard divine,
Thy love of Tasso, should have cut the knot
Which ties thee to thy tyrants; and thy lot
Is shameful to the nations,—most of all,   150
Albion! to thee: the Ocean queen should not
Abandon Ocean's children; in the fall
Of Venice think of thine, despite thy watery wall.

XVIII

I loved her from my boyhood—she to me
Was as a fairy city of the heart,
Rising like water-columns from the sea—
Of Joy the sojourn, and of Wealth the mart;
And Otway, Radcliffe, Schiller, Shakespeare's art,
Had stamped her image in me, and even so,
Although I found her thus, we did not part;   160
Perchance even dearer in her day of woe,
Than when she was a boast, a marvel, and a show.

XIX

I can repeople with the past—and of
The present there is still for eye and thought,
And meditation chastened down, enough;
And more, it may be, than I hoped or sought;
And of the happiest moments which were wrought
Within the web of my existence, some
From thee, fair Venice! have their colours caught:
There are some feelings Time can not benumb,   170
Nor Torture shake, or mine would now be cold and dumb.

XX

But, from their nature, will the Tannen grow
Loftiest on loftiest and least sheltered rocks,
Rooted in barrenness, where nought below
Of soil supports them 'gainst the Alpine shocks
Of eddying storms; yet springs the trunk, and mocks
The howling tempest, till its height and frame
Are worthy of the mountains from whose blocks
Of bleak, gray granite into life it came,
And grew a giant tree;—the Mind may grow the same.   180

XXI

Existence may be borne, and the deep root
Of life and sufferance make its firm abode
In bare and desolated bosoms: mute
The camel labours with the heaviest load,
And the wolf dies in silence,—not bestowed
In vain should such example be; if they,
Things of ignoble or of savage mood,
Endure and shrink not, we of nobler clay
May temper it to bear,—it is but for a day.

XXII

All suffering doth destroy, or is destroyed,   190
Even by the sufferer—and, in each event,
Ends:—Some, with hope replenished and rebuoyed,
Return to whence they came—with like intent,
And weave their web again; some, bowed and bent,

Wax gray and ghastly, withering ere their time,
And perish with the reed on which they leant;
Some seek devotion—toil—war—good or crime,
According as their souls were formed to sink or climb.

XXIII

But ever and anon of griefs subdued
There comes a token like a Scorpion's sting,   200
Scarce seen, but with fresh bitterness imbued;
And slight withal may be the things which bring
Back on the heart the weight which it would fling
Aside for ever: it may be a sound—
A tone of music—summer's eve—or spring—
A flower—the wind—the Ocean—which shall wound,
Striking the electric chain wherewith we are darkly bound;

XXIV

And how and why we know not, nor can trace
Home to its cloud this lightning of the mind,
But feel the shock renewed, nor can efface   210
The blight and blackening which it leaves behind,
Which out of things familiar, undesigned,
When least we deem of such, calls up to view
The Spectres whom no exorcism can bind,
The cold—the changed—perchance the dead, anew—
The mourned—the loved—the lost—too many! yet how few!

XXV

But my Soul wanders; I demand it back
To meditate amongst decay, and stand
A ruin amidst ruins; there to track
Fall'n states and buried greatness, o'er a land   220
Which *was* the mightiest in its old command,
And *is* the loveliest, and must ever be
The master-mould of Nature's heavenly hand;
Wherein were cast the heroic and the free,—
The beautiful—the brave—the Lords of earth and sea,

XXVI

The Commonwealth of Kings—the Men of Rome!
And even since, and now, fair Italy!
Thou art the Garden of the World, the Home
Of all Art yields, and Nature can decree;
Even in thy desert, what is like to thee?   230
Thy very weeds are beautiful—thy waste
More rich than other climes' fertility;
Thy wreck a glory—and thy ruin graced
With an immaculate charm which cannot be defaced.

XXVII

The Moon is up, and yet it is not night—
Sunset divides the sky with her—a sea
Of glory streams along the Alpine height
Of blue Friuli's mountains; Heaven is free
From clouds, but of all colours seems to be,—
Melted to one vast Iris of the West,—   240
Where the Day joins the past Eternity;
While, on the other hand, meek Dian's crest
Floats through the azure air—an island of the blest!

XXVIII

A single star is at her side, and reigns
With her o'er half the lovely heaven; but still
Yon sunny Sea heaves brightly, and remains
Rolled o'er the peak of the far Rhætian hill,
As Day and Night contending were, until
Nature reclaimed her order:—gently flows
The deep-dyed Brenta, where their hues instil   250
The odorous purple of a new-born rose,
Which streams upon her stream, and glassed within it glows,

XXIX

Filled with the face of heaven, which, from afar,
Comes down upon the waters! all its hues,
From the rich sunset to the rising star,
Their magical variety diffuse:
And now they change—a paler Shadow strews

Its mantle o'er the mountains; parting Day
Dies like the Dolphin, whom each pang imbues
With a new colour as it gasps away—   260
The last still loveliest, till—'tis gone—and all is gray.

X X X

There is a tomb in Arqua;—reared in air,
Pillared in their sarcophagus, repose
The bones of Laura's lover: here repair
Many familiar with his well-sung woes,
The Pilgrims of his Genius. He arose
To raise a language, and his land reclaim
From the dull yoke of her barbaric foes:
Watering the tree which bears his Lady's name
With his melodious tears, he gave himself to Fame.   270

X X X I

They keep his dust in Arqua, where he died—
The mountain-village where his latter days
Went down the vale of years; and 'tis their pride—
An honest pride—and let it be their praise,
To offer to the passing stranger's gaze
His mansion and his sepulchre—both plain
And venerably simple—such as raise
A feeling more accordant with his strain
Than if a Pyramid formed his monumental fane.

X X X I I

And the soft quiet hamlet where he dwelt   280
Is one of that complexion which seems made
For those who their mortality have felt,
And sought a refuge from their hopes decayed
In the deep umbrage of a green hill's shade,
Which shows a distant prospect far away
Of busy cities, now in vain displayed,
For they can lure no further; and the ray
Of a bright Sun can make sufficient holiday.

XXXIII

Developing the mountains, leaves, and flowers,
And shining in the brawling brook, where-by,   290
Clear as its current, glide the sauntering hours
With a calm languor, which, though to the eye
Idlesse it seem, hath its morality.
If from society we learn to live,
'Tis Solitude should teach us how to die;
It hath no flatterers—Vanity can give
No hollow aid; alone—man with his God must strive:

XXXIV

Or, it may be, with Demons, who impair
The strength of better thoughts, and seek their prey
In melancholy bosoms—such as were   300
Of moody texture from their earliest day,
And loved to dwell in darkness and dismay,
Deeming themselves predestined to a doom
Which is not of the pangs that pass away;
Making the Sun like blood, the Earth a tomb,
The tomb a hell—and Hell itself a murkier gloom.

XXXV

Ferrara! in thy wide and grass-grown streets,
Whose symmetry was not for solitude,
There seems as 'twere a curse upon the Seats
Of former Sovereigns, and the antique brood   310
Of Este, which for many an age made good
Its strength within thy walls, and was of yore
Patron or Tyrant, as the changing mood
Of petty power impelled, of those who wore
The wreath which Dante's brow alone had worn before.

XXXVI

And Tasso is their glory and their shame—
Hark to his strain! and then survey his cell!
And see how dearly earned Torquato's fame,
And where Alfonso bade his poet dwell:
The miserable Despot could not quell   320

The insulted mind he sought to quench, and blend
With the surrounding maniacs, in the hell
Where he had plunged it. Glory without end
Scattered the clouds away—and on that name attend

XXXVII

The tears and praises of all time, while thine
Would rot in its oblivion—in the sink
Of worthless dust, which from thy boasted line
Is shaken into nothing—but the link
Thou formest in his fortunes bids us think
Of thy poor malice, naming thee with scorn: 330
Alfonso! how thy ducal pageants shrink
From thee! if in another station born,
Scarce fit to be the slave of him thou mad'st to mourn:

XXXVIII

Thou! formed to eat, and be despised, and die,
Even as the beasts that perish—save that thou
Hadst a more splendid trough and wider sty:
He! with a glory round his furrowed brow,
Which emanated then, and dazzles now,
In face of all his foes, the Cruscan quire,
And Boileau, whose rash envy could allow   340
No strain which shamed his country's creaking lyre,
That whetstone of the teeth—Monotony in wire!

XXXIX

Peace to Torquato's injured shade! 'twas his
In life and death to be the mark where Wrong
Aimed with her poisoned arrows,—but to miss.
Oh, Victor unsurpassed in modern song!
Each year brings forth its millions—but how long
The tide of Generations shall roll on,
And not the whole combined and countless throng
Compose a mind like thine? though all in one   350
Condensed their scattered rays—they would not form a Sun.

XL

Great as thou art, yet paralleled by those,
Thy countrymen, before thee born to shine,
The Bards of Hell and Chivalry: first rose
The Tuscan Father's Comedy Divine;
Then, not unequal to the Florentine,
The southern Scott, the minstrel who called forth
A new creation with his magic line,
And, like the Ariosto of the North,
Sang Ladye-love and War, Romance and Knightly Worth.   360

XLI

The lightning rent from Ariosto's bust
The iron crown of laurel's mimicked leaves;
Nor was the ominous element unjust,
For the true laurel-wreath which Glory weaves
Is of the tree no bolt of thunder cleaves,
And the false semblance but disgraced his brow;
Yet still, if fondly Superstition grieves,
Know, that the lightning sanctifies below
Whate'er it strikes;—yon head is doubly sacred now.

XLII

Italia! oh, Italia! thou who hast   370
The fatal gift of Beauty, which became
A funeral dower of present woes and past—
On thy sweet brow is sorrow ploughed by shame,
And annals graved in characters of flame.
Oh, God! that thou wert in thy nakedness
Less lovely or more powerful, and couldst claim
Thy right, and awe the robbers back, who press
To shed thy blood, and drink the tears of thy distress;

XLIII

Then might'st thou more appal—or, less desired,   380
Be homely and be peaceful, undeplored
For thy destructive charms; then, still untired,
Would not be seen the arméd torrents poured
Down the deep Alps; nor would the hostile horde

Of many-nationed spoilers from the Po
Quaff blood and water; nor the stranger's sword
Be thy sad weapon of defence—and so,
Victor or vanquished, thou the slave of friend or foe.

XLIV

Wandering in youth, I traced the path of him,
The Roman friend of Rome's least-mortal mind,
The friend of Tully: as my bark did skim   390
The bright blue waters with a fanning wind,
Came Megara before me, and behind
Ægina lay—Piræus on the right,
And Corinth on the left; I lay reclined
Along the prow, and saw all these unite
In ruin—even as he had seen the desolate sight;

XLV

For Time hath not rebuilt them, but upreared
Barbaric dwellings on their shattered site,
Which only make more mourned and more endeared
The few last rays of their far-scattered light,   400
And the crushed relics of their vanished might.
The Roman saw these tombs in his own age,
These sepulchres of cities, which excite
Sad wonder, and his yet surviving page
The moral lesson bears, drawn from such pilgrimage.

XLVI

That page is now before me, and on mine
His Country's ruin added to the mass
Of perished states he mourned in their decline,
And I in desolation: all that *was*
Of then destruction *is*; and now, alas!   410
Rome—Rome imperial, bows her to the storm,
In the same dust and blackness, and we pass
The skeleton of her Titanic form,
Wrecks of another world, whose ashes still are warm.

XLVII

Yet, Italy! through every other land
Thy wrongs should ring—and shall—from side to side;
Mother of Arts! as once of Arms! thy hand
Was then our Guardian, and is still our Guide;
Parent of our Religion! whom the wide
Nations have knelt to for the keys of Heaven!   420
Europe, repentant of her parricide,
Shall yet redeem thee, and, all backward driven,
Roll the barbarian tide, and sue to be forgiven.

XLVIII

But Arno wins us to the fair white walls,
Where the Etrurian Athens claims and keeps
A softer feeling for her fairy halls:
Girt by her theatre of hills, she reaps
Her corn, and wine, and oil—and Plenty leaps
To laughing life, with her redundant Horn.
Along the banks where smiling Arno sweeps   430
Was modern Luxury of Commerce born,
And buried Learning rose, redeemed to a new Morn.

XLIX

There, too, the Goddess loves in stone, and fills
The air around with Beauty—we inhale
The ambrosial aspect, which, beheld, instils
Part of its immortality—the veil
Of heaven is half undrawn—within the pale
We stand, and in that form and face behold
What Mind can make, when Nature's self would fail;
And to the fond Idolaters of old   440
Envy the innate flash which such a Soul could mould:

L

We gaze and turn away, and know not where,
Dazzled and drunk with Beauty, till the heart
Reels with its fulness; there—for ever there—
Chained to the chariot of triumphal Art,

We stand as captives, and would not depart.
Away!—there need no words, nor terms precise,
The paltry jargon of the marble mart,
Where Pedantry gulls Folly—we have eyes:
Blood—pulse—and breast confirm the Dardan Shepherd's
    prize.   450

LI

Appear'dst thou not to Paris in this guise?
Or to more deeply blest Anchises? or,
In all thy perfect Goddess-ship, when lies
Before thee thy own vanquished Lord of War?
And gazing in thy face as toward a star,
Laid on thy lap, his eyes to thee upturn,
Feeding on thy sweet cheek! while thy lips are
With lava kisses melting while they burn,
Showered on his eyelids, brow, and mouth, as from an urn!

LII

Glowing, and circumfused in speechless love—   460
Their full divinity inadequate
That feeling to express, or to improve—
The Gods become as mortals—and man's fate
Has moments like their brightest; but the weight
Of earth recoils upon us;—let it go!
We can recall such visions, and create,
From what has been, or might be, things which grow
Into thy statue's form, and look like gods below.

LIII

I leave to learnéd fingers, and wise hands,
The Artist and his Ape, to teach and tell   470
How well his Connoisseurship understands
The graceful bend, and the voluptuous swell:
Let these describe the undescribable:
I would not their vile breath should crisp the stream
Wherein that Image shall for ever dwell—
The unruffled mirror of the loveliest dream
That ever left the sky on the deep soul to beam.

L I V

In Santa Croce's holy precincts lie
Ashes which make it holier, dust which is
Even in itself an immortality,   480
Though there were nothing save the past, and this,
The particle of those sublimities
Which have relapsed to chaos:—here repose
Angelo's—Alfieri's bones—and his,
The starry Galileo, with his woes;
Here Machiavelli's earth returned to whence it rose.

L V

These are four minds, which, like the elements,
Might furnish forth creation:—Italy!
Time, which hath wronged thee with ten thousand rents
Of thine imperial garment, shall deny   490
And hath denied, to every other sky,
Spirits which soar from ruin:—thy Decay
Is still impregnate with divinity,
Which gilds it with revivifying ray;
Such as the great of yore, Canova is to-day.

L V I

But where repose the all Etruscan three—
Dante, and Petrarch, and, scarce less than they,
The Bard of Prose, creative Spirit! he
Of the Hundred Tales of Love—where did they lay
Their bones, distinguished from our common clay   500
In death as life? Are they resolved to dust,
And have their Country's Marbles nought to say?
Could not her quarries furnish forth one bust?
Did they not to her breast their filial earth entrust?

L V I I

Ungrateful Florence! Dante sleeps afar,
Like Scipio, buried by the upbraiding shore:
Thy factions, in their worse than civil war,
Proscribed the Bard whose name for evermore
Their children's children would in vain adore

With the remorse of ages; and the crown   510
Which Petrarch's laureate brow supremely wore,
Upon a far and foreign soil had grown—
His life, his Fame—his Grave, though rifled—not thine own.

LVIII

Boccaccio to his parent earth bequeathed
His dust,—and lies it not her Great among,
With many a sweet and solemn requiem breathed
O'er him who formed the Tuscan's siren tongue?
That music in itself, whose sounds are song,
The poetry of speech? No;—even his tomb
Uptorn, must bear the hyæna bigot's wrong,   520
No more amidst the meaner dead find room,
Nor claim a passing sigh, because it told for *whom!*

LVIX

And Santa Croce wants their mighty dust;
Yet for this want more noted, as of yore
The Cæsar's pageant, shorn of Brutus' bust,
Did but of Rome's best Son remind her more:
Happier Ravenna! on thy hoary shore,
Fortress of falling Empire! honoured sleeps
The immortal Exile;—Arqua, too, her store
Of tuneful relics proudly claims and keeps,   530
While Florence vainly begs her banished dead and weeps.

LX

What is her Pyramid of precious stones?
Of porphyry, jasper, agate, and all hues
Of gem and marble, to encrust the bones
Of merchant-dukes? the momentary dews
Which, sparkling to the twilight stars, infuse
Freshness in the green turf that wraps the dead,
Whose names are Mausoleums of the Muse,
Are gently prest with far more reverent tread
Than ever paced the slab which paves the princely head.   540

LXI

There be more things to greet the heart and eyes
In Arno's dome of Art's most princely shrine,
Where Sculpture with her rainbow Sister vies;
There be more marvels yet—but not for mine;
For I have been accustomed to entwine
My thoughts with Nature, rather, in the fields,
Than Art in galleries: though a work divine
Calls for my Spirit's homage, yet it yields
Less than it feels, because the weapon which it wields

LXII

Is of another temper, and I roam   550
By Thrasimene's lake, in the defiles
Fatal to Roman rashness, more at home;
For there the Carthaginian's warlike wiles
Come back before me, as his skill beguiles
The host between the mountains and the shore,
Where Courage falls in her despairing files,
And torrents, swoll'n to rivers with their gore,
Reek through the sultry plain, with legions scattered o'er,

LXIII

Like to a forest felled by mountain winds:
And such the storm of battle on this day,   560
And such the frenzy, whose convulsion blinds
To all save Carnage, that, beneath the fray,
An Earthquake reeled unheededly away!
None felt stern Nature rocking at his feet,
And yawning forth a grave for those who lay
Upon their bucklers for a winding sheet—
Such is the absorbing hate when warring nations meet!

LXIV

The Earth to them was as a rolling bark
Which bore them to Eternity—they saw
The Ocean round, but had no time to mark   570
The motions of their vessel; Nature's law,
In them suspended, recked not of the awe

Which reigns when mountains tremble, and the birds
Plunge in the clouds for refuge, and withdraw
From their down-toppling nests; and bellowing herds
Stumble o'er heaving plains—and Man's dread hath no words.

LXV

Far other scene is Thrasimene now;
Her lake a sheet of silver, and her plain
Rent by no ravage save the gentle plough;
Her agéd trees rise thick as once the slain   580
Lay where their roots are; but a brook hath ta'en—
A little rill of scanty stream and bed—
A name of blood from that day's sanguine rain;
And Sanguinetto tells ye where the dead
Made the earth wet, and turned the unwilling waters red.

LXVI

But thou, Clitumnus! in thy sweetest wave
Of the most living crystal that was e'er
The haunt of river-Nymph, to gaze and lave
Her limbs where nothing hid them, thou dost rear
Thy grassy banks whereon the milk-white steer   590
Grazes—the purest God of gentle waters!
And most serene of aspect, and most clear;
Surely that stream was unprofaned by slaughters—
A mirror and a bath for Beauty's youngest daughters!

LXVII

And on thy happy shore a Temple still,
Of small and delicate proportion, keeps,
Upon a mild declivity of hill,
Its memory of thee; beneath it sweeps
Thy current's calmness; oft from out it leaps
The finny darter with the glittering scales,   600
Who dwells and revels in thy glassy deeps;
While, chance, some scattered water-lily sails
Down where the shallower wave still tells its bubbling tales.

LXVIII

Pass not unblest the Genius of the place!
If through the air a Zephyr more serene
Win to the brow, 'tis his; and if ye trace
Along his margin a more eloquent green,
If on the heart the freshness of the scene
Sprinkle its coolness, and from the dry dust
Of weary life a moment lave it clean   610
With Nature's baptism,—'tis to him ye must
Pay orisons for this suspension of disgust.

LXIX

The roar of waters!—from the headlong height
Velino cleaves the wave-worn precipice;
The fall of waters! rapid as the light
The flashing mass foams shaking the abyss;
The Hell of Waters! where they howl and hiss,
And boil in endless torture; while the sweat
Of their great agony, wrung out from this
Their Phlegethon, curls round the rocks of jet   620
That gird the gulf around, in pitiless horror set,

LXX

And mounts in spray the skies, and thence again
Returns in an unceasing shower, which round,
With its unemptied cloud of gentle rain,
Is an eternal April to the ground,
Making it all one emerald:—how profound
The gulf! and how the Giant Element
From rock to rock leaps with delirious bound,
Crushing the cliffs, which, downward worn and rent
With his fierce footsteps, yield in chasms a fearful vent   630

LXXI

To the broad column which rolls on, and shows
More like the fountain of an infant sea
Torn from the womb of mountains by the throes
Of a new world, than only thus to be
Parent of rivers, which flow gushingly,

With many windings, through the vale:—Look back!
Lo! where it comes like an Eternity,
As if to sweep down all things in its track,
Charming the eye with dread,—a matchless cataract,

LXXII

Horribly beautiful! but on the verge,   640
From side to side, beneath the glittering morn,
An Iris sits, amids the infernal surge,
Like Hope upon a death-bed, and, unworn
Its steady dyes, while all around is torn
By the distracted waters, bears serene
Its brilliant hues with all their beams unshorn:
Resembling, 'mid the torture of the scene,
Love watching Madness with unalterable mien.

LXXIII

Once more upon the woody Apennine—
The infant Alps, which—had I not before   650
Gazed on their mightier Parents, where the pine
Sits on more shaggy summits, and where roar
The thundering Lauwine—might be worshipped more:
But I have seen the soaring Jungfrau rear
Her never-trodden snow, and seen the hoar
Glaciers of bleak Mont Blanc both far and near—
And in Chimari heard the Thunder-Hills of fear,

LXXIV

Th' Acroceraunian mountains of old name;
And on Parnassus seen the Eagles fly
Like Spirits of the spot, as 'twere for fame,   660
For still they soared unutterably high:
I've looked on Ida with a Trojan's eye;
Athos—Olympus—Ætna—Atlas—made
These hills seem things of lesser dignity;
All, save the lone Soracte's height, displayed
Not *now* in snow, which asks the lyric Roman's aid

LXXV

For our remembrance, and from out the plain
Heaves like a long-swept wave about to break,
And on the curl hangs pausing: not in vain
May he, who will, his recollections rake,   670
And quote in classic raptures, and awake
The hills with Latin echoes—I abhorred
Too much, to conquer for the Poet's sake,
The drilled dull lesson, forced down word by word
In my repugnant youth, with pleasure to record

LXXVI

Aught that recalls the daily drug which turned
My sickening memory; and, though Time hath taught
My mind to meditate what then it learned,
Yet such the fixed inveteracy wrought
By the impatience of my early thought,   680
That, with the freshness wearing out before
My mind could relish what it might have sought,
If free to choose, I cannot now restore
Its health—but what it then detested, still abhor.

LXXVII

Then farewell, Horace—whom I hated so,
Not for thy faults, but mine: it is a curse
To understand, not feel thy lyric flow,
To comprehend, but never love thy verse;
Although no deeper Moralist rehearse
Our little life, nor Bard prescribe his art,   690
Nor livelier Satirist the conscience pierce,
Awakening without wounding the touched heart,
Yet fare thee well—upon Soracte's ridge we part.

LXXVIII

Oh, Rome! my Country! City of the Soul!
The orphans of the heart must turn to thee,
Lone Mother of dead Empires! and control
In their shut breasts their petty misery.
What are our woes and sufferance? Come and see

The cypress—hear the owl—and plod your way
O'er steps of broken thrones and temples—Ye!   700
Whose agonies are evils of a day—
A world is at our feet as fragile as our clay.

LXXIX

The Niobe of nations! there she stands,
Childless and crownless, in her voiceless woe;
An empty urn within her withered hands,
Whose holy dust was scattered long ago;
The Scipios' tomb contains no ashes now;
The very sepulchres lie tenantless
Of their heroic dwellers: dost thou flow,
Old Tiber! through a marble wilderness?   710
Rise, with thy yellow waves, and mantle her distress.

LXXX

The Goth, the Christian—Time—War—Flood, and Fire,
Have dealt upon the seven-hilled City's pride;
She saw her glories star by star expire,
And up the steep barbarian Monarchs ride,
Where the car climbed the Capitol; far and wide
Temple and tower went down, nor left a site:—
Chaos of ruins! who shall trace the void,
O'er the dim fragments cast a lunar light,
And say, "here was, or is," where all is doubly night?   720

LXXXI

The double night of ages, and of her,
Night's daughter, Ignorance, hath wrapt and wrap
All round us; we but feel our way to err:
The Ocean hath his chart, the Stars their map,
And Knowledge spreads them on her ample lap;
But Rome is as the desert—where we steer
Stumbling o'er recollections; now we clap
Our hands, and cry "Eureka!" "it is clear"—
When but some false Mirage of ruin rises near.

LXXXII

Alas! the lofty city! and, alas,   730
The trebly hundred triumphs! and the day
When Brutus made the dagger's edge surpass
The Conqueror's sword in bearing fame away!
Alas, for Tully's voice, and Virgil's lay,
And Livy's pictured page!—but these shall be
Her resurrection; all beside—decay.
Alas, for Earth, for never shall we see
That brightness in her eye she bore when Rome was free!

LXXXIII

Oh, thou, whose chariot rolled on Fortune's wheel,
Triumphant Sylla! Thou, who didst subdue   740
Thy country's foes ere thou wouldst pause to feel
The wrath of thy own wrongs, or reap the due
Of hoarded vengeance till thine Eagles flew
O'er prostrate Asia;—thou, who with thy frown
Annihilated senates;—Roman, too,
With all thy vices—for thou didst lay down
With an atoning smile a more than earthly crown,

LXXXIV

Thy dictatorial wreath—couldst thou divine
To what would one day dwindle that which made
Thee more than mortal? and that so supine,   750
By aught than Romans, Rome should thus be laid?—
She who was named Eternal, and arrayed
Her warriors but to conquer—she who veiled
Earth with her haughty shadow, and displayed,
Until the o'er-canopied horizon failed,
Her rushing wings—Oh! she who was Almighty hailed!

LXXXV

Sylla was first of victors; but our own,
The sagest of usurpers, Cromwell!—he
Too swept off senates while he hewed the throne
Down to a block—immortal rebel! See   760
What crimes it costs to be a moment free,

And famous through all ages! but beneath
His fate the moral lurks of destiny;
His day of double victory and death
Beheld him win two realms, and happier yield his breath.

LXXXVI

The third of the same Moon whose former course
Had all but crowned him, on the selfsame day
Deposed him gently from his throne of force,
And laid him with the Earth's preceding clay.
And showed not Fortune thus how fame and sway,   770
And all we deem delightful, and consume
Our souls to compass through each arduous way,
Are in her eyes less happy than the tomb?
Were they but so in Man's, how different were his doom!

LXXXVII

And thou, dread Statue! yet existent in
The austerest form of naked majesty—
Thou who beheldest, 'mid the assassins' din,
At thy bathed base the bloody Cæsar lie,
Folding his robe in dying dignity—
An offering to thine altar from the Queen   780
Of gods and men, great Nemesis! did he die,
And thou, too, perish, Pompey? have ye been
Victors of countless kings, or puppets of a scene?

LXXXVIII

And thou, the thunder-stricken nurse of Rome!
She-wolf! whose brazen-imaged dugs impart
The milk of conquest yet within the dome
Where, as a monument of antique art,
Thou standest:—Mother of the mighty heart,
Which the great Founder sucked from thy wild teat,
Scorched by the Roman Jove's ethereal dart,   790
And thy limbs black with lightning—dost thou yet
Guard thine immortal cubs, nor thy fond charge forget?

LXXXIX

Thou dost;—but all thy foster-babes are dead—
The men of iron—and the World hath reared
Cities from out their sepulchres: men bled
In imitation of the things they feared,
And fought and conquered, and the same course steered,
At apish distance; but as yet none have,
Nor could, the same supremacy have neared,
Save one vain Man, who is not in the grave—   800
But, vanquished by himself, to his own slaves a slave—

XC

The fool of false dominion—and a kind
Of bastard Cæsar, following him of old
With steps unequal; for the Roman's mind
Was modelled in a less terrestrial mould,
With passions fiercer, yet a judgment cold,
And an immortal instinct which redeemed
The frailties of a heart so soft, yet bold—
Alcides with the distaff now he seemed
At Cleopatra's feet,—and now himself he beamed,   810

XCI

And came—and saw—and conquered! But the man
Who would have tamed his Eagles down to flee,
Like a trained falcon, in the Gallic van,
Which he, in sooth, long led to Victory,
With a deaf heart which never seemed to be
A listener to itself, was strangely framed;
With but one weakest weakness—Vanity—
Coquettish in ambition—still he aimed—
At what? can he avouch, or answer what he claimed?

XCII

And would be all or nothing—nor could wait   820
For the sure grave to level him; few years
Had fixed him with the Cæsars in his fate,
On whom we tread: For *this* the conqueror rears
The Arch of Triumph! and for this the tears

And blood of earth flow on as they have flowed,
An universal Deluge, which appears
Without an Ark for wretched Man's abode,
And ebbs but to reflow!—Renew thy rainbow, God!

XCIII

What from this barren being do we reap?
Our senses narrow, and our reason frail,   830
Life short, and truth a gem which loves the deep,
And all things weighed in Custom's falsest scale;
Opinion an Omnipotence,—whose veil
Mantles the earth with darkness, until right
And wrong are accidents, and Men grow pale
Lest their own judgments should become too bright,
And their free thoughts be crimes, and Earth have too much light.

XCIV

And thus they plod in sluggish misery,
Rotting from sire to son, and age to age,
Proud of their trampled nature, and so die,   840
Bequeathing their hereditary rage
To the new race of inborn slaves, who wage
War for their chains, and rather than be free,
Bleed gladiator-like, and still engage
Within the same Arena where they see
Their fellows fall before, like leaves of the same tree.

XCV

I speak not of men's creeds—they rest between
Man and his maker—but of things allowed,
Averred, and known, and daily, hourly seen—
The yoke that is upon us doubly bowed,   850
And the intent of Tyranny avowed,
The edict of Earth's rulers, who are grown
The apes of him who humbled once the proud,
And shook them from their slumbers on the throne;
Too glorious, were this all his mighty arm had done.

XCVI

Can tyrants but by tyrants conquered be,
And Freedom find no Champion and no Child,
Such as Columbia saw arise when she
Sprung forth a Pallas, armed and undefiled?
Or must such minds be nourished in the wild,   860
Deep in the unpruned forest, 'midst the roar
Of cataracts, where nursing Nature smiled
On infant Washington? Has Earth no more
Such seeds within her breast, or Europe no such shore?

XCVII

But France got drunk with blood to vomit crime;
And fatal have her Saturnalia been
To Freedom's cause, in every age and clime;
Because the deadly days which we have seen,
And vile Ambition, that built up between
Man and his hopes an adamantine wall,   870
And the base pageant last upon the scene,
Are grown the pretext for the eternal thrall
Which nips Life's tree, and dooms man's worst—his second fall.

XCVIII

Yet, Freedom! yet thy banner, torn but flying,
Streams like the thunder-storm *against* the wind!
Thy trumpet voice, though broken now and dying,
The loudest still the Tempest leaves behind;
Thy tree hath lost its blossoms, and the rind,
Chopped by the axe, looks rough and little worth,
But the sap lasts,—and still the seed we find   880
Sown deep, even in the bosom of the North;
So shall a better spring less bitter fruit bring forth.

XCIX

There is a stern round tower of other days,
Firm as a fortress, with its fence of stone,
Such as an army's baffled strength delays,
Standing with half its battlements alone,
And with two thousand years of ivy grown,

The garland of Eternity, where wave
The green leaves over all by Time o'erthrown;—
What was this tower of strength? within its cave   890
What treasure lay so locked, so hid?—A woman's grave

C

But who was she, the Lady of the dead,
Tombed in a palace? Was she chaste and fair?
Worthy a king's—or more—a Roman's bed?
What race of Chiefs and Heroes did she bear?
What daughter of her beauties was the heir?
How lived—how loved—how died she? Was she not
So honoured—and conspicuously there,
Where meaner relics must not dare to rot,
Placed to commemorate a more than mortal lot?   900

C I

Was she as those who love their lords, or they
Who love the lords of others? such have been
Even in the olden time, Rome's annals say.
Was she a matron of Cornelia's mien,
Or the light air of Egypt's graceful Queen,
Profuse of joy—or 'gainst it did she war,
Inveterate in virtue? Did she lean
To the soft side of the heart, or wisely bar
Love from amongst her griefs?—for such the affections are.

C I I

Perchance she died in youth—it may be, bowed   910
With woes far heavier than the ponderous tomb
That weighed upon her gentle dust: a cloud
Might gather o'er her beauty, and a gloom
In her dark eye, prophetic of the doom
Heaven gives its favourites—early death—yet shed
A sunset charm around her, and illume
With hectic light, the Hesperus of the dead,
Of her consuming cheek the autumnal leaflike red.

CIII

Perchance she died in age—surviving all,
Charms—kindred—children—with the silver gray   920
On her long tresses, which might yet recall,
It may be, still a something of the day
When they were braided, and her proud array
And lovely form were envied, praised, and eyed
By Rome—But whither would Conjecture stray?
Thus much alone we know—Metella died,
The wealthiest Roman's wife: Behold his love or pride!

CIV

I know not why—but standing thus by thee
It seems as if I had thine inmate known,
Thou Tomb! and other days come back on me   930
With recollected music, though the tone
Is changed and solemn, like the cloudy groan
Of dying thunder on the distant wind;
Yet, could I seat me by this ivied stone
Till I had bodied, forth the heated mind,
Forms from the floating wreck which Ruin leaves behind;

CV

And from the planks, far shattered o'er the rocks,
Built me a little bark of hope, once more
To battle with the Ocean and the shocks
Of the loud breakers, and the ceaseless roar   940
Which rushes on the solitary shore
Where all lies foundered that was ever dear:
But could I gather from the wave-worn shore
Enough for my rude boat,—where should I steer?
There woos no home, nor hope, nor life, save what is here.

CVI

Then let the Winds howl on! their harmony
Shall henceforth be my music, and the Night
The sound shall temper with the owlets' cry,
As I now hear them, in the fading light

Dim o'er the bird of darkness' native site,   950
Answering each other on the Palatine,
With their large eyes, all glistening gray and bright,
And sailing pinions.—Upon such a shrine
What are our petty griefs?—let me not number mine.

CVII

Cypress and ivy, weed and wallflower grown
Matted and massed together—hillocks heaped
On what were chambers—arch crushed, column strown
In fragments—choked up vaults, and frescos steeped
In subterranean damps, where the owl peeped,
Deeming it midnight:—Temples—Baths—or Halls?   960
Pronounce who can: for all that Learning reaped
From her research hath been, that these are walls—
Behold the Imperial Mount! 'tis thus the Mighty falls.

CVIII

There is the moral of all human tales;
'Tis but the same rehearsal of the past,
First Freedom, and then Glory—when that fails,
Wealth—Vice—Corruption,—Barbarism at last:—
And History, with all her volumes vast,
Hath but *one* page,—'tis better written here,
Where gorgeous Tyranny hath thus amassed   970
All treasures, all delights, that Eye or Ear,
Heart, Soul could seek—Tongue ask—Away with words! draw
    near

CIX

Admire—exult—despise—laugh—weep,—for here
There is such matter for all feeling:—Man!
Thou pendulum betwixt a smile and tear,
Ages and Realms are crowded in this span,
This mountain, whose obliterated plan
The pyramid of Empires pinnacled,
Of Glory's gewgaws shining in the van
Till the Sun's rays with added flame were filled!   980
Where are its golden roofs? where those who dared to build?

C X

Tully was not so eloquent as thou,
Thou nameless column with the buried base!
What are the laurels of the Cæsar's brow?
Crown me with ivy from his dwelling-place.
Whose arch or pillar meets me in the face,
Titus' or Trajan's? No—'tis that of Time:
Triumph, arch, pillar, all he doth displace
Scoffing; and apostolic statues climb
To crush the Imperial urn, whose ashes slept sublime,   990

C X I

Buried in air, the deep blue sky of Rome,
And looking to the stars: they had contained
A Spirit which with these would find a home,
The last of those who o'er the whole earth reigned,
The Roman Globe—for, after, none sustained,
But yielded back his conquests:—he was more
Than a mere Alexander, and, unstained
With household blood and wine, serenely wore
His sovereign virtues—still we Trajan's name adore.

C X I I

Where is the rock of Triumph, the high place   1000
Where Rome embraced her heroes?—where the steep
Tarpeian?—fittest goal of Treason's race,
The Promontory whence the Traitor's Leap
Cured all ambition? Did the conquerors heap
Their spoils here? Yes; and in yon field below,
A thousand years of silenced factions sleep—
The Forum, where the immortal accents glow,
And still the eloquent air breathes—burns with Cicero!

C X I I I

The field of Freedom—Faction—Fame—and Blood:
Here a proud people's passions were exhaled,   1010
From the first hour of Empire in the bud
To that when further worlds to conquer failed;
But long before had Freedom's face been veiled,

And Anarchy assumed her attributes;
Till every lawless soldier, who assailed,
Trod on the trembling Senate's slavish mutes,
Or raised the venal voice of baser prostitutes.

CXIV

Then turn we to her latest Tribune's name,
From her ten thousand tyrants turn to thee,
Redeemer of dark centuries of shame—   1020
The friend of Petrarch—hope of Italy—
Rienzi! last of Romans! While the tree
Of Freedom's withered trunk puts forth a leaf,
Even for thy tomb a garland let it be—
The Forum's champion, and the people's chief—
Her new-born Numa thou—with reign, alas! too brief.

CXV

Egeria! sweet creation of some heart
Which found no mortal resting-place so fair
As thine ideal breast; whate'er thou art
Or wert,—a young Aurora of the air,   1030
The nympholepsy of some fond despair—
Or—it might be—a Beauty of the earth,
Who found a more than common Votary there
Too much adoring—whatsoe'er thy birth,
Thou wert a beautiful Thought, and softly bodied forth.

CXVI

The mosses of thy Fountain still are sprinkled
With thine Elysian water-drops; the face
Of thy cave-guarded Spring, with years unwrinkled,
Reflects the meek-eyed Genius of the place,
Whose green, wild margin now no more erase   1040
Art's works; nor must the delicate waters sleep
Prisoned in marble—bubbling from the base
Of the cleft statue, with a gentle leap
The rill runs o'er—and, round—fern, flowers, and ivy, creep

CXVII

Fantastically tangled: the green hills
Are clothed with early blossoms—through the grass
The quick-eyed lizard rustles—and the bills
Of summer-birds sing welcome as ye pass;
Flowers fresh in hue, and many in their class,
Implore the pausing step, and with their dyes   1050
Dance in the soft breeze in a fairy mass;
The sweetness of the Violet's deep blue eyes,
Kissed by the breath of heaven, seems coloured by its skies.

CXVIII

Here didst thou dwell, in this enchanted cover,
Egeria! thy all heavenly bosom beating
For the far footsteps of thy mortal lover;
The purple Midnight veiled that mystic meeting
With her most starry canopy—and seating
Thyself by thine adorer, what befel?
This cave was surely shaped out for the greeting   1060
Of an enamoured Goddess, and the cell
Haunted by holy Love—the earliest Oracle!

CXIX

And didst thou not, thy breast to his replying,
Blend a celestial with a human heart;
And Love, which dies as it was born, in sighing,
Share with immortal transports? could thine art
Make them indeed immortal, and impart
The purity of Heaven to earthly joys,
Expel the venom and not blunt the dart—
The dull satiety which all destroys—   1070
And root from out the soul the deadly weed which cloys?

CXX

Alas! our young affections run to waste,
Or water but the desert! whence arise
But weeds of dark luxuriance, tares of haste,
Rank at the core, though tempting to the eyes,

Flowers whose wild odours breathe but agonies,
And trees whose gums are poison; such the plants
Which spring beneath her steps as Passion flies
O'er the World's wilderness, and vainly pants
For some celestial fruit forbidden to our wants.   1080

CXXI

Oh, Love! no habitant of earth thou art—
An unseen Seraph, we believe in thee,—
A faith whose martyrs are the broken heart,—
But never yet hath seen, nor e'er shall see
The naked eye, thy form, as it should be;
The mind hath made thee, as it peopled Heaven,
Even with its own desiring phantasy,
And to a thought such shape and image given,
As haunts the unquenched soul—parched—wearied—wrung—
    and riven.

CXXII

Of its own beauty is the mind diseased,   1090
And fevers into false creation:—where,
Where are the forms the sculptor's soul hath seized?
In him alone. Can Nature show so fair?
Where are the charms and virtues which we dare
Conceive in boyhood and pursue as men,
The unreached Paradise of our despair,
Which o'er-informs the pencil and the pen,
And overpowers the page where it would bloom again?

CXXIII

Who loves, raves—'tis youth's frenzy—but the cure
Is bitterer still, as charm by charm unwinds   1100
Which robed our idols, and we see too sure
Nor Worth nor Beauty dwells from out the mind's
Ideal shape of such; yet still it binds—
The fatal spell, and still it draws us on,
Reaping the whirlwind from the oft-sown winds;
The stubborn heart, its alchemy begun,
Seems ever near the prize—wealthiest when most undone.

CXXIV

We wither from our youth, we gasp away—
Sick—sick; unfound the boon—unslaked the thirst,
Though to the last, in verge of our decay,   1110
Some phantom lures, such as we sought at first—
But all too late,—so are we doubly curst.
Love, Fame, Ambition, Avarice—'tis the same,
Each idle—and all ill—and none the worst—
For all are meteors with a different name,
And Death the sable smoke where vanishes the flame.

CXXV

Few—none—find what they love or could have loved,
Though accident, blind contact, and the strong
Necessity of loving, have removed
Antipathies—but to recur, ere long,   1120
Envenomed with irrevocable wrong;
And Circumstance, that unspiritual God
And Miscreator, makes and helps along
Our coming evils with a crutch-like rod,
Whose touch turns Hope to dust,—the dust we all have trod.

CXXVI

Our life is a false nature—'tis not in
The harmony of things,—this hard decree,
This uneradicable taint of Sin,
This boundless Upas, this all-blasting tree,
Whose root is Earth—whose leaves and branches be   1130
The skies which rain their plagues on men like dew—
Disease, death, bondage—all the woes we see,
And worse, the woes we see not—which throb through
The immedicable soul, with heart-aches ever new.

CXXVII

Yet let us ponder boldly—'tis a base
Abandonment of reason to resign
Our right of thought—our last and only place
Of refuge; this, at least, shall still be mine:
Though from our birth the faculty divine

Is chained and tortured—cabined, cribbed, confined,　　　　1140
And bred in darkness, lest the Truth should shine
Too brightly on the unpreparéd mind,
The beam pours in—for Time and Skill will couch the blind.

CXXVIII

Arches on arches! as it were that Rome,
Collecting the chief trophies of her line,
Would build up all her triumphs in one dome,
Her Coliseum stands; the moonbeams shine
As 'twere its natural torches—for divine
Should be the light which streams here,—to illume
This long-explored but still exhaustless mine　　　　1150
Of Contemplation; and the azure gloom
Of an Italian night, where the deep skies assume

CXXIX

Hues which have words and speak to ye of Heaven,
Floats o'er this vast and wondrous monument,
And shadows forth its glory. There is given
Unto the things of earth, which Time hath bent,
A Spirit's feeling, and where he hath leant
His band, but broke his scythe, there is a power
And magic in the ruined battlement,
For which the Palace of the present hour　　　　1160
Must yield its pomp, and wait till Ages are its dower.

CXXX

Oh, Time! the Beautifier of the dead,
Adorner of the ruin—Comforter
And only Healer when the heart hath bled;—
Time! the Corrector where our judgments err,
The test of Truth, Love—sole philosopher,
For all beside are sophists—from thy thrift,
Which never loses though it doth defer—
Time, the Avenger! unto thee I lift
My hands, and eyes, and heart, and crave of thee a gift:　　　　1170

CXXXI

Amidst this wreck, where thou hast made a shrine
And temple more divinely desolate—
Among thy mightier offerings here are mine,
Ruins of years—though few, yet full of fate:—
If thou hast ever seen me too elate,
Hear me not; but if calmly I have borne
Good, and reserved my pride against the hate
Which shall not whelm me, let me not have worn
This iron in my soul in vain—shall *they* not mourn?

CXXXII

And Thou, who never yet of human wrong   1180
Left the unbalanced scale, great Nemesis!
Here, where the ancient paid thee homage long—
Thou, who didst call the Furies from the abyss,
And round Orestes bade them howl and hiss
For that unnatural retribution—just,
Had it but been from hands less near—in this
Thy former realm, I call thee from the dust!
Dost thou not hear my heart?—Awake! thou shalt, and must.

CXXXIII

It is not that I may not have incurred,
For my ancestral faults or mine, the wound   1190
I bleed withal; and, had it been conferred
With a just weapon, it had flowed unbound;
But now my blood shall not sink in the ground—
To thee I do devote it—*Thou* shalt take
The vengeance, which shall yet be sought and found—
Which if *I* have not taken for the sake—
But let that pass—I sleep—but Thou shalt yet awake.

CXXXIV

And if my voice break forth, 'tis not that now
I shrink from what is suffered: let him speak
Who hath beheld decline, upon my brow,   1200
Or seen my mind's convulsion leave it weak;
But in this page a record will I seek.

Not in the air shall these my words disperse,
Though I be ashes; a far hour shall wreak
The deep prophetic fulness of this verse,
And pile on human heads the mountain of my curse!

CXXXV

That curse shall be Forgiveness.—Have I not—
Hear me, my mother Earth! behold it, Heaven!—
Have I not had to wrestle with my lot?
Have I not suffered things to be forgiven?   1210
Have I not had my brain seared, my heart riven,
Hopes sapped, name blighted, Life's life lied away?
And only not to desperation driven,
Because not altogether of such clay
As rots into the souls of those whom I survey.

CXXXVI

From mighty wrongs to petty perfidy
Have I not seen what human things could do?
From the loud roar of foaming calumny
To the small whisper of the as paltry few—
And subtler venom of the reptile crew,   1220
The Janus glance of whose significant eye,
Learning to lie with silence, would *seem* true—
And without utterance, save the shrug or sigh,
Deal round to happy fools its speechless obloquy.

CXXXVII

But I have lived, and have not lived in vain:
My mind may lose its force, my blood its fire,
And my frame perish even in conquering pain;
But there is that within me which shall tire
Torture and Time, and breathe when I expire;
Something unearthly, which they deem not of,   1230
Like the remembered tone of a mute lyre,
Shall on their softened spirits sink, and move
In hearts all rocky now the late remorse of Love.

CXXXVIII

The seal is set.—Now welcome, thou dread Power
Nameless, yet thus omnipotent, which here
Walk'st in the shadow of the midnight hour
With a deep awe, yet all distinct from fear;
Thy haunts are ever where the dead walls rear
Their ivy mantles, and the solemn scene
Derives from thee a sense so deep and clear   1240
That we become a part of what has been,
And grow upon the spot—all-seeing but unseen.

CXXXIX

And here the buzz of eager nations ran,
In murmured pity, or loud-roared applause,
As man was slaughtered by his fellow man.
And wherefore slaughtered? wherefore, but because
Such were the bloody Circus' genial laws,
And the imperial pleasure.—Wherefore not?
What matters where we fall to fill the maws
Of worms—on battle-plains or listed spot?   1250
Both are but theatres—where the chief actors rot.

CXL

I see before me the Gladiator lie:
He leans upon his hand—his manly brow
Consents to death, but conquers agony,
And his drooped head sinks gradually low—
And through his side the last drops, ebbing slow
From the red gash, fall heavy, one by one,
Like the first of a thunder-shower; and now
The arena swims around him—he is gone,
Ere ceased the inhuman shout which hailed the wretch who
    won.   1260

CXLI

He heard it, but he heeded not—his eyes
Were with his heart—and that was far away;
He recked not of the life he lost nor prize,

But where his rude hut by the Danube lay—
There were his young barbarians all at play,
There was their Dacian mother—he, their sire,
Butchered to make a Roman holiday—
All this rushed with his blood—Shall he expire
And unavenged?—Arise! ye Goths, and glut your ire!

CXLII

But here, where Murder breathed her bloody steam;—   1270
And here, where buzzing nations choked the ways,
And roared or murmured like a mountain stream
Dashing or winding as its torrent strays;
Here, where the Roman million's blame or praise
Was Death or Life—the playthings of a crowd—
My voice sounds much—and fall the stars' faint rays
On the arena void—seats crushed—walls bowed—
And galleries, where my steps seem echoes strangely loud.

CXLIII

A Ruin—yet what Ruin! from its mass
Walls—palaces—half-cities, have been reared;   1280
Yet oft the enormous skeleton ye pass,
And marvel where the spoil could have appeared.
Hath it indeed been plundered, or but cleared?
Alas! developed, opens the decay,
When the colossal fabric's form is neared:
It will not bear the brightness of the day,
Which streams too much on all—years—man—have reft away.

CXLIV

But when the rising moon begins to climb
Its topmost arch, and gently pauses there—
When the stars twinkle through the loops of Time,   1290
And the low night-breeze waves along the air
The garland-forest, which the gray walls wear,
Like laurels on the bald first Cæsar's head—
When the light shines serene but doth not glare—
Then in this magic circle raise the dead;—
Heroes have trod this spot—'tis on their dust ye tread.

CXLV

"While stands the Coliseum, Rome shall stand:
When falls the Coliseum, Rome shall fall;
And when Rome falls—the World." From our own land
Thus spake the pilgrims o'er this mighty wall   1300
In Saxon times, which we are wont to call
Ancient; and these three mortal things are still
On their foundations, and unaltered all—
Rome and her Ruin past Redemption's skill—
The World—the same wide den—of thieves, or what ye will.

CXLVI

Simple, erect, severe, austere, sublime—
Shrine of all saints and temple of all Gods,
From Jove to Jesus—spared and blest by Time—
Looking tranquillity, while falls or nods
Arch—empire—each thing round thee—and Man plods   1310
His way through thorns to ashes—glorious Dome!
Shalt thou not last? Time's scythe and Tyrants' rods
Shiver upon thee—sanctuary and home
Of Art and Piety—Pantheon!—pride of Rome!

CXLVII

Relic of nobler days, and noblest arts!
Despoiled yet perfect! with thy circle spreads
A holiness appealing to all hearts;
To Art a model—and to him who treads
Rome for the sake of ages, Glory sheds
Her light through thy sole aperture; to those   1320
Who worship, here are altars for their beads—
And they who feel for Genius may repose
Their eyes on honoured forms, whose busts around them close.

CXLVIII

There is a dungeon, in whose dim drear light
What do I gaze on? Nothing—Look again!
Two forms are slowly shadowed on my sight—
Two insulated phantoms of the brain:
It is not so—I see them full and plain—
An old man, and a female young and fair,

Fresh as a nursing mother, in whose vein   1330
The blood is nectar:—but what doth she there,
With her unmantled neck, and bosom white and bare?

CXLIX

Full swells the deep pure fountain of young life,
Where *on* the heart and *from* the heart we took
Our first and sweetest nurture—when the wife,
Blest into mother, in the innocent look,
Or even the piping cry of lips that brook
No pain and small suspense, a joy perceives
Man knows not—when from out its cradled nook
She sees her little bud put forth its leaves—   1340
What may the fruit be yet?—I know not—Cain was Eve's.

CL

But here Youth offers to Old Age the food,
The milk of his own gift: it is her Sire
To whom she renders back the debt of blood
Born with her birth:—No—he shall not expire
While in those warm and lovely veins the fire
Of health and holy feeling can provide
Great Nature's Nile, whose deep stream rises higher
Than Egypt's river:—from that gentle side
Drink—drink, and live—Old Man! Heaven's realm holds no
    such tide.   1350

CLI

The starry fable of the Milky Way
Has not thy story's purity; it is
A constellation of a sweeter ray,
And sacred Nature triumphs more in this
Reverse of her decree, than in the abyss
Where sparkle distant worlds:—Oh, holiest Nurse!
No drop of that clear stream its way shall miss
To thy Sire's heart, replenishing its source
With life, as our freed souls rejoin the Universe.

CLII

Turn to the Mole which Hadrian reared on high,   1360
Imperial mimic of old Egypt's piles,
Colossal copyist of deformity—
Whose travelled phantasy from the far Nile's
Enormous model, doomed the artist's toils
To build for Giants, and for his vain earth,
His shrunken ashes, raise this Dome: How smiles
The gazer's eye with philosophic mirth,
To view the huge design which sprung from such a birth!

CLIII

But lo! the Dome—the vast and wondrous Dome,
To which Diana's marvel was a cell—   1370
Christ's mighty shrine above His martyr's tomb!
I have beheld the Ephesian's miracle—
Its columns strew the wilderness, and dwell
The hyæna and the jackal in their shade;
I have beheld Sophia's bright roofs swell
There glittering mass i' the Sun, and have surveyed
Its sanctuary the while the usurping Moslem prayed;

CLIV

But thou, of temples old, or altars new,
Standest alone—with nothing like to thee—
Worthiest of God, the Holy and the True!   1380
Since Zion's desolation, when that He
Forsook his former city, what could be,
Of earthly structures, in His honour piled,
Of a sublimer aspect? Majesty—
Power—Glory—Strength—and Beauty all are aisled
In this eternal Ark of worship undefiled.

CLV

Enter: its grandeur overwhelms thee not;
And why? it is not lessened—but thy mind,
Expanded by the Genius of the spot,
Has grown colossal, and can only find   1390
A fit abode wherein appear enshrined

Thy hopes of Immortality—and thou
Shalt one day, if found worthy, so defined
See thy God face to face, as thou dost now
His Holy of Holies—nor be blasted by his brow.

CLVI

Thou movest—but increasing with the advance,
Like climbing some great Alp, which still doth rise,
Deceived by its gigantic elegance—
Vastness which grows but grows to harmonize—
All musical in its immensities;   1400
Rich marbles, richer painting—shrines where flame
The lamps of gold—and haughty dome which vies
In air with Earth's chief structures, though their frame
Sits on the firm-set ground—and this the clouds must claim.

CLVII

Thou seest not all—but piecemeal thou must break,
To separate contemplation, the great whole;
And as the Ocean many bays will make
That ask the eye—so here condense thy soul
To more immediate objects, and control
Thy thoughts until thy mind hath got by heart   1410
Its eloquent proportions, and unroll
In mighty graduations, part by part,
The Glory which at once upon thee did not dart,

CLVIII

Not by its fault—but thine: Our outward sense
Is but of gradual grasp—and as it is
That what we have of feeling most intense
Outstrips our faint expression; even so this
Outshining and o'erwhelming edifice
Fools our fond gaze, and greatest of the great
Defies at first our Nature's littleness,   1420
Till, growing with its growth, we thus dilate
Our Spirits to the size of that they contemplate.

CLIX

Then pause and be enlightened; there is more
In such a survey than the sating gaze
Of wonder pleased, or awe which would adore
The worship of the place, or the mere praise
Of Art and its great Masters, who could raise
What former time, nor skill, nor thought could plan:
The fountain of Sublimity displays
Its depth, and thence may draw the mind of Man   1430
Its golden sands, and learn what great Conceptions can.

CLX

Or, turning to the Vatican, go see
Laocoön's torture dignifying pain—
A Father's love and Mortal's agony
With an Immortal's patience blending:—Vain
The struggle—vain, against the coiling strain
And gripe, and deepening of the dragon's grasp,
The Old Man's clench; the long envenomed chain
Rivets the living links,—the enormous Asp
Enforces pang on pang, and stifles gasp on gasp.   1440

CLXI

Or view the Lord of the unerring bow,
The God of Life, and Poesy, and Light—
The Sun in human limbs arrayed, and brow
All radiant from his triumph in the fight;
The shaft hath just been shot—the arrow bright
With an Immortal's vengeance—in his eye
And nostril beautiful Disdain, and Might
And Majesty, flash their full lightnings by,
Developing in that one glance the Deity.

CLXII

But in his delicate form—a dream of Love,   1450
Shaped by some solitary Nymph, whose breast
Longed for a deathless lover from above,
And maddened in that vision—are exprest
All that ideal Beauty ever blessed

The mind with in its most unearthly mood,
When each conception was a heavenly Guest—
A ray of Immortality—and stood,
Starlike, around, until they gathered to a God!

CLXIII

And if it be Prometheus stole from Heaven
The fire which we endure—it was repaid   1460
By him to whom the energy was given
Which this poetic marble hath arrayed
With an eternal Glory—which, if made
By human hands, is not of human thought—
And Time himself hath hallowed it, nor laid
One ringlet in the dust—nor hath it caught
A tinge of years, but breathes the flame with which 'twas wrought.

CLXIV

But where is he, the Pilgrim of my Song,
The Being who upheld it through the past?
Methinks he cometh late and tarries long.   1470
He is no more—these breathings are his last—
His wanderings done—his visions ebbing fast,
And he himself as nothing:—if he was
Aught but a phantasy, and could be classed
With forms which live and suffer—let that pass—
His shadow fades away into Destruction's mass,

CLXV

Which gathers shadow—substance—life, and all
That we inherit in its mortal shroud—
And spreads the dim and universal pall
Through which all things grow phantoms; and the cloud   1480
Between us sinks and all which ever glowed,
Till Glory's self is twilight, and displays
A melancholy halo scarce allowed
To hover on the verge of darkness—rays
Sadder than saddest night, for they distract the gaze,

CLXVI

And send us prying into the abyss,
To gather what we shall be when the frame
Shall be resolved to something less than this—
Its wretched essence; and to dream of fame,
And wipe the dust from off the idle name   1490
We never more shall hear,—but never more,
Oh, happier thought! can we be made the same:—
It is enough in sooth that *once* we bore
These fardels of the heart—the heart whose sweat was gore.

CLXVII

Hark! forth from the abyss a voice proceeds,
A long low distant murmur of dread sound,
Such as arises when a nation bleeds
With some deep and immedicable wound;—
Through storm and darkness yawns the rending ground—
The gulf is thick with phantoms, but the Chief   1500
Seems royal still, though with her head discrowned,
And pale, but lovely, with maternal grief
She clasps a babe, to whom her breast yields no relief.

CLXVIII

Scion of Chiefs and Monarchs, where art thou?
Fond Hope of many nations, art thou dead?
Could not the Grave forget thee, and lay low
Some less majestic, less belovéd head?
In the sad midnight, while thy heart still bled,
The mother of a moment, o'er thy boy,
Death hushed that pang for ever: with thee fled   1510
The present happiness and promised joy
Which filled the Imperial Isles so full it seemed to cloy.

CLXIX

Peasants bring forth in safety.—Can it be,
Oh thou that wert so happy, so adored!
Those who weep not for Kings shall weep for thee,
And Freedom's heart, grown heavy, cease to hoard
Her many griefs, for *one*?—for she had poured

Her orisons for thee, and o'er thy head
Beheld her Iris.—Thou, too, lonely Lord,
And desolate Consort—vainly wert thou wed!　　　　1520
The husband of a year! the father of the dead!

CLXX

Of sackcloth was thy wedding garment made;
Thy bridal's fruit is ashes: in the dust
The fair-haired Daughter of the Isles is laid,
The love of millions! How we did entrust
Futurity to her! and, though it must
Darken above our bones, yet fondly deemed
Our children should obey her child, and blessed
Her and her hoped-for seed, whose promise seemed
Like stars to shepherds' eyes:—'twas but a meteor beamed.　　　　1530

CLXXI

Woe unto us—not her—for she sleeps well:
The fickle reek of popular breath, the tongue
Of hollow counsel, the false oracle,
Which from the birth of Monarchy hath rung
Its knell in princely ears, till the o'erstung
Nations have armed in madness—the strange fate
Which tumbles mightiest sovereigns, and hath flung
Against their blind omnipotence a weight
Within the opposing scale, which crushes soon or late,—

CLXXII

These might have been her destiny—but no—　　　　1540
Our hearts deny it: and so young, so fair,
Good without effort, great without a foe;
But now a Bride and Mother—and now *there!*
How many ties did that stern moment tear!
From thy Sire's to his humblest subject's breast
Is linked the electric chain of that despair,
Whose shock was as an Earthquake's, and opprest
The land which loved thee so that none could love thee best

CLXXIII

Lo, Nemi! navelled in the woody hills
So far, that the uprooting Wind which tears   1550
The oak from his foundation, and which spills
The Ocean o'er its boundary, and bears
Its foam against the skies, reluctant spares
The oval mirror of thy glassy lake;
And calm as cherished hate, its surface wears
A deep cold settled aspect nought can shake,
All coiled into itself and round, as sleeps the snake.

CLXXIV

And near, Albano's scarce divided waves
Shine from a sister valley;—and afar
The Tiber winds, and the broad Ocean laves   1560
The Latian coast where sprung the Epic war,
"Arms and the Man," whose re-ascending star
Rose o'er an empire:—but beneath thy right
Tully reposed from Rome;—and where yon bar
Of girdling mountains intercepts the sight
The Sabine farm was tilled, the weary Bard's delight.

CLXXV

But I forget.—My Pilgrim's shrine is won,
And he and I must part,—so let it be,—
His task and mine alike are nearly done;
Yet once more let us look upon the Sea;   1570
The Midland Ocean breaks on him and me,
And from the Alban Mount we now behold
Our friend of youth, that Ocean, which when we
Beheld it last by Calpe's rock unfold
Those waves, we followed on till the dark Euxine rolled

CLXXVI

Upon the blue Symplegades: long years—
Long, though not very many—since have done
Their work on both; some suffering and some tears
Have left us nearly where we had begun:
Yet not in vain our mortal race hath run—   1580

We have had our reward—and it is here,
That we can yet feel gladdened by the Sun,
And reap from Earth—Sea—joy almost as dear
As if there were no Man to trouble what is clear.

CLXXVII

Oh! that the Desert were my dwelling-place,
With one fair Spirit for my minister,
That I might all forget the human race,
And, hating no one, love but only her!
Ye elements!—in whose ennobling stir
I feel myself exalted—Can ye not   1590
Accord me such a Being? Do I err
In deeming such inhabit many a spot?
Though with them to converse can rarely be our lot.

CLXXVIII

There is a pleasure in the pathless woods,
There is a rapture on the lonely shore,
There is society, where none intrudes,
By the deep Sea, and Music in its roar:
I love not Man the less, but Nature more,
From these our interviews, in which I steal
From all I may be, or have been before,   1600
To mingle with the Universe, and feel
What I can ne'er express—yet can not all conceal.

CLXXIX

Roll on, thou deep and dark blue Ocean—roll!
Ten thousand fleets sweep over thee in vain;
Man marks the earth with ruin—his control
Stops with the shore;—upon the watery plain
The wrecks are all thy deed, nor doth remain
A shadow of man's ravage, save his own,
When, for a moment, like a drop of rain,
He sinks into thy depths with bubbling groan—   1610
Without a grave—unknelled, uncoffined, and unknown.

CLXXX

His steps are not upon thy paths,—thy fields
Are not a spoil for him,—thou dost arise
And shake him from thee; the vile strength he wields
For Earth's destruction thou dost all despise,
Spurning him from thy bosom to the skies—
And send'st him, shivering in thy playful spray
And howling, to his Gods, where haply lies
His petty hope in some near port or bay,
And dashest him again to Earth:—there let him lay.   1620

CLXXXI

The armaments which thunderstrike the walls
Of rock-built cities, bidding nations quake,
And Monarchs tremble in their Capitals,
The oak Leviathans, whose huge ribs make
Their clay creator the vain title take
Of Lord of thee, and Arbiter of War—
These are thy toys, and, as the snowy flake,
They melt into thy yeast of waves, which mar
Alike the Armada's pride, or spoils of Trafalgar.

CLXXXII

Thy shores are empires, changed in all save thee—   1630
Assyria—Greece—Rome—Carthage—what are they?
Thy waters washed them power while they were free,
And many a tyrant since; their shores obey
The stranger, slave, or savage; their decay
Has dried up realms to deserts:—not so thou,
Unchangeable save to thy wild waves' play;
Time writes no wrinkle on thine azure brow—
Such as Creation's dawn beheld, thou rollest now.

CLXXXIII

Thou glorious mirror, where the Almighty's form
Glasses itself in tempests; in all time,   1640
Calm or convulsed—in breeze, or gale, or storm—
Icing the Pole, or in the torrid clime
Dark-heaving—boundless, endless, and sublime—

The image of Eternity—the throne
Of the Invisible; even from out thy slime
The monsters of the deep are made—each Zone
Obeys thee—thou goest forth, dread, fathomless, alone.

CLXXXIV

And I have loved thee, Ocean! and my joy
Of youthful sports was on thy breast to be
Borne, like thy bubbles, onward: from a boy   1650
I wantoned with thy breakers—they to me
Were a delight; and if the freshening sea
Made them a terror—'twas a pleasing fear,
For I was as it were a Child of thee,
And trusted to thy billows far and near,
And laid my hand upon thy mane—as I do here.

CLXXXV

My task is done—my song hath ceased—my theme
Has died into an echo; it is fit
The spell should break of this protracted dream.
The torch shall be extinguished which hath lit   1660
My midnight lamp—and what is writ, is writ,—
Would it were worthier! but I am not now
That which I have been—and my visions flit
Less palpably before me—and the glow
Which in my Spirit dwelt is fluttering, faint, and low.

CLXXXVI

Farewell! a word that must be, and hath been—
A sound which makes us linger;—yet—farewell!
Ye! who have traced the Pilgrim to the scene
Which is his last—if in your memories dwell
A thought which once was his—if on ye swell   1670
A single recollection—not in vain
He wore his sandal-shoon, and scallop-shell;
Farewell! with *him* alone may rest the pain,
If such there were—with *you*, the Moral of his Strain.

SHORTER
POEMS

Early Poems

On Leaving Newstead Abbey

"Why dost thou build the hall, Son of the winged days?
Thou lookest from thy tower to-day: yet a few years, and the
blast of the desert comes: it howls in thy empty court."

—Ossian

1

Through thy battlements, Newstead, the hollow winds whistle:
    Thou, the hall of my Fathers, art gone to decay;
In thy once smiling garden, the hemlock and thistle
    Have choak'd up the rose which late bloom'd in the way.

2

Of the mail-cover'd Barons, who, proudly, to battle,
    Led their vassals from Europe to Palestine's plain,
The escutcheon and shield, which with ev'ry blast rattle,
    Are the only sad vestiges now that remain.

3

No more doth old Robert, with harp-stringing numbers,
    Raise a flame, in the breast, for the war-laurell'd wreath;
Near Askalon's towers, John of Horistan slumbers,
    Unnerv'd is the hand of his minstrel, by death.

10

4

Paul and Hubert too sleep in the valley of Cressy;
    For the safety of Edward and England they fell:
My Fathers! the tears of your country redress ye:
    How you fought! how you died! still her annals can tell.

5

On Marston, with Rupert, 'gainst traitors contending,
    Four brothers enrich'd, with their blood, the bleak field;
For the rights of a monarch their country defending,
    Till death their attachment to royalty seal'd.   20

6

Shades of heroes, farewell! your descendant departing
    From the seat of his ancestors, bids you adieu!
Abroad, or at home, your remembrance imparting
    New courage, he'll think upon glory and you.

7

Though a tear dim his eye at this sad separation,
    'Tis nature, not fear, that excites his regret;
Far distant he goes, with the same emulation,
    The fame of his fathers he ne'er can forget.

8

That fame, and that memory, still will he cherish;
    He vows that he ne'er will disgrace your renown: 30
Like you will he live, or like you will he perish;
    When decay'd, may he mingle his dust with your own!
                        1803. [First publ., December 1806.]

THE FIRST KISS OF LOVE

"Α βάρβιτος δὲ χορδαῖς
Ερωτα μοῦνον ἠχεῖ."
            —ANACREON

1

Away with your fictions of flimsy romance,
    Those tissues of falsehood which Folly has wove;

Give me the mild beam of the soul-breathing glance,
  Or the rapture which dwells on the first kiss of love.

2

Ye rhymers, whose bosoms with fantasy glow,
  Whose pastoral passions are made for the grove;
From what blest inspiration your sonnets would flow,
  Could you ever have tasted the first kiss of love!

3

If Apollo should e'er his assistance refuse,
  Or the Nine be dispos'd from your service to rove,   10
Invoke them no more, bid adieu to the Muse,
  And try the effect, of the first kiss of love.

4

I hate you, ye cold compositions of art,
  Though prudes may condemn me, and bigots reprove;
I court the effusions that spring from the heart,
  Which throbs, with delight, to the first kiss of love.

5

Your shepherds, your flocks, those fantastical themes,
  Perhaps may amuse, yet they never can move:
Arcadia displays but a region of dreams;
  What are visions like these, to the first kiss of love?   20

6

Oh! cease to affirm that man, since his birth,
  From Adam, till now, has with wretchedness strove;
Some portion of Paradise still is on earth,
  And Eden revives, in the first kiss of love.

7

When age chills the blood, when our pleasures are past—
  For years fleet away with the wings of the dove—
The dearest remembrance will still be the last,
  Our sweetest memorial, the first kiss of love.

            December 23, 1806. [*First publ., January 1807.*]

TO WOMAN

Woman! experience might have told me
That all must love thee, who behold thee:
Surely experience might have taught
Thy firmest promises are nought;
But, plac'd in all thy charms before me,
All I forget, but to *adore* thee.
Oh memory! thou choicest blessing,
When join'd with hope, when still possessing;
But how much curst by every lover
When hope is fled, and passion's over.   10
Woman, that fair and fond deceiver,
How prompt are striplings to believe her!
How throbs the pulse, when first we view
The eye that rolls in glossy blue,
Or sparkles black, or mildly throws
A beam from under hazel brows!
How quick we credit every oath,
And hear her plight the willing troth!
Fondly we hope 'twill last for aye,
When, lo! she changes in a day.   20
This record will for ever stand,
"Woman, thy vows are trac'd in sand."
                              [*First publ., December 1806.*]

REPLY TO SOME VERSES OF J. M. B. PIGOT, ESQ.,

ON THE CRUELTY OF HIS MISTRESS

1

Why, Pigot, complain
Of this damsel's disdain,
Why thus in despair do you fret?
For months you may try,
Yet, believe me, a *sigh*
Will never obtain a *coquette.*

2

Would you teach her to love?
For a time seem to rove;
At first she may *frown* in a *pet;*
But leave her awhile,
She shortly will smile,
And then you may *kiss* your *coquette.*

3

For such are the airs
Of these fanciful fairs,
They think all our *homage* a *debt:*
Yet a partial neglect
Soon takes an effect,
And humbles the proudest *coquette.*

4

Dissemble your pain,
And lengthen your chain,
And seem her *hauteur* to *regret;*
If again you shall sigh,
She no more will deny,
That *yours* is the rosy *coquette.*

5

If still, from false pride,
Your pangs she deride,
This whimsical virgin forget;
Some *other* admire,
Who will *melt* with your *fire,*
And laugh at the *little coquette.*

6

For *me,* I adore
Some *twenty* or more,
And love them most dearly; but yet,
Though my heart they enthral,
I'd abandon them all,
Did they act like your blooming *coquette.*

7

No longer repine,
Adopt this design,
And break through her slight-woven net!
Away with despair,   **40**
No longer forbear
To fly from the captious *coquette*.

8

Then quit her, my friend!
Your bosom defend,
Ere quite with her snares you're beset:
Lest your deep-wounded heart,
When incens'd by the smart
Should lead you to *curse* the *coquette*.

October 27, 1806. [*First publ., December 1806.*]

To the Sighing Strephon

1

Your pardon, my friend,
If my rhymes did offend,
Your pardon, a thousand times o'er;
From friendship I strove,
Your pangs to remove,
But, I swear, I will do so no more.

2

Since your *beautiful* maid,
Your flame has repaid,
No more I your folly regret;
She's now most divine,   **10**
And I bow at the shrine,
Of this quickly reformèd coquette.

3

Yet still, I must own,
I should never have known,

From *your verses,* what else she deserv'd,
    Your pain seem'd so great,
    I pitied your fate,
As your fair was so dev'lish reserv'd.

4

    Since the balm-breathing kiss
    Of this magical Miss,
Can such wonderful transports produce;
    Since the *"world you forget,*
    When your lips once have met,"
My counsel will get but abuse.

5

    You say, "When I rove,
    I know nothing of love;"
'Tis true, I am given to range;
    If I rightly remember,
    I've lov'd a good number;
Yet there's pleasure, at least, in a change.

6

    I will not advance,
    By the rules of romance,
To humour a whimsical fair;
    Though a smile may delight,
    Yet a *frown* will *affright,*
Or drive me to dreadful despair.

7

    While my blood is thus warm,
    I ne'er shall reform,
To mix in the Platonists' school;
    Of this I am sure,
    Was my Passion so pure,
Thy *Mistress* would think me a fool.

20

30

40

8

And if I should shun,
Every *woman* for *one*,
Whose *image* must fill my whole breast;
Whom I must *prefer,*
And *sigh* but for *her,*
What an *insult* 'twould be to the *rest!*

9

Now Strephon, good-bye;
I cannot deny,
Your *passion* appears most *absurd;*
Such *love* as you plead,
Is *pure* love, indeed,
For it *only* consists in the *word.*

[*First publ., December 1806.*]

LACHIN Y GAIR

1

Away, ye gay landscapes, ye gardens of roses!
  In you let the minions of luxury rove;
Restore me the rocks, where the snow-flake reposes,
  Though still they are sacred to freedom and love:
Yet, Caledonia, belov'd are thy mountains,
  Round their white summits though elements war;
Though cataracts foam 'stead of smooth-flowing fountains,
  I sigh for the valley of dark Loch na Garr.

2

Ah! there my young footsteps in infancy wander'd:
  My cap was the bonnet, my cloak was the plaid;
On chieftains, long perish'd, my memory ponder'd,
  As daily I strode through the pine-cover'd glade;
I sought not my home, till the day's dying glory
  Gave place to the rays of the bright polar star;
For fancy was cheer'd by traditional story,
  Disclos'd by the natives of dark Loch na Garr.

50

10

3

"Shades of the dead! have I not heard your voices
    Rise on the night-rolling breath of the gale?"
Surely, the soul of the hero rejoices,
    And rides on the wind, o'er his own Highland vale!   20
Round Loch na Garr, while the stormy mist gathers,
    Winter presides in his cold icy car:
Clouds, there, encircle the forms of my Fathers;
    They dwell in the tempests of dark Loch na Garr.

4

"Ill starr'd, though brave, did no visions foreboding
    Tell you that fate had forsaken your cause?"
Ah! were you destined to die at Culloden,
    Victory crown'd not your fall with applause:
Still were you happy, in Death's earthy slumber,
    You rest with your clan, in the caves of Braemar;   30
The Pibroch resounds, to the piper's loud number,
    Your deeds, on the echoes of dark Loch na Garr.

5

Years have roll'd on, Loch na Garr, since I left you,
    Years must elapse, ere I tread you again:
Nature of verdure and flowers has bereft you,
    Yet still are you dearer than Albion's plain:
England! thy beauties are tame and domestic,
    To one who has rov'd on the mountains afar:
Oh! for the crags that are wild and majestic,
    The steep, frowning glories of dark Loch na Garr.   40
                [*First publ., June 1807.*]

TO ROMANCE

1

Parent of golden dreams, Romance!
    Auspicious Queen of childish joys,
Who lead'st along, in airy dance,
    Thy votive train of girls and boys;

At length, in spells no longer bound,
    I break the fetters of my youth;
No more I tread thy mystic round,
    But leave thy realms for those of Truth.

2

And yet 'tis hard to quit the dreams
    Which haunt the unsuspicious soul,   10
Where every nymph a goddess seems,
    Whose eyes through rays immortal roll;
While Fancy holds her boundless reign,
    And all assume a varied hue;
When Virgins seem no longer vain,
    And even Woman's smiles are true.

3

And must we own thee, but a name,
    And from thy hall of clouds descend?
Nor find a Sylph in every dame,
    A Pylades in every friend?   20
But leave, at once, thy realms of air
    To mingling bands of fairy elves;
Confess that Woman's false as fair,
    And friends have feeling for—themselves?

4

With shame, I own, I've felt thy sway;
    Repentant, now thy reign is o'er;
No more thy precepts I obey,
    No more on fancied pinions soar;
Fond fool! to love a sparkling eye,
    And think that eye to truth was dear;   30
To trust a passing wanton's sigh,
    And melt beneath a wanton's tear!

5

Romance! disgusted with deceit,
    Far from thy motley court I fly,
Where Affectation holds her seat,

And sickly Sensibility;
Whose silly tears can never flow
For any pangs excepting thine;
Who turns aside from real woe,
To steep in dew thy gaudy shrine.   **40**

6

Now join with sable Sympathy,
With cypress crown'd, array'd in weeds,
Who heaves with thee her simple sigh,
Whose breast for every bosom bleeds;
And call thy sylvan female choir,
To mourn a Swain for ever gone,
Who once could glow with equal fire,
But bends not now before thy throne.

7

Ye genial Nymphs, whose ready tears
On all occasions swiftly flow;   **50**
Whose bosoms heave with fancied fears,
With fancied flames and phrenzy glow;
Say, will you mourn my absent name,
Apostate from your gentle train?
An infant Bard, at least, may claim
From you a sympathetic strain.

8

Adieu, fond race! a long adieu!
The hour of fate is hovering nigh;
E'en now the gulf appears in view,
Where unlamented you must lie: **60**
Oblivion's blackening lake is seen,
Convuls'd by gales you cannot weather,
Where you, and eke your gentle queen,
Alas! must perish altogether.

[*First publ., June 1807.*]

TO A LADY

[*Addressed to Mrs. Chaworth Musters, the "Mary" who was the great love of Byron's adolescence.*]

1

Oh! had my Fate been join'd with thine,
　　As once this pledge appear'd a token,
These follies had not, then, been mine,
　　For, then, my peace had not been broken.

2

To thee, these early faults I owe,
　　To thee, the wise and old reproving:
They know my sins, but do not know
　　'Twas thine to break the bonds of loving.

3

For once my soul, like thine, was pure,
　　And all its rising fires could smother;　　　　10
But, now, thy vows no more endure,
　　Bestow'd by thee upon another.

4

Perhaps, his peace I could destroy,
　　And spoil the blisses that await him;
Yet let my Rival smile in joy,
　　For thy dear sake, I cannot hate him.

5

Ah! since thy angel form is gone,
　　My heart no more can rest with any;
But what it sought in thee alone,
　　Attempts, alas! to find in many.　　　　20

6

Then, fare thee well, deceitful Maid!
　　'Twere vain and fruitless to regret thee;
Nor Hope, nor Memory yield their aid,
　　But Pride may teach me to forget thee.

7

Yet all this giddy waste of years,
    This tiresome round of palling pleasures;
These varied loves, these matrons' fears,
    These thoughtless strains to Passion's measures—

8

If thou wert mine, had all been hush'd:—
    This cheek, now pale from early riot,
With Passion's hectic ne'er had flush'd,
    But bloom'd in calm domestic quiet.

30

9

Yes, once the rural Scene was sweet,
    For Nature seem'd to smile before thee;
And once my Breast abhorr'd deceit,—
    For then it beat but to adore thee.

1 0

But, now, I seek for other joys—
    To think, would drive my soul to madness;
In thoughtless throngs, and empty noise,
    I conquer half my Bosom's sadness.

40

1 1

Yet, even in these, a thought will steal,
    In spite of every vain endeavour;
And fiends might pity what I feel—
    To know that thou art lost for ever.

[*First publ., June 1807.*]

"I WOULD I WERE A CARELESS CHILD"

1

I would I were a careless child,
    Still dwelling in my Highland cave,
Or roaming through the dusky wild,
    Or bounding o'er the dark blue wave;
The cumbrous pomp of Saxon pride,
    Accords not with the freeborn soul,

Which loves the mountain's craggy side,
    And seeks the rocks where billows roll.

2

Fortune! take back these cultur'd lands,
    Take back this name of splendid sound!   10
I hate the touch of servile hands,
    I hate the slaves that cringe around:
Place me among the rocks I love,
    Which sound to Ocean's wildest roar;
I ask but this—again to rove
    Through scenes my youth hath known before.

3

Few are my years, and yet I feel
    The World was ne'er design'd for me:
Ah! why do dark'ning shades conceal
    The hour when man must cease to be?   20
Once I beheld a splendid dream,
    A visionary scene of bliss:
Truth!—wherefore did thy hated beam
    Awake me to a world like this?

4

I lov'd—but those I lov'd are gone;
    Had friends—my early friends are fled.
How cheerless feels the heart alone,
    When all its former hopes are dead!
Though gay companions, o'er the bowl
    Dispel awhile the sense of ill;   30
Though Pleasure stirs the maddening soul,
    The heart—the heart—is lonely still.

5

How dull! to hear the voice of those
    Whom Rank or Chance, whom Wealth or Power,
Have made, though neither friends nor foes,
    Associates of the festive hour.
Give me again a faithful few,
    In years and feelings still the same,

And I will fly the midnight crew,
    Where boist'rous Joy is but a name.   40

6

And Woman, lovely Woman! thou,
    My hope, my comforter, my all!
How cold must be my bosom now,
    When e'en thy smiles begin to pall!
Without a sigh would I resign,
    This busy scene of splendid Woe,
To make that calm contentment mine,
    Which Virtue knows, or seems to know.

7

Fain would I fly the haunts of men—
    I seek to shun, not hate mankind;   50
My breast requires the sullen glen,
    Whose gloom may suit a darken'd mind.
Oh! that to me the wings were given,
    Which bear the turtle to her nest!
Then would I cleave the vault of Heaven,
    To flee away, and be at rest.

                              [First publ., 1808.]

"WHEN I ROV'D A YOUNG HIGHLANDER"

1

When I rov'd a young Highlander o'er the dark heath,
    And climb'd thy steep summit, oh Morven of snow!
To gaze on the torrent that thunder'd beneath,
    Or the mist of the tempest that gather'd below;
Untutor'd by science, a stranger to fear,
    And rude as the rocks, where my infancy grew,
No feeling, save one, to my bosom was dear;
    Need I say, my sweet Mary, 'twas centered in you?

2

Yet it could not be Love, for I knew not the name,—
    What passion can dwell in the heart of a child?   10

But, still, I perceive an emotion the same
　　As I felt, when a boy, on the crag-cover'd wild:
One image, alone, on my bosom impress'd,
　　I lov'd my bleak regions, nor panted for new;
And few were my wants, for my wishes were bless'd,
　　And pure were my thoughts, for my soul was with you.

3

I arose with the dawn, with my dog as my guide,
　　From mountain to mountain I bounded along;
I breasted the billows of Dee's rushing tide,
　　And heard at a distance the Highlander's song:　　　　20
At eve, on my heath-cover'd couch of repose,
　　No dreams, save of Mary, were spread to my view;
And warm to the skies my devotions arose,
　　For the first of my prayers was a blessing on you.

4

I left my bleak home, and my visions are gone;
　　The mountains are vanish'd, my youth is no more;
As the last of my race, I must wither alone,
　　And delight but in days, I have witness'd before:
Ah! splendour has rais'd, but embitter'd my lot;
　　More dear were the scenes which my infancy knew:　　30
Though my hopes may have fail'd, yet they are not forgot,
　　Though cold is my heart, still it lingers with you.

5

When I see some dark hill point its crest to the sky,
　　I think of the rocks that o'ershadow Colbleen;
When I see the soft blue of a love-speaking eye,
　　I think of those eyes that endear'd the rude scene;
When, haply, some light-waving locks I behold,
　　That faintly resemble my Mary's in hue,
I think on the long flowing ringlets of gold,
　　The locks that were sacred to beauty, and you.　　　　40

6

Yet the day may arrive, when the mountains once more
    Shall rise to my sight, in their mantles of snow;
But while these soar above me, unchang'd as before,
    Will Mary be there to receive me?—ah, no!
Adieu, then, ye hills, where my childhood was bred!
    Thou sweet flowing Dee, to thy waters adieu!
No home in the forest shall shelter my head,—
    Ah! Mary, what home could be mine, but with you?

[*First publ., 1808.*]

MISCELLANEOUS AND OCCASIONAL POEMS

FRAGMENT

WRITTEN SHORTLY AFTER THE MARRIAGE OF MISS CHAWORTH
[*Byron spent much of his time in 1803 and 1804 at Annesley Hall courting his cousin Mary Chaworth, who married John Musters in August 1805.*]

1

Hills of Annesley, Bleak and Barren,
    Where my thoughtless Childhood stray'd,
How the northern Tempests, warring,
    Howl above thy tufted Shade!

2

Now no more, the Hours beguiling,
    Former favourite Haunts I see;
Now no more my Mary smiling,
    Makes ye seem a Heaven to Me.

                    1805. [*First publ. 1830.*]

LINES INSCRIBED UPON A CUP FORMED FROM A SKULL

*[The skull was found in the garden of Newstead Abbey, Byron's es-
tate. "A strange fancy seized me," Byron told Thomas Medwin, "of
having it mounted as a drinking-cup. I accordingly sent it to town,
and it returned with a very high polish, and of a mottled colour like
tortoise-shell." Byron and his friends dressed in monkish gowns,
filled the cup with claret, and passed it around amid much hilarity.]*

1

Start not—nor deem my spirit fled:
　　In me behold the only skull,
From which, unlike a living head,
　　Whatever flows is never dull.

2

I liv'd, I lov'd, I quaff'd, like thee:
　　I died: let the earth my bones resign;
Fill up—thou canst not injure me;
　　The worm hath fouler lips than thine.

3

Better to hold the sparkling grape,
　　Than nurse the earth-worm's slimy brood;　　　10
And circle in the goblet's shape
　　The drink of Gods, than reptiles' food.

4

Where once my wit, perchance, hath shone,
　　In aid of others' let me shine;
And when, alas! our brains are gone,
　　What nobler substitute than wine?

5

Quaff while thou canst: another race,
　　When thou and thine, like me, are sped,
May rescue thee from Earth's embrace,
　　And rhyme and revel with the dead.　　　20

6

Why not? since through life's little day
  Our heads such sad effects produce;
Redeem'd from worms and wasting clay,
  This chance is theirs, to be of use.
          Newstead Abbey, 1808. [*First publ., 1814.*]

INSCRIPTION ON THE MONUMENT OF A NEWFOUNDLAND DOG

[*Byron's dog, "Boatswain," died November 18, 1808, and was buried in a vault in the garden at Newstead Abbey. In a will drawn up in 1811 (later changed), Byron expressed a wish to be buried in the same vault.*]

When some proud son of man returns to earth,
Unknown to glory, but upheld by birth,
The sculptor's art exhausts the pomp of woe
And storied urns record who rest below:
When all is done, upon the tomb is seen,
Not what he was, but what he should have been:
But the poor dog, in life the firmest friend,
The first to welcome, foremost to defend,
Whose honest heart is still his master's own,
Who labours, fights, lives, breathes for him alone,   10
Unhonour'd falls unnotic'd all his worth—
Denied in heaven the soul he held on earth:
While Man, vain insect! hopes to be forgiven,
And claims himself a sole exclusive Heaven.
Oh Man! thou feeble tenant of an hour,
Debas'd by slavery, or corrupt by power,
Who knows thee well must quit thee with disgust,
Degraded mass of animated dust!
Thy love is lust, thy friendship all a cheat,
Thy smiles hypocrisy, thy words deceit!   20
By nature vile, ennobled but by name,
Each kindred brute might bid thee blush for shame.
Ye! who perchance behold its simple urn,

Pass on—it honours none you wish to mourn:
To mark a Friend's remains these stones arise;
I never knew but one—and here he lies.
    Newstead Abbey, October 30, 1808. [*First publ., 1809.*]

"WELL! THOU ART HAPPY"

[*Byron dined at Annesley Hall with Mary Chaworth Musters and her husband and was much affected when her small daughter was brought into the room, for he had been greatly attached to Mary Chaworth before her marriage.*]

1

Well! thou art happy, and I feel
    That I should thus be happy too;
For still my heart regards thy weal
    Warmly, as it was wont to do.

2

Thy husband's blest—and 'twill impart
    Some pangs to view his happier lot:
But let them pass—Oh! how my heart
    Would hate him if he lov'd thee not!

3

When late I saw thy favourite child,
    I thought my jealous heart would break;   10
But when the unconscious infant smil'd,
    I kiss'd it for its mother's sake.

4

I kiss'd it,—and repress'd my sighs
    Its father in its face to see;
But then it had its mother's eyes,
    And they were all to love and me.

5

Mary, adieu! I must away;
    While thou art blest I'll not repine;

But near thee I can never stay;
    My heart would soon again be thine.   20

6

I deem'd that Time, I deem'd that Pride,
    Had quench'd at length my boyish flame;
Nor knew, till seated by thy side,
    My heart in all,—save hope,—the same.

7

Yet was I calm: I knew the time
    My breast would thrill before thy look;
But now to tremble were a crime—
    We met,—and not a nerve was shook.

8

I saw thee gaze upon my face,
    Yet meet with no confusion there: 30
One only feeling could'st thou trace;
    The sullen calmness of despair.

9

Away! away! my early dream,
    Remembrance never must awake:
Oh! where is Lethe's fabled stream?
    My foolish heart be still, or break.
            November 2, 1808. [First publ., 1809.]

TO A LADY

ON BEING ASKED MY REASON FOR
QUITTING ENGLAND IN THE SPRING
[*To Mrs. Chaworth Musters.*]

1

When Man, expell'd from Eden's bowers,
    A moment linger'd near the gate,
Each scene recall'd the vanish'd hours,
    And bade him curse his future fate.

2

But, wandering on through distant climes,
   He learnt to bear his load of grief;
Just gave a sigh to other times,
   And found in busier scenes relief.

3

Thus, Lady! will it be with me,
   And I must view thy charms no more;   10
For, while I linger near to thee,
   I sigh for all I knew before.

4

In flight I shall be surely wise,
   Escaping from temptation's snare;
I cannot view my Paradise
   Without the wish of dwelling there.
             December 2, 1808. [*First publ., 1809.*]

STANZAS WRITTEN IN PASSING THE AMBRACIAN GULF

[*This and the following poem were inspired by Byron's memory of Mrs. Constance Spencer Smith, whom he had met at Malta.*]

1

Through cloudless skies, in silvery sheen,
   Full beams the moon on Actium's coast:
And on these waves, for Egypt's queen,
   The ancient world was won and lost.

2

And now upon the scene I look,
   The azure grave of many a Roman;
Where stern Ambition once forsook
   His wavering crown to follow *Woman*

3

Florence! whom I will love as well
   (As ever yet was said or sung,   10

Since Orpheus sang his spouse from Hell)
    Whilst *thou* art *fair* and *I* am *young;*

4

Sweet Florence! those were pleasant times,
    When worlds were staked for Ladies' eyes:
Had bards as many realms as rhymes,
    Thy charms might raise new Antonies,

5

Though Fate forbids such things to be,
    Yet, by thine eyes and ringlets curled!
I cannot *lose* a *world* for thee,
    But would not lose *thee* for a World.   20
           November 14, 1809. [*First publ., 1812.*]

"THE SPELL IS BROKE, THE CHARM IS FLOWN!"

WRITTEN AT ATHENS, JANUARY 16, 1810

The spell is broke, the charm is flown!
    Thus is it with Life's fitful fever:
We madly smile when we should groan;
    Delirium is our best deceiver.
Each lucid interval of thought
    Recalls the woes of Nature's charter;
And *He* that acts as *wise men ought,*
    But *lives*—as saints have died—a martyr.
              [*First publ., 1812.*]

THE GIRL OF CADIZ

[*This poem, written during Byron's first pilgrimage, originally was inserted in the manuscript of* Childe Harold, *Canto I. Byron probably recognized that it was out of tone with that poem and substituted the stanzas "To Inez."*]

1

Oh never talk again to me
    Of northern climes and British ladies;
It has not been your lot to see,
    Like me, the lovely Girl of Cadiz.
Although her eye be not of blue,
    Nor fair her locks, like English lasses,
How far its own expressive hue
    The languid azure eye surpasses!

2

Prometheus-like from heaven she stole
    The fire that through those silken lashes   10
In darkest glances seems to roll,
    From eyes that cannot hide their flashes:
And as along her bosom steal
    In lengthened flow her raven tresses,
You'd swear each clustering lock could feel,
    And curled to give her neck caresses.

3

Our English maids are long to woo,
    And frigid even in possession;
And if their charms be fair to view,
    Their lips are slow at Love's confession;   20
But, born beneath a brighter sun,
    For love ordained the Spanish maid is,
And who,—when fondly, fairly won,—
    Enchants you like the Girl of Cadiz?

4

The Spanish maid is no coquette,
    Nor joys to see a lover tremble,

And if she love, or if she hate,
    Alike she knows not to dissemble.
Her heart can ne'er be bought or sold—
    Howe'er it beats, it beats sincerely;   **30**
And, though it will not bend to gold,
    'Twill love you long and love you dearly.

5

The Spanish girl that meets your love
    Ne'er taunts you with a mock denial,
For every thought is bent to prove
    Her passion in the hour of trial.
When thronging foemen menace Spain,
    She dares the deed and shares the danger;
And should her lover press the plain,
    She hurls the spear, her love's avenger.   **40**

6

And when, beneath the evening star,
    She mingles in the gay Bolero,
Or sings to her attuned guitar
    Of Christian knight or Moorish hero,
Or counts her beads with fairy hand
    Beneath the twinkling rays of Hesper,
Or joins Devotion's choral band,
    To chaunt the sweet and hallowed vesper;—

7

In each, her charms the heart must move
    Of all who venture to behold her;   **50**
Then let not maids less fair reprove
    Because her bosom is not colder:
Through many a clime 'tis mine to roam
    Where many a soft and melting maid is,
But none abroad, and few at home,
    May match the dark-eyed Girl of Cadiz.
                1809. [*First publ., 1832.*]

WRITTEN AFTER SWIMMING FROM SESTOS TO ABYDOS

[*Byron swam across the Hellespont in an hour and ten minutes on May 3, 1810.*]

1

If, in the month of dark December,
    Leander, who was nightly wont
(What maid will not the tale remember?)
    To cross thy stream, broad Hellespont!

2

If, when the wintry tempest roared,
    He sped to Hero, nothing loth,
And thus of old thy current poured,
    Fair Venus! how I pity both!

3

For *me*, degenerate modern wretch,
    Though in the genial month of May   10
My dripping limbs I faintly stretch,
    And think I've done a feat to-day.

4

But since he crossed the rapid tide,
    According to the doubtful story,
To woo,—and—Lord knows what beside,
    And swam for Love, as I for Glory;

5

'Twere hard to say who fared the best:
    Sad mortals! thus the Gods still plague you!
He lost his labour, I my jest:
    For he was drowned, and I've the ague.   20
            May 9, 1810. [*First publ., 1812.*]

"MAID OF ATHENS, ERE WE PART"

Ζωή μου, σᾶς ἀγαπῶ.

[*Philhellenic enthusiasm has exalted this sentimental lyric far beyond its merits as a poem and has made it one of the best known and most popular of all Byron's verses on Greek themes. It was inspired by Theresa Macri, daughter of a former British Consul from whose widow Byron rented rooms when he was in Athens in 1810. Theresa was then under thirteen.*]

1

Maid of Athens, ere we part,
Give, oh give me back my heart!
Or, since that has left my breast,
Keep it now, and take the rest!
Hear my vow before I go,
Ζωή μου, σᾶς ἀγαπῶ.

2

By those tresses unconfined,
Wooed by each Ægean wind;
By those lids whose jetty fringe
Kiss thy soft cheeks blooming tinge;   10
By those wild eyes like the roe,
Ζωή μου, σᾶς ἀγαπῶ.

3

By that lip I long to taste;
By that zone-encircled waist;
By all the token-flowers that tell
What words can never speak so well;
By Love's alternate joy and woe,
Ζωή μου, σᾶς ἀγαπῶ.

4

Maid of Athens! I am gone:
Think of me, sweet! when alone.   20
Though I fly to Istambol,
Athens holds my heart and soul:

Can I cease to love thee? No!
Ζωή μον, σᾶς ἀγαπῶ.

Athens, 1810. [First publ., 1812.]

FAREWELL TO MALTA

Adieu, ye joys of La Valette!
Adieu, Sirocco, sun, and sweat!
Adieu, thou palace rarely entered!
Adieu, ye mansions where—I've ventured!
Adieu, ye curséd streets of stairs!
(How surely he who mounts them swears!)
Adieu, ye merchants often failing!
Adieu, thou mob for ever railing!
Adieu, ye packets—without letters!
Adieu, ye fools—who ape your betters!   10
Adieu, thou damned'st quarantine,
That gave me fever, and the spleen!
Adieu that stage which makes us yawn, Sirs,
Adieu his Excellency's dancers!
Adieu to Peter—whom no fault's in,
But could not teach a colonel waltzing;
Adieu, ye females fraught with graces!
Adieu red coats, and redder faces!
Adieu the supercilious air
Of all that strut *en militaire!*   20
I go—but God knows when, or why,
To smoky towns and cloudy sky,
To things (the honest truth to say)
As bad—but in a different way.

Farewell to these, but not adieu
Triumphant sons of truest blue!
While either Adriatic shore,
And fallen chiefs, and fleets no more,
And nightly smiles, and daily dinners,
Proclaim you war and women's winners.   30
Pardon my Muse, who apt to prate is,

And take my rhyme—because 'tis "gratis."
And now I've got to Mrs. Fraser,
Perhaps you think I mean to praise her—
And were I vain enough to think
My praise was worth this drop of ink,
A line—or two—were no hard matter,
As here, indeed, I need not flatter:
But she must be content to shine
In better praises than in mine,   40
With lively air, and open heart,
And fashion's ease, without its art;
Her hours can gaily glide along,
Nor ask the aid of idle song.

And now, O Malta! since thou'st got us,
Thou little military hot-house!
I'll not offend with words uncivil,
And wish thee rudely at the Devil,
But only stare from out my casement,
And ask, "for what is such a place meant?"   50
Then, in my solitary nook,
Return to scribbling, or a book,
Or take my physic while I'm able
(Two spoonsful hourly, by this label),
Prefer my nightcap to my beaver,
And bless my stars I've got a fever.
                    May 26, 1811. [*First publ., 1816.*]

NEWSTEAD ABBEY

1

In the dome of my Sires as the clear moonbeam falls
Through Silence and Shade o'er its desolate walls,
It shines from afar like the glories of old;
It gilds, but it warms not—'tis dazzling, but cold.

2

Let the Sunbeam be bright for the younger of days:
'Tis the light that should shine on a race that decays,

When the Stars are on high and the dews on the ground,
And the long shadow lingers the ruin around.

3

And the step that o'erechoes the gray floor of stone
Falls sullenly now, for 'tis only my own;   10
And sunk are the voices that sounded in mirth,
And empty the goblet, and dreary the hearth.

4

And vain was each effort to raise and recall
The brightness of old to illumine our Hall;
And vain was the hope to avert our decline,
And the fate of my fathers had faded to mine.

5

And theirs was the wealth and the fulness of Fame,
And mine to inherit too haughty a name;
And theirs were the times and the triumphs of yore,
And mine to regret, but renew them no more.   20

6

And Ruin is fixed on my tower and my wall,
Too hoary to fade, and too massy to fall;
It tells not of Time's or the tempest's decay,
But the wreck of the line that have held it in sway.
                    August 26, 1811. [*First publ., 1878.*]

EPISTLE TO A FRIEND

IN ANSWER TO SOME LINES EXHORTING THE AUTHOR TO BE
CHEERFUL, AND TO "BANISH CARE"

[*The friend was probably the Rev. Francis Hodgson, who had tried
to cheer Byron and bring him out of his dark mood caused by the
death of his mother and several close friends in succession.*]

"Oh! banish care"—such ever be
The motto of *thy* revelry!
Perchance of *mine,* when wassail nights

Renew those riotous delights,
Wherewith the children of Despair
Lull the lone heart, and "banish care."
But not in Morn's reflecting hour,
When present, past, and future lower,
When all I loved is changed or gone,
Mock with such taunts the woes of one,   10
Whose every thought—but let them pass—
Thou know'st I am not what I was.
But, above all, if thou wouldst hold
Place in a heart that ne'er was cold,
By all the powers that men revere,
By all unto thy bosom dear,
Thy joys below, thy hopes above,
Speak—speak of anything but Love.

   'Twere long to tell, and vain to hear,
The tale of one who scorns a tear;   20
And there is little in that tale
Which better bosoms would bewail.
But mine has suffered more than well
'Twould suit philosophy to tell.
I've seen my bride another's bride,—
Have seen her seated by his side,—
Have seen the infant, which she bore,
Wear the sweet smile the mother wore,
When she and I in youth have smiled,
As fond and faultless as her child;—   30
Have seen her eyes, in cold disdain,
Ask if I felt no secret pain;
And *I* have acted well my part,
And made my cheek belie my heart,
Returned the freezing glance she gave,
Yet felt the while *that* woman's slave;—
Have kissed, as if without design,
The babe which ought to have been mine,
And showed, alas! in each caress
Time had not made me love the less.   40

But let this pass—I'll whine no more,
Nor seek again an eastern shore;
The world befits a busy brain,—
I'll hie me to its haunts again.
But if, in some succeeding year,
When Britain's "May is in the sere,"
Thou hear'st of one, whose deepening crimes
Suit with the sablest of the times,
Of one, whom love nor pity sways,
Nor hope of fame, nor good men's praise;   50
One, who in stern Ambition's pride,
Perchance not blood shall turn aside;
One ranked in some recording page
With the worst anarchs of the age,
Him wilt thou *know*—and *knowing* pause,
Nor with the *effect* forget the cause.

Newstead Abbey, October 11, 1811. [*First publ., 1830.*]

To Thyrza

[*The "Thyrza" of this and the following four poems is now known
to be John Edleston, a Cambridge chorister to whom Byron became
strongly attached and whose death in 1811 was the occasion of
more than half a dozen poems of the deepest melancholy.*]

Without a stone to mark the spot,
    And say, what Truth might well have said,
By all, save one, perchance forgot,
    Ah! wherefore art thou lowly laid?
By many a shore and many a sea
    Divided, yet beloved in vain;
The Past, the Future fled to thee,
    To bid us meet—no—ne'er again!
Could this have been—a word, a look,
    That softly said, "We part in peace,"   10
Had taught my bosom how to brook,
    With fainter sighs, thy soul's release.

And didst thou not—since Death for thee
    Prepared a light and pangless dart—
Once long for him thou ne'er shalt see,
    Who held, and holds thee in his heart?
Oh! who like him had watched thee here?
    Or sadly marked thy glazing eye,
In that dread hour ere Death appear,
    When silent Sorrow fears to sigh,   20
Till all was past? But when no more
    'Twas thine to reck of human woe,
Affection's heart-drops, gushing o'er,
    Had flowed as fast—as now they flow.
Shall they not flow, when, many a day,
    In these, to me, deserted towers—
Ere called but for a time away—
    Affection's mingling tears were ours?
Ours too the glance none saw beside;
    The smile none else might understand;   30
The whispered thought of hearts allied,
    The pressure of the thrilling hand;
The kiss, so guiltless and refined,
    That Love each warmer wish forebore;
Those eyes proclaimed so pure a mind,
    Ev'n Passion blushed to plead for more—
The tone, that taught me to rejoice,
    When prone, unlike thee, to repine;
The song, celestial from thy voice,
    But sweet to me from none but thine;   40
The pledge we wore—*I* wear it still,
    But where is thine?—Ah! where art thou?
Oft have I borne the weight of ill,
    But never bent beneath till now!
Well hast thou left in Life's best bloom
    The cup of Woe for me to drain;
If rest alone be in the tomb,
    I would not wish thee here again:
But if in worlds more blest than this

Thy virtues seek a fitter sphere,   50
Impart some portion of thy bliss,
 To wean me from mine anguish here.
Teach me—too early taught by thee!
 To bear, forgiving and forgiven:
On earth thy love was such to me;
 It fain would form my hope in Heaven!

    October 11, 1811. [*First publ., 1812.*]

"AWAY, AWAY, YE NOTES OF WOE!"

1

Away, away, ye notes of Woe!
 Be silent, thou once soothing Strain,
Or I must flee from hence—for, oh!
 I dare not trust those sounds again.
To me they speak of brighter days—
 But lull the chords, for now, alas!
I must not think, I may not gaze,
 On what I *am*—on what I *was.*

2

The voice that made those sounds more sweet
 Is hushed, and all their charms are fled;   10
And now their softest notes repeat
 A dirge, an anthem o'er the dead!
Yes, Thyrza! yes, they breathe of thee,
 Belovéd dust! since dust thou art;
And all that once was Harmony
 Is worse than discord to my heart!

3

'Tis silent all!—but on my ear
 The well remembered Echoes thrill;
I hear a voice I would not hear,
 A voice that now might well be still: 20
Yet oft my doubting Soul 'twill shake;
 Ev'n Slumber owns its gentle tone,

Till Consciousness will vainly wake
   To listen, though the dream be flown.

4

Sweet Thyrza! waking as in sleep,
   Thou art but now a lovely dream;
A Star that trembled o'er the deep,
   Then turned from earth its tender beam.
But he who through Life's dreary way
   Must pass, when Heaven is veiled in wrath,   30
Will long lament the vanished ray
   That scattered gladness o'er his path.
            December 8, 1811. [*First publ., 1812.*]

"ONE STRUGGLE MORE, AND I AM FREE"

1

One struggle more, and I am free
   From pangs that rend my heart in twain;
One last long sigh to Love and thee,
   Then back to busy life again.
It suits me well to mingle now
   With things that never pleased before:
Though every joy is fled below,
   What future grief can touch me more?

2

Then bring me wine, the banquet bring;
   Man was not formed to live alone: 10
I'll be that light unmeaning thing
   That smiles with all, and weeps with none.
It was not thus in days more dear,
   It never would have been, but thou
Hast fled, and left me lonely here;
   Thou'rt nothing,—all are nothing now.

3

In vain my lyre would lightly breathe!
   The smile that Sorrow fain would wear

But mocks the woe that lurks beneath,
  Like roses o'er a sepulchre.   20
Though gay companions o'er the bowl
  Dispel awhile the sense of ill;
Though Pleasure fires the maddening soul,
  The Heart,—the Heart is lonely still!

4

On many a lone and lovely night
  It soothed to gaze upon the sky;
For then I deemed the heavenly light
  Shone sweetly on thy pensive eye:
And oft I thought at Cynthia's noon,
  When sailing o'er the Ægean wave,   30
"Now Thyrza gazes on that moon"—
  Alas, it gleamed upon her grave!

5

When stretched on Fever's sleepless bed,
  And sickness shrunk my throbbing veins,
" 'Tis comfort still," I faintly said,
  "That Thyrza cannot know my pains:"
Like freedom to the time-worn slave—
  A boon 'tis idle then to give—
Relenting Nature vainly gave
  My life, when Thyrza ceased to live!   40

6

My Thyrza's pledge in better days,
  When Love and Life alike were new!
How different now thou meet'st my gaze!
  How tinged by time with Sorrow's hue!
The heart that gave itself with thee
  Is silent—ah, were mine as still!
Though cold as e'en the dead can be,
  It feels, it sickens with the chill.

7

Thou bitter pledge! thou mournful token!
  Though painful, welcome to my breast!   50

Still, still, preserve that love unbroken,
    Or break the heart to which thou'rt pressed.
Time tempers Love, but not removes,
    More hallowed when its Hope is fled:
Oh! what are thousand living loves
    To that which cannot quit the dead?
                [First publ., 1812.]

EUTHANASIA

1

When Time, or soon or late, shall bring
    The dreamless sleep that lulls the dead,
Oblivion! may thy languid wing
    Wave gently o'er my dying bed!

2

No band of friends or heirs be there,
    To weep, or wish, the coming blow:
No maiden, with dishevelled hair,
    To feel, or feign, decorous woe.

3

But silent let me sink to Earth,
    With no officious mourners near   10
I would not mar one hour of mirth,
    Nor startle Friendship with a fear.

4

Yet Love, if Love in such an hour
    Could nobly check its useless sighs,
Might then exert its latest power
    In her who lives, and him who dies.

5

'Twere sweet, my Psyche! to the last
    Thy features still serene to see:
Forgetful of its struggles past,
    E'en Pain itself should smile on thee.   20

6

But vain the wish—for Beauty still
    Will shrink, as shrinks the ebbing breath;
And Woman's tears, produced at will,
    Deceive in life, unman in death.

7

Then lonely be my latest hour,
    Without regret, without a groan;
For thousands Death hath ceased to lower,
    And pain been transient or unknown.

8

"Aye, but to die, and go," alas!
    Where all have gone, and all must go!   30
To be the nothing that I was
    Ere born to life and living woe!

9

Count o'er the joys thine hours have seen,
    Count o'er thy days from anguish free,
And know, whatever thou hast been,
    'Tis something better not to be.
                [*First publ., 1812.*]

"AND THOU ART DEAD, AS YOUNG AND FAIR"

"Heu, quanto minus est cum reliquis versari quam tui meminisse!"

1

And thou art dead, as young and fair
    As aught of mortal birth;
And form so soft, and charms so rare,
    Too soon returned to Earth!
Though Earth received them in her bed,
And o'er the spot the crowd may tread
    In carelessness or mirth,
There is an eye which could not brook
A moment on that grave to look.

2

I will not ask where thou liest low,
 Nor gaze upon the spot;
There flowers or weeds at will may grow,
 So I behold them not:
It is enough for me to prove
That what I loved, and long must love,
 Like common earth can rot;
To me there needs no stone to tell,
'Tis Nothing that I loved so well.

10

3

Yet did I love thee to the last
 As fervently as thou,
Who didst not change through all the past,
 And canst not alter now.
The love where Death has set his seal,
Nor age can chill, nor rival steal,
 Nor falsehood disavow:
And, what were worse, thou canst not see
Or wrong, or change, or fault in me.

20

4

The better days of life were ours;
 The worst can be but mine:
The sun that cheers, the storm that lowers,
 Shall never more be thine.
The silence of that dreamless sleep
I envy now too much to weep;
 Nor need I to repine,
That all those charms have passed away
I might have watched through long decay.

30

5

The flower in ripened bloom unmatched
 Must fall the earliest prey;
Though by no hand untimely snatched,
 The leaves must drop away:
And yet it were a greater grief

40

To watch it withering, leaf by leaf,
 Than see it plucked to-day;
Since earthly eye but ill can bear
To trace the change to foul from fair.

6

I know not if I could have borne
 To see thy beauties fade;
The night that followed such a morn
 Had worn a deeper shade:
Thy day without a cloud hath passed,   50
And thou wert lovely to the last;
 Extinguished, not decayed;
As stars that shoot along the sky
Shine brightest as they fall from high.

7

As once I wept, if I could weep,
 My tears might well be shed,
To think I was not near to keep
 One vigil o'er thy bed;
To gaze, how fondly! on thy face,
To fold thee in a faint embrace,   60
 Uphold thy drooping head;
And show that love, however vain,
Nor thou nor I can feel again.

8

Yet how much less it were to gain,
 Though thou hast left me free,
The loveliest things that still remain,
 Than thus remember thee!
The all of thine that cannot die
Through dark and dread Eternity
 Returns again to me,   70
And more thy buried love endears
Than aught, except its living years.
    February 1812. [*First publ., 1812.*]

LINES TO A LADY WEEPING

[*First published in* The Morning Chronicle, *March 7, 1812,
anonymously. Byron refers to a famous incident at a banquet at
Carlton House, February 22, 1812, when the Princess Charlotte
wept because her father, the Prince Regent, had repudiated his for-
mer political associates. There was a great furor when the poem ap-
peared in 1814 under Byron's name in the volume containing* The
Corsair.]

Weep, daughter of a royal line,
    A Sire's disgrace, a realm's decay;
Ah! happy if each tear of thine
    Could wash a Father's fault away!
Weep—for thy tears are Virtue's tears—
    Auspicious to these suffering Isles;
And be each drop in future years
    Repaid thee by thy People's smiles!
                March 1812.

"REMEMBER THEE! REMEMBER THEE!"

[*Addressed to Lady Caroline Lamb, who had written in one of
Byron's books in his absence, "Remember me!"*]

1

Remember thee! remember thee!
    Till Lethe quench Life's burning stream
Remorse and Shame shall cling to thee,
    And haunt thee like a feverish dream!

2

Remember thee! Aye, doubt it not.
    Thy husband too shall think of thee:
By neither shalt thou be forgot,
    Thou *false* to him, thou *fiend* to me!
                [*First publ., 1824.*]

"THOU ART NOT FALSE, BUT THOU ART FICKLE"

1

Thou art not false, but thou art fickle,
　　To those thyself so fondly sought;
The tears that thou hast forced to trickle
　　Are doubly bitter from that thought:
'Tis this which breaks the heart thou grievest,
Too well thou lov'st—*too soon* thou leavest.

2

The wholly false the *heart* despises,
　　And spurns deceiver and deceit;
But she who not a thought disguises,
　　Whose love is as sincere as sweet,—　　　　　10
When *she* can change who loved so truly,
It *feels* what mine has *felt* so newly.

3

To dream of joy and wake to sorrow
　　Is doomed to all who love or live;
And if, when conscious on the morrow,
　　We scarce our Fancy can forgive,
That cheated us in slumber only,
To leave the waking soul more lonely,

4

What must they feel whom no false vision
　　But truest, tenderest Passion warmed?　　　　20
Sincere, but swift in sad transition:
　　As if a dream alone had charmed?
Ah! sure such *grief* is *Fancy's* scheming,
And all thy *Change* can be but *dreaming!*
　　　　　　　　　　　[*First publ., 1814.*]

SONNET, TO GENEVRA

[*This sonnet and the following one were addressed to Lady Frances Webster. In contrast to these sentiments see "When we two parted" and the accompanying note.*]

Thine eyes' blue tenderness, thy long fair hair,
   And the wan lustre of thy features—caught,
   From contemplation—where serenely wrought,
Seems Sorrow's softness charmed from its despair—
Have thrown such speaking sadness in thine air,
   That—but I know thy blesséd bosom fraught
   With mines of unalloyed and stainless thought—
I should have deemed thee doomed to earthly care.
With such an aspect, by his colours blent,
   When from his beauty-breathing pencil born,   10
(Except that *thou* hast nothing to repent)
   The Magdalen of Guido saw the morn—
Such seem'st thou—but how much more excellent!
   With nought Remorse can claim—nor Virtue scorn.
          December 17, 1813. [*First publ., 1814.*]

SONNET, TO THE SAME

Thy cheek is pale with thought, but not from woe,
   And yet so lovely, that if Mirth could flush
   Its rose of whiteness with the brightest blush,
My heart would wish away that ruder glow:
And dazzle not thy deep-blue eyes—but, oh!
   While gazing on them sterner eyes will gush,
   And into mine my mother's weakness rush,
Soft as the last drops round Heaven's airy bow,
For, through thy long dark lashes low depending,
   The soul of melancholy Gentleness   10
Gleams like a Seraph from the sky descending,
   Above all pain, yet pitying all distress;
At once such majesty with sweetness blending,
   I worship more, but cannot love thee less.
          December 17, 1813. [*First publ., 1814.*]

ODE TO NAPOLEON BUONAPARTE

"Expende Annibalem:—quot libras in duce summo Invenies?"
—JUVENAL, *Sat.* x. line 147.

"The Emperor Nepos was acknowledged by the *Senate*, by the *Italians*, and by the Provincials of *Gaul*; his moral virtues, and military talents, were loudly celebrated; and those who derived any private benefit from his government announced, in prophetic strains, the restoration of the public felicity.... By this shameful abdication, he protracted his life about five years, in a very ambiguous state, between an Emperor and an Exile, till !!!"

—GIBBON'S *DECLINE AND FALL*, two vols., notes by Milman, I, 979.

I

'Tis done—but yesterday a King!
    And armed with Kings to strive—
And now thou art a nameless thing:
    So abject—yet alive!
Is this the man of thousand thrones,
Who strewed our earth with hostile bones,
    And can he thus survive?
Since he, miscalled the Morning Star,
Nor man nor fiend hath fallen so far.

II

Ill-minded man! why scourge thy kind   10
    Who bowed so low the knee?
By gazing on thyself grown blind,
    Thou taught'st the rest to see.
With might unquestioned,—power to save,—
Thine only gift hath been the grave
    To those that worshipped thee;
Nor till thy fall could mortals guess
Ambition's less than littleness!

III

Thanks for that lesson—it will teach
    To after-warriors more   20
Than high Philosophy can preach,
    And vainly preached before.

That spell upon the minds of men
Breaks never to unite again,
   That led them to adore
Those Pagod things of sabre-sway,
With fronts of brass, and feet of clay.

IV

The triumph, and the vanity,
   The rapture of the strife—
The earthquake-voice of Victory,   30
   To thee the breath of life;
The sword, the sceptre, and that sway
Which man seemed made but to obey,
   Wherewith renown was rife—
All quelled!—Dark Spirit! what must be
The madness of thy memory!

V

The Desolator desolate!
   The Victor overthrown!
The Arbiter of others' fate
   A Suppliant for his own!   40
Is it some yet imperial hope
That with such change can calmly cope?
   Or dread of death alone!
To die a Prince—or live a slave—
Thy choice is most ignobly brave!

VI

He who of old would rend the oak,
   Dreamed not of the rebound;
Chained by the trunk he vainly broke—
   Alone—how looked he round?
Thou, in the sternness of thy strength,   50
An equal deed hast done at length,
   And darker fate hast found:
He fell, the forest prowlers' prey;
But thou must eat thy heart away!

VII

The Roman, when his burning heart
  Was slaked with blood of Rome,
Threw down the dagger—dared depart,
  In savage grandeur, home.—
He dared depart in utter scorn
Of men that such a yoke had borne,
  Yet left him such a doom!
His only glory was that hour
Of self-upheld abandoned power.

VIII

The Spaniard, when the lust of sway
  Had lost its quickening spell,
Cast crowns for rosaries away,
  An empire for a cell;
A strict accountant of his beads,
A subtle disputant on creeds,
  His dotage trifled well:
Yet better had he neither known—
A bigot's shrine, nor despot's throne.

IX

But thou—from thy reluctant hand
  The thunderbolt is wrung—
Too late thou leav'st the high command
  To which thy weakness clung;
All Evil Spirit as thou art,
It is enough to grieve the heart
  To see thine own unstrung;
To think that God's fair world hath been
The footstool of a thing so mean;

X

And Earth hath spilt her blood for him,
  Who thus can hoard his own!
And Monarchs bowed the trembling limb,
  And thanked him for a throne!

Fair Freedom! we may hold thee dear,
When thus thy mightiest foes their fear
   In humblest guise have shown.
Oh! ne'er may tyrant leave behind
A brighter name to lure mankind!   90

XI

Thine evil deeds are writ in gore,
   Nor written thus in vain—
Thy triumphs tell of fame no more,
   Or deepen every stain:
If thou hadst died as Honour dies,
Some new Napoleon might arise,
   To shame the world again—
But who would soar the solar height,
To set in such a starless night?

XII

Weighed in the balance, hero dust   100
   Is vile as vulgar clay;
Thy scales, Mortality! are just
   To all that pass away:
But yet, methought, the living great
Some higher sparks should animate,
   To dazzle and dismay:
Nor deemed Contempt could thus make mirth
Of these, the Conquerors of the earth.

XIII

And she, proud Austria's mournful flower,
   Thy still imperial bride;   110
How bears her breast the torturing hour?
   Still clings she to thy side?
Must she too bend, must she too share
Thy late repentance, long despair,
   Thou throneless Homicide?
If still she loves thee, hoard that gem,—
'Tis worth thy vanished diadem!

XIV

Then haste thee to thy sullen Isle,
   And gaze upon the sea;
That element may meet thy smile—   120
   It ne'er was ruled by thee!
Or trace with thine all idle hand,
In loitering mood upon the sand,
   That Earth is now as free!
That Corinth's pedagogue hath now
Transferred his by-word to thy brow.

XV

Thou Timour! in his captive's cage
   What thoughts will there be thine,
While brooding in thy prisoned rage?
   But one—"The world *was* mine!"   130
Unless, like he of Babylon,
All sense is with thy sceptre gone,
   Life will not long confine
That spirit poured so widely forth—
So long obeyed—so little worth!

XVI

Or, like the thief of fire from heaven,
   Wilt thou withstand the shock?
And share with him, the unforgiven,
   His vulture and his rock!
Foredoomed by God—by man accurst,   140
And that last act, though not thy worst,
   The very Fiend's arch mock;
He in his fall preserved his pride,
And, if a mortal, had as proudly died!

XVII

There was a day—there was an hour,
   While earth was Gaul's—Gaul thine—
When that immeasurable power
   Unsated to resign

Had been an act of purer fame
Than gathers round Marengo's name,   150
    And gilded they decline,
Through the long twilight of all time,
Despite some passing clouds of crime.

XVIII

But thou, forsooth, must be a King
    And don the purple vest,
As if that foolish robe could wring
    Remembrance from thy breast.
Where is that faded garment? Where
The gewgaws thou wert fond to wear,
    The star, the string, the crest?   160
Vain froward child of Empire! say,
Are all thy playthings snatched away?

XIX

Where may the wearied eye repose
    When gazing on the Great;
Where neither guilty glory glows,
    Nor despicable state?
Yes—One—the first—the last—the best—
The Cincinnatus of the West,
    Whom Envy dared not hate,
Bequeathed the name of Washington   170
To make man blush there was but one!
            [First publ., April 16, 1814.]

STANZAS FOR MUSIC

[Addressed to Byron's half sister Augusta Leigh.]

1

I speak not, I trace not, I breathe not thy name,
There is grief in the sound, there is guilt in the fame:
But the tear which now burns on my cheek may impart
The deep thoughts that dwell in that silence of heart.

2

Too brief for our passion, too long for our peace,
Were those hours—can their joy or their bitterness cease?
We repent, we abjure, we will break from our chain,—
We will part, we will fly to—unite it again!

3

Oh! thine be gladness, and mine be the guilt!
Forgive me, adored one!—forsake, if thou wilt;— 10
But the heart which is thine shall expire undebased,
And *man* shall not break it—whatever *thou* mayst.

4

And stern to the haughty, but humble to thee,
This soul, in its bitterest blackness, shall be:
And our days seem as swift, and our moments more sweet,
With thee by my side, than with worlds at our feet.

5

One sigh of thy sorrow, one look of thy love,
Shall turn me or fix, shall reward or reprove;
And the heartless may wonder at all I resign—
Thy lip shall reply, not to them, but to *mine*. 20
               May 4, 1814. [*First publ., 1829*]

STANZAS FOR MUSIC

"O lachrymarum fons, tenero sacros
Ducentium ortus ex animo: quater
    Felix! In imo qui scatentem
      Pector te, pia Nympha sensit."
          —GRAY'S *POEMATA*.

[*Written after he had received news of the death of his Harrow
friend the Duke of Dorset.*]

1

There's not a joy the world can give like that it takes away,
When the glow of early thought declines in Feeling's dull decay;

'Tis not on Youth's smooth cheek the blush alone, which fades so fast,
But the tender bloom of heart is gone, ere Youth itself be past.

2

Then the few whose spirits float above the wreck of happiness
Are driven o'er the shoals of guilt or ocean of excess:
The magnet of their course is gone, or only points in vain
The shore to which their shivered sail shall never stretch again.

3

Then the mortal coldness of the soul like Death itself comes
   down;
It cannot feel for others' woes, it dare not dream its own;   10
That heavy chill has frozen o'er the fountain of our tears,
And though the eye may sparkle still, 'tis where the ice appears.

4

Though wit may flash from fluent lips, and mirth distract the breast,
Through midnight hours that yield no more their former hope of
   rest;
'Tis but as ivy-leaves around the ruined turret wreath,
All green and wildly fresh without, but worn and grey beneath.

5

Oh, could I feel as I have felt,—or be what I have been,
Or weep as I could once have wept, o'er many a vanished scene;
As springs, in deserts found, seem sweet, all brackish though they be,
So, midst the withered waste of life, those tears would flow to
   me.   20

                March 1815. [First publ., 1816.]

STANZAS FOR MUSIC

[*Probably addressed to John Edleston. See Marchand,* Byron: A
Biography, I, *313n.*]

1

There be none of Beauty's daughters
   With a magic like thee;

And like music on the waters
  Is thy sweet voice to me:
When, as if it sound were causing
The charméd Ocean's pausing,
The waves lie still and gleaming,
And the lulled winds seem dreaming:

2

And the Midnight Moon is weaving
  Her bright chain o'er the deep;   10
Whose breast is gently heaving,
  As an infant's asleep:
So the spirit bows before thee,
To listen and adore thee;
With a full but soft emotion,
Like the swell of Summer's ocean.

[First publ., 1816.]

DARKNESS

[*This poem, which registers the depths of Byron's melancholy in the summer of 1816, should be compared with the pious and sentimental handling of the same theme by Thomas Campbell in "The Last Man." It is characteristic that Byron should have pictured man under a dying sun reverting to the savagery from which he sprang, and that he should have ascribed the only selfless devotion in that dying world to a dog.*]

I had a dream, which was not all a dream.
The bright sun was extinguished, and the stars
Did wander darkling in the eternal space,
Rayless, and pathless, and the icy Earth
Swung blind and blackening in the moonless air;
Morn came and went—and came, and brought no day,
And men forgot their passions in the dread
Of this their desolation; and all hearts
Were chilled into a selfish prayer for light:
And they did live by watchfires—and the thrones,   10

The palaces of crownéd kings—the huts,
The habitations of all things which dwell,
Were burnt for beacons; cities were consumed,
And men were gathered round their blazing homes
To look once more into each other's face;
Happy were those who dwelt within the eye
Of the volcanoes, and their mountain-torch:
A fearful hope was all the World contained;
Forests were set on fire—but hour by hour
They fell and faded—and the crackling trunks   20
Extinguished with a crash—and all was black.
The brows of men by the despairing light
Wore an unearthly aspect, as by fits
The flashes fell upon them; some lay down
And hid their eyes and wept; and some did rest
Their chins upon their clenchéd hands, and smiled;
And others hurried to and fro, and fed
Their funeral piles with fuel, and looked up
With mad disquietude on the dull sky,
The pall of a past World; and then again   30
With curses cast them down upon the dust,
And gnashed their teeth and howled: the wild birds shrieked,
And, terrified, did flutter on the ground
And flap their useless wings; the wildest brutes
Came tame and tremulous; and vipers crawled
And twined themselves among the multitude,
Hissing, but stingless—they were slain for food:
And War, which for a moment was no more,
Did glut himself again:—a meal was bought
With blood, and each sate sullenly apart   40
Gorging himself in gloom: no Love was left;
All earth was but one thought—and that was Death,
Immediate and inglorious; and the pang
Of famine fed upon all entrails—men
Died, and their bones were tombless as their flesh;
The meagre by the meagre were devoured,
Even dogs assailed their masters, all save one,
And he was faithful to a corse, and kept

The birds and beasts and famished men at bay,
Till hunger clung them, or the dropping dead   50
Lured their lank jaws; himself sought out no food,
But with a piteous and perpetual moan,
And a quick desolate cry, licking the hand
Which answered not with a caress—he died.
The crowd was famished by degrees; but two
Of an enormous city did survive,
And they were enemies: they met beside
The dying embers of an altar-place
Where had been heaped a mass of holy things
For an unholy usage; they raked up,   60
And shivering scraped with their cold skeleton hands
The feeble ashes, and their feeble breath
Blew for a little life, and made a flame
Which was mockery; then they lifted up
Their eyes as it grew lighter, and beheld
Each other's aspects—saw, and shrieked, and died—
Even of their mutual hideousness they died,
Unknowing who he was upon whose brow
Famine had written Fiend. The World was void,
The populous and the powerful was a lump,   70
Seasonless, herbless, treeless, manless, lifeless—
A lump of death—a chaos of hard clay.
The rivers, lakes, and ocean all stood still,
And nothing stirred within their silent depths;
Ships sailorless lay rotting on the sea,
And their masts fell down piecemeal: as they dropped
They slept on the abyss without a surge
The waves were dead; the tides were in their grave,
The Moon, their mistress, had expired before;
The winds were withered in the stagnant air,   80
And the clouds perished; Darkness had no need
Of aid from them—She was the Universe.

Diodati, July 1816. [First publ., 1816.]

CHURCHILL'S GRAVE

A FACT LITERALLY RENDERED

[*Charles Churchill (1731–1764), the satirical poet. Byron visited his grave in Dover before sailing for Ostend, April 25, 1816.*]

I stood beside the grave of him who blazed
 The Comet of a season, and I saw
The humblest of all sepulchres, and gazed
 With not the less of sorrow and of awe
On that neglected turf and quiet stone,
With name no clearer than the names unknown,
Which lay unread around it; and I asked
 The Gardener of that ground, why it might be
That for this plant strangers his memory tasked,
 Through the thick deaths of half a century;   10
And thus he answered—"Well, I do not know
Why frequent travellers turn to pilgrims so;
He died before my day of Sextonship,
 And I had not the digging of this grave."
And is this all? I thought,—and do we rip
 The veil of Immortality, and crave
I know not what of honour and of light
Through unborn ages, to endure this blight?
So soon, and so successless? As I said,
The Architect of all on which we tread,   20
For Earth is but a tombstone, did essay
To extricate remembrance from the clay,
Whose minglings might confuse a Newton's thought,
 Were it not that all life must end in one,
Of which we are but dreamers;—as he caught
 As 'twere the twilight of a former Sun,
Thus spoke he,—"I believe the man of whom
You wot, who lies in this selected tomb,
Was a most famous writer in his day,
And therefore travellers step from out their way   30
To pay him honour,—and myself whate'er
 Your honour pleases:"—then most pleased I shook
 From out my pocket's avaricious nook

Some certain coins of silver, which as 'twere
Perforce I gave this man, though I could spare
So much but inconveniently:—Ye smile,
I see ye, ye profane ones! All the while,
Because my homely phrase the truth would tell.
You are the fool, not I—for I did dwell
With a deep thought, and with a softened eye,   40
On that old Sexton's natural homily,
In which there was Obscurity and Fame,—
The Glory and the Nothing of a Name.

Diodati, 1816. [*First publ., 1816.*]

PROMETHEUS

[*Byron had been fascinated by the defiant Titan since as a school-
boy he translated the* Prometheus Vinctus *of Aeschylus. As a
symbol of revolt against tyranny and oppression Prometheus en-
tered into most of the Byronic heroes. Byron said in* Don Juan *that
he was "born for opposition." But here Prometheus, though praised
for his efforts to render less "The sum of human wretchedness," is
rather a reminder of man's indomitable mind, the only consolation
for his "funereal destiny."*]

I

Titan! to whose immortal eyes
    The sufferings of mortality,
    See in their sad reality,
Were not as things that gods despise;
What was the pity's recompense?
A silent suffering, and intense;
The rock, the vulture, and the chain,
All that the proud can feel of pain,
The agony they do not show,
The suffocating sense of woe,   10
    Which speaks but in its loneliness,
And then is jealous lest the sky
Should have a listener, nor will sigh
    Until its voice is echoless.

II

Titan! To thee the strife was given
  Between the suffering and the will,
  Which torture where they cannot kill;
And the inexorable Heaven,
And the deaf tyranny of Fate,
The ruling principle of Hate,   20
Which for its pleasure doth create
The things it may annihilate,
Refused thee even the boon to die:
The wretched gift Eternity
Was thine—and thou hast borne it well.
All that The Thunderer wrung from thee
Was but the Menace which flung back
On him the torments of thy rack;
The fate thou didst so well forsee,
But would not to appease him tell;   30
And in thy Silence was his Sentence,
And in his Soul a vain repentance,
And evil dread so ill dissembled,
That in his hand the lightnings trembled.

III

Thy Godlike crime was to be kind,
  To render with thy precepts less
  The sum of human wretchedness,
And strengthen Man with his own mind;
But baffled as thou wert from high,
Still in thy patient energy,   40
In the endurance, and repulse
  Of thine impenetrable Spirit,
Which Earth and Heaven could not convulse,
  A mighty lesson we inherit:
Thou art a symbol and a sign
  To Mortals of their fate and force;
Like thee, Man is in part divine,
  A troubled stream from a pure source;
And Man in portions can foresee

His own funereal destiny;   50
His wretchedness, and his resistance,
And his sad unallied existence:
To which his Spirit may oppose
Itself—an equal to all woes—
　　And a firm will, and a deep sense,
Which even in torture can descry
　　Its own concentered recompense,
Triumphant where it dares defy,
And making Death Victory.
　　　　　Diodati, July 1816. [*First publ., 1816.*]

A FRAGMENT

Could I remount the river of my years
To the first fountain of our smiles and tears,
I would not trace again the stream of hours
Between their outworn banks of withered flowers,
But bid it flow as now—until it glides
Into the number of the nameless tides.

　　　　　　　* * * * *

What is this Death?—a quiet of the heart?
The whole of that of which we are a part?
For Life is but a vision—what I see
Of all which lives alone is Life to me,   10
And being so—the absent are the dead,
Who haunt us from tranquillity, and spread
A dreary shroud around us, and invest
With sad remembrancers our hours of rest.
　　The absent are the dead—for they are cold,
And ne'er can be what once we did behold;
And they are changed, and cheerless,—or if yet
The unforgotten do not all forget,
Since thus divided—equal must it be
If the deep barrier be of earth, or sea;   20
If may be both—but one day end it must
In the dark union of insensate dust.
　　The under-earth inhabitants—are they

But mingled millions decomposed to clay?
The ashes of a thousand ages spread
Wherever Man has trodden or shall tread?
Or do they in their silent cities dwell
Each in his incommunicative cell?
Or have their own language? and a sense
Of breathless being?—darkened and intense   30
As Midnight in her solitude?—Oh Earth!
Where are the past?—and wherefore had they birth?
The dead are thy inheritors—and we
But bubbles on thy surface; and the key
Of thy profundity is in the Grave,
The ebon portal of thy peopled cave,
Where I would walk in spirit, and behold
Our elements resolved to things untold,
And fathom hidden wonders, and explore
The essence of great bosoms now no more.   40

* * * * *

Diodati, July 1816. [First publ., 1830.]

Sonnet to Lake Leman

Rousseau—Voltaire—our Gibbon—and De Staël—
   Leman! these names are worthy of thy shore,
   Thy shore of names like these! Wert thou no more,
Their memory thy remembrance would recall:
To them thy banks were lovely as to all,
   But they have made them lovelier, for the lore
   Of mighty minds doth hallow in the core
Of human hearts the ruin of a wall
   Where dwelt the wise and wondrous; but by *thee*
How much more, Lake of Beauty! do we feel,   10
   In sweetly gliding o'er thy crystal sea,
The wild glow of that not ungentle zeal,
   Which of the Heirs of Immortality
Is proud, and makes the breath of Glory real!
            Diodati, July, 1816. [First publ., 1816.]

ON SAM ROGERS

[Written in 1818 and not intended for publication. Byron admired the poetry of Rogers and was friendly with him while in London, but he suspected him of being a scandal-monger. The verses, "Question" and "Answer," were first published in Fraser's Magazine *in 1833 while Rogers was still living.]*

QUESTION

Nose and Chin that make a knocker,
Wrinkles that would puzzle Cocker;
Mouth that marks the envious Scorner,
With a Scorpion in each corner
Curling up his tail to sting you,
In the place that most may wring you;
Eyes of lead-like hue and gummy,
Carcase stolen from some mummy,
Bowels—(but they were forgotten,
Save the Liver, and that's rotten),   10
Skin all sallow, flesh all sodden,
Form the Devil would frighten G—d in.
Is't a Corpse stuck up for show,
Galvanized at times to go?
With the Scripture has't connection,
New proof of the Resurrection?
Vampire, Ghost, or Goul (*sic*), what is it?
I would walk ten miles to miss it.

ANSWER

Many passengers arrest one,
To demand the same free question.   20
Shorter's my reply and franker,—
That's the Bard, and Beau, and Banker:
Yet, if you could bring about
Just to turn him inside out,
Satan's self would seem less sooty,

And his present aspect—Beauty.
Mark that (as he masks the bilious)
Air so softly supercilious,
Chastened bow, and mock humility,
Almost sickened to Servility: 30
Hear his tone (which is to talking
That which creeping is to walking—
Now on all fours, now on tiptoe):
Hear the tales he lends his lip to—
Little hints of heavy scandals—
Every friend by turns he handles:
All that women or that men do
Glides forth in an inuendo (*sic*)—
Clothed in odds and ends of humour,
Herald of each paltry rumour—   40
From divorces down to dresses,
Woman's frailties, Man's excesses:
All that life present of evil
Make for him a constant revel.
You're his foe—for that he fears you,
And in absence blasts and sears you;
You're his friend—for that he hates you,
First obliges, and then baits you,
Darting on the opportunity
When to do it with impunity: 50
You are neither—then he'll flatter,
Till he finds some trait for satire;
Hunts your weak point out, then shows it,
Where it injures, to expose it
In the mode that's most insidious,
Adding every trait that's hideous—
From the bile, whose blackening river
Rushes through his Stygian liver.
Then he thinks himself a lover—
Why? I really can't discover,   60
In his mind, age, face, or figure;
Viper broth might give him vigour:

Let him keep the cauldron steady,
He the venom has already.

For his faults—he has but *one*;
'Tis but Envy, when all's done:
He but pays the pain he suffers,
Clipping, like a pair of Snuffers,
Light that ought to burn the brighter
For his temporary blighter.   70
He's the Cancer of his Species,
And will eat himself to pieces,—
Plague personfied and Famine,—
Devil, whose delight is damning.
For his merits—don't you know 'em?
Once he wrote a pretty Poem.

                                             1818.

STANZAS TO THE PO

[*These stanzas were conceived in April 1819, while Byron was in Venice and not on the Po. There has been much confusion concerning them, partly because the Countess Teresa Guiccioli, to whom they were addressed, tried to confuse the issue after Byron's death, for she didn't want it to be known that they referred to her. There seems little doubt, however, that they express Byron's sincere feelings with regard to his involvement with Teresa, whom he had met in Venice in April, and whose husband in carrying her back to Ravenna had stopped at an estate at the mouth of the Po. The verses were actually written down on June 1, just before Byron left to join the Countess in Ravenna. On June 8, 1820, Byron wrote to Hobhouse: "You say the Po verses are fine; I thought so little of them, that they lay by me a year uncopied, but they were written in* red-hot *earnest and that makes them good." The poem was first published by Medwin in 1824. There is an unpublished manuscript version in Byron's hand in the Berg Collection in the New York Public Library which differs considerably from the published one, especially in the last eight lines, which read:*

My heart is all meridian, were it not
  I had not suffered now, nor should I be
Despite old tortures ne'er to be forgot
  The slave again—Oh! Love! at least of thee!
'Tis vain to struggle, I have struggled long
  To love again no more as once I loved.
Oh! Time! why leave this earliest Passion strong?
  To tear a heart which pants to be unmoved?]

1

River, that rollest by the ancient walls,
  Where dwells the Lady of my love, when she
Walks by thy brink, and there, perchance, recalls
  A faint and fleeting memory of me:

2

What if thy deep and ample stream should be
  A mirror of my heart, where she may read
The thousand thoughts I now betray to thee,
  Wild as thy wave, and headlong as thy speed!

3

What do I say—a mirror of my heart?
  Are not thy waters sweeping, dark, and strong?   10
Such as my feelings were and are, thou art;
  And such as thou art were my passions long.

4

Time may have somewhat tamed them,—not for ever;
  Thou overflow'st thy banks, and not for aye
Thy bosom overboils, congenial river!
  Thy floods subside, and mine have sunk away:

5

But left long wrecks behind, and now again,
  Borne in our old unchanged career, we move;
Thou tendest wildly onwards to the main,
  And I—to loving *one* I should not love.   20

6

The current I behold will sweep beneath
  Her native walls, and murmur at her feet;
Her eyes will look on thee, when she shall breathe
  The twilight air, unharmed by summer's heat.

7

She will look on thee,—I have looked on thee,
  Full of that thought: and, from that moment, ne'er
Thy waters could I dream of, name, or see,
  Without the inseparable sigh for her!

8

Her bright eyes will be imaged in thy stream,—
  Yes! They will meet the wave I gaze on now: 30
Mine cannot witness, even in a dream,
  That happy wave repass me in its flow!

9

The wave that bears my tears returns no more:
  Will she return by whom that wave shall sweep?—
Both treat thy banks, both wander on thy shore,
  I by thy source, she by the dark-blue deep.

1 0

But that which keepeth us apart is not
  Distance, nor depth of wave, nor space of earth,
But the distraction of a various lot,
  As various as the climates of our birth.   40

1 1

A stranger loves the Lady of the land,
  Born far beyond the mountains, but his blood
Is all meridian, as if never fanned
  By the black wind that chills the polar flood.

1 2

My blood is all meridian; were it not,
  I had not left my clime, nor should I be,
In spite of tortures, ne'er to be forgot,
  A slave again of love,—at least of thee.

1 3

'Tis vain to struggle—let me perish young—
 Live as I lived, and love as I have loved;   **50**
To dust if I return, from dust I sprung,
 And then, at least, my heart can ne'er be moved.

            June 1819.

STANZAS

[*Written in Venice, December 1, 1819, when Byron was debating whether to return to England or to rejoin the Countess Guiccioli in Ravenna.*]

1

Could Love for ever
Run like a river,
And Time's endeavour
 Be tried in vain—
No other pleasure
With this could measure;
And like a treasure
 We'd hug the chain.
But since our sighing
Ends not in dying,   **10**
And, formed for flying,
 Love plumes his wing;
Then for this reason
Let's love a season;
But let that season be only Spring.

2

When lovers parted
Feel broken-hearted,
And, all hopes thwarted,
 Expect to die;
A few years older,   **20**
Ah! how much colder
They might behold her
 For whom they sigh!

When linked together,
In every weather,
They pluck Love's feather
   From out his wing—
He'll stay forever,
But sadly shiver
Without his plumage, when past the Spring.   **30**

3

Like Chiefs of Faction,
His life is action—
A formal paction
   That curbs his reign,
Obscures his glory,
Despot no more, he
Such territory
   Quits his disdain.
Still, still advancing
With banners glancing,   **40**
His power enhancing,
   He must move on—
Repose but cloys him,
Retreat destroys him,
Love brooks not a degraded throne.

4

Wait not, fond lover!
 Till years are over,
And then recover
   As from a dream.
While each bewailing   **50**
The other's failing
With wrath and railing,
   All hideous seem—
While first decreasing,
Yet not quite ceasing,
Wait not till teasing,
   All passion blight:
If once diminished

Love's reign is finished—
Then part in friendship,—and bid good-night.   60

5

So shall Affection
To recollection
The dear connection
   Bring back with joy:
You had not waited
Till, tired or hated,
Your passions sated
   Began to cloy.
Your last embraces
Leave no cold traces—   70
The same fond faces
   As through the past:
And eyes, the mirrors
Of your sweet errors,
Reflect but rapture—not least though last.

6

True, separations
Ask more than patience;
What desperations
   From such have risen!
But yet remaining,   80
What is't but chaining
Hearts which, once waning,
   Beat 'gainst their prison?
Time can but cloy love,
And use destroy love:
The wingéd boy, Love,
   Is but for boys—
You'll find it torture
Though sharper, shorter,
To wean, and not wear out your joys.   90
        December 1, 1819. [*First publ., 1832.*]

STANZAS WRITTEN ON THE ROAD
BETWEEN FLORENCE AND PISA

1

Oh talk not to me of a name great in story—
The days of our Youth are the days of our glory;
And the myrtle and ivy of sweet two-and-twenty
Are worth all your laurels, though ever so plenty.

2

What are garlands and crowns to the brow that is wrinkled?
'Tis but as a dead flower with May-dew be-sprinkled:
Then away with all such from the head that is hoary,
What care I for the wreaths that can *only* give glory?

3

OH FAME!—if I e'er took delight in thy praises,
'Twas less for the sake of thy high-sounding phrases,   10
Than to see the bright eyes of the dear one discover,
She thought that I was not unworthy to love her.

4

There chiefly sought thee, *there* only I found thee;
Her Glance was the best of the rays that surround thee,
When it sparkled o'er aught that was bright in my story,
I knew it was Love, and I felt it was Glory.

November 6, 1821. [*First publ., 1830.*]

ARISTOMENES

CANTO FIRST

1

The Gods of old are silent on their shore,
Since the great Pan expired, and through the roar
Of the Ionian waters broke a dread
Voice which proclaimed "the Mighty Pan is dead."
How much died with him! false or true—the dream
Was beautiful which peopled every stream

With more than finny tenants, and adorned
The woods and waters with coy nymphs that scorned
Pursuing Deities, or in the embrace
Of gods brought forth the high heroic race   10
Whose names are on the hills and oe'r the seas.

Cephalonia, September 10, 1823. [First publ., 1903.]

LAST WORDS ON GREECE

What are to me those honours or renown
   Past or to come, a new-born people's cry?
Albeit for such I could despise a crown
   Of aught save laurel, or for such could die.
I am a fool of passion, and a frown
   Of thine to me is as an adder's eye
To the poor bird whose pinion fluttering down
   Wafts unto death the breast it bore so high:
Such is this maddening fascination grown,
   So strong thy magic or so weak am I.   10

[First publ., February 1887.]

ON THIS DAY I COMPLETE MY THIRTY-SIXTH YEAR

1

'T is time this heart should be unmoved,
   Since others it hath ceased to move:
Yet, though I cannot be beloved,
   Still let me love!

2

My days are in the yellow leaf;
   The flowers and fruits of Love are gone;
The worm, the canker, and the grief
   Are mine alone!

3

The fire that on my bosom preys
   Is lone as some Volcanic isles;   10

No torch is kindled at its blaze—
    A funeral pile.

4

The hope, the fear, the zealous care,
    The exalted portion of the pain
And power of love, I cannot share,
    But wear the chain.

5

But 't is not *thus*—and 't is not *here*—
    Such thoughts should take my soul, nor *now*
Where Glory decks the hero's bier,
    Or binds his brow.   20

6

The Sword, the Banner, and the Field,
    Glory and Greece, around me see!
The Spartan, borne upon his shield,
    Was not more free.

7

Awake! (not Greece—she *is* awake!)
    Awake, my spirit! Think through *whom*
Thy life-blood tracks its parent lake,
    And then strike home!

8

Tread those reviving passions down,
    Unworthy manhood!—unto thee   30
Indifferent should the smile or frown
    Of Beauty be.

9

If thou regret'st thy youth, *why live?*
    The land of honourable death
Is here:—up to the Field, and give
    Away thy breath!

1 0

Seek out—less often sought than found—
    A soldier's grave, for thee the best;
Then look around, and choose thy ground,
    And take thy Rest.   40
              Missolonghi, January 22, 1824.
            [*First publ., October 29, 1824.*]

[LOVE AND DEATH]

[*Probably the last poem Byron wrote, addressed (as were also the
"Last Words on Greece" and the poem on his thirty-sixth birthday)
to the Greek boy Lukas Chalandritsanos, whom Byron took from
Cephalonia to Missolonghi as a page.*]

1

I watched thee when the foe was at our side,
    Ready to strike at him—or thee and me,
Were safety hopeless—rather than divide
    Aught with one loved save love and liberty.

2

I watched thee on the breakers, when the rock,
    Received our prow, and all was storm and fear,
And bade thee cling to me through every shock;
    This arm would be thy bark, or breast thy bier.

3

I watched thee when the fever glazed thine eyes,
    Yielding my couch and stretched me on the ground   10
When overworn with watching, ne'er to rise
    From thence if thou an early grave hadst found.

4

They earthquake came, and rocked the quivering wall,
    And men and nature reeled as if with wine.
Whom did I seek around the tottering hall?
    For thee. Whose safety first provide for? Thine.

5

And when convulsive throes denied my breath
  The faintest utterance to my fading thought,
To thee—to thee—e'en in the gasp of death
  My spirit turned, oh! oftener than it ought.   20

6

Thus much and more; and yet thou lov'st me not,
  And never wilt! Love dwells not in our will.
Nor can I blame thee, though it be my lot
  To strongly, wrongly, vainly love thee still.

[*First publ., February 1887.*]

HEBREW MELODIES

ADVERTISEMENT

The subsequent poems were written at the request of my friend, the Hon. Douglas Kinnaird, for a Selection of Hebrew Melodies and have been published, with the music, arranged by Mr. Braham and Mr. Nathan.

January 1815.

"SHE WALKS IN BEAUTY"

[*Written after returning from a ball at Lady Sitwell's where he had seen the beautiful Lady Wilmot Horton in mourning with numerous spangles on her dress. Published with the* Hebrew Melodies *but not properly one of them.*]

I

She walks in Beauty, like the night
  Of cloudless climes and starry skies;
And all that's best of dark and bright
  Meet in her aspect and her eyes:
Thus mellowed to that tender light
  Which Heaven to gaudy day denies.

II

One shade the more, one ray the less,
   Had half impaired the nameless grace
Which waves in every raven tress,
   Or softly lightens o'er her face;   10
Where thoughts serenely sweet express,
   How pure, how dear their dwelling-place.

III

And on that cheek, and o'er that brow,
   So soft, so calm, yet eloquent,
The smiles that win, the tints that glow,
   But tell of days in goodness spent,
A mind at peace with all below,
   A heart whose love is innocent!
                              June 12, 1814.

"THE HARP THE MONARCH MINSTREL SWEPT"

I

The Harp the Monarch Minstrel swept,
   The King of men, the loved of Heaven!
Which Music hallowed while she wept
   O'er tones her heart of hearts had given—
Redoubled be her tears, its chords are riven!
   It softened men of iron mould,
      It gave them virtues not their own;
   No ear so dull, no soul so cold,
      That felt not—fired not to the tone,
Till David's Lyre grew mightier than his Throne!   10

II

It told the triumphs of our King,
   It wafted glory to our God;
It made our gladdened valleys ring,
   The cedars bow, the mountains nod;
Its sound aspired to Heaven and there abode!

Since then, though heard on earth no more,
   Devotion and her daughter Love
Still bid the bursting spirit soar
   To sounds that seem as from above,
In dreams that day's broad light can not remove.   20

"IF THAT HIGH WORLD"

I

If that high world, which lies beyond
   Our own, surviving Love endears;
If there the cherished heart be fond,
   The eye the same, except in tears—
How welcome those untrodden spheres!
   How sweet this very hour to die!
To soar from earth and find all fears
   Lost in thy light—Eternity!

II

It must be so: 'tis not for self
   That we so tremble on the brink;   10
And striving to o'erleap the gulf,
   Yet cling to Being's severing link.
Oh! in that future let us think
   To hold, each heart, the heart that shares;
With them the immortal waters drink,
   And, soul in soul, grow deathless theirs!

"THE WILD GAZELLE"

I

The wild gazelle on Judah's hills
   Exulting yet may bound,
And drink from all the living rills
   That gush on holy ground;
Its airy step and glorious eye
May glance in tameless transport by:—

II

A step as fleet, an eye more bright,
   Hath Judah witnessed there;
And o'er her scenes of lost delight
   Inhabitants more fair.
The cedars wave on Lebanon,
But Judah's statelier maids are gone!

10

III

More blest each palm that shades those plains
   Than Israel's scattered race;
For, taking root, it there remains
   In solitary grace:
It cannot quit its place of birth,
It will not live in other earth.

IV

But we must wander witheringly,
   In other lands to die;
And where our fathers' ashes be,
   Our own may never lie:
Our temple hath not left a stone,
And Mockery sits on Salem's throne.

20

"OH! WEEP FOR THOSE"

I

Oh! weep for those that wept by Babel's stream,
Whose shrines are desolate, whose land a dream;
Weep for the harp of Judah's broken shell;
Mourn—where their God hath dwelt the godless dwell!

II

And where shall Israel lave her bleeding feet?
And when shall Zion's song again seem sweet?
And Judah's melody once more rejoice
The hearts that leaped before its heavenly voice?

III

Tribes of the wandering foot and weary breast,
How shall ye flee away and be at rest!   10
The wild-dove hath her nest, the fox his cave,
Mankind their country—Israel but the grave!

"ON JORDAN'S BANKS"

I

On Jordan's banks the Arab's camels stray,
On Sion's hill the False One's votaries pray,
The Baal-adorer bows on Sinai's steep—
Yet there—even there—Oh God! thy thunders sleep:

II

There—where thy finger scorched the tablet stone!
There—where thy shadow to thy people shone!
Thy glory shrouded in its garb of fire:
Thyself—none living see and not expire!

III

Oh! in the lightning let thy glance appear;
Sweep from his shivered hand the oppressor's spear!   10
How long by tyrants shall thy land be trod?
How long thy temple worshipless, Oh God?

JEPHTHA'S DAUGHTER

I

Since our Country, our God—Oh, my Sire!
Demand that thy Daughter expire;
Since thy triumph was bought by the vow—
Strike the bosom that's bared for thee now!

II

And the voice of my mourning is o'er,
And the mountains behold me no more:
If the hand that I love lay me low,
There cannot be pain in the blow!

III

And of this, oh, my Father! be sure—
That the blood of thy child is as pure   10
As the blessing I beg ere it flow,
And the last thought that soothes me below.

IV

Though the virgins of Salem lament,
Be the judge and the hero unbent!
I have won the great battle for thee,
And my Father and Country are free!

V

When this blood of thy giving hath gushed,
When the voice that thou lovest is hushed,
Let my memory still be thy pride,
And forget not I smiled as I died!   20

"OH! SNATCHED AWAY IN BEAUTY'S BLOOM"

I

Oh! snatched away in Beauty's bloom,
On thee shall press no ponderous tomb;
But on thy turf shall roses rear
Their leaves, the earliest of the year;
And the wild cypress wave in tender gloom:

II

And oft by yon blue gushing stream
Shall Sorrow lean her drooping head,
And feed deep thought with many a dream,
And lingering pause and lightly tread;
Fond wretch! As if her step disturbed the dead!   10

III

Away! we know that tears are vain,
That Death nor heeds nor hears distress:
Will this unteach us to complain?
Or make one mourner weep the less?

And thou—who tell'st me to forget—
Thy looks are wan, thine eyes are wet.

"MY SOUL IS DARK"

I

My soul is dark—Oh! quickly string
    The harp I yet can brook to hear;
And let thy gentle fingers fling
    Its melting murmurs o'er mine ear.
If in this heart a hope be dear,
    That sound shall charm it forth again:
If in these eyes there lurk a tear
    'Twill flow, and cease to burn my brain.

II

But bid the strain be wild and deep,
    Nor let thy notes of joy be first: 10
I tell thee, minstrel, I must weep,
    Or else this heavy heart will burst;
For it hath been by sorrow nursed,
    And ached in sleepless silence long;
And now 'tis doomed to know the worst,
    And break at once—or yield to song.

"I SAW THEE WEEP"

I

I saw thee weep—the big bright tear
    Came o'er that eye of blue;
And then, methought, it did appear
    A violet dropping dew:
I saw thee smile—the sapphire's blaze
    Beside thee ceased to shine;
It could not match the living rays
    That filled that glance of thine.

II

As clouds from yonder sun receive
   A deep and mellow dye,
Which scarce the shade of coming eve
   Can banish from the sky,
Those smiles unto the moodiest mind
   Their own pure joy impart;
Their sunshine leaves a glow behind
   That lightens o'er the heart.

10

"THY DAYS ARE DONE"

I

Thy days are done, thy fame begun;
   Thy country's strains record
The triumphs of her chosen Son,
   The slaughters of his sword!
The deeds he did, the fields he won,
   The freedom he restored!

II

Though thou art fall'n, while we are free
   Thou shalt not taste of death!
The generous blood that flowed from thee
   Disdained to sink beneath:
Within our veins its currents be,
   Thy spirit on our breath!

10

III

Thy name, our charging hosts along,
   Shall be the battle-word!
Thy fall, the theme of choral song
   From virgin voices poured!
To weep would do thy glory wrong:
   Thou shalt not be deplored.

SONG OF SAUL BEFORE HIS LAST BATTLE

I

Warriors and Chiefs! should the shaft or the sword
Pierce me in leading the host of the Lord,
Heed not the corse, though a King's, in your path:
Bury your steel in the bosoms of Gath!

II

Thou who art bearing my buckler and bow,
Should the soldiers of Saul look away from the foe,
Stretch me that moment in blood at thy feet!
Mine be the doom which they dared not to meet.

III

Farewell to others, but never we part,
Heir to my Royalty—Son of my heart!   10
Bright is the diadem, boundless the sway,
Or kingly the death, which awaits us to-day!

Seaham, 1815.

SAUL

I

Thou whose spell can raise the dead,
   Bid the Prophet's form appear:—
"Samuel, raise thy buried head!
   King, behold the phantom Seer!"
Earth yawned; he stood the centre of a cloud:
Light changed its hue, retiring from his shroud.
Death stood all glassy in his fixéd eye;
His hand was withered, and his veins were dry;
His foot, in bony whiteness, glittered there,
Shrunken and sinewless, and ghastly bare;   10
From lips that moved not and unbreathing frame,
Like caverned winds, the hollow accents came.
Saul saw, and fell to earth, as falls the oak
At once, and blasted by the thunder-stroke.

11

"Why is my sleep disquieted?
Who is he that calls the dead?
Is it thou, O King? Behold,
Bloodless are these limbs, and cold:
Such are mine; and such shall be
Thine to-morrow, when with me: 20
Ere the coming day is done,
Such shalt thou be—such thy Son.
Fare thee well, but for a day,
Then we mix our mouldering clay.
Thou—thy race, lie pale and low,
Pierced by shafts of many a bow;
And the falchion by thy side
To thy heart thy hand shall guide:
Crownless—breathless—headless fall,
Son and Sire—the house of Saul!"   30

Seaham, February, 1815.

"ALL IS VANITY, SAITH THE PREACHER"

I

Fame, Wisdom, Love, and Power were mine,
    And Health and Youth possessed me;
My goblets blushed from every vine,
    And lovely forms caressed me;
I sunned my heart in Beauty's eyes,
    And felt my soul grow tender;
All Earth can give, or mortal prize,
    Was mine of regal splendour.

II

I strive to number o'er what days
    Remembrance can discover,   10
Which all that Life or Earth displays
    Would lure me to live over.

There rose no day, there rolled no hour
    Of pleasure unembittered;
And not a trapping decked my Power
    That galled not while it glittered.

III

The serpent of the field, by art
    And spells, is won from harming;
But that which coils around the heart,
    Oh! who hath power of charming?   20
It will not list to Wisdom's lore,
    Nor Music's voice can lure it;
But there it stings for evermore
    The soul that must endure it.
                   Seaham, 1815.

"WHEN COLDNESS WRAPS THIS SUFFERING CLAY"

I

When coldness wraps this suffering clay,
    Ah! whither strays the immortal mind?
It cannot die, it cannot stay,
    But leaves its darkened dust behind.
Then, unembodied, doth it trace
    By steps each planet's heavenly way?
Or fill at once the realms of space,
    A thing of eyes, that all survey?

II

Eternal—boundless,—undecayed,
    A thought unseen, but seeing all,
All, all in earth, or skies displayed,   10
    Shall it survey, shall it recall:
Each fainter trace that Memory holds
    So darkly of departed years,
In one broad glance the Soul beholds,
    And all, that was, at once appears.

III

Before Creation peopled earth,
 Its eye shall roll through chaos back;
And where the farthest heaven had birth,
 The Spirit trace its rising track.   20
And where the future mars or makes,
 Its glance dilate o'er all to be,
While sun is quenched—or System breaks,
 Fixed in its own Eternity.

IV

Above or Love—Hope—Hate—or Fear,
 It lives all passionless and pure:
An age shall fleet like earthly year;
 Its years as moments shall endure.
Away—away—without a wing,
 O'er all—through all—its thought shall fly, 30
A nameless and eternal thing,
 Forgetting what it was to die.

         Seaham, 1815.

VISION OF BELSHAZZAR

I

The King was on his throne,
 The Satraps thronged the hall:
A thousand bright lamps shone
 O'er that high festival.
A thousand cups of gold,
 In Judah deemed divine—
Jehovah's vessels hold
 The godless Heathen's wine!

II

In that same hour and hall,
 The fingers of a hand   10
Came forth against the wall,
 And wrote as if on sand:

The fingers of a man;—
    A solitary hand
Along the letters ran,
    And traced them like a wand.

III

The monarch saw, and shook,
    And bade no more rejoice;
All bloodless waxed his look,
    And tremulous his voice.   20
"Let the men of lore appear,
    The wisest of the earth,
And expound the words of fear,
    Which mar our royal mirth."

IV

Chaldea's seers are good,
    But here they have no skill;
And the unknown letters stood
    Untold and awful still.
And Babel's men of age
    Are wise and deep in lore;   30
But now they were not sage,
    They saw—but knew no more.

V

A captive in the land,
    A stranger and a youth,
He heard the King's command,
    He saw that writing's truth.
The lamps around were bright,
    The prophecy in view;
He read it on that night,—
    The morrow proved it true.   40

VI

"Belshazzar's grave is made,
    His kingdom passed away,
He, in the balance weighed,

Is light and worthless clay;
    The shroud, his robe of state,
        His canopy the stone;
    The Mede is at his gate!
        The Persian on his throne!"

"SUN OF THE SLEEPLESS!"

Sun of the sleepless! melancholy star!
Whose tearful beam glows tremulously far,
That show'st the darkness thou canst not dispel,
How like art thou to Joy remembered well!
So gleams the past, the light of other days,
Which shines, but warms not with its powerless rays:
A night-beam, Sorrow watcheth to behold,
Distinct, but distant—clear—but, oh how cold!

"WERE MY BOSOM AS FALSE AS THOU DEEM'ST IT TO BE"

I

Were my bosom as false as thou deem'st it to be,
I need not have wandered from far Galilee;
It was but abjuring my creed to efface
The curse which, thou say'st, is the crime of my race.

II

If the bad never triumph, then God is with thee!
If the slave only sin—thou art spotless and free!
If the Exile on earth is an Outcast on high,
Live on in thy faith—but in mine I will die.

III

I have lost for that faith more than thou canst bestow
As the God who permits thee to prosper doth know;   10
In his hand is my heart and my hope—and in thine
The land and the life which for him I resign.

                                        Seaham, 1815.

HEROD'S LAMENT FOR MARIAMNE

I

Oh, Mariamne! now for thee
    The heart for which thou bled'st is bleeding;
Revenge is lost in Agony
    And wild Remorse to rage succeeding.
Oh, Mariamne! where art thou?
    Thou canst not hear my bitter pleading:
Ah! could'st thou—thou would'st pardon now,
    Though Heaven were to my prayer unheeding.

II

And is she dead?—and did they dare
    Obey my Frenzy's jealous raving?   10
My Wrath but doomed my own despair:
    The sword that smote her 's o'er me waving—
But thou art cold, my murdered Love!
    And this dark heart is vainly craving
For her who soars alone above,
    And leaves my soul, unworthy saving.

III

She's gone, who shared my diadem;
    She sunk, with her my joys entombing;
I swept that flower from Judah's stem,
    Whose leaves for me alone were blooming;   20
And mine's the guilt, and mine the hell,
    This bosom's desolation dooming;
And I have earned those tortures well,
    Which unconsumed are still consuming!

January 15, 1815.

ON THE DAY OF THE
DESTRUCTION OF JERUSALEM
BY TITUS

I

From the last hill that looks on thy once holy dome,
I beheld thee, oh Sion! when rendered to Rome:
'Twas thy last sun went down, and the flames of thy fall
Flashed back on the last glance I gave to thy wall.

II

I looked for thy temple—I looked for my home,
And forgot for a moment my bondage to come;
I beheld but the death-fire that fed on thy fane,
And the fast-fettered hands that made vengeance in vain.

III

On many an eve, the high spot whence I gazed
Had reflected the last beam of day as it blazed;   10
While I stood on the height, and beheld the decline
Of the rays from the mountain that shone on thy shrine.

IV

And now on that mountain I stood on that day,
But I marked not the twilight beam melting away;
Oh! would that the lightning had glared in its stead,
And the thunderbolt burst on the Conqueror's head!

V

But the Gods of the Pagan shall never profane
The shrine where Jehovah disdained not to reign;
And scattered and scorned as thy people may be,
Our worship, oh Father! is only for thee.   20

1815.

By the Rivers of Babylon We
Sat Down and Wept

I

We sate down and wept by the waters
   Of Babel, and thought of the day
When our foe, in the hue of his slaughters,
   Made Salem's high places his prey;
And Ye, oh her desolate daughters!
   Were scattered all weeping away.

II

While sadly we gazed on the river
   Which rolled on in freedom below,
They demanded the song; but, oh never
   That triumph the Stranger shall know!   10
May this right hand be withered for ever,
   Ere it string our high harp for the foe!

III

On the willow that harp is suspended,
   Oh Salem! its sound should be free;
And the hour when thy glories were ended
   But left me that token of thee:
And ne'er shall its soft tones be blended
   With the voice of the Spoiler by me!
                    January 15, 1813.

The Destruction of
Sennacherib

I

The Assyrian came down like the wolf on the fold,
And his cohorts were gleaming in purple and gold;
And the sheen of their spears was like stars on the sea,
When the blue wave rolls nightly on deep Galilee.

II

Like the leaves of the forest when Summer is green,
That host with their banners at sunset were seen:
Like the leaves of the forest when Autumn hath blown,
That host on the morrow lay withered and strown.

III

For the angel of Death spread his wings on the blast,
And breathed in the face of the foe as he passed;   10
And the eyes of the sleepers waxed deadly and chill,
And their hearts but once heaved—and for ever grew still!

IV

And there lay the steed with his nostril all wide,
But through it there rolled not the breath of his pride;
And the foam of his gasping lay white on the turf,
And cold as the spray of the rock-beating surf.

V

And there lay the rider distorted and pale,
With the dew on his brow, and the rust on his mail:
And the tents were all silent—the banners alone—
The lances unlifted—the trumpet unblown.   20

VI

And the widows of Ashur are loud in their wail,
And the idols are broke in the temple of Baal;
And the might of the Gentile, unsmote by the sword,
Hath melted like snow in the glance of the Lord!

Seaham, February 17, 1815.

"A SPIRIT PASSED BEFORE ME"

FROM JOB

I

A Spirit passed before me: I beheld
The face of Immortality unveiled—
Deep Sleep came down on every eye save mine—
And there it stood,—all formless—but divine:
Along my bones the creeping flesh did quake;
And as my damp hair stiffened, thus it spake:

II

"Is man more just than God? Is man more pure
Than he who deems even Seraphs insecure?
Creatures of clay—vain dwellers in the dust!
The moth survives you, and are ye more just?   10
Things of a day! you wither ere the night,
Heedless and blind to Wisdom's wasted light!"

"BY THE WATERS OF BABYLON"

I

In the valley of waters we wept on the day
When the host of the Stranger made Salem his prey;
And our heads on our bosoms all droopingly lay,
And our hearts were so full of the land far away!

II

The song they demanded in vain—it lay still
In our souls as the wind that hath died on the hill—
They called for the harp—but our blood they shall spill
Ere our right hands shall teach them one tone of their skill.

III

All stringlessly hung in the willow's sad tree,
As dead as her dead-leaf, those mute harps must be: 10
Our hands may be fettered—our tears still are free
For our God—and our Glory—and Sion, Oh *Thee!*

                                        1815. [*First publ., 1829.*]

DOMESTIC PIECES

FARE THEE WELL

[Lady Byron left her husband on January 16, 1816, assigning no reason, and the real causes of the separation are still unknown. These verses were written March 18 without the intention of publication, but Byron was foolish enough to have fifty copies printed for private circulation on April 7. Of course copies got out and on April 21 it was published by Leigh Hunt in the Examiner *and brought a good deal of execration on Byron's head.]*

> "Alas! they had been friends in youth;
> But whispering tongues can poison truth:
> And Constancy lives in realms above;
> And Life is thorny; and youth is vain:
> And to be wroth with one we love,
> Doth work like madness in the brain;
> . . . . . .
> But never either found another
> To free the hollow heart from painting—
> They stood aloof, the scars remaining,
> Like cliffs which had been rent asunder;
> A dreary sea now flows between,
> But neither heat, nor frost, nor thunder,

> Shall wholly do away, I ween,
> The marks of that which once hath been."
>
> —COLERIDGE'S *CHRISTABEL.*

Fare thee well! and if for ever,
   Still for ever, fare *thee well:*
Even though unforgiving, never
   'Gainst thee shall my heart rebel.
Would that breast were bared before thee
   Where thy head so oft hath lain,
While that placid sleep came o'er thee
   Which thou ne'er canst know again:
Would that breast, by thee glanced over,
   Every inmost thought could show!   10
Then thou would'st at last discover
   'Twas not well to spurn it so.
Though the world for this commend thee—
   Though it smile upon the blow,
Even its praises must offend thee,
   Founded on another's woe:
Though my many faults defaced me,
   Could no other arm be found,
Than the one which once embraced me,
   To inflict a cureless wound?   20
Yet, oh yet, thyself deceive not—
   Love may sink by slow decay,
But by sudden wrench, believe not
   Hearts can thus be torn away:
Still thine own its life retaineth—
   Still must mine, though bleeding, beat;
And the undying thought which paineth
   Is—that we no more may meet.
These are words of deeper sorrow
   Than the wail above the dead;   30
Both shall live—but every morrow
   Wake us from a widowed bed.
And when thou would'st solace gather—

When our child's first accents flow—
  Wilt thou teach her to say "Father!"
    Though his care she must forgo?
When her little hands shall press thee—
  · When her lip to thine is pressed—
Think of him whose prayer shall bless thee—
    Think of him thy love *had* blessed!   40
Should her lineaments resemble
  Those thou never more may'st see,
Then thy heart will softly tremble
    With a pulse yet true to me.
All my faults perchance thou knowest—
  All my madness—none can know;
All my hopes—where'er thou goest—
    Wither—yet with *thee* they go.
Every feeling hath been shaken;
  Pride—which not a world could bow—   50
Bows to thee—by thee forsaken,
    Even my soul forsakes me now.
But 'tis done—all words are idle—
  Words from me are vainer still;
But the thoughts we cannot bridle
    Force their way without the will.
Fare thee well! thus disunited—
  Torn from every nearer tie—
Seared in heart—and lone—and blighted—
    More than this I scarce can die.   60

STANZAS TO AUGUSTA

[*This and the following poem were addressed to Byron's half-sister Augusta Leigh, praising her for standing by him during the trying days of his separation from Lady Byron.*]

When all around grew drear and dark,
  And Reason half withheld her ray—
And Hope but shed a dying spark

Which more misled my lonely way;
In that deep midnight of the mind,
    And that internal strife of heart,
When dreading to be deemed too kind,
    The weak despair—the cold depart;
When Fortune changed—and Love fled far,
    And Hatred's shafts flew thick and fast,   10
Thou wert the solitary star
    Which rose and set not to the last.
Oh! blest be thine unbroken light!
    That watched me as a Seraph's eye,
And stood between me and the night,
    For ever shining sweetly nigh.
And when the cloud upon us came,
    Which strove to blacken o'er thy ray—
Then purer spread its gentle flame,
    And dashed the darkness all away.   20
Still may thy Spirit dwell on mine,
    And teach it what to brave or brook—
There's more in one soft word of thine
    Than in the world's defied rebuke.
Thou stood'st, as stands a lovely tree,
    That still unbroke, though gently bent,
Still waves with fond fidelity
    Its boughs above a monument.
The winds might rend—the skies might pour,
    But there thou wert—and still wouldst be   30
Devoted in the stormiest hour
    To shed thy weeping leaves o'er me.
But thou and thine shall know no blight,
    Whatever fate on me may fall;
For Heaven in sunshine will requite
    The kind—and thee the most of all.
Then let the ties of baffled love
    Be broken—thine will never break;
Thy heart can feel—but will not move;
    Thy soul, though soft, will never shake.   40
And these, when all was lost beside,

Were found and still are fixed in thee;—
And bearing still a breast so tried,
Earth is no desert—ev'n to me.

[First publ., 1816.]

STANZAS TO AUGUSTA

I

Though the day of my Destiny's over,
And the star of my Fate hath declined,
Thy soft heart refused to discover
The faults which so many could find;
Though thy Soul with my grief was acquainted,
It shrunk not to share it with me,
And the Love which my Spirit hath painted
It never hath found but in *Thee.*

II

Then when Nature around me is smiling,
The last smile which answers to mine,   10
I do not believe it beguiling,
Because it reminds me of thine;
And when winds are at war with the ocean,
As the breasts I believed in with me,
If their billows excite an emotion,
It is that they bear me from *Thee.*

III

Though the rock of my last Hope is shivered,
And its fragments are sunk in the wave,
Though I feel that my soul is delivered
To Pain—it shall not be its slave.   20
There is many a pang to pursue me:
They may crush, but they shall not contemn—
They may torture, but shall not subdue me—
'Tis of *Thee* that I think—not of them.

IV

Though human, thou didst not deceive me,
  Though woman, thou didst not forsake,
Though loved, thou forborest to grieve me,
  Though slandered, thou never couldst shake,—
Though trusted, thou didst not disclaim me,
  Though parted, it was not to fly,   30
Though watchful, 'twas not to defame me,
  Nor, mute, that the world might belie.

V

Yet I blame not the World, nor despise it,
  Nor the war of the many with one;
If my Soul was not fitted to prize it,
  'Twas folly not sooner to shun:
And if dearly that error hath cost me,
  And more than I once could foresee,
I have found that, whatever it lost me,
  It could not deprive me of *Thee*.   40

VI

From the wreck of the past, which hath perished,
  Thus much I at least may recall,
It hath taught me that what I most cherished
  Deserved to be dearest of all:
In the Desert a fountain is springing,
  In the wide waste there still is a tree,
And a bird in the solitude singing,
  Which speaks to my spirit of *Thee*.
                    July 24, 1816. [*First publ., 1816.*]

THE DREAM

[The sentimental self-revelation of this poem makes it unique among Byron's autobiographical poems. The details of his unsuccessful wooing of Mary Chaworth are etched in realistic bitterness and self-pity.]

I

Our life is twofold: Sleep hath its own world,
A boundary between the things misnamed
Death and existence: Sleep hath its own world,
And a wide realm of wild reality,
And dreams in their development have breath,
And tears, and tortures, and the touch of Joy;
They leave a weight upon our waking thoughts,
They take a weight from off our waking toils,
They do divide our being; they become
A portion of ourselves as of our time,   10
And look like heralds of Eternity;
They pass like spirits of the past,—they speak
Like Sibyls of the future; they have power—
The tyranny of pleasure and of pain;
They make us what we were not—what they will,
And shake us with the vision that's gone by,
The dread of vanished shadows—Are they so?
Is not the past all shadow—What are they?
Creations of the mind?—The mind can make
Substance, and people planets of its own   20
With beings brighter than have been, and give
A breath to forms which can outlive all flesh.
I would recall a vision which I dreamed
Perchance in sleep—for, in itself, a thought,
A slumbering thought, is capable of years,
And curdles a long life into one hour.

II

I saw two beings in the hues of youth
Standing upon a hill, a gentle hill,
Green and of mild declivity, the last
As 'twere the cape of a long ridge of such,   30

Save that there was no sea to lave its base,
But a most living landscape, and the wave
Of woods and cornfields, and the abodes of men
Scattered at intervals, and wreathing smoke
Arising from such rustic roofs;—the hill
Was crowned with a peculiar diadem
Of trees, in circular array, so fixed,
Not by the sport of nature, but of man:
These two, a maiden and a youth, were there
Gazing—the one on all that was beneath   40
Fair as herself—but the Boy gazed on her;
And both were young, and one was beautiful:
And both were young—yet not alike in youth.
As the sweet moon on the horizon's verge,
The Maid was on the eve of Womanhood;
The Boy had fewer summers, but his heart
Had far outgrown his years, and to his eye
There was but one belovéd face on earth,
And that was shining on him: he had looked
Upon it till it could not pass away;   50
He had no breath, no being, but in hers;
She was his voice; he did not speak to her,
But trembled on her words; she was his sight,
For his eye followed hers, and saw with hers,
Which coloured all his objects:—he had ceased
To live within himself; she was his life,
The ocean to the river of his thoughts,
Which terminated all; upon a tone,
A touch of hers, his blood would ebb and flow,
And his cheek change tempestuously—his heart   60
Unknowing of its cause of agony.
But she in these fond feelings had no share:
Her sighs were not for him; to her he was
Even as a brother—but no more; 'twas much,
For brotherless she was, save in the name
Her infant friendship had bestowed on him;
Herself the solitary scion left
Of a time-honoured race.—It was a name

Which pleased him, and yet pleased him not—and why?
Time taught him a deep answer—when she loved   70
Another: even *now* she loved another,
And on the summit of that hill she stood
Looking afar if yet her lover's steed
Kept pace with her expectancy, and flew.

III

A change came o'er the spirit of my dream.
There was an ancient mansion, and before
Its walls there was a steed caparisoned:
Within an antique Oratory stood
The Boy of whom I spake;—he was alone,
And pale, and pacing to and fro: anon   80
He sate him down, and seized a pen, and traced
Words which I could not guess of; then he leaned
His bowed head on his hands, and shook as 'twere
With a convulsion—then arose again,
And with his teeth and quivering hands did tear
What he had written, but he shed no tears.
And he did calm himself, and fix his brow
Into a kind of quiet: as he paused,
The Lady of his love re-entered there;
She was serene and smiling then, and yet   90
She knew she was by him beloved—she knew,
For quickly comes such knowledge, that his heart
Was darkened with her shadow, and she saw
That he was wretched, but she saw not all.
He rose, and with a cold and gentle grasp
He took her hand; a moment o'er his face
A tablet of unutterable thoughts
Was traced, and then it faded, as it came;
He dropped the hand he held, and with slow steps
Retired, but not as bidding her adieu,   100
For they did part with mutual smiles; he passed
From out the massy gate of that old Hall,
And mounting on his steed he went his way;
And ne'er repassed that hoary threshold more.

IV

A change came o'er the spirit of my dream.
The Boy was sprung to manhood: in the wilds
Of fiery climes he made himself a home,
And his Soul drank their sunbeams: he was girt
With strange and dusky aspects; he was not
Himself like what he had been; on the sea   110
And on the shore he was a wanderer;
There was a mass of many images
Crowded like waves upon me, but he was
A part of all; and in the last he lay
Reposing from the noontide sultriness,
Couched among fallen columns, in the shade
Of ruined walls that had survived the names
Of those who reared them; by his sleeping side
Stood camels grazing, and some goodly steeds
Were fastened near a fountain; and a man   120
Clad in a flowing garb did watch the while,
While many of his tribe slumbered around:
And they were canopied by the blue sky,
So cloudless, clear, and purely beautiful,
That God alone was to be seen in Heaven.

V

A change came o'er the spirit of my dream.
The Lady of his love was wed with One
Who did not love her better:—in her home,
A thousand leagues from his,—her native home,
She dwelt, begirt with growing Infancy,   130
Daughters and sons of Beauty,—but behold!
Upon her face there was the tint of grief,
The settled shadow of an inward strife,
And an unquiet drooping of the eye,
As if its lid were charged with unshed tears.
What could her grief be?—she had all she loved,
And he who had so loved her was not there
To trouble with bad hopes, or evil wish,
Or ill-repressed affliction, her pure thoughts.

What could her grief be?——she had loved him not,   140
Nor given him cause to deem himself beloved,
Nor could he be a part of that which preyed
Upon her mind——a spectre of the past.

V I

A change came o'er the spirit of my dream.
The Wanderer was returned.——I saw him stand
Before an Altar——with a gentle bride;
Her face was fair, but was not that which made
The Starlight of his Boyhood;——as he stood
Even at the altar, o'er his brow there came
The self-same aspect, and the quivering shock   150
That in the antique Oratory shook
His bosom in its solitude; and then——
As in that hour——a moment o'er his face
The tablet of unutterable thoughts
Was traced,——and then it faded as it came,
And he stood calm and quiet, and he spoke
The fitting vows, but heard not his own words,
And all things reeled around him; he could see
Not that which was, nor that which should have been——
But the old mansion, and the accustomed hall,   160
And the remembered chambers, and the place,
The day, the hour, the sunshine, and the shade,
All things pertaining to that place and hour,
And her who was his destiny, came back
And thrust themselves between him and the light:
What business had they there at such a time?

V I I

A change came o'er the spirit of my dream.
The Lady of his love;——Oh! she was changed
As by the sickness of the soul; her mind
Had wandered from its dwelling, and her eyes   170
They had not their own lustre, but the look
Which is not of the earth; she was become
The Queen of a fantastic realm; her thoughts

Were combinations of disjointed things;
And forms, impalpable and unperceived
Of others' sight, familiar were to hers.
And this the world calls frenzy; but the wise
Have a far deeper madness—and the glance
Of melancholy is a fearful gift;
What is it but the telescope of truth?   180
Which strips the distance of its fantasies,
And brings life near in utter nakedness,
Making the cold reality too real!

VIII

A change came o'er the spirit of my dream.
The Wanderer was alone as heretofore,
The beings which surrounded him were gone,
Or were at war with him; he was a mark
For blight and desolation, compassed round
With Hatred and Contention; Pain was mixed
In all which was served up to him, until,   190
Like to the Pontic monarch of old days,
He fed on poisons, and they had no power,
But were a kind of nutriment; he lived
Through that which had been death to many men,
And made him friends of mountains: with the stars
And the quick Spirit of the Universe
He held his dialogues; and they did teach
To him the magic of their mysteries;
To him the book of Night was opened wide,
And voices from the deep abyss revealed   200
A marvel and a secret—Be it so.

IX

My dream was past; it had no further change.
It was of a strange order, that the doom
Of these two creatures should be thus traced out
Almost like a reality—the one
To end in madness—both in misery.

July 1816. [*First publ., 1816.*]

JEUX D'ESPRIT AND
EPHEMERAL VERSES

LINES TO MR. HODGSON

WRITTEN ON BOARD THE LISBON PACKET

[*Included in a letter to the Rev. Francis Hodgson on the eve of Byron's departure on his first pilgrimage to the Near East.*]

1

Huzza! Hodgson, we are going,
   Our embargo's off at last;
Favourable breezes blowing
   Bend the canvas o'er the mast.
From aloft the signal's streaming,
   Hark! the farewell gun is fired;
Women screeching, tars blaspheming,
   Tell us that our time's expired.
      Here's a rascal
      Come to task all,
   Prying from the Custom-house,
      Trunks unpacking,
      Cases cracking—
   Not a corner for a mouse
'Scapes unsearched amid the racket,
Ere we sail on board the Packet.

10

2

Now our boatmen quit their mooring,
    And all hands must ply the oar;
Baggage from the quay is lowering,
    We're impatient, push from shore.   20
"Have a care! that case holds liquor—
    Stop the boat—I'm sick—oh Lord!"
"Sick, Ma'am, damme, you'll be sicker,
    Ere you've been an hour on board."
            Thus are screaming
            Men and women,
        Gemmen, ladies, servants, Jacks;
            Here entangling,
            All are wrangling,
        Stuck together close as wax.—   30
Such the general noise and racket,
Ere we reach the Lisbon Packet.

3

Now we've reached her, lo! the Captain,
    Gallant Kidd, commands the crew;
Passengers their berths are clapt in,
    Some to grumble, some to spew.
"Hey day! call you that a cabin?
    Why 'tis hardly three feet square:
Not enough to stow Queen Mab in—
    Who the deuce can harbour there?"   40
        "Who, sir? plenty—
        Nobles twenty
    Did at once my vessel fill."—
        "Did they? Jesus,
        How you squeeze us!
    Would to God they did so still:
Then I'd 'scape the heat and racket
Of the good ship, Lisbon Packet."

4

Fletcher! Murray! Bob! where are you?
    Stretched along the deck like logs—   50

Bear a hand, you jolly tar, you!
　　Here's a rope's end for the dogs.
Hobhouse muttering fearful curses,
　　As the hatchway down he rolls,
Now his breakfast, now his verses,
　　Vomits forth—and damns our souls.
　　　　"Here's a stanza
　　　　On Braganza—
Help!"—"A couplet?"—"No, a cup
　　　　Of warm water—"　　　　　　　　　　　　60
　　　　"What's the matter?"
　　"Zounds! my liver's coming up;
I shall not survive the racket
Of this brutal Lisbon Packet."

　　　　　　　　5
Now at length we're off for Turkey,
　　Lord knows when we shall come back!
Breezes foul and tempests murky
　　May unship us in a crack.
But, since Life at most a jest is,
　　As philosophers allow,　　　　　　　　　　70
Still to laugh by far the best is,
　　Then laugh on—as I do now.
　　　　Laugh at all things,
　　　　Great and small things,
Sick or well, at sea or shore;
　　　　While we're quaffing,
　　　　Let's have laughing—
Who the devil cares for more?—
Some good wine! and who would lack it,
Ev'n on board the Lisbon Packet?　　　　　　80
Falmouth Roads, June 30, 1809. [*First publ., 1830.*]

Translation of the Nurse's Dole in the *Medea* of Euripides

[*A parody translation of some lines of the* Medea *of Euripides, included in a letter to Henry Drury, June 17, 1810.*]

Oh how I wish that an embargo
Had kept in port the good ship Argo!
Who, still unlaunched from Grecian docks,
Had never passed the Azure rocks;
But now I fear her trip will be a
Damned business for my Miss Medea, etc.

June 1810. [*First publ., 1830.*]

Windsor Poetics

LINES COMPOSED ON THE OCCASION OF HIS ROYAL
HIGHNESS THE PRINCE REGENT BEING SEEN STANDING
BETWEEN THE COFFINS OF HENRY VIII AND
CHARLES I, IN THE ROYAL VAULT AT WINDSOR

Famed for contemptuous breach of sacred ties,
By headless Charles see heartless Henry lies;
Between them stands another sceptred thing—
It moves, it reigns—in all but name, a king:
Charles to his people, Henry to his wife,
—In him the double tyrant starts to life:
Justice and Death have mixed their dust in vain,
Each royal Vampire wakes to life again.
Ah, what can tombs avail!—since these disgorge
The blood and dust of both—to mould a George.

[*First publ., 1819.*]

"So we'll go no more a-roving"

[*To Thomas Moore, February 28, 1817. Byron says that he had been up late too many nights at the Carnival in Venice.*]

1

So we'll go no more a-roving
   So late into the night,
Though the heart be still as loving,
   And the moon be still as bright.

2

For the sword outwears its sheath,
   And the soul wears out the breast,
And the heart must pause to breathe,
   And Love itself have rest.

3

Though the night was made for loving,
   And the day returns too soon,
Yet we'll go no more a-roving
   By the light of the moon.

[*First publ., 1830.*]

10

VERSICLES

[*To Thomas Moore, March 25, 1817.* The Missionary of the Andes *is by W. L. Bowles;* Ilderim, *by H. Gally Knight;* Margaret of Anjou *by Margaret Holford;* Waterloo and other Poems, *by Byron's friend, J. Wedderburn Webster;* Glenarvon, a Novel, *by Lady Caroline Lamb, who pictured Byron in the book, quoting one of his devastating letters to her after their* liaison *had broken up.*]

I read the "Christabel";
   Very well:
I read the "Missionary";
   Pretty—very:
I tried at "Ilderim";
   Ahem!

I read a sheet of "Marg'ret of *Anjou*";
   Can you?
I turned a page of Webster's "Waterloo";
   Pooh! pooh!
I looked at Wordsworth's milk-white "Rylstone Doe";
   Hillo!
I read "Glenarvon," too, by Caro Lamb;
   God damn!

                    [*First publ., 1830.*]

TO MR. MURRAY

[*To John Murray, March 25, 1817. See note to previous poem.*]

To hook the reader, you, John Murray,
   Have published "Anjou's Margaret,"
Which won't be sold off in a hurry
   (At least, it has not been as yet);
And then, still further to bewilder him,
   Without remorse, you set up "Ilderim";
   So mind you don't get into debt,—
Because—as how—if you should fail,
These books would be but baddish bail.
And mind you do *not* let escape   10
   These rhymes to *Morning Post* or Perry,
Which would be *very* treacherous—*very,*
And get me into such a scrape!
   For, firstly, I should have to sally,
   All in my little boat, against a *Galley;*
And, should I chance to slay the Assyrian wight,
Have next to combat with the female Knight:
And pricked to death expire upon her needle,
A sort of end which I should take indeed ill!

                    [*First publ., 1830.*]

TO THOMAS MOORE

[*To Thomas Moore, July 10, 1817.*]

1

My boat is on the shore,
    And my bark is on the sea;
But, before I go, Tom Moore,
    Here's a double health to thee!

2

Here's a sigh to those who love me,
    And a smile to those who hate;
And, whatever sky's above me,
    Here's a heart for every fate.

3

Though the Ocean roar around me,
    Yet it still shall bear me on;   10
Though a desert should surround me,
    It hath springs that may be won.

4

Were't 't the last drop in the well,
    As I gasped upon the brink,
Ere my fainting spirit fell,
    'Tis to thee that I would drink.

5

With that water, as this wine,
    The libation I would pour
Should be—peace with thine and mine,
    And a health to thee, Tom Moore.   20
[*First publ., January 8, 1821.*]

EPISTLE FROM MR. MURRAY
TO DR. POLIDORI

[*To John Murray, August 21, 1817. Murray had asked Byron to*
write him a "delicate declension" of the play sent him by the touchy
and vain Dr. John Polidori, who had been Byron's physician when
he left England in April 1816.]

Dear Doctor, I have read your play,
Which is a good one in its way,—
Purges the eyes, and moves the bowels,
And drenches handkerchiefs like towels
With tears, that, in a flux of grief,
Afford hysterical relief
To shattered nerves and quickened pulses,
Which your catastrophe convulses.
    I like your moral and machinery;
Your plot, too, has such scope for Scenery!   10
Your dialogue is apt and smart;
The play's concoction full of art;
Your hero raves, your heroine cries,
All stab, and every body dies.
In short, your tragedy would be
The very thing to hear and see:
And for a piece of publication,
If I decline on this occasion,
It is not that I am not sensible
To merits in themselves ostensible,   20
But—and I grieve to speak it—plays
Are drugs—mere drugs, Sir—now-a-days.
I had a heavy loss by *Manuel*—
Too lucky if it prove not annual,—
And Sotheby, with his *Orestes*,
(Which, by the way, the old Bore's best is),
Has lain so very long on hand,
That I despair of all demand;
I've advertised, but see my books,
Or only watch my Shopman's looks;—   30

Still *Ivan, Ina,* and such lumber,
My back-shop glut, my shelves encumber.
    There's Byron, too, who once did better,
Has sent me, folded in a letter,
A sort of—it's no more a drama
Than *Darnley, Ivan,* or *Kehama;*
So altered since last year his pen is,
I think he's lost his wits at Venice.
Or drained his brains away as stallion
To some dark-eyed and warm Italian;   40
In short, Sir, what with one and t'other,
I dare not venture on another.
I write in haste; excuse each blunder;
The Coaches through the street so thunder!
My room's so full—we've Gifford here
Reading MS., with Hookham Frere,
Pronouncing on the nouns and particles,
Of some of our forthcoming Articles.
    The *Quarterly*—Ah, Sir, if you
Had but the genius to review!—   50
A smart Critique upon St. Helena,
Or if you only would but tell in a
Short compass what—but to resume;
As I was saying, Sir, the Room—
The Room's so full of wits and bards,
Crabbes, Campbells, Crokers, Freres, and Wards
And others, neither bards nor wits:
My humble tenement admits
All persons in the dress of Gent.,
From Mr. Hammond to Dog Dent.   60
    A party dines with me to-day,
All clever men, who make their way:
Crabbe, Malcolm, Hamilton, and Chantrey,
Are all partakers of my pantry.
They're at this moment in discussion
On poor De Staël's late dissolution.
Her book, they say, was in advance—
Pray Heaven, she tell the truth of France!

'Tis said she certainly was married
To Rocca, and had twice miscarried,   70
No—not miscarried, I opine,—
But brought to bed at forty-nine.
Some say she died a Papist; some
Are of opinion that's a Hum;
I don't know that—the fellows Schlegel,
Are very likely to inveigle
A dying person in compunction
To try th' extremity of Unction.
But peace be with her! for a woman
Her talents surely were uncommon,   80
Her Publisher (and Public too)
The hour of her demise may rue—
For never more within his shop he—
Pray—was not she interred at Coppet?
Thus run our time and tongues away;—
But, to return, Sir, to your play:
Sorry, Sir, but I cannot deal,
Unless 'twere acted by O'Neill.
My hands are full—my head so busy,
I'm almost dead—and always dizzy;   90
   And so, with endless truth and hurry,
   Dear Doctor, I am yours,

                        John Murray.

        August 21, 1817. [First publ., 1830.
  Lines 67–82 first publ., 1900; lines 39–40, 1950.]

EPISTLE TO MR. MURRAY

[*To John Murray, January 8, 1818. Byron was sending the fourth
canto of* Childe Harold *by his friend Hobhouse.*]

1

My dear Mr. Murray,
You're in a damned hurry
   To set up this ultimate Canto;
But (if they don't rob us)

You'll see Mr. Hobhouse
   Will bring it safe in his portmanteau.

2

For the Journal you hint of,
As ready to print off,
   No doubt you do right to commend it;
But as yet I have writ off
The devil a bit of
   Our "Beppo":—when copied, I'll send it.

3

In the mean time you've "Galley"
Whose verses all tally,
   Perhaps you may say he's a Ninny,
But if you abashed are
Because of *Alashtar*,
   He'll piddle another *Phrosine*.

4

Then you've Sotheby's Tour,—
No great things, to be sure,—
   You could hardly begin with a less work;
For the pompous rascallion,
Who don't speak Italian
   Nor French, must have scribbled by guesswork.

5

No doubt he's a rare man
Without knowing German
   Translating his way up Parnassus,
And now, still absurder,
He meditates Murder,
   As you'll see in the trash he calls *Tasso's*.

6

But you've others, his betters,
The real men of letters,
   Your Orators—Critics—and Wits—
And I'll bet that your Journal

(Pray is it diurnal?)
     Will pay with your luckiest hits.

7

You can make any loss up
With "Spence" and his gossip,
     A work which must surely succeed;
Then Queen Mary's Epistle-craft,   40
With the new "Fytte" of "Whistlecraft,"
     Must make people purchase and read.

8

Then you've General Gordon,
Who girded his sword on,
     To serve with a Muscovite Master,
And help him to polish
A nation so owlish,
     They thought shaving their beards a disaster.

9

For the man, *"poor and shrewd,"*
With whom you'd conclude   50
     A compact without more delay,
Perhaps some such pen is
Still extant in Venice;
     But please, Sir, to mention *your pay.*

1 0

Now tell me some news
Of your friends and the Muse,
     Of the Bar, or the Gown, or the House,
From Canning, the tall wit,
To Wilmot, the small wit,
     Ward's creeping Companion and *Louse,*   60

1 1

Who's so damnably bit
With fashion and Wit,
     That he crawls on the surface like Vermin,
But an Insect in both,—

By his Intellect's growth,
   Of what size you may quickly determine.

       1 2

Now, I'll put out my taper
(I've finished my paper
   For these stanzas you see on the *brink* stand)
There's a whore on my right   70
For I rhyme best at Night
   When a C-t is tied close to my Inkstand.

       1 3

It was Mahomet's notion
That comical motion
   Increased his "devotion in prayer"—
If that tenet holds good
In a prophet it should
   In a poet be equally fair.

       1 4

For, in rhyme or in love
(Which both come from above)   80
   I'll *stand* with our "Tommy" or "Sammy"
But the Sopha and lady
Are both of them ready
   And so, here's "good night to you damnee!"
           Venice, January 8, 1818.
[*First publ., 1830. Stanzas 3, 5, 6, 10, 11, first publ., 1900;*
           stanzas 12, 13, 14, 1957.]

TO MR. MURRAY

       1

Strahan, Tonson, Lintot of the times,
Patron and publisher of rhymes,
For thee the bard up Pindus climbs,
          My Murray.

2

To thee, with hope and terror dumb,
The unfledged MS. authors come;
Thou printest all—and sellest some—
                    My Murray.

3

Upon thy table's baize so green
The last new Quarterly is seen,—   10
But where is thy new Magazine,
                    My Murray?

4

Along thy sprucest bookshelves shine
The works thou deemest most divine—
The Art of Cookery, and mine,
                    My Murray.

5

Tours, travels, Essays, too, I wist,
And Sermons, to thy mill bring grist;
And then thou hast the *Navy List,*
                    My Murray.   20

6

And Heaven forbid I should conclude,
Without "the Board of Longitude,"
Although this narrow paper would,
                    My Murray.
            Venice, April 11, 1818. [*First publ., 1830.*]

EPIGRAM

FROM THE FRENCH OF RULHIÈRES

[*To John Murray, August 12, 1819. Byron says the stanzas were
written on some Frenchwoman. He gives a translation.*]

If for silver, or for gold,
    You could melt ten thousand pimples

Into half a dozen dimples,
 Then your face we might behold,
  Looking, doubtless, much more snugly,
  Yet even *then* 'twould be damned ugly.
     [*First publ., 1830.*]

EPILOGUE

1

There's something in a stupid ass,
 And something in a heavy dunce;
But never since I went to school
 I heard or saw so damned a fool
As William Wordsworth is for once.

2

And now I've seen so great a fool
 As William Wordsworth is for once;
I really wish that Peter Bell
 And he who wrote it were in hell,
For writing nonsense for the nonce.   10

3

It saw the "light in ninety-eight,"
 Sweet babe of one and twenty years!
And then he gives it to the nation
 And deems himself of Shakespeare's peers!

4

He gives the perfect work to light!
 Will Wordsworth, if I might advise,
Content you with the praise you get
 From Sir George Beaumont, Baronet,
And with your place in the Excise!   20
    1819. [*First published, 1888.*]

ON MY WEDDING-DAY

[*To Thomas Moore, January 2, 1820, the anniversary of Byron's
wedding.*]

> Here's a happy New Year! but with reason
>   I beg you'll permit me to say—
> Wish me *many* returns of the *Season*,
>   But as *few* as you please of the *Day*.
>   [*First publ., 1830.*]

MY BOY HOBBIE O

[*This song, sent to John Murray, March 23, 1820, almost caused
a breach in Byron's friendship with John Cam Hobhouse, who had
been committed to Newgate Prison for several weeks for a parlia-
mentary "breach of privilege."*]

New Song to the tune of

> "*Whare hae ye been a' day,
>   My boy Tammy O?
> Courting o' a young thing
>   Just come frae her Mammie O.*"

1

> How came you in Hob's pound to cool,
>   My boy Hobbie O?
> Because I bade the people pull
>   The House into the Lobby O.

2

> What did the House upon this call,
>   My boy Hobbie O?
> They voted me to Newgate all,
>   Which is an awkward Jobby O.

3

Who are now the people's men,
  My boy Hobbie O?
There's I and Burdett—Gentlemen,
  And blackguard Hunt and Cobby O.

10

4

You hate the house—*why* canvass, then?
  My boy Hobbie O?
Because I would reform the den
  As member for the Mobby O.

5

Wherefore do you hate the Whigs,
  My boy Hobbie O?
Because they want to run their rigs,
  As under Walpole Bobby O.

20

6

But when we at Cambridge were
  My boy Hobbie O,
If my memory don't err
  You founded a Whig Clubbie O.

7

When to the mob you make a speech,
  My boy Hobbie O,
How do you keep without their reach
  The watch within your fobby O?

8

But never mind such petty things,
  My boy Hobbie O;
God save the people—damn all Kings,
  So let us Crown the Mobby O!
      Yours truly,
            (Signed) *INFIDUS SCURRA.*
            [*First publ., March 1887.*]

30

LINES

ADDRESSED BY LORD BYRON TO MR. HOBHOUSE ON
HIS ELECTION FOR WESTMINSTER

[*To John Murray, April 9, 1820. Byron's friend Hobhouse, after
serving time in Newgate Prison for a breach of parliamentary
privilege, was returned to the House of Commons from Westminster,
having gained prestige by his fearless espousal of radical and popu-
lar causes.*]

Would you go to the house by the true gate,
    Much faster than ever Whig Charley went;
Let Parliament send you to Newgate,
    And Newgate will send you to Parliament.
                [*First publ., 1821.*]

EPIGRAM

[*To Thomas Moore, June 22, 1821.*]

The world is a bundle of hay,
    Mankind are the asses who pull;
Each tugs it a different way,—
    And the greatest of all is John Bull!
                [*First publ., 1830.*]

JOHN KEATS

[*To John Murray, July 30, 1821.*]

Who killed John Keats?
    "I," says the Quarterly,
    So savage and Tartarly;
" 'T was one of my feats."

Who shot the arrow?
    "The poet-priest Milman"
    (So ready to kill man)
"Or Southey, or Barrow."
              [*First publ., 1830.*]

SATIRES

ENGLISH BARDS, AND
SCOTCH REVIEWERS

A SATIRE BY LORD BYRON

"I had rather be a kitten, and cry, mew!
Than one of these same metre ballad-mongers."
—SHAKESPEARE.

"Such shameless Bards we have; and yet 'tis true,
There are as mad, abandon'd Critics, too."
—POPE.

[*As early as October, 1807, Byron had been at work on a satire on contemporary writers in the general style of Pope. It was to be called* British Bards. *Then after Lord Brougham had written a severe criticism of Byron's* Hours of Idleness *in the* Edinburgh Review *of January, 1808, Byron revised the satire and published it anonymously in March, 1809. Believing Francis Jeffrey, the editor of the* Edinburgh Review, *to be the author of the offending article, he added many lines abusing him. The first edition had 696 lines. The second edition, enlarged to 1050 lines, was prepared for the press before he left England in June and published in the same year during his absence with his name on the title page. Two more editions were published in 1810, but before a fifth edition (containing 1070 lines) could appear Byron suppressed the poem, having in the meantime made friends with Lord Holland, Thomas Moore, and many others whom he had ridiculed in the satire, and having regretted almost from the first publication many of his snap judgments and unfair assessments of his contemporaries. To his chagrin, however, pirated editions continued to be published throughout his life. The first three paragraphs of the Preface printed here appeared first in the second edition.*]

PREFACE

ALL MY FRIENDS, learned and unlearned, have urged me not to publish this Satire with my name. If I were to be "turned from the career of my humour by quibbles quick, and paper bullets of the brain," I should have complied with their counsel. But I am not to be terrified by abuse, or bullied by reviewers, with or without arms. I can safely say that I have attacked none *personally*, who did not commence on the offensive. An Author's works are public property: he who purchases may judge, and publish his opinion if he pleases; and the Authors I have endeavoured to commemorate may do by me as I have done by them. I dare say they will succeed better in condemning my scribblings, than in mending their own. But my object is not to prove that I can write well, but, if *possible*, to make others write better.

As the Poem has met with far more success than I expected, I have endeavoured in this Edition to make some additions and alterations, to render it more worthy of public perusal.

In the First Edition of this Satire, published anonymously, fourteen lines on the subject of Bowles's Pope were written by, and inserted at the request of, an ingenious friend of mine, who has now in the press a volume of Poetry. In the present Edition they are erased, and some of my own substituted in their stead; my only reason for this being that which I conceive would operate with any other person in the same manner,—a determination not to publish with my name any production, which was not entirely and exclusively my own composition.

With regard to the real talents of many of the poetical persons whose performances are mentioned or alluded to in the following pages, it is presumed by the Author that there can be little difference of opinion in the Public at large; though, like other sectaries, each has his separate tabernacle of proselytes, by whom his abilities are over-rated, his faults overlooked, and his metrical canons received without scruple and without consideration. But the unquestionable possession of considerable genius by several of the writers here censured renders their mental prostitution more to be regretted. Imbecility may be pitied, or, at worst, laughed at and forgotten; perverted powers demand the most decided reprehension. No one can wish more than the Author that some known and able writer had undertaken their exposure, but Mr *Gifford* has devoted himself to Massinger, and, in the absence of the regular physician, a country practitioner may, in cases of absolute necessity, be allowed to prescribe his nostrum to prevent the extension of so deplorable an epidemic, provided there be no quackery in his treatment of the malady. A caustic is here offered; as it is to be feared nothing short of actual cautery can recover the numerous patients afflicted with the present prevalent and distressing *rabies* for rhyming.—As to the *Edinburgh Reviewers,* it would indeed require an Hercules to crush the Hydra; but if the Author succeeds in merely "bruising one of the heads of the serpent," though his own hand should suffer in the encounter, he will be amply satisfied.

Still must I hear?—shall hoarse FITZGERALD bawl
His creaking couplets in a tavern hall,
And I not sing, lest, haply, Scotch Reviews
Should dub me scribbler, and denounce my *Muse?*
Prepare for rhyme—I'll publish, right or wrong;
Fools are my theme, let Satire be my song.

    Oh! Nature's noblest gift—my grey goose-quill!
Slave of my thoughts, obedient to my will,
Torn from thy parent bird to form a pen,
That mighty instrument of little men!   10
The pen! foredoomed to aid the mental throes
Of brains that labour, big with Verse or Prose;
Though Nymphs forsake, and Critics may deride,
The Lover's solace, and the Author's pride.
What Wits! what Poets dost thou daily raise!
How frequent is thy use, how small thy praise!
Condemned at length to be forgotten quite,
With all the pages which 'twas thine to write.
But thou, at least, mine own especial pen!
Once laid aside, but now assumed again,   20
Our task complete, like Hamet's shall be free;
Though spurned by others, yet beloved by me:
Then let us soar to-day; no common theme,
No Eastern vision, no distempered dream
Inspires—our path, though full of thorns, is plain;
Smooth be the verse, and easy be the strain.

    When Vice triumphant holds her sov'reign sway,
Obeyed by all who nought beside obey;
When Folly, frequent harbinger of crime,
Bedecks her cap with bells of every Clime;   30
When knaves and fools combined o'er all prevail,
And weigh their Justice in a Golden Scale;
E'en then the boldest start from public sneers,
Afraid of Shame, unknown to other fears,
More darkly sin, by Satire kept in awe,
And shrink from Ridicule, though not from Law.

Such is the force of Wit! but not belong
To me the arrows of satiric song;
The royal vices of our age demand
A keener weapon, and a mightier hand.   40
Still there are follies, e'en for me to chase,
And yield at least amusement in the race:
Laugh when I laugh, I seek no other fame,
The cry is up, and scribblers are my game:
Speed, Pegasus!—ye strains of great and small,
Ode! Epic! Elegy!—have at you all!
I, too, can scrawl, and once upon a time
I poured along the town a flood of rhyme,
A schoolboy freak, unworthy praise or blame;
I printed—older children do the same.   50
'Tis pleasant, sure, to see one's name in print;
A Book's a Book, altho' there's nothing in't.
Not that a Title's sounding charm can save
Or scrawl or scribbler from an equal grave:
This LAMB must own, since his patrician name
Failed to preserve the spurious Farce from shame.
No matter, GEORGE continues still to write,
Tho' now the name is veiled from public sight.
Moved by the great example, I pursue
The self-same road, but make my own review: 60
Not seek great JEFFREY'S, yet like him will be
Self-constituted Judge of Poesy.

A man must serve his time to every trade
Save Censure—Critics all are ready made.
Take hackneyed jokes from MILLER, got by rote,
With just enough of learning to misquote;
A mind well skilled to find, or forge a fault;
A turn for punning—call it Attic salt;
To JEFFREY go, be silent and discreet,
His pay is just ten sterling pounds per sheet: 70
Fear not to lie, 'twill seem a *sharper* hit;
Shrink not from blasphemy, 'twill pass for wit;

Care not for feeling—pass your proper jest,
And stand a Critic, hated yet caressed.

And shall we own such judgment? no—as soon
Seek roses in December—ice in June;
Hope constancy in wind, or corn in chaff,
Believe a woman or an epitaph,
Or any other thing that's false, before
You trust in Critics, who themselves are sore;   80
Or yield one single thought to be misled
By JEFFREY'S heart, or LAMB'S Bœotian head.
To these young tyrants, by themselves misplaced,
Combined usurpers on the Throne of Taste;
To these, when Authors bend in humble awe,
And hail their voice as Truth, their word as Law;
While these are Censors, 'twould be sin to spare;
While such are Critics, why should I forbear?
But yet, so near all modern worthies run,
'Tis doubtful whom to seek, or whom to shun;   90
Nor know we when to spare, or where to strike,
Our Bards and Censors are so much alike.

Then should you ask me, why I venture o'er
The path which POPE and GIFFORD trod before;
If not yet sickened, you can still proceed;
Go on; my rhyme will tell you as you read.
"But hold!" exclaims a friend,—"here's some neglect:
This—that—and t'other line seem incorrect."
What then? the self-same blunder Pope has got,
And careless Dryden—"Aye, but Pye has not:"—   100
Indeed!—'tis granted, faith!—but what care I?
Better to err with POPE, than shine with PYE.

Time was, ere yet in these degenerate days
Ignoble themes obtained mistaken praise,
When Sense and Wit and Poesy allied,
No fabled Graces, flourished side by side;
From the same fount their inspiration drew,

And, reared by Taste, bloomed fairer as they grew.
Then, in this happy Isle, a POPE'S pure strain
Sought the rapt soul to charm, nor sought in vain;   110
A polished nation's praise aspired to claim,
And raised the people's, as the poet's fame.
Like him great DRYDEN poured the tide of song,
In stream less smooth, indeed, yet doubly strong.
Then CONGREVE'S scenes could cheer, or OTWAY'S melt;
For Nature then an English audience felt—
But why these names, or greater still, retrace,
When all to feebler Bards resign their place?
Yet to such times our lingering looks are cast,
When taste and reason with those times are past.   120
Now look around, and turn each trifling page,
Survey the precious works that please the age;
This truth at least let Satire's self allow,
No dearth of Bards can be complained of now.
The loaded Press beneath her labour groans,
And Printers' devils shake their weary bones;
While SOUTHEY'S Epics cram the creaking shelves,
And LITTLE'S Lyrics shine in hot-pressed twelves.
Thus saith the *Preacher:* "Nought beneath the sun
Is new," yet still from change to change we run.   130
What varied wonders tempt us as they pass!
The Cow-pox, Tractors, Galvanism, and Gas,
In turns appear, to make the vulgar stare,
Till the swoln bubble bursts—and all is air!
Nor less new schools of Poetry arise,
Where dull pretenders grapple for the prize:
O'er Taste awhile these Pseudo-bards prevail;
Each country Book-club bows the knee to Baal,
And, hurling lawful Genius from the throne,
Erects a shrine and idol of its own;   140
Some leaden calf—but whom it matters not,
From soaring SOUTHEY, down to groveling STOTT.

    Behold! in various throngs the scribbling crew,
For notice eager, pass in long review:

Each spurs his jaded Pegasus apace,
And Rhyme and Blank maintain an equal race;
Sonnets on sonnets crowd, and ode on ode;
And Tales of Terror jostle on the road;
Immeasurable measures move along;
To strange, mysterious Dulness still the friend,   150
For simpering Folly loves a varied song,
Admires the strain she cannot comprehend.
Thus Lays of Minstrels—may they be the last!—
On half-strung harps whine mournful to the blast,
While mountain spirits prate to river sprites,
That dames may listen to the sound at nights;
And goblin brats, of Gilpin Horner's brood
Decoy young Border-nobles through the wood,
And skip at every step, Lord knows how high,
And frighten foolish babes, the Lord knows why;   160
While high-born ladies in their magic cell,
Forbidding Knights to read who cannot spell,
Despatch a courier to a wizard's grave,
And fight with honest men to shield a knave.

  Next view in state, proud prancing on his roan,
The golden-crested haughty Marmion,
Now forging scrolls, now foremost in the fight,
Not quite a Felon, yet but half a Knight,
The gibbet or the field prepared to grace—
A mighty mixture of the great and base.   170
And think'st thou, SCOTT! by vain conceit perchance,
On public taste to foist thy stale romance,
Though MURRAY with his MILLER may combine
To yield thy muse just half-a-crown per line?
No! when the sons of song descend to trade,
Their bays are sear, their former laurels fade,
Let such forgo the poet's sacred name,
Who rack their brains for lucre, not for fame:
Still for stern Mammon may they toil in vain!
And sadly gaze on gold they cannot gain!   180
Such be their meed, such still the just reward

Of prostituted Muse and hireling bard!
For this we spurn Apollo's venal son,
And bid a long "good night to Marmion."

    These are the themes that claim our plaudits now;
These are the Bards to whom the Muse must bow;
While MILTON, DRYDEN, POPE, alike forgot,
Resign their hallowed Bays to WALTER SCOTT.

    The time has been, when yet the Muse was young,
When HOMER swept the lyre, and MARO sung,   190
An Epic scarce ten centuries could claim,
While awe-struck nations hailed the magic name:
The work of each immortal Bard appears
The single wonder of a thousand years.
Empires have mouldered from the face of earth,
Tongues have expired with those who gave them birth,
Without the glory such a strain can give,
As even in ruin bids the language live.
Not so with us, though minor Bards content,
On one great work a life of labour spent: 200
With eagle pinion soaring to the skies,
Behold the Ballad-monger SOUTHEY rise!
To him let CAMOËNS, MILTON, TASSO yield,
Whose annual strains, like armies, take the field.
First in the ranks see Joan of Arc advance,
The scourge of England and the boast of France!
Though burnt by wicked BEDFORD for a witch,
Behold her statue placed in Glory's niche;
Her fetters burst, and just released from prison,
A virgin Phœnix from her ashes risen.   210
Next see tremendous Thalaba come on,
Arabia's monstrous, wild, and wond'rous son;
Domdaniel's dread destroyer, who o'erthrew
More mad magicians than the world e'er knew.
Immortal Hero! all thy foes o'ercome,
For ever reign—the rival of Tom Thumb!
Since startled Metre fled before thy face,

Well wert thou doomed the last of all thy race!
Well might triumphant Genii bear thee hence,
Illustrious conqueror of common sense!   220
Now, last and greatest, Madoc spreads his sails,
Cacique in Mexico, and Prince in Wales;
Tells us strange tales, as other travellers do,
More old than Mandeville's, and not so true.
Oh, SOUTHEY! SOUTHEY! cease thy varied song!
A bard may chaunt too often and too long:
As thou art strong in verse, in mercy spare!
A fourth, alas! were more than we could bear.
But if, in spite of all the world can say,
Thou still wilt verseward plod thy weary way;   230
If still in Berkeley-Ballads most uncivil,
Thou wilt devote old women to the devil,
The babe unborn thy dread intent may rue:
"God help thee," SOUTHEY, and thy readers too.

  Next comes the dull disciple of thy school,
That mild apostate from poetic rule,
The simple WORDSWORTH, framer of a lay
As soft as evening in his favourite May,
Who warns his friend "to shake off toil and trouble,
And quit his books, for fear of growing double";   240
Who, both by precept and example, shows
That prose is verse, and verse is merely prose;
Convincing all, by demonstration plain,
Poetic souls delight in prose insane;
And Christmas stories tortured into rhyme
Contain the essence of the true sublime.
Thus, when he tells the tale of Betty Foy,
The idiot mother of "an idiot Boy";
A moon-struck, silly lad, who lost his way,
And, like his bard, confounded night with day;   250
So close on each pathetic part he dwells,
And each adventure so sublimely tells,
That all who view the "idiot in his glory"
Conceive the Bard the hero of the story.

Shall gentle COLERIDGE pass unnoticed here,
To turgid ode and tumid stanza dear?
Though themes of innocence amuse him best,
Yet still Obscurity's a welcome guest.
If Inspiration should her aid refuse
To him who takes a Pixy for a muse,　　　　　　　　260
Yet none in lofty numbers can surpass
The bard who soars to elegize an ass:
So well the subject suits his noble mind,
He brays, the Laureate of the long-eared kind.

Oh! wonder-working LEWIS! Monk, or Bard,
Who fain would make Parnassus a churchyard!
Lo! wreaths of yew, not laurel, bind thy brow,
Thy Muse a Sprite, Apollo's sexton thou!
Whether on ancient tombs thou tak'st thy stand,
By gibb'ring spectres hailed, thy kindred band;　　270
Or tracest chaste descriptions on thy page,
To please the females of our modest age;
All hail, M.P.! from whose infernal brain
Thin-sheeted phantoms glide, a grisly train;
At whose command "grim women" throng in crowds,
And kings of fire, of water, and of clouds,
With "small grey men,"—"wild yagers," and what not,
To crown with honour thee and WALTER SCOTT:
Again, all hail! if tales like thine may please,
St. Luke alone can vanquish the disease:　　　　　280
Even Satan's self with thee might dread to dwell,
And in thy skull discern a deeper Hell.

Who in soft guise, surrounded by a choir
Of virgins melting, not to Vesta's fire,
With sparkling eyes, and cheek by passion flushed
Strikes his wild lyre, whilst listening dames are hushed?
'Tis LITTLE! young Catullus of his day,
As sweet, but as immoral, in his Lay!
Grieved to condemn, the Muse must still be just,
Nor spare melodious advocates of lust.　　　　　290

Pure is the flame which o'er her altar burns;
From grosser incense with disgust she turns:
Yet, kind to youth, this expiation o'er,
She bids thee, "mend thy line, and sin no more."

For thee, translator of the tinsel song,
To whom such glittering ornaments belong,
Hibernian STRANGFORD! with thine eyes of blue,
And boasted locks of red or auburn hue,
Whose plaintive strain each love-sick Miss admires,
And o'er harmonious fustion half expires,   300
Learn, if thou canst, to yield thine author's sense,
Nor vend thy sonnets on a false pretence.
Think'st thou to gain thy verse a higher place,
By dressing Camoëns in a suit of lace?
Mend, STRANGFORD! mend thy morals and thy taste;
Be warm, but pure; be amorous, but be chaste:
Cease to deceive; thy pilfered harp restore,
Nor teach the Lusian Bard to copy MOORE.

Behold—Ye Tarts!—one moment spare the text!—
HAYLEY'S last work, and worst—until his next;   310
Whether he spin poor couplets into plays,
Or damn the dead with purgatorial praise,
His style in youth or age is still the same,
For ever feeble and for ever tame.
Triumphant first see "Temper's Triumphs" shine!
At least I'm sure they triumphed over mine.
Of "Music's Triumphs," all who read may swear
That luckless Music never triumphed there.

Moravians, rise! bestow some meet reward
On dull devotion—Lo! the Sabbath Bard,   320
Sepulchral GRAHAME, pours his notes sublime
In mangled prose, nor e'en aspires to rhyme;
Breaks into blank the Gospel of St. Luke,
And boldly pilfers from the Pentateuch;

And, undisturbed by conscientious qualms,
Perverts the Prophets, and purloins the Psalms.

    Hail, Sympathy! thy soft idea brings
A thousand visions of a thousand things,
And shows, still whimpering through three-score of years,
The maudlin prince of mournful sonneteers.   330
And art thou not their prince, harmonious BOWLES!
Thou first, great oracle of tender souls?
Whether thou sing'st with equal ease, and grief,
The fall of empires, or a yellow leaf;
Whether thy muse most lamentably tells
What merry sounds proceed from Oxford bells,
Or, still in bells delighting, finds a friend
In every chime that jingled from Ostend;
Ah! how much juster were thy Muse's hap,
If to thy bells thou would'st but add a cap!   340
Delightful BOWLES! still blessing and still blest,
All love thy strain, but children like it best.
'Tis thine, with gentle LITTLE's moral song,
To soothe the mania of the amorous throng!
With thee our nursery damsels shed their tears,
Ere Miss as yet completes her infant years:
But in her teens thy whining powers are vain;
She quits poor BOWLES for LITTLE's purer strain.
Now to soft themes thou scornest to confine
The lofty numbers of a harp like thine;   350
"Awake a louder and a loftier strain,"
Such as none heard before, or will again!
Where all discoveries jumbled from the flood,
Since first the leaky ark reposed in mud,
By more or less, are sung in very book,
From Captain Noah down to Captain Cook.
Nor this alone—but, pausing on the road,
The Bard sighs forth a gentle episode,
And gravely tells—attend, each beauteous Miss!—
When first Madeira trembled to a kiss.   360
BOWLES! in thy memory let this precept dwell,

Stick to thy Sonnets, Man!—at least they sell.
But if some new-born whim, or larger bribe,
Prompt thy crude brain, and claim thee for a scribe:
If 'chance some bard, though once by dunces feared,
Now, prone in dust, can only be revered;
If POPE, whose fame and genius, from the first,
Have foiled the best of critics, needs the worst,
Do thou essay: each fault, each failing scan;
The first of poets was, alas! but man.   370
Rake from each ancient dunghill ev'ry pearl,
Consult Lord Fanny, and confide in CURLL;
Let all the scandals of a former age
Perch on thy pen, and flutter o'er thy page;
Affect a candour which thou canst not feel,
Clothe envy in the garb of honest zeal;
Write, as if St. John's soul could still inspire,
And do from hate what MALLET did for hire.
Oh! hadst thou lived in that congenial time,
To rave with DENNIS, and with RALPH to rhyme—   380
Thronged with the rest around his living head,
Not raised thy hoof against the lion dead,
A meet reward had crowned thy glorious gains,
And linked thee to the Dunciad for thy pains.

　　Another Epic! Who inflicts again
More books of blank upon the sons of men?
Bœotian COTTLE, rich Bristowa's boast,
Imports old stories from the Cambrian coast,
And sends his goods to market—all alive!
Lines forty thousand, Cantos twenty-five!   390
Fresh fish from Hippocrene! who'll buy? who'll buy?
The precious bargain's cheap—in faith, not I.
Your turtle-feeder's verse must needs be flat,
Though Bristol bloat him with the verdant fat;
If Commerce fills the purse, she clogs the brain,
And AMOS COTTLE strikes the Lyre in vain.
In him an author's luckless lot behold!
Condemned to make the books which once he sold.

Oh, AMOS COTTLE!—Phœbus! what a name
To fill the speaking trump of future fame!—   400
Oh, AMOS COTTLE! for a moment think
What meagre profits spring from pen and ink!
When thus devoted to poetic dreams,
Who will peruse thy prostituted reams?
Oh! pen perverted! paper misapplied!
Had COTTLE still adorned the counter's side,
Bent o'er the desk, or, born to useful toils,
Been taught to make the paper which he soils,
Ploughed, delved, or plied the oar with lusty limb,
He had not sung of Wales, nor I of him.   410

   As Sisyphus against the infernal steep
Rolls the huge rock whose motions ne'er may sleep,
So up thy hill, ambrosial Richmond! heaves
Dull MAURICE all his granite weight of leaves:
Smooth, solid monuments of mental pain!
The petrifactions of a plodding brain,
That, ere they reach the top, fall lumbering back again.

   With broken lyre and cheek serenely pale,
Lo! sad Alcæus wanders down the vale;
Though fair they rose, and might have bloomed at last,   420
His hopes have perished by the northern blast:
Nipped in the bud by Caledonian gales,
His blossoms wither as the blast prevails!
O'er his lost works let *classic* SHEFFIELD weep;
May no rude hand disturb their early sleep!

   Yet say! why should the Bard, at once, resign
His claim to favour from the sacred Nine?
For ever startled by the mingled howl
Of Northern Wolves, that still in darkness prowl;
A coward Brood, which mangle as they prey,   430
By hellish instinct, all that cross their way:
Agéd or young, the living or the dead,
No mercy find—these harpies must be fed.

Why do the injured unresisting yield
The calm possession of their native field?
Why tamely thus before their fangs retreat,
Nor hunt the blood-hounds back to Arthur's Seat?

Health to immortal JEFFREY! once, in name,
England could boast a judge almost the same;
In soul so like, so merciful, yet just,   440
Some think that Satan has resigned his trust,
And given the Spirit to the world again,
To sentence Letters, as he sentenced men.
With hand less mighty, but with heart as black,
With voice as willing to decree the rack;
Bred in the Courts betimes, though all that law
As yet have taught him is to find a flaw,—
Since well instructed in the patriot school
To rail at party, though a party tool—
Who knows? if chance his patrons should restore   450
Back to the sway they forfeited before,
His scribbling toils some recompense may meet,
And raise this Daniel to the Judgment-Seat.
Let JEFFREY'S shade indulge the pious hope,
And greeting thus, present him with a rope:
"Heir to my virtues! man of equal mind!
Skilled to condemn as to traduce mankind,
This cord receive! for thee reserved with care,
To wield in judgment, and at length to wear."

Health to great JEFFREY! Heaven preserve his life,   460
To flourish on the fertile shores of Fife,
And guard it sacred in its future wars,
Since authors sometimes seek the field of Mars!
Can none remember that eventful day,
That ever-glorious, almost fatal fray,
When LITTLE'S leadless pistol met his eye,
And Bow-street Myrmidons stood laughing by?
Oh, day disastrous! on her firm-set rock,
Dunedin's castle felt a secret shock;

Dark rolled the sympathetic waves of Forth,   470
Low groaned the startled whirlwinds of the north;
TWEED ruffled half his waves to form a tear,
The other half pursued his calm career;
ARTHUR'S steep summit nodded to its base,
The surly Tolbooth scarcely kept her place.
The Tolbooth felt—for marble sometimes can,
On such occasions, feel as much as man—
The Tolbooth felt defrauded of his charms,
If JEFFREY died, except within her arms:
Nay last, not least, on that portentous morn,   480
The sixteenth story, where himself was born,
His patrimonial garret, fell to ground,
And pale Edina shuddered at the sound:
Strewed were the streets around with milk-white reams,
Flowed all the Canongate with inky streams;
This of his candour seemed the sable dew,
That of his valour showed the bloodless hue;
And all with justice deemed the two combined
The mingled emblems of his mighty mind.
But Caledonia's goddess hovered o'er   490
The field, and saved him from the wrath of MOORE;
From either pistol snatched the vengeful lead,
And straight restored it to her favourite's head;
That head, with greater than magnetic power,
Caught it, as Danäe caught the golden shower,
And, though the thickening dross will scarce refine,
Augments its ore, and is itself a mine.
"My son," she cried, "ne'er thirst for gore again,
Resign the pistol and resume the pen;
O'er politics and poesy preside,   500
Boast of thy country, and Britannia's guide!
For long as Albion's heedless sons submit,
Or Scottish taste decides on English wit,
So long shall last thine unmolested reign,
Nor any dare to take thy name in vain.
Behold, a chosen band shall aid thy plan,
And own thee chieftain of the critic clan.

First in the oat-fed phalanx shall be seen
The travelled Thane, Athenian Aberdeen.
HERBERT shall wield THOR'S hammer, and sometimes,   510
In gratitude, thou'lt praise his rugged rhymes.
Smug SYDNEY, too, thy bitter page shall seek,
And classic HALLAM, much renowned for Greek;
SCOTT may perchance his name and influence lend
And paltry PILLANS shall traduce his friend;
While gay Thalia's luckless votary, LAMB,
Damned like the Devil—Devil-like will damn.
Known be thy name! unbounded be thy sway!
Thy HOLLAND'S banquets shall each toil repay!
While grateful Britain yields the praise she owes   520
To HOLLAND'S hirelings and to Learning's foes.
Yet mark one caution ere thy next Review
Spread its light wings of Saffron and of Blue,
Beware lest blundering BROUGHAM destroy the sale,
Turn Beef to Bannocks, Cauliflowers to Kail."
Thus having said, the kilted Goddess kissed
Her son, and vanished in a Scottish mist.

   Then prosper, JEFFREY! pertest of the train
Whom Scotland pampers with her fiery grain!
Whatever blessing waits a genuine Scot,   530
In double portion swells thy glorious lot;
For thee Edina culls her evening sweets,
And showers their odours on thy candid sheets,
Whose Hue and Fragrance to thy work adhere—
This scents its pages, and that gilds its rear.
Lo! blushing Itch, coy nymph, enamoured grown,
Forsakes the rest, and cleaves to thee alone,
And, too unjust to other Pictish men,
Enjoys thy person, and inspires thy pen!

   Illustrious HOLLAND! hard would be his lot,   540
His hirelings mentioned, and himself forgot!
HOLLAND, with HENRY PETTY at his back,
The whipper-in and huntsman of the pack.

Blest be the banquets spread at Holland House,
Where Scotchmen feed, and Critics may carouse!
Long, long beneath that hospitable roof
Shall Grub-street dine, while duns are kept aloof.
See honest HALLAM lay aside his fork,
Resume his pen, review his Lordship's work,
And, grateful for the dainties on his plate,   550
Declare his landlord can at least translate!
Dunedin! view thy children with delight,
They write for food—and feed because they write:
And lest, when heated with the unusual grape,
Some glowing thoughts should to the press escape,
And tinge with red the female reader's cheek.
My lady skims the cream of each critique;
Breathes o'er the page her purity of soul,
Reforms each error, and refines the whole.

    Now to the Drama turn—Oh! motley sight!   560
What precious scenes the wondering eyes invite:
Puns, and a Prince within a barrel pent,
And DIBDIN'S nonsense yield complete content.
Though now, thank Heaven! the Rosciomania's o'er,
And full-grown actors are endured once more;
Yet what avail their vain attempts to please,
While British critics suffer scenes like these;
While REYNOLDS vents his *"dammes!"* "poohs!" and "zounds!"
And common-place and common sense confounds?
While KENNEY'S "World"—ah! where is KENNEY'S wit?—   570
Tires the sad gallery, lulls the listless Pit;
And BEAUMONT'S pilfered Caratach affords
A tragedy complete in all but words?
Who but must mourn, while these are all the rage,
The degradation of our vaunted stage?
Heavens! is all sense of shame and talent gone?
Have we no living Bard of merit?—none?
Awake, GEORGE COLMAN! CUMBERLAND, awake!
Ring the alarum bell! let folly quake!
Oh! SHERIDAN! if aught can move thy pen,   580

Let Comedy assume her throne again;
Abjure the mummery of German schools;
Leave new Pizarros to translating fools;
Give, as thy last memorial to the age,
One classic drama, and reform the stage.
Gods! o'er those boards shall Folly rear her head,
Where GARRICK trod, and SIDDONS lives to tread?
On those shall Farce display Buffoonery's mask,
And HOOK conceal his heroes in a cask?
Shall sapient managers new scenes produce   590
From CHERRY, SKEFFINGTON, and Mother Goose?
While SHAKESPEARE, OTWAY, MASSINGER, forgot,
On stalls must moulder, or in closets rot?
Lo! with what pomp the daily prints proclaim
The rival candidates for Attic fame!
In grim array though LEWIS' spectres rise,
Still SKEFFINGTON and GOOSE divide the prize.
And, sure, *great* SKEFFINGTON must claim our praise,
For skirtless coats and skeletons of plays
Renowned alike; whose genius ne'er confines   600
Her flight to garnish Greenwood's gay designs;
Nor sleeps with "Sleeping Beauties," but anon
In five facetious acts comes thundering on;
While poor John Bull, bewildered with the scene,
Stares, wondering what the devil it can mean;
But as some hands applaud, a venal few!
Rather than sleep, why, John applauds it too.

    Such are we now. Ah! wherefore should we turn
To what our fathers were, unless to mourn?
Degenerate Britons! are ye dead to shame,   610
Or, kind to dulness, do you fear to blame?
Well may the nobles of our present race
Watch each distortion of a NALDI's face;
Well may they smile on Italy's buffoons,
And worship CATALANI's pantaloons,
Since their own Drama yields no fairer trace
Of wit than puns, of humour than grimace.

Then let Ausonia, skilled in every art
To soften manners, but corrupt the heart,
Pour her exotic follies o'er the town,   620
To sanction Vice, and hunt Decorum down:
Let wedded strumpets languish o'er DESHAYES,
And bless the promise which his form displays;
While Gayton bounds before th' enraptured looks
Of hoary Marquises, and stripling Dukes:
Let high-born lechers eye the lively Presle
Twirl her light limbs, that spurn the needless veil;
Let Angiolini bare her breast of snow,
Wave the white arm, and point the pliant toe;
Collini trill her love-inspiring song,   630
Strain her fair neck, and charm the listening throng!
Whet not your scythe, Suppressors of our Vice!
Reforming Saints! too delicately nice!
By whose decrees, our sinful souls to save,
No Sunday tankards foam, no barbers shave;
And beer undrawn, and beards unmown, display
Your holy reverence for the Sabbath-day.

Or hail at once the patron and the pile
Of vice and folly, Greville and Argyle!
Where yon proud palace, Fashion's hallowed fane,   640
Spreads wide her portals for the motley train,
Behold the new Petronius of the day,
Our arbiter of pleasure and of play!
There the hired eunuch, the Hesperian choir,
The melting lute, the soft lascivious lyre,
The song from Italy, the step from France,
The midnight orgy, and the mazy dance,
The smile of beauty, and the flush of wine,
For fops, fools, gamesters, knaves, and Lords combine:
Each to his humour—Comus all allows;   650
Champagne, dice, music—or your neighbour's spouse.
Talk not to us, ye starving sons of trade!
Of piteous ruin, which ourselves have made;
In Plenty's sunshine Fortune's minions bask,

Nor think of Poverty, except "en masque,"
When for the night some lately titled ass
Appears the beggar which his grandsire was.
The curtain dropped, the gay Burletta o'er,
The audience take their turn upon the floor:
Now round the room the circling dow'gers sweep,   660
Now in loose waltz the thin-clad daughters leap;
The first in lengthened line majestic swim,
The last display the free unfettered limb!
Those for Hibernia's lusty sons repair
With art the charms which Nature could not spare;
These after husbands wing their eager flight,
Nor leave much mystery for the nuptial night.

    Oh! blest retreats of infamy and ease,
Where, all forgotten but the power to please,
Each maid may give a loose to genial thought,   670
Each swain may teach new systems, or be taught:
There the blithe youngster, just returned from Spain,
Cuts the light pack, or calls the rattling main;
The jovial Caster's set, and seven's the Nick,
Or—done!—a thousand on the coming trick!
If, mad with loss, existence 'gins to tire,
And all your hope or wish is to expire,
Here's POWELL'S pistol ready for your life,
And, kinder still, two PAGETS for your wife:
Fit consummation of an earthly race   680
Begun in folly, ended in disgrace,
While none but menials o'er the bed of death,
Wash thy red wounds, or watch thy wavering breath:
Traduced by liars, and forgot by all,
The mangled victim of a drunken brawl,
To live like CLODIUS, and like FALKLAND fall.

    Truth! rouse some genuine Bard, and guide his hand
To drive this pestilence from out the land.
E'en I—least thinking of a thoughtless throng,

Just skilled to know the right and choose the wrong,   690
Freed at that age when Reason's shield is lost,
To fight my course through Passion's countless host,
Whom every path of Pleasure's flow'ry way
Has lured in turn, and all have led astray—
E'en I must raise my voice, e'en I must feel
Such scenes, such men, destroy the public weal:
Altho' some kind, censorious friend will say,
"What art thou better, meddling fool, than they?"
And every Brother Rake will smile to see
That miracle, a Moralist in me.   700
No matter—when some Bard in virtue strong,
GIFFORD perchance, shall raise the chastening song,
Then sleep my pen for ever! and my voice
Be only heard to hail him, and rejoice,
Rejoice, and yield my feeble praise, though I
May feel the lash that Virtue must apply.

    As for the smaller fry, who swarm in shoals
From silly HAFIZ up to simple BOWLES,
Why should we call them from their dark abode,
In broad St. Gile's or in Tottenham-Road?   710
Or (since some men of fashion nobly dare
To scrawl in verse) from Bond-street or the Square?
If things of Ton their harmless lays indite,
Most wisely doomed to shun the public sight,
What harm? in spite of every critic elf,
Sir T. may read his stanzas to himself;
MILES ANDREWS still his strength in couplets try,
And live in prologues, though his dramas die.
Lords too are Bards: such things at times befall,
And 'tis some praise in Peers to write at all.   720
Yet, did or Taste or Reason sway the times,
Ah! who would take their titles with their rhymes?
ROSCOMMON! SHEFFIELD! with your spirits fled,
No future laurels deck a noble head;
No Muse will cheer, with renovating smile,
The paralytic puling of CARLISLE.

The puny schoolboy and his early lay
Men pardon, if his follies pass away;
But who forgives the Senior's ceaseless verse,
Whose hairs grow hoary as his rhymes grow worse?   730
What heterogeneous honours deck the Peer!
Lord, rhymester, petit-maître, pamphleteer!
So dull in youth, so drivelling in his age,
His scenes alone had damned our sinking stage;
But Managers for once cried, "Hold, enough!"
Nor drugged their audience with the tragic stuff.
Yet at their judgment let his Lordship laugh,
And case his volumes in congenial calf;
Yes! doff that covering, where Morocco shines,
And hang a calf-skin on those recreant lines.   740

    With you, ye Druids! rich in native lead,
Who daily scribble for your daily bread:
With you I war not: GIFFORD'S heavy hand
Has crushed, without remorse, your numerous band.
On "All the Talents" vent your venal spleen;
Want is your plea, let Pity be your screen.
Let Monodies on Fox regale your crew,
And Melville's Mantle prove a Blanket too!
One common Lethe waits each hapless Bard,
And, peace be with you! 'tis your best reward.   750
Such damning fame as Dunciads only give
Could bid your lines beyond a morning live;
But now at once your fleeting labours close,
With names of greater note in blest repose.
Far be't from me unkindly to upbraid
The lovely ROSA'S prose in masquerade,
Whose strains, the faithful echoes of her mind,
Leave wondering comprehension far behind.
Though CRUSCA'S bards no more our journals fill,
Some stragglers skirmish round the columns still;   760
Last of the howling host which once was Bell's,
MATILDA snivels yet, and HAFIZ yells;

And MERRY'S metaphors appear anew,
Chained to the signature of O. P. Q.

When some brisk youth, the tenant of a stall,
Employs a pen less pointed than his awl,
Leaves his snug shop, forsakes his store of shoes,
St. Crispin quits, and cobbles for the Muse,
Heavens! how the vulgar stare! how crowds applaud!
How ladies read, and Literati laud!   770
If, 'chance, some wicked wag should pass his jest,
'Tis sheer ill-nature—don't the world know best?
Genius must guide when wits admire the rhyme,
And CAPEL LOFFT declares 'tis quite sublime.
Hear, then, ye happy sons of needless trade!
Swains! quit the plough, resign the useless spade!
Lo! BURNS and BLOOMFIELD, nay, a greater far,
GIFFORD was born beneath an adverse star,
Forsook the labours of a servile state,
Stemmed the rude storm, and triumphed over Fate: 780
Then why no more? if Phœbus smiled on you,
BLOOMFIELD! why not on brother Nathan too?
Him too the Mania, not the Muse, has seized;
Not inspiration, but a mind diseased:
And now no Boor can seek his last abode,
No common be inclosed without an ode.
Oh! since increased refinement deigns to smile
On Britain's sons, and bless our genial Isle,
Let Poesy go forth, pervade the whole,
Alike the rustic, and mechanic soul!   790
Ye tuneful cobblers! still your notes prolong,
Compose at once a slipper and a song;
So shall the fair your handywork peruse,
Your sonnets sure shall please—perhaps your shoes.
May Moorland weavers boast Pindaric skill,
And tailors' lays be longer than their bill!
While punctual beaux reward the grateful notes,
And pay for poems—when they pay for coats.

To the famed throng now paid the tribute due,
Neglected Genius! let me turn to you.   800
Come forth, oh CAMPBELL! give thy talents scope;
Who dares aspire if thou must cease to hope?
And thou, melodious ROGERS! rise at last,
Recall the pleasing memory of the past;
Arise! let blest remembrance still inspire,
And strike to wonted tones thy hallowed lyre;
Restore Apollo to his vacant throne,
Assert thy country's honour and thine own.
What! must deserted Poesy still weep
Where her last hopes with pious COWPER sleep?   810
Unless, perchance, from his cold bier she turns,
To deck the turf that wraps her minstrel, BURNS!
No! though Contempt hath marked the spurious brood,
The race who rhyme from folly, or for food,
Yet still some genuine sons 'tis hers to boast,
Who, least affecting, still affect the most:
Feel as they write, and write but as they feel—
Bear witness GIFFORD, SOTHEBY, MACNEIL.

"Why slumbers GIFFORD?" once was asked in vain;
Why slumbers GIFFORD? let us ask again.   820
Are there no follies for his pen to purge?
Are there no fools whose backs demand the scourge?
Are there no sins for Satire's Bard to greet?
Stalks not gigantic Vice in every street?
Shall Peers or Princes tread Pollution's path,
And 'scape alike the Law's, and Muse's wrath,
Nor blaze with guilty glare through future time,
Eternal beacons of consummate crime?
Arouse thee, GIFFORD! be thy promise claimed,
Make bad men better, or at least ashamed.   830

Unhappy WHITE! while life was in its spring,
And thy young Muse just waved her joyous wing,
The Spoiler swept that soaring Lyre away,
Which else had sounded an immortal lay.

Oh! what a noble heart was here undone,
When Science' self destroyed her favourite son!
Yes, she too much indulged thy fond pursuit,
She sowed the seeds, but Death has reaped the fruit.
'Twas thine own Genius gave the final blow,
And helped to plant the wound that laid thee low: 840
So the struck Eagle, stretched upon the plain,
No more through rolling clouds to soar again,
Viewed his own feather on the fatal dart,
And winged the shaft that quivered in his heart;
Keen were his pangs, but keener far to feel
He nursed the pinion which impelled the steel;
While the same plumage that had warmed his nest
Drank the last life-drop of his bleeding breast.

    There be who say, in these enlightened days,
That splendid lies are all the poet's praise;   850
That strained Invention, ever on the wing,
Alone impels the modern Bard to sing:
'Tis true, that all who rhyme—nay, all who write,
Shrink from that fatal word to Genius—Trite;
Yet Truth sometimes will lend her noblest fires,
And decorate the verse herself inspires:
This fact in Virtue's name let CRABBE attest:
Though Nature's sternest Painter, yet the best.

    And here let SHEE and Genius find a place,
Whose pen and pencil yield an equal grace;   860
To guide whose hand the sister Arts combine,
And trace the Poet's or the Painter's line;
Whose magic touch can bid the canvas glow,
Or pour the easy rhyme's harmonious flow;
While honours, doubly merited, attend
The Poet's rival, but the Painter's friend.

    Blest is the man who dares approach the bower
Where dwelt the Muses at their natal hour;

Whose steps have pressed, whose eye has marked afar,
The clime that nursed the sons of song and war,   870
The scenes which Glory still must hover o'er,
Her place of birth, her own Achaian shore.
But doubly blest is he whose heart expands
With hallowed feelings for those classic lands;
Who rends the veil of ages long gone by,
And views their remnants with a poet's eye!
WRIGHT! 'twas thy happy lot at once to view
Those shores of glory, and to sing them too;
And, sure, no common Muse inspired thy pen
To hail the land of Gods and Godlike men.   880

    And you, associate Bards! who snatched to light
Those gems too long withheld from modern sight;
Whose mingling taste combined to cull the wreath
While Attic flowers Aonian odours breathe,
And all their renovated fragrance flung,
To grace the beauties of your native tongue;
Now let those minds, that nobly could transfuse
The glorious Spirit of the Grecian Muse,
Though soft the echo, scorn a borrowed tone:
Resign Achaia's lyre, and strike your own.   890

    Let these, or such as these, with just applause,
Restore the Muse's violated laws;
But not in flimsy DARWIN's pompous chime,
That mighty master of unmeaning rhyme,
Whose gilded cymbals, more adorned than clear,
The eye delighted, but fatigued the ear,
In show the simple lyre could once surpass,
But now, worn down, appear in native brass;
While all his train of hovering sylphs around
Evaporate his similes and sound: 900
Him let them shun, with him let tinsel die:
False glare attracts, but more offends the eye.

Yet let them not to vulgar WORDSWORTH stoop,
The meanest object of the lowly group,
Whose verse, of all but childish prattle void,
Seems blessed harmony to LAMB and LLOYD:
Let them—but hold, my Muse, nor dare to teach
A strain far, far beyond thy humble reach:
The native genius with their being given
Will point the path, and peal their notes to heaven. 910

And thou, too, SCOTT! resign to minstrels rude
The wilder Slogan of a Border feud:
Let others spin their meagre lines for hire;
Enough for Genius, if itself inspire!
Let SOUTHEY sing, altho' his teeming muse,
Prolific every spring, be too profuse;
Let simple WORDSWORTH chime his childish verse,
And brother COLERIDGE lull the babe at nurse;
Let Spectre-mongering LEWIS aim, at most,
To rouse the Galleries, or to raise a ghost; 920
Let MOORE still sigh; let STRANGFORD steal from MOORE,
And swear that CAMOËNS sang such notes of yore;
Let HAYLEY hobble on, MONTGOMERY rave,
And godly GRAHAME chant a stupid stave;
Let sonneteering BOWLES his strains refine,
And whine and whimper to the fourteenth line;
Let STOTT, CARLISLE, MATILDA, and the rest
Of Grub Street, and of Grosvenor Place the best,
Scrawl on, till Death release us from the strain,
Or Common Sense assert her rights again; 930
But Thou, with powers that mock the aid of praise,
Should'st leave to humbler Bards ignoble lays:
Thy country's voice, the voice of all the Nine,
Demand a hallowed harp—that harp is thine.
Say! will not Caledonia's annals yield
The glorious record of some nobler field,
Than the vile foray of a plundering clan,
Whose proudest deeds disgrace the name of man?

Or Marmion's acts of darkness, fitter food
For SHERWOOD'S outlaw tales of ROBIN HOOD?   940
Scotland! still proudly claim thy native Bard,
And be thy praise his first, his best reward!
Yet not with thee alone his name should live,
But own the vast renown a world can give;
Be known, perchance, when Albion is no more,
And tell the tale of what she was before;
To future times her faded fame recall,
And save her glory, though his country fall.

Yet what avails the sanguine Poet's hope,
To conquer ages, and with time to cope?   950
New eras spread their wings, new nations rise,
And other Victors fill th' applauding skies;
A few brief generations fleet along,
Whose sons forget the Poet and his song:
E'en now, what once-loved Minstrels scarce may claim
The transient mention of a dubious name!
When Fame's loud trump hath blown its noblest blast,
Though long the sound, the echo sleeps at last;
And Glory, like the Phœnix midst her fires,
Exhales her odours, blazes, and expires.   960

Shall hoary Granta call her sable sons,
Expert in science, more expert at puns?
Shall these approach the Muse? ah, no! she flies,
Even from the tempting ore of Seaton's prize;
Though Printers condescend the press to soil
With rhyme by HOARE, and epic blank by HOYLE:—
Not him whose page, if still upheld by whist,
Requires no sacred theme to bid us list.
Ye! who in Granta's honours would surpass,
Must mount her Pegasus, a full-grown ass;   970
A foal well worthy of her ancient Dam,
Whose Helicon is duller than her Cam.

There CLARKE, still striving piteously "to please,"
Forgetting doggerel leads not to degrees,
A would-be Satirist, a hired Buffoon,
A monthly scribbler of some low lampoon,
Condemned to drudge, the meanest of the mean,
And furbish falsehoods for a magazine,
Devotes to scandal his congenial mind;
Himself a living libel on mankind.   980

Oh dark asylum of a Vandal race!
At once the boast of learning, and disgrace!
So lost to Phœbus, that nor HODGSON'S verse
Can make thee better, nor poor HEWSON'S worse.
But where fair Isis rolls her purer wave,
The partial Muse delighted loves to lave;
On her green banks a greener wreath she wove,
To crown the Bards that haunt her classic grove;
Where RICHARDS wakes a genuine poet's fires,
And modern Britons glory in their Sires.   990

For me, who, thus unasked, have dared to tell
My country, what her sons should know too well,
Zeal for her honour bade me here engage
The host of idiots that infest her age;
No just applause her honoured name shall lose,
As first in freedom, dearest to the Muse.
Oh! would thy bards but emulate thy fame,
And rise more worthy, Albion, of thy name!
What Athens was in science, Rome in power,
What Tyre appeared in her meridian hour,   1000
'Tis thine at once, fair Albion! to have been—
Earth's chief Dictatress, Ocean's lovely Queen:
But Rome decayed, and Athens strewed the plain,
And Tyre's proud piers lie shattered in the main;
Like these, thy strength may sink in ruin hurled,
And Britain fall, the bulwark of the world.
But let me cease, and dread Cassandra's fate,

With warning ever scoffed at, till too late;
To themes less lofty still my lay confine,
And urge thy Bards to gain a name like thine.   1010

　　Then, hapless Britain! be thy rulers blest,
The Senate's oracles, the people's jest!
Still hear thy motley orators dispense
The flowers of rhetoric, though not of sense,
While CANNING'S colleagues hate him for his wit,
And old dame PORTLAND fills the place of PITT.

　　Yet once again, adieu! ere this the sail
That wafts me hence is shivering in the gale;
And Afric's coast and Calpe's adverse height,
And Stamboul's minarets must greet my sight: 1020
Thence shall I stray through Beauty's native clime,
Where Kaff is clad in rocks, and crowned with snows sublime.
But should I back return, no tempting press
Shall drag my journal from the desk's recess;
Let coxcombs, printing as they come from far,
Snatch his own wreath of Ridicule from Carr;
Let ABERDEEN and ELGIN still pursue
The shade of fame through regions of Virtù;
Waste useless thousands on their Phidian freaks,
Misshapen monuments and maimed antiques;   1030
And make their grand saloons a general mart
For all the mutilated blocks of art:
Of Dardan tours let Dilettanti tell,
I leave topography to rapid GELL;
And, quite content, no more shall interpose
To stun the public ear—at least with Prose.

　　Thus far I've held my undisturbed career,
Prepared for rancour, steeled 'gainst selfish fear;
This thing of rhyme I ne'er disdained to own—
Though not obtrusive, yet not quite unknown: 1040
My voice was heard again, though not so loud,

My page, though nameless, never disavowed;
And now at once I tear the veil away:—
Cheer on the pack! the Quarry stands at bay,
Unscared by all the din of MELBOURNE house,
By LAMB's resentment, or by HOLLAND's spouse,
By JEFFREY's harmless pistol, HALLAM's rage,
Edina's brawny sons and brimstone page.
Our men in buckram shall have blows enough,
And feel they too are "penetrable stuff ":   1050
And though I hope not hence unscathed to go,
Who conquers me shall find a stubborn foe.
The time hath been, when no harsh sound would fall
From lips that now may seem imbued with gall;
Nor fools nor follies tempt me to despise
The meanest thing that crawled beneath my eyes:
But now, so callous grown, so changed since youth,
I've learned to think, and sternly speak the truth;
Learned to deride the critic's starch decree,
And break him on the wheel he meant for me;   1060
To spurn the rod a scribbler bids me kiss,
Nor care if courts and crowds applaud or hiss:
Nay more, though all my rival rhymesters frown,
I too can hunt a Poetaster down;
And, armed in proof, the gauntlet cast at once
To Scotch marauder, and to Southern dunce.
Thus much I've dared; if my incondite lay
Hath wronged these righteous times, let others say:
This, let the world, which knows not how to spare,
Yet rarely blames unjustly, now declare.   1070

POSTSCRIPT TO THE SECOND EDITION

I have been informed, since the present edition went to the press, that my trusty and well-beloved cousins, the Edinburgh Reviewers, are preparing a most vehement critique on my poor, gentle, *unresisting* Muse, whom they have already so be-deviled with their ungodly ribaldry;

"Tantæne animis cœlestibus Iræ!"

I suppose I must say of JEFFREY as Sir ANDREW AGUECHEEK saith, "an I had known he was so cunning of fence, I had seen him damned ere I had fought him." What a pity it is that I shall be beyond the Bosphorus before the next number has passed the Tweed! But I yet hope to light my pipe with it in Persia.

My Northern friends have accused me, with justice, of personality towards their great literary Anthropophagus, JEFFREY; but what else was to be done with him and his dirty pack, who feed by "lying and slandering," and slake their thirst by "evil speaking"? I have adduced facts already well known, and of JEFFREY's mind I have stated my free opinion, nor has he thence sustained any injury:—what scavenger was ever soiled by being pelted with mud? It may be said that I quit England because I have censured there "persons of honour and wit about town"; but I am coming back again, and their vengeance will keep hot till my return. Those who know me can testify that my motives for leaving England are very different from fears, literary or personal: those who do not, may one day be convinced. Since the publication of this thing, my name has not been concealed; I have been mostly in London, ready to answer for my transgressions, and in daily expectation of sundry cartels; but, alas! "the age of chivalry is over," or, in the vulgar tongue, there is no spirit now-a-days.

There is a youth ycleped Hewson Clarke (subaudi *esquire*), a sizer of Emmanuel College, and, I believe, a denizen of Berwick-upon-Tweed, whom I have introduced in these pages to much better company than he has been accustomed to meet; he is, notwithstanding, a very sad dog, and for no reason that I can discover, except a personal quarrel with a bear, kept by me at Cambridge to sit for a fellowship, and whom the jealousy of his Trinity contemporaries prevented from success, has been abusing me, and, what is worse, the defenceless innocent above mentioned, in the *Satirist* for one year and some months. I am utterly unconscious of having given him any provocation; indeed, I am guiltless of having heard his name, till coupled with the *Satirist*. He has therefore no reason to complain, and I dare say that, like Sir Fretful Plagiary, he is rather *pleased* than otherwise. I have now mentioned all who have done me the honour to notice me and mine, that is, my bear and my book, except the editor of the *Satirist*, who, it seems, is a gentleman—God wot! I wish he could impart a little of his gentility to his subordinate scribblers. I hear that Mr. JERNINGHAM is about to take up the cudgels for his Mæcenas, Lord Carlisle. I hope not: he was one of the few, who, in the very short intercourse I had with him, treated me with kindness when a boy; and whatever he may say or do, "pour on, I will endure." I have nothing further to add, save a general note of thanksgiving to readers, purchasers, and publishers, and in the words of *Scott,* I wish

> "To all and each a fair good night,
> And rosy dreams and slumbers light."

THE VISION OF JUDGMENT

By Quevedo Redivivus, Suggested by the Composition So Entitled by the Author of "Wat Tyler"

"A Daniel come to judgment! yea, a Daniel!
I thank thee, Jew, for teaching me that word."

PREFACE

It hath been wisely said, that "One fool makes many;" and it hath been poetically observed—

"[That] fools rush in where angels fear to tread."
—POPE'S *Essay on Criticism.*

If Mr. Southey had not rushed in where he had no business, and where he never was before, and never will be again, the following poem would not have been written. It is not impossible that it may be as good as his own, seeing that it cannot, by any species of stupidity, natural or acquired, be *worse*. The gross flattery, the dull impudence, the renegado intolerance, and impious cant, of the poem by the author of "Wat Tyler," are something so stupendous as to form the sublime of himself—containing the quintessence of his own attributes.

So much for his poem—a word on his preface. In this preface it has pleased the magnanimous Laureate to draw the picture of a supposed "Satanic School," the which he doth recommend to the notice of the legislature; thereby adding to his other laurels the ambition of those of an informer. If there exists anywhere, except in his imagination, such a School, is he not sufficiently armed against it by his own intense vanity? The truth is that there are certain writers whom Mr. S. imagines, like Scrub, to have "talked of *him;* for they laughed consumedly."

I think I know enough of most of the writers to whom he is supposed to allude, to assert, that they, in their individual capacities, have done more good, in the charities of life, to their fellow-creatures, in any one year, than Mr. Southey has done harm to himself by his absurdities in his whole life; and this is saying a great deal. But I have a few questions to ask.

1stly, Is Mr. Southey the author of *Wat Tyler?*

2ndly, Was he not refused a remedy at law by the highest judge of his beloved England, because it was a blasphemous and seditious publication?

3rdly, Was he not entitled by William Smith, in full parliament, "a rancorous renegado?"

4thly, Is he not poet laureate, with his own lines on Martin the regicide staring him in the face?

And, 5thly, Putting the four preceding items together, with what conscience dare *he* call the attention of the laws to the publications of others, be they what they may?

I say nothing of the cowardice of such a proceeding; its meanness speaks for itself; but I wish to touch upon the *motive,* which is neither more nor less than that Mr. S. has been laughed at a little in some recent publications, as he was of yore in the *Antijacobin,* by his present patrons. Hence all this "skimble scamble stuff " about "Satanic," and so forth. However, it is worthy of him—*"qualis ab incepto."*

If there is anything obnoxious to the political opinions of a portion of the public in the following poem, they may thank Mr. Southey. He might have written hexameters, as he has written everything else, for aught that the writer cared—had they been upon another subject. But to attempt to canonise a monarch, who, whatever were his household virtues, was neither a successful nor a patriot king,—inasmuch as several years of his reign passed in war with America and Ireland, to say nothing of the aggression upon France—like all other exaggeration, necessarily begets opposition. In whatever manner he may be spoken of in this new *Vision,* his *public* career will not be more favourably transmitted by history. Of his private virtues (although a little expensive to the nation) there can be no doubt.

With regard to the supernatural personages treated of, I can only say that I know as much about them, and (as an honest man) have a better right to talk of them than Robert Southey. I have also treated them more tolerantly. The way in which that poor insane creature, the Laureate, deals about his judgments in the next world, is like his own judgment in this. If it was not completely ludicrous, it would be something worse. I don't think that there is much more to say at present.

QUEVEDO REDIVIVUS.

P.S.—It is possible that some readers may object, in these objectionable times, to the freedom with which saints, angels, and spiritual persons discourse in this *Vision*. But, for precedents upon such points, I must refer him to Fielding's *Journey from this World to the next*, and to the Visions of myself, the said Quevedo, in Spanish or translated. The reader is also requested to observe, that no doctrinal tenets are insisted upon or discussed; that the person of the Deity is carefully withheld from sight, which is more than can be said for the Laureate, who hath thought proper to make him talk, not "like a school-divine," but like the unscholarlike Mr. Southey. The whole action passes on the outside of heaven; and Chaucer's *Wife of Bath,* Pulci's *Morgante Maggiore,* Swift's *Tale of a Tub,* and the other works above referred to, are cases in point of the freedom with which saints, etc., may be permitted to converse in works not intended to be serious.

Q.R.

*** Mr. Southey being, as he says, a good Christian and vindictive, threatens, I understand, a reply to this our answer. It is to be hoped that his visionary faculties will in the meantime have acquired a little more judgment, properly so called: otherwise he will get himself into new dilemmas. These apostate jacobins furnish rich rejoinders. Let him take a specimen. Mr. Southey laudeth grievously "one Mr. Landor," who cultivates much private renown in the shape of Latin verses; and not long ago, the poet laureate dedicated to him, it appeareth, one of his fugitive lyrics, upon the strength of a poem called *"Gebir."* Who could suppose, that in this same Gebir the aforesaid Savage Landor (for such is his grim cognomen) putteth into the infernal regions no less a person than the hero of his friend Mr. Southey's heaven,—yea, even George the Third! See also how personal Savage becometh, when he hath a mind. The following is his portrait of our late gracious sovereign:—

(Prince Gebir having descended into the infernal regions, the shades of his royal ancestors are, at his request, called up to his view; and he exclaims to his ghostly guide)—

> " 'Aroar, what wretch that nearest us? what wretch
> Is that with eyebrows white and slanting brow?
> Listen! him yonder who, bound down supine,
> Shrinks yelling from that sword there, engine-hung;
> He too amongst my ancestors! I hate
> The despot, but the dastard I despise.
> Was he our countryman?'
>   'Alas, O king!
> Iberia bore him, but the breed accurst
> Inclement winds blew blighting from north-east.'
> 'He was a warrior then, nor feared the gods?'
> 'Gebir, he feared the Demons, not the gods,
> Though them indeed his daily face adored;
> And was no warrior, yet the thousand lives
> Squandered, as stones to exercise a sling,
> And the tame cruelty and cold caprice—
>   Oh madness of mankind! addressed, adored!' "
>
>   *Gebir* [*Works, etc., 1876, vii. 17*].

I omit noticing some edifying Ithyphallics of Savagius, wishing to keep the proper veil over them, if his grave but somewhat indiscreet worshipper will suffer it; but certainly these teachers of "great moral lessons" are apt to be found in strange company.

I

Saint Peter sat by the celestial gate:
    His keys were rusty, and the lock was dull,
So little trouble had been given of late;
    Not that the place by any means was full,
But since the Gallic-era "eighty-eight"
    The Devils had ta'en a longer, stronger pull,

And "a pull altogether," as they say
At sea—which drew most souls another way.

II

The Angels all were singing out of tune,
    And hoarse with having little else to do,   10
Excepting to wind up the sun and moon,
    Or curb a runaway young star or two,
Or wild colt of a comet, which too soon
    Broke out of bounds o'er the ethereal blue,
Splitting some planet with its playful tail,
As boats are sometimes by a wanton whale.

III

The Guardian Seraphs had retired on high,
    Finding their charges past all care below;
Terrestrial business filled nought in the sky
    Save the Recording Angel's black bureau;   20
Who found, indeed, the facts to multiply
    With such rapidity of vice and woe,
That he had stripped off both his wings in quills,
And yet was in arrear of human ills.

IV

His business so augmented of late years,
    That he was forced, against his will, no doubt,
(Just like those cherubs, earthly ministers,)
    For some resource to turn himself about,
And claim the help of his celestial peers,
    To aid him ere he should be quite worn out   30
By the increased demand for his remarks:
Six Angels and twelve Saints were named his clerks.

V

This was a handsome board—at least for Heaven;
    And yet they had even then enough to do,
So many Conquerors' cars were daily driven,
    So many kingdoms fitted up anew;
Each day, too, slew its thousands six or seven,

Till at the crowning carnage, Waterloo,
They threw their pens down in divine disgust—
The page was so besmeared with blood and dust.   40

VI

This by the way; 'tis not mine to record
    What Angels shrink from: even the very Devil
On this occasion his own work abhorred,
    So surfeited with the infernal revel:
Though he himself had sharpened every sword,
    It almost quenched his innate thirst of evil.
(Here Satan's sole good work deserves insertion—
'Tis, that he has both Generals in reversion.)

VII

Let's skip a few short years of hollow peace,
    Which peopled earth no better, Hell as wont,   50
And Heaven none—they form the tyrant's lease,
    With nothing but new names subscribed upon 't;
'Twill one day finish: meantime they increase,
    "With seven heads and ten horns," and all in front,
Like Saint John's foretold beast; but ours are born
Less formidable in the head than horn.

VIII

In the first year of Freedom's second dawn
    Died George the Third; although no tyrant, one
Who shielded tyrants, till each sense withdrawn
    Left him nor mental nor external sun: 60
A better farmer ne'er brushed dew from lawn,
    A worse king never left a realm undone!
He died—but left his subjects still behind,
One half as mad—and t'other no less blind.

IX

He died! his death made no great stir on earth:
    His burial made some pomp; there was profusion
Of velvet—gilding—brass—and no great dearth
    Of aught but tears—save those shed by collusion:

For these things may be bought at their true worth;
    Of elegy there was the due infusion—   70
Bought also; and the torches, cloaks and banners,
Heralds, and relics of old Gothic manners,

            x

Formed a sepulchral melodrame. Of all
    The fools who flocked to swell or see the show,
Who cared about the corpse? The funeral
    Made the attraction, and the black the woe.
There throbbed not there a thought which pierced the pall;
    And when the gorgeous coffin was laid low,
It seemed the mockery of hell to fold
The rottenness of eighty years in gold.   80

           x i

So mix his body with the dust! It might
    Return to what it *must* far sooner, were
The natural compound left alone to fight
    Its way back into earth, and fire, and air;
But the unnatural balsams merely blight
    What Nature made him at his birth, as bare
As the mere million's base unmummied clay—
Yet all his spices but prolong decay.

           x i i

He's dead—and upper earth with him has done;
    He's buried; save the undertaker's bill,   90
Or lapidary scrawl, the world is gone
    For him, unless he left a German will:
But where's the proctor who will ask his son?
    In whom his qualities are reigning still,
Except that household virtue, most uncommon,
Of constancy to a bad, ugly woman.

           x i i i

"God save the king!" It is a large economy
    In God to save the like; but if he will
Be saving, all the better; for not one am I

Of those who think damnation better still: 100
I hardly know too if not quite alone am I
    In this small hope of bettering future ill
By circumscribing, with some slight restriction,
The eternity of Hell's hot jurisdiction.

XIV

I know this is unpopular; I know
    'Tis blasphemous; I know one may be damned
For hoping no one else may e'er be so;
    I know my catechism; I know we're crammed
With the best doctrines till we quite o'erflow;
    I know that all save England's Church have shammed,   110
And that the other twice two hundred churches
And synagogues have made a *damned* bad purchase.

XV

God help us all! God help me too! I am,
    God knows, as helpless as the Devil can wish,
And not a whit more difficult to damn,
    Than is to bring to land a late-hooked fish,
Or to the butcher to purvey the lamb;
    Not that I'm fit for such a noble dish,
As one day will be that immortal fry
Of almost every body born to die.   120

XVI

Saint Peter sat by the celestial gate,
    And nodded o'er his keys: when, lo! there came
A wondrous noise he had not heard of late—
    A rushing sound of wind, and stream, and flame;
In short, a roar of things extremely great,
    Which would have made aught save a Saint exclaim;
But he, with first a start and then a wink,
Said, "There's another star gone out, I think!"

XVII

But ere he could return to his repose,
    A Cherub flapped his right wing o'er his eyes—   130

At which Saint Peter yawned, and rubbed his nose:
   "Saint porter," said the angel, "prithee rise!"
Waving a goodly wing, which glowed, as glows
   An earthly peacock's tail, with heavenly dyes:
To which the saint replied, "Well, what's the matter?
Is Lucifer come back with all this clatter?"

XVIII

"No," quoth the Cherub: "George the Third is dead."
   "And who *is* George the Third?" replied the apostle:
"What George? What Third?" "The King of England," said
   The angel. "Well! he won 't find kings to jostle   140
Him on his way; but does he wear his head?
   Because the last we saw here had a tustle,
And ne'er would have got into Heaven's good graces,
Had he not flung his head in all our faces.

XIX

"He was—if I remember—King of France;
   That head of his, which could not keep a crown
On earth, yet ventured in my face to advance
   A claim to those of martyrs—like my own:
If I had had my sword, as I had once
   When I cut ears off, I had cut him down;   150
But having but my *keys,* and not my brand,
I only knocked his head from out his hand.

XX

"And then he set up such a headless howl,
   That all the Saints came out and took him in;
And there he sits by Saint Paul, check by jowl;
   That fellow Paul—the parvenù! The skin
Of Saint Bartholomew, which makes his cowl
   In heaven, and upon earth redeemed his sin,
So as to make a martyr, never sped
Better than did this weak and wooden head.   160

XXI

"But had it come up here upon its shoulders,
    There would have been a different tale to tell:
The fellow-feeling in the Saint's beholders
    Seems to have acted on them like a spell;
And so this very foolish head Heaven solders
    Back on its trunk: it may be very well,
And seems the custom here to overthrow
Whatever has been wisely done below."

XXII

The Angel answered, "Peter! do not pout:
    The King who comes has head and all entire,   170
And never knew much what it was about—
    He did as doth the puppet—by its wire,
And will be judged like all the rest, no doubt:
    My business and your own is not to inquire
Into such matters, but to mind our cue—
Which is to act as we are bid to do."

XXIII

While thus they spake, the angelic caravan,
    Arriving like a rush of mighty wind,
Cleaving the fields of space, as doth the swan
    Some silver stream (say Ganges, Nile, or Inde,   180
Or Thames, or Tweed), and midst them an old man
    With an old soul, and both extremely blind,
Halted before the gate, and, in his shroud,
Seated their fellow-traveller on a cloud.

XXIV

But bringing up the rear of this bright host
    A Spirit of a different aspect waved
His wings, like thunder-clouds above some coast
    Whose barren beach with frequent wrecks is paved;
His brow was like the deep when tempest-tossed;
    Fierce and unfathomable thoughts engraved   190
Eternal wrath on his immortal face,
And *where* he gazed a gloom pervaded space.

XXV

As he drew near, he gazed upon the gate
　　Ne'er to be entered more by him or Sin,
With such a glance of supernatural hate,
　　As made Saint Peter wish himself within;
He pottered with his keys at a great rate,
　　And sweated through his Apostolic skin:
Of course his perspiration was but ichor,
Or some such other spiritual liquor.　　　　　200

XXVI

The very Cherubs huddled all together,
　　Like birds when soars the falcon; and they felt
A tingling to the tip of every feather,
　　And formed a circle like Orion's belt
Around their poor old charge; who scarce knew whither
　　His guards had led him, though they gently dealt
With Royal Manes (for by many stories,
And true, we learn the Angels all are Tories).

XXVII

As things were in this posture, the gate flew
　　Asunder, and the flashing of its hinges　　　　210
Flung over space an universal hue
　　Of many-coloured flame, until its tinges
Reached even our speck of earth, and made a new
　　Aurora borealis spread its fringes
O'er the North Pole; the same seen, when ice-bound,
By Captain Parry's crew, in "Melville's Sound."

XXVIII

And from the gate thrown open issued beaming
　　A beautiful and mighty Thing of Light,
Radiant with glory, like a banner streaming
　　Victorious from some world-o'erthrowing fight:　　　220
My poor comparisons must needs be teeming
　　With earthly likenesses, for here the night
Of clay obscures our best conceptions, saving
Johanna Southcote, or Bob Southey raving.

XXIX

'Twas the Archangel Michael: all men know
    The make of Angels and Archangels, since
There's scarce a scribbler has not one to show,
    From the fiends' leader to the Angels' Prince.
There also are some altar-pieces, though
    I really can't say that they much evince   230
One's inner notions of immortal spirits;
But let the connoisseurs explain *their* merits.

XXX

Michael flew forth in glory and in good;
    A goodly work of him from whom all Glory
And Good arise; the portal past—he stood;
    Before him the young Cherubs and Saints hoary—
(I say *young,* begging to be understood
    By looks, not years; and should be very sorry
To state, they were not older than St. Peter,
But merely that they seemed a little sweeter).   240

XXXI

The Cherubs and the Saints bowed down before
    That arch-angelic Hierarch, the first
Of Essences angelical who wore
    The aspect of a god; but this ne'er nursed
Pride in his heavenly bosom, in whose core
    No thought, save for his Maker's service, durst
Intrude—however glorified and high,
He knew him but the Viceroy of the sky.

XXXII

He and the sombre, silent Spirit met—
    They knew each other both for good and ill;   250
Such was their power, that neither could forget
    His former friend and future foe; but still
There was a high, immortal, proud regret
    In either's eye, as if 'twere less their will
Than destiny to make the eternal years
Their date of war, and their "Champ Clos" the spheres.

XXXIII

But here they were in neutral space: we know
    From Job, that Satan hath the power to pay
A heavenly visit thrice a-year or so;
    And that the "Sons of God," like those of clay,   260
Must keep him company; and we might show
    From the same book, in how polite a way
The dialogue is held between the Powers
Of Good and Evil—but 'twould take up hours.

XXXIV

And this is not a theologic tract,
    To prove with Hebrew and with Arabic,
If Job be allegory or a fact,
    But a true narrative; and thus I pick
From out the whole but such and such an act
    As sets aside the slightest thought of trick.   270
'Tis every tittle true, beyond suspicion,
And accurate as any other vision.

XXXV

The spirits were in neutral space, before
    The gate of Heaven; like eastern thresholds is
The place where Death's grand cause is argued o'er
    And souls despatched to that world or to this;
And therefore Michael and the other wore
    A civil aspect: though they did not kiss,
Yet still between his Darkness and his Brightness
There passed a mutual glance of great politeness.   280

XXXVI

The Archangel bowed, not like a modern beau,
    But with a graceful oriental bend,
Pressing one radiant arm just where below
    The heart in good men is supposed to tend;
He turned as to an equal, not too low,
    But kindly; Satan met his ancient friend
With more hauteur, as might an old Castilian
Poor Noble meet a mushroom rich civilian.

XXXVII

He merely bent his diabolic brow
        An instant; and then raising it, he stood   290
In act to assert his right or wrong, and show
        Cause why King George by no means could or should
Make out a case to be exempt from woe
        Eternal, more than other kings, endued
With better sense and hearts, whom History mentions,
Who long have "paved Hell with their good intentions."

XXXVIII

Michael began: "What wouldst thou with this man,
        Now dead, and brought before the Lord? What ill
Hath he wrought since his mortal race began,
        That thou canst claim him? Speak! and do thy will,   300
If it be just: if in this earthly span
        He hath been greatly failing to fulfil
His duties as a king and mortal, say,
And he is thine; if not—let him have way."

XXXIX

"Michael!" replied the Prince of Air, "even here
        Before the gate of Him thou servest, must
I claim my subject: and will make appear
        That as he was my worshipper in dust,
So shall he be in spirit, although dear
        To thee and thine, because nor wine nor lust   310
Were of his weaknesses; yet on the throne
He reigned o'er millions to serve me alone.

XL

"Look to *our* earth, or rather *mine*; it was,
        Once, more thy master's: but I triumph not
In this poor planet's conquest; nor, alas!
        Need he thou servest envy me my lot:
With all the myriads of bright worlds which pass
        In worship round him, he may have forgot
Yon weak creation of such paltry things:
I think few worth damnation save their kings,   320

XLI

"And these but as a kind of quit-rent, to
    Assert my right as Lord: and even had
I such an inclination, 'twere (as you
    Well know) superfluous; they are grown so bad,
That Hell has nothing better left to do
    Than leave them to themselves: so much more mad
And evil by their own internal curse,
Heaven cannot make them better, nor I worse.

XLII

"Look to the earth, I said, and say again:
    When this old, blind, mad, helpless, weak, poor worm   330
Began in youth's first bloom and flush to reign,
    The world and he both wore a different form,
And much of earth and all the watery plain
    Of Ocean called him king: through many a storm
His isles had floated on the abyss of Time;
For the rough virtues chose them for their clime.

XLIII

"He came to his sceptre young; he leaves it old:
    Look to the state in which he found his realm,
And left it; and his annals too behold,
    How to a minion first he gave the helm;   340
How grew upon his heart a thirst for gold,
    The beggar's vice, which can but overwhelm
The meanest hearts; and for the rest, but glance
Thine eye along America and France.

XLIV

" 'Tis true, he was a tool from first to last
    (I have the workmen safe); but as a tool
So let him be consumed. From out the past
    Of ages, since mankind have known the rule
Of monarchs—from the bloody rolls amassed
    Of Sin and Slaughter—from the Cæsars' school,   350
Take the worst pupil; and produce a reign
More drenched with gore, more cumbered with the slain.

XLV

"He ever warred with freedom and the free:
    Nations as men, home subjects, foreign foes,
So that they uttered the word 'Liberty!'
    Found George the Third their first opponent. Whose
History was ever stained as his will be
    With national and individual woes?
I grant his household abstinence; I grant
His neutral virtues, which most monarchs want;   360

XLVI

"I know he was a constant consort; own
    He was a decent sire, and middling lord.
All this is much, and most upon a throne;
    As temperance, if at Apicius' board,
Is more than at an anchorite's supper shown.
    I grant him all the kindest can accord;
And this was well for him, but not for those
Millions who found him what Oppression chose.

XLVII

"The New World shook him off; the Old yet groans
    Beneath what he and his prepared, if not   370
Completed: he leaves heirs on many thrones
    To all his vices, without what begot
Compassion for him—his tame virtues; drones
    Who sleep, or despots who have now forgot
A lesson which shall be retaught them, wake
Upon the thrones of earth; but let them quake!

XLVIII

"Five millions of the primitive, who hold
    The faith which makes ye great on earth, implored
A *part* of that vast *all* they held of old,—
    Freedom to worship—not alone your Lord,   380
Michael, but you, and you, Saint Peter! Cold
    Must be your souls, if you have not abhorred
The foe to Catholic participation
In all the license of a Christian nation.

XLIX

"True! he allowed them to pray God; but as
    A consequence of prayer, refused the law
Which would have placed them upon the same base
    With those who did not hold the Saints in awe."
But here Saint Peter started from his place
    And cried, "You may the prisoner withdraw: 390
Ere Heaven shall ope her portals to this Guelph,
While I am guard, may I be damned myself!

L

"Sooner will I with Cerberus exchange
    My office (and *his* is no sinecure)
Than see this royal Bedlam-bigot range
    The azure fields of Heaven, of that be sure!"
"Saint!" replied Satan, "you do well to avenge
    The wrongs he made your satellites endure;
And if to this exchange you should be given,
I'll try to coax *our* Cerberus up to heaven!"   400

LI

Here Michael interposed: "Good Saint! And Devil!
    Pray, not so fast; you both outrun discretion.
Saint Peter! you were wont to be more civil:
    Satan! Excuse this warmth of his expression,
And condescension to the vulgar's level:
    Even Saints sometimes forget themselves in session.
Have you got more to say?"—"No."—"If you please,
I'll trouble you to call your witnesses."

LII

Then Satan turned and waved his swarthy hand,
    Which stirred with its electric qualities   410
Clouds farther off than we can understand,
    Although we find him sometimes in our skies;
Infernal thunder shook both sea and land
    In all the planets—and Hell's batteries
Let off the artillery, which Milton mentions
As one of Satan's most sublime inventions.

LIII

This was a signal unto such damned souls
   As have the privilege of their damnation
Extended far beyond the mere controls
   Of worlds past, present, or to come; no station   420
Is theirs particularly in the rolls
   Of Hell assigned; but where their inclination
Or business carries them in search of game,
They may range freely—being damned the same.

LIV

They are proud of this—as very well they may,
   It being a sort of knighthood, or gilt key
Stuck in their loins; or like to an "entré"
   Up the back stairs, or such free-masonry.
I borrow my comparisons from clay,
   Being clay myself. Let not those spirits be   430
Offended with such base low likenesses;
We know their posts are nobler far than these.

LV

When the great signal ran from Heaven to Hell—
   About ten million times the distance reckoned
From our sun to its earth, as we can tell
   How much time it takes up, even to a second,
For every ray that travels to dispel
   The fogs of London, through which, dimly beaconed,
The weathercocks are gilt some thrice a year,
If that the *summer* is not too severe: 440

LVI

I say that I can tell—'twas half a minute;
   I know the solar beams take up more time
Ere, packed up for their journey, they begin it;
   But then their Telegraph is less sublime,
And if they ran a race, they would not win it
   'Gainst Satan's couriers bound for their own clime.
The sun takes us some years for every ray
To reach its goal—the Devil not half a day.

LVII

Upon the verge of space, about the size
    Of half-a-crown, a little speck appeared   **450**
(I've seen a something like it in the skies
    In the Ægean, ere a squall); it neared,
And, growing bigger, took another guise;
    Like an aërial ship it tacked, and steered,
Or *was* steered (I am doubtful of the grammar
Of the last phrase, which makes the stanza stammer;

LVIII

But take your choice): and then it grew a cloud;
    And so it was—a cloud of witnesses.
But such a cloud! No land ere saw a crowd
    Of locusts numerous as the heavens saw these;   **460**
They shadowed with their myriads Space; their loud
    And varied cries were like those of wild geese,
(If nations may be likened to a goose),
And realised the phrase of "Hell broke loose."

LIX

Here crashed a sturdy oath of stout John Bull,
    Who damned away his eyes as heretofore:
There Paddy brogued "By Jasus!"—"What's your wull?"
    The temperate Scot exclaimed: the French ghost swore
In certain terms I shan't translate in full,
    As the first coachman will; and 'midst the war,   **470**
The voice of Jonathan was heard to express,
"*Our* President is going to war, I guess."

LX

Besides there were the Spaniard, Dutch, and Dane;
    In short, an universal shoal of shades
From Otaheite's isle to Salisbury Plain,
    Of all climes and professions, years and trades,
Ready to swear against the good king's reign,
    Bitter as clubs in cards are against spades:
All summoned by this grand "subpœna," to
Try if kings mayn't be damned like me or you.   **480**

LXI

When Michael saw his host, he first grew pale,
　　As Angels can; next, like Italian twilight,
He turned all colours—as a peacock's tail,
　　Or sunset streaming through a Gothic skylight
In some old abbey, or a trout not stale,
　　Or distant lightning on the horizon *by* night,
Or a fresh rainbow, or a grand review
Of thirty regiments in red, green, and blue.

LXII

Then he addressed himself to Satan: "Why—
　　My good old friend, for such I deem you, though　　490
Our different parties make us fight so shy,
　　　　I ne'er mistake you for a *personal* foe;
Our difference is *political,* and I
　　　　Trust that, whatever may occur below,
You know my great respect for you: and this
Makes me regret whate'er you do amiss—

LXIII

"Why, my dear Lucifer, would you abuse
　　My call for witnesses? I did not mean
That you should half of Earth and Hell produce;
　　　　'Tis even superfluous, since two honest, clean,　　500
True testimonies are enough: we lose
　　　　Our Time, nay, our Eternity, between
The accusation and defence: if we
Hear both, 'twill stretch our immortality."

LXIV

Satan replied, "To me the matter is
　　Indifferent, in a personal point of view:
I can have fifty better souls than this
　　　　With far less trouble than we have gone through
Already; and I merely argued his
　　　　Late Majesty of Britain's case with you　　510
Upon a point of form: you may dispose
Of him; I've kings enough below, God knows!"

LXV

Thus spoke the Demon (late called "multi-faced"
    By multo-scribbling Southey). "Then we'll call
One or two persons of the myriads placed
    Around our congress, and dispense with all
The rest," quoth Michael: "Who may be so graced
    As to speak first? there's choice enough—who shall
It be?" Then Satan answered, "There are many;
But you may choose Jack Wilkes as well as any."   520

LXVI

A merry, cock-eyed, curious-looking Sprite
    Upon the instant started from the throng,
Dressed in a fashion now forgotten quite;
    For all the fashions of the flesh stick long
By people in the next world; where unite
    All the costumes since Adam's, right or wrong,
From Eve's fig-leaf down to the petticoat,
Almost as scanty, of days less remote.

LXVII

The Spirit looked around upon the crowds
    Assembled, and exclaimed, "My friends of all   530
The spheres, we shall catch cold amongst these clouds;
    So let's to business: why this general call?
If those are freeholders I see in shrouds,
    And 'tis for an election that they bawl,
Behold a candidate with unturned coat!
Saint Peter, may I count upon your vote?"

LXVIII

"Sir," replied Michael, "you mistake; these things
    Are of a former life, and what we do
Above is more august; to judge of kings
    Is the tribunal met: so now you know."   540
"Then I presume those gentlemen with wings,"
    Said Wilkes, "are Cherubs; and that soul below
Looks much like George the Third, but to my mind
A good deal older—bless me! is he blind?"

LXIX

"He is what you behold him, and his doom
    Depends upon his deeds," the Angel said;
"If you have aught to arraign in him, the tomb
    Gives licence to the humblest beggar's head
To lift itself against the loftiest."—"Some,"
    Said Wilkes, "don't wait to see them laid in lead,   550
For such a liberty—and I, for one,
Have told them what I thought beneath the sun."

LXX

"*Above* the sun repeat, then, what thou hast
    To urge against him," said the Archangel. "Why,"
Replied the Spirit, "since old scores are past,
    Must I turn evidence? In faith, not I.
Besides, I beat him hollow at the last,
    With all his Lords and Commons: in the sky
I don't like ripping up old stories, since
His conduct was but natural in a prince.   560

LXXI

"Foolish, no doubt, and wicked, to oppress
    A poor unlucky devil without a shilling;
But then I blame the man himself much less
    Than Bute and Grafton, and shall be unwilling
To see him punished here for their excess,
    Since they were both damned long ago, and still in
Their place below: for me, I have forgiven,
And vote his *habeas corpus* into Heaven."

LXXII

"Wilkes," said the Devil, "I understand all this;
    You turned to half a courtier ere you died,   570
And seem to think it would not be amiss
    To grow a whole one on the other side
Of Charon's ferry; you forget that *his*
    Reign is concluded; whatso'er betide,
He won't be sovereign more: you've lost your labour,
For at the best he will but be your neighbour.

LXXIII

"However, I knew what to think of it,
    When I beheld you in your jesting way,
Flitting and whispering round about the spit
    Where Belial, upon duty for the day,   580
With Fox's lard was basting William Pitt,
    His pupil; I knew what to think, I say:
That fellow even in Hell breeds farther ills;
I'll have him *gagged*—'twas one of his own Bills.

LXXIV

"Call Junius!" From the crowd a shadow stalked,
    And at the name there was a general squeeze,
So that the very ghosts no longer walked
    In comfort, at their own aërial ease,
But were all rammed, and jammed (but to be balked,
    As we shall see), and jostled hands and knees,   590
Like wind compressed and pent within a bladder,
Or like a human colic, which is sadder.

LXXV

The shadow came—a tall, thin, grey-haired figure,
    That looked as it had been a shade on earth;
Quick in its motions, with an air of vigour,
    But nought to mark its breeding or its birth;
Now it waxed little, then again grew bigger,
    With now an air of gloom, or savage mirth;
But as you gazed upon its features, they
Changed every instant—to *what*, none could say.   600

LXXVI

The more intently the ghosts gazed, the less
    Could they distinguish whose the features were;
The Devil himself seemed puzzled even to guess;
    They varied like a dream—now here, now there;
And several people swore from out the press,
    They knew him perfectly; and one could swear
He was his father; upon which another
Was sure he was his mother's cousin's brother:

LXXVII

Another, that he was a duke, or knight,
   An orator, a lawyer, or a priest,   610
A nabob, a man-midwife; but the wight
    Mysterious changed his countenance at least
As oft as they their minds: though in full sight
   He stood, the puzzle only was increased;
The man was a phantasmagoria in
Himself—he was so volatile and thin.

LXXVIII

The moment that you had pronounced him *one*,
   Presto! his face changed, and he was another;
And when that change was hardly well put on,
   It varied, till I don't think his own mother   620
(If that he had a mother) would her son
   Have known, he sifted so from one to t'other;
Till guessing from a pleasure grew a task,
At this epistolary "Iron Mask."

LXXIX

For sometimes he like Cerberus would seem—
   "Three gentlemen at once" (as sagely says
Good Mrs. Malaprop); then you might deem
   That he was not even *one;* now many rays
Were flashing round him; and now a thick steam
   Hid him from sight—like fogs on London days: 630
Now Burke, now Tooke, he grew to people's fancies,
And certes often like Sir Philip Francis.

LXXX

I've an hypothesis—'tis quite my own;
   I never let it out till now, for fear
Of doing people harm about the throne,
   And injuring some minister or peer,
On whom the stigma might perhaps be blown;
   It is—my gentle public, lend thine ear!
'Tis, that what Junius we are wont to call,
Was *really—truly*—nobody at all.   640

LXXXI

I don't see wherefore letters should not be
  Written without hands, since we daily view
Them written without heads; and books, we see,
  Are filled as well without the latter too:
And really till we fix on somebody
  For certain sure to claim them as his due,
Their author, like the Niger's mouth, will bother
The world to say if *there* be mouth or author.

LXXXII

"And who and what art thou?" the Archangel said.
  "For *that* you may consult my title-page,"   650
Replied this mighty shadow of a shade:
  "If I have kept my secret half an age,
I scarce shall tell it now."—"Canst thou upbraid,"
  Continued Michael, "George Rex, or allege
Aught further?" Junius answered, "You had better
First ask him for *his* answer to my letter:

LXXXIII

"My charges upon record will outlast
  The brass of both his epitaph and tomb."
"Repent'st thou not," said Michael, "of some past
  Exaggeration? something which may doom   660
Thyself if false, as him if true? Thou wast
  Too bitter—is it not so?—in thy gloom
Of passion?"—"Passion!" cried the phantom dim,
"I loved my country, and I hated him.

LXXXIV

"What I have written, I have written: let
  The rest be on his head or mine!" So spoke
Old *"Nominis Umbra";* and while speaking yet,
  Away he melted in celestial smoke.
Then Satan said to Michael, "Don't forget
  To call George Washington, and John Horne Tooke,   670
And Franklin;"—but at this time there was heard
A cry for room, though not a phantom stirred.

LXXXV

At length with jostling, elbowing, and the aid
  Of Cherubim appointed to that post,
The devil Asmodeus to the circle made
  His way, and looked as if his journey cost
Some trouble. When his burden down he laid,
  "What's this?" cried Michael; "why, 'tis not a ghost?"
"I know it," quoth the Incubus; "but he
Shall be one, if you leave the affair to me.   680

LXXXVI

"Confound the renegado! I have sprained
  My left wing, he's so heavy; one would think
Some of his works about his neck were chained.
  But to the point; while hovering o'er the brink
Of Skiddaw (where as usual it still rained),
  I saw a taper, far below me, wink,
And stooping, caught this fellow at a libel—
No less on History—than the Holy Bible.

LXXXVII

"The former is the Devil's scripture, and
  The latter yours, good Michael: so the affair   690
Belongs to all of us, you understand.
  I snatched him up just as you see him there,
And brought him off for sentence out of hand:
  I've scarcely been ten minutes in the air—
At least a quarter it can hardly be:
I dare say that his wife is still at tea."

LXXXVIII

Here Satan said, "I know this man of old,
  And have expected him for some time here;
A sillier fellow you will scarce behold,
  Or more conceited in his petty sphere: 700
But surely it was not worth while to fold
  Such trash below yiour wing, Asmodeus dear:
We had the poor wretch safe (without being bored
With carriage) coming of his own accord.

LXXXIX

"But since he's here, let's see what he had done."
    "Done!" cried Asmodeus, "he anticipates
The very business you are now upon,
    And scribbles as if head clerk to the Fates.
Who knows to what his ribaldry may run,
    When such an ass as this, like Balaam's, prates?   710
"Let's hear," quoth Michael, "what he has to say:
You know we're bound to that in every way."

XC

Now the Bard, glad to get an audience, which
    By no means often was his case below,
Began to cough, and hawk, and hem, and pitch
    His voice into that awful note of woe
To all unhappy hearers within reach
    Of poets when the tide of rhyme's in flow;
But stuck fast with his first hexameter,
Not one of all whose gouty feet would stir.   720

XCI

But ere the spavined dactyls could be spurred
    Into recitative, in great dismay
Both Cherubim and Seraphim were heard
    To murmur loudly through their long array;
And Michael rose ere he could get a word
    Of all his foundered verse under way,
And cried, "For God's sake stop, my friend! 'twere best—
'Non Di, non homines'—you know the rest."

XCII

A general bustle spread throughout the throng
    Which seemed to hold all verse in detestation;   730
The Angels had of course enough of song
    When upon service; and the generation
Of ghosts had heard too much in life, not long
    Before, to profit by a new occasion:
The Monarch, mute till then, exclaimed, "What! what!
Pye come again? No more—no more of that!"

XCIII

The tumult grew; an universal cough
   Convulsed the skies, as during a debate,
When Castlereagh has been up long enough
   (Before he was first minister of state,
                     740
I mean—the *slaves hear now*); some cried "Off, off!"
   As at a farce; till, grown quite deperate.
The Bard Saint Peter prayed to interpose
(Himself an author) only for his prose.

XCIV

The varlet was not an ill-favoured knave;
   A good deal like a vulture in the face,
With a hook nose and a hawk's eye, which gave
   A smart and sharper-looking sort of grace
To his whole aspect, which, though rather grave,
Was by no means so ugly as his case;
                     750
But that, indeed, was hopeless as can be,
Quite a poetic felony *"de se."*

XCV

Then Michael blew his trump, and stilled the noise
   With one still greater, as is yet the mode
On earth besides; except some grumbling voice,
   Which now and then will make a slight inroad
Upon decorous silence, few will twice
   Lift up their lungs when fairly overcrowed
And now the Bard could plead his own bad cause,
With all the attitudes of self-applause.
                     760

XCVI

He said—(I only give the heads)—he said,
   He meant no harm in scribbling; 'twas his way
Upon all topics; 'twas, besides, his bread,
   Of which he buttered both sides; 'twould delay
Too long the assembly (he was pleased to dread),
   And take up rather more time than a day,
To name his works—he would but cite a few—
"Wat Tyler"—"Rhymes on Blenheim"—"Waterloo."

XCVII

He had written praises of a Regicide;
    He had written praises of all kings whatever;   770
He had written for republics far and wide,
    And then against them bitterer than ever;
For pantisocracy he once had cried
    Aloud, a scheme less moral than 'twas clever;
Then grew a hearty anti-jacobin—
Had turned his coat—and would have turned his skin.

XCVIII

He had sung against all battles, and again
    In their high praise and glory; he had called
Reviewing "the ungentle craft," and then
    Became as base a critic as e'er crawled—   780
Fed, paid, and pampered by the very men
    By whom his muse and morals had been mauled:
He had written much blank verse, and blanker prose,
And more of both than any body knows.

XCIX

He had written Wesley's life:—here turning round
    To Satan, "Sir, I'm ready to write yours,
In two octavo volumes, nicely bound,
    With notes and preface, all that most allures
The pious purchaser; and there's no ground
    For fear, for I can choose my own reviewers: 790
So let me have the proper documents,
That I may add you to my other saints."

C

Satan bowed, and was silent. "Well, if you,
    With amiable modesty, decline
My offer, what say's Michael? There are few
    Whose memoirs could be rendered more divine.
Mine is a pen of all work; not so new
    As it was once, but I would make you shine
Like your own trumpet. By the way, my own
Has more of brass in it, and is as well blown.   800

CI

"But talking about trumpets, here's my 'Vision'!
    Now you shall judge, all people—yes—you shall
Judge with my judgment! and by my decision
    Be guided who shall enter heaven or fall.
I settle all these things by intuition,
    Times present, past, to come—Heaven—Hell—and all,
Like King Alfonso. When I thus see double,
I save the Deity some worlds of trouble."

CII

He ceased, and drew forth an MS.; and no
    Persuasion on the part of Devils, Saints,   810
Or Angels, now could stop the torrent; so
    He read the first three lines of the contents;
But at the fourth, the whole spiritual show
    Had vanished, with variety of scents,
Ambrosial and sulphureous, as they sprang,
Like lightning, off from his "melodious twang."

CIII

Those grand heroics acted as a spell;
    The Angels stopped their ears and plied their pinions;
The Devils ran howling, deafened, down to Hell;
    The ghosts fled, gibbering, for their own dominions—   820
(For 'tis not yet decided where they dwell,
    And I leave every man to his opinions);
Michael took refuge in his trump—but, lo!
His teeth were set on edge, he could not blow!

CIV

Saint Peter, who has hitherto been known
    For an impetuous saint, upraised his keys,
And at the fifth line knocked the poet down;
    Who fell like Phaeton, but more at ease,
Into his lake, for there he did not drown;
    A different web being by the Destinies   830
Woven for the Laureate's final wreath, when'er
Reform shall happen either here or there.

CV

He first sank to the bottom—like his works,
　　But soon rose to the surface like himself;
For all corrupted things are buoyed like corks,
　　By their own rottenness, light as an elf,
Or wisp that flits o'er a morass: he lurks,
　　It may be, still, like dull books on a shelf,
In his own den, to scrawl some "Life" or Vision,"
As Welborn says—"The Devil turned precisian."　　　　840

CVI

As for the rest, to come to the conclusion
　　Of this true dream, the telescope is gone
Which kept my optics free form all delusion,
　　And showed me what I in my turn have shown;
All I saw farther, in the last confusion,
　　Was, that King George slipped into Heaven for one;
And when the tumult dwindled to a calm,
I left him practising the hundredth psalm.

R[avenn]a, October 4, 1821.
[First publ., October 22, 1822.]

From DON JUAN

[*Byron began this mock-epic, after the success of* Beppo, *with the idea of "being a little quietly facetious upon every thing," but he soon saw its possibilities for the expression of every thought and mood, serious as well as comic. He deliberately selected a hero who, according to the conventional Spanish legend, was a cruel libertine and rake and made him into something like an idealized concept of his own youth, innocent and well meaning even when he was corrupted by society and experience. But the story of Juan's adventures serves only as an excuse to put him in different situations and environments that will allow the most pungent digressional comment. Some of the most entertaining episodes are in the first three cantos, which include Juan's innocent seduction by Julia, and the idyllic love of Juan and Haidée on a Greek island. But the less well known pictures in the later cantos of Juan among the "bores and bored" in English high society are drawn with equal brilliance.*]

DEDICATION

I

Bob Southey! You're a poet—Poet-laureate,
   And representative of all the race;

Although 't is true that you turned out a Tory at
    Last,—yours has lately been a common case;
And now, my Epic Renegade! what are ye at?
    With all the Lakers, in and out of place?
A nest of tuneful persons, to my eye
Like "four and twenty Blackbirds in a pye;

II

"Which pye being opened they began to sing,"
    (This old song and new simile holds good),   10
"A dainty dish to set before the King,"
    Or Regent, who admires such kind of food;—
And Coleridge, too, has lately taken wing,
    But like a hawk encumbered with his hood,—
Explaining Metaphysics to the nation—
I wish he would explain his Explanation.

III

You, Bob! are rather insolent, you know,
    At being disappointed in your wish
To supersede all warblers here below,
    And be the only Blackbird in the dish;   20
And then you overstrain yourself, or so,
    And tumble downward like the flying fish
Gasping on deck, because you soar too high, Bob,
And fall, for lack of moisture, quite a-dry, Bob!

IV

And Wordsworth, in a rather long "Excursion,"
    (I think the quarto holds five hundred pages),
Has given a sample from the vasty version
    Of his new system to perplex the sages;
'T is poetry—at least by his assertion,
    And may appear so when the dog-star rages—   30
And he who understands it would be able
To add a story to the Tower of Babel.

V

You—Gentlemen! by dint of long seclusion
　　From better company, have kept your own
At Keswick, and, through still continued fusion
　　Of one another's minds, at last have grown
To deem as a most logical conclusion,
　　That Poesy has wreaths for you alone:
There is a narrowness in such a notion,
Which makes me wish you'd change your lakes for Ocean.　　40

V I

I would not imitate the petty thought,
　　Nor coin my self-love to so base a vice,
For all the glory your conversion brought,
　　Since gold alone should not have been its price.
You have your salary; was 't for that you wrought?
　　And Wordsworth has his place in the Excise.
You 're shabby fellows—true—but poets still,
And duly seated on the Immortal Hill.

V I I

Your bays may hide the baldness of your brows—
　　Perhaps some virtuous blushes;—let them go—　　50
To you I envy neither fruit nor boughs—
　　And for the fame you would engross below,
The field is universal, and allows
　　Scope to all such as feel the inherent glow:
Scott, Rogers, Campbell, Moore, and Crabbe, will try
'Gainst you the question with posterity.

V I I I

For me, who, wandering with pedestrian Muses,
　　Contend not with you on the wingéd steed,
I wish your fate may yield ye, when she chooses,
　　The fame you envy, and the skill you need;　　60
And, recollect, a poet nothing loses
　　In giving to his brethren their full meed
Of merit—and complaint of present days
Is not the certain path to future praise.

IX

He that reserves his laurels for posterity
    (Who does not often claim the bright reversion)
Has generally no great crop to spare it, he
    Being only injured by his own assertion;
And although here and there some glorious rarity
    Arise like Titan from the sea's immersion,   70
The major part of such appellants go
To—God knows where—for no one else can know.

X

If, fallen in evil days on evil tongues,
    Milton appealed to the Avenger, Time,
If Time, the Avenger, execrates his wrongs,
    And makes the word "Miltonic" mean *"Sublime,"*
He deigned not to belie his soul in songs,
    Nor turn his very talent to a crime;
He did not loathe the Sire to laud the Son,
But closed the tyrant-hater he begun.   80

XI

Think'st thou, could he—the blind Old Man—arise
    Like Samuel from the grave, to freeze once more
The blood of monarchs with his prophecies,
    Or be alive again—again all hoar
With time and trials, and those helpless eyes,
    And heartless daughters—worn—and pale—and poor;
Would *he* adore a sultan? *he* obey
The intellectual eunuch Castlereagh?*

---

*Or—
        "Would *he* subside into a hackney Laureate—
        A scribbling, self-sold, soul-hired scorned Iscariot?"
I doubt if "Laureate" and "Iscariot" be good rhymes, but must say, as Ben Jonson did to Sylvester, who challenged him to rhyme with—
        "I, John Sylvester,
        Lay with your sister."
Jonson answered—"I, Ben Jonson, lay with your wife." Sylvester answered,—"That is not rhyme."—"No," said Ben Jonson; "but it is *true.*" [Byron's note.]

XII

Cold-blooded, smooth-faced, placid miscreant!
 Dabbling its sleek young hands in Erin's gore,   90
And thus for wider carnage taught to pant,
 Transferred to gorge upon a sister shore,
The vulgarest tool that Tyranny could want,
 With just enough of talent, and no more,
To lengthen fetters by another fixed,
And offer poison long already mixed.

XIII

An orator of such set trash of phrase
 Ineffably—legitimately vile,
That even its grossest flatterers dare not praise,
 Nor foes—all nations—condescend to smile,— 100
Nor even a sprightly blunder's spark can blaze
 From that Ixion grindstone's ceaseless toil,
That turns and turns to give the world a notion
Of endless torments and perpetual motion.

XIV

A bungler even in its disgusting trade,
 And botching, patching, leaving still behind
Something of which its masters are afraid—
 States to be curbed, and thoughts to be confined,
Conspiracy or Congress to be made—
 Cobbling at manacles for all mankind— 110
A tinkering slave-maker, who mends old chains,
With God and Man's abhorrence for its gains.

XV

If we may judge of matter by the mind,
 Emasculated to the marrow *It*
Hath but two objects, how to serve, and bind,
 Deeming the chain it wears even men may fit,
Eutropius of its many masters,—blind
 To worth as freedom, wisdom as to wit,
Fearless—because *no* feeling dwells in ice,
Its very courage stagnates to a vice. 120

XVI

Where shall I turn me not to *view* its bonds,
  For I will never *feel* them?—Italy!
Thy late reviving Roman soul desponds
  Beneath the lie this State-thing breathed o'er thee.—
Thy clanking chain, and Erin's yet green wounds,
  Have voices—tongues to cry aloud for me.
Europe has slaves—allies—kings—armies still—
And Southey lives to sing them very ill.

XVII

Meantime, Sir Laureate, I proceed to dedicate,
  In honest simple verse, this song to you.
And, if in flattering strains I do not predicate,
  'T is that I still retain my "buff and blue;"*
My politics as yet are all to educate:
  Apostasy 's so fashionable, too,
To keep *one* creed 's a task grown quite Herculean;
Is it not so, my Tory, ultra-Julian?

[*Venice, September 16, 1818.*]

130

CANTO THE FIRST†

I

I want a hero: an uncommon want,
  When every year and month sends forth a new one,
Till, after cloying the gazettes with cant,
  The age discovers he is not the true one;
Of such as these I should not care to vaunt,
  I'll therefore take our ancient friend Don Juan—
We all have seen him, in the pantomime,
Sent to the Devil somewhat ere his time.

---

*[Charles James Fox and the Whig Club of his time adopted a uniform of blue and buff. Hence the livery of the *Edinburgh Review*.]

†[Begun at Venice, September 6; finished November 1, 1818.]

II

Vernon, the butcher Cumberland, Wolfe, Hawke,
    Prince Ferdinand, Granby, Burgoyne, Keppel, Howe,   10
Evil and good, have had their tithe of talk,
    And filled their sign-posts then, like Wellesley now;
Each in their turn like Banquo's monarchs stalk,
    Followers of Fame, "nine farrow" of that sow:
France, too, had Buonaparté and Dumourier
Recorded in the Moniteur and Courier.

III

Barnave, Brissot, Condorcet, Mirabeau,
    Petion, Clootz, Danton, Marat, La Fayette
Were French, and famous people, as we know;
    And there were others, scarce forgotten yet,   20
Joubert, Hoche, Marceau, Lannes, Desaix, Moreau,
    With many of the military set,
Exceedingly remarkable at times,
But not at all adapted to my rhymes.

IV

Nelson was once Britannia's god of War,
    And still should be so, but the tide is turned;
There 's no more to be said of Trafalgar,
    'T is with our hero quietly inurned;
Because the army 's grown more popular,
    At which the naval people are concerned;   30
Besides, the Prince is all for the land-service,
Forgetting Duncan, Nelson, Howe, and Jervis.

V

Brave men were living before Agamemnon
    And since, exceeding valorous and sage,
A good deal like him too, though quite the same none;
    But then they shone not on the poet's page,
And so have been forgotten:—I condemn none,
    But can't find any in the present age
Fit for my poem (that is, for my new one);
So, as I said, I'll take my friend Don Juan.   40

VI

Most epic poets plunge *"in medias res"*
· (Horace makes this the heroic turnpike road),
And then your hero tells, whene'er you please,
What went before—by way of episode,
While seated after dinner at his ease,
Beside his mistress in some soft abode,
Palace, or garden, paradise, or cavern,
Which serves the happy couple for a tavern.

VII

That is the usual method, but not mine—
My way is to begin with the beginning;   50
The regularity of my design
Forbids all wandering as the worst of sinning,
And therefore I shall open with a line
(Although it cost me half an hour in spinning),
Narrating somewhat of Don Juan's father,
And also of his mother, if you'd rather.

VIII

In Seville was he born, a pleasant city,
Famous for oranges and women,—he
Who has not seen it will be much to pity,
So says the proverb—and I quite agree;   60
Of all the Spanish towns is none more pretty,
Cadiz perhaps—but that you soon may see;—
Don Juan's parents lived beside the river,
A noble stream, and called the Guadalquivir.

IX

His father's name was José—*Don,* of course,—
A true Hidalgo, free from every stain
Of Moor or Hebrew blood, he traced his source
Through the most Gothic gentlemen of Spain;
A better cavalier ne'er mounted horse,
Or, being mounted, e'er got down again,   70
Than José, who begot our hero, who
Begot—but that's to come——Well, to renew:

X

His mother was a learnéd lady, famed
    For every branch of every science known—
In every Christian language ever named,
    With virtues equalled by her wit alone:
She made the cleverest people quite ashamed,
    And even the good with inward envy groan,
Finding themselves so very much exceeded,
In their own way, by all the things that she did.   80

X I

Her memory was a mine: she knew by heart
    All Calderon and greater part of Lopé,
So, that if any actor missed his part,
    She could have served him for the prompter's copy;
For her Feinagle's were an useless art,
    And he himself obliged to shut up shop—he
Could never make a memory so fine as
That which adorned the brain of Donna Inez.

X I I

Her favourite science was the mathematical,
    Her noblest virtue was her magnanimity,   90
Her wit (she sometimes tried at wit) was Attic all,
    Her serious sayings darkened to sublimity;
In short, in all things she was fairly what I call
    A prodigy—her morning dress was dimity,
Her evening silk, or, in the summer, muslin,
And other stuffs, with which I won't stay puzzling.

X I I I

She knew the Latin—that is, "the Lord's prayer,"
    And Greek—the alphabet—I 'm nearly sure;
She read some French romances here and there,
    Although her mode of speaking was not pure;   100
For native Spanish she had no great care,
    At least her conversation was obscure;
Her thoughts were theorems, her words a problem,
As if she deemed that mystery would ennoble 'em.

XIV

She liked the English and the Hebrew tongue,
    And said there was analogy between 'em;
She proved it somehow out of sacred song,
    But I must leave the proofs to those who 've seen 'em;
But this I heard her say, and can't be wrong,
    And all may think which way their judgments lean 'em,   110
" 'T is strange—the Hebrew noun which means 'I am,'
The English always use to govern d—n."

XV

Some women use their tongues—she *looked* a lecture,
    Each eye a sermon, and her brow a homily,
An all-in-all sufficient self-director,
    Like the lamented late Sir Samuel Romilly,
The Law's expounder, and the State's corrector,
    Whose suicide was almost an anomaly—
One sad example more, that "All is vanity,"—
(The jury brought their verdict in "Insanity!")   120

XVI

In short, she was a walking calculation,
    Miss Edgeworth's novels stepping from their covers,
Or Mrs. Trimmer's books on education,
    Or "Cœlebs' Wife" set out in quest of lovers,
Morality's prim personification,
    In which not Envy's self a flaw discovers;
To others' share let "female errors fall,"
For she had not even one—the worst of all.

XVII

Oh! she was perfect past all parallel—
    Of any modern female saint's comparison;   130
So far above the cunning powers of Hell,
    Her Guardian Angel had given up his garrison;
Even her minutest motions went as well
    As those of the best time-piece made by Harrison:
In virtues nothing earthly could surpass her,
Save thine "incomparable oil," Macassar!

XVIII

Perfect she was, but as perfection is
    Insipid in this naughty world of ours,
Where our first parents never learned to kiss
    Till they were exiled from their earlier bowers,   140
Where all was peace, and innocence, and bliss,
    (I wonder how they got through the twelve hours),
Don José, like a lineal son of Eve,
Went plucking various fruit without her leave.

XIX

He was a mortal of the careless kind,
    With no great love for learning, or the learned,
Who chose to go where'er he had a mind,
    And never dreamed his lady was concerned;
The world, as usual, wickedly inclined
    To see a kingdom or a house o'erturned,   150
Whispered he had a mistress, some said *two*.
But for domestic quarrels *one* will do.

XX

Now Donna Inez had, with all her merit,
    A great opinion of her own good qualities;
Neglect, indeed, requires a saint to bear it,
    And such, indeed, she was in her moralities;
But then she had a devil of a spirit,
    And sometimes mixed up fancies with realities,
And let few opportunities escape
Of getting her liege lord into a scrape.   160

XXI

This was an easy matter with a man
    Oft in the wrong, and never on his guard;
And even the wisest, do the best they can,
    Have moments, hours, and days, so unprepared,
That you might "brain them with their lady's fan;"
    And sometimes ladies hit exceeding hard,
And fans turn into falchions in fair hands,
And why and wherefore no one understands.

XXII

'T is pity learnéd virgins ever wed
    With persons of no sort of education,   170
Or gentlemen, who, though well born and bred,
    Grow tired of scientific conversation:
I don't choose to say much upon this head,
    I 'm a plain man, and in a single station,
But—Oh! ye lords of ladies intellectual,
Inform us truly, have they not hen-pecked you all?

XXIII

Don José and his lady quarrelled—*why*,
    Not any of the many could divine,
Though several thousand people chose to try,
    'T was surely no concern of theirs nor mine;   180
I loathe that low vice—curiosity;
    But if there 's anything in which I shine,
'T is in arranging all my friends' affairs,
Not having, of my own, domestic cares.

XXIV

And so I interfered, and with the best
    Intentions, but their treatment was not kind;
I think the foolish people were possessed,
    For neither of them could I ever find,
Although their porter afterwards confessed—
    But that's no matter, and the worst 's behind,   190
For little Juan o'er me threw, down stairs,
A pail of housemaid's water unawares.

XXV

A little curly-headed, good-for-nothing,
    And mischief-making monkey from his birth;
His parents ne'er agreed except in doting
    Upon the most unquiet imp on earth;
Instead of quarrelling, had they been but both in
    Their senses, they 'd have sent young master forth
To school, or had him soundly whipped at home,
To teach him manners for the time to come.   200

XXVI

Don José and the Donna Inez led
   For some time an unhappy sort of life,
Wishing each other, not divorced, but dead;
   They lived respectably as man and wife,
Their conduct was exceedingly well-bred,
   And gave no outward signs of inward strife,
Until at length the smothered fire broke out,
And put the business past all kind of doubt.

XXVII

For Inez called some druggists and physicians,
   And tried to prove her loving lord was *mad,*   210
But as he had some lucid intermissions,
   She next decided he was only *bad;*
Yet when they asked her for her depositions,
   No sort of explanation could be had,
Save that her duty both to man and God
Required this conduct—which seemed very odd.

XXVIII

She kept a journal, where his faults were noted,
   And opened certain trunks of books and letters,
All which might, if occasion served, be quoted;
   And then she had all Seville for abettors,   220
Besides her good old grandmother (who doted);
   The hearers of her case became repeaters,
Then advocates, inquisitors, and judges,
Some for amusement, others for old grudges.

XXIX

And then this best and meekest woman bore
   With such serenity her husband's woes,
Just as the Spartan ladies did of yore,
   Who saw their spouses killed, and nobly chose
Never to say a word about them more—
   Calmly she heard each calumny that rose,   230
And saw *his* agonies with such sublimity,
That all the world exclaimed, "What magnanimity!"

XXX

No doubt this patience, when the world is damning us,
    Is philosophic in our former friends;
'T is also pleasant to be deemed magnanimous,
    The more so in obtaining our own ends;
And what the lawyers call a *"malus animus"*
    Conduct like this by no means comprehends:
Revenge in person 's certainly no virtue,
But then 't is not *my* fault, if *others* hurt you.   240

XXXI

And if our quarrels should rip up old stories,
    And help them with a lie or two additional,
I 'm not to blame, as you well know—no more is
    Any one else—they were become traditional;
Besides, their resurrection aids our glories
    By contrast, which is what we just were wishing all:
And Science profits by this resurrection—
Dead scandals form good subjects for dissection.

XXXII

Their friends had tried at reconciliation,
    Then their relations, who made matters worse.   250
('T were hard to tell upon a like occasion
    To whom it may be best to have recourse—
I can't say much for friend or yet relation):
    The lawyers did their utmost for divorce,
But scarce a fee was paid on either side
Before, unluckily, Don José died.

XXXIII

He died: and most unluckily, because,
    According to all hints I could collect
From Counsel learnéd in those kind of laws,
    (Although their talk 's obscure and circumspect)   260
His death contrived to spoil a charming cause;
    A thousand pities also with respect
To public feeling, which on this occasion
Was manifested in a great sensation.

XXXIV

But ah! he died; and buried with him lay
  The public feeling and the lawyers' fees:
His house was sold, his servants sent away,
  A Jew took one of his two mistresses,
A priest the other—at least so they say:
  I asked the doctors after his disease— 270
He died of the slow fever called the tertian,
And left his widow to her own aversion.

XXXV

Yet José was an honourable man,
  That I must say, who knew him very well;
Therefore his frailties I' ll no further scan,
  Indeed there were not many more to tell:
And if his passions now and then outran
  Discretion, and were not so peaceable
As Numa's (who was also named Pompilius),
He had been ill brought up, and was born bilious. 280

XXXVI

Whate'er might be his worthlessness or worth,
  Poor fellow! he had many things to wound him.
Let 's own—since it can do no good on earth—
  It was a trying moment that which found him
Standing alone beside his desolate hearth,
  Where all his household gods lay shivered round him:
No choice was left his feelings or his pride,
Save Death or Doctors' Commons—so he died.

XXXVII

Dying intestate, Juan was sole heir
  To a chancery suit, and messuages, and lands, 290
Which, with a long minority and care,
  Promised to turn out well in proper hands:
Inez became sole guardian, which was fair,
  And answered but to Nature's just demands;
An only son left with an only mother
Is brought up much more wisely than another.

XXXVIII

Sagest of women, even of widows, she
    Resolved that Juan should be quite a paragon,
And worthy of the noblest pedigree,
    (His Sire was of Castile, his Dam from Aragon):   300
Then, for accomplishments of chivalry,
    In case our Lord the King should go to war again,
He learned the arts of riding, fencing, gunnery,
And how to scale a fortress—or a nunnery.

XXXIX

But that which Donna Inez most desired,
    And saw into herself each day before all
The learnéd tutors whom for him she hired,
    Was, that his breeding should be strictly moral:
Much into all his studies she inquired,
    And so they were submitted first to her, all,   310
Arts, sciences—no branch was made a mystery
To Juan's eyes, excepting natural history.

XL

The languages, especially the dead,
    The sciences, and most of all the abstruse,
The arts, at least all such as could be said
    To be the most remote from common use,
In all these he was much and deeply read:
    But not a page of anything that 's loose,
Or hints continuation of the species,
Was ever suffered, lest he should grow vicious.   320

XLI

His classic studies made a little puzzle,
    Because of filthy loves of gods and goddesses,
Who in the earlier ages raised a bustle,
    But never put on pantaloons or bodices;
His reverend tutors had at times a tussle,
    And for their Æneids, Iliads, and Odysseys,
Were forced to make an odd sort of apology,
For Donna Inez dreaded the Mythology.

XLII

Ovid 's a rake, as half his verses show him,
    Anacreon's morals are a still worse sample,   330
Catullus scarcely has a decent poem,
    I don't think Sappho's Ode a good example,
Although Longinus tells us there is no hymn
    Where the Sublime soars forth on wings more ample;
But Virgil's songs are pure, except that horrid one
Beginning with *"Formosum Pastor Corydon."*

XLIII

Lucretius' irreligion is too strong
    For early stomachs, to prove wholesome food;
I can't help thinking Juvenal was wrong,
    Although no doubt his real intent was good,   340
For speaking out so plainly in his song,
    So much indeed as to be downright rude;
And then what proper person can be partial
To all those nauseous epigrams of Martial?

XLIV

Juan was taught from out the best edition,
    Expurgated by learnéd men, who place,
Judiciously, from out the schoolboy's vision,
    The grosser parts; but, fearful to deface
Too much their modest bard by this omission,
    And pitying sore his mutilated case,   350
They only add them all in an appendix,
Which saves, in fact, the trouble of an index;

XLV

For there we have them all "at one fell swoop,"
    Instead of being scattered through the pages;
They stand forth marshalled in a handsome troop,
    To meet the ingenuous youth of future ages,
Till some less rigid editor shall stoop
    To call them back into their separate cages,
Instead of standing staring all together,
Like garden gods—and not so decent either.   360

XLVI

The Missal too (it was the family Missal)
    Was ornamented in a sort of way
Which ancient mass-books often are, and this all
    Kinds of grotesques illumined; and how they,
Who saw those figures on the margin kiss all,
    Could turn their optics to the text and pray,
Is more than I know—But Don Juan's mother
Kept this herself, and gave her son another.

XLVII

Sermons he read, and lectures he endured,
    And homilies, and lives of all the saints;   370
To Jerome and to Chrysostom inured,
    He did not take such studies for restraints;
But how Faith is acquired, and then insured,
    So well not one of the aforesaid paints
As Saint Augustine in his fine Confessions,
Which make the reader envy his transgressions.

XLVIII

This, too, was a sealed book to little Juan—
    I can't but say that his mamma was right,
If such an education was the true one.
    She scarcely trusted him from out her sight;   380
Her maids were old, and if she took a new one,
    You might be sure she was a perfect fright;
She did this during even her husband's life—
I recommend as much to every wife.

XLIX

Young Juan waxed in goodliness and grace;
    At six a charming child, and at eleven
With all the promise of as fine a face
    As e'er to Man's maturer growth was given:
He studied steadily, and grew apace,
    And seemed, at least, in the right road to Heaven,   390
For half his days were passed at church, the other
Between his tutors, confessor, and mother.

L

At six, I said, he was a charming child,
  At twelve he was a fine, but quiet boy;
Although in infancy a little wild,
  They tamed him down amongst them: to destroy
His natural spirit not in vain they toiled,
  At least it seemed so; and his mother's joy
Was to declare how sage, and still, and steady,
Her young philosopher was grown already.   400

LI

I had my doubts, perhaps I have them still,
  But what I say is neither here nor there:
I knew his father well, and have some skill
  In character—but it would not be fair
From sire to son to augur good or ill:
  He and his wife were an ill-sorted pair—
But scandal 's my aversion—I protest
Against all evil speaking, even in jest.

LII

For my part I say nothing—nothing—but
  This I will say—my reasons are my own—   410
That if I had an only son to put
  To school (as God be praised that I have none),
'T is not with Donna Inez I would shut
  Him up to learn his catechism alone,
No—no—I'd send him out betimes to college,
For there it was I picked up my own knowledge.

LIII

For there one learns—'t is not for me to boast,
  Though I acquired—but I pass over *that,*
As well as all the Greek I since have lost:
  I say that there 's the place—but *"Verbum sat,"*   420
I think I picked up too, as well as most,
  Knowledge of matters—but no matter *what*—
I never married—but, I think, I know
That sons should not be educated so.

LIV

Young Juan now was sixteen years of age,
　　Tall, handsome, slender, but well knit: he seemed
Active, though not so sprightly, as a page;
　　And everybody but his mother deemed
Him almost man; but she flew in a rage
　　And bit her lips (for else she might have screamed)　　430
If any said so—for to be precocious
Was in her eyes a thing the most atrocious.

LV

Amongst her numerous acquaintance, all
　　Selected for discretion and devotion,
There was the Donna Julia, whom to call
　　Pretty were but to give a feeble notion
Of many charms in her as natural
　　As sweetness to the flower, or salt to Ocean,
Her zone to Venus, or his bow to Cupid,
(But this last simile is trite and stupid.)　　440

LVI

The darkness of her Oriental eye
　　Accorded with her Moorish origin;
(Her blood was not all Spanish; by the by,
　　In Spain, you know, this is a sort of sin;)
When proud Granada fell, and, forced to fly,
　　Boabdil wept: of Donna Julia's kin
Some went to Africa, some stayed in Spain—
Her great great grandmamma chose to remain.

LVII

She married (I forget the pedigree)
　　With an Hidalgo, who transmitted down　　450
His blood less noble than such blood should be;
　　At such alliances his sires would frown,
In that point so precise in each degree
　　That they bred *in and in*, as might be shown,
Marrying their cousins—nay, their aunts, and nieces,
Which always spoils the breed, if it increases.

LVIII

This heathenish cross restored the breed again,
  Ruined its blood, but much improved its flesh;
For from a root the ugliest in Old Spain
  Sprung up a branch as beautiful as fresh;   460
The sons no more were short, the daughters plain:
  But there's a rumour which I fain would hush,
'T is said that Donna Julia's grandmamma
Produced her Don more heirs at love than law.

LIX

However this might be, the race went on
  Improving still through every generation,
Until it centred in an only son,
  Who left an only daughter; my narration
May have suggested that this single one
  Could be but Julia (whom on this occasion   470
I shall have much to speak about), and she
Was married, charming, chaste, and twenty-three.

LX

Her eye (I'm very fond of handsome eyes)
  Was large and dark, suppressing half its fire
Until she spoke, then through its soft disguise
  Flashed an expression more of pride than ire,
And love than either; and there would arise
  A something in them which was not desire,
But would have been, perhaps, but for the soul
Which struggled through and chastened down the whole. 480

LXI

Her glossy hair was clustered o'er a brow
  Bright with intelligence, and fair, and smooth;
Her eyebrow's shape was like the aërial bow,
  Her cheek all purple with the beam of youth,
Mounting, at times, to a transparent glow,
  As if her veins ran lightning; she, in sooth,
Possessed an air and grace by no means common:
Her stature tall—I hate a dumpy woman.

LXII

Wedded she was some years, and to a man
    Of fifty, and such husbands are in plenty;   490
And yet, I think, instead of such a ONE
    'T were better to have TWO of five-and-twenty,
Especially in countries near the sun:
    And now I think on 't, *"mi vien in mente,"*
Ladies even of the most uneasy virtue
Prefer a spouse whose age is short of thirty.

LXIII

'T is a sad thing, I cannot choose but say,
    And all the fault of that indecent sun,
Who cannot leave alone our helpless clay,
    But will keep baking, broiling, burning on,   500
That howsoever people fast and pray,
    The flesh is frail, and so the soul undone:
What men call gallantry, and gods adultery,
Is much more common where the climate 's sultry.

LXIV

Happy the nations of the moral North!
    Where all is virtue, and the winter season
Sends sin, without a rag on, shivering forth
    ('T was snow that brought St. Anthony to reason);
Where juries cast up what a wife is worth,
    By laying whate'er sum, in mulct, they please on   510
The lover, who must pay a handsome price,
Because it is a marketable vice.

LXV

Alfonso was the name of Julia's lord,
    A man well looking for his years, and who
Was neither much beloved nor yet abhorred:
    They lived together as most people do,
Suffering each other's foibles by accord,
    And not exactly either *one* or *two;*
Yet he was jealous, though he did not show it,
For Jealousy dislikes the world to know it.   520

LXVI

Julia was—yet I never could see why—
    With Donna Inez quite a favourite friend;
Between their tastes there was small sympathy,
    For not a line had Julia ever penned:
Some people whisper (but, no doubt, they lie,
    For Malice still imputes some private end)
That Inez had, ere Don Alfonso's marriage,
Forgot with him her very prudent carriage;

LXVII

And that still keeping up the old connection,
    Which Time had lately rendered much more chaste,   530
She took his lady also in affection,
    And certainly this course was much the best:
She flattered Julia with her sage protection,
    And complimented Don Alfonso's taste;
And if she could not (who can?) silence scandal,
At least she left it a more slender handle.

LXVIII

I can't tell whether Julia saw the affair
    With other people's eyes, or if her own
Discoveries made, but none could be aware
    Of this, at least no symptom e'er was shown;   540
Perhaps she did not know, or did not care,
    Indifferent from the first, or callous grown:
I 'm really puzzled what to think or say,
She kept her counsel in so close a way.

LXIX

Juan she saw, and, as a pretty child,
    Caressed him often—such a thing might be
Quite innocently done, and harmless styled,
    When she had twenty years, and thirteen he;
But I am not so sure I should have smiled
    When he was sixteen, Julia twenty-three;   550
These few short years make wondrous alterations,
Particularly amongst sun-burnt nations.

LXX

Whate'er the cause might be, they had become
    Changed; for the dame grew distant, the youth shy,
Their looks cast down, their greetings almost dumb,
    And much embarrassment in either eye;
There surely will be little doubt with some
    That Donna Julia knew the reason why,
But as for Juan, he had no more notion
Than he who never saw the sea of Ocean.   560

LXXI

Yet Julia's very coldness still was kind,
    And tremulously gentle her small hand
Withdrew itself from his, but left behind
    A little pressure, thrilling, and so bland
And slight, so very slight, that to the mind
    'T was but a doubt; but ne'er magician's wand
Wrought change with all Armida's fairy art
Like what this light touch left on Juan's heart.

LXXII

And if she met him, though she smiled no more,
    She looked a sadness sweeter than her smile,   570
As if her heart had deeper thoughts in store
    She must not own, but cherished more the while
For that compression in its burning core;
    Even Innocence itself has many a wile,
And will not dare to trust itself with truth,
And Love is taught hypocrisy from youth.

LXXIII

But Passion most dissembles, yet betrays
    Even by its darkness; as the blackest sky
Foretells the heaviest tempest, it displays
    Its workings through the vainly guarded eye,   580
And in whatever aspect it arrays
    Itself, 't is still the same hypocrisy;
Coldness or Anger, even Disdain or Hate,
Are masks it often wears, and still too late.

LXXIV

Then there were sighs, the deeper for suppression,
    And stolen glances, sweeter for the theft,
And burning blushes, though for no transgression,
    Tremblings when met, and restlessness when left;
All these are little preludes to possession,
    Of which young Passion cannot be bereft,   590
And merely tend to show how greatly Love is
Embarrassed at first starting with a novice.

LXXV

Poor Julia's heart was in an awkward state;
    She felt it going, and resolved to make
The noblest efforts for herself and mate,
    For Honour's, Pride's, Religion's, Virtue's sake:
Her resolutions were most truly great,
    And almost might have made a Tarquin quake:
She prayed the Virgin Mary for her grace,
As being the best judge of a lady's case.   600

LXXVI

She vowed she never would see Juan more,
    And next day paid a visit to his mother,
And looked extremely at the opening door,
    Which, by the Virgin's grace, let in another;
Grateful she was, and yet a little sore—
    Again it opens, it can be no other,
'T is surely Juan now—No! I 'm afraid
That night the Virgin was no further prayed.

LXXVII

She now determined that a virtuous woman
    Should rather face and overcome temptation,   610
That flight was base and dastardly, and no man
    Should ever give her heart the least sensation,
That is to say, a thought beyond the common
    Preference, that we must feel, upon occasion,
For people who are pleasanter than others,
But then they only seem so many brothers.

LXXVIII

And even if by chance—and who can tell?
 The Devil 's so very sly—she should discover
That all within was not so very well,
 And, if still free, that such or such a lover   620
Might please perhaps, a virtuous wife can quell
 Such thoughts, and be the better when they 're over;
And if the man should ask, 't is but denial:
I recommend young ladies to make trial.

LXXIX

And, then, there are such things as Love divine,
 Bright and immaculate, unmixed and pure,
Such as the angels think so very fine,
 And matrons, who would be no less secure,
Platonic, perfect, "just such love as mine;"
 Thus Julia said—and thought so, to be sure; 630
And so I'd have her think, were *I* the man
On whom her reveries celestial ran.

LXXX

Such love is innocent, and may exist
 Between young persons without any danger.
A hand may first, and then a lip be kissed;
 For my part, to such doings I 'm a stranger,
But *hear* these freedoms form the utmost list
 Of all o'er which such love may be a ranger:
If people go beyond, 't is quite a crime,
But not my fault—I tell them all in time. 640

LXXXI

Love, then, but Love within its proper limits,
 Was Julia's innocent determination
In young Don Juan's favour, and to him its
 Exertion might be useful on occasion;
And, lighted at too pure a shrine to dim its
 Ethereal lustre, with what sweet persuasion
He might be taught, by Love and her together—
I really don't know what, nor Julia either.

LXXXII

Fraught with this fine intention, and well fenced
    In mail of proof—her purity of soul—   650
She, for the future, of her strength convinced,
    And that her honour was a rock, or mole,
Exceeding sagely from that hour dispensed
    With any kind of troublesome control;
But whether Julia to the task was equal
Is that which must be mentioned in the sequel.

LXXXIII

Her plan she deemed both innocent and feasible,
    And, surely, with a stripling of sixteen
Not Scandal's fangs could fix on much that 's seizable,
    Or if they did so, satisfied to mean   660
Nothing but what was good, her breast was peaceable—
    A quiet conscience makes one so serene!
Christians have burnt each other, quite persuaded
That all the Apostles would have done as they did.

LXXXIV

And if in the mean time her husband died,
    But Heaven forbid that such a thought should cross
Her brain, though in a dream! (and then she sighed)
    Never could she survive that common loss;
But just suppose that moment should betide,
    I only say suppose it—*inter nos:*   670
(This should be *entre nous,* for Julia thought
In French, but then the rhyme would go for nought.)

LXXXV

I only say, suppose this supposition:
    Juan being then grown up to man's estate
Would fully suit a widow of condition,
    Even seven years hence it would not be too late;
And in the interim (to pursue this vision)
    The mischief, after all, could not be great,
For he would learn the rudiments of Love,
I mean the *seraph* way of those above.   680

LXXXVI

So much for Julia! Now we 'll turn to Juan.
    Poor little fellow! he had no idea
Of his own case, and never hit the true one;
    In feelings quick as Ovid's Miss Medea,
He puzzled over what he found a new one,
    But not as yet imagined it could be a
Thing quite in course, and not at all alarming,
Which, with a little patience, might grow charming.

LXXXVII

Silent and pensive, idle, restless, slow,
    His home deserted for the lonely wood,   690
Tormented with a wound he could not know,
    His, like all deep grief, plunged in solitude:
I 'm fond myself of solitude or so,
    But then, I beg it may be understood,
By solitude I mean a Sultan's (not
A Hermit's), with a haram for a grot.

LXXXVIII

"Oh Love! in such a wilderness as this,
    Where Transport and Security entwine,
Here is the Empire of thy perfect bliss,
    And here thou art a God indeed divine."   700
The bard I quote from does not sing amiss,
    With the exception of the second line,
For that same twining "Transport and Security"
Are twisted to a phrase of some obscurity.

LXXXIX

The Poet meant, no doubt, and thus appeals
    To the good sense and senses of mankind,
The very thing which everybody feels,
    As all have found on trial, or may find,
That no one likes to be disturbed at meals
    Or love.—I won't say more about "entwined"   710
Or "Transport," as we knew all that before,
But beg "Security" will bolt the door.

XC

Young Juan wandered by the glassy brooks,
    Thinking unutterable things; he threw
Himself at length within the leafy nooks
    Where the wild branch of the cork forest grew;
There poets find materials for their books,
    And every now and then we read them through,
So that their plan and prosody are eligible,
Unless, like Wordsworth, they prove unintelligible.   720

XCI

He, Juan (and not Wordsworth), so pursued
    His self-communion with his own high soul,
Until his mighty heart, in its great mood,
    Had mitigated part, though not the whole
Of its disease; he did the best he could
    With things not very subject to control,
And turned, without perceiving his condition,
Like Coleridge, into a metaphysician.

XCII

He thought about himself, and the whole earth,
    Of man the wonderful, and of the stars,   730
And how the deuce they ever could have birth;
    And then he thought of earthquakes, and of wars,
How many miles the moon might have in girth,
    Of air-balloons, and of the many bars
To perfect knowledge of the boundless skies;—
And then he thought of Donna Julia's eyes.

XCIII

In thoughts like these true Wisdom may discern
    Longings sublime, and aspirations high,
Which some are born with, but the most part learn
    To plague themselves withal, they know not why: 740
'T was strange that one so young should thus concern
    His brain about the action of the sky;
If *you* think 't was Philosophy that this did,
I can't help thinking puberty assisted.

XCIV

He pored upon the leaves, and on the flowers,
    And heard a voice in all the winds; and then
He thought of wood-nymphs and immortal bowers,
    And how the goddesses came down to men:
He missed the pathway, he forgot the hours,
    And when he looked upon his watch again,   750
He found how much old Time had been a winner—
He also found that he had lost his dinner.

XCV

Sometimes he turned to gaze upon his book,
    Boscan, or Garcilasso;—by the wind
Even as the page is rustled while we look,
    So by the poesy of his own mind
Over the mystic leaf his soul was shook,
    As if 't were one whereon magicians bind
Their spells, and give them to the passing gale,
According to some good old woman's tale.   760

XCVI

Thus would he while his lonely hours away
    Dissatisfied, not knowing what he wanted;
Nor glowing reverie, nor poet's lay,
    Could yield his spirit that for which it panted,
A bosom whereon he his head might lay,
    And hear the heart beat with the love it granted,
With——several other things, which I forget,
Or which, at least, I need not mention yet.

XCVII

Those lonely walks, and lengthening reveries,
    Could not escape the gentle Julia's eyes;   770
She saw that Juan was not at his ease;
    But that which chiefly may, and must surprise,
Is, that the Donna Inez did not tease
    Her only son with question or surmise;
Whether it was she did not see, or would not,
Or, like all very clever people, could not.

XCVIII

This may seem strange, but yet 't is very common;
    For instance—gentlemen, whose ladies take
Leave to o'erstep the written rights of Woman,
    And break the——Which commandment is 't they break?   780
(I have forgot the number, and think no man
    Should rashly quote, for fear of a mistake;)
I say, when these same gentlemen are jealous,
They make some blunder, which their ladies tell us.

XCIX

A real husband always is suspicious,
    But still no less suspects in the wrong place,
Jealous of some one who had no such wishes,
    Or pandering blindly to his own disgrace,
By harbouring some dear friend extremely vicious;
    The last indeed 's infallibly the case: 790
And when the spouse and friend are gone off wholly,
He wonders at their vice, and not his folly.

C

Thus parents also are at times short-sighted:
    Though watchful as the lynx, they ne'er discover,
The while the wicked world beholds delighted,
    Young Hopeful's mistress, or Miss Fanny's lover,
Till some confounded escapade has blighted
    The plan of twenty years, and all is over;
And then the mother cries, the father swears,
And wonders why the devil he got heirs.   800

CI

But Inez was so anxious, and so clear
    Of sight, that I must think, on this occasion,
She had some other motive much more near
    For leaving Juan to this new temptation,
But what that motive was, I sha'n't say here;
    Perhaps to finish Juan's education,
Perhaps to open Don Alfonso's eyes,
In case he thought his wife too great a prize.

CII

It was upon a day, a summer's day;—
    Summer 's indeed a very dangerous season,   810
And so is spring about the end of May;
    The sun, no doubt, is the prevailing reason;
But whatsoe'er the cause is, one may say
    And stand convicted of more truth than treason,
That there are months which nature grows more merry in,—
March has its hares, and May must have its heroine.

CIII

'T was on a summer's day—the sixth of June:
    I like to be particular in dates,
Not only of the age, and year, but moon;
    They are a sort of post-house, where the Fates   820
Change horses, making History change its tune,
    Then spur away o'er empires and o'er states,
Leaving at last not much besides chronology,
Excepting the post-obits of theology.

CIV

'T was on the sixth of June, about the hour
    Of half-past six—perhaps still nearer seven—
When Julia sate within as pretty a bower
    As e'er held houri in that heathenish heaven
Described by Mahomet, and Anacreon Moore,
    To whom the lyre and laurels have been given,   830
With all the trophies of triumphant song—
He won them well, and may he wear them long!

CV

She sate, but not alone; I know not well
    How this same interview had taken place,
And even if I knew, I should not tell—
    People should hold their tongues in any case;
No matter how or why the thing befell,
    But there were she and Juan, face to face—
When two such faces are so, 't would be wise,
But very difficult, to shut their eyes.   840

CVI

How beautiful she looked! her conscious heart
 Glowed in her cheek, and yet she felt no wrong:
Oh Love! how perfect is thy mystic art,
 Strengthening the weak, and trampling on the strong!
How self-deceitful is the sagest part
 Of mortals whom thy lure hath led along!—
The precipice she stood on was immense,
So was her creed in her own innocence.

CVII

She thought of her own strength, and Juan's youth,
 And of the folly of all prudish fears,   850
Victorious Virtue, and domestic Truth,
 And then of Don Alfonso's fifty years:
I wish these last had not occurred, in sooth,
 Because that number rarely much endears,
And through all climes, the snowy and the sunny,
Sounds ill in love, whate'er it may in money.

CVIII

When people say, "I 've told you *fifty* times,"
 They mean to scold, and very often do;
When poets say, "I 've written *fifty* rhymes,"
 They make you dread that they 'll recite them too;   860
In gangs of *fifty*, thieves commit their crimes;
 At *fifty* love for love is rare, 't is true,
But then, no doubt, it equally as true is,
A good deal may be bought for *fifty* Louis.

CIX

Julia had honour, virtue, truth, and love
 For Don Alfonso; and she inly swore,
By all the vows below to Powers above,
 She never would disgrace the ring she wore,
Nor leave a wish which wisdom might reprove;
 And while she pondered this, besides much more,   870
One hand on Juan's carelessly was thrown,
Quite by mistake—she thought it was her own;

CX

Unconsciously she leaned upon the other,
    Which played within the tangles of her hair;
And to contend with thoughts she could not smother
    She seemed by the distraction of her air.
'T was surely very wrong in Juan's mother
    To leave together this imprudent pair,
She who for many years had watched her son so—
I'm very certain *mine* would not have done so.   880

CXI

The hand which still held Juan's, by degrees
    Gently, but palpably confirmed its grasp,
As if it said, "Detain me, if you please;"
    Yet there 's no doubt she only meant to clasp
His fingers with a pure Platonic squeeze;
    She would have shrunk as from a toad, or asp,
Had she imagined such a thing could rouse
A feeling dangerous to a prudent spouse.

CXII

I cannot know what Juan thought of this,
    But what he did, is much what you would do;   890
His young lip thanked it with a grateful kiss,
    And then, abashed at its own joy, withdrew
In deep despair, lest he had done amiss,—
    Love is so very timid when 't is new:
She blushed, and frowned not, but she strove to speak,
And held her tongue, her voice was grown so weak.

CXIII

The sun set, and up rose the yellow moon:
    The Devil 's in the moon for mischief; they
Who called her CHASTE, methinks, began too soon
    Their nomenclature; there is not a day,   900
The longest, not the twenty-first of June,
    Sees half the business in a wicked way,
On which three single hours of moonshine smile—
And then she looks so modest all the while!

CXIV

There is a dangerous silence in that hour,
    A stillness, which leaves room for the full soul
To open all itself, without the power
    Of calling wholly back its self-control;
The silver light which, hallowing tree and tower,
    Sheds beauty and deep softness o'er the whole,   910
Breathes also to the heart, and o'er it throws
A loving languor, which is not repose.

CXV

And Julia sate with Juan, half embraced
    And half retiring from the glowing arm,
Which trembled like the bosom where 't was placed;
    Yet still she must have thought there was no harm,
Or else 't were easy to withdraw her waist;
    But then the situation had its charm,
And then——God knows what next—I can't go on;
I 'm almost sorry that I e'er begun.   920

CXVI

Oh Plato! Plato! you have paved the way,
    With your confounded fantasies, to more
Immoral conduct by the fancied sway
    Your system feigns o'er the controlless core
Of human hearts, than all the long array
    Of poets and romancers:—You 're a bore,
A charlatan, a coxcomb—and have been,
At best, no better than a go-between.

CXVII

And Julia's voice was lost, except in sighs,
    Until too late for useful conversation;   930
The tears were gushing from her gentle eyes,
    I wish, indeed, they had not had occasion;
But who, alas! can love, and then be wise?
    Not that Remorse did not oppose Temptation;
A little still she strove, and much repented,
And whispering "I will ne'er consent"—consented.

CXVIII

'T is said that Xerxes offered a reward
    To those who could invent him a new pleasure:
Methinks the requisition 's rather hard,
    And must have cost his Majesty a treasure: 940
For my part, I 'm a moderate-minded bard,
    Fond of a little love (which I call leisure);
I care not for new pleasures, as the old
Are quite enough for me, so they but hold.

CXIX

Oh Pleasure! you 're indeed a pleasant thing,
    Although one must be damned for you, no doubt:
I make a resolution every spring
    Of reformation, ere the year run out,
But somehow, this my vestal vow takes wing,
    Yet still, I trust, it may be kept throughout: 950
I'm very sorry, very much ashamed,
And mean, next winter, to be quite reclaimed.

CXX

Here my chaste Muse a liberty must take—
    Start not! still chaster reader—she 'll be nice hence-
Forward, and there is no great cause to quake;
    This liberty is a poetic licence,
Which some irregularity may make
    In the design, and as I have a high sense
Of Aristotle and the Rules, 't is fit
To beg his pardon when I err a bit.   960

CXXI

This licence is to hope the reader will
    Suppose from June the sixth (the fatal day,
Without whose epoch my poetic skill
    For want of facts would all be thrown away),
But keeping Julia and Don Juan still
    In sight, that several months have passed; we 'll say
'T was in November, but I 'm not so sure
About the day—the era 's more obscure.

CXXII

We 'll talk of that anon.—'T is sweet to hear
    At midnight on the blue and moonlit deep   970
The song and oar of Adria's gondolier,
    By distance mellowed, o'er the waters sweep;
'T is sweet to see the evening star appear;
    'T is sweet to listen as the night-winds creep
From leaf to leaf; 't is sweet to view on high
The rainbow, based on ocean, span the sky.

CXXIII

'T is sweet to hear the watch-dog's honest bark
    Bay deep-mouthed welcome as we draw near home;
'T is sweet to know there is an eye will mark
    Our coming, and look brighter when we come;   980
'T is sweet to be awakened by the lark,
    Or lulled by falling waters; sweet the hum
Of bees, the voice of girls, the song of birds,
The lisp of children, and their earliest words.

CXXIV

Sweet is the vintage, when the showering grapes
    In Bacchanal profusion reel to earth,
Purple and gushing: sweet are our escapes
    From civic revelry to rural mirth;
Sweet to the miser are his glittering heaps,
    Sweet to the father is his first-born's birth,   990
Sweet is revenge—especially to women—
Pillage to soldiers, prize-money to seamen.

CXXV

Sweet is a legacy, and passing sweet
    The unexpected death of some old lady,
Or gentleman of seventy years complete,
    Who 've made "us youth" wait too—too long
        already,
For an estate, or cash, or country seat,
    Still breaking, but with stamina so steady,
That all the Israelites are fit to mob its
Next owner for their double-damned post-obits.   1000

CXXVI

'T is sweet to win, no matter how, one's laurels,
　　By blood or ink; 't is sweet to put an end
To strife; 't is sometimes sweet to have our quarrels,
　　Particularly with a tiresome friend:
Sweet is old wine in bottles, ale in barrels;
　　Dear is the helpless creature we defend
Against the world; and dear the schoolboy spot
We ne'er forget, though there we are forgot.

CXXVII

But sweeter still than this, than these, than all,
　　Is first and passionate Love—it stands alone,　　　1010
Like Adam's recollection of his fall;
　　The Tree of Knowledge has been plucked—all 's known—
And Life yields nothing further to recall
　　Worthy of this ambrosial sin, so shown,
No doubt in fable, as the unforgiven
Fire which Prometheus filched for us from Heaven.

CXXVIII

Man 's a strange animal, and makes strange use
　　Of his own nature, and the various arts,
And likes particularly to produce
　　Some new experiment to show his parts;　　　1020
This is the age of oddities let loose,
　　Where different talents find their different marts;
You 'd best begin with truth, and when you 've lost your
Labour, there 's a sure market for imposture.

CXXIX

What opposite discoveries we have seen!
　　(Signs of true genius, and of empty pockets.)
One makes new noses, one a guillotine,
　　One breaks your bones, one sets them in their sockets;
But Vaccination certainly has been
　　A kind antithesis to Congreve's rockets,　　　1030
With which the Doctor paid off an old pox,
By borrowing a new one from an ox.

CXXX

Bread has been made (indifferent) from potatoes:
    And Galvanism has set some corpses grinning,
But has not answered like the apparatus
    Of the Humane Society's beginning,
By which men are unsuffocated gratis:
    What wondrous new machines have late been spinning!
I said the small-pox has gone out of late;
Perhaps it may be followed by the great.   1040

CXXXI

'T is said the great came from America;
    Perhaps it may set out on its return,—
The population there so spreads, they say
    'T is grown high time to thin it in its turn,
With war, or plague, or famine—any way,
    So that civilisation they may learn;
And which in ravage the more loathsome evil is—
Their real *lues,* or our pseudo-syphilis?

CXXXII

This is the patent age of new inventions
    For killing bodies, and for saving souls,   1050
All propagated with the best intentions;
    Sir Humphry Davy's lantern, by which coals
Are safely mined for in the mode he mentions,
    Tombuctoo travels, voyages to the Poles
Are ways to benefit mankind, as true,
Perhaps, as shooting them at Waterloo.

CXXXIII

Man 's a phenomenon, one knows not what,
    And wonderful beyond all wondrous measure;
'T is pity though, in this sublime world, that
    Pleasure 's a sin, and sometimes Sin 's a pleasure;   1060
Few mortals know what end they would be at,
    But whether Glory, Power, or Love, or Treasure,
The path is through perplexing ways, and when
The goal is gained, we die, you know—and then——

CXXXIV

What then?—I do not know, no more do you—
  And so good night.—Return we to our story:
'T was in November, when fine days are few,
  And the far mountains wax a little hoary,
And clap a white cape on their mantles blue;
  And the sea dashes round the promontory,   1070
And the loud breaker boils against the rock,
And sober suns must set at five o'clock.

CXXXV

'T was, as the watchmen say, a cloudy night;
  No moon, no stars, the wind was low or loud
By gusts, and many a sparkling hearth was bright
  With the piled wood, round which the family crowd;
There 's something cheerful in that sort of light,
  Even as a summer sky's without a cloud;
I 'm fond of fire, and crickets, and all that,
A lobster salad, and champagne, and chat.   1080

CXXXVI

'T was midnight—Donna Julia was in bed,
  Sleeping, most probably,—when at her door
Arose a clatter might awake the dead,
  If they had never been awoke before,
And that they have been so we all have read,
  And are to be so, at the least, once more;—
The door was fastened, but with voice and fist
First knocks were heard, then "Madam—Madam—hist!

CXXXVII

"For God's sake, Madam—Madam—here 's my master,
  With more than half the city at his back—   1090
Was ever heard of such a curst disaster!
  'T is not my fault—I kept good watch—Alack!
Do pray undo the bolt a little faster—
  They 're on the stair just now, and in a crack
Will all be here; perhaps he yet may fly—
Surely the window 's not so *very* high!"

CXXXVIII

By this time Don Alfonso was arrived,
   With torches, friends, and servants in great number;
The major part of them had long been wived,
   And therefore paused not to disturb the slumber   1100
Of any wicked woman, who contrived
   By stealth her husband's temples to encumber:
Examples of this kind are so contagious,
Were *one* not punished, *all* would be outrageous.

CXXXIX

I can't tell how, or why, or what suspicion
   Could enter into Don Alfonso's head;
But for a cavalier of his condition
   It surely was exceedingly ill-bred,
Without a word of previous admonition,
   To hold a levee round his lady's bed,   1110
And summon lackeys, armed with fire and sword,
To prove himself the thing he most abhorred.

CXL

Poor Donna Julia! starting as from sleep,
   (Mind—that I do not say—she had not slept),
Began at once to scream, and yawn, and weep;
   Her maid, Antonia, who was an adept,
Contrived to fling the bed-clothes in a heap,
   As if she had just now from out them crept:
I can't tell why she should take all this trouble
To prove her mistress had been sleeping double.   1120

CXLI

But Julia mistress, and Antonia maid,
   Appeared like two poor harmless women, who
Of goblins, but still more of men afraid,
   Had thought one man might be deterred by two,
And therefore side by side were gently laid,
   Until the hours of absence should run through,
And truant husband should return, and say,
"My dear,—I was the first who came away."

CXLII

Now Julia found at length a voice, and cried,
   "In Heaven's name, Don Alfonso, what d' ye mean?   1130
Has madness seized you? would that I had died
   Ere such a monster's victim I had been!
What may this midnight violence betide,
   A sudden fit of drunkenness or spleen?
Dare you suspect me, whom the thought would kill?
Search, then, the room!"—Alfonso said, "I will."

CXLIII

He searched, *they* searched, and rummaged everywhere,
   Closet and clothes' press, chest and window-seat,
And found much linen, lace, and several pair
   Of stockings, slippers, brushes, combs, complete,   1140
With other articles of ladies fair,
   To keep them beautiful, or leave them neat:
Arras they pricked and curtains with their swords,
And wounded several shutters, and some boards.

CXLIV

Under the bed they searched, and there they found—
   No matter what—it was not that they sought;
They opened windows, gazing if the ground
   Had signs or footmarks, but the earth said nought;
And then they stared each others' faces round:
   'T is odd, not one of all these seekers thought,   1150
And seems to me almost a sort of blunder,
Of looking *in* the bed as well as under.

CXLV

During this inquisition Julia's tongue
   Was not asleep—"Yes, search and search," she cried,
"Insult on insult heap, and wrong on wrong!
   It was for this that I became a bride!
For this in silence I have suffered long
   A husband like Alfonso at my side;
But now I'll bear no more, nor here remain,
If there be law or lawyers in all Spain.   1160

CXLVI

"Yes, Don Alfonso! husband now no more,
    If ever you indeed deserved the name,
Is 't worthy of your years?—you have threescore—
    Fifty, or sixty, it is all the same—
Is 't wise or fitting, causeless to explore
    For facts against a virtuous woman's fame?
Ungrateful, perjured, barbarous Don Alfonso,
How dare you think your lady would go on so?

CXLVII

"Is it for this I have disdained to hold
    The common privileges of my sex?   1170
That I have chosen a confessor so old
    And deaf, that any other it would vex,
And never once he has had cause to scold,
    But found my very innocence perplex
So much, he always doubted I was married—
How sorry you will be when I've miscarried!

CXLVIII

"Was it for this that no Cortejo e'er
    I yet have chosen from out the youth of Seville?
Is it for this I scarce went anywhere,
    Except to bull-fights, mass, play, rout, and revel?   1180
Is it for this, whate'er my suitors were,
    I favoured none—nay, was almost uncivil?
Is it for this that General Count O'Reilly,
Who took Algiers, declares I used him vilely?

CXLIX

"Did not the Italian *Musico* Cazzani
    Sing at my heart six months at least in vain?
Did not his countryman, Count Corniani,
    Call me the only virtuous wife in Spain?
Were there not also Russians, English, many?
    The Count Strongstroganoff I put in pain,   1190
And Lord Mount Coffeehouse, the Irish peer,
Who killed himself for love (with wine) last year.

CL

"Have I not had two bishops at my feet?
    The Duke of Ichar, and Don Fernan Nunez;
And is it thus a faithful wife you treat?
    I wonder in what quarter now the moon is:
I praise your vast forbearance not to beat
    Me also, since the time so opportune is—
Oh, valiant man! with sword drawn and cocked trigger,
Now, tell me, don't you cut a pretty figure?   1200

CLI

"Was it for this you took your sudden journey,
    Under pretence of business indispensable
With that sublime of rascals your attorney,
    Whom I see standing there, and looking sensible
Of having played the fool? though both I spurn, he
    Deserves the worst, his conduct 's less defensible,
Because, no doubt, 't was for his dirty fee,
And not from any love to you nor me.

CLII

"If he comes here to take a deposition,
    By all means let the gentleman proceed;   1210
You've made the apartment in a fit condition:—
    There's pen and ink for you, sir, when you need—
Let everything be noted with precision,
    I would not you for nothing should be fee'd—
But, as my maid's undressed, pray turn your spies out."
"Oh!" sobbed Antonia, "I could tear their eyes out."

CLIII

"There is the closet, there the toilet, there
    The antechamber—search them under, over;
There is the sofa, there the great arm-chair,
    The chimney—which would really hold a lover.   1220
I wish to sleep, and beg you will take care
    And make no further noise, till you discover
The secret cavern of this lurking treasure—
And when 't is found, let me, too, have that pleasure.

CLIV

"And now, Hidalgo! now that you have thrown
    Doubt upon me, confusion over all,
Pray have the courtesy to make it known
    Who is the man you search for? how d' ye call
Him? what 's his lineage? let him but be shown—
    I hope he 's young and handsome—is he tall?   1230
Tell me—and be assured, that since you stain
My honour thus, it shall not be in vain.

CLV

"At least, perhaps, he has not sixty years,
    At that age he would be too old for slaughter,
Or for so young a husband's jealous fears—
    (Antonia! let me have a glass of water.)
I am ashamed of having shed these tears,
    They are unworthy of my father's daughter;
My mother dreamed not in my natal hour,
That I should fall into a monster's power.   1240

CLVI

"Perhaps 't is of Antonia you are jealous,
    You saw that she was sleeping by my side,
When you broke in upon us with your fellows:
    Look where you please—we 've nothing, sir, to hide;
Only another time, I trust, you 'll tell us,
    Or for the sake of decency abide
A moment at the door, that we may be
Dressed to receive so much good company.

CLVII

"And now, sir, I have done, and say no more;
    The little I have said may serve to show   1250
The guileless heart in silence may grieve o'er
    The wrongs to whose exposure it is slow:—
I leave you to your conscience as before,
    'T will one day ask you *why* you used me so?
God grant you feel not then the bitterest grief!—
Antonia! where 's my pocket-handkerchief?"

CLVIII

She ceased, and turned upon her pillow; pale
   She lay, her dark eyes flashing through their tears,
Like skies that rain and lighten; as a veil,
   Waved and o'ershading her wan cheek, appears   1260
Her streaming hair; the black curls strive, but fail
   To hide the glossy shoulder, which uprears
Its snow through all;—her soft lips lie apart,
And louder than her breathing beats her heart.

CLIX

The Senhor Don Alfonso stood confused;
   Antonia bustled round the ransacked room,
And, turning up her nose, with looks abused
   Her master, and his myrmidons, of whom
Not one, except the attorney, was amused;
   He, like Achates, faithful to the tomb,   1270
So there were quarrels, cared not for the cause,
Knowing they must be settled by the laws.

CLX

With prying snub-nose, and small eyes, he stood,
   Following Antonia's motions here and there,
With much suspicion in his attitude;
   For reputations he had little care;
So that a suit or action were made good,
   Small pity had he for the young and fair,
And ne'er believed in negatives, till these
Were proved by competent false witnesses.   1280

CLXI

But Don Alfonso stood with downcast looks,
   And, truth to say, he made a foolish figure;
When, after searching in five hundred nooks,
   And treating a young wife with so much rigour,
He gained no point, except some self-rebukes,
   Added to those his lady with such vigour
Had poured upon him for the last half-hour,
Quick, thick, and heavy—as a thunder-shower.

CLXII

At first he tried to hammer an excuse,
   To which the sole reply was tears, and sobs,   1290
And indications of hysterics, whose
   Prologue is always certain throes, and throbs,
Gasps, and whatever else the owners choose:
   Alfonso saw his wife, and thought of Job's;
He saw too, in perspective, her relations,
And then he tried to muster all his patience.

CLXIII

He stood in act to speak, or rather stammer,
   But sage Antonia cut him short before
The anvil of his speech received the hammer,
   With "Pray, sir, leave the room, and say no more,   1300
Or madam dies."—Alfonso muttered, "D—n her,"
   But nothing else, the time of words was o'er;
He cast a rueful look or two, and did,
He knew not wherefore, that which he was bid.

CLXIV

With him retired his *"posse comitatus,"*
   The attorney last, who lingered near the door
Reluctantly, still tarrying there as late as
   Antonia let him—not a little sore
At this most strange and unexplained *"hiatus"*
   In Don Alfonso's facts, which just now wore   1310
An awkward look; as he revolved the case,
The door was fastened in his legal face.

CLXV

No sooner was it bolted, than—Oh Shame!
   Oh Sin! Oh Sorrow! and Oh Womankind!
How can you do such things and keep your fame,
   Unless this world, and t' other too, be blind?
Nothing so dear as an unfilched good name!
   But to proceed—for there is more behind:
With much heartfelt reluctance be it said,
Young Juan slipped, half-smothered, from the bed.   1320

CLXVI

He had been hid—I don't pretend to say
    How, nor can I indeed describe the where—
Young, slender, and packed easily, he lay,
    No doubt, in little compass, round or square;
But pity him I neither must nor may
    His suffocation by that pretty pair;
'T were better, sure, to die so, than be shut
With maudlin Clarence in his Malmsey butt.

CLXVII

And, secondly, I pity not, because
    He had no business to commit a sin,   1330
Forbid by heavenly, fined by human laws;—
    At least 't was rather early to begin,
But at sixteen the conscience rarely gnaws
    So much as when we call our old debts in
At sixty years, and draw the accompts of evil,
And find a deuced balance with the Devil.

CLXVIII

Of his position I can give no notion:
    'T is written in the Hebrew Chronicle,
How the physicians, leaving pill and potion,
    Prescribed, by way of blister, a young belle,   1340
When old King David's blood grew dull in motion,
    And that the medicine answered very well;
Perhaps 't was in a different way applied,
For David lived, but Juan nearly died.

CLXIX

What 's to be done? Alfonso will be back
    The moment he has sent his fools away.
Antonia's skill was put upon the rack,
    But no device could be brought into play—
And how to parry the renewed attack?
    Besides, it wanted but few hours of day: 1350
Antonia puzzled; Julia did not speak,
But pressed her bloodless lip to Juan's cheek.

CLXX

He turned his lip to hers, and with his hand
    Called back the tangles of her wandering hair;
Even then their love they could not all command,
    And half forgot their danger and despair:
Antonia's patience now was at a stand—
    "Come, come, 't is no time now for fooling there,"
She whispered, in great wrath—"I must deposit
This pretty gentleman within the closet: 1360

CLXXI

"Pray, keep your nonsense for some luckier night—
    Who can have put my master in this mood?
What will become on 't—I 'm in such a fright,
    The Devil 's in the urchin, and no good—
Is this a time for giggling? this a plight?
    Why, don't you know that it may end in blood?
You 'll lose your life, and I shall lose my place,
My mistress all, for that half-girlish face.

CLXXII

"Had it but been for a stout cavalier
    Of twenty-five or thirty—(Come, make haste)   1370
But for a child, what piece of work is here!
    I really, madam, wonder at your taste—
(Come, sir, get in)—my master must be near.
    There, for the present, at the least he's fast,
And, if we can but till the morning keep
Our counsel—(Juan, mind, you must not sleep)."

CLXXIII

Now, Don Alfonso entering, but alone,
    Closed the oration of the trusty maid:
She loiter'd, and he told her to be gone,
    An order somewhat sullenly obey'd;   1380
However, present remedy was none,
    And no great good seem'd answer'd if she staid:
Regarding both with slow and sidelong view,
She snuff'd the candle, curtsied, and withdrew.

CLXXIV

Alfonso paused a minute—then begun
    Some strange excuses for his late proceeding;
He would not justify what he had done,
    To say the best, it was extreme ill-breeding;
But there were ample reasons for it, none
    Of which he specified in this his pleading: 1390
His speech was a fine sample, on the whole,
Of rhetoric, which the learn'd call *"rigmarole."*

CLXXV

Julia said nought; though all the while there rose
    A ready answer, which at once enables
A matron, who her husband's foible knows,
    By a few timely words to turn the tables,
Which if it does not silence still must pose,
    Even if it should comprise a pack of fables;
'T is to retort with firmness, and when he
Suspects with *one,* do you reproach with *three.*   1400

CLXXVI

Julia, in fact, had tolerable grounds,
    Alfonso's loves with Inez were well known;
But whether 't was that one's own guilt confounds,
    But that can't be, as has been often shown,
A lady with apologies abounds;
    It might be that her silence sprang alone
From delicacy to Don Juan's ear,
To whom she knew his mother's fame was dear.

CLXXVII

There might be one more motive, which makes two;
    Alfonso ne'er to Juan had alluded,   1410
Mention'd his jealousy, but never who
    Had been the happy lover, he concluded,
Conceal'd amongst his premises; 't is true,
    His mind the more o'er this its mystery brooded;
To speak of Inez now were, one may say,
Like throwing Juan in Alfonso's way.

CLXXVIII

A hint, in tender cases, is enough;
    Silence is best, besides there is a *tact*
(That modern phrase appears to me sad stuff,
    But it will serve to keep my verse compact)
Which keeps, when push'd by questions rather rough,
    A lady always distant from the fact—
The charming creatures lie with such a grace,
There's nothing so becoming to the face.

CLXXIX

They blush, and we believe them; at least I
    Have always done so; 't is of no great use,
In any case, attempting a reply,
    For then their eloquence grows quite profuse;
And when at length they 're out of breath, they sigh,
    And cast their languid eyes down, and let loose
A tear or two, and then we make it up;
And then—and then—and then—sit down and sup.

CLXXX

Alfonso closed his speech, and begged her pardon,
    Which Julia half withheld, and then half granted,
And laid conditions he thought very hard on,
    Denying several little things he wanted:
He stood like Adam lingering near his garden,
    With useless penitence perplexed and haunted;
Beseeching she no further would refuse,
When, lo! he stumbled o'er a pair of shoes.

CLXXXI

A pair of shoes!—what then? not much, if they
    Are such as fit with ladies' feet, but these
(No one can tell how much I grieve to say)
    Were masculine; to see them, and to seize,
Was but a moment's act.—Ah! well-a-day!
    My teeth begin to chatter, my veins freeze!
Alfonso first examined well their fashion,
And then flew out into another passion.

CLXXXII

He left the room for his relinquished sword,
　　And Julia instant to the closet flew.　　　　　　　　1450
"Fly, Juan, fly! for Heaven's sake—not a word—
　　The door is open—you may yet slip through
The passage you so often have explored—
　　Here is the garden-key—Fly—fly—Adieu!
Haste—haste! I hear Alfonso's hurrying feet—
Day has not broke—there's no one in the street."

CLXXXIII

None can say that this was not good advice,
　　The only mischief was, it came too late;
Of all experience 't is the usual price,
　　A sort of income-tax laid on by fate:　　　　　　　　1460
Juan had reached the room-door in a trice,
　　And might have done so by the garden-gate,
But met Alfonso in his dressing-gown,
Who threatened death—so Juan knocked him down.

CLXXXIV

Dire was the scuffle, and out went the light;
　　Antonia cried out "Rape!" and Julia "Fire!"
But not a servant stirred to aid the fight.
　　Alfonso, pommelled to his heart's desire,
Swore lustily he 'd be revenged this night;
　　And Juan, too, blasphemed an octave higher;　　　　1470
His blood was up: though young, he was a Tartar,
And not at all disposed to prove a martyr.

CLXXXV

Alfonso's sword had dropped ere he could draw it,
　　And they continued battling hand to hand,
For Juan very luckily ne'er saw it;
　　His temper not being under great command,
If at that moment he had chanced to claw it,
　　Alfonso's days had not been in the land
Much longer.—Think of husbands', lovers' lives!
And how ye may be doubly widows—wives!　　　　　　1480

CLXXXVI

Alfonso grappled to detain the foe,
    And Juan throttled to get away,
And blood ('t was from the nose) began to flow;
    At last, as they more faintly wrestling lay,
Juan contrived to give an awkward blow,
    And then his only garment quite gave way;
He fled, like Joseph, leaving it; but there,
I doubt, all likeness ends between the pair.

CLXXXVII

Lights came at length, and men, and maids, who found
    An awkward spectacle their eyes before;   1490
Antonia in hysterics, Julia swooned,
    Alfonso leaning, breathless, by the door;
Some half-torn drapery scattered on the ground,
    Some blood, and several footsteps, but no more:
Juan the gate gained, turned the key about,
And liking not the inside, locked the out.

CLXXXVIII

Here ends this canto.—Need I sing, or say,
    How Juan, naked, favoured by the night,
Who favours what she should not, found his way,
    And reached his home in an unseemly plight?   1500
The pleasant scandal which arose next day,
    The nine days' wonder which was brought to light,
And how Alfonso sued for a divorce,
Were in the English newspapers, of course.

CLXXXIX

If you would like to see the whole proceedings,
    The depositions, and the Cause at full,
The names of all the witnesses, the pleadings
    Of Counsel to nonsuit, or to annul,
There's more than one edition, and the readings
    Are various, but they none of them are dull: 1510
The best is that in short-hand ta'en by Gurney,
Who to Madrid on purpose made a journey.

CXC

But Donna Inez, to divert the train
  Of one of the most circulating scandals
That had for centuries been known in Spain,
  At least since the retirement of the Vandals,
First vowed (and never had she vowed in vain)
  To Virgin Mary several pounds of candles;
And then, by the advice of some old ladies,
She sent her son to be shipped off from Cadiz.   1520

CXCI

She had resolved that he should travel through
  All European climes, by land or sea,
To mend his former morals, and get new,
  Especially in France and Italy—
(At least this is the thing most people do.)
  Julia was sent into a convent—she
Grieved—but, perhaps, her feelings may be better
Shown in the following copy of her Letter:—

CXCII

"They tell me 't is decided you depart:
  'T is wise—'t is well, but not the less a pain;   1530
I have no further claim on your young heart,
  Mine is the victim, and would be again:
To love too much has been the only art
  I used;—I write in haste, and if a stain
Be on this sheet, 't is not what it appears;
My eyeballs burn and throb, but have no tears.

CXCIII

"I loved, I love you, for this love have lost
  State, station, Heaven, Mankind's, my own esteem,
And yet can not regret what it hath cost,
  So dear is still the memory of that dream;   1540
Yet, if I name my guilt, 't is not to boast,
  None can deem harshlier of me than I deem:
I trace this scrawl because I cannot rest—
I 've nothing to reproach, or to request.

CXCIV

"Man's love is of man's life a thing apart,
    'T is a Woman's whole existence; Man may range
The Court, Camp, Church, the Vessel, and the Mart;
    Sword, Gown, Gain, Glory, offer in exchange
Pride, Fame, Ambition, to fill up his heart,
    And few there are whom these can not estrange;   1550
Men have all these resources, We but one,
To love again, and be again undone.

CXCV

"You will proceed in pleasure, and in pride,
    Beloved and loving many; all is o'er
For me on earth, except some years to hide
    My shame and sorrow deep in my heart's core:
These I could bear, but cannot cast aside
    The passion which still rages as before,—
And so farewell—forgive me, love me—No,
That word is idle now—but let it go.   1560

CXCVI

"My breast has been all weakness, is so yet;
    But still I think I can collect my mind;
My blood still rushes where my spirit 's set,
    As roll the waves before the settled wind;
My heart is feminine, nor can forget—
    To all, except one image, madly blind;
So shakes the needle, and so stands the pole,
As vibrates my fond heart to my fixed soul.

CXCVII

"I have no more to say, but linger still,
    And dare not set my seal upon this sheet,   1570
And yet I may as well the task fulfil,
    My misery can scarce be more complete;
I had not lived till now, could sorrow kill;
    Death shuns the wretch who fain the blow would meet,
And I must even survive this last adieu,
And bear with life, to love and pray for you!"

CXCVIII

This note was written upon gilt-edged paper
   With a neat little crow-quill, slight and new;
Her small white hand could hardly reach the taper,
   It trembled as magnetic needles do,   1580
And yet she did not let one tear escape her;
   The seal a sun-flower; *"Elle vous suit partout,"*
The motto cut upon a white cornelian;
The wax was superfine, its hue vermilion.

CXCIX

This was Don Juan's earliest scrape; but whether
   I shall proceed with his adventures is
Dependent on the public altogether;
   We 'll see, however, what they say to this:
Their favour in an author's cap 's a feather,
   And no great mischief 's done by their caprice;   1590
And if their approbation we experience,
Perhaps they'll have some more about a year hence.

CC

My poem 's epic, and is meant to be
   Divided in twelve books; each book containing,
With Love, and War, a heavy gale at sea,
   A list of ships, and captains, and kings reigning,
New characters; the episodes are three:
   A panoramic view of Hell 's in training,
After the style of Virgil and of Homer,
So that my name of Epic 's no misnomer.   1600

CCI

All these things will be specified in time,
   With strict regard to Aristotle's rules,
The *Vade Mecum* of the true sublime,
   Which makes so many poets, and some fools:
Prose poets like blank-verse, I 'm fond of rhyme,
   Good workmen never quarrel with their tools;

I 've got new mythological machinery,
And very handsome supernatural scenery.

CCII

There 's only one slight difference between
    Me and my epic brethren gone before,   1610
And here the advantage is my own, I ween
    (Not that I have not several merits more,
But this will more peculiarly be seen);
    They so embellish, that 't is quite a bore
Their labyrinth of fables to thread through,
Whereas this story 's actually true.

CCIII

If any person doubt it, I appeal
    To History, Tradition, and to Facts,
To newspapers, whose truth all know and feel,
    To plays in five, and operas in three acts;   1620
All these confirm my statement a good deal,
    But that which more completely faith exacts
Is, that myself, and several now in Seville,
Saw Juan's last elopement with the Devil.

CCIV

If ever I should condescend to prose,
    I 'll write poetical commandments, which
Shall supersede beyond all doubt all those
    That went before; in these I shall enrich
My text with many things that no one knows,
    And carry precept to the highest pitch: 1630
I 'll call the work "Longinus o'er a Bottle,
Or, Every Poet his *own* Aristotle."

CCV

Thou shalt believe in Milton, Dryden, Pope;
    Thou shalt not set up Wordsworth, Coleridge, Southey;
Because the first is crazed beyond all hope,
    The second drunk, the third so quaint and mouthy:

With Crabbe it may be difficult to cope,
    And Campbell's Hippocrene is somewhat drouthy:
Thou shalt not steal from Samuel Rogers, nor
Commit—flirtation with the muse of Moore.   1640

CCVI

Thou shalt not covet Mr. Sotheby's Muse,
    His Pegasus, nor anything that 's his;
Thou shalt not bear false witness like "the Blues"—
    (There 's *one,* at least, is very fond of this);
Thou shalt not write, in short, but what I choose:
    This is true criticism, and you may kiss—
Exactly as you please, or not,—the rod;
But if you don't, I 'll lay it on, by G—d!

CCVII

If any person should presume to assert
    This story is not moral, first, I pray,   1650
That they will not cry out before they 're hurt,
    Then that they 'll read it o'er again, and say
(But, doubtless, nobody will be so pert)
    That this is not a moral tale, though gay:
Besides, in Canto Twelfth, I mean to show
The very place where wicked people go.

CCVIII

If, after all, there should be some so blind
    To their own good this warning to despise,
Led by some tortuosity of mind,
    Not to believe my verse and their own eyes,   1660
And cry that they "the moral cannot find,"
    I tell him, if a clergyman, he lies;
Should captains the remark, or critics, make,
They also lie too—under a mistake.

CCIX

The public approbation I expect,
    And beg they 'll take my word about the moral,

Which I with their amusement will connect
    (So children cutting teeth receive a coral);
Meantime they 'll doubtless please to recollect
    My epical pretensions to the laurel: 1670
For fear some prudish readers should grow skittish,
I 've bribed my Grandmother's Review—the British.

CCX

I sent it in a letter to the Editor,
    Who thanked me duly by return of post—
I 'm for a handsome article his creditor;
    Yet, if my gentle Muse he please to roast,
And break a promise after having made it her,
    Denying the receipt of what it cost,
And smear his page with gall instead of honey,
All I can say is—that he had the money.   1680

CCXI

I think that with this holy *new* alliance
    I may ensure the public, and defy
All other magazines of art or science,
    Daily, or monthly, or three monthly; I
Have not essayed to multiply their clients,
    Because they tell me 't were in vain to try,
And that the Edinburgh Review and Quarterly
Treat a dissenting author very martyrly.

CCXII

"Non ego hoc ferrem calidus juventá
    Consule Planco," Horace said, and so   1690
Say I; by which quotation there is meant a
    Hint that some six or seven good years ago
(Long ere I dreamt of dating from the Brenta)
    I was most ready to return a blow,
And would not brook at all this sort of thing
In my hot youth—when George the Third was King.

CCXIII

But now at thirty years my hair is grey—
   (I wonder what it will be like at forty?
I thought of a peruke the other day—)
   My heart is not much greener; and, in short, I   1700
Have squandered my whole summer while 't was May,
   And feel no more the spirit to retort; I
Have spent my life, both interest and principal,
And deem not, what I deemed—my soul invincible.

CCXIV

No more—no more—Oh! never more on me
   The freshness of the heart can fall like dew,
Which out of all the lovely things we see
   Extracts emotions beautiful and new,
Hived in our bosoms like the bag o' the bee.
   Think'st thou the honey with those objects grew?   1710
Alas! 't was not in them, but in thy power
To double even the sweetness of a flower.

CCXV

No more—no more—Oh! never more, my heart,
   Canst thou be my sole world, my universe!
Once all in all, but now a thing apart,
   Thou canst not be my blessing or my curse:
The illusion 's gone for ever, and thou art
   Insensible, I trust, but none the worse,
And in thy stead I 've got a deal of judgment,
Though Heaven knows how it ever found a lodgment.   1720

CCXVI

My days of love are over; me no more
   The charms of maid, wife, and still less of widow,
Can make the fool of which they made before,—
   In short, I must not lead the life I did do;
The credulous hope of mutual minds is o'er,
   The copious use of claret is forbid too,
So for a good old-gentlemanly vice,
I think I must take up with avarice.

CCXVII

Ambition was my idol, which was broken
  Before the shrines of Sorrow, and of Pleasure;   1730
And the two last have left me many a token
  O'er which reflection may be made at leisure:
Now, like Friar Bacon's Brazen Head, I've spoken,
  "Time is, Time was, Time's past."—a chymic treasure
Is glittering Youth, which I have spent betimes—
My heart in passion, and my head on rhymes.

CCXVIII

What is the end of Fame? 't is but to fill
  A certain portion of uncertain paper:
Some liken it to climbing up a hill,
  Whose summit, like all hills', is lost in vapour;   1740
For this men write, speak, preach, and heroes kill,
  And bards burn what they call their "midnight taper,"
To have, when the original is dust,
A name, a wretched picture and worse bust.

CCXIX

What are the hopes of man? Old Egypt's King
  Cheops erected the first Pyramid
And largest, thinking it was just the thing
  To keep his memory whole, and mummy hid;
But somebody or other rummaging,
  Burglariously broke his coffin's lid: 1750
Let not a monument give you or me hopes.
Since not a pinch of dust remains of Cheops.

CCXX

But I, being fond of true philosophy,
  Say very often to myself, "Alas!
All things that have been born were born to die,
  And flesh (which Death mows down to hay) is grass;
You've passed your youth not so unpleasantly,
  And if you had it o'er again—'t would pass—
So thank your stars that matters are no worse,
And read your Bible, sir, and mind your purse."   1760

CCXXI

But for the present, gentle reader! and
    Still gentler purchaser! the Bard—that's I—
Must, with permission, shake you by the hand,
    And so—"your humble servant, and Good-bye!"
We meet again, if we should understand
    Each other; and if not, I shall not try
Your patience further than by this short sample—
'T were well if others followed my example.

CCXXII

"Go, little Book, from this my solitude!
    I cast thee on the waters—go thy ways!   1770
And if, as I believe, thy vein be good,
    The World will find thee after many days."
When Southey's read, and Wordsworth understood,
    I can't help putting in my claim to praise—
The four first rhymes are Southey's every line:
For God's sake, reader! take them not for mine.

                                    [*November 1, 1818.*]

FRAGMENT ON THE BACK
OF THE MS. OF CANTO I

I would to Heaven that I were so much clay,
    As I am blood, bone, marrow, passion, feeling—
Because at least the past were passed away,
    And for the future—(but I write this reeling,
Having got drunk exceedingly to-day,
    So that I seem to stand upon the ceiling)
I say—the future is a serious matter—
And so—for God's sake—hock and soda-water!

CANTO THE SECOND*

. . .

XII

I can't but say it is an awkward sight
    To see one's native land receding through 90
The growing waters; it unmans one quite,
    Especially when life is rather new:
I recollect Great Britain's coast looks white,
    But almost every other country's blue,
When gazing on them, mystified by distance,
We enter on our nautical existence.

. . .

XVII

And Juan wept, and much he sighed and thought,
    While his salt tears dropped into the salt sea, 130
"Sweets to the sweet;" (I like so much to quote;
    You must excuse this extract,—'t is where she,
The Queen of Denmark, for Ophelia brought
    Flowers to the grave); and, sobbing often, he
Reflected on his present situation,
And seriously resolved on reformation.

XVIII

"Farewell, my Spain! a long farewell!" he cried,
    "Perhaps I may revisit thee no more,
But die, as many an exiled heart hath died,
    Of its own thirst to see again thy shore: 140
Farewell, where Guadalquivir's waters glide!
    Farewell, my mother! and, since all is o'er,
Farewell, too, dearest Julia!—(here he drew
Her letter out again, and read it through.)

XIX

"And oh! if e'er I should forget, I swear—
    But that's impossible, and cannot be—

*[Begun at Venice, December 13, 1818; finished January 20, 1819.]

Sooner shall this blue Ocean melt to air,
  Sooner shall Earth resolve itself to sea,
Than I resign thine image, oh, my fair!
  Or think of anything, excepting thee;   150
A mind diseased no remedy can physic—
(Here the ship gave a lurch, and he grew sea-sick.)

X X

"Sooner shall Heaven kiss earth—(here he fell sicker)
  Oh, Julia! what is every other woe?—
(For God's sake let me have a glass of liquor;
  Pedro, Battista, help me down below.)
Julia, my love!—(you rascal, Pedro, quicker)—
  Oh, Julia!—(this curst vessel pitches so)—
Belovéd Julia, hear me still beseeching!"
(Here he grew inarticulate with retching.)   160

X X I

He felt that chilling heaviness of heart,
  Or rather stomach, which, alas! attends,
Beyond the best apothecary's art,
  The loss of Love, the treachery of friends,
Or death of those we dote on, when a part
  Of us dies with them as each fond hope ends:
No doubt he would have been much more pathetic,
But the sea acted as a strong emetic.

X X I I

Love's a capricious power: I've known it hold
  Out through a fever caused by its own heat,   170
But be much puzzled by a cough and cold,
  And find a quinsy very hard to treat;
Against all noble maladies he's bold,
  But vulgar illnesses don't like to meet,
Nor that a sneeze should interrupt his sigh,
Nor inflammations redden his blind eye.

X X I I I

But worst of all is nausea, or a pain
  About the lower region of the bowels;

Love, who heroically breathes a vein,
    Shrinks from the application of hot towels,   180
And purgatives are dangerous to his reign,
    Sea-sickness death: his love was perfect, how else
Could Juan's passion, while the billows roar,
Resist his stomach, ne'er at sea before?

XXIV

The ship, called the most holy "Trinidada,"*
    Was steering duly for the port Leghorn;
For there the Spanish family Moncada
    Were settled long ere Juan's sire was born:
They were relations, and for them he had a
    Letter of introduction, which the morn   190
Of his departure had been sent him by
His Spanish friends for those in Italy.

XXV

His suite consisted of three servants and
    A tutor, the licentiate Pedrillo,
Who several languages did understand,
    But now lay sick and speechless on his pillow
And, rocking in his hammock, longed for land,
    His headache being increased by every billow;
And the waves oozing through the port-hole made
His berth a little damp, and him afraid.   200

. . .

XXXIV

There's nought, no doubt, so much the spirit calms
    As rum and true religion: thus it was,
Some plundered, some drank spirits, some sung psalms,
    The high wind made the treble, and as bass

*[With regard to the charges about the Shipwreck, I think that I told you and Mr. Hobhouse, years ago, that there was not a *single circumstance* of it *not* taken from *fact*; not, indeed, from any *single* shipwreck, but all from *actual* facts of different wrecks."—Letter to Murray, August 23, 1821. In the *Monthly Magazine,* vol. liii. (August, 1821, pp. 19–22, and September, 1821, pp. 105–109), Byron's indebtedness to Sir G. Dalzell's *Shipwrecks and Disasters at Sea* (1821, 8vo) is pointed out, and the parallel passages are printed in full.]

The hoarse harsh waves kept time; fright cured the qualms
　　Of all the luckless landsmen's sea-sick maws:　　　　　　270
Strange sounds of wailing, blasphemy, devotion,
Clamoured in chorus to the roaring Ocean.

　　　　　　　　　　xxxv

Perhaps more mischief had been done, but for
　　Our Juan, who, with sense beyond his years,
Got to the spirit-room, and stood before
　　It with a pair of pistols; and their fears,
As if Death were more dreadful by his door
　　Of fire than water, spite of oaths and tears,
Kept still aloof the crew, who, ere they sunk,
Thought it would be becoming to die drunk.　　　　　　280

　　　　　　　　　　xxxvi

"Give us more grog," they cried, "for it will be
　　All one an hour hence." Juan answered, "No!
'T is true that Death awaits both you and me,
　　But let us die like men, not sink below
Like brutes:"—and thus his dangerous post kept he,
　　And none liked to anticipate the blow;
And even Pedrillo, his most reverend tutor,
Was for some rum a disappointed suitor.

　　　　　　　　. . .

　　　　　　　　　　LI

At half-past eight o'clock, booms, hencoops, spars,
　　And all things, for a chance, had been cast loose,
That still could keep afloat the struggling tars,
　　For yet they strove, although of no great use:
There was no light in heaven but a few stars,
　　The boats put off o'ercrowded with their crews;
She gave a heel, and then a lurch to port,
And, going down head foremost—sunk, in short.

　　　　　　　　　　LII

Then rose from sea to sky the wild farewell—
　　Then shrieked the timid, and stood still the brave,—　　　　410

Then some leaped overboard with dreadful yell,
    As eager to anticipate their grave;
And the sea yawned around her like a hell,
    And down she sucked with her the whirling wave,
Like one who grapples with his enemy,
And strives to strangle him before he die.

LIII

And first one universal shriek there rushed,
    Louder than the loud Ocean, like a crash
Of echoing thunder; and then all was hushed,
    Save the wild wind and the remorseless dash   420
Of billows; but at intervals there gushed,
    Accompanied by a convulsive splash,
A solitary shriek, the bubbling cry
Of some strong swimmer in his agony.

LIV

The boats, as stated, had got off before,
    And in them crowded several of the crew;
And yet their present hope was hardly more
    Than what it had been, for so strong it blew
There was slight chance of reaching any shore;
    And then they were too many, though so few—   430
Nine in the cutter, thirty in the boat,
Were counted in them when they got afloat.

LV

All the rest perished; near two hundred souls
    Had left their bodies; and what's worse, alas!
When over Catholics the Ocean rolls,
    They must wait several weeks before a mass
Takes off one peck of purgatorial coals,
    Because, till people know what's come to pass,
They won't lay out their money on the dead—
It costs three francs for every mass that's said.   440

LVI

Juan got into the long-boat, and there
    Contrived to help Pedrillo to a place;
It seemed as if they had exchanged their care,
    For Juan wore the magisterial face
Which courage gives, while poor Pedrillo's pair
    Of eyes were crying for their owner's case:
Battista, though, (a name called shortly Tita),
Was lost by getting at some aqua-vita.

LVII

Pedro, his valet, too, he tried to save,
    But the same cause, conducive to his loss,   450
Left him so drunk, he jumped into the wave,
    As o'er the cutter's edge he tried to cross,
And so he found a wine-and-watery grave;
    They could not rescue him although so close,
Because the sea ran higher every minute,
And for the boat—the crew kept crowding in it.

LVIII

A small old spaniel,—which had been Don José's,
    His father's, whom he loved, as ye may think,
For on such things the memory reposes
    With tenderness—stood howling on the brink,   460
Knowing, (dogs have such intellectual noses!)
    No doubt, the vessel was about to sink;
And Juan caught him up, and ere he stepped
Off threw him in, then after him he leaped.

. . .

LXX

The fourth day came, but not a breath of air,
    And Ocean slumbered, like an unweaned child:
The fifth day, and their boat lay floating there,
    The sea and sky were blue, and clear, and mild—
With their one oar (I wish they had had a pair)
    What could they do? and Hunger's rage grew wild:

So Juan's spaniel, spite of his entreating,
Was killed, and portioned out for present eating.   560

LXXI

On the sixth day they fed upon his hide,
   And Juan, who had still refused, because
The creature was his father's dog that died,
   Now feeling all the vulture in his jaws,
With some remorse received (though first denied)
   As a great favour one of the fore-paws,
Which he divided with Pedrillo, who
Devoured it, longing for the other too.

LXXII

The seventh day, and no wind—the burning sun
   Blistered and scorched, and, stagnant on the sea,   570
They lay like carcasses; and hope was none,
   Save in the breeze that came not: savagely
They glared upon each other—all was done,
   Water, and wine, and food,—and you might see
The longings of the cannibal arise
(Although they spoke not) in their wolfish eyes.

LXXIII

At length one whispered his companion, who
   Whispered another, and thus it went round,
And then into a hoarser murmur grew,
   An ominous, and wild, and desperate sound;   580
And when his comrade's thought each sufferer knew,
   'T was but his own, suppressed till now, he found:
And out they spoke of lots for flesh and blood,
And who should die to be his fellow's food.

LXXIV

But ere they came to this, they that day shared
   Some leathern caps, and what remained of shoes;
And then they looked around them, and despaired,
   And none to be the sacrifice would choose;

At length the lots were torn up, and prepared,
    But of materials that must shock the Muse—   590
Having no paper, for the want of better,
They took by force from Juan Julia's letter.

LXXV

The lots were made, and marked, and mixed, and handed,
    In silent horror, and their distribution
Lulled even the savage hunger which demanded,
    Like the Promethean vulture, this pollution;
None in particular had sought or planned it,
    'T was Nature gnawed them to this resolution,
By which none were permitted to be neuter—
And the lot fell on Juan's luckless tutor.   600

LXXVI

He but requested to be bled to death:
    The surgeon had his instruments, and bled
Pedrillo, and so gently ebbed his breath,
    You hardly could perceive when he was dead.
He died as born, a Catholic in faith,
    Like most in the belief in which they're bred,
And first a little crucifix he kissed,
And then held out his jugular and wrist.

LXXVII

The surgeon, as there was no other fee.
    Had his first choice of morsels for his pains;   610
But being thirstiest at the moment, he
    Preferred a draught from the fast-flowing veins.
Part was divided, part thrown in the sea,
    And such things as the entrails and the brains
Regaled two sharks, who followed o'er the billow—
The sailors ate the rest of poor Pedrillo.

. . . .

LXXXIII

And if Pedrillo's fate should shocking be,
    Remember Ugolino condescends

To eat the head of his arch-enemy
 The moment after he politely ends   660
His tale: if foes be food in Hell, at sea
 'T is surely fair to dine upon our friends,
When Shipwreck's short allowance grows too scanty,
Without being much more horrible than Dante.

. . .

CIII

As they drew nigh the land, which now was seen
 Unequal in its aspect here and there,
They felt the freshness of its growing green,
 That waved in forest-tops, and smoothed the air,   820
And fell upon their glazed eyes like a screen
 From glistening waves, and skies so hot and bare—
Lovely seemed any object that should sweep
Away the vast—salt—dread—eternal Deep.

CIV

The shore looked wild, without a trace of man,
 And girt by formidable waves; but they
Were mad for land, and thus their course they ran,
 Though right ahead the roaring breakers lay:
A reef between them also now began
 To show its boiling surf and bounding spray,   830
But finding no place for their landing better,
They ran the boat for shore,—and overset her.

CV

But in his native stream, the Guadalquivir,
 Juan to lave his youthful limbs was wont;
And having learnt to swim in that sweet river,
 Had often turned the art to some account:
A better swimmer you could scarce see ever,
 He could, perhaps, have passed the Hellespont,
As once (a feat on which ourselves we prided)
Leander, Mr. Ekenhead, and I did.   840

CVI

So here, though faint, emaciated, and stark,
   He buoyed his boyish limbs, and strove to ply
With the quick wave, and gain, ere it was dark,
   The beach which lay before him, high and dry:
The greatest danger here was from a shark,
   That carried off his neighbour by the thigh;
As for the other two, they could not swim,
So nobody arrived on shore but him.

. . .

CXII

His eyes he opened, shut, again unclosed,
   For all was doubt and dizziness; he thought   890
He still was in the boat, and had but dozed,
   And felt again with his despair o'erwrought,
And wished it Death in which he had reposed,
   And then once more his feelings back were brought,
And slowly by his swimming eyes was seen
A lovely female face of seventeen.

CXIII

'T was bending close o'er his, and the small mouth
   Seemed almost prying into his for breath;
And chafing him, the soft warm hand of youth
   Recalled his answering spirits back from Death: 900
And, bathing his chill temples, tried to soothe
   Each pulse to animation, till beneath
Its gentle touch and trembling care, a sigh
To these kind efforts made a low reply.

CXIV

Then was the cordial poured, and mantle flung
   Around his scarce-clad limbs; and the fair arm
Raised higher the faint head which o'er it hung;
   And her transparent cheek, all pure and warm,
Pillowed his death-like forehead; then she wrung
   His dewy curls, long drenched by every storm;   910

And watched with eagerness each throb that drew
A sigh from his heaved bosom—and hers, too.

CXV

And lifting him with care into the cave,
   The gentle girl, and her attendant,—one
Young, yet her elder, and of brow less grave,
   And more robust of figure,—then begun
To kindle fire, and as the new flames gave
   Light to the rocks that roofed them, which the sun
Had never seen, the maid, or whatsoe'er
She was, appeared distinct, and tall, and fair.   920

CXVI

Her brow was overhung with coins of gold,
   That sparkled o'er the auburn of her hair—
Her clustering hair, whose longer locks were rolled
   In braids behind; and though her stature were
Even of the highest for a female mould,
   They nearly reached her heel; and in her air
There was a something which bespoke command,
As one who was a Lady in the land.

CXVII

Her hair, I said, was auburn; but her eyes
   Were black as Death, their lashes the same hue,   930
Of downcast length, in whose silk shadow lies
   Deepest attraction; for when to the view
Forth from its raven fringe the full glance flies,
   Ne'er with such force the swiftest arrow flew;
'T is as the snake late coiled, who pours his length,
And hurls at once his venom and his strength.

CXVIII

Her brow was white and low, her cheek's pure dye
   Like twilight rosy still with the set sun;
Short upper lip—sweet lips! that make us sigh
   Ever to have seen such; for she was one   940

Fit for the model of a statuary
    (A race of mere impostors, when all's done—
I've seen much finer women, ripe and real,
Than all the nonsense of their stone ideal).

. . .

CXXIV

I'll tell you who they were, this female pair,
    Lest they should seem Princesses in disguise;
Besides, I hate all mystery, and that air
    Of clap-trap, which your recent poets prize;
And so, in short, the girls they really were
    They shall appear before your curious eyes,   990
Mistress and maid; the first was only daughter
Of an old man, who lived upon the water.

CXXV

A fisherman he had been in his youth,
    And still a sort of fisherman was he;
But other speculations were, in sooth,
    Added to his connection with the sea,
Perhaps not so respectable, in truth:
    A little smuggling, and some piracy,
Left him, at last, the sole of many masters
Of an ill-gotten million of piastres.   1000

CXXVI

A fisher, therefore, was he,—though of men,
    Like Peter the Apostle, and he fished
For wandering merchant-vessels, now and then,
    And sometimes caught as many as he wished;
The cargoes he confiscated, and gain
    He sought in the slave-market too, and dished
Full many a morsel for that Turkish trade,
By which, no doubt, a good deal may be made.

CXXVII

He was a Greek, and on his isle had built
    (One of the wild and smaller Cyclades)   1010

A very handsome house from out his guilt,
　　And there he lived exceedingly at ease;
Heaven knows what cash he got, or blood he spilt,
　　A sad old fellow was he, if you please;
But this I know, it was a spacious building,
Full of barbaric carving, paint, and gilding.

CXXVIII

He had an only daughter, called Haidée,
　　The greatest heiress of the Eastern Isles;
Besides, so very beautiful was she,
　　Her dowry was as nothing to her smiles:　　　　1020
Still in her teens, and like a lovely tree
　　She grew to womanhood, and between whiles
Rejected several suitors, just to learn
How to accept a better in his turn.

CXXIX

And walking out upon the beach, below
　　The cliff, towards sunset, on that day she found,
Insensible,—not dead, but nearly so,—
　　Don Juan, almost famished, and half drowned;
But being naked, she was shocked, you know,
　　Yet deemed herself in common pity bound,　　　　1030
As far as in her lay, "to take him in,
A stranger" dying—with so white a skin.

CXXX

But taking him into her father's house
　　Was not exactly the best way to save,
But like conveying to the cat the mouse,
　　Or people in a trance into their grave;
Because the good old man had so much "νοῦς,"
　　Unlike the honest Arab thieves so brave,
He would have hospitably cured the stranger,
And sold him instantly when out of danger.　　　　1040

CXXXI

And therefore, with her maid, she thought it best
    (A virgin always on her maid relies)
To place him in the cave for present rest:
    And when, at last, he opened his black eyes,
Their charity increased about their guest;
    And their compassion grew to such a size,
It opened half the turnpike-gates to Heaven—
(St. Paul says, 't is the toll which must be given).

CXXXII

They made a fire,—but such a fire as they
    Upon the moment could contrive with such   1050
Materials as were cast up round the bay,—
    Some broken planks, and oars, that to the touch
Were nearly tinder, since, so long they lay,
    A mast was almost crumbled to a crutch;
But, by God's grace, here wrecks were in such plenty,
That there was fuel to have furnished twenty.

CXXXIII

He had a bed of furs, and a pelisse,
    For Haidée stripped her sables off to make
His couch; and, that he might be more at ease,
    And warm, in case by chance he should awake,   1060
They also gave a petticoat apiece,
    She and her maid,—and promised by daybreak
To pay him a fresh visit, with a dish
For breakfast, of eggs, coffee, bread, and fish.

CXXXIV

And thus they left him to his lone repose:
    Juan slept like a top, or like the dead,
Who sleep at last, perhaps (God only knows),
    Just for the present: and in his lulled head
Not even a vision of his former woes
    Throbbed in accursèd dreams, which sometimes spread   1070
Unwelcome visions of our former years,
Till the eye, cheated, opens thick with tears.

CXXXV

Young Juan slept all dreamless:—but the maid,
　　Who smoothed his pillow, as she left the den
Looked back upon him, and a moment stayed,
　　And turned, believing that he called again.
He slumbered; yet she thought, at least she said
　　(The heart will slip, even as the tongue and pen),
He had pronounced her name—but she forgot
That at this moment Juan knew it not.　　　　　1080

CXXXVI

And pensive to her father's house she went,
　　Enjoining silence strict to Zoe, who
Better than her knew what, in fact, she meant,
　　She being wiser by a year or two:
A year or two's an age when rightly spent,
　　And Zoe spent hers, as most women do,
In gaining all that useful sort of knowledge
Which is acquired in Nature's good old college.

CXXXVII

The morn broke, and found Juan slumbering still
　　Fast in his cave, and nothing clashed upon　　　1090
His rest; the rushing of the neighbouring rill,
　　And the young beams of the excluded Sun,
Troubled him not, and he might sleep his fill;
　　And need he had of slumber yet, for none
Had suffered more—his hardships were comparative
To those related in my grand-dad's "Narrative."

. . .

CXLII

And down the cliff the island virgin came,
　　And near the cave her quick light footsteps drew,　　　1130
While the Sun smiled on her with his first flame,
　　And young Aurora kissed her lips with dew,
Taking her for a sister; just the same
　　Mistake you would have made on seeing the two,
Although the mortal, quite as fresh and fair,
Had all the advantage, too, of not being air.

CXLIII

And when into the cavern Haidée stepped
　　All timidly, yet rapidly, she saw
That like an infant Juan sweetly slept;
　　And then she stopped, and stood as if in awe　　　　1140
(For sleep is awful), and on tiptoe crept
　　And wrapped him closer, lest the air, too raw,
Should reach his blood, then o'er him still as Death
Bent, with hushed lips, that drank his scarce-drawn breath.

CXLIV

And thus like to an Angel o'er the dying
　　Who die in righteousness, she leaned; and there
All tranquilly the shipwrecked boy was lying,
　　As o'er him lay the calm and stirless air:
But Zoe the meantime some eggs was frying,
　　Since, after all, no doubt the youthful pair　　　　1150
Must breakfast—and, betimes, lest they should ask it,
She drew out her provision from the basket.

CXLV

She knew that the best feelings must have victual,
　　And that a shipwrecked youth would hungry be;
Besides, being less in love, she yawned a little,
　　And felt her veins chilled by the neighbouring sea;
And so, she cooked their breakfast to a tittle;
　　I can't say that she gave them any tea,
But there were eggs, fruit, coffee, bread, fish, honey,
With Scio wine,—and all for love, not money.　　　　1160

CXLVI

And Zoe, when the eggs were ready, and
　　The coffee made, would fain have wakened Juan;
But Haidée stopped her with her quick small hand,
　　And without word, a sign her finger drew on
Her lip, which Zoe needs must understand;
　　And, the first breakfast spoilt, prepared a new one,
Because her mistress would not let her break
That sleep which seemed as it would ne'er awake.

CXLVII

For still he lay, and on his thin worn cheek
    A purple hectic played like dying day   1170
On the snow-tops of distant hills; the streak
    Of sufferance yet upon his forehead lay,
Where the blue veins looked shadowy, shrunk, and weak;
    And his black curls were dewy with the spray,
Which weighed upon them yet, all damp and salt,
Mixed with the stony vapours of the vault.

CXLVIII

And she bent o'er him, and he lay beneath,
    Hushed as the babe upon its mother's breast,
Drooped as the willow when no winds can breathe,
    Lulled like the depth of Ocean when at rest,   1180
Fair as the crowning rose of the whole wreath,
    Soft as the callow cygnet in its nest;
In short, he was a very pretty fellow,
Although his woes had turned him rather yellow.

CXLIX

He woke and gazed, and would have slept again,
    But the fair face which met his eyes forbade
Those eyes to close, though weariness and pain
    Had further sleep a further pleasure made:
For Woman's face was never formed in vain
    For Juan, so that even when he prayed   1190
He turned from grisly saints, and martyrs hairy,
To the sweet portraits of the Virgin Mary.

CL

And thus upon his elbow he arose,
    And looked upon the lady, in whose cheek
The pale contended with the purple rose,
    As with an effort she began to speak;
Her eyes were eloquent, her words would pose,
    Although she told him, in good modern Greek,
With an Ionian accent, low and sweet,
That he was faint, and must not talk, but eat.   1200

. . .

CLVIII

He ate, and he was well supplied; and she,
　　Who watched him like a mother, would have fed
Him past all bounds, because she smiled to see
　　Such appetite in one she had deemed dead:　　　　1260
But Zoe, being older than Haidée,
　　Knew (by tradition, for she ne'er had read)
That famished people must be slowly nurst,
And fed by spoonfuls, else they always burst.

CLIX

And so she took the liberty to state,
　　Rather by deeds than words, because the case
Was urgent, that the gentleman, whose fate
　　Had made her mistress quit her bed to trace
The sea-shore at this hour, must leave his plate,
　　Unless he wished to die upon the place—　　　　1270
She snatched it, and refused another morsel,
Saying, he had gorged enough to make a horse ill.

. . .

CLXIV

'T is pleasing to be schooled in a strange tongue
　　By female lips and eyes—that is, I mean,
When both the teacher and the taught are young,
　　As was the case, at least, where I have been;
They smile so when one's right, and when one's wrong.
　　They smile still more, and then there intervene　　　1310
Pressure of hands, perhaps even a chaste kiss;—
I learned the little that I know by this:

CLXV

That is, some words of Spanish, Turk, and Greek,
　　Italian not at all, having no teachers;
Much English I cannot pretend to speak,
　　Learning that language chiefly from its preachers,
Barrow, South, Tillotson, whom every week
　　I study, also Blair—the highest reachers
Of eloquence in piety and prose—
I hate your poets, so read none of those.　　　　1320

CLXVI

As for the ladies, I have nought to say,
   A wanderer from the British world of Fashion,
Where I, like other "dogs, have had my day,"
   Like other men, too, may have had my passion—
But that, like other things, has passed away,
   And all her fools whom I *could* lay the lash on:
Foes, friends, men, women, now are nought to me
But dreams of what has been, no more to be.

CLXVII

Return we to Don Juan. He begun
   To hear new words, and to repeat them; but   1330
Some feelings, universal as the Sun,
   Were such as could not in his breast be shut
More than within the bosom of a nun:
   He was in love,—as you would be, no doubt,
With a young benefactress,—so was she,
Just in the way we very often see.

CLXVIII

And every day by daybreak—rather early
   For Juan, who was somewhat fond of rest—
She came into the cave, but it was merely
   To see her bird reposing in his nest;   1340
And she would softly stir his locks so curly,
   Without disturbing her yet slumbering guest
Breathing all gently o'er his cheek and mouth,
As o'er a bed of roses the sweet South.

. . .

CLXXVII

It was a wild and breaker-beaten coast,
   With cliffs above, and a broad sandy shore,   1410
Guarded by shoals and rocks as by an host,
   With here and there a creek, whose aspect wore
A better welcome to the tempest-tost;
   And rarely ceased the haughty billow's roar,
Save on the dead long summer days, which make
The outstretched Ocean glitter like a lake.

CLXXVIII

And the small ripple spilt upon the beach
    Scarcely o'erpassed the cream of your champagne,
When o'er the brim the sparkling bumpers reach,
    That spring-dew of the spirit! the heart's rain!   1420
Few things surpass old wine; and they may preach
    Who please,—the more because they preach in vain,—
Let us have Wine and Woman, Mirth and Laughter,
Sermons and soda-water the day after.

CLXXIX

Man, being reasonable, must get drunk;
    The best of Life is but intoxication:
Glory, the Grape, Love, Gold, in these are sunk
    The hopes of all men, and of every nation;
Without their sap, how branchless were the trunk
    Of Life's strange tree, so fruitful on occasion!   1430
But to return,—Get very drunk, and when
You wake with headache—you shall see what then!

CLXXX

Ring for your valet—bid him quickly bring
    Some hock and soda-water, then you'll know
A pleasure worthy Xerxes the great king;
    For not the blest sherbet, sublimed with snow,
Nor the first sparkle of the desert-spring,
    Nor Burgundy in all its sunset glow,
After long travel, Ennui, Love, or Slaughter,
Vie with that draught of hock and soda-water!   1440

CLXXXI

The coast—I think it was the coast that I
    Was just describing—Yes, it *was* the coast—
Lay at this period quiet as the sky,
    The sands untumbled, the blue waves untossed,
And all was stillness, save the sea-bird's cry,
    And dolphin's leap, and little billow crossed
By some low rock or shelve, that made it fret
Against the boundary it scarcely wet.

CLXXXII

And forth they wandered, her sire being gone,
    As I have said, upon an expedition;   1450
And mother, brother, guardian, she had none,
    Save Zoe, who, although with due precision
She waited on her lady with the Sun,
    Thought daily service was her only mission,
Bringing warm water, wreathing her long tresses,
And asking now and then for cast-off dresses.

CLXXXIII

It was the cooling hour, just when the rounded
    Red sun sinks down behind the azure hill,
Which then seems as if the whole earth it bounded,
    Circling all Nature, hushed, and dim, and still,   1460
With the far mountain-crescent half surrounded
    On one side, and the deep sea calm and chill
Upon the other, and the rosy sky
With one star sparkling through it like an eye.

CLXXXIV

And thus they wandered forth, and hand in hand,
    Over the shining pebbles and the shells,
Glided along the smooth and hardened sand,
    And in the worn and wild receptacles
Worked by the storms, yet worked as it were planned
    In hollow halls, with sparry roofs and cells,   1470
They turned to rest; and, each clasped by an arm,
Yielded to the deep Twilight's purple charm.

CLXXXV

They looked up to the sky, whose floating glow
    Spread like a rosy Ocean, vast and bright;
They gazed upon the glittering sea below,
    Whence the broad Moon rose circling into sight;
They heard the waves' splash, and the wind so low,
    And saw each other's dark eyes darting light
Into each other—and, beholding this,
Their lips drew near, and clung into a kiss;   1480

CLXXXVI

A long, long kiss, a kiss of Youth, and Love,
    And Beauty, all concentrating like rays
Into one focus, kindled from above;
    Such kisses as belong to early days,
Where Heart, and Soul, and Sense, in concert move,
    And the blood's lava, and the pulse a blaze,
Each kiss a heart-quake,—for a kiss's strength,
I think, it must be reckoned by its length.

CLXXXVII

By length I mean duration; theirs endured
    Heaven knows how long—no doubt they never
        reckoned;   1490
And if they had, they could not have secured
    The sum of their sensations to a second:
They had not spoken, but they felt allured,
    As if their souls and lips each other beckoned,
Which, being joined, like swarming bees they clung—
Their hearts the flowers from whence the honey sprung.

CLXXXVIII

They were alone, but not alone as they
    Who shut in chambers think it loneliness;
The silent Ocean, and the starlight bay,
    The twilight glow, which momently grew less,   1500
The voiceless sands, and dropping caves, that lay
    Around them, made them to each other press,
As if there were no life beneath the sky
Save theirs, and that their life could never die.

CLXXXIX

They feared no eyes nor ears on the lone beach;
    They felt no terrors from the night; they were
All in all to each other: though their speech
    Was broken words, they *thought* a language there,—
And all the burning tongues the Passions teach
    Found in one sigh the best interpreter   1510
Of Nature's oracle—first love,—that all
Which Eve has left her daughters since her fall.

CXC

Haidée spoke not of scruples, asked no vows,
    Nor offered any; she had never heard
Of plight and promises to be a spouse,
    Or perils by a loving maid incurred;
She was all which pure Ignorance allows,
    And flew to her young mate like a young bird;
And, never having dreamt of falsehood, she
Had not one word to say of constancy.   1520

CXCI

She loved, and was belovéd—she adored,
    And she was worshipped after Nature's fashion—
Their intense souls, into each other poured,
    If souls could die, had perished in that passion,—
But by degrees their senses were restored,
    Again to be o'ercome, again to dash on;
And, beating 'gainst *his* bosom, Haidée's heart
Felt as if never more to beat apart.

CXCII

Alas! they were so young, so beautiful,
    So lonely, loving, helpless, and the hour   1530
Was that in which the Heart is always full,
    And, having o'er itself no further power,
Prompts deeds Eternity can not annul,
    But pays off moments in an endless shower
Of hell-fire—all prepared for people giving
Pleasure or pain to one another living.

CXCIII

Alas! for Juan and Haidée! they were
    So loving and so lovely—till then never,
Excepting our first parents, such a pair
    Had run the risk of being damned for ever: 1540
And Haidée, being devout as well as fair,
    And, doubtless, heard about the Stygian river,
And Hell and Purgatory—but forgot
Just in the very crisis she should not.

CXCIV

They look upon each other, and their eyes
    Gleam in the moonlight; and her white arm clasps
Round Juan's head, and his around her lies
    Half buried in the tresses which it grasps;
She sits upon his knee, and drinks his sighs,
    He hers, until they end in broken gasps;   1550
And thus they form a group that's quite antique,
Half naked, loving, natural, and Greek.

CXCV

And when those deep and burning moments passed,
    And Juan sunk to sleep within her arms,
She slept not, but all tenderly, though fast,
    Sustained his head upon her bosom's charms;
And now and then her eye to Heaven is cast,
    And then on the pale cheek her breast now warms,
Pillowed on her o'erflowing heart, which pants
With all it granted, and with all it grants.   1560

CXCVI

An infant when it gazes on a light,
    A child the moment when it drains the breast,
A devotee when soars the Host in sight,
    An Arab with a stranger for a guest,
A sailor when the prize has struck in fight,
    A miser filling his most hoarded chest,
Feel rapture; but not such true joy are reaping
As they who watch o'er what they love while sleeping.

CXCVII

For there it lies so tranquil, so beloved,
    All that it hath of Life with us is living;   1570
So gentle, stirless, helpless, and unmoved,
    And all unconscious of the joy 't is giving;
All it hath felt, inflicted, passed, and proved,
    Hushed into depths beyond the watcher's diving:
There lies the thing we love with all its errors
And all its charms, like Death without its terrors.

CXCVIII

The Lady watched her lover—and that hour
  Of Love's, and Night's, and Ocean's solitude
O'erflowed her soul with their united power;
  Amidst the barren sand and rocks so rude   1580
She and her wave-worn love had made their bower,
  Where nought upon their passion could intrude,
And all the stars that crowded the blue space
Saw nothing happier than her glowing face.

CXCIX

Alas! the love of Women! it is known
  To be a lovely and a fearful thing;
For all of theirs upon that die is thrown,
  And if 't is lost, Life hath no more to bring
To them but mockeries of the past alone,
  And their revenge is as the tiger's spring,   1590
Deadly, and quick, and crushing; yet, as real
Torture is theirs—what they inflict they feel.

CC

They are right; for Man, to man so oft unjust,
  Is always so to Women: one sole bond
Awaits them—treachery is all their trust;
  Taught to conceal their bursting hearts despond
Over their idol, till some wealthier lust
  Buys them in marriage—and what rests beyond?
A thankless husband—next, a faithless lover—
Then dressing, nursing, praying—and all 's over.   1600

CCI

Some take a lover, some take drams or prayers,
  Some mind their household, others dissipation,
Some run away, and but exchange their cares,
  Losing the advantage of a virtuous station;
Few changes e'er can better their affairs,
  Theirs being an unnatural situation,
From the dull palace to the dirty hovel:
Some play the devil, and then write a novel.

CCII

Haidée was Nature's bride, and knew not this;
  Haidée was Passion's child, born where the Sun   1610
Showers triple light, and scorches even the kiss
  Of his gazelle-eyed daughters; she was one
Made but to love, to feel that she was his
  Who was her chosen: what was said or done
Elsewhere was nothing. She had nought to fear,
Hope, care, nor love, beyond,—her heart beat *here*.

CCIII

And oh! that quickening of the heart, that beat!
  How much it costs us! yet each rising throb
Is in its cause as its effect so sweet,
  That Wisdom, ever on the watch to rob   1620
Joy of its alchemy, and to repeat
  Fine truths; even Conscience, too, has a tough job
To make us understand each good old maxim,
So good—I wonder Castlereagh don't tax 'em.

CCIV

And now 't was done—on the lone shore were plighted
  Their hearts; the stars, their nuptial torches, shed
Beauty upon the beautiful they lighted:
  Ocean their witness, and the cave their bed,
By their own feelings hallowed and united,
  Their priest was Solitude, and they were wed: 1630
And they were happy—for to their young eyes
Each was an angel, and earth Paradise.

CCV

Oh, Love! of whom great Cæsar was the suitor,
  Titus the master, Antony the slave,
Horace, Catullus, scholars—Ovid tutor—
  Sappho the sage blue-stocking, in whose grave
All those may leap who rather would be neuter—
  (Leucadia's rock still overlooks the wave)—
Oh, Love! thou art the very God of evil,
For, after all, we cannot call thee Devil.   1640

CCVI

Thou mak'st the chaste connubial state precarious,
   And jestest with the brows of mightiest men:
Cæsar and Pompey, Mahomet, Belisarius,
   Have much employed the Muse of History's pen:
Their lives and fortunes were extremely various,
   Such worthies Time will never see again;
Yet to these four in three things the same luck holds,
They all were heroes, conquerors, and cuckolds.

CCVII

Thou mak'st philosophers; there 's Epicurus
   And Aristippus, a material crew!   1650
Who to immoral courses would allure us
   By theories quite practicable too;
If only from the Devil they would insure us,
   How pleasant were the maxim (not quite new),
"Eat, drink, and love, what can the rest avail us?"
So said the royal sage Sardanapalus.

CCVIII

But Juan! had he quite forgotten Julia?
   And should he have forgotten her so soon?
I can't but say it seems to me most truly a
   Perplexing question; but, no doubt, the moon   1660
Does these things for us, and whenever newly a
   Strong palpitation rises, 't is her boon,
Else how the devil is it that fresh features
Have such a charm for us poor human creatures?

CCIX

I hate inconstancy—I loathe, detest,
   Abhor, condemn, abjure the mortal made
Of such quicksilver clay that in his breast
   No permanent foundation can be laid;
Love, constant love, has been my constant guest,
   And yet last night, being at a masquerade,   1670
I saw the prettiest creature, fresh from Milan,
Which gave me some sensations like a villain.

CCX

But soon Philosophy came to my aid,
    And whispered, "Think of every sacred tie!"
"I will, my dear Philosophy!" I said,
    "But then her teeth, and then, oh, Heaven! her eye!
I 'll just inquire if she be wife or maid,
    Or neither—out of curiosity."
"Stop!" cried Philosophy, with air so Grecian,
(Though she was masqued then as a fair Venetian;)   1680

CCXI

"Stop!" so I stopped.—But to return: that which
    Men call inconstancy is nothing more
Than admiration due where Nature's rich
    Profusion with young beauty covers o'er
Some favoured object; and as in the niche
    A lovely statue we almost adore,
This sort of adoration of the real
Is but a heightening of the *beau idéal*.

CCXII

'T is the perception of the Beautiful,
    A fine extension of the faculties,   1690
Platonic, universal, wonderful,
    Drawn from the stars, and filtered through the skies,
Without which Life would be extremely dull;
    In short, it is the use of our own eyes,
With one or two small senses added, just
To hint that flesh is formed of fiery dust.

CCXIII

Yet 't is a painful feeling, and unwilling,
    For surely if we always could perceive
In the same object graces quite as killing
    As when she rose upon us like an Eve,   1700
'T would save us many a heartache, many a shilling,
    (For we must get them anyhow, or grieve),

Whereas if one sole lady pleased for ever,
How pleasant for the heart, as well as liver!

CCXIV

The Heart is like the sky, a part of Heaven,
    But changes night and day, too, like the sky;
Now o'er it clouds and thunder must be driven,
    And Darkness and Destruction as on high:
But when it hath been scorched, and pierced, and riven,
    Its storms expire in water-drops; the eye   1710
Pours forth at last the Heart's blood turned to tears,
Which make the English climate of our years.

CCXV

The liver is the lazaret of bile,
    But very rarely executes its function,
For the first passion stays there such a while,
    That all the rest creep in and form a junction,
Like knots of vipers on a dunghill's soil—
    Rage, fear, hate, jealousy, revenge, compunction—
So that all mischiefs spring up from this entrail,
Like Earthquakes from the hidden fire called "central."   1720

CCXVI

In the mean time, without proceeding more
    In this anatomy, I've finished now
Two hundred and odd stanzas as before,
    That being about the number I'll allow
Each canto of the twelve, or twenty-four;
    And, laying down my pen, I make my bow,
Leaving Don Juan and Haidée to plead
For them and theirs with all who deign to read.

Canto the Third*

I

Hail, Muse! et cetera.—We left Juan sleeping,
  Pillowed upon a fair and happy breast,
And watched by eyes that never yet knew weeping,
  And loved by a young heart, too deeply blest
To feel the poison through her spirit creeping,
  Or know who rested there, a foe to rest,
Had soiled the current of her sinless years,
And turned her pure heart's purest blood to tears!

II

Oh, Love! what is it in this world of ours
  Which makes it fatal to be loved? Ah why   10
With cypress branches hast thou wreathed thy bowers,
  And made thy best interpreter a sigh?
As those who dote on odours pluck the flowers,
  And place them on their breast—but place to die—
Thus the frail beings we would fondly cherish
Are laid within our bosoms but to perish.

III

In her first passion Woman loves her lover,
  In all the others all she loves is Love,
Which grows a habit she can ne'er get over,
  And fits her loosely—like an easy glove,   20
As you may find, whene'er you like to prove her:
  One man alone at first her heart can move;
She then prefers him in the plural number,
Not finding that the additions much encumber.

IV

I know not if the fault be men's or theirs;
  But one thing's pretty sure; a woman planted
(Unless at once she plunge for life in prayers)—
  After a decent time must be gallanted;

*[November 30, 1819.]

Although, no doubt, her first of love affairs
    Is that to which her heart is wholly granted;   30
Yet there are some, they say, who have had *none,*
But those who have ne'er end with only *one.*

V

'T is melancholy, and a fearful sign
    Of human frailty, folly, also crime,
That Love and Marriage rarely can combine,
    Although they both are born in the same clime;
Marriage from Love, like vinegar from wine—
    A sad, sour, sober beverage—by Time
Is sharpened from its high celestial flavour
Down to a very homely household savour.   40

VI

There 's something of antipathy, as 't were,
    Between their present and their future state;
A kind of flattery that's hardly fair
    Is used until the truth arrives too late—
Yet what can people do, except despair?
    The same things change their names at such a rate;
For instance—Passion in a lover 's glorious,
But in a husband is pronounced uxorious.

VII

Men grow ashamed of being so very fond;
    They sometimes also get a little tired   50
(But that, of course, is rare), and then despond:
    The same things cannot always be admired,
Yet 't is "so nominated in the bond,"
    That both are tied till one shall have expired.
Sad thought! to lose the spouse that was adorning
Our days, and put one's servants into mourning.

VIII

There's doubtless something in domestic doings
    Which forms, in fact, true Love's antithesis;
Romances paint at full length people's wooings,

But only give a bust of marriages; 60
For no one cares for matrimonial cooings,
  There's nothing wrong in a connubial kiss:
Think you, if Laura had been Petrarch's wife,
He would have written sonnets all his life?

IX

All tragedies are finished by a death,
  All comedies are ended by a marriage;
The future states of both are left to faith,
  For authors fear description might disparage
The worlds to come of both, or fall beneath,
  And then both worlds would punish their miscarriage; 70
So leaving each their priest and prayer-book ready,
They say no more of Death or of the Lady.

X

The only two that in my recollection,
  Have sung of Heaven and Hell, or marriage, are
Dante and Milton, and of both the affection
  Was hapless in their nuptials, for some bar
Of fault or temper ruined the connection
  (Such things, in fact, it don't ask much to mar);
But Dante's Beatrice and Milton's Eve
Were not drawn from their spouses, you conceive. 80

XI

Some persons say that Dante meant Theology
  By Beatrice, and not a mistress—I,
Although my opinion may require apology,
  Deem this a commentator's phantasy,
Unless indeed it was from his own knowledge he
  Decided thus, and showed good reason why;
I think that Dante's more abstruse ecstatics
Meant to personify the Mathematics.

XII

Haidée and Juan were not married, but
   The fault was theirs, not mine: it is not fair,   90
Chaste reader, then, in any way to put
   The blame on me, unless you wish they were;
Then if you'd have them wedded, please to shut
   The book which treats of this erroneous pair,
Before the consequences grow too awful;
'T is dangerous to read of loves unlawful.

XIII

Yet they were happy,—happy in the illicit
   Indulgence of their innocent desires;
But more imprudent grown with every visit,
   Haidée forgot the island was her Sire's;   100
When we have what we like 't is hard to miss it,
   At least in the beginning, ere one tires;
Thus she came often, not a moment losing,
Whilst her piratical papa was cruising.

XIV

Let not his mode of raising cash seem strange,
   Although he fleeced the flags of every nation,
For into a Prime Minister but change
   His title, and 't is nothing but taxation;
But he, more modest, took an humbler range
   Of Life, and in an honester vocation   110
Pursued o'er the high seas his watery journey,
And merely practised as a sea-attorney.

. . .

XXXVII

He—being a man who seldom used a word
   Too much, and wishing gladly to surprise   290
(In general he surprised men with the sword)
   His daughter—had not sent before to advise
Of his arrival, so that no one stirred;
   And long he paused to re-assure his eyes,

In fact much more astonished than delighted,
To find so much good company invited.

XXXVIII

He did not know (alas! how men will lie)
    That a report (especially the Greeks)
Avouched his death (such people never die),
    And put his house in mourning several weeks,—   300
But now their eyes and also lips were dry;
    The bloom, too, had returned to Haidée's cheeks:
Her tears, too, being returned into their fount,
She now kept house upon her own account.

XXXIX

Hence all this rice, meat, dancing, wine, and fiddling,
    Which turned the isle into a place of pleasure;
The servants all were getting drunk or idling,
    A life which made them happy beyond measure.
Her father's hospitality seemed middling,
    Compared with what Haidée did with his treasure;   310
'T was wonderful how things went on improving,
While she had not one hour to spare from loving.

XL

Perhaps you think, in stumbling on this feast,
    He flew into a passion, and in fact
There was no mighty reason to be pleased;
    Perhaps you prophesy some sudden act,
The whip, the rack, or dungeon at the least,
    To teach his people to be more exact,
And that, proceeding at a very high rate,
He showed the royal *penchants* of a pirate.   320

XLI

You're wrong.—He was the mildest mannered man
    That ever scuttled ship or cut a throat;
With such true breeding of a gentleman,
    You never could divine his real thought;
No courtier could, and scarcely woman can

Gird more deceit within a petticoat;
Pity he loved adventurous life's variety,
He was so great a loss to good society.

. . .

LIII

He was a man of a strange temperament,
    Of mild demeanour though of savage mood,
Moderate in all his habits, and content
      With temperance in pleasure, as in food,   420
Quick to perceive, and strong to bear, and meant
      For something better, if not wholly good;
His Country's wrongs and his despair to save her
Had stung him from a slave to an enslaver.

LIV

The love of power, and rapid gain of gold,
    The hardness by long habitude produced,
The dangerous life in which he had grown old,
    The mercy he had granted oft abused,
The sights he was accustomed to behold,
      The wild seas, and wild men with whom he cruised,   430
Had cost his enemies a long repentance,
And made him a good friend, but bad acquaintance.

LV

But something of the spirit of old Greece
    Flashed o'er his soul a few heroic rays,
Such as lit onward to the Golden Fleece
    His predecessors in the Colchian days;
'T is true he had no ardent love for peace—
    Alas! his country showed no path to praise:
Hate to the world and war with every nation
He waged, in vengeance of her degradation.   440

. . .

LXVII

Haidée and Juan carpeted their feet
    On crimson satin, bordered with pale blue;   530

Their sofa occupied three parts complete
    Of the apartment—and appeared quite new;
The velvet cushions (for a throne more meet)
    Were scarlet, from whose glowing centre grew
A sun embossed in gold, whose rays of tissue,
Meridian-like, were seen all light to issue.

. . .

LXXVIII

And now they were diverted by their suite,
    Dwarfs, dancing girls, black eunuchs, and a poet,
Which made their new establishment complete;
    The last was of great fame, and liked to show it;   620
His verses rarely wanted their due feet—
    And for his theme—he seldom sung below it,
He being paid to satirise or flatter,
As the Psalm says, "inditing a good matter."

. . .

LXXXII

Their poet, a sad trimmer, but, no less,
    In company a very pleasant fellow,   650
Had been the favourite of full many a mess
    Of men, and made them speeches when half mellow;
And though his meaning they could rarely guess,
    Yet still they deigned to hiccup or to bellow
The glorious meed of popular applause,
Of which the first ne'er knows the second cause.

LXXXIII

But now being lifted into high society,
    And having picked up several odds and ends
Of free thoughts in his travels for variety,
    He deemed, being in a lone isle, among friends,   660
That, without any danger of a riot, he
    Might for long lying make himself amends;
And, singing as he sung in his warm youth,
Agree to a short armistice with Truth.

LXXXIV

He had travelled 'mongst the Arabs, Turks, and Franks,
    And knew the self-loves of the different nations;
And having lived with people of all ranks,
    Had something ready upon most occasions—
Which got him a few presents and some thanks.
    He varied with some skill his adulations;   670
To "do at Rome as Romans do," a piece
Of conduct was which *he* observed in Greece.

LXXXV

Thus, usually, when *he* was asked to sing,
    He gave the different nations something national;
'T was all the same to him—"God save the King,"
    Or "Ça ira," according to the fashion all:
His Muse made increment of anything.
    From the high lyric down to the low rational;
If Pindar sang horse-races, what should hinder
Himself from being as pliable as Pindar?   680

LXXXVI

In France, for instance, he would write a chanson;
    In England a six canto quarto tale;
In Spain he'd make a ballad or romance on
    The last war—much the same in Portugal;
In Germany, the Pegasus he 'd prance on
    Would be old Goethe's—(see what says De Staël);
In Italy he 'd ape the "Trecentisti;"
In Greece, he 'd sing some sort of hymn like this t' ye:

1

    The Isles of Greece, the Isles of Greece!
        Where burning Sappho loved and sung,   690
    Where grew the arts of War and Peace,
        Where Delos rose, and Phœbus sprung!
    Eternal summer gilds them yet,
    But all, except their Sun, is set.

2

The Scian and the Teian muse,
　　The Hero's harp, the Lover's lute,
Have found the fame your shores refuse:
　　Their place of birth alone is mute
To sounds which echo further west
Than your Sires' "Islands of the Blest." 700

3

The mountains look on Marathon—
　　And Marathon looks on the sea;
And musing there an hour alone,
　　I dreamed that Greece might still be free;
For standing on the Persians' grave,
I could not deem myself a slave.

4

A King sate on the rocky brow
　　Which looks o'er sea-born Salamis;
And ships, by thousands, lay below,
　　And men in nations;—all were his! 710
He counted them at break of day—
And, when the Sun set, where were they?

5

And where are they? and where art thou,
　　My Country? On thy voiceless shore
The heroic lay is tuneless now—
　　The heroic bosom beats no more!
And must thy Lyre, so long divine,
Degenerate into hands like mine?

6

'T is something, in the dearth of Fame,
　　Though linked among a fettered race, 720
To feel at least a patriot's shame,
　　Even as I sing, suffuse my face;
For what is left the poet here?
For Greeks a blush—for Greece a tear.

7

Must *we* but weep o'er days more blest?
    Must *we* but blush?—Our fathers bled.
Earth! render back from out thy breast
    A remnant of our Spartan dead!
Of the three hundred grant but three,
To make a new Thermopylæ!   730

8

What, silent still? and silent all?
    Ah! no;—the voices of the dead
Sound like a distant torrent's fall,
    And answer, "Let one living head,
But one arise,—we come, we come!"
'T is but the living who are dumb.

9

In vain—in vain: strike other chords;
    Fill high the cup with Samian wine!
Leave battles to the Turkish hordes,
    And shed the blood of Scio's vine!   740
Hark! rising to the ignoble call—
How answers each bold Bacchanal!

10

You have the Pyrrhic dance as yet,
    Where is the Pyrrhic phalanx gone?
Of two such lessons, why forget
    The nobler and the manlier one?
You have the letters Cadmus gave—
Think ye he meant them for a slave?

11

Fill high the bowl with Samian wine!
    We will not think of themes like these!   750
It made Anacreon's song divine:
    He served—but served Polycrates—
A Tyrant; but our masters then
Were still, at least, our countrymen.

12

The Tyrant of the Chersonese
  Was Freedom's best and bravest friend;
That tyrant was Miltiades!
  Oh! that the present hour would lend
Another despot of the kind!
Such chains as his were sure to bind.   760

13

Fill high the bowl with Samian wine!
  On Suli's rock, and Parga's shore,
Exists the remnant of a line
  Such as the Doric mothers bore;
And there, perhaps, some seed is sown,
The Heracleidan blood might own.

14

Trust not for freedom to the Franks—
  They have a king who buys and sells;
In native swords, and native ranks,
  The only hope of courage dwells;   770
But Turkish force, and Latin fraud,
Would break your shield, however broad.

15

Fill high the bowl with Samian wine!
  Our virgins dance beneath the shade—
I see their glorious black eyes shine;
  But gazing on each glowing maid,
My own the burning tear-drop laves,
To think such breasts must suckle slaves.

16

Place me on Sunium's marbled steep,
  Where nothing, save the waves and I,   780
May hear our mutual murmurs sweep;
  There, swan-like, let me sing and die:
A land of slaves shall ne'er be mine—
Dash down yon cup of Samian wine!

LXXXVII

Thus sung, or would, or could, or should have sung,
   The modern Greek, in tolerable verse;
If not like Orpheus quite, when Greece was young,
   Yet in these times he might have done much worse:
His strain displayed some feeling—right or wrong;
   And feeling, in a poet, is the source   790
Of others' feeling; but they are such liars,
And take all colours—like the hands of dyers.

LXXXVIII

But words are things, and a small drop of ink,
   Falling like dew, upon a thought, produces
That which makes thousands, perhaps millions, think;
   'T is strange, the shortest letter which man uses
Instead of speech, may form a lasting link
   Of ages; to what straits old Time reduces
Frail man, when paper—even a rag like this,
Survives himself, his tomb, and all that 's his!   800

LXXXIX

And when his bones are dust, his grave a blank,
   His station, generation, even his nation,
Become a thing, or nothing, save to rank
   In chronological commemoration,
Some dull MS. Oblivion long has sank,
   Or graven stone found in a barrack's station
In digging the foundation of a closet,
May turn his name up, as a rare deposit.

XC

And Glory long has made the sages smile;
   'T is something, nothing, words, illusion, wind—   810
Depending more upon the historian's style
   Than on the name a person leaves behind:
Troy owes to Homer what whist owes to Hoyle:
   The present century was growing blind
To the great Marlborough's skill in giving knocks,
Until his late Life by Archdeacon Coxe.

XCI

Milton 's the Prince of poets—so we say;
    A little heavy, but no less divine:
An independent being in his day—
    Learned, pious, temperate in love and wine;   820
But, his life falling into Johnson's way,
    We 're told this great High Priest of all the Nine
Was whipped at college—a harsh sire—odd spouse,
For the first Mrs. Milton left his house.

XCII

All these are, *certes,* entertaining facts,
    Like Shakespeare's stealing deer, Lord Bacon's bribes;
Like Titus' youth, and Cæsar's earliest acts;
    Like Burns (whom Doctor Currie well describes);
Like Cromwell's pranks;—but although Truth exacts
    These amiable descriptions from the scribes,   830
As most essential to their Hero's story,
They do not much contribute to his glory.

XCIII

All are not moralists, like Southey, when
    He prated to the world of "Pantisocracy;"
Or Wordsworth unexcised, unhired, who then
    Seasoned his pedlar poems with Democracy;
Or Coleridge long before his flighty pen
    Let to the Morning Post its aristocracy;
When he and Southey, following the same path,
Espoused two partners (milliners of Bath).   840

XCIV

Such names at present cut a convict figure,
    The very Botany Bay in moral geography;
Their loyal treason, renegado rigour,
    Are good manure for their more bare biography;
Wordsworth's last quarto, by the way, is bigger
    Than any since the birthday of typography;
A drowsy, frowzy poem, called the "Excursion,"
Writ in a manner which is my aversion.

XCV

He there builds up a formidable dyke
    Between his own and others' intellect;   850
But Wordsworth's poem, and his followers, like
    Joanna Southcote's Shiloh and her sect,
Are things which in this century don't strike
    The public mind,—so few are the elect;
And the new births of both their stale Virginities
Have proved but Dropsies, taken for Divinities.

XCVI

But let me to my story: I must own,
    If I have any fault, it is digression,
Leaving my people to proceed alone,
    While I soliloquize beyond expression: 860
But these are my addresses from the throne,
    Which put off business to the ensuing session:
Forgetting each omission is a loss to
The world, not quite so great as Ariosto.

XCVII

I know that what our neighbours call *"longueurs,"*
    (We've not so good a *word,* but have the *thing,*
In that complete perfection which insures
    An epic from Bob Southey every spring—)
Form not the true temptation which allures
    The reader; but 't would not be hard to bring   870
Some fine examples of the *Epopée,*
To prove its grand ingredient is *Ennui.*

XCVIII

We learn from Horace, "Homer sometimes sleeps;"
    We feel without him,—Wordsworth sometimes wakes,—
To show with what complacency he creeps,
    With his dear *"Waggoners,"* around his lakes.
He wishes for "a boat" to sail the deeps—
    Of Ocean?—No, of air; and then he makes
Another outcry for "a little boat,"
And drivels seas to set it well afloat.   880

XCIX

If he must fain sweep o'er the ethereal plain,
    And Pegasus runs restive in his "Waggon,"
Could he not beg the loan of Charles's Wain?
    Or pray Medea for a single dragon?
Or if, too classic for his vulgar brain,
    He feared his neck to venture such a nag on,
And he must needs mount nearer to the moon,
Could not the blockhead ask for a balloon?

C

"Pedlars," and "Boats," and "Waggons!" Oh! ye shades
    Of Pope and Dryden, are we come to this?   890
That trash of such sort not alone evades
    Contempt, but from the bathos' vast abyss
Floats scumlike uppermost, and these Jack Cades
    Of sense and song above your graves may hiss—
The "little boatman" and his *Peter Bell*
Can sneer at him who drew "Achitophel!"

CI

T' our tale.—The feast was over, the slaves gone,
    The dwarfs and dancing girls had all retired;
The Arab lore and Poet's song were done,
    And every sound of revelry expired;   900
The lady and her lover, left alone,
    The rosy flood of Twilight's sky admired;—
Ave Maria! o'er the earth and sea,
That heavenliest hour of Heaven is worthiest thee!

CII

Ave Maria! blesséd be the hour!
    The time, the clime, the spot, where I so oft
Have felt that moment in its fullest power
    Sink o'er the earth—so beautiful and soft—
While swung the deep bell in the distant tower,
    Or the faint dying day-hymn stole aloft,   910
And not a breath crept through the rosy air,
And yet the forest leaves seemed stirred with prayer.

CIII

Ave Maria! 't is the hour of prayer!
    Ave Maria! 't is the hour of Love!
Ave Maria! may our spirits dare
    Look up to thine and to thy Son's above!
Ave Maria! oh that face so fair!
    Those downcast eyes beneath the Almighty Dove—
What though 't is but a pictured image?—strike—
That painting is no idol,—'t is too like.   920

CIV

Some kinder casuists are pleased to say,
    In nameless print—that I have no devotion;
But set those persons down with me to pray,
    And you shall see who has the properest notion
Of getting into Heaven the shortest way;
    My altars are the mountains and the Ocean,
Earth—air—stars,—all that springs from the great Whole,
Who hath produced, and will receive the Soul.

CV

Sweet Hour of Twilight!—in the solitude
    Of the pine forest, and the silent shore   930
Which bounds Ravenna's immemorial wood,
    Rooted where once the Adrian wave flowed o'er,
To where the last Cæsarean fortress stood,
    Evergreen forest! which Boccaccio's lore
And Dryden's lay made haunted ground to me,
How have I loved the twilight hour and thee!

CVI

The shrill cicalas, people of the pine,
    Making their summer lives one ceaseless song,
Were the sole echoes, save my steed's and mine,
    And Vesper bell's that rose the boughs along;   940
The spectre huntsman of Onesti's line,
    His hell-dogs, and their chase, and the fair throng
Which learned from this example not to fly
From a true lover,—shadowed my mind's eye.

CVII

Oh, Hesperus! thou bringest all good things—
    Home to the weary, to the hungry cheer,
To the young bird the parent's brooding wings,
    The welcome stall to the o'erlaboured steer;
Whate'er of peace about our hearthstone clings,
    Whate'er our household gods protect of dear,   950
Are gathered round us by thy look of rest;
Thou bring'st the child, too, to the mother's breast.

CVIII

Soft Hour! which wakes the wish and melts the heart
    Of those who sail the seas, on the first day
When they from their sweet friends are torn apart;
    Or fills with love the pilgrim on his way
As the far bell of Vesper makes him start,
    Seeming to weep the dying day's decay;
Is this a fancy which our reason scorns?
Ah! surely Nothing dies but Something mourns!   960

CIX

When Nero perished by the justest doom
    Which ever the Destroyer yet destroyed,
Amidst the roar of liberated Rome,
    Of nations freed, and the world overjoyed,
Some hands unseen strewed flowers upon his tomb:
    Perhaps the weakness of a heart not void
Of feeling for some kindness done, when Power
Had left the wretch an uncorrupted hour.

CX

But I'm digressing; what on earth has Nero,
    Or any such like sovereign buffoons,   970
To do with the transactions of my hero,
    More than such madmen's fellow man—the moon's?
Sure my invention must be down at zero,
    And I grown one of many "Wooden Spoons"
Of verse, (the name with which we Cantabs please
To dub the last of honours in degrees).

C X I

I feel this tediousness will never do—
    'T is being *too* epic, and I must cut down
(In copying) this long canto into two;
    They 'll never find it out, unless I own   980
The fact, excepting some experienced few;
    And then as an improvement 't will be shown:
I 'll prove that such the opinion of the critic is
From Aristotle *passim.*—See ΠΟΙΗΤΙΚΗΣ.

CANTO THE FOURTH

I

Nothing so difficult as a beginning
    In poesy, unless perhaps the end;
For oftentimes when Pegasus seems winning
    The race, he sprains a wing, and down we tend,
Like Lucifer when hurled from Heaven for sinning;
    Our sin the same, and hard as his to mend,
Being Pride, which leads the mind to soar too far,
Till our own weakness shows us what we are.

I I

But Time, which brings all beings to their level,
    And sharp Adversity, will teach at last   10
Man,—and, as we would hope,—perhaps the Devil,
    That neither of their intellects are vast:
While Youth's hot wishes in our red veins revel,
    We know not this—the blood flows on too fast;
But as the torrent widens towards the Ocean,
We ponder deeply on each past emotion.

I I I

As boy, I thought myself a clever fellow,
    And wished that others held the same opinion;
They took it up when my days grew more mellow,
    And other minds acknowledged my dominion: 20
Now my sere Fancy "falls into the yellow

Leaf," and Imagination droops her pinion,
And the sad truth which hovers o'er my desk
Turns what was once romantic to burlesque.

IV

And if I laugh at any mortal thing,
    'T is that I may not weep; and if I weep,
'T is that our nature cannot always bring
    Itself to apathy, for we must steep
Our hearts first in the depths of Lethe's spring,
    Ere what we least wish to behold will sleep: 30
Thetis baptized her mortal son in Styx;
A mortal mother would on Lethe fix.

V

Some have accused me of a strange design
    Against the creed and morals of the land,
And trace it in this poem every line:
    I don't pretend that I quite understand
My own meaning when I would be *very* fine;
    But the fact is that I have nothing planned,
Unless it were to be a moment merry—
A novel word in my vocabulary.   40

. . .

XII

"Whom the gods love die young," was said of yore,
    And many deaths do they escape by this: 90
The death of friends, and that which slays even more—
    The death of Friendship, Love, Youth, all that is,
Except mere breath: and since the silent shore
    Awaits at last even those who longest miss
The old Archer's shafts, perhaps the early grave
Which men weep over may be meant to save.

XIII

Haidée and Juan thought not of the dead—
    The Heavens, and Earth, and Air, seemed made for them:

They found no fault with Time, save that he fled;
    They saw not in themselves aught to condemn: 100
Each was the other's mirror, and but read
    Joy sparkling in their dark eyes like a gem;
And knew such brightness was but the reflection
Of their exchanging glances of affection.

XIV

The gentle pressure, and the thrilling touch,
    The least glance better understood than words,
Which still said all, and ne'er could say too much;
    A language, too, but like to that of birds,
Known but to them, at least appearing such
    As but to lovers a true sense affords;   110
Sweet playful phrases, which would seem absurd
To those who have ceased to hear such, or ne'er heard—

XV

All these were theirs, for they were children still,
    And children still they should have ever been;
They were not made in the real world to fill
    A busy character in the dull scene,
But like two beings born from out a rill,
    A Nymph and her belovéd, all unseen
To pass their lives in fountains and on flowers,
And never know the weight of human hours.   120

. . .

XXVI

Juan and Haidée gazed upon each other
    With swimming looks of speechless tenderness,
Which mixed all feelings—friend, child, lover, brother—
    All that the best can mingle and express
When two pure hearts are poured in one another,
    And love too much, and yet can not love less;
But almost sanctify the sweet excess
By the immortal wish and power to bless.

XXVII

Mixed in each other's arms, and heart in heart,
　　Why did they not then die?—they had lived too long　　210
Should an hour come to bid them breathe apart;
　　Years could but bring them cruel things or wrong;
The World was not for them—nor the World's art
　　For beings passionate as Sappho's song;
Love was born *with* them, *in* them, so intense,
It was their very Spirit—not a sense.

XXVIII

They should have lived together deep in woods,
　　Unseen as sings the nightingale; they were
Unfit to mix in these thick solitudes
　　Called social, haunts of Hate, and Vice, and Care:　　220
How lonely every freeborn creature broods!
　　The sweetest song-birds nestle in a pair;
The eagle soars alone; the gull and crow
Flock o'er their carrion, just like men below.

XXIX

Now pillowed cheek to cheek, in loving sleep,
　　Haidée and Juan their siesta took,
A gentle slumber, but it was not deep,
　　For ever and anon a something shook
Juan, and shuddering o'er his frame would creep;
　　And Haidée's sweet lips murmured like a brook　　230
A wordless music, and her face so fair
Stirred with her dream, as rose-leaves with the air.

XXX

Or as the stirring of a deep clear stream
　　Within an Alpine hollow, when the wind
Walks o'er it, was she shaken by the dream,
　　The mystical Usurper of the mind—
O'erpowering us to be whate'er may seem
　　Good to the soul which we no more can bind;
Strange state of being! (for 't is still to be)
Senseless to feel, and with sealed eyes to see.　　240

. . .

XLII

Lambro presented, and one instant more
    Had stopped this Canto, and Don Juan's breath,   330
When Haidée threw herself her boy before;
    Stern as her sire: "On me," she cried, "let Death
Descend—the fault is mine; this fatal shore
    He found—but sought not. I have pledged my faith;
I love him—I will die with him: I knew
Your nature's firmness—know your daughter's too."

XLIII

A minute past, and she had been all tears,
    And tenderness, and infancy; but now
She stood as one who championed human fears—
    Pale, statue-like, and stern, she wooed the blow;   340
And tall beyond her sex, and their compeers,
    She drew up to her height, as if to show
A fairer mark; and with a fixed eye scanned
Her Father's face—but never stopped his hand.

XLIV

He gazed on her, and she on him; 't was strange
    How like they looked! the expression was the same;
Serenely savage, with a little change
    In the large dark eye's mutual-darted flame;
For she, too, was as one who could avenge,
    If cause should be—a Lioness, though tame.   350
Her Father's blood before her Father's face
Boiled up, and proved her truly of his race.

XLV

I said they were alike, their features and
    Their stature, differing but in sex and years;
Even to the delicacy of their hand
    There was resemblance, such as true blood wears;
And now to see them, thus divided, stand
    In fixed ferocity, when joyous tears
And sweet sensations should have welcomed both,
Shows what the passions are in their full growth.   360

XLVI

The father paused a moment, then withdrew
    His weapon, and replaced it; but stood still,
And looking on her, as to look her through,
    "Not *I*," he said, "have sought this stranger's ill;
Not *I* have made this desolation: few
    Would bear such outrage, and forbear to kill;
But I must do my duty—how thou hast
Done thine, the present vouches for the past.

XLVII

"Let him disarm; or, by my father's head,
    His own shall roll before you like a ball!"   370
He raised his whistle, as the word he said,
    And blew; another answered to the call,
And rushing in disorderly, though led,
    And armed from boot to turban, one and all,
Some twenty of his train came, rank on rank;
He gave the word,—"Arrest or slay the Frank."

XLVIII

Then, with a sudden movement, he withdrew
    His daughter; while compressed within his clasp,
'Twixt her and Juan interposed the crew;
    In vain she struggled in her father's grasp—   380
His arms were like a serpent's coil: then flew
    Upon their prey, as darts an angry asp,
The file of pirates—save the foremost, who
Had fallen, with his right shoulder half cut through.

XLIX

The second had his cheek laid open; but
    The third, a wary, cool old sworder, took
The blows upon his cutlass, and then put
    His own well in; so well, ere you could look,
His man was floored, and helpless at his foot,
    With the blood running like a little brook   390
From two smart sabre gashes, deep and red—
One on the arm, the other on the head.

L

And then they bound him where he fell, and bore
　　Juan from the apartment: with a sign
Old Lambro bade them take him to the shore,
　　Where lay some ships which were to sail at nine.
They laid him in a boat, and plied the oar
　　Until they reached some galliots, placed in line;
On board of one of these, and under hatches,
They stowed him, with strict orders to the watches.　　**400**

LI

The world is full of strange vicissitudes,
　　And here was one exceedingly unpleasant:
A gentleman so rich in the world's goods,
　　Handsome and young, enjoying all the present,
Just at the very time when he least broods
　　On such a thing, is suddenly to sea sent,
Wounded and chained, so that he cannot move,
And all because a lady fell in love.

. . .

LVIII

The last sight which she saw was Juan's gore,
　　And he himself o'ermastered and cut down;
His blood was running on the very floor
　　Where late he trod, her beautiful, her own;　　**460**
Thus much she viewed an instant and no more,—
　　Her struggles ceased with one convulsive groan;
On her Sire's arm, which until now scarce held
Her writhing, fell she like a cedar felled.

LIX

A vein had burst, and her sweet lips' pure dyes
　　Were dabbled with the deep blood which ran o'er;
And her head drooped, as when the lily lies
　　O'ercharged with rain: her summoned handmaids bore
Their lady to her couch with gushing eyes;
　　Of herbs and cordials they produced their store,　　**470**
But she defied all means they could employ,
Like one Life could not hold, nor Death destroy.

LX

Days lay she in that state unchanged, though chill—
    With nothing livid, still her lips were red;
She had no pulse, but Death seemed absent still;
    No hideous sign proclaimed her surely dead;
Corruption came not in each mind to kill
    All hope; to look upon her sweet face bred
New thoughts of Life, for it seemed full of soul—
She had so much, Earth could not claim the whole.   480

. . .

LXIX

Twelve days and nights she withered thus; at last,
    Without a groan, or sigh, or glance, to show
A parting pang, the spirit from her passed:
    And they who watched her nearest could not know
The very instant, till the change that cast
    Her sweet face into shadow, dull and slow,   550
Glazed o'er her eyes—the beautiful, the black—
Oh! to possess such lustre—and then lack!

LXX

She died, but not alone; she held, within,
    A second principle of Life, which might
Have dawned a fair and sinless child of sin;
    But closed its little being without light,
And went down to the grave unborn, wherein
    Blossom and bough lie withered with one blight;
In vain the dews of Heaven descend above
The bleeding flower and blasted fruit of Love.   560

LXXI

Thus lived—thus died she; never more on her
    Shall Sorrow light, or Shame. She was not made
Through years or moons the inner weight to bear,
    Which colder hearts endure till they are laid
By age in earth: her days and pleasures were
    Brief, but delightful—such as had not staid

Long with her destiny; but she sleeps well
By the sea-shore, whereon she loved to dwell.

LXXII

That isle is now all desolate and bare,
    Its dwellings down, its tenants passed away;   570
None but her own and Father's grave is there,
    And nothing outward tells of human clay;
Ye could not know where lies a thing so fair,
    No stone is there to show, no tongue to say,
What was; no dirge, except the hollow sea's,
Mourns o'er the beauty of the Cyclades.

LXXIII

But many a Greek maid in a loving song
    Sighs o'er her name; and many an islander
With her Sire's story makes the night less long;
    Valour was his, and Beauty dwelt with her: 580
If she loved rashly, her life paid for wrong—
    A heavy price must all pay who thus err,
In some shape; let none think to fly the danger,
For soon or late Love is his own avenger.

. . .

CANTO THE SEVENTH*

I

O Love! O Glory! what are ye who fly
    Around us ever, rarely to alight?
There's not a meteor in the polar sky
    Of such transcendent and more fleeting flight.

*["These [the seventh and eighth] Cantos contain a full detail (like the storm in Canto Second) of the siege and assault of Ismael, with much of sarcasm on those butchers in large business, your mercenary soldiery. . . . With these things and these fellows it is necessary, in the present clash of philosophy and tyranny, to throw away the scabbard. I know it is against fearful odds; but the battle must be fought; and it will be eventually for the good of mankind, whatever it may be for the individual who risks himself."—Letter to Moore, August 8, 1822, *Letters*, 1901, vi. 101.]

Chill, and chained to cold earth, we lift on high
    Our eyes in search of either lovely light;
A thousand and a thousand colours they
Assume, then leave us on our freezing way.

II

And such as they are, such my present tale is,
    A nondescript and ever-varying rhyme,   10
A versified Aurora Borealis,
    Which flashes o'er a waste and icy clime.
When we know what all are, we must bewail us,
    But ne'ertheless I hope it is no crime
To laugh at *all* things—for I wish to know
What, after *all*, are *all* things—but a *show?*

III

They accuse me—*Me*—the present writer of
    The present poem—of—I know not what—
A tendency to under-rate and scoff
    At human power and virtue, and all that;   20
And this they say in language rather rough.
    Good God! I wonder what they would be at!
I say no more than hath been said in Danté's
Verse, and by Solomon and by Cervantes;

IV

By Swift, by Machiavel, by Rochefoucault,
    By Fénélon, by Luther, and by Plato;
By Tillotson, and Wesley, and Rousseau,
    Who knew this life was not worth a potato.
'T is not their fault, nor mine, if this be so,—
    For my part, I pretend not to be Cato,   30
Nor even Diogenes.—We live and die,
But which is best, *you* know no more than I.

V

Socrates said, our only knowledge was
    "To know that nothing could be known;" a pleasant
Science enough, which levels to an ass

Each man of wisdom, future, past, or present.
Newton (that proverb of the mind), alas!
  Declared, with all his grand discoveries recent,
That he himself felt only "like a youth
Picking up shells by the great ocean—Truth."   40

V I

Ecclesiastes said, "that all is vanity"—
  Most modern preachers say the same, or show it
By their examples of true Christianity:
  In short, all know, or very soon may know it;
And in this scene of all-confessed inanity,
  By Saint, by Sage, by Preacher, and by Poet,
Must I restrain me, through the fear of strife,
From holding up the nothingness of Life?

V I I

Dogs, or men!—for I flatter you in saying
  That ye are dogs—your betters far—ye may   50
Read, or read not, what I am now essaying
  To show ye what ye are in every way.
As little as the moon stops for the baying
  Of wolves, will the bright Muse withdraw one ray
From out her skies—then howl your idle wrath!
While she still silvers o'er your gloomy path.

V I I I

"Fierce loves and faithless wars"—I am not sure
  If this be the right reading—'t is no matter;
The fact 's about the same, I am secure;
  I sing them both, and am about to batter   60
A town which did a famous siege endure,
  And was beleaguered both by land and water
By Souvaroff, or Anglicè Suwarrow,
Who loved blood as an alderman loves marrow.

. . .

CANTO THE NINTH

I

Oh, Wellington! (or "Villainton"—for Fame
    Sounds the heroic syllables both ways;
France could not even conquer your great name,
    But punned it down to this facetious phrase—
Beating or beaten she will laugh the same,)
    You have obtained great pensions and much praise:
Glory like yours should any dare gainsay,
Humanity would rise, and thunder "Nay!"

II

I don't think that you used Kinnaird quite well
    In Marinèt's affair—in fact, 't was shabby,   10
And like some other things won't do to tell
    Upon your tomb in Westminster's old Abbey.
Upon the rest 't is not worth while to dwell,
    Such tales being for the tea-hours of some tabby;
But though your years as *man* tend fast to zero,
In fact your Grace is still but a *young Hero.*

III

Though Britain owes (and pays you too) so much,
    Yet Europe doubtless owes you greatly more:
You have repaired Legitimacy's crutch,
    A prop not quite so certain as before: 20
The Spanish, and the French, as well as Dutch,
    Have seen, and felt, how strongly you *restore;*
And Waterloo has made the world your debtor
(I wish your bards would sing it rather better).

IV

You are "the best of cut-throats:"—do not start;
    The phrase is Shakespeare's, and not misapplied:—
War 's a brain-spattering, windpipe-slitting art,
    Unless her cause by right be sanctified.
If you have acted *once* a generous part,
    The World, not the World's masters, will decide,   30

And I shall be delighted to learn who,
Save you and yours, have gained by Waterloo?

V

I am no flatterer—you 've supped full of flattery:
    They say you like it too—'t is no great wonder.
He whose whole life has been assault and battery,
    At last may get a little tired of thunder;
And swallowing eulogy much more than satire, he
    May like being praised for every lucky blunder,
Called "Saviour of the Nations"—not yet saved,—
And "Europe's Liberator"—still enslaved.   40

VI

I 've done. Now go and dine from off the plate
    Presented by the Prince of the Brazils,
And send the sentinel before your gate
    A slice or two from your luxurious meals:
He fought, but has not fed so well of late.
    Some hunger, too, they say the people feels:—
There is no doubt that you deserve your ration,
But pray give back a little to the nation.

VII

I don't mean to reflect—a man so great as
    You, my lord Duke! is far above reflection: 50
The high Roman fashion, too, of Cincinnatus,
    With modern history has but small connection:
Though as an Irishman you love potatoes,
    You need not take them under your direction;
And half a million for your Sabine farm
Is rather dear!—I 'm sure I mean no harm.

VIII

Great men have always scorned great recompenses:
    Epaminondas saved his Thebes, and died,
Not leaving even his funeral expenses:
    George Washington had thanks, and nought beside,   60
Except the all-cloudless glory (which few men's is)

To free his country: Pitt too had his pride,
And as a high-souled Minister of state is
Renowned for ruining Great Britain gratis.

IX

Never had mortal man such opportunity,
    Except Napoleon, or abused it more:
You might have freed fallen Europe from the unity
    Of Tyrants, and been blest from shore to shore:
And *now*—what *is* your fame? Shall the Muse tune it ye?
    Now—that the rabble's first vain shouts are o'er?   70
Go! hear it in your famished country's cries!
Behold the World! and curse your victories!

X

As these new cantos touch on warlike feats,
    To *you* the unflattering Muse deigns to inscribe
Truths, that you will not read in the Gazettes,
    But which 't is time to teach the hireling tribe
Who fatten on their country's gore, and debts,
    Must be recited—and without a bribe.
You *did great* things, but not being *great* in mind,
Have left *undone* the *greatest*—and mankind.   80

. . .

XVI

"To be, or not to be?"—Ere I decide,
    I should be glad to know that which *is being*.
'T is true we speculate both far and wide,
    And deem, because we *see,* we are *all-seeing:*
For my part, I 'll enlist on neither side,
    Until I see both sides for once agreeing.
For me, I sometimes think that Life is Death,
Rather than Life a mere affair of breath.

XVII

"Que scaise-je?" was the motto of Montaigne,
    As also of the first academicians: 130
That all is dubious which man may attain,

Was one of their most favourite positions.
  There 's no such thing as certainty, that 's plain
    As any of Mortality's conditions;
So little do we know what we 're about in
This world, I doubt if doubt itself be doubting.

XVIII

It is a pleasant voyage perhaps to float,
  Like Pyrrho, on a sea of speculation;
But what if carrying sail capsize the boat?
  Your wise men don't know much of navigation;   140
And swimming long in the abyss of thought
  Is apt to tire: a calm and shallow station
Well nigh the shore, where one stoops down and gathers
Some pretty shell, is best for moderate bathers.

XIX

"But Heaven," as Cassio says, "is above all—
  No more of this, then, let us pray!" We have
Souls to save, since Eve's slip and Adam's fall,
  Which tumbled all mankind into the grave,
Besides fish, beasts, and birds. "The sparrow's fall
  Is special providence," though how *it* gave   150
Offence, we know not; probably it perched
Upon the tree which Eve so fondly searched.

XX

Oh! ye immortal Gods! what is Theogony?
  Oh! thou, too, mortal man! what is Philanthropy?
Oh! World, which was and is, what is Cosmogony?
  Some people have accused me of Misanthropy;
And yet I know no more than the mahogany
  That forms this desk, of what they mean;—*Lykanthropy*
I comprehend, for without transformation
Men become wolves on any slight occasion.   160

XXI

But I, the mildest, meekest of mankind,
  Like Moses, or Melancthon, who have ne'er

Done anything exceedingly unkind,—
 And (though I could not now and then forbear
Following the bent of body or of mind)
 Have always had a tendency to spare,—
Why do they call me Misanthrope? Because
They hate me, not I them.—and here we 'll pause.

XXII

'T is time we should proceed with our good poem,—
 For I maintain that it is really good,   170
Not only in the body but the proem,
 However little both are understood
Just now,—but by and by the Truth will show 'em
 Herself in her sublimest attitude:
And till she doth, I fain must be content
To share her beauty and her banishment.

XXIII

Our hero (and, I trust, kind reader! yours)
 Was left upon his way to the chief city
Of the immortal Peter's polished boors,
 Who still have shown themselves more brave than witty. 180
I know its mighty Empire now allures
 Much flattery—even Voltaire's, and that 's a pity.
For me, I deem an absolute autocrat
Not a barbarian, but much worse than that.

XXIV

And I will war, at least in words (and—should
 My chance so happen—deeds), with all who war
With Thought;—and of Thought's foes by far most rude,
 Tyrants and sycophants have been and are.
I know not who may conquer: if I could
 Have such a prescience, it should be no bar 190
To this my plain, sworn, downright detestation
Of every despotism in every nation.

XXV

It is not that I adulate the people:
  Without *me,* there are demagogues enough,
And infidels, to pull down every steeple,
  And set up in their stead some proper stuff.
Whether they may sow scepticism to reap Hell,
  As is the Christian dogma rather rough,
I do not know;—I wish men to be free
As much from mobs as kings—from you as me.   200

XXVI

The consequence is, being of no party,
  I shall offend all parties:—never mind!
My words, at least, are more sincere and hearty
  Than if I sought to sail before the wind.
He who has nought to gain can have small art: he
  Who neither wishes to be bound nor bind,
May still expatiate freely, as will I,
Nor give my voice to slavery's jackal cry.

· · ·

CANTO THE ELEVENTH

*[Juan has come to England as an emissary of Catherine the
Great.]*

I

When Bishop Berkeley said "There was no matter,"
  And proved it—'t was no matter what he said:
They say his system 't is in vain to batter,
  Too subtle for the airiest human head;
And yet who can believe it? I would shatter
  Gladly all matters down to stone or lead,
Or adamant, to find the World a spirit,
And wear my head, denying that I wear it.

II

What a sublime discovery 't was to make the
  Universe universal egotism,   10

That all 's ideal—*all ourselves!*—I 'll stake the
    World (be it what you will) that *that 's* no schism.
Oh Doubt!—if thou be'st Doubt, for which some take thee,
    But which I doubt extremely—thou sole prism
Of the Truth's rays, spoil not my draught of spirit!
Heaven's brandy, though our brain can hardly bear it.

III

For ever and anon comes Indigestion
    (Not the most "dainty Ariel"), and perplexes
Our soarings with another sort of question:
    And that which after all my spirit vexes,   20
Is, that I find no spot where Man can rest eye on,
    Without confusion of the sorts and sexes,
Of Beings, Stars, and this unriddled wonder,
The World, which at the worst 's a *glorious* blunder—

IV

If it be chance—or, if it be according
    To the old text, still better:—lest it should
Turn out so, we 'll say nothing 'gainst the wording,
    As several people think such hazards rude.
They 're right; our days are too brief for affording
    Space to dispute what *no one* ever could   30
Decide, and *everybody one day* will
Know very clearly—or at least lie still.

V

And therefore will I leave off metaphysical
    Discussion, which is neither here nor there:
If I agree that what is, is; then this I call
    Being quite perspicuous and extremely fair;
The truth is, I 've grown lately rather phthisical:
    I don't know what the reason is—the air
Perhaps; but as I suffer from the shocks
Of illness, I grow much more orthodox.   40

V I

The first attack at once proved the Divinity
    (But *that* I never doubted, nor the Devil);
The next, the Virgin's mystical virginity;
    The third, the usual Origin of Evil;
The fourth at once established the whole Trinity
    On so uncontrovertible a level,
That I devoutly wished the three were four—
On purpose to believe so much the more.

. . .

X X X V

Juan presented in the proper place,
    To proper placemen, every Russ credential;
And was received with all the due grimace
    By those who govern in the mood potential,
Who, seeing a handsome stripling with smooth face,
    Thought (what in state affairs is most essential),
That they as easily might *do* the youngster,
As hawks may pounce upon a woodland songster.   280

X X X V I

They erred, as agéd men will do; but by
    And by we 'll talk of that; and if we don't,
'T will be because our notion is not high
    Of politicians and their double front,
Who live by lies, yet dare not boldly lie:—
    Now what I love in women is, they won't
Or can't do otherwise than lie—but do it
So well, the very Truth seems falsehood to it.

X X X V I I

And, after all, what is a lie? 'T is but
    The truth in masquerade; and I defy   290
Historians—heroes—lawyers—priests, to put
    A fact without some leaven of a lie.
The very shadow of true Truth would shut
    Up annals—revelations—poesy,
And prophecy—except it should be dated
Some years before the incidents related.

XXXVIII

Praised be all liars and all lies! Who now
    Can tax my mild Muse with misanthropy?
She rings the World's "Te Deum," and her brow
    Blushes for those who will not:—but to sigh   300
Is idle; let us like most others bow,
    Kiss hands—feet—any part of Majesty,
After the good example of "Green Erin,"
Whose shamrock now seems rather worse for wearing.

XXXIX

Don Juan was presented, and his dress
    And mien excited general admiration—
I don't know which was more admired or less:
    One monstrous diamond drew much observation,
Which Catherine in a moment of *"ivresse"*
    (In Love or Brandy's fervent fermentation),   310
Bestowed upon him, as the public learned;
And, to say truth, it had been fairly earned.

XL

Besides the ministers and underlings,
    Who must be courteous to the accredited
Diplomatists of rather wavering Kings,
    Until their royal riddle 's fully read,
The very clerks,—those somewhat dirty springs
    Of Office, or the House of Office, fed
By foul corruption into streams,—even they
Were hardly rude enough to earn their pay: 320

. . .

XLVI

He was a bachelor, which is a matter
    Of import both to virgin and to bride,
The former's hymeneal hopes to flatter;
    And (should she not hold fast by Love or Pride)
'T is also of some moment to the latter: 365
    A rib 's a thorn in a wed gallant's side,

Requires decorum, and is apt to double
The horrid sin—and what 's still worse, the trouble.

. . .

XLVIII

Fair virgins blushed upon him; wedded dames
    Bloomed also in less transitory hues;
For both commodities dwell by the Thames,
    The painting and the painted; Youth, Ceruse,   380
Against his heart preferred their usual claims,
    Such as no gentleman can quite refuse:
Daughters admired his dress, and pious mothers
Inquired his income, and if he had brothers.

. . .

LIV

However, he did pretty well, and was
    Admitted as an aspirant to all
The coteries, and, as in Banquo's glass,
    At great assemblies or in parties small,
He saw ten thousand living authors pass,
    That being about their average numeral;   430
Also the eighty "greatest living poets,"
As every paltry magazine can show *it 's.*

LV

In twice five years the "greatest living poet,"
    Like to the champion in the fisty ring,
Is called on to support his claim, or show it,
    Although 't is an imaginary thing.
Even I—albeit I 'm sure I did not know it,
    Nor sought of foolscap subjects to be king,—
Was reckoned, a considerable time,
The grand Napoleon of the realms of rhyme.   440

LVI

But Juan was my Moscow, and Faliero
    My Leipsic, and my Mont Saint Jean seems Cain:

La Belle Alliance of dunces down at zero,
    Now that the Lion 's fallen, may rise again:
But I will fall at least as fell my Hero;
    Nor reign at all, or as a *monarch* reign;
Or to some lonely isle of gaolers go,
With turncoat Southey for my turnkey Lowe.

LVII

Sir Walter reigned before me; Moore and Campbell
    Before and after; but now grown more holy,   450
The Muses upon Sion's hill must ramble
    With poets almost clergymen, or wholly;
And Pegasus has a psalmodic amble
    Beneath the very Reverend Rowley Powley,
Who shoes the glorious animal with stilts,
A modern Ancient Pistol—"by these hilts!"

LVIII

Still he excels that artificial hard
    Labourer in the same vineyard, though the vine
Yields him but vinegar for his reward.—
    That neutralised dull Dorus of the Nine;   460
That swarthy Sporus, neither man nor bard;
    That ox of verse, who *ploughs* for every line:—
Cambyses' roaring Romans beat at least
The howling Hebrews of Cybele's priest.—

LIX

Then there 's my gentle Euphues,—who, they say,
    Sets up for being a sort of *moral me;*
He 'll find it rather difficult some day
    To turn out both, or either, it may be.
Some persons think that Coleridge hath the sway;
    And Wordsworth has supporters, two or three;   470
And that deep-mouthed Bœotian "Savage Landor"
Has taken for a swan rogue Southey's gander.

LX

John Keats, who was killed off by one critique,
    Just as he really promised something great,

If not intelligible, without Greek
    Contrived to talk about the gods of late,
Much as they might have been supposed to speak.
    Poor fellow! His was an untoward fate;
'T is strange the mind, that very fiery particle,
Should let itself be snuffed out by an article.   480

. . .

LXIV

My Juan, whom I left in deadly peril
    Amongst live poets and *blue* ladies, passed
With some small profit through that field so sterile,
    Being tired in time—and, neither least nor last,
Left it before he had been treated very ill;
    And henceforth found himself more gaily classed   510
Amongst the higher spirits of the day,
The Sun's true son, no vapour, but a ray.

LXV

His morns he passed in business—which dissected,
    Was, like all business, a laborious nothing
That leads to lassitude, the most infected
    And Centaur Nessus garb of mortal clothing,
And on our sofas makes us lie dejected,
    And talk in tender horrors of our loathing
All kinds of toil, save for our country's good—
Which grows no better, though 't is time it should.   520

LXVI

His afternoons he passed in visits, luncheons,
    Lounging and boxing; and the twilight hour
In riding round those vegetable puncheons
    Called "Parks," where there is neither fruit nor flower
Enough to gratify a bee's slight munchings;
    But after all it is the only "bower"
(In Moore's phrase) where the fashionable fair
Can form a slight acquaintance with fresh air.

. . .

CANTO THE TWELFTH

· · ·

XXXIX

Oh, pardon my digression—or at least
    Peruse! 'T is always with a moral end
That I dissert, like grace before a feast:
    For like an agéd aunt, or tiresome friend,
A rigid guardian, or a zealous priest,
    My Muse by exhortation means to mend   310
All people, at all times, and in most places,
Which puts my Pegasus to these grave paces.

XL

But now I 'm going to be immoral; now
    I mean to show things really as they are,
Not as they ought to be: for I avow,
    That till we see what 's what in fact, we 're far
From much improvement with that virtuous plough
    Which skims the surface, leaving scarce a scar
Upon the black loam long manured by Vice,
Only to keep its corn at the old price.   320

· · ·

XLIV

Moreover I 've remarked (and I was once
    A slight observer in a modest way),
And so may every one except a dunce,
    That ladies in their youth a little gay,
Besides their knowledge of the World, and sense
    Of the sad consequence of going astray,   350
Are wiser in their warnings 'gainst the woe
Which the mere passionless can never know.

· · ·

LIV

But now I will begin my poem. 'T is
    Perhaps a little strange, if not quite new,

That from the first of Cantos up to this
    I 've not begun what we have to go through.
These first twelve books are merely flourishes,
    Preludios, trying just a string or two   430
Upon my lyre, or making the pegs sure;
And when so, you shall have the overture.

L V

My Muses do not care a pinch of rosin
    About what 's called success, or not succeeding:
Such thoughts are quite below the strain they have chosen;
    'T is a "great moral lesson" they are reading.
I thought, at setting off, about two dozen
    Cantos would do; but at Apollo's pleading,
If that my Pegasus should not be foundered,
I think to canter gently through a hundred.   440

L V I

Don Juan saw that Microcosm on stilts,
    Yclept the Great World; for it is the least,
Although the highest: but as swords have hilts
    By which their power of mischief is increased,
When Man in battle or in quarrel tilts,
    Thus the low world, north, south, or west, or east,
Must still obey the high—which is their handle,
Their Moon, their Sun, their gas, their farthing candle.

L V I I

He had many friends who had many wives, and was
    Well looked upon by both, to that extent   450
Of friendship which you may accept or pass,
    It does nor good nor harm; being merely meant
To keep the wheels going of the higher class,
    And draw them nightly when a ticket 's sent;
And what with masquerades, and fêtes, and balls,
For the first season such a life scarce palls.

LVIII

A young unmarried man, with a good name
   And fortune, has an awkward part to play;
For good society is but a game,
   "The royal game of Goose," as I may say,   460
Where everybody has some separate aim,
   An end to answer, or a plan to lay—
The single ladies wishing to be double,
The married ones to save the virgins trouble.

LIX

I don't mean this as general, but particular
   Examples may be found of such pursuits:
Though several also keep their perpendicular
   Like poplars, with good principles for roots;
Yet many have a method more *reticular*—
   "Fishers for men," like Sirens with soft lutes: 470
For talk six times with the same single lady,
And you may get the wedding-dresses ready.

LX

Perhaps you 'll have a letter from the mother,
   To say her daughter's feelings are trepanned;
Perhaps you 'll have a visit from the brother,
   All strut, and stays, and whiskers, to demand
What "your intentions are?"—One way or other
   It seems the virgin's heart expects your hand:
And between pity for her case and yours,
You 'll add to Matrimony's list of cures.   480

LXI

I 've known a dozen weddings made even *thus,*
   And some of them high names: I have also known
Young men who—though they hated to discuss
   Pretensions which they never dreamed to have shown—
Yet neither frightened by a female fuss,
   Nor by mustachios moved, were let alone,
And lived, as did the broken-hearted fair,
In happier plight than if they formed a pair.

LXII

There 's also nightly, to the uninitiated,
    A peril—not indeed like Love or Marriage,   490
But not the less for this to be depreciated:
    It is—I meant and mean not to disparage
The show of Virtue even in the vitiated—
    It adds an outward grace unto their carriage—
But to denounce the amphibious sort of harlot,
Couleur de rose, who 's neither white nor scarlet.

LXIII

Such is your cold coquette, who can't say "No,"
    And won't say "Yes," and keeps you on and off-ing
On a lee-shore, till it begins to blow—
    Then sees your heart wrecked, with an inward scoffing.   500
This works a world of sentimental woe,
    And sends new Werters yearly to their coffin;
But yet is merely innocent flirtation,
Not quite adultery, but adulteration.

LXIV

"Ye gods, I grow a talker!" Let us prate.
    The next of perils, though I place it *stern*est,
Is when, without regard to Church or State,
    A wife makes or takes love in upright earnest.
Abroad, such things decide few women's fate—
    (Such, early Traveller! is the truth thou learnest)—   510
But in old England, when a young bride errs,
Poor thing! Eve's was a trifling case to hers.

LXV

For 't is a low, newspaper, humdrum, lawsuit
    Country, where a young couple of the same ages
Can't form a friendship, but the world o'erawes it.
    Then there 's the vulgar trick of those d—d damages!
A verdict—grievous foe to those who cause it!—
    Forms a sad climax to romantic homages;
Besides those soothing speeches of the pleaders,
And evidences which regale all readers.   520

LXVI

But they who blunder thus are raw beginners;
    A little genial sprinkling of hypocrisy
Has saved the fame of thousand splendid sinners,
    The loveliest oligarchs of our Gynocracy;
You may see such at all the balls and dinners,
    Among the proudest of our aristocracy,
So gentle, charming, charitable, chaste—
And all by having *tact* as well as taste.

LXVII

Juan, who did not stand in the predicament
    Of a mere novice, had one safeguard more;   530
For he was sick——no, 't was not the word *sick* I meant—
    But he had seen so much good love before,
That he was not in heart so very weak;—I meant
    But thus much, and no sneer against the shore
Of white cliffs, white necks, blue eyes, bluer stockings—
Tithes, taxes, duns—and doors with double knockings.

LXVIII

But coming young from lands and scenes romantic,
    Where lives, not lawsuits, must be risked for Passion
And Passion's self must have a spice of frantic,
    Into a country where 't is half a fashion,   540
Seemed to him half commercial, half pedantic,
    Howe'er he might esteem this moral nation:
Besides (alas! his taste—forgive and pity!)
At *first* he did not think the women pretty.

· · ·

CANTO THE THIRTEENTH[*]

I

I now mean to be serious;—it is time,
    Since Laughter now-a-days is deemed too serious;

[*][February 12, 1823.]

A jest at Vice by Virtue 's called a crime,
  And critically held as deleterious:
Besides, the sad 's a source of the sublime,
  Although, when long, a little apt to weary us;
And therefore shall my lay soar high and solemn,
As an old temple dwindled to a column.

I I

The Lady Adeline Amundeville
  ('T is an old Norman name, and to be found
In pedigrees, by those who wander still
  Along the last fields of that Gothic ground)
Was high-born, wealthy by her father's will,
  And beauteous, even where beauties most abound,
In Britain—which, of course, true patriots find
The goodliest soil of Body and of Mind.

. . .

V I I

Rough Johnson, the great moralist, professed,
  Right honestly, "he liked an honest hater!"—
The only truth that yet has been confessed
  Within these latest thousand years or later.
Perhaps the fine old fellow spoke in jest:—
  For my part, I am but a mere spectator,
And gaze where'er the palace or the hovel is,
Much in the mode of Goethe's Mephistopheles;

V I I I

But neither love nor hate in much excess;
  Though 't was not once so. If I sneer sometimes,
It is because I cannot well do less,
  And now and then it also suits my rhymes.
I should be very willing to redress
  Men's wrongs, and rather check than punish crimes,
Had not Cervantes, in that too true tale
Of Quixote, shown how all such efforts fail.

10

50

60

IX

Of all tales 't is the saddest—and more sad,
 Because it makes us smile: his hero 's right,
And still pursues the right;—to curb the bad
 His only object, and 'gainst odds to fight
His guerdon: 't is his virtue makes him mad!
 But his adventures form a sorry sight;—   70
A sorrier still is the great moral taught
By that real Epic unto all who have thought.

X

Redressing injury, revenging wrong,
 To aid the damsel and destroy the caitiff;
Opposing singly the united strong,
 From foreign yoke to free the helpless native:—
Alas! must noblest views, like an old song,
 Be for mere Fancy's sport a theme creative,
A jest, a riddle, Fame through thin and thick sought!
And Socrates himself but Wisdom's Quixote?   80

XI

Cervantes smiled Spain's chivalry away;
 A single laugh demolished the right arm
Of his own country;—seldom since that day
 Has Spain had heroes. While Romance could charm,
The World gave ground before her bright array;
 And therefore have his volumes done such harm,
That all their glory, as a composition,
Was dearly purchased by his land's perdition.

XII

I 'm "at my old lunes"—digression, and forget
 The Lady Adeline Amundeville;   90
The fair most fatal Juan ever met,
 Although she was not evil nor meant ill;
But Destiny and Passion spread the net
 (Fate is a good excuse for our own will),
And caught them;—what do they *not* catch, methinks?
But I 'm not Œdipus, and Life 's a Sphinx.

. . .

XIV

Chaste was she, to Detraction's desperation,
    And wedded unto one she had loved well—
A man known in the councils of the Nation,
    Cool, and quite English, imperturbable,
Though apt to act with fire upon occasion,
    Proud of himself and her: the World could tell
Nought against either, and both seemed secure—
She in her virtue, he in his hauteur.

XV

It chanced some diplomatical relations,
    Arising out of business, often brought
Himself and Juan in their mutual stations
    Into close contact. Though reserved, nor caught
By specious seeming, Juan's youth, and patience,
    And talent, on his haughty spirit wrought,
And formed a basis of esteem, which ends
In making men what Courtesy calls friends.

XVI

And thus Lord Henry, who was cautious as
    Reserve and Pride could make him, and full slow
In judging men—when once his judgment was
    Determined, right or wrong, on friend or foe,
Had all the pertinacity Pride has,
    Which knows no ebb to its imperious flow,
And loves or hates, disdaining to be guided,
Because its own good pleasure hath decided.

. . .

XXII

He liked the gentle Spaniard for his gravity;
    He almost honoured him for his docility;
Because, though young, he acquiesced with suavity,
    Or contradicted but with proud humility.
He knew the World, and would not see depravity

110

120

170

In faults which sometimes show the soil's fertility,
    If that the weeds o'erlive not the first crop—
For then they are very difficult to stop.

. . .

XXXIV

There also was of course in Adeline
    That calm patrician polish in the address,
Which ne'er can pass the equinoctial line
    Of anything which Nature would express;
Just as a Mandarin finds nothing fine,—
    At least his manner suffers not to guess,   270
That anything he views can greatly please:
Perhaps we have borrowed this from the Chinese—

XXXV

Perhaps from Horace: his *"Nil admirari"*
    Was what he called the "Art of Happiness"—
An art on which the artists greatly vary,
    And have not yet attained to much success.
However, 't is expedient to be wary:
    Indifference, certes, don't produce distress;
And rash Enthusiasm in good society
Were nothing but a moral inebriety.   280

XXXVI

But Adeline was not indifferent: for
    (*Now* for a common-place!) beneath the snow,
As a Volcano holds the lava more
    Within—*et cætera*. Shall I go on?—No!
I hate to hunt down a tired metaphor,
    So let the often-used Volcano go.
Poor thing! How frequently, by me and others,
It hath been stirred up till its smoke quite smothers!

XXXVII

I 'll have another figure in a trice:—
    What say you to a bottle of champagne?   290
Frozen into a very vinous ice,

Which leaves few drops of that immortal rain,
Yet in the very centre, past all price,
   About a liquid glassful will remain;
And this is stronger than the strongest grape
Could e'er express in its expanded shape:

XXXVIII

'T is the whole spirit brought to a quintessence;
   And thus the chilliest aspects may concentre
A hidden nectar under a cold presence.
   And such are many—though I only meant her   300
From whom I now deduce these moral lessons,
   On which the Muse has always sought to enter.
And your cold people are beyond all price,
When once you 've broken their confounded ice.

XXXIX

But after all they are a North-West Passage
   Unto the glowing India of the soul;
And as the good ships sent upon that message
   Have not exactly ascertained the Pole
(Though Parry's efforts look a lucky presage),
   Thus gentlemen may run upon a shoal;   310
For if the Pole 's not open, but all frost
(A chance still), 't is a voyage or vessel lost.

. . .

XLII

The English winter—ending in July,
   To recommence in August—now was done.   330
'T is the postilion's paradise: wheels fly;
   On roads, East, South, North, West, there is a run.
But for post-horses who finds sympathy?
   Man's pity 's for himself, or for his son,
Always premising that said son at college
Has not contracted much more debt than knowledge.

. . .

L

Lord Henry and the Lady Adeline
    Departed like the rest of their compeers,
The peerage, to a mansion very fine;
    The Gothic Babel of a thousand years.
None than themselves could boast a longer line,
    Where Time through heroes and through beauties steers;
And oaks as olden as their pedigree
Told of their Sires—a tomb in every tree.   400

. . .

LV

To Norman Abbey whirled the noble pair,—
    An old, old Monastery once, and now
Still older mansion—of a rich and rare
    Mixed Gothic, such as artists all allow
Few specimens yet left us can compare
    Withal: it lies, perhaps, a little low,
Because the monks preferred a hill behind,
To shelter their devotion from the wind.   440

. . .

LXVII

Huge halls, long galleries, spacious chambers, joined
    By no quite lawful marriage of the arts,   530
Might shock a connoisseur; but when combined,
    Formed a whole which, irregular in parts,
Yet left a grand impression on the mind,
    At least of those whose eyes are in their hearts:
We gaze upon a giant for his stature,
Nor judge at first if all be true to nature.

LXVIII

Steel Barons, molten the next generation
    To silken rows of gay and gartered Earls,
Glanced from the walls in goodly preservation:
    And Lady Marys blooming into girls,   540
With fair long locks, had also kept their station:
    And Countesses mature in robes and pearls:

Also some beauties of Sir Peter Lely,
Whose drapery hints we may admire them freely.

LXIX

Judges in very formidable ermine
    Were there, with brows that did not much invite
The accused to think their lordships would determine
    His cause by leaning much from might to right:
Bishops, who had not left a single sermon;
    Attorneys-general, awful to the sight,   550
As hinting more (unless our judgments warp us)
Of the "Star Chamber" than of "Habeas Corpus."

. . .

LXXIV

But, reader, thou hast patient been of late,
    While I, without remorse of rhyme, or fear,
Have built and laid out ground at such a rate,
    Dan Phœbus takes me for an auctioneer.
That Poets were so from their earliest date,
    By Homer's "Catalogue of ships" is clear;   590
But a mere modern must be moderate—
I spare you then the furniture and plate.

LXXV

The mellow Autumn came, and with it came
    The promised party, to enjoy its sweets.
The corn is cut, the manor full of game;
    The pointer ranges, and the sportsman beats
In russet jacket:—lynx-like in his aim;
    Full grows his bag, and wonder*ful* his feats.
Ah, nutbrown partridges! Ah, brilliant pheasants!
And ah, ye poachers!—'T is no sport for peasants.   600

LXXVI

An English Autumn, though it hath no vines,
    Blushing with Bacchant coronals along
The paths o'er which the far festoon entwines
    The red grape in the sunny lands of song,

Hath yet a purchased choice of choicest wines;
    The Claret light, and the Madeira strong.
If Britain mourn her bleakness, we can tell her,
The very best of vineyards is the cellar.

LXXVII

Then, if she hath not that serene decline
    Which makes the southern Autumn's day appear   610
As if 't would to a second Spring resign
    The season, rather than to Winter drear,—
Of in-door comforts still she hath a mine,—
    The sea-coal fires, the "earliest of the year;"
Without doors, too, she may compete in mellow,
As what is lost in green is gained in yellow.

LXXVIII

And for the effeminate *villeggiatura*—
    Rife with more horns than hounds—she hath the chase,
So animated that it might allure a
    Saint from his beads to join the jocund race: 620
Even Nimrod's self might leave the plains of Dura,
    And wear the Melton jacket for a space:
If she hath no wild boars, she hath a tame
Preserve of bores, who ought to be made game.

LXXIX

The noble guests, assembled at the Abbey,
    Consisted of—we give the sex the *pas*—
The Duchess of Fitz-Fulke; the Countess Crabby,
    The Ladies Scilly, Busey;—Miss Eclat,
Miss Bombazeen, Miss Mackstay, Miss O'Tabby,
    And Mrs. Rabbi, the rich banker's squaw;   630
Also the honourable Mrs. Sleep,
Who looked a white lamb, yet was a black sheep:

LXXX

With other Countesses of Blank—but rank;
    At once the "lie" and the *élite* of crowds;

Who pass like water filtered in a tank,
　　All purged and pious from their native clouds;
Or paper turned to money by the Bank:
　　No matter how or why, the passport shrouds
The *passée* and the past; for good society
Is no less famed for tolerance than piety,—　　　　640

. . .

LXXXIV

There was Parolles, too, the legal bully,
　　Who limits all his battles to the Bar
And Senate: when invited elsewhere, truly,
　　He shows more appetite for words than war.
There was the young bard Rackrhyme, who had newly
　　Come out and glimmered as a six weeks' star.　　670
There was Lord Pyrrho, too, the great freethinker;
And Sir John Pottledeep, the mighty drinker.

LXXXV

There was the Duke of Dash, who was a—duke,
　　"Aye, every inch a" duke; there were twelve peers
Like Charlemagne's—and all such peers in *look*
　　And *intellect,* that neither eyes nor ears
For commoners had ever them mistook.
　　There were the six Miss Rawbolds—pretty dears!
All song and sentiment; whose hearts were set
Less on a convent than a coronet.　　　　680

LXXXVI

There were four Honourable Misters, whose
　　Honour was more before their names than after;
There was the *preux Chevalier de la Ruse,*
　　Whom France and Fortune lately deigned to waft here,
Whose chiefly harmless talent was to amuse;
　　But the clubs found it rather serious laughter,
Because—such was his magic power to please—
The dice seemed charmed, too, with his repartees.

LXXXVII

There was Dick Dubious, the metaphysician,
    Who loved philosophy and a good dinner;   690
Angle, the *soi-disant* mathematician;
    Sir Henry Silvercup, the great race-winner.
There was the Reverend Rodomont Precisian,
    Who did not hate so much the sin as sinner:
And Lord Augustus Fitz-Plantagenet,
Good at all things, but better at a bet.

LXXXVIII

There was Jack Jargon, the gigantic guardsman;
    And General Fireface, famous in the field,
A great tactician, and no less a swordsman,
    Who ate, last war, more Yankees than he killed.   700
There was the waggish Welsh Judge, Jefferies Hardsman,
    In his grave office so completely skilled,
That when a culprit came for condemnation,
He had his Judge's joke for consolation.

. . .

XCIV

If all these seem an heterogeneous mass
    To be assembled at a country seat,
Yet think, a specimen of every class
    Is better than a humdrum tête-à-tête.
The days of Comedy are gone, alas!
    When Congreve's fool could vie with Molière's *bête:*   750
Society is smoothed to that excess,
That manners hardly differ more than dress.

XCV

Our ridicules are kept in the back-ground—
    Ridiculous enough, but also dull;
Professions, too, are no more to be found
    Professional; and there is nought to cull
Of Folly's fruit; for though your fools abound,
    They 're barren, and not worth the pains to pull.

Society is now one polished horde,
Formed of two mighty tribes, the *Bores* and *Bored*.   760

. . .

XCIX

Lord Henry and his lady were the hosts;
    The party we have touched on were the guests.
Their table was a board to tempt even ghosts
    To pass the Styx for more substantial feasts.
I will not dwell upon *ragoûts* or roasts,
    Albeit all human history attests   790
That happiness for Man—the hungry sinner!—
Since Eve ate apples, much depends on dinner.

C

Witness the lands which "flowed with milk and honey,"
    Held out unto the hungry Israelites:
To this we have added since, the love of money,
    The only sort of pleasure which requites.
Youth fades, and leaves our days no longer sunny;
    We tire of mistresses and parasites;
But oh, ambrosial cash! Ah! who would lose thee?
When we no more can use, or even abuse thee!   800

CI

The gentlemen got up betimes to shoot,
    Or hunt: the young, because they liked the sport—
The first thing boys like after play and fruit;
    The middle-aged, to make the day more short;
For *ennui* is a growth of English root,
    Though nameless in our language:—we retort
The fact for words, and let the French translate
That awful yawn which sleep can not abate.

CII

The elderly walked through the library,
    And tumbled books, or criticised the pictures,   810
Or sauntered through the gardens piteously,

And made upon the hot-house several strictures,
Or rode a nag which trotted not too high,
   Or on the morning papers read their lectures,
Or on the watch their longing eyes would fix,
Longing at sixty for the hour of six.

C I I I

But none were *gêné:* the great hour of union
   Was rung by dinner's knell; till then all were
Masters of their own time—or in communion,
   Or solitary, as they chose to bear   820
The hours, which how to pass is but to few known.
   Each rose up at his own, and had to spare
What time he chose for dress, and broke his fast
When, where, and how he chose for that repast.

C I V

The ladies—some rouged, some a little pale—
   Met the morn as they might. If fine, they rode,
Or walked; if foul, they read, or told a tale,
   Sung, or rehearsed the last dance from abroad;
Discussed the fashion which might next prevail,
   And settled bonnets by the newest code,   830
Or crammed twelve sheets into one little letter,
To make each correspondent a new debtor.

C V

For some had absent lovers, all had friends;
   The earth has nothing like a she epistle,
And hardly Heaven—because it never ends—
   I love the mystery of a female missal,
Which, like a creed, ne'er says all it intends,
   But full of cunning as Ulysses' whistle,
When he allured poor Dolon:—you had better
Take care what you reply to such a letter.   840

C V I

Then there were billiards; cards, too, but *no* dice;—
   Save in the clubs no man of honour plays;—

Boats when 't was water, skating when 't was ice,
  And the hard frost destroyed the scenting days:
And angling, too, that solitary vice,
  Whatever Izaak Walton sings or says:
The quaint, old, cruel coxcomb, in his gullet
Should have a hook, and a small trout to pull it.

CVII

With evening came the banquet and the wine;
  The conversazione—the duet   850
Attuned by voices more or less divine
  (My heart or head aches with the memory yet).
The four Miss Rawbolds in a glee would shine;
  But the two youngest loved more to be set
Down to the harp—because to Music's charms
They added graceful necks, white hands and arms.

CVIII

Sometimes a dance (though rarely on field days,
  For then the gentlemen were rather tired)
Displayed some sylph-like figures in its maze;
  Then there was small-talk ready when required;   860
Flirtation—but decorous; the mere praise
  Of charms that should or should not be admired.
The hunters fought their fox-hunt o'er again,
And then retreated soberly—at ten.

CIX

The politicians, in a nook apart,
  Discussed the World, and settled all the spheres:
The wits watched every loophole for their art,
  To introduce a *bon-mot* head and ears;
Small is the rest of those who would be smart,
  A moment's good thing may have cost them years   870
Before they find an hour to introduce it;
And then, even *then,* some bore may make them lose it.

CX

But all was gentle and aristocratic
  In this our party; polished, smooth, and cold,

As Phidian forms cut out of marble Attic.
　　There now are no Squire Westerns, as of old;
And our Sophias are not so emphatic,
　　But fair as then, or fairer to behold:
We have no accomplished blackguards, like Tom Jones,
But gentlemen in stays, as stiff as stones.　　　　　　880

. . .

CANTO THE FOURTEENTH

I

If from great Nature's or our own abyss
　　Of Thought we could but snatch a certainty,
Perhaps Mankind might find the path they miss—
　　But then 't would spoil much good philosophy.
One system eats another up, and this
　　Much as old Saturn ate his progeny;
For when his pious consort gave him stones
In lieu of sons, of these he made no bones.

II

But System doth reverse the Titan's breakfast,
　　And eats her parents, albeit the digestion　　　　10
Is difficult. Pray tell me, can you make fast,
　　After due search, your faith to any question?
Look back o'er ages, ere unto the stake fast
　　You bind yourself, and call some mode the best one.
Nothing more true than *not* to trust your senses;
And yet what are your other evidences?

III

For me, I know nought; nothing I deny,
　　Admit—reject—contemn: and what know *you*,
Except perhaps that you were born to die?
　　And both may after all turn out untrue.　　　　20
An age may come, Font of Eternity,
　　When nothing shall be either old or new.

Death, so called, is a thing which makes men weep,
And yet a third of Life is passed in sleep.

IV

A sleep without dreams, after a rough day
 Of toil, is what we covet most; and yet
How clay shrinks back from more quiescent clay!
 The very Suicide that pays his debt
At once without instalments (an old way
 Of paying debts, which creditors regret),   30
Lets out impatiently his rushing breath,
Less from disgust of Life than dread of Death.

. . .

XIII

Besides, my Muse by no means deals in fiction:
 She gathers a repertory of facts,
Of course with some reserve and slight restriction,
 But mostly sings of human things and acts—   100
And that 's one cause she meets with contradiction;
 For too much truth, at first sight, ne'er attracts;
And were her object only what 's called Glory,
With more ease too she 'd tell a different story.

XIV

Love—War—a tempest—surely there 's variety;
 Also a seasoning slight of lucubration;
A bird's-eye view, too, of that wild, Society;
 A slight glance thrown on men of every station.
If you have nought else, here 's at least satiety,
 Both in performance and in preparation;   110
And though these lines should only line portmanteaus,
Trade will be all the better for these Cantos.

. . .

XXXI

Juan—in this respect, at least, like saints—
 Was all things unto people of all sorts,

And lived contentedly, without complaints,
    In camps, in ships, in cottages, or courts—
Born with that happy soul which seldom faints,   245
    And mingling modestly in toils or sports.
He likewise could be most things to all women,
Without the coxcombry of certain *she* men.

. . .

XLI

No marvel then he was a favourite;
    A full-grown Cupid, very much admired;
A little spoilt, but by no means so quite;
    At least he kept his vanity retired.
Such was his tact, he could alike delight
    The chaste, and those who are not so much inspired.
The Duchess of Fitz-Fulke, who loved *tracasserie,*
Began to treat him with some small *agacerie.*

XLII

She was a fine and somewhat full-blown blonde,
    Desirable, distinguished, celebrated   330
For several winters in the grand, *grand Monde:*
    I 'd rather not say what might be related
Of her exploits, for this were ticklish ground;
    Besides there might be falsehood in what 's stated:
Her late performance had been a dead set
At Lord Augustus Fitz-Plantagenet.

. . .

LXI

The Lady Adeline resolved to take
    Such measures as she thought might best impede
The farther progress of this sad mistake.
    She thought with some simplicity indeed;
But Innocence is bold even at the stake,
    And simple in the World, and doth not need
Nor use those palisades by dames erected,
Whose virtue lies in never being detected.

LXII

It was not that she feared the very worst:
  His Grace was an enduring, married man,   490
And was not likely all at once to burst
  Into a scene, and swell the clients' clan
Of Doctors' Commons; but she dreaded first
  The magic of her Grace's talisman,
And next a quarrel (as he seemed to fret)
With Lord Augustus Fitz-Plantagenet.

LXIII

Her Grace, too, passed for being an *intrigante,*
  And somewhat *méchante* in her amorous sphere;
One of those pretty, precious plagues, which haunt
  A lover with caprices soft and dear,   500
That like to *make* a quarrel, when they can't
  Find one, each day of the delightful year:
Bewitching, torturing, as they freeze or glow,
And—what is worst of all—won't let you go:

LXIV

The sort of thing to turn a young man's head,
  Or make a Werter of him in the end.
No wonder then a purer soul should dread
  This sort of chaste *liaison* for a friend;
It were much better to be wed or dead,
  Than wear a heart a Woman loves to rend.   510
'T is best to pause, and think, ere you rush on,
If that a *bonne fortune* be really *bonne.*

LXV

And first, in the overflowing of her heart,
  Which really knew or thought it knew no guile,
She called her husband now and then apart,
  And bade him counsel Juan. With a smile
Lord Henry heard her plans of artless art
  To wean Don Juan from the Siren's wile;
And answered, like a statesman or a prophet,
In such guise that she could make nothing of it.   520

LXVI

Firstly, he said, "he never interfered
    In anybody's business but the King's:"
Next, that "he never judged from what appeared,
    Without strong reason, of those sort of things:"
Thirdly, that "Juan had more brain than beard,
    And was not to be held in leading strings;"
And fourthly, what need hardly be said twice,
"That good but rarely came from good advice."

LXVII

And, therefore, doubtless to approve the truth
    Of the last axiom, he advised his spouse   530
To leave the parties to themselves, forsooth—
    At least as far as *bienséance* allows:
That time would temper Juan's faults of youth;
    That young men rarely made monastic vows;
That Opposition only more attaches—
But here a messenger brought in despatches:

LXVIII

And being of the council called "the Privy,"
    Lord Henry walked into his cabinet,
To furnish matter for some future Livy
    To tell how he reduced the Nation's debt;   540
And if their full contents I do not give ye,
    It is because I do not know them yet;
But I shall add them in a brief appendix,
To come between mine Epic and its index.

LXIX

But ere he went, he added a slight hint,
    Another gentle common-place or two,
Such as are coined in Conversation's mint,
    And pass, for want of better, though not new:
Then broke his packet, to see what was in 't,
    And having casually glanced it through,   550
Retired: and, as he went out, calmly kissed her,
Less like a young wife than an agéd sister.

. . .

LXXXVI

She loved her Lord, or thought so; but *that* love
    Cost her an effort, which is a sad toil,
The stone of Sisyphus, if once we move
    Our feelings 'gainst the nature of the soil.
She had nothing to complain of, or reprove,   685
    No bickerings, no connubial turmoil:
Their union was a model to behold,
Serene and noble,—conjugal, but cold.

. . .

XCI

She knew not her own heart; then how should I?
    I think not she was *then* in love with Juan:
If so, she would have had the strength to fly
    The wild sensation, unto her a new one:
She merely felt a common sympathy
    (I will not say it was a false or true one)
In him, because she thought he was in danger,—
Her husband's friend—her own—young—and a stranger.

XCII

She was, or thought she was, his friend—and this
    Without the farce of Friendship, or romance   730
Of Platonism, which leads so oft amiss
    Ladies who have studied Friendship but in France
Or Germany, where people *purely* kiss.
    To thus much Adeline would not advance;
But of such friendship as Man's may to Man be
She was as capable as Woman can be.

XCIII

No doubt the secret influence of the Sex
    Will there, as also in the ties of blood,
An innocent predominance annex,
    And tune the concord to a finer mood.   740
If free from Passion, which all Friendship checks,
    And your true feelings fully understood,
No friend like to a woman Earth discovers,
So that you have not been nor will be lovers.

XCIV

Love bears within its breast the very germ
 Of Change; and how should this be otherwise?
That violent things more quickly find a term
 Is shown through Nature's whole analogies;
And how should the most fierce of all be firm?
 Would you have endless lightning in the skies?   750
Methinks Love's very title says enough:
How should "the *tender* passion" e'er be *tough?*

. . .

XCVII

Whether Don Juan and chaste Adeline
 Grew friends in this or any other sense,   770
Will be discussed hereafter, I opine:
 At present I am glad of a pretence
To leave them hovering, as the effect is fine,
 And keeps the atrocious reader in *suspense:*
The surest way—for ladies and for books—
To bait their tender—or their tenter—hooks.

. . .

CI

'T is strange,—but true; for Truth is always strange—
 Stranger than fiction: if it could be told,
How much would novels gain by the exchange!
 How differently the World would men behold!
How oft would Vice and Virtue places change!   805
 The new world would be nothing to the old,
If some Columbus of the moral seas
Would show mankind their Souls' antipodes.

. . .

CANTO THE FIFTEENTH

. . .

VI

The Lady Adeline, right honourable,
    And honoured, ran a risk of growing less so;
For few of the soft sex are very stable
    In their resolves—alas! that I should say so;
They differ as wine differs from its label,   45
    When once decanted;—I presume to guess so,
But will not swear: yet both upon occasion,
Till old, may undergo adulteration.

. . .

XI

Some parts of Juan's history, which Rumour,
    That live Gazette, had scattered to disfigure,
She had heard; but Women hear with more good humour
    Such aberrations than we men of rigour:
Besides, his conduct, since in England, grew more
    Strict, and his mind assumed a manlier vigour:
Because he had, like Alcibiades,
The art of living in all climes with ease.

XII

His manner was perhaps the more seductive,
    Because he ne'er seemed anxious to seduce;   90
Nothing affected, studied, or constructive
    Of coxcombry or conquest: no abuse
Of his attractions marred the fair perspective,
    To indicate a Cupidon broke loose,
And seem to say, "Resist us if you can"—
Which makes a Dandy while it spoils a Man.

XIII

They are wrong—that's not the way to set about it;
    As, if they told the truth, could well be shown.
But, right or wrong, Don Juan was without it;
    In fact, his manner was his own alone: 100

Sincere he was—at least you could not doubt it,
  In listening merely to his voice's tone.
The Devil hath not in all his quiver's choice
An arrow for the Heart like a sweet voice.

XIV

By nature soft, his whole address held off
  Suspicion: though not timid, his regard
Was such as rather seemed to keep aloof,
  To shield himself than put *you* on your guard:
Perhaps 't was hardly quite assured enough,
  But Modesty 's at times its own reward,   110
Like Virtue; and the absence of pretension
Will go much farther than there 's need to mention.

XV

Serene, accomplished, cheerful but not loud;
  Insinuating without insinuation;
Observant of the foibles of the crowd,
  Yet ne'er betraying this in conversation;
Proud with the proud, yet courteously proud,
  So as to make them feel he knew his station
And theirs:—without a struggle for priority,
He neither brooked nor claimed superiority—   120

XVI

That is, with Men: with Women he was what
  They pleased to make or take him for; and their
Imagination 's quite enough for that:
  So that the outline 's tolerably fair,
They fill the canvas up—and *"verbum sat."*
  If once their phantasies be brought to bear
Upon an object, whether sad or playful,
They can transfigure brighter than a Raphael.

XVII

Adeline, no deep judge of character,
  Was apt to add a colouring from her own: 130

'T is thus the Good will amiably err,
    And eke the Wise, as has been often shown.
Experience is the chief philosopher,
    But saddest when his science is well known:
And persecuted Sages teach the Schools
Their folly in forgetting there are fools.

XVIII

Was it not so, great Locke? and greater Bacon?
    Great Socrates? And thou, Diviner still,
Whose lot it is by Man to be mistaken,
    And thy pure creed made sanction of all ill?   140
Redeeming Worlds to be by bigots shaken,
    How was thy toil rewarded? We might fill
Volumes with similar sad illustrations,
But leave them to the conscience of the nations.

XIX

I perch upon an humbler promontory,
    Amidst Life's infinite variety:
With no great care for what is nicknamed Glory,
    But speculating as I cast mine eye
On what may suit or may not suit my story,
    And never straining hard to versify,   150
I rattle on exactly as I 'd talk
With anybody in a ride or walk.

XX

I don't know that there may be much ability
    Shown in this sort of desultory rhyme;
But there 's a conversational facility,
    Which may round off an hour upon a time.
Of this I 'm sure at least, there 's no servility
    In mine irregularity of chime,
Which rings what 's uppermost of new or hoary,
Just as I feel the *Improvvisatore*.   160

XXI

"*Omnia vult* belle *Matho dicere—dic aliquando*
　　Et bene, *dic* neutrum, *dic aliquando* male."
The first is rather more than mortal can do;
　　The second may be sadly done or gaily;
The third is still more difficult to stand to;
　　The fourth we hear, and see, and say too, daily:
The whole together is what I could wish
To serve in this conundrum of a dish.

XXII

A modest hope—but Modesty 's my forte,
　　And Pride my feeble:—let us ramble on.　　　　　　　170
I meant to make this poem very short,
　　But now I can't tell where it may not run.
No doubt, if I had wished to pay my court
　　To critics, or to hail the *setting* sun
Of Tyranny of all kinds, my concision
Were more;—but I was born for opposition.

. . .

XXVII

We 'll do our best to make the best on 't:—March!
　　March, my Muse! If you cannot fly, yet flutter;　　　210
And when you may not be sublime, be arch,
　　Or starch, as are the edicts statesmen utter.
We surely may find something worth research:
　　Columbus found a new world in a cutter,
Or brigantine, or pink, of no great tonnage,
While yet America was in her non-age.

XXVIII

When Adeline, in all her growing sense
　　Of Juan's merits and his situation,
Felt on the whole an interest intense,—
　　Partly perhaps because a fresh sensation,　　　　　220
Or that he had an air of innocence,
　　Which is for Innocence a sad temptation,—

As Women hate half measures, on the whole,
She 'gan to ponder how to save his soul.

XXIX

She had a good opinion of Advice,
   Like all who give and eke receive it gratis,
For which small thanks are still the market price,
   Even where the article at highest rate is:
She thought upon the subject twice or thrice,
   And morally decided—the best state is   230
For Morals—Marriage; and, this question carried,
She seriously advised him to get married.

XXX

Juan replied, with all becoming deference,
   He had a predilection for that tie;
But that, at present, with immediate reference
   To his own circumstances, there might lie
Some difficulties, as in his own preference,
   Or that of her to whom he might apply:
That still he 'd wed with such or such a lady,
If that they were not married all already.   240

. . .

XL

But Adeline determined Juan's wedding
   In her own mind, and that 's enough for Woman:
But then, with whom? There was the sage Miss Reading,
   Miss Raw, Miss Flaw, Miss Showman, and Miss Knowman,
And the two fair co-heiresses Giltbedding.
   She deemed his merits something more than common:
All these were unobjectionable matches,
And might go on, if well wound up, like watches.   320

XLI

There was Miss Millpond, smooth as summer's sea,
   That usual paragon, an only daughter,
Who seemed the cream of Equanimity,

Till skimmed—and then there was some milk and water,
With a slight shade of blue too, it might be,
  Beneath the surface; but what did it matter?
Love 's riotous, but Marriage should have quiet,
And being consumptive, live on a milk diet.

XLII

And then there was the Miss Audacia Shoestring,
  A dashing *demoiselle* of good estate,   330
Whose heart was fixed upon a star or blue string;
  But whether English Dukes grew rare of late,
Or that she had not harped upon the true string,
  By which such Sirens can attract our great,
She took up with some foreign younger brother,
A Russ or Turk—the one 's as good as t' other.

XLIII

And then there was—but why should I go on,
  Unless the ladies should go off?—there was
Indeed a certain fair and fairy one,
  Of the best class, and better than her class,—   340
Aurora Raby, a young star who shone
  O'er Life, too sweet an image for such glass,
A lovely being, scarcely formed or moulded,
A rose with all its sweetest leaves yet folded;

XLIV

Rich, noble, but an orphan—left an only
  Child to the care of guardians good and kind—
But still her aspect had an air so lonely;
  Blood is not water; and where shall we find
Feelings of Youth like those which overthrown lie
  By Death, when we are left, alas! behind,   350
To feel, in friendless palaces, a home
Is wanting, and our best ties in the tomb?

XLV

Early in years, and yet more infantine
  In figure, she had something of Sublime

In eyes which sadly shone, as Seraphs' shine.
    All Youth—but with an aspect beyond Time;
Radiant and grave—as pitying Man's decline;
    Mournful—but mournful of another's crime,
She looked as if she sat by Eden's door,
And grieved for those who could return no more.   360

. . .

XLVIII

Now it so happened, in the catalogue
    Of Adeline, Aurora was omitted,
Although her birth and wealth had given her vogue,
    Beyond the charmers we have already cited;   380
Her beauty also seemed to form no clog
    Against her being mentioned as well fitted,
By many virtues, to be worth the trouble
Of single gentlemen who would be double.

XLIX

And this omission, like that of the bust
    Of Brutus at the pageant of Tiberius,
Made Juan wonder, as no doubt he must.
    This he expressed half smiling and half serious;
When Adeline replied with some disgust,
    And with an air, to say the least, imperious,   390
She marvelled "what he saw in such a baby
As that prim, silent, cold Aurora Raby?"

. . .

LV

Little Aurora deemed she was the theme
    Of such discussion. She was there a guest;
A beauteous ripple of the brilliant stream
    Of Rank and Youth, though purer than the rest,
Which flowed on for a moment in the beam
    Time sheds a moment o'er each sparkling crest.
Had she known this, she would have calmly smiled—
She had so much, or little, of the child.   440

LVI

The dashing and proud air of Adeline
    Imposed not upon her: she saw her blaze
Much as she would have seen a glow-worm shine,
    Then turned unto the stars for loftier rays.
Juan was something she could not divine,
    Being no Sibyl in the new world's ways;
Yet she was nothing dazzled by the meteor,
Because she did not pin her faith on feature.

LVII

His fame too,—for he had that kind of fame
    Which sometimes plays the deuce with Womankind,   450
A heterogeneous mass of glorious blame,
    Half virtues and whole vices being combined;
Faults which attract because they are not tame;
    Follies tricked out so brightly that they blind:—
These seals upon her wax made no impression,
Such was her coldness or her self-possession.

. . .

LXXXIII

Aurora, who in her indifference
    Confounded him in common with the crowd
Of flatterers, though she deemed he had more sense
    Than whispering foplings, or than witlings loud—   660
Commenced (from such slight things will great commence)
    To feel that flattery which attracts the proud
Rather by deference than compliment,
And wins even by a delicate dissent.

LXXXIV

And then he had good looks;—that point was carried
    Nem. con. amongst the women, which I grieve
To say leads oft to *crim. con.* with the married—
    A case which to the juries we may leave,
Since with digressions we too long have tarried.
    Now though we know of old that looks deceive,   670

And always have done,—somehow these good looks
Make more impression than the best of books.

LXXXV

Aurora, who looked more on books than faces,
    Was very young, although so very sage,
Admiring more Minerva than the Graces,
    Especially upon a printed page,
But Virtue's self, with all her tightest laces,
    Has not the natural stays of strict old age;
And Socrates, that model of all duty,
Owned to a *penchant*, though discreet, for beauty.   680

LXXXVI

And girls of sixteen are thus far Socratic,
    But innocently so, as Socrates;
And really, if the Sage sublime and Attic
    At seventy years had phantasies like these,
Which Plato in his dialogues dramatic
    Has shown, I know not why they should displease
In virgins—always in a modest way,
Observe,—for that with me 's a *sine quâ*.

LXXXVII

Also observe, that, like the great Lord Coke
    (See Littleton), whene'er I have expressed   690
Opinions two, which at first sight may look
    Twin opposites, the second is the best.
Perhaps I have a third too, in a nook,
    Or none at all—which seems a sorry jest:
But if a writer should be quite consistent,
How could he possibly show things existent?

LXXXVIII

If people contradict themselves, can I
    Help contradicting them, and everybody,
Even my veracious self?—But that 's a lie:
    I never did so, never will—how should I?   700

He who doubts all things nothing can deny:
   Truth's fountains may be clear—her streams are muddy,
And cut through such canals of contradiction,
That she must often navigate o'er fiction.

LXXXIX

Apologue, Fable, Poesy, and Parable,
   Are false, but may be rendered also true,
By those who sow them in a land that 's arable:
   'T is wonderful what Fable will not do!
'T is said it makes Reality more bearable:
   But what 's Reality? Who has its clue?   710
Philosophy? No; she too much rejects.
Religion? *Yes;* but which of all her sects?

XC

Some millions must be wrong, that 's pretty clear;
   Perhaps it may turn out that all were right.
God help us! Since we have need on our career
   To keep our holy beacons always bright,
'T is time that some new prophet should appear,
   Or *old* indulge man with a second sight.
Opinions wear out in some thousand years,
Without a small refreshment from the spheres.   720

XCI

But here again, why will I thus entangle
   Myself with Metaphysics? None can hate
So much as I do any kind of wrangle;
   And yet, such is my folly, or my fate,
I always knock my head against some angle
   About the present, past, or future state:
Yet I wish well to Trojan and to Tyrian,
For I was bred a moderate Presbyterian.

XCII

But though I am a temperate theologian,
   And also meek as a metaphysician,   730

Impartial between Tyrian and Trojan,
   As Eldon on a lunatic commission,—
In politics my duty is to show John
   Bull something of the lower world's condition.
It makes my blood boil like the springs of Hecla,
To see men let these scoundrel Sovereigns break law.

. . .

CANTO THE SIXTEENTH

. . .

XX

As Juan mused on mutability,
   Or on his Mistress—terms synonymous—
No sound except the echo of his sigh
   Or step ran sadly through that antique house;
When suddenly he heard, or thought so, nigh,
   A supernatural agent—or a mouse,
Whose little nibbling rustle will embarrass
Most people as it plays along the arras.   160

XXI

It was no mouse—but lo! a monk, arrayed
   In cowl and beads, and dusky garb, appeared,
Now in the moonlight, and now lapsed in shade,
   With steps that trod as heavy, yet unheard;
His garments only a slight murmur made;
   He moved as shadowy as the Sisters weird,
But slowly; and as he passed Juan by,
Glanced, without pausing, on him a bright eye.

XXII

Juan was petrified; he had heard a hint
   Of such a Spirit in these halls of old,   170
But thought, like most men, that there was nothing in 't
   Beyond the rumour which such spots unfold,
Coined from surviving Superstition's mint,

Which passes ghosts in currency like gold,
But rarely seen, like gold compared with paper.
And did he see this? or was it a vapour?

XXIII

Once, twice, thrice passed, repassed—the thing of air,
    Or earth beneath, or Heaven, or t' other place;
And Juan gazed upon it with a stare,
    Yet could not speak or move; but, on its base   180
As stands a statue, stood: he felt his hair
    Twine like a knot of snakes around his face;
He taxed his tongue for words, which were not granted,
To ask the reverend person what he wanted.

XXIV

The third time, after a still longer pause,
    The shadow passed away—but where? the hall
Was long, and thus far there was no great cause
    To think his vanishing unnatural:
Doors there were many, through which, by the laws
    Of physics, bodies whether short or tall   190
Might come or go; but Juan could not state
Through which the Spectre seemed to evaporate.

XXV

He stood—how long he knew not, but it seemed
    An age—expectant, powerless, with his eyes
Strained on the spot where first the figure gleamed
    Then by degrees recalled his energies,
And would have passed the whole off as a dream,
    But could not wake; he was, he did surmise,
Waking already, and returned at length
Back to his chamber, shorn of half his strength.   200

. . .

XXX

And when he walked down into the Saloon,
    He sate him pensive o'er a dish of tea,

Which he perhaps had not discovered soon,
  Had it not happened scalding hot to be,
Which made him have recourse unto his spoon;
  So much *distrait* he was, that all could see
That something was the matter—Adeline
The first—but *what* she could not well divine.   240

XXXI

She looked, and saw him pale, and turned as pale
  Herself; then hastily looked down, and muttered
Something, but what 's not stated in my tale.
  Lord Henry said, his muffin was ill buttered;
The Duchess of Fitz-Fulke played with her veil,
  And looked at Juan hard, but nothing uttered.
Aurora Raby with her large dark eyes
Surveyed him with a kind of calm surprise.

XXXII

But seeing him all cold and silent still,
  And everybody wondering more or less,   250
Fair Adeline inquired, "If he were ill?"
  He started, and said, "Yes—no—rather—yes."
The family physician had great skill,
  And being present, now began to express
His readiness to feel his pulse and tell
The cause, but Juan said, he was "quite well."

. . .

XXXV

Then Henry turned to Juan, and addressed
  A few words of condolence on his state:
"You look," quoth he, "as if you had had your rest
  Broke in upon by the Black Friar of late."
"What Friar?" said Juan; and he did his best
  To put the question with an air sedate,
Or careless; but the effort was not valid
To hinder him from growing still more pallid.   280

XXXVI

"Oh! have you never heard of the Black Friar?
    The Spirit of these walls?"—"In truth not I."
"Why Fame—but Fame you know 's sometimes a liar—
    Tells an odd story, of which by and by:
Whether with time the Spectre has grown shyer,
    Or that our Sires had a more gifted eye
For such sights, though the tale is half believed,
The Friar of late has not been oft perceived.

. . .

LV

And then, the mid-day having worn to one,
    The company prepared to separate;
Some to their several pastimes, or to none,
    Some wondering 't was so early, some so late.
There was a goodly match too, to be run
    Between some greyhounds on my Lord's estate,
And a young race-horse of old pedigree,
Matched for the spring, whom several went to see.

LVI

There was a picture-dealer who had brought
    A special Titian, warranted original,   490
So precious that it was not to be bought,
    Though Princes the possessor were besieging all—
The King himself had cheapened it, but thought
    The civil list he deigns to accept (obliging all
His subjects by his gracious acceptation)—
Too scanty, in these times of low taxation.

LVII

But as Lord Henry was a connoisseur,—
    The friend of Artists, if not Arts,—the owner,
With motives the most classical and pure,
    So that he would have been the very donor,   500
Rather than seller, had his wants been fewer,
    So much he deemed his patronage an honour,

Had brought the *capo d'opera*, not for sale,
But for his judgment—never known to fail.

LVIII

There was a modern Goth, I mean a Gothic
   Bricklayer of Babel, called an architect,
Brought to survey these grey walls which, though so thick,
   Might have from Time acquired some slight defect;
Who, after rummaging the Abbey through thick
   And thin, produced a plan whereby to erect   510
New buildings of correctest conformation,
And throw down old—which he called *restoration*.

. . .

LXI

There were two poachers caught in a steel trap,
   Ready for gaol, their place of convalescence;   530
There was a country girl in a close cap
   And scarlet cloak (I hate the sight to see, since—
Since—since—in youth, I had the sad mishap—
   But luckily I have paid few parish fees since):
That scarlet cloak, alas! unclosed with rigour,
Presents the problem of a double figure.

LXII

A reel within a bottle is a mystery,
   One can't tell how it e'er got in or out;
Therefore the present piece of natural history
   I leave to those who are fond of solving doubt;   540
And merely state, though not for the Consistory,
   Lord Henry was a Justice, and that Scout
The constable, beneath a warrant's banner,
Had bagged this poacher upon Nature's manor.

LXIII

Now Justices of Peace must judge all pieces
   Of mischief of all kinds, and keep the game
And morals of the country from caprices

Of those who have not a licence for the same;
And of all things, excepting tithes and leases,
   Perhaps these are most difficult to tame: 550
Preserving partridges and pretty wenches
Are puzzles to the most precautious benches.

      . . .

       X C V

But Adeline was occupied by fame
   This day; and watching, witching, condescending
To the consumers of fish, fowl, and game,
   And dignity with courtesy so blending,
As all must blend whose part it is to aim
   (Especially as the sixth year is ending)
At their lord's, son's, or similar connection's
Safe conduct through the rocks of re-elections.

       X C V I

Though this was most expedient on the whole
   And usual—Juan, when he cast a glance   810
On Adeline while playing her grand *rôle,*
   Which she went through as though it were a dance,
Betraying only now and then her soul
   By a look scarce perceptibly askance
(Of weariness or scorn), began to feel
Some doubt how much of Adeline was *real;*

       X C V I I

So well she acted all and every part
   By turns—with that vivacious versatility,
Which many people take for want of heart.
   They err—'t is merely what is called mobility,   820
A thing of temperament and not of art,
   Though seeming so, from its supposed facility;
And false—though true; for, surely, they're sincerest
Who are strongly acted on by what is nearest.

       X C V I I I

This makes your actors, artists, and romancers,
   Heroes sometimes, though seldom—sages never:

But speakers, bards, diplomatists, and dancers,
    Little that 's great, but much of what is clever;
Most orators, but very few financiers,
    Though all Exchequer Chancellors endeavour,   830
Of late years, to dispense with Cocker's rigours,
And grow quite figurative with their figures.

. . .

CVII

The Ghost at least had done him this much good,
    In making him as silent as a ghost,
If in the circumstances which ensued
    He gained esteem where it was worth the most;   900
And, certainly, Aurora had renewed
    In him some feelings he had lately lost,
Or hardened; feelings which, perhaps ideal,
Are so divine, that I must deem them real:—

CVIII

The love of higher things and better days;
    The unbounded hope, and heavenly ignorance
Of what is called the World, and the World's ways;
    The moments when we gather from a glance
More joy than from all future pride or praise,
    Which kindle manhood, but can ne'er entrance   910
The Heart in an existence of its own,
Of which another's bosom is the zone.

CIX

Who would not sigh Aἴ αἴ τὰν Κυθέρειαν
    That *hath* a memory, or that *had* a heart?
Alas! *her* star must fade like that of Dian:
    Ray fades on ray, as years on years depart.
Anacreon only had the soul to tie an
    Unwithering myrtle round the unblunted dart
Of Eros: but though thou hast played us many tricks,
Still we respect thee, *"Alma Venus Genetrix!"*   920

CX

And full of sentiments, sublime as billows
    Heaving between this World and Worlds beyond,
Don Juan, when the midnight hour of pillows
    Arrived, retired to his; but to despond
Rather than rest. Instead of poppies, willows
    Waved o'er his couch; he meditated, fond
Of those sweet bitter thoughts which banish sleep,
And make the worldling sneer, the youngling weep.

CXI

The night was as before: he was undrest,
    Saving his night-gown, which is an undress;   930
Completely *sans culotte*, and without vest;
    In short, he hardly could be clothed with less:
But apprehensive of his spectral guest,
    He sate with feelings awkward to express
(By those who have not had such visitations),
Expectant of the Ghost's fresh operations.

CXII

And not in vain he listened;—Hush! what's that?
    I see—I see—Ah, no!—'t is not—yet 't is—
Ye powers! it is the—the—the—Pooh! the cat!
    The Devil may take that stealthy pace of his!   940
So like a spiritual pit-a-pat,
    Or tiptoe of an amatory Miss,
Gliding the first time to a *rendezvous*,
And dreading the chaste echoes of her shoe.

CXIII

Again—what is 't? The wind? No, no,—this time
    It is the sable Friar as before,
With awful footsteps regular as rhyme,
    Or (as rhymes may be in these days) much more.
Again through shadows of the night sublime,
    When deep sleep fell on men, and the World wore   950
The starry darkness round her like a girdle
Spangled with gems—the Monk made his blood curdle.

CXIV

A noise like to wet fingers drawn on glass,
 Which sets the teeth on edge; and a slight clatter,
Like showers which on the midnight gusts will pass,
 Sounding like very supernatural water,
Came over Juan's ear, which throbbed, alas!
 For Immaterialism 's a serious matter;
So that even those whose faith is the most great
In Souls immortal, shun them *tête-à-tête*.   960

CXV

Were his eyes open?—Yes! and his mouth too.
 Surprise has this effect—to make one dumb,
Yet leave the gate which Eloquence slips through
 As wide as if a long speech were to come.
Nigh and more nigh the awful echoes drew,
 Tremendous to a mortal tympanum:
His eyes were open, and (as was before
Stated) his mouth. What opened next?—the door.

CXVI

It opened with a most infernal creak,
 Like that of Hell. "Lasciate ogni speranza,   970
Voi, ch'entrate!" The hinge seemed to speak,
 Dreadful as Dante's *rima*, or this stanza;
Or—but all words upon such themes are weak:
 A single shade 's sufficient to entrance a
Hero—for what is Substance to a Spirit?
Or how is 't *Matter* trembles to come near it?

CXVII

The door flew wide, not swiftly,—but, as fly
 The sea-gulls, with a steady, sober flight—
And then swung back; nor close—but stood awry,
 Half letting in long shadows on the light,   980
Which still in Juan's candlesticks burned high,
 For he had two, both tolerably bright,
And in the doorway, darkening darkness, stood
The sable Friar in his solemn hood.

CXVIII

Don Juan shook, as erst he had been shaken
   The night before; but being sick of shaking,
He first inclined to think he had been mistaken;
   And then to be ashamed of such mistaking;
His own internal ghost began to awaken
   Within him, and to quell his corporal quaking—   990
Hinting that Soul and Body on the whole
Were odds against a disembodied Soul.

CXIX

And then his dread grew wrath, and his wrath fierce,
   And he arose, advanced—the Shade retreated;
But Juan, eager now the truth to pierce,
   Followed, his veins no longer cold, but heated,
Resolved to thrust the mystery *carte* and *tierce*,
   At whatsoever risk of being defeated:
The Ghost stopped, menaced, then retired, until
He reached the ancient wall, then stood stone still.   1000

CXX

Juan put forth one arm—Eternal powers!
   It touched no soul, nor body, but the wall,
On which the moonbeams fell in silvery showers,
   Chequered with all the tracery of the Hall;
He shuddered, as no doubt the bravest cowers
   When he can't tell what 't is that doth appal.
How odd, a single hobgoblin's nonentity
Should cause more fear than a whole host's identity!

CXXI

But still the Shade remained: the blue eyes glared,
   And rather variably for stony death;   1010
Yet one thing rather good the grave had spared,
   The Ghost had a remarkably sweet breath:
A straggling curl showed he had been fair-haired;
   A red lip, with two rows of pearls beneath,
Gleamed forth, as through the casement's ivy shroud
The Moon peeped, just escaped from a grey cloud.

CXXII

And Juan, puzzled, but still curious, thrust
   His other arm forth—Wonder upon wonder!
It pressed upon a hard but glowing bust,
   Which beat as if there was a warm heart under.   1020
He found, as people on most trials must,
   That he had made at first a silly blunder,
And that in his confusion he had caught
Only the wall, instead of what he sought.

CXXIII

The Ghost, if Ghost it were, seemed a sweet soul
   As ever lurked beneath a holy hood:
A dimpled chin, a neck of ivory, stole
   Forth into something much like flesh and blood;
Back fell the sable frock and dreary cowl,
   And they revealed—alas! that e'er they should!   1030
In full, voluptuous, but *not o'er*grown bulk,
The phantom of her frolic Grace—Fitz-Fulke!*

CANTO THE SEVENTEENTH†

. . .

V

There is a common-place book argument,
   Which glibly glides from every tongue;
When any dare a new light to present,
   "If you are right, then everybody 's wrong"!
Suppose the converse of this precedent
   So often urged, so loudly and so long;
"If you are wrong, then everybody 's right"!
Was ever everybody yet so quite?   40

VI

Therefore I would solicit free discussion
   Upon all points—no matter what, or whose—

*[End of Canto 16. B. My. 6, 1823.—*MS.*]
†[May 8, 1823.—*MS.*]

Because as Ages upon Ages push on,
    The last is apt the former to accuse
Of pillowing its head on a pin-cushion,
    Heedless of pricks because it was obtuse:
What was a paradox becomes a truth or
A something like it—witness Luther!

VII

The Sacraments have been reduced to two,
    And Witches unto none, though somewhat late   50
Since burning agéd women (save a few—
    Not witches only b—ches—who create
Mischief in families, as some know or knew,
    Should still be singed, but lightly, let me state,)
Has been declared an act of inurbanity,
Malgré Sir Matthew Hales's great humanity.

VIII

Great Galileo was debarred the Sun,
    Because he fixed it; and, to stop his talking,
How Earth could round the solar orbit run,
    Found his own legs embargoed from mere walking: 60
The man was well-nigh dead, ere men begun
    To think his skull had not some need of caulking;
But now, it seems, he's right—his notion just:
No doubt a consolation to his dust.

IX

Pythagoras, Locke, Socrates—but pages
    Might be filled up, as vainly as before,
With the sad usage of all sorts of sages,
    Who in his life-time, each, was deemed a Bore!
The loftiest minds outrun their tardy ages:
    This they must bear with and, perhaps, much more;   70
The wise man 's sure when he no more can share it, he
Will have a firm Post Obit on posterity.

X

If such doom waits each intellectual Giant,
     We little people in our lesser way,
In Life's small rubs should surely be more pliant,
     And so for one will I—as well I may—
Would that I were less bilious—but, oh, fie on 't!
     Just as I make my mind up every day,
To be a *"totus, teres,"* Stoic, Sage,
The wind shifts and I fly into a rage.   80

X I

Temperate I am—yet never had a temper;
     Modest I am—yet with some slight assurance;
Changeable too—yet somehow *"Idem semper:"*
     Patient—but not enamoured of endurance;
Cheerful—but, sometimes, rather apt to whimper:
     Mild—but at times a sort of *"Hercules furens:"*
So that I almost think that the same skin
For one without—has two or three within.

X I I

Our Hero was, in Canto the Sixteenth,
     Left in a tender moonlight situation,   90
Such as enables Man to show his strength
     Moral or physical: on this occasion
Whether his virtue triumphed—or, at length,
     His vice—for he was of a kindling nation—
Is more than I shall venture to describe;—
Unless some Beauty with a kiss should bribe.

X I I I

I leave the thing a problem, like all things:—
     The morning came—and breakfast, tea and toast,
Of which most men partake, but no one sings.
     The company whose birth, wealth, worth, has cost   100
My trembling Lyre already several strings,
     Assembled with our hostess, and mine host;
The guests dropped in—the last but one, Her Grace,
The latest, Juan, with his virgin face.

XIV

Which best it is to encounter—Ghost, or none,
    'Twere difficult to say—but Juan looked
As if he had combated with more than one,
    Being wan and worn, with eyes that hardly brooked
The light, that through the Gothic window shone:
    Her Grace, too, had a sort of air rebuked—   110
Seemed pale and shivered, as if she had kept
A vigil, or dreamt rather more than slept.

TALES

THE GIAOUR

A FRAGMENT OF A TURKISH TALE

[*Byron's Oriental tales have some realism of detail, for the author had lived in the Near East and knew much of costumes and customs, but these tales are melodramatic in the extreme. They were very popular in his own day both for their dark hints of autobiography and their picturesque description. The chief interest for the modern reader, aside from the revelation of Byronic character, rests in their "purple passages" on Greece, some of which are included here. The Giaour, as Byron took care to hint, had some factual basis. It was rumored that while at Athens he had rescued a girl, who, according to Turkish custom, as a punishment for infidelity, had been sewed in a sack and was to be cast into the sea. The passage quoted is a picture of Greece under the Turkish yoke, a death in life.*]

No breath of air to break the wave
That rolls below the Athenian's grave,
That tomb which, gleaming o'er the cliff,
First greets the homeward-veering skiff
High o'er the land he saved in vain:
When shall such Hero live again?

* * * * *

Fair clime! where every season smiles
Benignant o'er those blesséd isles,
Which, seen from far Colonna's height,
Make glad the heart that hails the sight,   10
And lend to loneliness delight.
There mildly dimpling, Ocean's cheek
Reflects the tints of many a peak
Caught by the laughing tides that lave
These Edens of the Eastern wave:
And if at times a transient breeze
Break the blue crystal of the seas,
Or sweep one blossom from the trees,
How welcome is each gentle air
That wakes and wafts the odours there!   20
For there the Rose, o'er crag or vale,
Sultana of the Nightingale,

   The maid for whom his melody,

  His thousand songs are heard on high,
Blooms blushing to her lover's tale:
His queen, the garden queen, his Rose,
Unbent by winds, unchilled by snows,
Far from the winters of the west,
By every breeze and season blest,
Returns the sweets by Nature given   30
In softest incense back to Heaven;
And grateful yields that smiling sky
Her fairest hue and fragrant sigh.
And many a summer flower is there,
And many a shade that Love might share,
And many a grotto, meant for rest,
That holds the pirate for a guest;
Whose bark in sheltering cove below
Lurks for the passing peaceful prow,
Till the gay mariner's guitar   40
Is heard, and seen the Evening Star;
Then stealing with the muffled oar,
Far shaded by the rocky shore,
Rush the night-prowlers on the prey,

And turn to groans his roundelay.
Strange—that where Nature loved to trace,
As if for Gods, a dwelling place,
And every charm and grace hath mixed
Within the Paradise she fixed,
There man, enamoured of distress,   50
Should mar it into wilderness,
And trample, brute-like, o'er each flower
That tasks not one laborious hour;
Nor claims the culture of his hand
To bloom along the fairy land,
But springs as to preclude his care,
And sweetly woos him—but to spare!
Strange—that where all is Peace beside,
There Passion riots in her pride,
And Lust and Rapine wildly reign   60
To darken o'er the fair domain.
It is as though the Fiends prevailed
Against the Seraphs they assailed,
And, fixed on heavenly thrones, should dwell
The freed inheritors of Hell;
So soft the scene, so formed for joy,
So curst the tyrants that destroy!

   He who hath bent him o'er the dead
Ere the first day of Death is fled,
The first dark day of Nothingness,   70
The last of Danger and Distress,
(Before Decay's effacing fingers
Have swept the lines where Beauty lingers,)
And marked the mild angelic air,
The rapture of Repose that's there,
The fixed yet tender traits that streak
The languor of the placid cheek,
And—but for that sad shrouded eye,
   That fires not, wins not, weeps not, now,
   And but for that chill, changeless brow,   80
Where cold Obstruction's apathy

Appals the gazing mourner's heart,
As if to him it could impart
The doom he dreads, yet dwells upon;
Yes, but for these and these alone,
Some moments, aye, one treacherous hour,
He still might doubt the Tyrant's power;
So fair, so calm, so softly sealed,
The first, last look by Death revealed!
Such is the aspect of this shore: 90
'Tis Greece, but living Greece no more!
So coldly sweet, so deadly fair,
We start, for Soul is wanting there.
Hers is the loveliness in death,
That parts not quite with parting breath;
But beauty with that fearful bloom,
That hue which haunts it to the tomb,
Expression's last receding ray,
A gilded Halo hovering round decay,
The farewell beam of Feeling past away!   100
Spark of that flame, perchance of heavenly birth,
Which gleams, but warms no more its cherished earth!

   Clime of the unforgotten brave!
Whose land from plain to mountain-cave
Was Freedom's home or Glory's grave!
Shrine of the mighty! can it be,
That this is all remains of thee?
Approach, thou craven crouching slave:
   Say, is not this Thermopylæ?
These waters blue that round you lave,—   110
   Oh servile offspring of the free—
Pronounce, what sea, what shore is this?
The gulf, the rock of Salamis!
These scenes, their story not unknown,
Arise, and make again your own;
Snatch from the ashes of your Sires
The embers of their former fires;
And he who in the strife expires

Will add to theirs a name of fear
That Tyranny shall quake to hear,   120
And leave his sons a hope, a fame,
They too will rather die than shame:
For Freedom's battle once begun,
Bequeathed by bleeding Sire to Son,
Though baffled oft is ever won.
Bear witness, Greece, thy living page!
Attest it many a deathless age!
While kings, in dusty darkness hid,
Have left a nameless pyramid,
Thy Heroes, though the general doom   130
Hath swept the column from their tomb,
A mightier monument command,
The mountains of their native land!
There points thy Muse to stranger's eye
The graves of those that cannot die!
'Twere long to tell, and sad to trace,
Each step from Splendour to Disgrace;
Enough—no foreign foe could quell
Thy soul, till from itself it fell;
Yet—Self-abasement paved the way   140
To villain-bonds and despot sway.

What can he tell who treads thy shore?
    No legend of thine olden time,
No theme on which the Muse might soar
High as thine own in days of yore,
    When man was worthy of thy clime.
The hearts within thy valleys bred,
The fiery souls that might have led
    Thy sons to deeds sublime,
Now crawl from cradle to the Grave,   150
Slaves—nay, the bondsmen of a Slave,
    And callous, save to crime;
Stained with each evil that pollutes
Mankind, where least above the brutes;
Without even savage virtue blest,

Without one free or valiant breast,
Still to the neighbouring ports they waft
Proverbial wiles, and ancient craft;
In this the subtle Greek is found,
For this, and this alone, renowned,   160
In vain might Liberty invoke
The spirit to its bondage broke,
Or raise the neck that courts the yoke:
No more her sorrows I bewail,
Yet this will be a mournful tale,
And they who listen may believe,
Who heard it first had cause to grieve.
                    * * * * *
    Far, dark, along the blue sea glancing,
The shadows of the rocks advancing
Start on the Fisher's eye like boat   170
Of island-pirate or Mainote;
And fearful for his light caïque,
He shuns the near but doubtful creek:
Though worn and weary with his toil,
And cumbered with his scaly spoil,
Slowly, yet strongly, plies the oar,
Till Port Leone's safer shore
Receives him by the lovely light
That best becomes an Eastern night.
                    * * * * *
    Who thundering comes on blackest steed,   180
With slackened bit and hoof of speed?
Beneath the clattering iron's sound
The caverned Echoes wake around
In lash for lash, and bound for bound;
The foam that streaks the courser's side
Seems gathered from the Ocean-tide:
Though weary waves are sunk to rest,
There's none within his rider's breast;
And though to-morrow's tempest lower,
'Tis calmer than thy heart, young Giaour!   190
I know thee not, I loathe thy race,

But in thy lineaments I trace
What Time shall strengthen, not efface:
Though young and pale, that sallow front
Is scathed by fiery Passion's brunt;
Though bent on earth thine evil eye,
As meteor-like thou glidest by,
Right well I view and deem thee one
Whom Othman's sons should slay or shun.

On—on he hastened, and he drew   200
My gaze of wonder as he flew:
Though like a Demon of the night
He passed, and vanished from my sight,
His aspect and his air impressed
A troubled memory on my breast,
And long upon my startled ear
Rung his dark courser's hoofs of fear.
He spurs his steed; he nears the steep,
That, jutting, shadows o'er the deep;
He winds around; he hurries by;   210
The rock relieves him from mine eye;
For, well I ween, unwelcome he
Whose glance is fixed on those that flee;
And not a star but shines too bright
On him who takes such timeless flight.
He wound along; but ere he passed
One glance he snatched, as if his last,
A moment checked his wheeling steed,
A moment breathed him from his speed,
A moment on his stirrup stood—   220
Why looks he o'er the olive wood?
The Crescent glimmers on the hill,
The Mosque's high lamps are quivering still:
Though too remote for sound to wake
In echoes of the far tophaike,
The flashes of each joyous peal
Are seen to prove the Moslem's zeal.
To-night, set Rhamazani's sun;

To-night, the Bairam feast's begun;
To-night—but who and what art thou   230
Of foreign garb and fearful brow?
And what are these to thine or thee,
That thou shouldst either pause or flee?
He stood—some dread was on his face,
Soon Hatred settled in its place:
It rose not with the reddening flush
Of transient Anger's hasty blush,
But pale as marble o'er the tomb,
Whose ghastly whiteness aids its gloom.
His brow was bent, his eye was glazed;   240
He raised his arm, and fiercely raised,
And sternly shook his hand on high,
As doubting to return or fly;
Impatient of his flight delayed,
Here loud his raven charger neighed—
Down glanced that hand, and grasped his blade;
That sound had burst his waking dream,
As Slumber starts at owlet's scream.
The spur hath lanced his courser's sides;
Away—away—for life he rides: 250
Swift as the hurled on high jerreed
Springs to the touch his startled steed;
The rock is doubled, and the shore
Shakes with the clattering tramp no more;
The crag is won, no more is seen
His Christian crest and haughty mien.
'Twas but an instant he restrained
That fiery barb so sternly reined;
'Twas but a moment that he stood,
Then sped as if by Death pursued;   260
But in that instant o'er his soul
Winters of Memory seemed to roll,
And gather in that drop of time
A life of pain, an age of crime.
O'er him who loves, or hates, or fears,
Such moment pours the grief of years:

What felt *he* then, at once opprest
By all that most distracts the breast?
That pause, which pondered o'er his fate,
Oh, who its dreary length shall date!   270
Though in Time's record nearly nought,
It was Eternity to Thought!
For infinite as boundless space
The thought that Conscience must embrace,
Which in itself can comprehend
Woe without name, or hope, or end.

    The hour is past, the Giaour is gone;
And did he fly or fall alone?
Woe to that hour he came or went!
The curse for Hassan's sin was sent   280
To turn a palace to a tomb;
He came, he went, like the Simoom,
That harbinger of Fate and gloom,
Beneath whose widely-wasting breath
The very cypress droops to death—
Dark tree, still sad when others' grief is fled,
The only constant mourner o'er the dead!

    The steed is vanished from the stall;
No serf is seen in Hassan's hall;
The lonely Spider's thin gray pall   290
Waves slowly widening o'er the wall;
The Bat builds in his Haram bower,
And in the fortress of his power
The owl usurps the beacon-tower;
The wild-dog howls o'er the fountain's brim,
With baffled thirst, and famine, grim;
For the stream had shrunk from its marble bed,
Where the weeds and the desolate dust are spread.
'Twas sweet of yore to see it play
And chase the sultriness of day,   300
As springing high the silver dew

In whirls fantastically flew,
And flung luxurious coolness round
The air, and verdure o'er the ground.
'Twas sweet, when cloudless stars were bright,
To view the wave of watery light,
And hear its melody by night.
And oft had Hassan's Childhood played
Around the verge of that cascade;
And oft upon his mother's breast   310
That sound had harmonized his rest;
And oft had Hassan's Youth along
Its bank been soothed by Beauty's song;
And softer seemed each melting tone
Of Music mingled with its own.
But ne'er shall Hassan's Age repose
Along the brink at Twilight's close:
The stream that filled that font is fled—
The blood that warmed his heart is shed!
And here no more shall human voice   320
Be heard to rage, regret, rejoice.
The last sad note that swelled the gale
Was woman's wildest funeral wail:
That quenched in silence, all is still,
But the lattice that flaps when the wind is shrill:
Though raves the gust, and floods the rain,
No hand shall close its clasp again.
On desert sands 'twere joy to scan
The rudest steps of fellow man,
So here the very voice of Grief   330
Might wake an Echo like relief—
At least 'twould say, "All are not gone;
There lingers Life, though but in one"—
For many a gilded chamber's there,
Which Solitude might well forbear,
Within that dome as yet Decay
Hath slowly worked her cankering way—
But gloom is gathered o'er the gate,

Nor there the Fakir's self will wait;
Nor there will wandering Dervise stay,   340
For Bounty cheers not his delay;
Nor there will weary stranger halt
To bless the sacred "bread and salt."
Alike must Wealth and Poverty
Pass heedless and unheeded by
For Courtesy and Pity died
With Hassan on the mountain side.
His roof, that refuge unto men,
Is Desolation's hungry den.
The guest flies the hall, and the vassal from labour,   350
Since his turban was cleft by the infidel's sabre!

           * * * * *

    I hear the sound of coming feet,
But not a voice mine ear to greet;
More near—each turban I can scan,
And silver-sheathèd ataghan;
The foremost of the band is seen
An Emir by his garb of green:
    "Ho! who art thou?"—"This low salam
Replies of Moslem faith I am.
The burthen ye so gently bear,   360
Seems one that claims your utmost care,
And, doubtless, holds some precious freight—
My humble bark would gladly wait."

    "Thou speakest sooth: thy skiff unmoor,
And waft us from the silent shore;
Nay, leave the sail still furled, and ply
The nearest oar that's scattered by,
And midway to those rocks where sleep
The channelled waters dark and deep.
Rest from your task—so—bravely done,   370
Our course has been right swiftly run;
Yet 'tis the longest voyage, I trow,
That one of— ...

* * * * *"

Sullen it plunged, and slowly sank,
The calm wave rippled to the bank;
I watched it as it sank, methought
Some motion from the current caught
Bestirred it more,—'twas but the beam
That checkered o'er the living stream:
I gazed, till vanishing from view,   380
Like lessening pebble it withdrew;
Still less and less, a speck of white
That gemmed the tide, then mocked the sight;
And all its hidden secrets sleep,
Known but to Genii of the deep,
Which, trembling in their coral caves,
They dare not whisper to the waves.

* * * * *

As rising on its purple wing
The insect queen of Eastern spring,
O'er emerald meadows of Kashmeer   390
Invites the young pursuer near,
And leads him on from flower to flower
A weary-chase and wasted hour,
Then leaves him, as it soars on high,
With panting heart and tearful eye:
So Beauty lures the full-grown child,
With hue as bright, and wing as wild:
A chase of idle hopes and fears,
Begun in folly, closed in tears.
If won, to equal ills betrayed,   400
Woe waits the insect and the maid;
A life of pain, the loss of peace,
From infant's play, and man's caprice:
The lovely toy so fiercely sought
Hath lost its charm by being caught,
For every touch that wooed its stay
Hath brushed its brightest hues away,
Till charm, and hue, and beauty gone,
'Tis left to fly or fall alone.

With wounded wing, or bleeding breast, 410
Ah! where shall either victim rest?
Can this with faded pinion soar
From rose to tulip as before?
Or Beauty, blighted in an hour,
find joy within her broken bower?
No: gayer insects fluttering by
Ne'er droop the wing o'er those that die,
And lovelier things have mercy shown
To every failing but their own,
And every woe a tear can claim 420
Except an erring Sister's shame.

* * * * *

The Mind, that broods o'er guilty woes,
    Is like the Scorpion girt by fire;
In circle narrowing as it glows,
The flame around their captive close,
Till inly searched by thousand throes,
    And maddening in her ire,
One sad and sole relief she knows—
The sting she nourished for her foes,
Whose venom never yet was vain, 430
Gives but one pang, and cures all pain,
And darts into her desperate brain:
So do the dark in soul expire,
Or live like Scorpion girt by fire;
So writhes the mind Remorse hath riven,
Unfit for earth, undoomed for heaven,
Darkness above, despair beneath,
Around it flame, within it death!

* * * * *

    Black Hassan from the Haram flies,
Nor bends on woman's form his eyes; 440
The unwonted chase each hour employs,
Yet shares he not the hunter's joys.
Not thus was Hassan wont to fly
When Leila dwelt in his Serai.
Doth Leila there no longer dwell?

That tale can only Hassan tell:
Strange rumours in our city say
Upon that eve she fled away
When Rhamazan's last sun was set
And flashing from each Minaret   450
Millions of lamps proclaimed the feast
Of Bairam through the boundless East.
'Twas then she went as to the bath,
Which Hassan vainly searched in wrath;
For she was flown her master's rage
In likeness of a Georgian page,
And far beyond the Moslem's power
Had wronged him with the faithless Giaour.
Somewhat of this had Hassan deemed;
But still so fond, so fair she seemed,   460
Too well he trusted to the slave
Whose treachery deserved a grave:
And on that eve had gone to Mosque,
And thence to feast in his Kiosk.
Such is the tale his Nubians tell,
Who did not watch their charge too well;
But others say, that on that night,
By pale Phingari's trembling light,
The Giaour upon his jet-black steed
Was seen, but seen alone to speed   470
With bloody spur along the shore,
Nor maid nor page behind him bore.
                    * * * * *
Her eye's dark charm 'twere vain to tell,
But gaze on that of the Gazelle,
It will assist thy fancy well;
As large, as languishingly dark,
But Soul beamed forth in every spark
That darted from beneath the lid,
Bright as the jewel of Giamschid.
Yea, *Soul,* and should our prophet say   480
That form was nought but breathing clay,

By Alla! I would answer nay;
Though on Al-Sirat's arch I stood,
Which totters o'er the fiery flood,
With Paradise within my view,
And all his Houris beckoning through.
Oh! who young Leila's glance could read
And keep that portion of his creed
Which saith that woman is but dust,
A soulless toy for tyrant's lust?   490
On her might Muftis gaze, and own
That through her eye the Immortal shone;
On her fair cheek's unfading hue
The young pomegranate's blossoms strew
Their bloom in blushes ever new;
Her hair in hyacinthine flow,
When left to roll its folds below,
As midst her handmaids in the hall
She stood superior to them all,
Hath swept the marble where her feet   500
Gleamed whiter than the mountain sleet
Ere from the cloud that gave it birth
It fell, and caught one stain of earth.
The cygnet nobly walks the water;
So moved on earth Circassia's daughter,
The loveliest bird of Franguestan!
As rears her crest the ruffled Swan,
    And spurns the wave with wings of pride,
When pass the steps of stranger man
    Along the banks that bound her tide;   510
Thus rose fair Leila's whiter neck:——
Thus armed with beauty would she check
Intrusion's glance, till Folly's gaze
Shrunk from the charms it meant to praise.
Thus high and graceful was her gait;
Her heart as tender to her mate;
Her mate—stern Hassan, who was he?
Alas! that name was not for thee!

* * * * *

Stern Hassan hath a journey ta'en
With twenty vassals in his train,   520
Each armed, as best becomes a man,
With arquebuss and ataghan;
The chief before, as decked for war,
Bears in his belt the scimitar
Stained with the best of Arnaut blood,
When in the pass the rebels stood,
And few returned to tell the tale
Of what befell in Parne's vale.
The pistols which his girdle bore
Were those that once a Pasha wore,   530
Which still, though gemmed and bossed with gold,
Even robbers tremble to behold.
'Tis said he goes to woo a bride
More true than her who left his side;
The faithless slave that broke her bower,
And—worse than faithless—for a Giaour!

* * * * *

The Sun's last rays are on the hill,
And sparkle in the fountain rill,
Whose welcome waters, cool and clear,
Draw blessings from the mountaineer: 540
Here may the loitering merchant Greek
Find that repose 'twere vain to seek
In cities lodged too near his lord,
And trembling for his secret hoard—
Here may he rest where none can see,
In crowds a slave, in deserts free;
And with forbidden wine may stain
The bowl a Moslem must not drain.

* * * * *

The foremost Tartar's in the gap,
Conspicuous by his yellow cap;   550
The rest in lengthening line the while
Wind slowly through the long defile:
Above, the mountain rears a peak,

Where vultures whet the thirsty beak,
And theirs may be a feast to-night,
Shall tempt them down ere morrow's light;
Beneath, a river's wintry stream
Has shrunk before the summer beam,
And left a channel bleak and bare,
Save shrubs that spring to perish there: 560
Each side the midway path there lay
Small broken crags of granite gray,
By time, or mountain lightning, riven
From summits clad in mists of heaven;
For where is he that hath beheld
The peak of Liakura unveiled?

            * * * * *

    They reach the grove of pine at last;
"Bismillah! now the peril's past;
For yonder view the opening plain,
And there we'll prick our steeds amain:"   570
The Chiaus spake, and as he said,
A bullet whistled o'er his head;
The foremost Tartar bites the ground!
    Scarce had they time to check the rein,
Swift from their steeds the riders bound;
    But three shall never mount again:
Unseen the foes that gave the wound,
    The dying ask revenge in vain.
With steel unsheathed, and carbine bent,
Some o'er their courser's harness leant,   580
    Half sheltered by the steed;
Some fly beneath the nearest rock,
And there await the coming shock,
    Nor tamely stand to bleed
Beneath the shaft of foes unseen,
Who dare not quit their craggy screen.
Stern Hassan only from his horse
Disdains to light, and keeps his course,
Till fiery flashes in the van
Proclaim too sure the robber-clan   590

Have well secured the only way
Could now avail the promised prey;
Then curled his very beard with ire,
And glared his eye with fiercer fire;
"Though far and near the bullets hiss,
I've scaped a bloodier hour than this."
And now the foe their covert quit,
And call his vassals to submit;
But Hassan's frown and furious word
Are dreaded more than hostile sword,   600
Nor of his little band a man
Resigned carbine or ataghan,
Nor raised the craven cry, Amaun!
In fuller sight, more near and near,
The lately ambushed foes appear,
And, issuing from the grove, advance
Some who on battle-charger prance.
Who leads them on with foreign brand
Far flashing in his red right hand?
" 'Tis he! 'tis he! I know him now;   610
I know him by his pallid brow;
I know him by the evil eye
That aids his envious treachery;
I know him by his jet-black barb;
Though now arrayed in Arnaut garb,
Apostate from his own vile faith,
It shall not save him from the death:
'Tis he! well met in any hour,
Lost Leila's love—accurséd Giaour!"

    As rolls the river into Ocean,   620
In sable torrent wildly streaming;
    As the sea-tide's opposing motion,
In azure column proudly gleaming,
Beats back the current many a rood,
In curling foam and mingling flood,
While eddying whirl, and breaking wave,
Roused by the blast of winter, rave;

Through sparkling spray, in thundering clash.
The lightnings of the waters flash
In awful whiteness o'er the shore,   630
That shines and shakes beneath the roar;
Thus—as the stream and Ocean greet,
With waves that madden as they meet—
Thus join the bands, whom mutual wrong,
And fate, and fury, drive along.
The bickering sabres' shivering jar;
    And pealing wide or ringing near
    Its echoes on the throbbing ear,
The deathshot hissing from afar;
The shock, the shout, the groan of war,   640
    Reverberate along that vale,
    More suited to the shepherd's tale:
Though few the numbers—theirs the strife.
That neither spares nor speaks for life!
Ah! fondly youthful hearts can press,
To seize and share the dear caress;
But Love itself could never pant
For all that Beauty sighs to grant
With half the fervour Hate bestows
Upon the last embrace of foes,   650
When grappling in the fight they fold
Those arms that ne'er shall lose their hold:
Friends meet to part; Love laughs at faith;
True foes, once met, are joined till death!
                    * * * * *

    With sabre shivered to the hilt,
Yet dripping with the blood he spilt;
Yet strained within the severed hand
Which quivers round that faithless brand;
His turban far behind him rolled,
And cleft in twain its firmest fold: 660
His flowing robe by falchion torn,
And crimson as those clouds of morn
That, streaked with dusky red, portend
The day shall have a stormy end;

A stain on every bush that bore
A fragment of his palampore;
His breast with wounds unnumbered riven,
His back to earth, his face to Heaven,
Fall'n Hassan lies—his unclosed eye
Yet lowering on his enemy,   670
As if the hour that sealed his fate
Surviving left his quenchless hate;
And o'er him bends that foe with brow
As dark as his that bled below.

* * * * *

"Yes, Leila sleeps beneath the wave,
But his shall be a redder grave;
Her spirit pointed well the steel
Which taught that felon heart to feel.
He called the Prophet, but his power
Was vain against the vengeful Giaour: 680
He called on Alla—but the word
Arose unheeded or unheard.
Thou Paynim fool! could Leila's prayer
Be passed, and thine accorded there?
I watched my time, I leagued with these,
The traitor in his turn to seize;
My wrath is wreaked, the deed is done,
And now I go,—but go alone."

* * * * *

* * * * *

The browsing camels' bells are tinkling:
His mother looked from her lattice high—   690
    She saw the dews of eve besprinkling
The pasture green beneath her eye,
    She saw the planets faintly twinkling:
" 'Tis twilight—sure his train is nigh."
She could not rest in the garden-bower,
But gazed through the grate of his steepest tower.
"Why comes he not? his steeds are fleet,
Nor shrink they from the summer heat;

Why sends not the Bridegroom his promised gift?
Is his heart more cold, or his barb less swift?   700
Oh, false reproach! yon Tartar now
Has gained our nearest mountain's brow,
And warily the steep descends,
And now within the valley bends;
And he bears the gift at his saddle bow—
How could I deem his courser slow?
Right well my largess shall repay
His welcome speed, and weary way."
The Tartar lighted at the gate,
But scarce upheld his fainting weight!   710
His swarthy visage spake distress,
But this might be from weariness;
His garb with sanguine spots was dyed,
But these might be from his courser's side;
He drew the token from his vest—
Angel of Death! 'Tis Hassan's cloven crest!
His calpac rent—his caftan red—
"Lady, a fearful bride thy Son hath wed:
Me, not from mercy, did they spare,
But this empurpled pledge to bear.   720
Peace to the brave! whose blood is spilt:
Woe to the Giaour! for his the guilt."

     * * * * *

  A Turban carved in coarsest stone,
A Pillar with rank weeds o'ergrown,
Whereon can now be scarcely read
The Koran verse that mourns the dead,
Point out the spot where Hassan fell
A victim in that lonely dell.
There sleeps as true as Osmanlie
As e'er at Mecca bent the knee;   730
As ever scorned forbidden wine,
Or prayed with face towards the shrine,
In orisons resumed anew
At solemn sound of "Alla Hu!"
Yet died he by a stranger's hand,

And stranger in his native land;
Yet died he as in arms he stood,
And unavenged, at least in blood.
But him the maids of Paradise
   Impatient to their halls invite,   740
And the dark heaven of Houris' eyes
   On him shall glance for ever bright;
They come—their kerchiefs green they wave,
And welcome with a kiss the brave!
Who falls in battle 'gainst a Giaour
Is worthiest an immortal bower.

     * * * * *

   But thou, false Infidel! shall writhe
Beneath avenging Monkir's scythe;
And from its torments 'scape alone
To wander round lost Eblis' throne;   750
And fire unquenched, unquenchable,
Around, within, thy heart shall dwell;
Nor ear can hear nor tongue can tell
The tortures of that inward hell!
But first, on earth as Vampire sent,
Thy corse shall from its tomb be rent:
Then ghastly haunt thy native place,
And suck the blood of all thy race;
There from thy daughter, sister, wife,
At midnight drain the stream of life;   760
Yet loathe the banquet which perforce
Must feed thy livid living corse:
Thy victims ere they yet expire
Shall know the demon for their sire,
As cursing thee, thou cursing them,
Thy flowers are withered on the stem.
But one that for thy crime must fall,
The youngest, most beloved of all,
Shall bless thee with a *father's* name—
That word shall wrap thy heart in flame!   770
Yet must thou end thy task, and mark
Her cheek's last tinge, her eye's last spark,

And the last glassy glance must view
Which freezes o'er its lifeless blue;
Then with unhallowed hand shalt tear
The tresses of her yellow hair,
Of which in life a lock when shorn
Affection's fondest pledge was worn,
But now is borne away by thee,
Memorial of thine agony!   780
Wet with thine own best blood shall drip
Thy gnashing tooth and haggard lip;
Then stalking to thy sullen grave,
Go—and with Gouls and Afrits rave;
Till these in horror shrink away
From Sceptre more accursed than they!

        * * * * *

"How name ye yon lone Caloyer?
   His features I have scanned before
In mine own land: 'tis many a year,
   Since, dashing by the lonely shore,   790
I saw him urge as fleet a steed
As ever served a horseman's need.
But once I saw that face, yet then
It was so marked with inward pain,
I could not pass it by again;
It breathes the same dark spirit now,
As death were stamped upon his brow.

" 'Tis twice three years at summer tide
   Since first among our freres he came;
And here it soothes him to abide   800
   For some dark deed he will not name.
But never at our Vesper prayer,
Nor e'er before Confession chair
Kneels he, nor recks he when arise
Incense or anthem to the skies,
But broods within his cell alone,
His faith and race alike unknown.
The sea from Paynim land he crost,

And here ascended from the coast;
Yet seems he not of Othman race,　　　　　　　810
But only Christian in his face:
I'd judge him some stray renegade,
Repentant of the change he made,
Save that he shuns our holy shrine,
Nor tastes the sacred bread and wine.
Great largess to these walls he brought,
And thus our Abbot's favour bought;
But were I Prior, not a day
Should brook such stranger's further stay,
Or pent within our penance cell　　　　　　　820
Should doom him there for aye to dwell.
Much in his visions mutters he
Of maiden whelmed beneath the sea;
Of sabres clashing, foemen flying,
Wrongs avenged, and Moslem dying.
On cliff he hath been known to stand
And rave as to some bloody hand
Fresh severed from its parent limb,
Invisible to all but him,
Which beckons onward to his grave,　　　　　　830
And lures to leap into the wave."

* * * * *

* * * * *

Dark and unearthly is the scowl
That glares beneath his dusky cowl:
The flash of that dilating eye
Reveals too much of times gone by;
Though varying, indistinct its hue,
Oft will his glance the gazer rue,
For in it lurks that nameless spell,
Which speaks, itself unspeakable,
A spirit yet unquelled and high,　　　　　　　840
That claims and keeps ascendancy;
And like the bird whose pinions quake,
But cannot fly the gazing snake,
Will others quail beneath his look,

Nor 'scape the glance they scarce can brook:
From him the half-affrighted Friar
When met alone would fain retire,
As if that eye and bitter smile
Transferred to others fear and guile:
Not oft to smile descendeth he,   850
And when he doth 'tis sad to see
That he but mocks at Misery.
How that pale lip will curl and quiver!
Then fix once more as if for ever;
As if his sorrow or disdain
Forbade him e'er to smile again.
Well were it so—such ghastly mirth
From joyaunce ne'er derived its birth.
But sadder still it were to trace
What once were feelings in that face: 860
Time hath not yet the features fixed,
But brighter traits with evil mixed;
And there are hues not always faded,
Which speak a mind not all degraded
Even by the crimes through which it waded:
The common crowd but see the gloom
Of wayward deeds, and fitting doom;
The close observer can espy
A noble soul, and lineage high:
Alas! though both bestowed in vain,   870
Which Grief could change, and Guilt could stain,
It was no vulgar tenement
To which such lofty gifts were lent,
And still with little less than dread
On such the sight is riveted.
The roofless cot, decayed and rent,
    Will scarce delay the passer-by;
The tower by war or tempest bent,
While yet may frown one battlement,
    Demands and daunts the stranger's eye;   880
Each ivied arch, and pillar lone,
Pleads haughtily for glories gone!

"His floating robe around him folding,
    Slow sweeps he through the columned aisle;
With dread beheld, with gloom beholding
    The rites that sanctify the pile.
But when the anthem shakes the choir,
And kneel the monks, his steps retire;
By yonder lone and wavering torch
His aspect glares within the porch;   890
There will he pause till all is done—
And hear the prayer, but utter none.
See—by the half-illumined wall
His hood fly back, his dark hair fall,
That pale brow wildly wreathing round,
As if the Gorgon there had bound
The sablest of the serpent-braid
That o'er her fearful forehead strayed:
For he declines the convent oath,
And leaves those locks unhallowed growth,   900
But wears our garb in all beside;
And, not from piety but pride,
Gives wealth to walls that never heard
Of his one holy vow nor word.
Lo!—mark ye, as the harmony
Peals louder praises to the sky,
That livid cheek, that stony air
Of mixed defiance and despair!
Saint Francis, keep him from the shrine!
Else may we dread the wrath divine   910
Made manifest by awful sign.
If ever evil angel bore
The form of mortal, such he wore:
By all my hope of sins forgiven,
Such looks are not of earth nor heaven!"

    To Love the softest hearts are prone,
But such can ne'er be all his own;
Too timid in his woes to share,

Too meek to meet, or brave despair;
And sterner hearts alone may feel   920
The wound that Time can never heal.
The rugged metal of the mine
Must burn before its surface shine,
But plunged within the furnace-flame,
It bends and melts—though still the same;
Then tempered to thy want, or will,
'Twill serve thee to defend or kill—
A breast-plate for thine hour of need,
Or blade to bid thy foeman bleed;
But if a dagger's form it bear,   930
Let those who shape its edge, beware!
Thus Passion's fire, and Woman's art,
Can turn and tame the sterner heart;
From these its form and tone are ta'en,
And what they make it, must remain,
But break—before it bend again.

* * * * *
* * * * *

If solitude succeed to grief,
Release from pain is slight relief;
The vacant bosom's wilderness
Might thank the pang that made it less.   940
We loathe what none are left to share:
Even bliss—'twere woe alone to bear;
The heart once left thus desolate
Must fly at last for ease—to hate.
It is as if the dead could feel
The icy worm around them steal,
And shudder, as the reptiles creep
To revel o'er their rotting sleep,
Without the power to scare away
The cold consumers of their clay!   950
It is as if the desert bird,
    Whose beak unlocks her bosom's stream
    To still her famished nestlings' scream,
Nor mourns a life to them transferred,

Should rend her rash devoted breast,
And find them flown her empty nest.
The keenest pangs the wretched find
    Are rapture to the dreary void—
The leafless desert of the mind,
    The waste of feelings unemployed.   960
Who would be doomed to gaze upon
A sky without a cloud or sun?
Less hideous far the tempest's roar,
Than ne'er to brave the billows more—
Thrown, when the war of winds is o'er,
A lonely wreck on Fortune's shore,
'Mid sullen calm, and silent bay,
Unseen to drop by dull decay;—
Better to sink beneath the shock
Than moulder piecemeal on the rock!   970
      * * * * *

"Father! thy days have passed in peace,
    'Mid counted beads, and countless prayer;
To bid the sins of others cease,
    Thyself without a crime or care,
Save transient ills that all must bear,
Has been thy lot from youth to age;
And thou wilt bless thee from the rage
Of passions fierce and uncontrolled,
Such as thy penitents unfold,
Whose secret sins and sorrows rest   980
Within thy pure and pitying breast.
My days, though few, have passed below
In much of Joy, but more of Woe;
Yet still in hours of love or strife,
I've 'scaped the weariness of Life:
Now leagued with friends, now girt by foes,
I loathed the languor of repose.
Now, nothing left to love or hate,
No more with hope or pride elate,
I'd rather be the thing that crawls   990
Most noxious o'er a dungeon's walls,

Than pass my dull, unvarying days,
Condemned to meditate and gaze.
Yet, lurks a wish within my breast
For rest—but not to feel 'tis rest.
Soon shall my Fate that wish fulfil;
    And I shall sleep without the dream
Of what I was, and would be still,
    Dark as to thee my deeds may seem:
My memory now is but the tomb   1000
Of joys long dead; my hope, their doom:
Though better to have died with those
Than bear a life of lingering woes.
My spirit shrunk not to sustain
The searching throes of ceaseless pain;
Nor sought the self-accorded grave
Of ancient fool and modern knave:
Yet death I have not feared to meet;
And in the field it had been sweet,
Had Danger wooed me on to move   1010
The slave of Glory, not of Love.
I've braved it—not for Honour's boast;
I smile at laurels won or lost;
To such let others carve their way,
For high renown, or hireling pay:
But place again before my eyes
Aught that I deem a worthy prize—
The maid I love, the man I hate—
And I will hunt the steps of fate,
To save or slay, as these require,   1020
Through rending steel, and rolling fire:
Nor needst thou doubt this speech from one
Who would but do—what he *hath* done.
Death is but what the haughty brave,
The weak must bear, the wretch must crave;
Then let life go to Him who gave:
I have not quailed to Danger's brow
When high and happy—need I *now?*

* * * * *

"I loved her, Friar! nay, adored—
    But these are words that all can use—   1030
I proved it more in deed than word;
There's blood upon that dinted sword,
    A stain its steel can never lose:
'Twas shed for her, who died for me,
    It warmed the heart of one abhorred:
Nay, start not—no—nor bend thy knee,
    Nor midst my sin such act record;
Thou wilt absolve me from the deed,
For he was hostile to thy creed!
The very name of Nazarene   1040
Was wormwood to his Paynim spleen.
Ungrateful fool! since but for brands
Well wielded in some hardy hands,
And wounds by Galileans given—
The surest pass to Turkish heaven—
For him his Houris still might wait
Impatient at the Prophet's gate.
I loved her—Love will find its way
Through paths where wolves would fear to prey;
And if it dares enough, 'twere hard   1050
If Passion met not some reward—
No matter how, or where or why,
I did not vainly seek, nor sigh:
Yet sometimes, with remorse, in vain
I wish she had not loved again.
She died—I dare not tell thee how;
But look—'tis written on my brow!
There read of Cain the curse and crime,
In characters unworn by Time:
Still, ere thou dost condemn me, pause;   1060
Not mine the act, though I the cause.
Yet did he but what I had done
Had she been false to more than one.
Faithless to him—he gave the blow;
But true to me—I laid him low:
Howe'er deserved her doom might be

Her treachery was truth to me;
To me she gave her heart, that all
Which Tyranny can ne'er enthrall;
And I, alas! too late to save!   1070
Yet all I then could give, I gave—
'Twas some relief—our foe a grave.
His death sits lightly; but her fate
Has made me—what thou well mayst hate.

   His doom was sealed—he knew it well,
Warned by the voice of stern Taheer,
Deep in whose darkly boding ear
The deathshot pealed of murder near,
   As filed the troop to where they fell!
He died too in the battle broil,   1080
A time that heeds nor pain nor toil;
One cry to Mahomet for aid,
One prayer to Alla all he made.
He knew and crossed me in the fray—
I gazed upon him where he lay,
And watched his spirit ebb away:
Though pierced like pard by hunter's steel,
He felt not half that now I feel.
I searched, but vainly searched, to find
The workings of a wounded mind;   1090
Each feature of that sullen corse
Betrayed his rage, but no remorse.
Oh, what had Vengeance given to trace
Despair upon his dying face!—
The late repentance of that hour
When Penitence hath lost her power
To tear one terror from the grave,
And will not soothe, and cannot save.
       * * * * *

"The cold in clime are cold in blood,
   Their love can scarce deserve the name;   1100
But mine was like the lava flood
   That boils in Ætna's breast of flame.
I cannot prate in puling strain

Of Ladye-love, and Beauty's chain:
If changing cheek, and scorching vein,
Lips taught to writhe, but not complain,
If bursting heart, and maddening brain,
And daring deed, and vengeful steel,
And all that I have felt and feel,
Betoken love—that love was mine,   1110
And shown by many a bitter sign.
'Tis true, I could not whine nor sigh,
I knew but to obtain or die.
I die—but first I have possessed,
And come what may, I *have been* blessed.
Shall I the doom I sought upbraid?
No—reft of all, yet undismayed
But for the thought of Leila slain,
Give me the pleasure with the pain,
So would I live and love again.   1120
I grieve, but not, my holy Guide!
For him who dies, but her who died:
She sleeps beneath the wandering wave—
Ah! had she but an earthly grave,
This breaking heart and throbbing head
Should seek and share her narrow bed.
She was a form of Life and Light,
That, seen, became a part of sight;
And rose, where'er I turned mine eye,
The Morning-star of Memory!   1130

"Yes, Love indeed is light from Heaven;
    A spark of that immortal fire
With angels shared, by Alla given,
    To lift from earth our low desire.
Devotion wafts the mind above,
But Heaven itself descends in Love—
A feeling from the Godhead caught,
To wean from self each sordid thought;
A ray of Him who formed the whole—
A Glory circling round the soul!   1140

I grant *my* love imperfect, all
That mortals by the name miscall:
Then deem it evil, what thou wilt—
But say, oh say, *hers* was not Guilt!
She was my Life's unerring Light:
That quenched—what beam shall break my night?
Oh! would it shone to lead me still,
Although to death or deadliest ill!
Why marvel ye, if they who lose
    This present joy, this future hope,   1150
    No more with sorrow meekly cope;
In phrensy then their fate accuse;
In madness do those fearful deeds
    That seem to add but Guilt to Woe?
Alas! the breast that inly bleeds
    Hath nought to dread from outward blow:
Who falls from all he knows of bliss,
Cares little into what abyss.
Fierce as the gloomy vulture's now
    To thee, old man, my deeds appear: 1160
I read abhorrence on thy brow,
    And this too was I born to bear!
'Tis true, that, like that bird of prey,
With havock have I marked my way:
But this was taught me by the dove,
To die—and know no second love.
This lesson yet hath man to learn,
Taught by the thing he dares to spurn:
The bird that sings within the brake,
The swan that swims upon the lake,   1170
One mate, and one alone, will take.
And let the fool still prone to range,
And sneer on all who cannot change,
Partake his jest with boasting boys;
I envy not his varied joys,
But deem such feeble, heartless man,
Less than yon solitary swan,—
Far, far beneath the shallow maid

He left believing and betrayed.
Such shame at least was never mine—   1180
Leila! each thought was only thine!
My good, my guilt, my weal, my woe,
My hope on high—my all below.
Earth holds no other like to thee,
Or, if it doth, in vain for me:
For worlds I dare not view the dame
Resembling thee, yet not the same.
The very crimes that mar my youth,
This bed of death—attest my truth!
'Tis all too late—thou wert, thou art   1190
The cherished madness of my heart!

"And she was lost—and yet I breathed,
    But not the breath of human life:
A serpent round my heart was wreathed,
    And stung my every thought to strife.
Alike all time—abhorred all place—
Shuddering I shrank from Nature's face,
Where every hue that charmed before
The blackness of my bosom wore.
The rest thou dost already know,   1200
And all my sins, and half my woe.
But talk no more of penitence;
Thou seest I soon shall part from hence;
And if thy holy tale were true,
The deed that's done canst *thou* undo?
Think me not thankless—but this grief
Looks not to priesthood for relief.
My soul's estate in secret guess:
But wouldst thou pity more, say less.
When thou canst bid my Leila live,   1210
Then will I sue thee to forgive;
Then plead my cause in that high place
Where purchased masses proffer grace.
Go, when the hunter's hand hath wrung
From forest-cave her shrieking young,

And calm the lonely lioness:
But soothe not—mock not *my* distress!

"In earlier days, and calmer hours,
    When heart with heart delights to blend,
Where bloom my native valley's bowers,   1220
    I had—Ah! have I now—a friend!
To him this pledge I charge thee send,
    Memorial of a youthful vow;
I would remind him of my end:
    Though souls absorbed like mine allow
Brief thought to distant Friendship's claim,
Yet dear to him my blighted name.
'Tis strange—he prophesied my doom,
    And I have smiled—I then could smile—
When Prudence would his voice assume,   1230
    And warn—I recked not what—the while:
But now Remembrance whispers o'er
Those accents scarcely marked before.
Say—that his bodings came to pass,
    And he will start to hear their truth,
    And wish his words had not been sooth:
Tell him—unheeding as I was,
    Through many a busy bitter scene
    Of all our golden youth had been,
In pain, my faltering tongue had tried   1240
To bless his memory—ere I died;
But Heaven in wrath would turn away,
If Guilt should for the guiltless pray.
I do not ask him not to blame,
Too gentle he to wound my name;
And what have I to do with Fame?
I do not ask him not to mourn,
Such cold request might sound like scorn;
And what than Friendship's manly tear
May better grace a brother's bier?   1250
But bear this ring, his own of old,
And tell him—what thou dost behold!

The withered frame, the ruined mind,
The wrack by passion left behind,
A shrivelled scroll, a scattered leaf,
Seared by the autumn blast of Grief!
* * * * *
"Tell me no more of Fancy's gleam,
No, Father, no, 'twas not a dream;
Alas! the dreamer first must sleep,—
I only watched, and wished to weep;   1260
But could not, for my burning brow
Throbbed to the very brain as now:
I wished but for a single tear,
As something welcome, new, and dear:
I wished it then, I wish it still;
Despair is stronger than my will.
Waste not thine orison—despair
Is mightier than thy pious prayer:
I would not, if I might, be blest;
I want no Paradise, but rest.   1270
'Twas then—I tell thee—Father! then
I saw her; yes, she lived again,
And shining in her white symar,
As through yon pale gray cloud the star
Which now I gaze on, as on her,
Who looked and looks far lovelier;
Dimly I view its trembling spark;
To-morrow's night shall be more dark;
And I, before its rays appear,
That lifeless thing the living fear.   1280
I wander—Father! for my soul
Is fleeting towards the final goal.
I saw her—Friar! and I rose
Forgetful of our former woes;
And rushing from my couch, I dart,
And clasp her to my desperate heart;
I clasp—what is it that I clasp?
No breathing form within my grasp,
No heart that beats reply to mine—

Yet, Leila! yet the form is thine!   1290
And art thou, dearest, changed so much
As meet my eye, yet mock my touch?
Ah! were thy beauties e'er so cold,
I care not—so my arms enfold
The all they ever wished to hold.
Alas! around a shadow prest
They shrink upon my lonely breast;
Yet still 'tis there! In silence stands,
And beckons with beseeching hands!
With braided hair, and bright-black eye—   1300
I knew 'twas false—she could not die!
But *he* is dead! within the dell
I saw him buried where he fell;
He comes not—for he cannot break
From earth;—why then art *thou* awake?
They told me wild waves rolled above
The face I view—the form I love;
They told me—'twas a hideous tale!—
I'd tell it, but my tongue would fail:
If true, and from thine ocean-cave   1310
Thou com'st to claim a calmer grave,
Oh! pass thy dewy fingers o'er
This brow that then will burn no more;
Or place them on my hopeless heart:
But, Shape or Shade! whate'er thou art,
In mercy ne'er again depart!
Or farther with thee bear my soul
Than winds can waft or waters roll!
                        * * * * *

"Such is my name, and such my tale.
    Confessor! to thy secret ear   1320
I breathe the sorrows I bewail,
    And thank thee for the generous tear
This glazing eye could never shed.
Then lay me with the humblest dead,
And, save the cross above my head,
Be neither name nor emblem spread,

By prying stranger to be read,
Or stay the passing pilgrim's tread."
He passed—nor of his name and race
He left a token or a trace,   1330
Save what the Father must not say
Who shrived him on his dying day:
This broken tale was all we knew
Of her he loved, or him he slew.

[*First publ., December 27, 1813.*]

From THE BRIDE OF ABYDOS

A TURKISH TALE

[The opening lines of The Bride of Abydos *set the tone for the tale of dark deeds and forbidden love in the "clime of the East."]*

CANTO THE FIRST

I

Know ye the land where the cypress and myrtle
   Are emblems of deeds that are done in their clime?
Where the rage of the vulture, the love of the turtle,
   Now melt into sorrow, now madden to crime?
Know ye the land of the cedar and vine,
Where the flowers ever blossom, the beams ever shine;
Where the light wings of Zephyr, oppressed with perfume,
Wax faint o'er the gardens of Gúl in her bloom;
Where the citron and olive are fairest of fruit,
And the voice of the nightingale never is mute;   10
Where the tints of the earth, and the hues of the sky,
In colour though varied, in beauty may vie,
And the purple of Ocean is deepest in dye;
Where the virgins are soft as the roses they twine,
And all, save the spirit of man, is divine—

'T is the clime of the East—'t is the land of the Sun—
Can he smile on such deeds as his children have done?
Oh! wild as the accents of lovers' farewell
Are the hearts which they bear, and the tales which they tell.

. . .

From THE CORSAIR

A TALE

[*This tale of a benevolent pirate, a man "of loneliness and mystery,"
had an unprecedented popularity in Byron's day, selling 10,000
copies on the day of publication. The passage here quoted, the de-
scription of a sunset as seen from the Acropolis at Athens, was first
written by Byron in 1811 as a prelude to his* Curse of Minerva
but was later transferred to the opening of the third canto of The
Corsair.]

. . .

CANTO THE THIRD

"—come vedi, ancor non m'abbandona."
—DANTE, *INFERNO,* V. 105.

I

Slow sinks, more lovely ere his race be run,
Along Morea's hills the setting Sun;   1170
Not, as in Northern climes, obscurely bright,
But one unclouded blaze of living light!
O'er the hushed deep the yellow beam he throws,
Gilds the green wave, that trembles as it glows.
On old Ægina's rock, and Idra's isle,
The God of gladness sheds his parting smile;

O'er his own regions lingering, loves to shine,
Though there his altars are no more divine.
Descending fast the mountain shadows kiss
Thy glorious gulf, unconquered Salamis!   1180
Their azure arches through the long expanse
More deeply purpled meet his mellowing glance,
And tenderest tints, along their summits driven,
Mark his gay course, and own the hues of Heaven;
Till, darkly shaded from the land and deep,
Behind his Delphian cliff he sinks to sleep.

On such an eve, his palest beam he cast,
When—Athens! here thy Wisest looked his last.
How watched thy better sons his farewell ray,
That closed their murdered Sage's latest day!   1190
Not yet—not yet—Sol pauses on the hill—
The precious hour of parting lingers still;
But sad his light to agonizing eyes,
And dark the mountain's once delightful dyes:
Gloom o'er the lovely land he seemed to pour,
The land, where Phœbus never frowned before:
But ere he sunk below Cithæron's head,
The cup of woe was quaffed—the Spirit fled;
The Soul of him who scorned to fear or fly—
Who lived and died, as none can live or die!   1200

But lo! from high Hymettus to the plain,
The Queen of night asserts her silent reign:
No murky vapour, herald of the storm,
Hides her fair face, nor girds her glowing form;
With cornice glimmering as the moon-beams play,
There the white column greets her grateful ray,
And bright around with quivering beams beset,
Her emblem sparkles o'er the Minaret:
The groves of olive scattered dark and wide
Where meek Cephisus pours his scanty tide;   1210
The cypress saddening by the sacred Mosque,
The gleaming turret of the gay Kiosk;

And, dun and sombre 'mid the holy calm,
Near Theseus' fane yon solitary palm,
All tinged with varied hues arrest the eye—
And dull were his that passed them heedless by.

Again the Ægean, heard no more afar,
Lulls his chafed breast from elemental war;
Again his waves in milder tints unfold
Their long array of sapphire and of gold,   1220
Mixed with the shades of many a distant isle,
That frown—where gentler Ocean seems to smile.
                    · · ·

The Prisoner of Chillon

[*The poem was written in the summer of 1816, after Byron and Shelley had made a trip by boat to the head of Lake Geneva and had visited the Chateau of Chillon. Though Byron's account is based on a story of François Bonivard which he picked up on the spot and which is inaccurate both as to historical events and characters, it has not failed to be one of the most gripping of his poetic tales, for which reason probably it is the most widely known. Bonivard was once incarcerated in the dungeon of Chillon for four years (1532–1536) for his political activities against Duke Charles III of Savoy, but so far as is known no brothers died with him. He was not chained but walked about so much that he wore a path in the rock.*]

SONNET ON CHILLON

Eternal Spirit of the chainless Mind!
    Brightest in dungeons, Liberty! thou art:
    For there thy habitation is the heart—
The heart which love of thee alone can bind;
And when thy sons to fetters are consigned—
    To fetters, and the damp vault's dayless gloom,
    Their country conquers with their martyrdom,
And Freedom's fame finds wings on every wind.

Chillon! thy prison is a holy place,
  And thy sad floor an altar—for 'twas trod,
Until his very steps have left a trace
  Worn, as if thy cold pavement were a sod,
By Bonnivard!—May none those marks efface!
For they appeal from tyranny to God.

ADVERTISEMENT

When this poem was composed, I was not sufficiently aware of the history of Bonnivard, or I should have endeavoured to dignify the subject by an attempt to celebrate his courage and his virtues. With some account of his life I have been furnished, by the kindness of a citizen of that republic, which is still proud of the memory of a man worthy of the best age of ancient freedom:—

"François de Bonnivard, fils de Louis de Bonnivard, originaire de Seyssel et Seigneur de Lunes, naquit en 1496. Il fit ses études à Turin: en 1510 Jean Aimé de Bonnivard, son oncle, lui résigna le Prieuré de St. Victor, qui aboutissoit aux murs de Genève, et qui formait un bénéfice considérable....

"Ce grand homme—(Bonnivard mérite ce titre par la force de son âme, la droiture de son cœur, la noblesse de ses intentions, la sagesse de ses conseils, le courage de ses démarches, l'étendue de ses connaissances, et la vivacité de son esprit),—ce grand homme, qui excitera l'admiration de tous ceux qu'une vertu héroïque peut encore émouvoir, inspirera encore la plus vive reconnaissance dans les cœurs des Génevois qui aiment Genève. Bonnivard en fut toujours un des plus fermes appuis: pour assurer la liberté de notre République, il ne craignit pas de perdre souvent la sienne; il oublia son repos; il méprisa ses richesses; il ne négligea rien pour affermir le bonheur d'une patrie qu'il honora de son choix: dès ce moment il la chérit comme le plus zélé de ses citoyens; il la servit avec l'intrépidité d'un héros, et il écrivit son Histoire avec la naïveté d'un philosophe et la chaleur d'un patriote.

"Il dit dans le commencement de son Histoire de Genève, que, *dès qu'il eut commencé de lire l'histoire des nations, il se sentit entraîné par son goût pour les Républiques, dont il épousa toujours les intérêts:* c'est ce goût pour la liberté qui lui fit sans doute adopter Genève pour sa patrie....

"Bonnivard, encore jeune, s'annonça hautement comme le défenseur de Genève contre le Duc de Savoye et l'Evêque....

"En 1519, Bonnivard devient le martyr de sa patrie: Le Duc de Savoye étant entré dans Genève avec cinq cents hommes, Bonnivard craint le ressentiment du Duc; il voulut se retirer à Fribourg pour en éviter les suites; mais il fut trahi par deux hommes qui l'accompagnaient, et conduit par ordre du Prince à Grolée, où il resta prisonnier pendant deux ans. Bonnivard était malheureux dans ses voyages: comme ses malheurs n'avaient point ralenti son zèle pour Genève, il était toujours un ennemi redoutable pour ceux qui la menaçaient, et par conséquent il devait être exposé à leurs coups. Il fut rencontré en 1530 sur le Jura par des voleurs, qui le dépouillèrent, et qui le mirent encore entre les mains du Duc de Savoye: ce Prince le fit enfermer dans le Château de Chillon, où il resta sans être interrogé jusques en 1536; il fut alors delivré par les Bernois, qui s'emparèrent du Pays-de-Vaud.

"Bonnivard, en sortant de sa captivité, eut le plaisir de trouver Genève libre et réformée: la République s'empressa de lui témoigner sa reconnaissance, et de le dédommager des maux qu'il avoit soufferts; elle le reçut Bourgeois de la ville au mois de Juin, 1536; elle lui donna la maison habitée autrefois par le Vicaire-Général, et elle lui assigna une pension de deux cents écus d'or tant qu'il séjournerait à Genève. Il fut admis dans le Conseil des Deux-Cent en 1537.

"Bonnivard n'a pas fini d'être utile: après avoir travaillé à rendre Genève libre, il réussit à la rendre tolérante. Bonnivard engagea le Conseil à accorder [aux ecclésiastiques et aux paysans] un tems suffisant pour examiner les propositions qu'on leur faisait; il réussit par sa douceur; on prêche toujours le Christianisme avec succès quand on le prêche avec charité....

"Bonnivard fut savant: ses manuscrits, qui sont dans la bibliothèque publique, prouvent qu'il avait bien lu les auteurs classiques Latins, et qu'il avait approfondi la théologie et l'histoire. Ce grand homme aimait les sciences, et il croyait qu'elles pouvaient faire la gloire de Genève; aussi il ne négligea rien pour les fixer dans cette ville naissante; en 1551 il donna sa bibliothèque au public; elle fut le commencement de notre bibliothèque publique; et ces livres sont en partie les rares et belles éditions du quinzième siècle qu'on voit dans notre collection. Enfin, pendant la même année, ce bon patriote institua la République son héritière, à condition qu'elle employerait ses biens à entretenir le collège dont on projettait la fondation.

"Il paraît que Bonnivard mourut en 1570; mais on ne peut l'assurer, parce qu'il y a une lacune dans le Nécrologe depuis le mois de Juillet, 1570, jusques en 1571."—[*Histoire Littéraire de Genève,* par Jean Sénebier (1741–1809), 1786, i. 131–137.]

I

My hair is grey, but not with years,
Nor grew it white
In a single night,
As men's have grown from sudden fears:
My limbs are bowed, though not with toil,
But rusted with a vile repose,
For they have been a dungeon's spoil,
And mine has been the fate of those
To whom the goodly earth and air
Are banned, and barred—forbidden fare;   10
But this was for my father's faith
I suffered chains and courted death;
That father perished at the stake
For tenets he would not forsake;
And for the same his lineal race
In darkness found a dwelling place;
We were seven—who now are one,
Six in youth, and one in age,
Finished as they had begun,
Proud of Persecution's rage;   20
One in fire, and two in field,
Their belief with blood have sealed,
Dying as their father died,
For the God their foes denied;—
Three were in a dungeon cast,
Of whom this wreck is left the last.

II

There are seven pillars of Gothic mould,
In Chillon's dungeons deep and old,
There are seven columns, massy and grey,
Dim with a dull imprisoned ray,   30
A sunbeam which hath lost its way,
And through the crevice and the cleft
Of the thick wall is fallen and left;
Creeping o'er the floor so damp,
Like a marsh's meteor lamp:
And in each pillar there is a ring,
    And in each ring there is a chain;
That iron is a cankering thing,
    For in these limbs its teeth remain,
With marks that will not wear away,   40
Till I have done with this new day,
Which now is painful to these eyes,
Which have not seen the sun so rise
For years—I cannot count them o'er,
I lost their long and heavy score
When my last brother dropped and died,
And I lay living by his side.

III

They chained us each to a column stone,
And we were three—yet, each alone;
We could not move a single pace,   50
We could not see each other's face,
But with that pale and livid light
That made us strangers in our sight:
And thus together—yet apart,
Fettered in hand, but joined in heart,
'Twas still some solace in the dearth
Of the pure elements of earth,
To hearken to each other's speech,
And each turn comforter to each
With some new hope, or legend old,   60
Or song heroically bold;

But even these at length grew cold.
Our voices took a dreary tone,
An echo of the dungeon stone,
  A grating sound, not full and free,
  As they of yore were wont to be:
  It might be fancy—but to me
They never sounded like our own.

IV

I was the eldest of the three,
  And to uphold and cheer and rest   70
  I ought to do—and did my best—
And each did well in his degree.
  The youngest, whom my father loved,
Because our mother's brow was given
To him, with eyes as blue as heaven—
  For him my soul was sorely moved:
And truly might it be distressed
To see such bird in such a nest;
For he was beautiful as day—
  (When day was beautiful to me   80
  As to young eagles, being free)—
  A polar day, which will not see
A sunset till its summer's gone,
  Its sleepless summer of long light,
The snow-clad offspring of the sun:
  And thus he was as pure and bright,
And in his natural spirit gay,
With tears for naught but others' ills,
And then they flowed like mountain rills,
Unless he could assuage the woe   90
Which he abhorred to view below.

V

The other was as pure of mind,
But formed to combat with his kind;
Strong in his frame, and of a mood
Which 'gainst the world in war had stood.

And perished in the foremost rank
    With joy:—but not in chains in pine:
His spirit withered with their clank,
    I saw it silently decline—
    And so perchance in sooth did mine: 100
But yet I forced it on to cheer
Those relics of a home so dear.
He was a hunter of the hills,
    Had followed there the deer and wolf
    To him this dungeon was a gulf,
And fettered feet the worst of ills.

VI

    Lake Leman lies by Chillon's walls:
A thousand feet in depth below
Its massy waters meet and flow;
Thus much the fathom-line was sent   110
From Chillon's snow-white battlement,
    Which round about the wave inthralls:
A double dungeon wall and wave
Have made—and like a living grave.
Below the surface of the lake
The dark vault lies wherein we lay:
We heard it ripple night and day;
    Sounding o'er our heads it knocked;
And I have felt the winter's spray
Wash through the bars when winds were high   120
And wanton in the happy sky;
    And then the very rock hath rocked,
    And I have felt it shake, unshocked,
Because I could have smiled to see
The death that would have set me free.

VII

I said my nearer brother pined,
I said his mighty heart declined,
He loathed and put away his food;
It was not that 'twas coarse and rude,

For we were used to hunter's fare,   130
And for the like had little care:
The milk drawn from the mountain goat
Was changed for water from the moat,
Our bread was such as captives' tears
Have moistened many a thousand years,
Since man first pent his fellow men
Like brutes within an iron den;
But what were these to us or him?
These wasted not his heart or limb;
My brother's soul was of that mould   140
Which in a palace had grown cold,
Had his free breathing been denied
The range of the steep mountain's side;
But why delay the truth?—he died.
I saw, and could not hold his head,
Nor reach his dying hand—nor dead,—
Though hard I strove, but strove in vain,
To rend and gnash my bonds in twain.
He died—and they unlocked his chain,
And scooped for him a shallow grave   150
Even from the cold earth of our cave.
I begged them, as a boon, to lay
His corse in dust whereon the day
Might shine—it was a foolish thought,
But then within my brain it wrought,
That even in death his freeborn breast
In such a dungeon could not rest.
I might have spared my idle prayer—
They coldly laughed—and laid him there:
The flat and turfless earth above   160
The being we so much did love;
His empty chain above it leant,
Such Murder's fitting monument!

VIII

But he, the favourite and the flower,
Most cherished since his natal hour,

His mother's image in fair face,
The infant love of all his race,
His martyred father's dearest thought,
My latest care, for whom I sought
To hoard my life, that his might be   170
Less wretched now, and one day free;
He, too, who yet had held untired
A spirit natural or inspired—
He, too, was struck, and day by day
Was withered on the stalk away.
Oh, God! it is a fearful thing
To see the human soul take wing
In any shape, in any mood:
I've seen it rushing forth in blood,
I've seen it on the breaking ocean   180
Strive with a swoln convulsive motion,
I've seen the sick and ghastly bed
Of Sin delirious with its dread:
But these were horrors—this was woe
Unmixed with such—but sure and slow:
He faded, and so calm and meek,
So softly worn, so sweetly weak,
So tearless, yet so tender—kind,
And grieved for those he left behind;
With all the while a cheek whose bloom   190
Was as a mockery of the tomb,
Whose tints as gently sunk away
As a departing rainbow's ray;
An eye of most transparent light,
That almost made the dungeon bright;
And not a word of murmur—not
A groan o'er his untimely lot,—
A little talk of better days,
A little hope my own to raise,
For I was sunk in silence—lost   200
In this last loss, of all the most;
And then the sighs he would suppress
Of fainting Nature's feebleness,

More slowly drawn, grew less and less:
I listened, but I could not hear;
I called, for I was wild with fear;
I knew 'twas hopeless, but my dread
Would not be thus admonishéd;
I called, and thought I heard a sound—
I burst my chain with one strong bound,   210
And rushed to him:—I found him not,
I only stirred in this black spot,
I only lived, *I* only drew
The accurséd breath of dungeon-dew;
The last, the sole, the dearest link
Between me and the eternal brink,
Which bound me to my failing race,
Was broken in this fatal place.
One on the earth, and one beneath—
My brothers—both had ceased to breathe!   220
I took that hand which lay so still,
Alas! my own was full as chill;
I had not strength to stir, or strive,
But felt that I was still alive—
A frantic feeling, when we know
That what we love shall ne'er be so.
    I know not why
    I could not die,
I had no earthly hope—but faith,
And that forbade a selfish death.   230

IX

What next befell me then and there
    I know not well—I never knew—
First came the loss of light, and air,
    And then of darkness too:
I had no thought, no feeling—none—
Among the stones I stood a stone,
And was, scarce conscious what I wist,
As shrubless crags within the mist;
For all was blank, and bleak, and grey;

It was not night—it was not day; 240
It was not even the dungeon-light,
So hateful to my heavy sight,
But vacancy absorbing space,
And fixedness—without a place;
There were no stars—no earth—no time—
No check—no change—no good—no crime—
But silence, and a stirless breath
Which neither was of life nor death;
A sea of stagnant idleness,
Blind, boundless, mute, and motionless! 250

X

A light broke in upon my brain,—
    It was the carol of a bird;
It ceased, and then it came again,
    The sweetest song ear ever heard,
And mine was thankful till my eyes
Ran over with the glad surprise,
And they that moment could not see
I was the mate of misery;
But then by dull degrees came back
My senses to their wonted track; 260
I saw the dungeon walls and floor
Close slowly round me as before,
I saw the glimmer of the sun
Creeping as it before had done,
But through the crevice where it came
That bird was perched, as fond and tame,
    And tamer than upon the tree;
A lovely bird, with azure wings,
And song that said a thousand things,
    And seemed to say them all for me! 270
I never saw its like before,
I ne'er shall see its likeness more:
It seemed like me to want a mate,
But was not half so desolate,
And it was come to love me when

None lived to love me so again,
And cheering from my dungeon's brink,
Had brought me back to feel and think.
I know not if it late were free,
   Or broke its cage to perch on mine,   280
But knowing well captivity,
   Sweet bird! I could not wish for thine!
Or if it were, in wingéd guise,
A visitant from Paradise;
For—Heaven forgive that thought! the while
Which made me both to weep and smile—
I sometimes deemed that it might be
My brother's soul come down to me;
But then at last away it flew,
And then 'twas mortal well I knew,   290
For he would never thus have flown—
And left me twice so doubly lone,—
Lone—as the corse within its shroud,
Lone—as a solitary cloud,
   A single cloud on a sunny day,
While all the rest of heaven is clear,
A frown upon the atmosphere,
That hath no business to appear
   When skies are blue, and earth is gay.

X I

A kind of change came in my fate,   300
My keepers grew compassionate;
I know not what had made them so,
They were inured to sights of woe,
But so it was:—my broken chain
With links unfastened did remain,
And it was liberty to stride
Along my cell from side to side,
And up and down, and then athwart,
And tread it over every part;
And round the pillars one by one,   310
Returning where my walk begun,

Avoiding only, as I trod,
My brothers' graves without a sod;
For if I thought with heedless tread
My step profaned their lowly bed,
My breath came gaspingly and thick,
And my crushed heart felt blind and sick.

XII

I made a footing in the wall,
    It was not therefrom to escape,
For I had buried one and all,   320
    Who loved me in a human shape;
And the whole earth would henceforth be
A wider prison unto me:
No child—no sire—no kin had I,
No partner in my misery;
I thought of this, and I was glad,
For thought of them had made me mad;
But I was curious to ascend
To my barred windows, and to bend
Once more, upon the mountains high,   330
The quiet of a loving eye.

XIII

I saw them—and they were the same,
They were not changed like me in frame;
I saw their thousand years of snow
On high—their wide long lake below,
And the blue Rhone in fullest flow;
I heard the torrents leap and gush
O'er channelled rock and broken bush;
I saw the white-walled distant town,
And whiter sails go skimming down;   340
And then there was a little isle,
Which in my very face did smile,
    The only one in view;
A small green isle, it seemed no more,
Scarce broader than my dungeon floor,

But in it there were three tall trees,
And o'er it blew the mountain breeze,
And by it there were waters flowing,
And on it there were young flowers growing,
   Of gentle breath and hue. 350
The fish swam by the castle wall,
And they seemed joyous each and all;
The eagle rode the rising blast,
Methought he never flew so fast
As then to me he seemed to fly;
And then new tears came in my eye,
And I felt troubled—and would fain
I had not left my recent chain;
And when I did descend again,
The darkness of my dim abode 360
Fell on me as a heavy load;
It was as is a new-dug grave,
Closing o'er one we sought to save,—
And yet my glance, too much opprest,
Had almost need of such a rest.

XIV

It might be months, or years, or days—
   I kept no count, I took no note—
I had no hope my eyes to raise,
   And clear them of their dreary mote;
At last men came to set me free; 370
   I asked not why, and recked not where;
It was at length the same to me,
Fettered or fetterless to be,
   I learned to love despair.
And thus when they appeared at last,
And all my bonds aside were cast,
These heavy walls to me had grown
A hermitage—and all my own!
And half I felt as they were come
To tear me from a second home: 380
With spiders I had friendship made,

And watched them in their sullen trade,
Had seen the mice by moonlight play,
And why should I feel less than they?
We were all inmates of one place,
And I, the monarch of each race,
Had power to kill—yet, strange to tell!
In quiet we had learned to dwell;
My very chains and I grew friends,
So much a long communion tends   390
To make us what we are;—even I
Regained my freedom with a sigh.

[*First publ., December 5, 1816.*]

BEPPO

A VENETIAN STORY

[*Based on a story then current in Venice. In a letter to John Murray, October 12, 1817, Byron says he has "written a poem (of 84 octave stanzas), humourous, in or after the excellent manner of Mr. Whistlecraft (whom I take to be Frere), on a Venetian anecdote which amused me." He himself never said more of this anecdote. Actually the story was told to Byron and his friend John Cam Hobhouse on the evening of August 29, 1817, at La Mira, on the Brenta just outside of Venice, where Marianna Segati—"pretty as an antelope," with "large black, Oriental eyes"—had established herself in Byron's house as his regular* amica. *It is perhaps ironically appropriate to the spirit of* Beppo *that it should have been told by the husband of Marianna, who, Hobhouse says, used to spend the weekends at La Mira to court another lady.*

This is the anecdote as Hobhouse recorded it in his diary: ". . . dine, ride, moonlight walk with B. Zagati [sic] at dinner told us two singular stories . . . [the second one concerns us here]. A Turk arrived at the Regina di Unghera [sic] inn at Venice and lodged there—he asked to speak to the mistress of the inn a buxom lady of 40 in keeping with several children and who had lost her husband many years before at sea—after some preliminaries my hostess went to the Turk who immediately shut the door and began questioning her about her family and her late husband—she told her loss—when the Turk asked if her husband had any particular mark about him she said—yes he had a scar on his shoulder—something like this said the Turk pulling down his robe—I am your husband—I have been to Turkey—I have made a large fortune and I make you three offers, either to quit your amoroso and come with me or to stay with your amoroso or to accept a pension and live alone." Hobhouse adds: The lady has not yet given an answer, but M. Zagati said—I'm sure I would not leave my amoroso for any husband—looking at B. This is too gross even for me."

In a little more than a month Byron had transformed this "gross" episode which amused him into the poetic irony of Beppo.]

Rosalind. Farewell, Monsieur Traveller; Look, you lisp, and wear strange suits: disable all the benefits of your own country; be out of love with your Nativity, and almost chide God for making you that countenance you are; or I will scarce think you have swam in a *Gondola.*

—As You Like It, act iv. sc. 1, lines 33–35.

Annotation of the Commentators.

That is, *been at Venice,* which was much visited by the young English gentlemen of those times, and was *then* what *Paris* is *now*—the seat of all dissoluteness.

—S.A.

I

'Tis known, at least it should be, that throughout
    All countries of the Catholic persuasion,
Some weeks before Shrove Tuesday comes about,
    The People take their fill of recreation,
And buy repentance, ere they grow devout,
    However high their rank, or low their station,
With fiddling, feasting, dancing, drinking, masquing,
And other things which may be had for asking.

II

The moment night with dusky mantle covers
    The skies (and the more duskily the better),
The Time less liked by husbands than by lovers
    Begins, and Prudery flings aside her fetter;
And Gaiety on restless tiptoe hovers,
    Giggling with all the gallants who beset her;   10

And there are songs and quavers, roaring, humming,
Guitars, and every other sort of strumming.

III

And there are dresses splendid, but fantastical,
    Masks of all times and nations, Turks and Jews,
And harlequins and clowns, with feats gymnastical,
    Greeks, Romans, Yankee-doodles, and Hindoos;
All kinds of dress, except the ecclesiastical,
    All people, as their fancies hit, may choose,
But no one in these parts may quiz the Clergy,—
Therefore take heed, ye Freethinkers! I charge ye.

IV

You'd better walk about begirt with briars,
    Instead of coat and small clothes, than put on
A single stitch reflecting upon friars,
    Although you swore it only was in fun;
They'd haul you o'er the coals, and stir the fires
    Of Phlegethon with every mother's son,
Nor say one mass to cool the cauldron's bubble
That boiled your bones, unless you paid them double.

V

But saving this, you may put on whate'er
    You like by way of doublet, cape, or cloak,
Such as in Monmouth-street, or in Rag Fair,
    Would rig you out in seriousness or joke;
And even in Italy such places are,
    With prettier name in softer accents spoke,
For, bating Covent Garden, I can hit on
No place that's called "Piazza" in Great Britain.

VI

This feast is named the Carnival, which being
    Interpreted, implies "farewell to flesh"—
So called, because the name and thing agreeing,
    Through Lent they live on fish both salt and fresh.
But why they usher Lent with so much glee in,
    Is more than I can tell, although I guess

'Tis as we take a glass with friends at parting,
In the Stage-Coach or Packet, just at starting.

VII

And thus they bid farewell to carnal dishes,
   And solid meats, and highly spiced ragouts,   50
To live for forty days on ill-dressed fishes,
   Because they have no sauces to their stews;
A thing which causes many "poohs" and "pishes,"
   And several oaths (which would not suit the Muse),
From travellers accustomed from a boy
To eat their salmon, at the least, with soy;

VIII

And therefore humbly I would recommend
   "The curious in fish-sauce," before they cross
The sea, to bid their cook, or wife, or friend,
   Walk or ride to the Strand, and buy in gross   60
(Or if set out beforehand, these may send
   By any means least liable to loss),
Ketchup, Soy, Chili-vinegar, and Harvey,
Or, by the Lord! a Lent will well nigh starve ye;

IX

That is to say, if your religion's Roman,
   And you at Rome would do as Romans do,
According to the proverb,—although no man,
   If foreign, is obliged to fast; and you,
If Protestant, or sickly, or a woman,
   Would rather dine in sin on a ragout—   70
Dine and be d—d! I don't mean to be coarse,
But that's the penalty, to say no worse.

X

Of all the places where the Carnival
   Was most facetious in the days of yore,
For dance, and song, and serenade, and ball,
   And Masque, and Mime, and Mystery, and more
Than I have time to tell now, or at all,

Venice the bell from every city bore,—
And at the moment when I fix my story,
That sea-born city was in all her glory.   80

XI

They've pretty faces yet, those same Venetians,
    Black eyes, arched brows, and sweet expressions still;
Such as of old were copied from the Grecians,
    In ancient arts by moderns mimicked ill;
And like so many Venuses of Titian's
    (The best's at Florence—see it, if ye will,)
They look when leaning over the balcony,
Or stepped from out a picture by Giorgione,

XII

Whose tints are Truth and Beauty at their best;
    And when you to Manfrini's palace go,   90
That picture (howsoever fine the rest)
    Is loveliest to my mind of all the show;
It may perhaps be also to *your* zest,
    And that's the cause I rhyme upon it so:
'Tis but a portrait of his Son, and Wife,
And self; but *such* a Woman! Love in Life!

XIII

Love in full life and length, not love ideal,
    No, nor ideal beauty, that fine name,
But something better still, so very real,
    That the sweet Model must have been the same;   100
A thing that you would purchase, beg, or steal,
    Wer't not impossible, besides a shame:
The face recalls some face, as 'twere with pain,
You once have seen, but ne'er will see again;

XIV

One of those forms which flit by us, when we
    Are young, and fix our eyes on every face;
And, oh! the Loveliness at times we see
    In momentary gliding, the soft grace,

The Youth, the Bloom, the Beauty which agree,
    In many a nameless being we retrace,   110
Whose course and home we knew not, nor shall know,
Like the lost Pleiad seen no more below.

X V

I said that like a picture by Giorgione
    Venetian women were, and so they *are*,
Particularly seen from a balcony,
    (For beauty's sometimes best set off afar)
And there, just like a heroine of Goldoni,
    They peep from out the blind, or o'er the bar;
And truth to say, they're mostly very pretty,
And rather like to show it, more's the pity!   120

X V I

For glances beget ogles, ogles sighs,
    Sighs wishes, wishes words, and words a letter,
Which flies on wings of light-heeled Mercuries,
    Who do such things because they know no better;
And then, God knows what mischief may arise,
    When Love links two young people in one fetter,
Vile assignations, and adulterous beds,
Elopements, broken vows, and hearts, and heads.

X V I I

Shakespeare described the sex in Desdemona
    As very fair, but yet suspect in fame,   130
And to this day from Venice to Verona
    Such matters may be probably the same,
Except that since those times was never known a
    Husband whom mere suspicion could inflame
To suffocate a wife no more than twenty,
Because she had a "Cavalier Servente."

X V I I I

Their jealousy (if they are ever jealous)
    Is of a fair complexion altogether,
Not like that sooty devil of Othello's
    Which smothers women in a bed of feather,   140

But worthier of these much more jolly fellows,
    When weary of the matrimonial tether
His head for such a wife no mortal bothers,
But takes at once another, or *another's.*

XIX

Didst ever see a Gondola? For fear
    You should not, I'll describe it you exactly:
'Tis a long covered boat that's common here,
    Carved at the prow, built lightly, but compactly,
Rowed by two rowers, each called "Gondolier,"
    It glides along the water looking blackly,   150
Just like a coffin clapt in a canoe,
Where none can make out what you say or do.

XX

And up and down the long canals they go,
    And under the Rialto shoot along,
By night and day, all paces, swift or slow,
    And round the theatres, a sable throng,
They wait in their dusk livery of woe,—
    But not to them do woeful things belong,
For sometimes they contain a deal of fun,
Like mourning coaches when the funeral's done.   160

XXI

But to my story.—'Twas some years ago,
    It may be thirty, forty, more or less,
The Carnival was at its height, and so
    Were all kinds of buffoonery and dress;
A certain lady went to see the show,
    Her real name I know not, nor can guess,
And so we'll call her Laura, if you please,
Because it slips into my verse with ease.

XXII

She was not old, nor young, nor at the years
    Which certain people call a *"certain age,"*   170
Which yet the most uncertain age appears,
    Because I never heard, nor could engage

A person yet by prayers, or bribes, or tears,
 To name, define by speech, or write on page,
The period meant precisely by that word,—
Which surely is exceedingly absurd.

XXIII

Laura was blooming still, had made the best
 Of Time, and Time returned the compliment,
And treated her genteelly, so that, dressed,
 She looked extremely well where'er she went;   180
A pretty woman is a welcome guest,
 And Laura's brow a frown had rarely bent;
Indeed, she shone all smiles, and seemed to flatter
Mankind with her black eyes for looking at her.

XXIV

She was a married woman; 'tis convenient,
 Because in Christian countries 'tis a rule
To view their little slips with eyes more lenient;
 Whereas if single ladies play the fool,
(Unless within the period intervenient
 A well-timed wedding makes the scandal cool)   190
I don't know how they ever can get over it,
Except they manage never to discover it.

XXV

Her husband sailed upon the Adriatic,
 And made some voyages, too, in other seas,
And when he lay in Quarantine for pratique
 (A forty days' precaution 'gainst disease),
His wife would mount, at times, her highest attic,
 For thence she could discern the ship with ease:
He was a merchant trading to Aleppo,
His name Giuseppe, called more briefly, Beppo.   200

XXVI

He was a man as dusky as a Spaniard,
 Sunburnt with travel, yet a portly figure;
Though coloured, as it were, within a tanyard,
 He was a person both of sense and vigour—

A better seaman never yet did man yard;
    And she, although her manner showed no rigour,
Was deemed a woman of the strictest principle,
So much as to be thought almost invincible.

XXVII

But several years elapsed since they had met;
    Some people thought the ship was lost, and some   210
That he had somehow blundered into debt,
    And did not like the thought of steering home;
And there were several offered any bet,
    Or that he would, or that he would not come;
For most men (till by losing rendered sager)
Will back their own opinions with a wager.

XXVIII

'Tis said that their last parting was pathetic,
    As partings often are, or ought to be,
And their presentiment was quite prophetic,
    That they should never more each other see,   220
(A sort of morbid feeling, half poetic,
    Which I have known occur in two or three,)
When kneeling on the shore upon her sad knee
He left this Adriatic Ariadne.

XXIX

And Laura waited long, and wept a little,
    And thought of wearing weeds, as well she might;
She almost lost all appetite for victual,
    And could not sleep with ease alone at night;
She deemed the window-frames and shutters brittle
    Against a daring housebreaker or sprite,   230
And so she thought it prudent to connect her
With a vice-husband, *chiefly* to *protect her*.

XXX

She chose, (and what is there they will not choose,
    If only you will but oppose their choice?)
Till Beppo should return from his long cruise,
    And bid once more her faithful heart rejoice,

A man some women like, and yet abuse—
    A Coxcomb was he by the public voice;
A Count of wealth, they said, as well as quality,
And in his pleasures of great liberality.   240

XXXI

And then he was a Count, and then he knew
    Music, and dancing, fiddling, French and Tuscan;
The last not easy, be it known to you,
    For few Italians speak the right Etruscan.
He was a critic upon operas, too,
    And knew all niceties of sock and buskin;
And no Venetian audience could endure a
Song, scene, or air, when he cried "seccatura!"

XXXII

His "bravo" was decisive, for that sound
    Hushed "Academie" sighed in silent awe;   250
The fiddlers trembled as he looked around,
    For fear of some false note's detected flaw;
The "Prima Donna's" tuneful heart would bound,
    Dreading the deep damnation of his "Bah!"
Soprano, Basso, even the Contra-Alto,
Wished him five fathom under the Rialto.

XXXIII

He patronised the Improvisatori,
    Nay, could himself extemporise some stanzas,
Wrote rhymes, sang songs, could also tell a story,
    Sold pictures, and was skilful in the dance as   260
Italians can be, though in this their glory
    Must surely yield the palm to that which France has;
In short, he was a perfect Cavaliero
And to his very valet seemed a hero.

XXXIV

Then he was faithful too, as well as amorous;
    So that no sort of female could complain,
Although they're now and then a little clamorous,
    He never put the pretty souls in pain;

His heart was one of those which most enamour us,
    Wax to receive, and marble to retain: 270
He was a lover of the good old school,
    Who still become more constant as they cool.

XXXV

No wonder such accomplishments should turn
    A female head, however sage and steady—
With scarce a hope that Beppo could return,
    In law he was almost as good as dead, he
Nor sent, nor wrote, nor showed the least concern,
    And she had waited several years already:
And really if a man won't let us know
That he's alive, he's *dead*—or should be so.   280

XXXVI

Besides, within the Alps, to every woman,
    (Although, God knows, it is a grievous sin,)
'Tis, I may say, permitted to have *two* men;
    I can't tell who first brought the custom in,
But "Cavalier Serventes" are quite common
    And no one notices or cares a pin;
And we may call this (not to say the worst)
A *second* marriage which corrupts the *first.*

XXXVII

The word was formerly a "Cicisbeo,"
    But *that* is now grown vulgar and indecent;   290
The Spaniards call the person a *"Cortejo,"*
    For the same mode subsists in Spain, though recent;
In short it reaches from the Po to Teio,
    And may perhaps at last be o'er the sea sent:
But Heaven preserve Old England from such courses!
Or what becomes of damage and divorces?

XXXVIII

However, I still think, with all due deference
    To the fair *single* part of the creation,
That married ladies should preserve the preference
    In *tête à tête* or general conversation—   300

And this I say without peculiar reference
    To England, France, or any other nation—
Because they know the world, and are at ease,
And being natural, naturally please.

XXXIX

'Tis true, your budding Miss is very charming,
    But shy and awkward at first coming out,
So much alarmed, that she is quite alarming,
    All Giggle, Blush—half Pertness, and half Pout;
And glancing at *Mamma,* for fear there's harm in
    What you, she, it, or they, may be about: 310
The Nursery still lisps out in all they utter—
Besides, they always smell of bread and butter.

XL

But "Cavalier Servente" is the phrase
    Used in politest circles to express
This supernumerary slave, who stays
    Close to the lady as a part of dress,
Her word the only law which he obeys.
    His is no sinecure, as you may guess;
Coach, servants, gondola, he goes to call,
And carries fan and tippet, gloves and shawl.   320

XLI

With all its sinful doings, I must say,
    That Italy's a pleasant place to me,
Who love to see the Sun shine every day,
    And vines (not nailed to walls) from tree to tree
Festooned, much like the back scene of a play,
    Or melodrame, which people flock to see,
When the first act is ended by a dance
In vineyards copied from the south of France.

XLII

I like on Autumn evenings to ride out,
    Without being forced to bid my groom be sure   330
My cloak is round his middle strapped about,
    Because the skies are not the most secure;

I know too that, if stopped upon my route,
  Where the green alleys windingly allure,
Reeling with *grapes* red wagons choke the way,—
In England 'twould be dung, dust, or a dray.

XLIII

I also like to dine on becaficas,
  To see the Sun set, sure he'll rise to-morrow,
Not through a misty morning twinkling weak as
  A drunken man's dead eye in maudlin sorrow,   340
But with all Heaven t'himself; the day will break as
  Beauteous as cloudless, nor be forced to borrow
That sort of farthing candlelight which glimmers
Where reeking London's smoky cauldron simmers.

XLIV

I love the language, that soft bastard Latin,
  Which melts like kisses from a female mouth,
And sounds as if it should be writ on satin,
  With syllables which breathe of the sweet South,
And gentle liquids gliding all so pat in,
  That not a single accent seems uncouth,   350
Like our harsh northern whistling, grunting guttural,
Which we're obliged to hiss, and spit, and sputter all.

XLV

I like the women too (forgive my folly!),
  From the rich peasant cheek of ruddy bronze,
And large black eyes that flash on you a volley
  Of rays that say a thousand things at once,
To the high Dama's brow, more melancholy,
  But clear, and with a wild and liquid glance,
Heart on her lips, and soul within her eyes,
Soft as her clime, and sunny as her skies.   360

XLVI

Eve of the land which still is Paradise!
  Italian Beauty didst thou not inspire
Raphael, who died in thy embrace, and vies
  With all we know of Heaven, or can desire,

In what he hath bequeathed us?—in what guise
    Though flashing from the fervour of the Lyre,
Would *words* describe thy past and present glow,
While yet Canova can create below?

XLVII

"England! with all thy faults I love thee still,"
    I said at Calais, and have not forgot it;   370
I like to speak and lucubrate my fill;
    I like the government (but that is not it);
I like the freedom of the press and quill;
    I like the Habeas Corpus (when we've got it);
I like a Parliamentary debate,
Particularly when 'tis not too late:

XLVIII

I like the taxes, when they're not too many;
    I like a seacoal fire, when not too dear;
I like a beef-steak, too, as well as any;
    Have no objection to a pot of beer;   380
I like the weather,—when it is not rainy,
    That is, I like two months of every year.
And so God save the Regent, Church, and King!
Which means that I like all and every thing.

XLIX

Our standing army, and disbanded seamen,
    Poor's rate, Reform, my own, the nation's debt,
Our little riots, just to show we're free men,
    Our trifling bankruptcies in the Gazette,
Our cloudy climate, and our chilly women,
    All these I can forgive, and those forget,   390
And greatly venerate our recent glories,
And wish they were not owing to the Tories.

L

But to my tale of Laura,—for I find
    Digression is a sin, that by degrees
Becomes exceeding tedious to my mind,
    And, therefore, may the reader too displease—

The gentle reader, who may wax unkind,
    And caring little for the Author's ease,
Insist on knowing what he means—a hard
And hapless situation for a Bard.   400

LI

Oh! that I had the art of easy writing
    What should be easy reading! could I scale
Parnassus, where the Muses sit inditing
    Those pretty poems never known to fail,
How quickly would I print (the world delighting)
    A Grecian, Syrian, or Assyrian tale;
And sell you, mixed with western Sentimentalism,
Some samples of the *finest Orientalism.*

LII

But I am but a nameless sort of person,
    (A broken Dandy lately on my travels)   410
And take for rhyme, to hook my rambling verse on,
    The first that Walker's Lexicon unravels,
And when I can't find that, I put a worse on,
    Not caring as I ought for critic's cavils;
I've half a mind to tumble down to prose,
But verse is more in fashion—so here goes!

LIII

The Count and Laura made their new arrangement,
    Which lasted, as arrangements sometimes do,
For half a dozen years without estrangement;
    They had their little differences, too;   420
Those jealous whiffs, which never any change meant;
    In such affairs there probably are few
Who have not had this pouting sort of squabble,
From sinners of high station to the rabble.

LIV

But, on the whole, they were a happy pair,
    As happy as unlawful love could make them;
The gentleman was fond, the lady fair,
    Their chains so slight, 'twas not worth while to break them:

The World beheld them with indulgent air;
    The pious only wished "the Devil take them!"   430
He took them not; he very often waits,
And leaves old sinners to be young ones' baits.

LV

But they were young: Oh! what without our Youth
    Would Love be! What would Youth be without Love!
Youth lends its joy, and sweetness, vigour, truth,
    Heart, soul, and all that seems as from above;
But, languishing with years, it grows uncouth—
    One of few things Experience don't improve;
Which is, perhaps, the reason why old fellows
Are always so preposterously jealous.   440

LVI

It was the Carnival, as I have said
    Some six and thirty stanzas back, and, so
Laura the usual preparations made,
    Which you do when your mind's made up to go
To-night to Mrs. Boehm's masquerade,
    Spectator, or partaker in the show;
The only difference known between the cases
Is—*here,* we have six weeks of "varnished faces."

LVII

Laura, when dressed, was (as I sang before)
    A pretty woman as was ever seen,   450
Fresh as the Angel o'er a new inn door,
    Or frontispiece of a new Magazine,
With all the fashions which the last month wore,
    Coloured, and silver paper leaved between
That and the title-page, for fear the Press
Should soil with parts of speech the parts of dress.

LVIII

They went to the Ridotto; 'tis a hall
    Where People dance, and sup, and dance again;
Its proper name, perhaps, were a masqued ball,
    But that's of no importance to my strain;   460

'Tis (on a smaller scale) like our Vauxhall,
    Excepting that it can't be spoilt by rain;
The company is "mixed" (the phrase I quote is
As much as saying, they're below your notice);

LIX

For a "mixed company" implies that, save
    Yourself and friends, and half a hundred more,
Whom you may bow to without looking grave,
    The rest are but a vulgar set, the bore
Of public places, where they basely brave
    The fashionable stare of twenty score   470
Of well-bred persons, called *"The World"*; but I,
Although I know them, really don't know why.

LX

This is the case in England; at least was
    During the dynasty of Dandies, now
Perchance succeeded by some other class
    Of imitated Imitators:—how
Irreparably soon decline, alas!
    The Demagogues of fashion: all below
Is frail; how easily the world is lost
By Love, or War, and, now and then,—by Frost!   480

LXI

Crushed was Napoleon by the northern Thor,
    Who knocked his army down with icy hammer,
Stopped by the *Elements*—like a Whaler—or
    A blundering novice in his new French grammar;
Good cause had he to doubt the chance of war,
    And as for Fortune—but I dare not d—n her,
Because, were I to ponder to Infinity,
The more I should believe in her Divinity.

LXII

She rules the present, past, and all to be yet,
    She gives us luck in lotteries, love, and marriage;   490
I cannot say that she's done much for me yet;
    Not that I mean her bounties to disparage,

We've not yet closed accounts, and we shall see yet
 How much she'll make amends for past miscarriage;
Meantime the Goddess I'll no more importune,
Unless to thank her when she's made my fortune.

LXIII

To turn,—and to return;—the Devil take it!
 This story slips for ever through my fingers,
Because, just as the stanza likes to make it,
 It needs must be—and so it rather lingers;   500
This form of verse began, I can't well break it,
 But must keep time and tune like public singers;
But if I once get through my present measure,
I'll take another when I'm next at leisure.

LXIV

They went to the Ridotto ('tis a place
 To which I mean to go myself to-morrow,
Just to divert my thoughts a little space
 Because I'm rather hippish, and may borrow
Some spirits, guessing at what kind of face
 May lurk beneath each mask; and as my sorrow 510
Slackens its pace sometimes, I'll make, or find,
Something shall leave it half an hour behind.)

LXV

Now Laura moves along the joyous crowd,
 Smiles in her eyes, and simpers on her lips;
To some she whispers, others speaks aloud;
 To some she curtsies, and to some she dips,
Complains of warmth, and, this complaint avowed,
 Her lover brings the lemonade she sips;
She then surveys, condemns, but pities still
Her dearest friends for being dressed so ill.   520

LXVI

One has false curls, another too much paint,
 A third—where did she buy that frightful turban?
A fourth's so pale she fears she's going to faint,
 A fifth's look's vulgar, dowdyish, and suburban,

A sixth's white silk has got a yellow taint,
　　A seventh's thin muslin surely will be her bane,
And lo! an eighth appears,—"I'll see no more!"
For fear, like Banquo's kings, they reach a score.

LXVII

Meantime, while she was thus at others gazing,
　　Others were levelling their looks at her;　　　　　530
She heard the men's half-whispered mode of praising,
　　And, till 'twas done, determined not to stir;
The women only thought it quite amazing
　　That, at her time of life, so many were
Admirers still,—but "Men are so debased—
Those brazen Creatures always suit their taste."

LXVIII

For my part, now, I ne'er could understand
　　Why naughty women—but I won't discuss
A thing which is a scandal to the land,
　　I only don't see why it should be thus;　　　　　540
And if I were but in a gown and band,
　　Just to entitle me to make a fuss,
I'd preach on this till Wilberforce and Romilly
Should quote in their next speeches from my homily.

LXIX

While Laura thus was seen and seeing, smiling,
　　Talking, she knew not why, and cared not what,
So that her female friends, with envy broiling,
　　Beheld her airs, and triumph, and all that;
And well-dressed males still kept before her filing,
　　And passing bowed and mingled with her chat;　　550
More than the rest one person seemed to stare
With pertinacity that's rather rare.

LXX

He was a Turk, the colour of mahogany;
　　And Laura saw him, and at first was glad,
Because the Turks so much admire philogyny,
　　Although their usage of their wives is sad;

'Tis said they use no better than a dog any
    Poor woman, whom they purchase like a pad:
They have a number, though they ne'er exhibit 'em,
Four wives by law, and concubines "ad libitum."   560

LXXI

They lock them up, and veil, and guard them daily,
    They scarcely can behold their male relations,
So that their moments do not pass so gaily
    As is supposed the case with northern nations;
Confinement, too, must make them look quite palely;
    And as the Turks abhor long conversations,
Their days are either passed in doing nothing,
Or bathing, nursing, making love, and clothing.

LXXII

They cannot read, and so don't lisp in criticism;
    Nor write, and so they don't affect the Muse;   570
Were never caught in epigram or witticism,
    Have no romances, sermons, plays, reviews,—
In Harams learning soon would make a pretty schism!
    But luckily these Beauties are no "Blues";
No bustling *Botherby* have they to show 'em
"That charming passage in the last new poem":

LXXIII

No solemn, antique gentleman of rhyme,
    Who having angled all his life for Fame,
And getting but a nibble at a time,
    Still fussily keeps fishing on, the same   580
Small "Triton of the minnows," the sublime
    Of Mediocrity, the furious tame,
The Echo's echo, usher of the school
Of female wits, boy bards—in short, a fool!

LXXIV

A stalking oracle of awful phrase,
    The approving *"Good!"* (by no means GOOD in law)
Humming like flies around the newest blaze,
    The bluest of bluebottles you e'er saw,

Teasing with blame, excruciating with praise,
　　Gorging the little fame he gets all raw,　　　　　　590
Translating tongues he knows not even by letter,
And sweating plays so middling, bad were better.

L X X V

One hates an author that's *all author*—fellows
　　In foolscap uniforms turned up with ink,
So very anxious, clever, fine, and jealous,
　　One don't know what to say to them, or think,
Unless to puff them with a pair of bellows;
　　Of Coxcombry's worst coxcombs e'en the pink
Are preferable to these shreds of paper,
These unquenched snuffings of the midnight taper.　　600

L X X V I

Of these same we see several, and of others,
　　Men of the World, who know the World like Men,
Scott, Rogers, Moore, and all the better brothers,
　　Who think of something else besides the pen;
But for the children of the "Mighty Mother's,"
　　The would-be wits, and can't-be gentlemen,
I leave them to their daily "tea is ready,"
Smug coterie, and literary lady.

L X X V I I

The poor dear Mussul*women* whom I mention
　　Have none of these instructive pleasant people,　　610
And *one* would seem to them a new invention,
　　Unknown as bells within a Turkish steeple;
I think 'twould almost be worth while to pension
　　(Though best-sown projects very often reap ill)
A missionary author—just to preach
Our Christian usage of the parts of speech.

L X X V I I I

No Chemistry for them unfolds her gases,
　　No Metaphysics are let loose in lectures,
No Circulating Library amasses
　　Religious novels, moral tales, and strictures　　620

Upon the living manners, as they pass us;
　　No Exhibition glares with annual pictures;
They stare not on the stars from out their attics,
　　Nor deal (thank God for that!) in Mathematics.

LXXIX

Why I thank God for that is no great matter,
　　I have my reasons, you no doubt suppose,
And as, perhaps, they would not highly flatter,
　　I'll keep them for my life (to come) in prose;
I fear I have a little turn for Satire,
　　And yet methinks the older that one grows　　　　630
Inclines us more to laugh than scold, though Laughter
Leaves us so doubly serious shortly after.

LXXX

Oh, Mirth and Innocence! Oh, Milk and Water!
　　Ye happy mixtures of more happy days!
In these sad centuries of sin and slaughter,
　　Abominable Man no more allays
His thirst with such pure beverage. No matter,
　　I love you both, and both shall have my praise:
Oh, for old Saturn's reign of sugar-candy!—
Meantime I drink to your return in brandy.　　　　640

LXXXI

Our Laura's Turk still kept his eyes upon her,
　　Less in the Mussulman than Christian way,
Which seems to say, "Madam, I do you honour,
　　And while I please to stare, you'll please to stay."
Could staring win a woman, this had won her,
　　But Laura could not thus be led astray;
She had stood fire too long and well, to boggle
Even at this Stranger's most outlandish ogle.

LXXXII

The morning now was on the point of breaking,
　　A turn of time at which I would advise　　　　650
Ladies who have been dancing, or partaking
　　In any other kind of exercise,

To make their preparation for forsaking
    The ball-room ere the Sun begins to rise,
Because when once the lamps and candles fail,
His blushes make them look a little pale.

LXXXIII

I've seen some balls and revels in my time,
    And stayed them over for some silly reason,
And then I looked (I hope it was no crime)
    To see what lady best stood out the season;   660
And though I've seen some thousands in their prime
    Lovely and pleasing, and who still may please on,
I never saw but one (the stars withdrawn)
Whose bloom could after dancing dare the Dawn.

LXXXIV

The name of this Aurora I'll not mention,
    Although I might, for she was nought to me
More than that patent work of God's invention,
    A charming woman, whom we like to see;
But writing names would merit reprehension,
    Yet if you like to find out this fair *She,*   670
At the next London or Parisian ball
You still may mark her cheek, out-blooming all.

LXXXV

Laura, who knew it would not do at all
    To meet the daylight after seven hours' sitting
Among three thousand people at a ball,
    To make her curtsey thought it right and fitting;
The Count was at her elbow with her shawl,
    And they the room were on the point of quitting,
When lo! those curséd Gondoliers had got
Just in the very place where they *should not.*   680

LXXXVI

In this they're like our coachmen, and the cause
    Is much the same—the crowd, and pulling, hauling,
With blasphemies enough to break their jaws,
    They make a never intermitted bawling.

At home, our Bow-street gem'men keep the laws,
 And here a sentry stands within your calling;
But for all that, there is a deal of swearing,
And nauseous words past mentioning or bearing.

LXXXVII

The Count and Laura found their boat at last,
 And homeward floated o'er the silent tide,   690
Discussing all the dances gone and past;
 The dancers and their dresses, too, beside;
Some little scandals eke; but all aghast
 (As to their palace-stairs the rowers glide)
Sate Laura by the side of her adorer,
When lo! the Mussulman was there before her!

LXXXVIII

"Sir," said the Count, with brow exceeding grave,
 "Your unexpected presence here will make
It necessary for myself to crave
 Its import? But perhaps 'tis a mistake;   700
I hope it is so; and, at once to waive
 All compliment, I hope so for *your* sake;
You understand my meaning, or you *shall*."
"Sir," (quoth the Turk) " 'tis no mistake at all:

LXXXIX

"That Lady is *my wife!*" Much wonder paints
 The lady's changing cheek, as well it might;
But where an Englishwoman sometimes faints,
 Italian females don't do so outright;
They only call a little on their Saints,
 And then come to themselves, almost, or quite;   710
Which saves much hartshorn, salts, and sprinkling faces,
And cutting stays, as usual in such cases.

XC

She said,—what could she say? Why, not a word;
 But the Count courteously invited in
The Stranger, much appeased by what he heard:
 "Such things, perhaps, we'd best discuss within,"

Said he; "don't let us make ourselves absurd
    In public, by a scene, nor raise a din,
For then the chief and only satisfaction
Will be much quizzing on the whole transaction."   720

XCI

They entered, and for Coffee called—it came,
    A beverage for Turks and Christians both,
Although the way they make it's not the same.
    Now Laura, much recovered, or less loth
To speak, cries "Beppo! what's your pagan name?
    Bless me! your beard is of amazing growth!
And how came you to keep away so long?
Are you not sensible 'twas very wrong?

XCII

"Are you *really, truly,* now a Turk?
    With any other women did you wive?   730
Is't true they use their fingers for a fork?
    Well, that's the prettiest Shawl—as I'm alive!
You'll give it me? They say you eat no pork.
    And how so many years did you contrive
To—Bless me! did I ever? No, I never
Saw a man grown so yellow! How's your liver?

XCIII

"Beppo! that beard of yours becomes you not;
    It shall be shaved before you're a day older:
Why do you wear it? Oh! I had forgot—
    Pray don't you think the weather here is colder?   740
How do I look? You shan't stir from this spot
    In that queer dress, for fear that some beholder
Should find you out, and make the story known.
How short your hair is! Lord! how grey it's grown!"

XCIV

What answer Beppo made to these demands
    Is more than I know. He was cast away
About where Troy stood once, and nothing stands;
    Became a slave of course, and for his pay

Had bread and bastinadoes, till some bands
 Of pirates landing in a neighbouring bay,   750
He joined the rogues and prospered, and became
A renegado of indifferent fame.

XCV

But he grew rich, and with his riches grew so
 Keen the desire to see his home again,
He thought himself in duty bound to do so,
 And not be always thieving on the main;
Lonely he felt, at times, as Robin Crusoe,
 And so he hired a vessel come from Spain,
Bound for Corfu: she was a fine polacca,
Manned with twelve hands, and laden with tobacco.   760

XCVI

Himself, and much (heaven knows how gotten!) cash,
 He then embarked, with risk of life and limb,
And got clear off, although the attempt was rash;
 He said that *Providence* protected him—
For my part, I say nothing—lest we clash
 In our opinions:—well—the ship was trim,
Set sail, and kept her reckoning fairly on,
Except three days of calm when off Cape Bonn.

XCVII

They reached the Island, he transferred his lading,
 And self and live stock to another bottom,   770
And passed for a true Turkey-merchant, trading
 With goods of various names—but I've forgot 'em.
However, he got off by this evading,
 Or else the people would perhaps have shot him;
And thus at Venice landed to reclaim
His wife, religion, house, and Christian name.

XCVIII

His wife received, the Patriarch re-baptized him,
 (He made the Church a present, by the way;)
He then threw off the garments which disguised him,

And borrowed the Count's smallclothes for a day: 780
His friends the more for his long absence prized him,
    Finding he'd wherewithal to make them gay,
With dinners, where he oft became the laugh of them,
For stories—but *I* don't believe the half of them.

XCIX

Whate'er his youth had suffered, his old age
    With wealth and talking made him some amends;
Though Laura sometimes put him in a rage,
    I've heard the Count and he were always friends.
My pen is at the bottom of a page,
    Which being finished, here the story ends: 790
'Tis to be wished it had been sooner done,
But stories somehow lengthen when begun.

[First publ., February 28, 1818.]

DRAMA

MANFRED

A DRAMATIC POEM

[Manfred, *the most poetic of Byron's speculative dramas, wrestles with the central problems of romantic aspiration and despair. "Cooped in clay," Manfred longs for the freedom of the spirit world. Like Faust he conjures spirits, but is disappointed that they can tell him nothing that he doesn't already know, for they are the creations of his own mind. In the end he reaches nearest to that spirit world in the assertion of the indomitable, though unhappy, mind of man.*]

> "There are more things in heaven and earth, Horatio,
> Than are dreamt of in your philosophy."
>
> [*HAMLET*, i., 5.]

DRAMATIS PERSONAE

MANFRED

CHAMOIS HUNTER

ABBOT OF ST. MAURICE

MANUEL

HERMAN

WITCH OF THE ALPS

ARIMANES

NEMESIS

THE DESTINIES

SPIRITS, ETC.

*The scene of the Drama is amongst the Higher Alps—partly in the Castle of
Manfred, and partly in the Mountains.*

ACT I

SCENE I—MANFRED *alone.—Scene, a Gothic Gallery.—Time, Midnight.*
MANFRED. The lamp must be replenished, but even then
    It will not burn so long as I must watch:
    My slumbers—if I slumber—are not sleep,
    But a continuance of enduring thought,
    Which then I can resist not: in my heart
    There is a vigil, and these eyes but close
    To look within; and yet I live, and bear
    The aspect and the form of breathing men.
    But Grief should be the Instructor of the wise;
    Sorrow is Knowledge: they who know the most   10
    Must mourn the deepest o'er the fatal truth—
    The Tree of Knowledge is not that of Life.
    Philosophy and Science, and the springs
    Of Wonder, and the wisdom of the World,
    I have essayed, and in my mind there is
    A power to make these subject to itself—
    But they avail not: I have done men good,
    And I have met with good even among men—
    But this availed not: I have had my foes,
    And none have baffled, many fallen before me—   20
    But this availed not:—Good—or evil—life—
    Powers, passions—all I see in other beings,
    Have been to me as rain unto the sands,
    Since that all-nameless hour. I have no dread,
    And feel the curse to have no natural fear,
    Nor fluttering throb that beats with hopes or wishes,
    Or lurking love of something on the earth.
    Now to my task.—

Mysterious Agency!
Ye Spirits of the unbounded Universe!
Whom I have sought in darkness and in light—   30
Ye, who do compass earth about, and dwell
In subtler essence—ye, to whom the tops
Of mountains inaccessible are haunts,
And Earth's and Ocean's caves familiar things—
I call upon ye by the written charm
Which gives me power upon you—Rise! Appear!

[*A pause.*

They come not yet.—Now by the voice of him
Who is the first among you—by this sign,
Which makes you tremble—by the claims of him
Who is undying,—Rise! Appear!——Appear!   40

[*A pause.*

If it be so.—Spirits of Earth and Air,
Ye shall not so elude me! By a power,
Deeper than all yet urged, a tyrant-spell,
Which had its birthplace in a star condemned,
The burning wreck of a demolished world,
A wandering hell in the eternal Space;
By the strong curse which is upon my Soul,
The thought which is within me and around me,
I do compel ye to my will.—Appear!

[*A star is seen at the darker end of the gallery;*
it is stationary; and a voice is heard singing.

FIRST SPIRIT

Mortal! to thy bidding bowed,   50
From my mansion in the cloud,
Which the breath of Twilight builds,
And the Summer's sunset gilds
With the azure and vermilion,
Which is mixed for my pavilion;
Though thy quest may be forbidden,
On a star-beam I have ridden,
To thine adjuration bowed:
Mortal—be thy wish avowed!

Voice of the SECOND SPIRIT

    Mont Blanc is the Monarch of mountains;   60
        They crowned him long ago
    On a throne of rocks, in a robe of clouds,
        With a Diadem of snow.
    Around his waist are forests braced,
        The Avalanche in his hand;
    But ere it fall, that thundering ball
        Must pause for my command.
    The Glacier's cold and restless mass
        Moves onward day by day;
    But I am he who bids it pass,   70
        Or with its ice delay.
    I am the Spirit of the place,
        Could make the mountain bow
    And quiver to his caverned base—
        And what with me would'st *Thou?*

Voice of the THIRD SPIRIT

    In the blue depth of the waters,
        Where the wave hath no strife,
    Where the Wind is a stranger,
        And the Sea-snake hath life,
    Where the Mermaid is decking   80
        Her green hair with shells,
    Like the storm on the surface
        Came the sound of thy spells;
    O'er my calm Hall of Coral
        The deep Echo rolled—
    To the Spirit of Ocean
        Thy wishes unfold!

FOURTH SPIRIT

    Where the slumbering Earthquake
        Lies pillowed on fire,
    And the lakes of bitumen   90
        Rose boilingly higher;
    Where the roots of the Andes
        Strike deep in the earth,
    As their summits to heaven

Shoot soaringly forth;
I have quitted my birthplace,
   Thy bidding to bide—
Thy spell hath subdued me,
   Thy will be my guide!

FIFTH SPIRIT

I am the rider of the wind,
   The stirrer of the storm;   100
The hurricane I left behind
   Is yet with lightning warm;
To speed to thee, o'er shore and sea
   I swept upon the blast:
The fleet I met sailed well—and yet
   'Twill sink ere night be past.

SIXTH SPIRIT

My dwelling is the shadow of the Night,
Why doth thy magic torture me with light?

SEVENTH SPIRIT

The Star which rules thy destiny   110
Was ruled, ere earth began, by me:
It was a World as fresh and fair
As e'er revolved round Sun in air;
Its course was free and regular,
Space bosomed not a lovelier star.
The Hour arrived—and it became
A wandering mass of shapeless flame,
A pathless Comet, and a curse,
The menace of the Universe;
Still rolling on with innate force,   120
Without a sphere, without a course,
A bright deformity on high,
The monster of the upper sky!
And Thou! beneath its influence born—
Thou worm! whom I obey and scorn—
Forced by a Power (which is not thine,
And lent thee but to make thee mine)
For this brief moment to descend,
Where these weak Spirits round thee bend

And parley with a thing like thee—   130
  What would'st thou, Child of Clay! with me?

The SEVEN SPIRITS

  Earth—ocean—air—night—mountains—winds—thy Star,
    Are at thy beck and bidding, Child of Clay!
  Before thee at thy quest their Spirits are—
    What would'st thou with us, Son of mortals—say?

MANFRED. Forgetfulness——

FIRST SPIRIT.   Of what—of whom—and why?

MANFRED. Of that which is within me; read it there—
  Ye know it—and I cannot utter it.

SPIRIT. We can but give thee that which we possess:
  Ask of us subjects, sovereignty, the power   140
  O'er earth—the whole, or portion—or a sign
  Which shall control the elements, whereof
  We are the dominators,—each and all,
  These shall be thine.

MANFRED.   Oblivion—self-oblivion!
  Can ye not wring from out the hidden realms
  Ye offer so profusely—what I ask?

SPIRIT. It is not in our essence, in our skill;
  But—thou may'st die.

MANFRED.   Will Death bestow it on me?

SPIRIT We are immortal, and do not forget;
  We are eternal; and to us the past   150
  Is, as the future, present. Art thou answered?

MANFRED. Ye mock me—but the Power which brought ye here
  Hath made you mine. Slaves, scoff not at my will!
  The Mind—the Spirit—the Promethean spark,
  The lightning of my being, is as bright,
  Pervading, and far darting as your own,
  And shall not yield to yours, though cooped in clay!
  Answer, or I will teach you what I am.

SPIRIT. We answer—as we answered; our reply
  Is even in thine own words.

MANFRED.   Why say ye so?   160

SPIRIT. If, as thou say'st, thine essence be as ours,

We have replied in telling thee, the thing
Mortals call death hath nought to do with us.
MANFRED. I then have called ye from your realms in vain;
Ye cannot, or ye will not, aid me.
SPIRIT.   Say—
What we possess we offer; it is thine:
Bethink ere thou dismiss us;—ask again;
Kingdom, and sway, and strength, and length of days—
MANFRED. Accursèd! what have I to do with days?
They are too long already.—Hence—begone!   170
SPIRIT. Yet pause: being here, our will would do thee service;
Bethink thee, is there then no other gift
Which we can make not worthless in thine eyes?
MANFRED. No, none: yet stay—one moment, ere we part,
I would behold ye face to face. I hear
Your voices, sweet and melancholy sounds,
As Music on the waters; and I see
The steady aspect of a clear large Star—
But nothing more. Approach me as ye are,
Or one—or all—in your accustomed forms.   180
SPIRIT. We have no forms, beyond the elements
Of which we are the mind and principle:
But choose a form—in that we will appear.
MANFRED. I have no choice; there is no form on earth
Hideous or beautiful to me. Let him,
Who is most powerful of ye, take such aspect
As unto him may seem most fitting—Come!
SEVENTH SPIRIT (*appearing in the shape of a beautiful female figure*).
Behold!
MANFRED.   Oh God! if it be thus, and *thou*
Art not a madness and a mockery,
I yet might be most happy. I will clasp thee,   190
And we again will be——

                                        [*The figure vanishes.*
                    My heart is crushed!
                                        [MANFRED *falls senseless.*
              (*A voice is heard in the Incantation which follows.*)

When the Moon is on the wave,
   And the glow-worm in the grass,
And the meteor on the grave,
   And the wisp on the morass;
When the falling stars are shooting,
And the answered owls are hooting,
And the silent leaves are still
In the shadow of the hill,
Shall my soul be upon thine,   200
With a power and with a sign.

Though thy slumber may be deep,
Yet thy Spirit shall not sleep;
There are shades which will not vanish,
There are thoughts thou canst not banish;
By a Power to thee unknown,
Thou canst never be alone;
Thou art wrapt as with a shroud,
Thou art gathered in a cloud;
And for ever shalt thou dwell   210
In the spirit of this spell.

Though thou seest me not pass by,
Thou shalt feel me with thine eye
As a thing that, though unseen,
Must be near thee, and hath been;
And when in that secret dread
Thou hast turned around thy head,
Thou shalt marvel I am not
As thy shadow on the spot,
And the power which thou dost feel   220
Shall be what thou must conceal.

And a magic voice and verse
Hath baptized thee with a curse;
And a Spirit of the air
Hath begirt thee with a snare;
In the wind there is a voice

Shall forbid thee to rejoice;
And to thee shall Night deny
All the quiet of her sky;
And the day shall have a sun,
Which shall make thee wish it done.

From thy false tears I did distil
An essence which hath strength to kill;
From thy own heart I then did wring
The black blood in its blackest spring;
From thy own smile I snatched the snake,
For there it coiled as in a brake;
From thy own lip I drew the charm
Which gave all these their chiefest harm;
In proving every poison known,
I found the strongest was thine own.

By the cold breast and serpent smile,
By thy unfathomed gulfs of guile,
By that most seeming virtuous eye,
By thy shut soul's hypocrisy;
By the perfection of thine art
Which passed for human thine own heart:
By thy delight in others' pain,
And by thy brotherhood of Cain,
I call upon thee! and compel
Thyself to be thy proper Hell!

And on thy head I pour the vial
Which doth devote thee to this trial;
Nor to slumber, nor to die,
Shall be in thy destiny;
Though thy death shall still seem near
To thy wish, but as a fear;
Lo! the spell now works around thee,
And the clankless chain hath bound thee;
O'er thy heart and brain together
Hath the word been passed—now wither!

230

240

250

260

SCENE II—*The Mountain of the Jungfrau.—Time, Morning.—*
MANFRED *alone upon the cliffs.*

MANFRED. The spirits I have raised abandon me,
The spells which I have studied baffle me,
The remedy I recked of tortured me:
I lean no more on superhuman aid;
It hath no power upon the past, and for
The future, till the past be gulfed in darkness,
It is not of my search.—My Mother Earth!
And thou fresh-breaking Day, and you, ye Mountains,
Why are ye beautiful? I cannot love ye.
And thou, the bright Eye of the Universe,   10
That openest over all, and unto all
Art a delight—thou shin'st not on my heart.
And you ye crags, upon whose extreme edge
I stand, and on the torrent's brink beneath
Behold the tall pines dwindled as to shrubs
In dizziness of distance; when a leap,
A stir, a motion, even a breath, would bring
My breast upon its rocky bosom's bed
To rest for ever—wherefore do I pause?
I feel the impulse—yet I do not plunge;   20
I see the peril—yet do not recede;
And my brain reels—and yet my foot is firm:
There is a power upon me which withholds,
And makes it my fatality to live,—
If it be life to wear within myself
This barrenness of Spirit, and to be
My own Soul's sepulchre, for I have ceased
To justify my deeds unto myself—
The last infirmity of evil. Aye,
Thou winged and cloud-cleaving minister,   30
                              [*An Eagle passes.*

Whose happy flight is highest into heaven,
Well may'st thou swoop so near me—I should be
The prey, and gorge thine eaglets; thou art gone
Where the eye cannot follow thee; but thine
Yet pierces downward, onward, or above,

With a pervading vision.—Beautiful!
How beautiful is all this visible world!
How glorious in its action and itself!
But we, who name ourselves its sovereigns, we,
Half dust, half deity, alike unfit   40
To sink or soar, with our mixed essence make
A conflict of its elements, and breathe
The breath of degradation and of pride,
Contending with low wants and lofty will,
Till our Mortality predominates,
And men are—what they name not to themselves,
And trust not to each other. Hark! the note,
                    [*The Shepherd's pipe in the distance is heard.*
The natural music of the mountain reed—
For here the patriarchal days are not
A pastoral fable—pipes in the liberal air,   50
Mixed with the sweet bells of the sauntering herd;
My soul would drink those echoes. Oh, that I were
The viewless spirit of a lovely sound,
A living voice, a breathing harmony,
A bodiless enjoyment—born and dying
With the blest tone which made me!
                              Enter from below a CHAMOIS HUNTER.
CHAMOIS HUNTER.   Even so
This way the Chamois leapt: her nimble feet
Have baffled me; my gains to-day will scarce
Repay my break-neck travail.—What is here?
Who seems not of my trade, and yet hath reached   60
A height which none even of our mountaineers,
Save our best hunters, may attain: his garb
Is goodly, his mien manly, and his air
Proud as a free-born peasant's, at this distance:—
I will approach him nearer.
MANFRED (*not perceiving the other*). To be thus—
Grey-haired with anguish, like these blasted pines,
Wrecks of a single winter, barkless, branchless,
A blighted trunk upon a cursèd root,
Which but supplies a feeling to Decay—

And to be thus, eternally but thus, 70
Having been otherwise! Now furrowed o'er
With wrinkles, ploughed by moments, not by years
And hours, all tortured into ages—hours
Which I outlive!—Ye toppling crags of ice!
Ye Avalanches, whom a breath draws down
In mountainous o'erwhelming, come and crush me!
I hear ye momently above, beneath,
Crash with a frequent conflict; but ye pass,
And only fall on things that still would live;
On the young flourishing forest, or the hut 80
And hamlet of the harmless villager.

CHAMOIS HUNTER. The mists begin to rise from up the valley;
I'll warn him to descend, or he may chance
To lose at once his way and life together.

MANFRED. The mists boil up around the glaciers; clouds
Rise curling fast beneath me, white and sulphury,
Like foam from the roused ocean of deep Hell,
Whose every wave breaks on a living shore,
Heaped with the damned like pebbles.—I am giddy.

CHAMOIS HUNTER. I must approach him cautiously; if near, 90
A sudden step will startle him, and he
Seems tottering already.

MANFRED.   Mountains have fallen,
Leaving a gap in the clouds, and with the shock
Rocking their Alpine brethren; filling up
The ripe green valleys with Destruction's splinters;
Damming the rivers with a sudden dash,
Which crushed the waters into mist, and made
Their fountains find another channel—thus,
Thus, in its old age, did Mount Rosenberg—
Why stood I not beneath it?

CHAMOIS HUNTER.   Friend! have a care, 100
Your next step may be fatal!—for the love
Of Him who made you, stand not on that brink!

MANFRED (*not hearing him*). Such would have been for me a fitting
        tomb;
My bones had then been quiet in their depth;

They had not then been strewn upon the rocks
For the wind's pastime—as thus—thus they shall be—
In this one plunge.—Farewell, ye opening Heavens!
Look not upon me thus reproachfully—
You were not meant for me—Earth! take these atoms!

[As MANFRED *is in act to spring from the cliff, the* CHAMOIS HUNTER
seizes and retains him with a sudden grasp.

CHAMOIS HUNTER. Hold, madman!—though aweary of thy life,   110
Stain not our pure vales with thy guilty blood:
Away with me—I will not quit my hold.

MANFRED. I am most sick at heart—nay, grasp me not—
I am all feebleness—the mountains whirl,
Spinning around me——I grow blind——What art thou?

CHAMOIS HUNTER. I'll answer that anon.—Away with me——
The clouds grow thicker——there—now lean on me—
Place your foot here—here, take this staff, and cling
A moment to that shrub—now give me your hand,
And hold fast my girdle—softly—well—   120
The Chalet will be gained within an hour:
Come on, we'll quickly find a surer footing,
And something like a pathway, which the torrent
Hath washed since winter.—Come, 'tis bravely done—
You should have been a hunter.—Follow me.

[*As they descend the rocks with difficulty, the scene closes.*

ACT II

SCENE I—*A Cottage among the Bernese Alps.*—MANFRED *and the*
CHAMOIS HUNTER.

CHAMOIS HUNTER. No—no—yet pause—thou must not yet go
      forth:
Thy mind and body are alike unfit
To trust each other, for some hours, at least;
When thou art better, I will be thy guide—
But whither?

MANFRED.   It imports not: I do know
My route full well, and need no further guidance.

CHAMOIS HUNTER. Thy garb and gait bespeak thee of high
    lineage—
  One of the many chiefs, whose castled crags
  Look o'er the lower valleys—which of these
  May call thee lord? I only know their portals;   10
  My way of life leads me but rarely down
  To bask by the huge hearths of those old halls,
  Carousing with the vassals; but the paths,
  Which step from out our mountains to their doors,
  I know from childhood—which of these is thine?
MANFRED. No matter.
CHAMOIS HUNTER.   Well, Sir, pardon me the question,
  And be of better cheer. Come, taste my wine;
  'Tis of an ancient vintage; many a day
  'T has thawed my veins among our glaciers, now
  Let it do thus for thine—Come, pledge me fairly!   20
MANFRED. Away, away! there's blood upon the brim!
  Will it then never—never sink in the earth?
CHAMOIS HUNTER. What dost thou mean? thy senses wander from
    thee.
MANFRED. I say 'tis blood—my blood! the pure warm stream
  Which ran in the veins of my fathers, and in ours
  When we were in our youth, and had one heart,
  And loved each other as we should not love,
  And this was shed: but still it rises up,
  Colouring the clouds, that shut me out from Heaven,
  Where thou art not—and I shall never be.   30
CHAMOIS HUNTER. Man of strange words, and some
    half-maddening sin,
  Which makes thee people vacancy, whate'er
  Thy dread and sufferance be, there's comfort yet—
  The aid of holy men, and heavenly patience——
MANFRED. Patience—and patience! Hence—that word was made
  For brutes of burthen, not for birds of prey!
  Preach it to mortals of a dust like thine,—
  I am not of thine order.
CHAMOIS HUNTER.   Thanks to Heaven!
  I would not be of thine for the free fame

Of William Tell; but whatsoe'er thine ill, 40
It must be borne, and these wild starts are useless.
MANFRED. Do I not bear it?—Look on me—I live.
CHAMOIS HUNTER. This is convulsion, and no healthful life.
MANFRED. I tell thee, man! I have lived many years,
Many long years, but they are nothing now
To those which I must number: ages—ages—
Space and eternity—and consciousness,
With the fierce thirst of death—and still unslaked!
CHAMOIS HUNTER. Why, on thy brow the seal of middle age
Hath scarce been set; I am thine elder far. 50
MANFRED. Think'st thou existence doth depend on time?
It doth; but actions are our epochs: mine
Have made my days and nights imperishable,
Endless, and all alike, as sands on the shore,
Innumerable atoms; and one desert,
Barren and cold, on which the wild waves break,
But nothing rests, save carcasses and wrecks,
Rocks, and the salt-surf weeds of bitterness.
CHAMOIS HUNTER. Alas! he's mad—but yet I must not leave him.
MANFRED. I would I were—for then the things I see 60
Would be but a distempered dream.
CHAMOIS HUNTER. What is it
That thou dost see, or think thou look'st upon?
MANFRED. Myself, and thee—a peasant of the Alps—
Thy humble virtues, hospitable home,
And spirit patient, pious, proud, and free;
Thy self-respect grafted on innocent thoughts;
Thy days of health, and nights of sleep: thy toils,
By danger dignified, yet guiltless; hopes
Of cheerful old age and a quiet grave,
With cross and garland over its green turf, 70
And thy grandchildren's love for epitaph!
This do I see—and then I look within—
It matters not—my Soul was scorched already!
CHAMOIS HUNTER. And would'st thou then exchange thy lot for
mine?
MANFRED. No, friend! I would not wrong thee, nor exchange

My lot with living being: I can bear—
However wretchedly, 'tis still to bear—
In life what others could not brook to dream,
But perish in their slumber.

CHAMOIS HUNTER.   And with this—
This cautious feeling for another's pain,   80
Canst thou be black with evil?—say not so.
Can one of gentle thoughts have wreaked revenge
Upon his enemies?

MANFRED.   Oh! no, no, no!
My injuries came down on those who loved me—
On those whom I best loved: I never quelled
An enemy, save in my just defence—
My wrongs were all on those I should have cherished—
But my embrace was fatal.

CHAMOIS HUNTER.   Heaven give thee rest!
And Penitence restore thee to thyself;
My prayers shall be for thee.

MANFRED.   I need them not,   90
But can endure thy pity. I depart—
'Tis time—farewell!—Here's gold, and thanks for thee—
No words—it is thy due.—Follow me not—
I know my path—the mountain peril's past:
And once again I charge thee, follow not!

                                        [*Exit* MANFRED.

SCENE II—*A lower Valley in the Alps.—A Cataract.*
Enter MANFRED.

It is not noon—the Sunbow's rays still arch
The torrent with the many hues of heaven,
And roll the sheeted silver's waving column
O'er the crag's headlong perpendicular,
And fling its line of foaming light along,
And to and fro, like the pale courser's tail,
The Giant steed, to be bestrode by Death,
As told in the Apocalypse. No eyes
But mine now drink this sight of loveliness;
I should be sole in his sweet solitude,   10

And with the Spirit of the place divide
The homage of these waters.—I will call her.

    [MANFRED *takes some of the water into the palm of his hand and flings it*
      into the air, muttering the adjuration. After a pause, the WITCH OF THE
            ALPS *rises beneath the arch of the sunbow of the torrent.*

Beautiful Spirit! with thy hair of light,
And dazzling eyes of glory, in whose form
The charms of Earth's least mortal daughters grow
To an unearthly stature, in an essence
Of purer elements; while the hues of youth,—
Carnationed like a sleeping Infant's cheek,
Rocked by the beating of her mother's heart,
Or the rose tints, which Summer's twilight leaves   20
Upon the lofty Glacier's virgin snow,
The blush of earth embracing with her Heaven,—
Tinge thy celestial aspect, and make tame
The beauties of the Sunbow which bends o'er thee.
Beautiful Spirit! in thy calm clear brow,
Wherein is glassed serenity of Soul,
Which of itself shows immortality,
I read that thou wilt pardon to a Son
Of Earth, whom the abstruser powers permit
At times to commune with them—if that he   30
Avail him of his spells—to call thee thus,
And gaze on thee a moment.

WITCH.   Son of Earth!
I know thee, and the Powers which give thee power!
I know thee for a man of many thoughts,
And deeds of good and ill, extreme in both,
Fatal and fated in thy sufferings.
I have expected this—what would'st thou with me?

MANFRED. To look upon thy beauty—nothing further.
The face of the earth hath maddened me, and I
Take refuge in her mysteries, and pierce   40
To the abodes of those who govern her—
But they can nothing aid me. I have sought
From them what they could not bestow, and now
I search no further.

WITCH.   What could be the quest
 Which is not in the power of the most powerful,
 The rulers of the invisible?
MANFRED.   A boon;—
 But why should I repeat it? 'twere in vain.
WITCH. I know not that; let thy lips utter it.
MANFRED. Well, though it torture me, 'tis but the same;
 My pang shall find a voice. From my youth upwards 50
 My Spirit walked not with the souls of men,
 Nor looked upon the earth with human eyes;
 The thirst of their ambition was not mine,
 The aim of their existence was not mine;
 My joys—my griefs—my passions—and my powers,
 Made me a stranger; though I wore the form,
 I had no sympathy with breathing flesh,
 Nor midst the Creatures of Clay that girded me
 Was there but One who—but of her anon.
 I said with men, and with the thoughts of men, 60
 I held but slight communion; but instead,
 My joy was in the wilderness,—to breathe
 The difficult air of the iced mountain's top,
 Where the birds dare not build—nor insect's wing
 Flit o'er the herbless granite; or to plunge
 Into the torrent, and to roll along
 On the swift whirl of the new-breaking wave
 Of river-stream, or ocean, in their flow.
 In these my early strength exulted; or
 To follow through the night the moving moon, 70
 The stars and their development; or catch
 The dazzling lightnings till my eyes grew dim;
 Or to look, list'ning, on the scattered leaves,
 While Autumn winds were at their evening song.
 These were my pastimes, and to be alone;
 For if the beings, of whom I was one,—
 Hating to be so,—crossed me in my path,
 I felt myself degraded back to them,
 And all was clay again. And then I dived,

In my lone wanderings, to the caves of Death,   80
Searching its cause in its effect; and drew
From withered bones, and skulls, and heaped up dust,
Conclusions most forbidden. Then I passed
The nights of years in sciences untaught,
Save in the old-time; and with time and toil,
And terrible ordeal, and such penance
As in itself hath power upon the air,
And spirits that do compass air and earth,
Space, and the peopled Infinite, I made
Mine eyes familiar with Eternity,   90
Such as, before me, did the Magi, and
He who from out their fountain-dwellings raised
Eros and Anteros, at Gadara,
As I do thee;—and with my knowledge grew
The thirst of knowledge, and the power and joy
Of this most bright intelligence, until——
WITCH. Proceed.
MANFRED.   Oh! I but thus prolonged my words,
Boasting these idle attributes, because
As I approach the core of my heart's grief—
But—to my task. I have not named to thee   100
Father or mother, mistress, friend, or being,
With whom I wore the chain of human ties;
If I had such, they seemed not such to me—
Yet there was One——
WITCH.   Spare not thyself—proceed.
MANFRED. She was like me in lineaments—her eyes—
Her hair—her features—all, to the very tone
Even of her voice, they said were like to mine;
But softened all, and tempered into beauty:
She had the same lone thoughts and wanderings,
The quest of hidden knowledge, and a mind   110
To comprehend the Universe: nor these
Alone, but with them gentler powers than mine,
Pity, and smiles, and tears—which I had not;
And tenderness—but that I had for her;

Humility—and that I never had.
Her faults were mine—her virtues were her own—
I loved her, and destroyed her!

WITCH.   With thy hand?

MANFRED. Not with my hand, but heart, which broke her heart;
It gazed on mine, and withered. I have shed
Blood, but not hers—and yet her blood was shed;   120
I saw—and could not stanch it.

WITCH.   And for this—
A being of the race thou dost despise—
The order, which thine own would rise above,
Mingling with us and ours,—thou dost forgo
The gifts of our great knowledge, and shrink'st back
To recreant mortality——Away!

MANFRED. Daughter of Air! I tell thee, since that hour—
But words are breath—look on me in my sleep,
Or watch my watchings—Come and sit by me!
My solitude is solitude no more,   130
But peopled with the Furies;—I have gnashed
My teeth in darkness till returning morn,
Then cursed myself till sunset;—I have prayed
For madness as a blessing—'tis denied me.
I have affronted Death—but in the war
Of elements the waters shrunk from me,
And fatal things passed harmless; the cold hand
Of an all-pitiless Demon held me back,
Back by a single hair, which would not break
In Fantasy, Imagination, all   140
The affluence of my soul—which one day was
A Crœsus in creation—I plunged deep,
But, like an ebbing wave, it dashed me back
Into the gulf of my unfathomed thought.
I plunged amidst Mankind—Forgetfulness
I sought in all, save where 'tis to be found—
And that I have to learn—my Sciences,
My long pursued and superhuman art,
Is mortal here: I dwell in my despair—
And live—and live for ever.

WITCH.   It may be   150
  That I can aid thee.
MANFRED.   To do this thy power
  Must wake the dead, or lay me low with them.
  Do so—in any shape—in any hour—
  With any torture—so it be the last.
WITCH. That is not in my province; but if thou
  Wilt swear obedience to my will, and do
  My bidding, it may help thee to thy wishes.
MANFRED. I will not swear—Obey! and whom? the Spirits
  Whose presence I command, and be the slave
  Of those who served me—Never!
WITCH.   Is this all?   160
  Hast thou no gentler answer?—Yet bethink thee,
  And pause ere thou rejectest.
MANFRED.   I have said it.
WITCH. Enough! I may retire then—say!
MANFRED.   Retire!
                                    [*The* WITCH *disappears.*
MANFRED (*alone*). We are the fools of Time and Terror: Days
  Steal on us, and steal from us; yet we live,
  Loathing our life, and dreading still to die.
  In all the days of this detested yoke—
  This heaving burthen, this accursed breath—
  This vital weight upon the struggling heart,
  Which sinks with sorrow, or beats quick with pain,   170
  Or joy that ends in agony or faintness—
  In all the days of past and future—for
  In life there is no present—we can number
  How few—how less than few—wherein the soul
  Forbears to pant for death, and yet draws back
  As from a stream in winter, though the chill
  Be but a moment's. I have one resource
  Still in my science—I can call the dead,
  And ask them what it is we dread to be:
  The sternest answer can but be the Grave,   180
  And that is nothing: if they answer not——
  The buried Prophet answered to the Hag

Of Endor; and the Spartan Monarch drew
From the Byzantine maid's unsleeping spirit
An answer and his destiny—he slew
That which he loved, unknowing what he slew,
And died unpardoned—though he called in aid
The Phyxian Jove, and in Phigalia roused
The Arcadian Evocators to compel
The indignant shadow to depose her wrath,   190
Or fix her term of vengeance—she replied
In words of dubious import, but fulfilled.
If I had never lived, that which I love
Had still been living; had I never loved
That which I love would still be beautiful,
Happy and giving happiness. What is she?
What is she now?—a sufferer for my sins—
A thing I dare not think upon—or nothing.
Within few hours I shall not call in vain—
Yet in this hour I dread the thing I dare: 200
Until this hour I never shrunk to gaze
On spirit, good or evil—now I tremble,
And feel a strange cold thaw upon my heart.
But I can act even what I most abhor,
And champion human fears.—The night approaches.

[*Exit.*

SCENE III—*The summit of the Jungfrau Mountain.*
Enter FIRST DESTINY.

The Moon is rising broad, and round, and bright;
And here on snows, where never human foot
Of common mortal trod, we nightly tread,
And leave no traces: o'er the savage sea,
The glassy ocean of the mountain ice,
We skim its rugged breakers, which put on
The aspect of a tumbling tempest's foam
Frozen in a moment—a dead Whirlpool's image:
And this most steep fantastic pinnacle,
The fretwork of some earthquake—where the clouds   10

Pause to repose themselves in passing by—
Is sacred to our revels, or our vigils;
Here do I wait my sisters, on our way
To the Hall of Arimanes—for to-night
Is our great festival—'tis strange they come not.

A Voice without, singing.

   The Captive Usurper,
    Hurled down from the throne,
   Lay buried in torpor,
    Forgotten and lone;
   I broke through his slumbers,   20
    I shivered his chain,
   I leagued him with numbers—
    He's Tyrant again!
With the blood of a million he'll answer my care,
With a nation's destruction—his flight and despair!

Second Voice, without.

The Ship sailed on, the Ship sailed fast,
But I left not a sail, and I left not a mask;
There is not a plank of the hull or the deck,
And there is not a wretch to lament o'er his wreck;
Save one, whom I held, as he swam, by the hair, 30
And he was a subject well worthy my care;
A traitor on land, and a pirate at sea—
But I saved him to wreak further havoc for me!

FIRST DESTINY, *answering.*

   The City lies sleeping;
    The morn, to deplore it,
   May dawn on it weeping:
    Sullenly, slowly,
   The black plague flew o'er it—
    Thousands lie lowly;
   Tens of thousands shall perish;   40
    The living shall fly from
   The sick they should cherish;
    But nothing can vanquish
   The touch that they die from.

     Sorrow and anguish,
    And evil and dread,
     Envelop a nation;
    The blest are the dead,
     Who see not the sight
    Of their own desolation;   50
     This work of a night—
This wreck of a realm—this deed of my doing—
For ages I've done, and shall still be renewing!

Enter the SECOND *and* THIRD DESTINIES.
The Three.

    Our hands contain the hearts of men,
     Our footsteps are their graves;
    We only give to take again
     The Spirits of our slaves!

FIRST DESTINY. Welcome!—Where's Nemesis?
SECOND DESTINY.   At some great work;
 But what I know not, for my hands were full.
THIRD DESTINY. Behold she cometh.

              Enter NEMESIS.

FIRST DESTINY.   Say, where hast thou been?—— 60
 My Sisters and thyself are slow to-night.
NEMESIS. I was detained repairing shattered thrones—
 Marrying fools, restoring dynasties—
 Avenging men upon their enemies,
 And making them repent their own revenge;
 Goading the wise to madness; from the dull
 Shaping out oracles to rule the world
 Afresh—for they were waxing out of date,
 And mortals dared to ponder for themselves,
 To weigh kings in the balance—and to speak 70
 Of Freedom, the forbidden fruit.—Away!
 We have outstayed the hour—mount we our clouds!

              [Exeunt.

SCENE IV—*The Hall of Arimanes.*—ARIMANES *on his Throne, a Globe of Fire, surrounded by the* SPIRITS.

Hymn of the SPIRITS.

Hail to our Master!—Prince of Earth and Air!
Who walks the clouds and waters—in his hand
The sceptre of the Elements, which tear
    Themselves to chaos at his high command!
He breatheth—and a tempest shakes the sea;
    He speaketh—and the clouds reply in thunder;
He gazeth—from his glance the sunbeams flee;
    He moveth—Earthquakes rend the world asunder.
Beneath his footsteps the Volcanoes rise;
    His shadow is the Pestilence: his path   10
The comets herald through the crackling skies;
    And Planets turn to ashes at his wrath.
To him War offers daily sacrifice;
    To him Death pays his tribute; Life is his,
With all its Infinite of agonies—
    And his the Spirit of whatever is!

                    Enter the DESTINIES *and* NEMESIS.

FIRST DESTINY. Glory to Arimanes! on the earth
His power increaseth—both my sisters did
His bidding, nor did I neglect my duty!
SECOND DESTINY. Glory to Arimanes! we who bow   20
The necks of men, bow down before his throne!
THIRD DESTINY. Glory to Arimanes! we await
    His nod!
NEMESIS.   Sovereign of Sovereigns! we are thine,
And all that liveth, more or less, is ours,
And most things wholly so; still to increase
Our power, increasing thine, demands our care,
And we are vigilant. Thy late commands
Have been fulfilled to the utmost.

                        Enter MANFRED.

A SPIRIT.   What is here?
A mortal!—Thou most rash and fatal wretch,
Bow down and worship!

SECOND SPIRIT.   I do know the man——   30
    A Magian of great power, and fearful skill!
THIRD SPIRIT. Bow down and worship, slave!——What, know'st thou
       not
    Thine and our Sovereign?——Tremble, and obey!
ALL THE SPIRITS. Prostrate thyself, and thy condemnéd clay,
    Child of the Earth! or dread the worst.
MANFRED.   I know it;
    And yet ye see I kneel not.
FOURTH SPIRIT.   'Twill be taught thee.
MANFRED. 'Tis taught already;——many a night on the earth,
    On the bare ground, have I bowed down my face,
    And strewed my head with ashes; I have known
    The fulness of humiliation——for   40
    I sunk before my vain despair, and knelt
    To my own desolation.
FIFTH SPIRIT.   Dost thou dare
    Refuse to Arimanes on his throne
    What the whole earth accords, beholding not
    The terror of his Glory?——Crouch! I say.
MANFRED. Bid *him* bow down to that which is above him,
    The overruling Infinite——the Maker
    Who made him not for worship——let him kneel,
    And we will kneel together.
THE SPIRITS.   Crush the worm!
    Tear him in pieces!——
FIRST DESTINY.   Hence! Avaunt!——he's mine.   50
    Prince of the Powers invisible! This man
    Is of no common order, as his port
    And presence here denote: his sufferings
    Have been of an immortal nature——like
    Our own; his knowledge, and his powers and will,
    As far as is compatible with clay,
    Which clogs the ethereal essence, have been such
    As clay hath seldom borne; his aspirations
    Have been beyond the dwellers of the earth,
    And they have only taught him what we know——   60
    That knowledge is not happiness, and science

But an exchange of ignorance for that
Which is another kind of ignorance.
This is not all—the passions, attributes
Of Earth and Heaven, from which no power nor being,
Nor breath from the worm upwards is exempt,
Have pierced his heart; and in their consequence
Made him a thing—which—I who pity not,
Yet pardon those who pity. He is mine—
And thine it may be; be it so, or not—   70
No other Spirit in this region hath
A soul like his—or power upon his soul.

NEMESIS. What doth he here then?

FIRST DESTINY.   Let *him* answer that.

MANFRED. Ye know what I have known; and without power
   I could not be amongst ye: but there are
   Powers deeper still beyond—I come in quest
   Of such, to answer unto what I seek.

NEMESIS. What would'st thou?

MANFRED.   *Thou canst not reply to me.*
   Call up the dead—my question is for them.

NEMESIS. Great Arimanes, doth thy will avouch   80
   The wishes of this mortal?

ARIMANES.   Yea.

NEMESIS.   Whom wouldst thou
   Uncharnel?

MANFRED.   One without a tomb—call up
   Astarte.

NEMESIS.

           Shadow! or Spirit!
             Whatever thou art,
          Which still doth inherit
            The whole or a part
        Of the form of thy birth,
            Of the mould of thy clay,
        Which returned to the earth,   90
            Re-appear to the day!
        Bear what thou borest,
            The heart and the form,

                    And the aspect thou worest
                         Redeem from the worm.
                    Appear!—Appear!—Appear!
                    Who sent thee there requires thee here!
                         [*The Phantom of* ASTARTE *rises and stands in the midst.*
MANFRED. Can this be death? there's bloom upon her cheek;
    But now I see it is no living hue,
    But a strange hectic—like the unnatural red   100
    Which Autumn plants upon the perished leaf,
    It is the same! Oh, God! that I should dread
    To look upon the same—Astarte!—No,
    I cannot speak to her—but bid her speak—
    Forgive me or condemn me.
NEMESIS.
                    By the Power which hath broken
                         The grave which enthralled thee,
                    Speak to him who hath spoken,
                         Or those who have called thee!
MANFRED.   She is silent,   110
    And in that silence I am more than answered.
NEMESIS. My power extends no further. Prince of Air!
    It rests with thee alone—command her voice.
ARIMANES. Spirit—obey this sceptre!
NEMESIS.   Silent still!
    She is not of our order, but belongs
    To the other powers. Mortal! thy quest is vain,
    And we are baffled also.
MANFRED.   Hear me, hear me—
    Astarte! my belovéd! speak to me:
    I have so much endured—so much endure—
    Look on me! the grave hath not changed thee more   120
    Than I am changed for Thee. Thou lovedst me
    Too much, as I loved thee: we were not made
    To torture thus each other—though it were
    The deadliest sin to love as we have loved.
    Say that thou loath'st me not—that I do bear
    This punishment for both—that thou wilt be
    One of the blesséd—and that I shall die;

For hitherto all hateful things conspire
To bind me in existence—in a life
Which makes me shrink from Immortality—   130
A future like the past. I cannot rest.
I know not what I ask, nor what I seek:
I feel but what thou art, and what I am;
And I would hear yet once before I perish
The voice which was my music—speak to me!
For I have called on thee in the still night,
Startled the slumbering birds from the hushed boughs,
And woke the mountain wolves, and made the caves
Acquainted with thy vainly echoed name,
Which answered me—many things answered me—   140
Spirits and men—but thou wert silent all.
Yet speak to me! I have outwatched the stars,
And gazed o'er heaven in vain in search of thee.
Speak to me! I have wandered o'er the earth,
And never found thy likeness—Speak to me!
Look on the fiends around—they feel for me:
I fear them not, and feel for thee alone.
Speak to me! though it be in wrath;—but say—
I reck not what—but let me hear thee once—
This once—once more!
PHANTOM OF ASTARTE.   Manfred!
MANFRED.   Say on, say on—   150
    I live but in the sound—it is thy voice!
PHANTOM. Manfred! to-morrow ends thine earthly ills.
    Farewell!
MANFRED.   Yet one word more—am I forgiven?
PHANTOM. Farewell!
MANFRED.   Say, shall we meet again?
PHANTOM.   Farewell!
MANFRED. One word for mercy! Say thou lovest me.
PHANTOM. Manfred!
                    [*The Spirit of* ASTARTE *disappears.*
NEMESIS.   She's gone, and will not be recalled:
    Her words will be fulfilled. Return to the earth.
A SPIRIT He is convulsed—This is to be a mortal,

And seek the things beyond mortality.

ANOTHER SPIRIT Yet, see, he mastereth himself, and makes   160
  His torture tributary to his will.
  Had he been one of us, he would have made
  An awful spirit.

NEMESIS.   Hast thou further question
  Of our great sovereign, or his worshippers?

MANFRED. None.

NEMESIS.   Then, for a time, farewell.

MANFRED.   We meet then!
  Where? On the earth?—

NEMESIS.   That will be seen hereafter.

MANFRED. Even as thou wilt: and for the grace accorded
  I now depart a debtor. Fare ye well!

                    [*Exit* MANFRED.
                    (*Scene closes.*)

ACT III

SCENE I—*A Hall in the Castle of Manfred.*

                       MANFRED *and* HERMAN.

MANFRED. What is the hour?

HERMAN.   It wants but one till sunset,
  And promises a lovely twilight.

MANFRED.   Say,
  Are all things so disposed of in the tower
  As I directed?

HERMAN.   All, my Lord, are ready:
  Here is the key and casket.

MANFRED.   It is well:
  Thou mayst retire.

                    [*Exit* HERMAN.

MANFRED (*alone*).   There is a calm upon me—
  Inexplicable stillness! which till now
  Did not belong to what I knew of life.
  If that I did not know Philosophy
  To be of all our vanities the motliest,   10
  The merest word that ever fooled the ear

From out the schoolman's jargon, I should deem
The golden secret, the sought "Kalon," found,
And seated in my soul. It will not last,
But it is well to have known it, though but once:
It hath enlarged my thoughts with a new sense,
And I within my tablets would note down
That there is such a feeling. Who is there?

Re-enter HERMAN.

HERMAN. My Lord, the Abbot of St. Maurice craves
To greet your presence.

Enter the ABBOT OF ST. MAURICE.

ABBOT.   Peace be with Count Manfred!   20
MANFRED. Thanks, holy father! Welcome to these walls;
Thy presence honours them, and blesseth those
Who dwell within them.
ABBOT.   Would it were so, Count!—
But I would fain confer with thee alone.
MANFRED. Herman, retire.—What would my reverend guest?

[*Exit* HERMAN.

ABBOT. Thus, without prelude:—Age and zeal—my office—
And good intent must plead my privilege;
Our near, though not acquainted neighbourhood,
May also be my herald. Rumours strange,
And of unholy nature, are abroad,   30
And busy with thy name—a noble name
For centuries: may he who bears it now
Transmit it unimpaired!
MANFRED.   Proceed,—I listen.
ABBOT. 'Tis said thou holdest converse with the things
Which are forbidden to the search of man;
That with the dwellers of the dark abodes,
The many evil and unheavenly spirits
Which walk the valley of the Shade of Death,
Thou communest. I know that with mankind,
Thy fellows in creation, thou dost rarely   40
Exchange thy thoughts, and that thy solitude
Is as an Anchorite's—were it but holy.
MANFRED. And what are they who do avouch these things?

ABBOT. My pious brethren—the scared peasantry—
  Even thy own vassals—who do look on thee
  With most unquiet eyes. Thy life's in peril!
MANFRED. Take it.
ABBOT.   I come to save, and not destroy:
  I would not pry into thy secret soul;
  But if these things be sooth, there still is time
  For penitence and pity: reconcile thee   50
  With the true church, and through the church to Heaven.
MANFRED. I hear thee. This is my reply—whate'er
  I may have been, or am, doth rest between
  Heaven and myself—I shall not choose a mortal
  To be my mediator—Have I sinned
  Against your ordinances? prove and punish!
ABBOT. My son! I did not speak of punishment,
  But penitence and pardon;—with thyself
  The choice of such remains—and for the last,
  Our institutions and our strong belief   60
  Have given me power to smooth the path from sin
  To higher hope and better thoughts; the first
  I leave to Heaven,—"Vengeance is mine alone!"
  So saith the Lord, and with all humbleness
  His servant echoes back the awful word.
MANFRED. Old man! there is no power in holy men,
  Nor charm in prayer, nor purifying form
  Of penitence, nor outward look, nor fast,
  Nor agony—nor, greater than all these,
  The innate tortures of that deep Despair,   70
  Which is Remorse without the fear of Hell,
  But all in all sufficient to itself
  Would make a hell of Heaven—can exorcise
  From out the unbounded spirit the quick sense
  Of its own sins—wrongs—sufferance—and revenge
  Upon itself; there is no future pang
  Can deal that justice on the self-condemned
  He deals on his own soul.
ABBOT.   All this is well;
  For this will pass away, and be succeeded

By an auspicious hope, which shall look up   80
With calm assurance to that blessed place,
Which all who seek may win, whatever be
Their earthly errors, so they be atoned:
And the commencement of atonement is
The sense of its necessity. Say on—
And all our church can teach thee shall be taught;
And all we can absolve thee shall be pardoned.
MANFRED. When Rome's sixth Emperor was near his last,
   The victim of a self-inflicted wound,
   To shun the torments of a public death   90
   From senates once his slaves, a certain soldier,
   With show of loyal pity, would have stanched
   The gushing throat with his officious robe;
   The dying Roman thrust him back, and said—
   Some empire still in his expiring glance—
   "It is too late—is this fidelity?"
ABBOT. And what of this?
MANFRED.   I answer with the Roman—
   "It is too late!"
ABBOT.   It never can be so,
   To reconcile thyself with thy own soul,
   And thy own soul with Heaven. Hast thou no hope?   100
   'Tis strange—even those who do despair above,
   Yet shape themselves some fantasy on earth,
   To which frail twig they cling, like drowning men.
MANFRED. Aye—father! I have had those early visions,
   And noble aspirations in my youth,
   To make my own mind of other men,
   The enlightener of nations; and to rise
   I knew not whither—it might be to fall;
   But fall, even as the mountain-cataract,
   Which having leapt from its more dazzling height,   110
   Even in the foaming strength of its abyss,
   (Which casts up misty columns that become
   Clouds raining from the re-ascended skies,)
   Lies low but mighty still.—But this is past,
   My thoughts mistook themselves.

ABBOT.   And wherefore so?

MANFRED. I could not tame my nature down; for he
    Must serve who fain would sway; and soothe, and sue,
    And watch all time, and pry into all place,
    And be a living Lie, who would become
    A mighty thing amongst the mean—and such   120
    The mass are; I disdained to mingle with
    A herd, though to be leader—and of wolves.
    The lion is alone, and so am I.

ABBOT. And why not live and act with other men?

MANFRED. Because my nature was averse from life;
    And yet not cruel; for I would not make,
    But find a desolation. Like the Wind,
    The red-hot breath of the most lone Simoom,
    Which dwells but in the desert, and sweeps o'er
    The barren sands which bear no shrubs to blast,   130
    And revels o'er their wild and arid waves,
    And seeketh not, so that it is not sought,
    But being met is deadly,—such hath been
    The course of my existence; but there came
    Things in my path which are no more.

ABBOT.   Alas!
    I 'gin to fear that thou art past all aid
    From me and from my calling; yet so young,
    I still would——

MANFRED.   Look on me! there is an order
    Of mortals on the earth, who do become
    Old in their youth, and die ere middle age,   140
    Without the violence of warlike death;
    Some perishing of pleasure—some of study—
    Some worn with toil, some of mere weariness,—
    Some of disease—and some insanity—
    And some of withered, or of broken hearts;
    For this last is a malady which slays
    More than are numbered in the lists of Fate,
    Taking all shapes, and bearing many names.
    Look upon me! for even of all these things

Have I partaken; and of all these things   150
One were enough; then wonder not that I
Am what I am, but that I ever was,
Or having been, that I am still on earth.

ABBOT. Yet, hear me still——

MANFRED.   Old man! I do respect
Thine order, and revere thine years; I deem
Thy purpose pious, but it is in vain:
Think me not churlish; I would spare thyself,
Far more than me, in shunning at this time
All further colloquy—and so—farewell.

                                    [*Exit* MANFRED.

ABBOT. This should have been a noble creature: he   160
Hath all the energy which would have made
A goodly frame of glorious elements,
Had they been wisely mingled; as it is,
It is an awful chaos—Light and Darkness—
And mind and dust—and passions and pure thoughts
Mixed, and contending without end or order,—
All dormant or destructive. He will perish—
And yet he must not—I will try once more,
For such are worth redemption; and my duty
Is to dare all things for a righteous end.   170
I'll follow him—but cautiously, though surely.

                                    [*Exit* ABBOT.

SCENE II—*Another Chamber.*

                            MANFRED *and* HERMAN.

HERMAN. My lord, you bade me wait on you at sunset:
He sinks behind the mountain.

MANFRED.   Doth he so?
I will look on him.

                [MANFRED *advances to the Window of the Hall.*
                Glorious Orb! the idol
Of early nature, and the vigorous race
Of undiseased mankind, the giant sons
Of the embrace of Angels, with a sex

More beautiful than they, which did draw down
The erring Spirits who can ne'er return.—
Most glorious Orb! that wert a worship, ere
The mystery of thy making was revealed!   10
Thou earliest minister of the Almighty,
Which gladdened, on their mountain tops, the hearts
Of the Chaldean shepherds, till they poured
Themselves in orisons! Thou material God!
And representative of the Unknown—
Who chose thee for his shadow! Thou chief Star!
Centre of many stars! which mak'st our earth
Endurable, and temperest the hues
And hearts of all who walk within thy rays!
Sire of the seasons! Monarch of the climes,   20
And those who dwell in them! for near or far,
Our inborn spirits have a tint of thee
Even as our outward aspects;—thou dost rise,
And shine, and set in glory. Fare thee well!
I ne'er shall see thee more. As my first glance
Of love and wonder was for thee, then take
My latest look: thou wilt not beam on one
To whom the gifts of life and warmth have been
Of a more fatal nature. He is gone—
I follow.

                                         [*Exit* MANFRED.

SCENE III—*The Mountains—The Castle of Manfred at some distance—
A Terrace before a Tower.—Time, Twilight.*

            HERMAN, MANUEL, *and other dependents of* MANFRED.
HERMAN. 'Tis strange enough! night after night, for years,
He hath pursued long vigils in this tower,
Without a witness. I have been within it,—
So have we all been oft-times; but from it,
Or its contents, it were impossible
To draw conclusions absolute, of aught
His studies tend to. To be sure, there is
One chamber where none enter: I would give

The fee of what I have to come these three years,
To pore upon its mysteries.

MANUEL.   'Twere dangerous;   10
   Content thyself with what thou know'st already.

HERMAN. Ah! Manuel! thou art elderly and wise,
   And couldst say much; thou hast dwelt within the castle—
   How many years is't?

MANUEL.   Ere Count Manfred's birth,
   I served his father, whom he nought resembles.

HERMAN. There be more sons in like predicament!
   But wherein do they differ?

MANUEL.   I speak not
   Of features or of form, but mind and habits;
   Count Sigismund was proud, but gay and free,—
   A warrior and a reveller; he dwelt not   20
   With books and solitude, nor made the night
   A gloomy vigil, but a festal time,
   Merrier than day; he did not walk the rocks
   And forests like a wolf, nor turn aside
   From men and their delights.

HERMAN.   Beshrew the hour,
   But those were jocund times! I would that such
   Would visit the old walls again; they look
   As if they had forgotten them.

MANUEL.   These walls
   Must change their chieftain first. Oh! I have seen
   Some strange things in them, Herman.

HERMAN.   Come, be friendly;   30
   Relate me some to while away our watch:
   I've heard thee darkly speak of an event
   Which happened hereabouts, by this same tower.

MANUEL. That was a night indeed! I do remember
   'Twas twilight, as it may be now, and such
   Another evening:—yon red cloud, which rests
   On Eigher's pinnacle, so rested then,—
   So like that it might be the same; the wind
   Was faint and gusty, and the mountain snows

Began to glitter with the climbing moon;   40
Count Manfred was, as now, within his tower,—
How occupied, we knew not, but with him
The sole companion of his wanderings
And watchings—her, whom of all earthly things
That lived, the only thing he seemed to love,—
As he, indeed, by blood was bound to do,
The Lady Astarte, his——
                 Hush! who comes here?

                                 Enter the ABBOT.

ABBOT. Where is your master?
HERMAN.   Yonder in the tower.
ABBOT. I must speak with him.
MANUEL.   'Tis impossible;
He is most private, and must not be thus   50
Intruded on.
ABBOT.   Upon myself I take
The forfeit of my fault, if fault there be—
But I must see him.
HERMAN.   Thou hast seen him once
This eve already.
ABBOT.   Herman! I command thee,
Knock, and apprize the Count of my approach.
HERMAN. We dare not.
ABBOT.   Then it seems I must be herald
Of my own purpose.
MANUEL.   Reverend father, stop—
I pray you pause.
ABBOT.   Who so?
MANUEL.   But step this way,
And I will tell you further.

                                   [*Exeunt.*

SCENE IV—*Interior of the Tower.*
MANFRED *alone.*

The stars are forth, the moon above the tops
Of the snow-shining mountains.—Beautiful!
I linger yet with Nature, for the Night

Hath been to me a more familiar face
Than that of man; and in her starry shade
Of dim and solitary loveliness,
I learned the language of another world.
I do remember me, that in my youth,
When I was wandering,—upon such a night
I stood within the Coliseum's wall, 10
'Midst the chief relics of almighty Rome;
The trees which grew along the broken arches
Waved dark in the blue midnight, and the stars
Shone through the rents of ruin; from afar
The watch-dog bayed beyond the Tiber; and
More near from out the Cæsar's palace came
The owl's long cry, and, interruptedly,
Of distant sentinels the fitful song
Begun and died upon the gentle wind.
Some cypresses beyond the time-worn breach 20
Appeared to skirt the horizon, yet they stood
Within a bowshot. Where the Cæsars dwelt,
And dwell the tuneless birds of night, amidst
A grove which springs through levelled battlements,
And twines its roots with the imperial hearths,
Ivy usurps the laurel's place of growth;—
But the gladiators' bloody Circus stands,
A noble wreck in ruinous perfection,
While Cæsar's chambers, and the Augustan halls,
Grovel on earth in indistinct decay.— 30
And thou didst shine, thou rolling Moon, upon
All this, and cast a wide and tender light,
Which softened down the hoar austerity
Of rugged desolation, and filled up,
As 'twere anew, the gaps of centuries;
Leaving that beautiful which still was so,
And making that which was not—till the place
Became religion, and the heart ran o'er
With silent worship of the Great of old,—
The dead, but sceptred, Sovereigns, who still rule 40
Our spirits from their urns.

              'Twas such a night!
'Tis strange that I recall it at this time;
But I have found our thoughts take wildest flight
Even at the moment when they should array
Themselves in pensive order.

                                  Enter the ABBOT.

ABBOT.   My good Lord!
I crave a second grace for this approach;
But yet let not my humble zeal offend
By its abruptness—all it hath of ill
Recoils on me; its good in the effect
May light upon your head—could I say *heart*—   50
Could I touch *that*, with words or prayers, I should
Recall a noble spirit which hath wandered,
But is not yet all lost.
MANFRED.   Thou know'st me not;
My days are numbered, and my deeds recorded:
Retire, or 'twill be dangerous—Away!
ABBOT. Thou dost not mean to menace me?
MANFRED.   Not I!
I simply tell thee peril is at hand,
And would preserve thee.
ABBOT.   What dost thou mean?
MANFRED.   Look there!
What dost thou see?
ABBOT.   Nothing.
MANFRED.   Look there, I say,
And steadfastly;—now tell me what thou see'st?   60
ABBOT. That which should shake me,—but I fear it not:
I see a dusk and awful figure rise,
Like an infernal god, from out the earth;
His face wrapt in a mantle, and his form
Robed as with angry clouds: he stands between
Thyself and me—but I do fear him not.
MANFRED. Thou hast no cause—he shall not harm thee—but
His sight may shock thine old limbs into palsy.
I say to thee—Retire!

ABBOT.   And I reply—
  Never—till I have battled with this fiend:—   70
  What doth he here?
MANFRED.   Why—aye—what doth he here?
  I did not send for him,—he is unbidden.
ABBOT. Alas! lost Mortal! what with guests like these
  Hast thou to do? I tremble for thy sake:
  Why doth he gaze on thee, and thou on him?
  Ah! he unveils his aspect: on his brow
  The thunder-scars are graven; from his eye
  Glares forth the immortality of Hell—
  Avaunt!—
MANFRED.   Pronounce—what is thy mission?
SPIRIT.   Come!
ABBOT. What art thou, unknown being? answer!—speak!   80
SPIRIT The genius of this mortal.—Come! 'tis time.
MANFRED. I am prepared for all things, but deny
  The power which summons me. Who sent thee here?
SPIRIT Thou'lt know anon—Come! come!
MANFRED.   I have commanded
  Things of an essence greater far than thine,
  And striven with thy masters. Get thee hence!
SPIRIT Mortal! thine hour is come—Away! I say.
MANFRED. I knew, and know my hour is come, but not
  To render up my soul to such as thee:
  Away! I'll die as I have lived—alone.   90
SPIRIT. Then I must summon up my brethren.—Rise!
                               [*Other* SPIRITS *rise up.*
ABBOT. Avaunt! ye evil ones!—Avaunt! I say,—
  Ye have no power where Piety hath power,
  And I do charge ye in the name—
SPIRIT   Old man!
  We know ourselves, our mission and thine order;
  Waste not thy holy words on idle uses—
  It were in vain: this man is forfeited.
  Once more—I summon him—Away! Away!
MANFRED. I do defy ye,—though I feel my soul

Is ebbing from me, yet I do defy ye; 100
Nor will I hence, while I have earthly breath
To breathe my scorn upon ye—earthly strength
To wrestle, though with spirits; what ye take
Shall be ta'en limb by limb.

SPIRIT.   Reluctant mortal!
Is this the Magian who would so pervade
The world invisible, and make himself
Almost our equal? Can it be that thou
Art thus in love with life? the very life
Which made thee wretched?

MANFRED.   Thou false fiend, thou liest!
My life is in its last hour,—*that* I know, 110
Nor would redeem a moment of that hour;
I do not combat against Death, but thee
And thy surrounding angels; my past power
Was purchased by no compact with thy crew,
But by superior science—penance, daring,
And length of watching, strength of mind, and skill
In knowledge of our Fathers—when the earth
Saw men and spirits walking side by side,
And gave ye no supremacy: I stand
Upon my strength—I do defy—deny— 120
Spurn back, and scorn ye!—

SPIRIT.   But thy many crimes
Have made thee——

MANFRED.   What are they to such as thee?
Must crimes be punished but by other crimes,
And greater criminals?—Back to thy hell!
Thou hast no power upon me, *that* I feel;
Thou never shalt possess me, *that* I know:
What I have done is done; I bear within
A torture which could nothing gain from thine:
The Mind which is immortal makes itself
Requital for its good or evil thoughts,— 130
Is its own origin of ill and end—
And its own place and time: its innate sense,

When stripped of this mortality, derives
No colour from the fleeting things without,
But is absorbed in sufferance or in joy,
Born from the knowledge of its own desert.
Thou didst not tempt me, and thou couldst not tempt me;
I have not been thy dupe, nor am thy prey—
But was my own destroyer, and will be
My own hereafter.—Back, ye baffled fiends!   140
The hand of Death is on me—but not yours!

                                 [*The* DEMONS *disappear.*

ABBOT. Alas! how pale thou art—thy lips are white—
And thy breast heaves—and in thy gasping throat
The accents rattle: give thy prayers to Heaven—
Pray—albeit but in thought,—but die not thus.
MANFRED. 'Tis over—my dull eyes can fix thee not;
But all things swim around me, and the earth
Heaves as it were beneath me. Fare thee well—
Give me thy hand.
ABBOT.   Cold—cold—even to the heart—
But yet one prayer—Alas! how fares it with thee?   150
MANFRED. Old man! 'tis not so difficult to die.

                                 [MANFRED *expires.*

ABBOT. He's gone—his soul hath ta'en its earthless flight;
Whither? I dread to think—but he is gone.

                         [*First publ., June 16, 1817.*]

NOTES

CHILDE HAROLD'S PILGRIMAGE

PREFACE

p. 6 *Mr. Scott:* Sir Walter Scott (1771–1832), Scottish poet and novelist, editor of *Minstrelsy of the Scottish Border* (1802).

Dr. Beattie: James Beattie (1735–1803), Scottish poet and essayist.

ADDITION TO THE PREFACE

p. 7 *Rolland:* Barthélemi Gabriel Rolland d'Erceville (1734–1794), French scholar.

Sainte-Palaye: Jean Baptiste de La Curne de Sainte-Palaye (1697–1781), French historian and lexicographer. Byron refers to his *Mémoires sur l'ancienne chevalrie* (1781).

Burke: Edmund Burke (1729–1797). Burke deplored the execution of Marie Antoinette in his *Reflections on the Revolution in France* (1790).

Bayard: Pierre Terrail, seigneur de Bayard (c.1473–1524), French soldier known as the Chevalier sans peur et sans reproche ("the knight without fear and without reproach").

Sir Joseph Banks: British explorer and naturalist (1743–1820), who sailed with Captain Cook (1768–1771). Banks was ridiculed for having supposedly made love to Queen Oberea of Tahiti in a canoe.

Timon: Misanthropic character in Shakespeare's *Timon of Athens.*

Zeluco: Wicked protagonist of the novel *Zeluco* (1786), by John Moore (1729–1802).

TO IANTHE
Ianthe: Lady Charlotte Harley (1801–1880), whom Byron met in 1812.
line 19 *Peri:* Beautiful spirit in Persian mythology; also a lovely graceful girl.

CANTO THE FIRST
line 1 *Hellas:* Greece.
line 6 *Delphi:* Ancient Greek town, location of the most important shrine and oracle of Apollo.
line 8 *weary Nine:* The nine Muses.
line 10 *Whilome:* Once upon a time (archaic). *Albion's isle:* England. "Albion" is the earliest-known name for England, used by the ancient Greeks.
line 14 *wight:* A creature, a human being.
line 19 *hight:* Called; named (archaic).
line 23 *losel:* One that is worthless.
line 36 *Eremite:* Religious recluse or hermit.
line 49 *ee:* Eye (archaic).
line 61 *Paphian girls:* Wanton; from the Greek town of Paphos, near where Aphrodite was thought to have risen from the sea.
line 72 *mote:* May, might (archaic).
line 77 *lemans:* Lovers, mistresses (archaic).
line 79 *feere:* Mate (archaic).
line 81 *Mammon:* Riches or avarice; portrayed as a false god in the Old Testament. *Seraphs:* Members of the highest order of angels.
line 99 *Paynim:* A pagan, or non-Christian (archaic). *Earth's central line:* The equator.

CHILDE HAROLD'S GOOD NIGHT
line 121 *sea-mew:* Seagull.
line 160 *French foeman:* French adversary; England is at war with Napoleonic France.
line 199 *Biscay's sleepless bay:* Bay of Biscay, located between France and Spain.
line 202 *Cintra:* Present-day Sintra, a region of Portugal near Lisbon.
line 203 *Tagus:* The Tagus river in Spain and Portugal.
line 205 *Lusian:* Portuguese.
line 215 *Gaul's:* France's.
line 216 *Lisboa:* Lisbon.
line 224 *Gaul's unsparing Lord:* Napoleon Bonaparte, who invaded Portugal in 1807 and Spain in 1808.
line 232 *surtout:* A man's long coat.
line 233 *shent:* Harmed (archaic).
line 241 *the Bard . . . unlocked Elysium's gates:* John Milton's epic poem *Paradise Lost.*

line 259 *Honorius:* Sixteenth-century Capuchin monk who lived for thirty years in a small pit and died at the age of ninety-five.

line 275 *Vathek! England's wealthiest son:* William Beckford (1760–1844), phenomenally wealthy author of *Vathek* (1786), a Gothic novel. Beckford lived for two years at Quinta da Monserrate, near Sintra.

line 290 *Foolscap:* The cap or hood, usually trimmed with bells; worn by jesters.

line 297 *Convention:* The Convention of Cintra, August 30, 1808. After the defeat of the French at Vimiero, the British and French signed an agreement that not only allowed the French troops to leave Portugal in safety and return home but also arranged for British ships to transport them. The convention provoked widespread outrage in England.

line 298 *Marialva's dome:* Residence of the Marquis of Marialva, an eighteenth century Portuguese nobleman.

line 305 *Lusitania's coast:* Portuguese coast; from the Roman name for Portugal.

line 333 *Mafra:* Town eighteen miles northwest of Lisbon; site of the National Palace.

line 334 *luckless queen:* Maria I (1734–1816), who suffered a mental breakdown after her husband's death in 1816.

line 338 *Babylonian Whore:* The Catholic Church.

line 363 *Tayo:* The Tagus river.

line 368 *the rocks:* The Pyrenees.

line 369 *a silver streamlet:* The Caia river.

line 379 *Guadiana:* The Guadiana river.

line 388 *Pelagio:* Pelayo (d. 737), Gothic chief who fought and defeated the Moslems; traditionally the first Christian king of Spain.

line 389 *Cava:* Daughter of Count Julian Cæsarini, who was allowed the Moors to invade Spain as an act of revenge over the violation of his daughter La Cava.

line 415 *clang of conflict:* The Battle of Talavera, July 27–28, 1809.

line 421 *Siroc:* The sirocco, an oppressive wind of the Northern Mediterranean coast; either dry and laden with dust from the north African deserts or hot and damp.

line 459 *Albuera:* The Battle of Albuera, May 16, 1811, in which the British defeated the French with great losses on both sides.

line 484 *Ilion, Tyre:* Ilion (Troy) was destroyed by the Greeks; Tyre by Muslims in 1291.

line 490 *rebeck:* Medieval stringed instrument.

line 509 *Godoy:* Manuel de Godoy (1767–1851), Spanish prime minister whose Convention of Fontainebleau with France in 1807 allied Spain with France against Portugal and precipitated France's invasion of Spain and Portugal.

line 510 *wittol:* A man who knows of and tolerates his wife's infidelity. King Charles IV's, Queen Maria Luisa, wife was Godoy's lover.

line 519 *Dragon's nest:* The city of Jaén, south of Madrid.

line 523 *badge of crimson hue:* A patriotic cockade worn by the Spaniards.

line 531 *Morena:* The Sierra Morena, the east-west mountain range in southern Spain.

line 535 *fosse:* Defensive trench or moat.

line 545 *the Scourger of the world:* Napoleon.

lines 558–61 *Spanish maid ... dared the deed of war:* The famous "Maid of Saragossa," Agostina Domenech, who kept firing during the 1808–1809 siege after all the men had been killed.

line 560 *Anlace:* A dagger.

line 607 *Houries:* Beautiful virgins of the Islamic paradise.

line 610 *Prophet's:* Muhammad's.

line 612 *Parnassus:* Greek mountain thought by the Romans to be the home of the Muses.

line 646 *Daphne's deathless plant:* The bay (laurel) tree. Seeking to escape from the unwelcome attentions of Apollo, Daphne was transformed into a tree.

lines 650–51 *Delphi ... Pythian:* The Greek island of Delphi was home to a famous oracle of Apollo.

line 667 *Queen who conquers all:* Aphrodite (Venus).

line 679 *kibes:* Chilblains, or inflamed hands and feet (Byron misuses the word; he means "heels").

line 700 *jade:* Worn-out horse.

line 702 *Thamis:* The Thames river.

line 706 *Bœotian:* Obtuse; philistine.

line 707 *worship of the solemn Horn:* drinking; from the use of hollow horns as cups.

line 733 *featly:* Nimbly.

line 802 *Duenna:* A lady in charge of the younger females in Portugal or Spain; chaperon.

line 813 *Lethe's stream:* In Greek mythology, a river in Hades, the waters of which cause forgetfulness.

TO INEZ

line 854 *fabled Hebrew Wanderer:* The Wandering Jew, in medieval Christian legend a Jew condemned to wander the earth until the Second Coming.

lines 873–74 *Cadiz . . . thy walls have stood:* The city was under siege by the French from February 1810 until August 1812.

line 880 *save Nobility:* In 1808, Don Francisco Solano Ortiz de Rozas, commander of the Spanish forces at Cadiz, was killed by a mob for refusing to attack the French.

line 914 *Pizarros:* Francisco Pizarro, and the other Spanish conquistadors who conquered the Incas and other inhabitants of South America and Mexico.

line 915 *Columbia's:* America's.

line 916 *Quito's sons:* The Incas.

line 919 *Barossa's fight:* Battle of Barrosa, March 5, 1811.

line 945 *fytte:* canto or stanza of a song or poem.

line 949 *moe:* More.

line 952 *Eld:* Antiquity.

CANTO THE SECOND

line 3 *Goddess of Wisdom:* Athena.

lines 3–4 *thy temple . . . despite of War:* Part of the Acropolis was destroyed by an explosion in 1687.

line 19 *Son of the Morning:* Inhabitant of the East.

line 55 *Athena's wisest son:* Socrates.

line 61 *Acheron:* river of woe in Hades.

line 66 *Sadducee:* Member of a Jewish sect that did not believe in resurrection or other doctrines not in the Law.

line 67 *Sophists:* Fifth-century Greek philosophers, known for their clever but often specious reasoning.

line 72 *Bactrian, Samian sage:* Zoroaster, Pythagoras.

line 73 *Thou:* John Edleston, beloved by Byron when the two were at Trinity College, Cambridge.

line 84 *son of Saturn:* Zeus.

line 92 *Pallas:* Athena.

line 94 *dull spoiler, who was he?:* Thomas Bruce, seventh Earl of Elgin, eleventh Earl of Kincardine, British ambassador to the Ottoman Empire, who removed marble sculptures, including the frieze from the Parthenon (thereafter known as the "Elgin Marbles") and shipped them to England.

line 95 *Caledonia:* Scotland.

line 100 *Pict's:* The Picts were ancient people of northern Britain, hence Scot's.

line 118 *Ægis:* The shield of Athena, which bore the head of Medusa.

line 119 *Alaric:* King of the Visigoths, who plundered Athens in 395 but spared the marbles of the Parthenon.

line 120 *Peleus' son:* Achilles.

line 155 *well-reeved:* Fastened with ropes.

line 185 *Arion:* Semilegendary Greek poet (seventh century B.C.).

line 190 *Calpe's:* Gibraltar's; Calpe is a mountain on the eastern end of the Strait of Gibraltar.

line 193 *Hecate's:* The Moon's; Hecate was a Greek goddess of fertility and magic associated with the Moon.

line 197 *Mauritania's:* Morocco's.

line 208 *laving:* Lapping against.

line 209 *Dian's:* Diana's; Diana or Artemis was associated with the Moon.

lines 235–36 *Eremite ... Athos:* Mount Athos was the site of an independent monastic community founded in the tenth century.

line 253 *Calypso's isles:* Byron here means Goza and Malta, although Calypso, the sea nymph and lover of Odysseus in *The Odyssey,* was actually supposed to have lived on the mythical island of Ogygia.

lines 259–60 *his boy essayed ... Stern Mentor urged:* Telemachus, searching for his father, Odysseus, found Calypso's island, and escaped from it when Mentor urged him to leap into the ocean.

line 261 *Nymph-Queen:* Calypso.

line 266 *Sweet Florence:* Mrs. Constance Spencer Smith, with whom Byron had a brief affair at Malta in 1809.

line 298 *kens:* Knows. *ween:* Think (archaic).

line 322 *ared:* Aired; expounded.

line 334 *Iskander:* Turkish name for Alexander the Great; Byron claims here that he was born in Albania.

line 336 *his namesake:* George Kastrioti (1405–1468), Albanian national hero; known as Skanderbeg. As a child was given to the Turks as a hostage, converted to Islam and was named Iskander; later became a Christian and repelled numerous Turkish invasions.

line 344 *Penelope:* Wife of Odysseus, who awaited his return from Troy for many years.

lines 345–46 *the mount ... Lesbian's grave:* The cliff from which the Greek poet Sappho of Lesbos leaped to her death when her love for Phaon was unrequited.

line 353 *Leucadia's cape:* cape Doukato on the Ionian island of Levkás, site of Sappho's leap.

line 356 *Actium—Lepanto—fatal Trafalgar:* Great naval battles. The Battle of Actium in 31 B.C. ended with Octavian's victory over Mark Antony and Cleopatra. Allied Christian forces defeated the Ottoman Turks in the Battle of Lepanto in 1571. Admiral Horatio Nelson's victory over Napoleon at the Battle of Trafalgar (October 21, 1805) prevented an invasion of England and established British naval supremacy for over a hundred years.

line 360 *bravo:* Hired killer.

line 371 *Pindus' inland peak:* Pindus Mountains, stretching from Albania to Greece.

line 389 *the circumcised:* Here, the Muslims.

lines 397–98 *Ambracia's gulf . . . for Woman:* Scene of the Battle of Actium, where the forces of Mark Antony and Cleopatra were defeated.

line 402 *second Cæsar's:* Octavian's.

line 407 *Illyria's vales:* Northwestern part of the Balkan peninsula.

line 411 *fair Tempe:* In Thessaly, Greece, traditionally beautiful and sacred to Apollo.

line 415 *Acherusia's lake:* Palus Acherusia ("Acherusian swamp"), today the Lake of Fusaro in Campania, Italy.

line 418 *Albania's Chief:* Ali Pasha (1741–1822), brigand and tyrant who became pasha of Janina, Greece, in 1788. Byron met him in 1809.

line 424 *Zitza:* Village near Janina.

line 438 *caloyer:* Monk of Eastern Orthodox church.

line 453 *Chinæra's Alps:* Possibly the Ceraunian Mountains in northwest Greece.

line 456 *Acheron:* Byron misidentifies the river Kalamas (the present-day Thýamis). The actual Acheron river (named after the river of Woe in Hades) is further south in Epirus.

line 458 *Pluto:* Roman god of the underworld.

line 459 *Elysium:* Paradise of heroes in Greek mythology.

line 460 *ne:* No.

line 461 *Yanina:* Janina, city in northwestern Greece.

line 466 *capote:* Long hooded cloak.

line 469 *Dodona:* Ancient sanctuary of Zeus (Jove) in Epirus, Greece.

line 487 *Tomerit:* Mount Tomarus.

line 488 *Laos:* The river Aóös.

line 492 *Tepalen:* Tepelenë, Albanian city.

line 498 *Chief of power:* Ali Pasha; see note to line 418.

line 502 *santons:* Muslim saint or hermit.

line 518 *Delhi:* Title of honor for a fierce fighter.

line 519 *glaive:* Sword.

line 520 *mutilated son:* Eunuch.

line 532 *Ramazani's fast:* Ramadan, the ninth month of the Islamic calendar, during which Muslims fast from dawn until sunset.

line 561 *Hafiz:* Hafez, great fourteenth-century Persian poet.

line 562 *Teian:* Anacreon, ancient Greek lyric poet, born c. 582 B.C., in Teos, Ionia.

line 618 *Acarnania:* District of ancient Greece on the Ionian Sea.

line 620 *Achelous:* The longest river in Greece; border between Acarnania and Aetolia.

line 621 *Ætolia:* District of ancient Greece to the east of Acarnania.

line 637 *Palikar:* Soldier.

line 649 *Tambourgi:* Drummer.

line 654 *snowy camese:* Camise; white shirt.

line 665 *Parga:* Port on the Ionian Sea.

line 677 *Previsa:* City taken from the French by Ali Pasha in 1797.

line 685 *Muchtar:* Mukhtar, son of Ali Pasha, sent to fight Russian invaders.

line 686 *Giaours:* Infidels, to Muslims.

line 689 *Selictar:* Sword bearer.

line 699 *Thermopylæ:* Site of famous battle, August 480 B.C., in which a small number of Greeks heroically held off invading Persians before being overwhelmed.

line 701 *Eurotas' banks:* River in Greece in region of ancient Sparta.

lines 702–3 *Phyle ... Thrasybulus:* Phyle, northwest of Athens, was the location of a fortress used by Thrasybulus, the Athenian general who freed Athens from the tyranny of the Thirty Tyrants in 403 B.C.

line 707 *carle:* Rude, rustic man.

line 726 *Helots:* A class of slaves in Sparta.

line 729 *The city won for Allah:* Constantinople, taken by Mehmed II (1453).

line 730 *Othman:* Ottoman Turk.

line 733 *Wahab's rebel brood:* Wahhabism was a puritanical Islamic movement originated by Muhammad ibn'Abd al-Wahhab. Members of the Wahhabi movement sacked Mecca in 1803 and Medina in 1804.

line 748 *Stamboul:* Old section of Istanbul.

line 749 *Sophia's shrine:* Hagia Sophia, or Church of the Holy Wisdom, completed in 537 under the Byzantine Emperor Justinian I.

line 755 *Bosphorous:* Bosporus, strait between Europe and Asia, dividing Istanbul.

line 765 *Caique:* Long, narrow boat.

line 776 *searment:* Cerement; shroud.

line 792 *Lacedemon's:* Sparta's.

line 793 *Thebes Epaminondas:* The Theban general and politician Epaminondas defeated Spartan forces at Leuctra in 371 B.C., ending Sparta's military dominance of the Greek states.

line 812 *Tritonia's:* Athena's.

line 822 *Hymettus:* Limestone mountain, famed for flowers and bees because of the Roman poet Ovid's description of it in *Ars amatoria* (c. 1 B.C.).

line 826 *Mendeli's marbles:* Mount Pentelicus, the marble of which was used for the buildings and monuments of Athens in the fourth and fifth centuries B.C.

line 836 *Marathon:* At the Battle of Marathon in 490 B.C., the Athenians repelled the first Persian invasion of Greece.

line 841 *Hellas':* Greece's.

line 846 *Mede:* One of an Indo-European people related to the Persians.

line 883 *Idlesse:* Idleness (archaic).

line 891 *Thou:* John Edleston.

lines 904–5 *stern Death! thou hast / The Parent, Friend, and now the more than friend:* Byron's mother died on August 1, 1811, his friend Charles Skinner Matthews drowned in the Cam river a few days later, and John Edleston had died of consumption in May, though Byron did not learn of Edleston's death until October.

line 926 *Eld:* Old age (archaic).

CANTO THE THIRD

lines 1–2 *Is thy face like thy mother's . . . Ada:* Anne Isabella (Annabella) Milbanke, Lady Byron (1792–1860). She married Byron on January 2, 1815, and separated from him, January 15, 1816, taking the five-week-old Augusta Ada with her, the future Augusta Ada Byron King, Countess of Lovelace (1815–1852). After the separation from his wife, Byron never saw his daughter again.

line 118 *Chaldean, he could watch the stars:* The Chaldeans, an ancient people who ruled in Babylonia, were early practicioners of astronomy.

line 145 *an Empire's:* Napoleon's.

line 153 *Fields! king-making Victory:* The Battle of Waterloo (June 18, 1815), resulted in Napoleon's final defeat. Byron alludes to the fact that Napoleon's fall strengthened and secured monarchies throughout Europe.

lines 179–80 *when the myrtle . . . Athens' tyrant Lord:* In 514 B.C., Harmodius and Aristogiton attempted to assassinate the tyrant brothers Hippias and Hipparchus, attacking them with daggers concealed in myrtle. They succeeded in killing Hipparchus, and their names and the myrtle-wreathed sword became emblems of resistance to tyranny.

line 181 *a sound of revelry:* This stanza describes a famous ball given by the Duchess of Richmond on the eve of the Battle of Quatre-Bras, three days before Waterloo.

line 200 *Brunswick's fated Chieftan:* Frederick, Duke of Brunswick (1771–1815), nephew of King George III of England, was killed on the front line at Quatre-Bras.

line 205 *Which stretched his father on a bloody bier:* Brunswick's father, Charles William Ferdinand, was killed in the Battle of Auerstädt in 1806.

line 226 *"Cameron's Gathering":* The war song of the Cameron clan.

line 227 *Lochiel:* Chief of the Camerons. *Albyn:* Gælic name for Scotland.

line 229 *pibroch:* A series of variations on a war song or dirge for highland bag-pipes.

line 234 *Evan's—Donald's:* Sir Even Cameron (1629–1719) fought against Oliver Cromwell and for James II. His grandson, Donald Cameron (1695–1748), was wounded while fighting for the Stuarts in the Jacobite re-bellion of 1745–46.

line 235 *Ardennes:* Byron mistakenly indentifies the woods of Soignes with the forest of Ardennes.

lines 254–56 *Yet one ... did his Sire some wrong:* Major Frederick Howard, Byron's second cousin, died at Waterloo. Byron had satirized Howard's fa-ther, the Earl of Carlisle, in his *English Bards, and Scotch Reviewers.*

line 307 *The Psalmist numbered out:* Alluding to Psalms, 90:10, "The days of our years are threescore years and ten; and if by reason of strength they be fourscore years, yet is their strength labor and sorrow; for it is soon cut off and we fly away."

line 316 *the greatest, nor the worst of men:* Napoleon.

line 366 *Philip's son:* Alexander the Great.

line 368 *Diogenes:* Ancient Greek Cynic philosopher, who was supposed to have searched in vain for an honest man.

line 476 *In one fond breast:* That of Byron's half sister, Augusta Leigh (1784–1851).

line 496 *castled Crag of Drachenfels:* The hill of Drachenfels ("Dragon's Rock") is crowned by a castle built in the twelfth century and destroyed by the French in the seventeenth. The hill was the legendary abode of the dragon killed by the Germanic hero Siegfried.

line 536 *Coblentz:* Koblenz, German city at the confluence of the Rhine and Mosel rivers.

line 541 *Marceau:* General François-Séverin Marceau-Desgraviers (1769–1796), military hero of the French Revolutionary wars, killed by a sharpshooter while fighting the Austrians.

line 554 *Ehrenbreitstein with her shattered wall:* Fortress blown up by the French in 1801 after a four-year siege, afterward rebuilt into one of the strongest fortresses in Europe.

line 601 *Morat:* The Battle of Morat occurred on June 22, 1476, and was a great victory for the Swiss against the invading Burgundians.

line 608 *Cannæ's carnage:* The Battle of Cannæ in 216 B.C. resulted in the vic-tory of Hannibal over Roman forces, with great slaughter.

line 616 *Draconic:* Draco was a seventh-century B.C. Athenian lawmaker whose legal code punished almost every crime with death.

line 624 *coeval:* of the same age or duration.

line 625 *Aventicum:* Ancient Roman capital of Helvetia (Switzerland).

lines 627–32 *Julia ... she could not save:* Princess Julia Alpinula, who was supposed to have tried in vain to save her father from a death sentence on a charge of treason and to have died soon after. However, Byron's information about her came from an epitaph which has since been exposed as a forgery. It is doubtful that such a woman actually existed.

line 644 *Lake Leman:* Lake Geneva.

line 725 *Rousseau:* Jean-Jacques Rousseau (1712–1778), French philosopher and novelist, was born in Geneva and lived there in his youth.

line 743 *Julie:* Heroine of Rousseau's novel *Julie, ou la Nouvelle Héloïse* (1761).

line 745 *the memorable kiss:* Byron refers to the long walk Rousseau took every morning (as he recounts in his *Confessions,* 1782–1788) to receive a kiss from the Comtesse d'Houdetot.

line 762 *Pythian's mystic cave:* Site of Apollo's oracle at Delphi.

lines 763–65 *Those oracles which set the world in flame ... this for France:* Byron refers to the inspirational effect of Rousseau's writings upon the French Revolution.

line 809 *Jura:* Mountain range located mostly in Switzerland.

line 848 *Cytherea's zone:* The girdle of Aphrodite, which magically inspired love.

line 900 *knoll:* Knell, or the sound made by a bell that is rung slowly, as for a death.

line 923 *Clarens:* Village on Lake Geneva, the site of Rousseau's novel *Julie, ou la Nouvelle Héloïse.*

line 986 *The one was fire and fickleness:* Voltaire (François-Marie Arouet) (1694–1778), French writer and satirist, who lived at an estate in Ferney from 1758 to 1777.

line 991 *Proteus:* In Greek mythology, Poseidon's herdsman, who could take any shape.

line 995 *The other, deep and slow:* Edward Gibbon (1737–1794), author of *The History of the Decline and Fall of the Roman Empire* (1776–1788), which he finished while he lived at Lausanne from 1783 to 1793. Byron employs Voltaire and Gibbon as heroic symbols of rational skepticism and freedom of thought.

line 1000 *lord of irony:* Gibbon's attitude toward Christianity in his *Decline and Fall* was notoriously skeptical.

line 1024 *the fierce Carthaginian almost won thee:* The Carthaginian general Hannibal almost conquered Rome in the third century B.C.

line 1057 *filed:* Defiled, corrupted.

CANTO THE FOURTH

p. 107 *John Hobhouse:* John Cam Hobhouse (1786–1869), Byron's closest friend, with whom he traveled on his grand tour, 1809–1810, 1816–1817.

p. 108 *Goldsmith's* Citizen of the World: Alludes to the satirical *The Citizen of the World; or, Letters from a Chinese Philosopher, Residing in London, to his Friends in the East* (1760–1762), by Oliver Goldsmith (1731–1774).

p. 109 *Canova, Monti . . . Vacca:* Eminent Italians. Byron mentions the sculptor Antonio Canova (1757–1822); the poets Vincenzo Monti (1754–1828); Ugo Foscolo (1778–1827), and Ippolito Pindemonte (1753–1828); the archæologist Ennius Visconti (1751–1818); the liberal patriot Michele Morelli (1790–1822); the politician and antiquarian Count Leopoldo Cicognara (1767–1834); the Countess Albrizzi, an author and an acquaintance of Byron's (1760–1836); Cardinal Giuseppe Mezzofanti (1774–1849), polyglot and linguist; Cardinal Angelo Mai (1782–1854), philologist; the classicist Andrea Mustoxidi (1785–1860); and the physicians Francesco Aglietti (1757–1836); and Andrea Vacca Berlinghieri (1772–1826).

line 1 *the "Bridge of Sighs":* The Ponti dei Sospiri, an enclosed bridge built around 1600 by Antonio Contino, connecting the Doge's Palace to Venice's prisons. (The Doge was the ruler of Venice.) The bridge was called the Bridge of Sighs because of the sighs of despair that came from the condemned prisoners who crossed it.

line 8 *wingéd Lion:* A symbol of Venice; a motif that recurs in the architecture and art of Venice.

line 10 *Cybele:* The "Great Mother of the Gods," an ancient deity associated with motherhood and wild nature. Because she was associated with cities, she was often depicted with a crown made of gates or towers.

line 19 *Tasso's echoes are no more:* Torquato Tasso (1544–1595) was the author of the epic poem *Gerusalemme liberta* (1581). In Byron's time Venetian gondoliers were famed for singing passages from Tasso's poem.

line 31 *Dogeless city:* Napoleon deposed the last doge in 1797.

line 33 *Rialto:* The Rialto Bridge spans the Grand Canal. *Shylock and the Moor:* Shakespeare's Shylock, from the *Merchant of Venice,* and Othello, from the tragedy of the same name.

line 34 *Pierre:* Character from Thomas Otway's (1652–1685) play *Venice Preserved* (1682).

line 85 *Spartan's epitaph:* Brasidas (d. 422 B.C.), Spartan general during the Peloponnesian War. The epitaph is supposed to have been his Brasidas's mother's remark when strangers praised her dead son.

line 93 *Bucentaur:* The Doge's ceremonial barge, wrecked by the French in 1797.

line 95 *St. Mark yet sees his Lion:* The winged lion was the symbol of Mark, the patron saint of Venice.

line 97 *the proud Place where an Emperor sued:* Piazza San Marco. The Holy Roman Emperor Frederick Barbarossa (c.1123–1190), who challenged papal authority, finally acknowledged Alexander III as the true Pope in the Peace of Venice (1177), receiving the Pope's kiss of peace in the Piazza San Marco in front of the Basilica.

line 100 *Suabian:* Barbarossa was Duke of Swabia.

lines 100–1 *the Austrian reigns— / An Emperor tramples:* Francis I of Austria, who ruled Venice from 1797 to 1805 and again after 1814.

line 106 *Lauwine:* Avalanche.

lines 107–8 *blind old Dandolo ... conquering foe:* Enrico Dandolo (1167–1205), elected doge of Venice at the age of eighty-five. He persuaded the knights of the Fourth Crusade to help Venice conquer Constantinople.

line 109 *his Steeds of brass:* Positioned high up on the façade of St. Mark's Basilica, overlooking the Piazza San Marco, were the four gilded bronze horses that Dandolo sent to Venice from Constantinople in 1204.

line 111 *Doria's menace:* Alluding to a conflict between Venice and Genoa, during which the Genoese commander, Peter Doria, was said to have demanded that the brass horses be bridled.

line 118 *Tyre:* The ancient city of Tyre in Phoenecia (present-day Lebanon) was known for its splendor.

line 123 *Ottomite:* Turk.

line 124 *Troy's rival, Candia:* Crete, lost by the Venetians until 1669, after having defended it for over twenty years.

line 127 *shivered:* Shattered.

lines 136–44 *When Athens' armies ... for Freedom and his strains:* The Syracusans defeated an invading Athenian army during the Peloponnesian War. Plutarch relates that some of the captured Athenians gained mercy from the Syracusans by reciting lines from Euripides. "Attic" here means "Athenian."

lines 158–59 *Otway ... Had stamped her image in me:* Refers to works that are set in Venice: Thomas Otway's play *Venice Preserved* (1682), Ann Radcliffe's Gothic novel *The Mysteries of Udolpho* (1794), Friedrich Schiller's *Der Geisterseher* (1789); and Shakespeare's *The Merchant of Venice* and *Othello*.

line 172 *Tannen:* A type of Alpine fir tree.

line 238 *Friuli:* Region of northeastern Italy.

line 247 *Rhætian:* Referring to an ancient Roman province.

line 250 *Brenta:* River flowing to the Gulf of Venice.

lines 259–60 *Dies like the Dolphin ... colour as it gasps away:* Dolphins were thought to change color as they died.

lines 262–64 *tomb in Arqua . . . Laura's lover:* The Italian lyric poet Petrarch (1304–1374), many of whose poems were addressed to his idealized beloved, Laura. He was thought to be the greatest scholar of his age and helped found the tradition of European humanism.

lines 310–11 *antique brood / Of Este:* A noble family prominent in the history of medieval and Renaissance Italy. Members of the family ruled Ferrara in northern Italy from the thirteenth to the sixteenth century.

lines 316–23 *Tasso is . . . Where he had plunged it:* Torquato Tasso was confined in the hospital of Santa Anna by order of Duke Alfonso II of Ferrara (whom he served as court poet) from 1579 to 1586. His confinement was evidently due to a real mental illness, but Byron endorses the romantic tradition that he was unjustly imprisoned.

line 339 *Cruscan quire:* The Accademia della Crusca, founded in 1582 in Florence, attempted to purify the Tuscan language. It had criticized Tasso's *Gerusalemme liberata.*

line 340 *Boileau:* Nicolas Boileau (1636–1711), French poet, literary critic, and proponent of the classical tradition.

lines 354–60 *Bards of Hell . . . Knightly Worth:* Dante Alighieri (1265–1321), author of *The Divine Comedy* (c.1308–1321). Sir Walter Scott (1771–1832), Scottish author of poetic and prose romances. Ludovico Ariosto (1474–1533), author of the epic poem *Orlando Furioso* (1516–1532), about Charlemagne's knights.

lines 389–90 *Roman friend . . . of Tully:* Servius Sulpicius Rufus (c.106–43 B.C.) was a friend of the Roman statesman and orator Marcus Tullius Cicero, also known as Tully (106–43 B.C.).

lines 392–94 *Megara . . . Corinth:* Places described in a famous letter from Sulpicius Rufus to Cicero.

lines 424–25 *Arno . . . Etrurian Athens:* The Arno River in Tuscany that flows through Florence, the Athens of the Renaissance.

line 433 *the Goddess loves in stone:* The Venus de Medici.

line 450 *the Dardan shepherd's prize:* Refers to the Judgment of Paris, in which Paris chose Aphrodite (over Hera and Athena) as the most beautiful goddess, awarding her the Apple of Discord.

line 452 *Anchises:* A Trojan shepherd and the father of Aeneas by Venus.

line 454 *thy own vanquished Lord of War:* Mars, Roman god of war and Venus's lover.

lines 478–86 *Santa Croce . . . Machiavelli's:* Church of the Franciscans in Florence where Michelangelo, the poet Vittorio Alfieri (1749–1803), Galileo, and Macchiavelli are buried.

lines 498–99 *Bard of Prose . . . Hundred Tales of Love:* Giovanni Boccaccio (1313–1375), author of the *Decameron* (1348–1353).

line 505 *afar:* Dante is buried in Ravenna.

line 506 *Like Scipio:* The embittered Roman general Scipio Africanus the Elder (236–184 or 183 B.C.), who defeated Hannibal in the Battle of Zama, was buried in Liternum rather than Rome, which he considered to be ungrateful to him.

line 507 *Thy factions, in their worse than civil war:* Dante was caught up in the political conflicts between the Guelfs and the Ghibellines (papal and imperial partisans, respectively), and was condemned to be burned at the stake, a verdict that sent him into exile from Florence.

line 513 *rifled:* Petrarch's tomb in Arqua was rifled in the seventeenth century.

line 523 *wants:* Lacks.

line 525 *Brutus:* Marcus Junius Brutus (85–42 B.C.), leader of the conspirators who assassinated Julius Cæsar.

line 542 *Arno's dome:* The Uffizi Palace.

lines 551–52 *Thrasimene's lake … Roman rashness:* Lago Trasimeno, near where the Carthaginian Hannibal defeated the Romans in 217 B.C.

line 586 *Clitumnus:* The Clitunno river.

line 604 *the Genius of the place:* The "genius loci," the pervading spirit or deity of a place.

line 613 *roar of waters:* The falls of Terni.

line 614 *Velino:* The Velino river.

line 620 *Phlegethon:* The river of fire in Hades.

line 654 *Jungfrau:* Swiss peak in the Benese Alps.

line 656 *Mont Blanc:* Highest peak in Europe, glacier-covered and located in the Alps.

line 657 *Chimari:* The Chamonix Valley, below Mont Blanc.

line 658 *Acroceraunian:* Of or pertaining to the high mountain range between Epirus and Macedonia.

lines 662–663 *Ida … Athos—Olympus—Ætna—Atlas:* Greek mountains.

lines 665–66 *Soracte's height … lyric Roman's aid:* Mountain in central Italy celebrated in the poetry of Horace and Virgil.

line 685 *Horace:* Quintus Horatius Flaccus (65–8 B.C.), Roman poet and satirist.

line 703 *Niobe:* In Greek mythology, Niobe boasted that her fourteen children were more numerous than the Titan Leto's and so she should be worshiped rather than Leto. To punish Niobe, Leto's children, Apollo and Artemis, slew all Niobe's children.

line 707 *Scipios' tomb:* The tomb of the Scipios was plundered in the eighteenth century.

line 710 *Tiber:* River flowing through Rome.

line 734 *Virgil:* Publius Vergilius Maro (70–19 B.C.), Roman poet and author of the *Aeneid.*

line 735 *Livy:* Titus Livius (59 B.C.–17 A.D.), Roman historian.

lines 740–45 *Sylla ... Annihilated senates:* Lucius Cornelius Sulla (138–78 B.C.), Roman general who fought a civil war and became a cruel dictator in 82 B.C.

line 764 *His day of double victory and death:* Cromwell won the battles of Dunbar (1650) and Worcester (1651) and died (1658) on the same day of the month September 3.

lines 775–78 *dread Statue ... bloody Cæsar:* Statue of Pompey, found in 1522, at whose base Caesar was thought to have been assassinated.

line 781 *Nemesis:* Greek goddess of vengeance.

line 782 *Pompey:* Gnæus Pompeius Magnus (106–48 B.C.), Roman statesman and general, part of a ruling triumvirate with Julius Cæsar and Marcius Lucinus Crassus. He was later defeated in battle by Cæsar and murdered in Egypt.

lines 784–89 *nurse of Rome ... wild teat:* The Capitoline Wolf (late sixth to early fifth century B.C.), ancient statue of a she-wolf suckling the twins, Romulus and Remus, legendary founders of Rome. The figures of the twins were not added to the statue until the sixteenth century.

line 800 *one vain Man:* Napoleon.

line 809 *Alcides with the distaff:* As a punishment for killing Iole's brother, Alcides (the Greek hero Heracles) was forced to wear women's clothes and spin fiber into thread for Omphale, Queen of Lydia. A distaff is a staff on which wool or flax is wound before spinning. Hercules with the distaff was a popular subject for seventeenth- and eighteenth-century painters.

line 853 *him who humbled once the proud:* Napoleon.

line 858 *Columbia:* The United States of America.

line 865 *France got drunk with blood:* Referring to the French Revolution (1789) and the Reign of Terror.

line 866 *Saturnalia:* Orgy, drunken revelry.

line 871 *the base pageant last upon the scene:* The Congress of Vienna (1814–15), which reorganized Europe after the Napoleonic Wars. Its chief participants were the victorious allies Austria, Prussia, Russia, and Great Britian.

line 881 *the North:* England.

lines 892–93 *Lady of the dead / Tombed in a palace:* Byron describes the huge Tomb of Cæcilia Metella, wife of the Triumvir Crassus. It was converted into a fortress and a palace adjoined it.

line 904 *Cornelia:* Mother of Tiberius and Gaius Sempronius Gracchus (the Gracchi), reformers of the second century B.C. She was reknowned for being highly cultured.

line 917 *Hesperus:* Venus, as the evening star.

line 951 *Palatine:* The Palatine Hill, upon which Rome was founded.

line 987 *Titus' or Trajan's:* Titus Flavius Vespasianus (39–81) and Marcus Ulpius Trajanus (53–117), Roman emperors.

line 989 *apostolic statues:* In 1587, statues of St. Peter and St. Paul were placed on top of the columns of Trajan and Marcus Aurelius, respectively, replacing the ancient Roman statues.

line 1000 *Where is the rock of Triumph:* The location of the Temple of Jupiter on the Capitoline Hill was unknown at the time Byron was writing.

line 1002 *Tarpeian . . . Treason's race:* Criminals were thrown to their deaths from the Tarpeian Rock in Rome. It was named after Tarpeia, a Roman woman who betrayed the city to the Sabines.

line 1022 *Rienzi:* Cola di Rienzo (1313–1354), Roman popular leader, sometimes depicted as a forerunner of Italian nationalism.

line 1026 *Numa:* Numa Pompilius, legendary king of Rome (715–673 B.C.), and successor to Romulus, aided in his rule by his consort, the nymph Egeria.

line 1030 *Aurora:* Goddess of the dawn.

line 1031 *nympholepsy:* A frenzy of emotion, as for something unattainable.

line 1036 *thy Fountain:* The Grotto of Egeria, near the Appian Way.

line 1129 *Upas:* A legendary tree in Java that poisoned the earth around it.

line 1143 *couch:* To remove a cataract.

lines 1183–84 *Furies . . . Orestes:* Horrifying female divinities that punished criminals, such as Orestes who killed his mother and her lover in order to avenge the murder of his father, Agamemnon.

line 1221 *Janus:* Roman god of beginnings and endings, often shown with two faces, one looking to the past, the other to the future.

line 1243 *here the buzz of eager nations:* the Colosseum.

lines 1252–55 *I see . . . head sinks:* Byron is describing the statue of the Dying Gaul in the Capitoline Museum.

line 1266 *Dacian:* From Dacia, a region roughly corresponding with modern Romania.

lines 1279–80 *from its mass . . . reared:* Stones from the Colosseum were used in the construction of other structures.

line 1293 *bald first Cæsar's head:* Suetonius states that Julius Cæsar was pleased that his laurel wreath concealed his baldness.

line 1314 *Pantheon:* Temple of all the gods in Rome. It was converted to a Christian church in 609.

lines 1324–50 *There is a dungeon . . . such tide:* The legend of the Caritas Romana ("Roman Charity"), told by the Roman historian Valerius Maximus, tells how the aged Cimon was in prison awaiting his execution and was forbidden food. To keep his from starving, his pregnant daughter, Pero, visited him in prison and secretly breast-fed him.

line 1351 *The starry fable of the Milky Way:* In Greek mythology, the Milky Way was formed when Hera pushed the suckling infant Heracles away from her breast and her milk sprayed out into space.

line 1360 *the Mole:* The mausoleum of Hadrian, now the Castle of St. Angelo. A mole, used in this sense, is a massive structure.

line 1361 *Egypt's piles:* The pyramids.

line 1366 *this Dome:* St. Peter's Basilica, completed in 1615 and until 1989 the largest church in Christendom.

line 1370 *Diana's marvel:* The Temple of Artemis at Ephesus, one of the seven wonders of the ancient world.

line 1375 *Sophia's bright roofs:* The Hagia Sophia in Constantinople.

line 1381 *Zion's desolation:* The destruction of the Temple of Solomon (586 B.C.).

line 1433 *Laocoön's torture:* Statue in the Vatican Museum, (attributed by Pliny the Elder to Agesander, Polydorus, and Athenodorus) that depicts the Laocoön and his two sons being killed by two sea serpents sent by Poseidon.

line 1441 *Or view the Lord of the unerring bow:* The Apollo Belvedere statue, by the Athenian sculptor Apollonius.

line 1459 *Prometheus:* In Greek mythology, the Titan who was punished by Zeus for stealing fire from the gods to give to mankind.

line 1468 *the Pilgrim of my Song:* Childe Harold.

line 1494 *fardels:* Burdens.

lines 1495–1503 *a voice . . . no relief:* Princess Charlotte Augusta (1796–1817), only child of George IV, who gave birth to a stillborn son on November 5, 1817. She herself died of postpartum hemorrhage hours later.

line 1513 *bring forth:* Give birth.

line 1518 *orisons:* Prayers.

line 1519 *her Iris:* Rainbow, symbol of hope.

lines 1525–26 *How we did entrust / Futurity to her:* Princess Charlotte was heir to the throne and was expected to be a more liberal monarch than her father.

line 1549 *Nemi:* Lake Nemi, a crater lake in central Italy.

line 1558 *Albano's:* Lake Albano's.

line 1561 *Latian:* Referring to Latium, a region of ancient Italy.

lines 1561–62 *Epic war / "Arms and the Man":* Virgil's *Aeneid;* "Arms and the Man" is a translation of part of the first line (which, as translated by John Dryden, reads: "Arms, and the man I sing, who, forc'd by fate, . . .").

line 1575 *Euxine:* The Black Sea.

line 1576 *Symplegades:* Two islands in the narrow entrance to the Black Sea. In the story of Jason and the Argonauts, they swung together and crushed any ship that tried to sail between them.

line 1620 *lay:* Byron's incorrect usage of the word here is a famous solecism.

lines 1628–29 *which mar / Alike the Armada's pride, or spoils of Trafalgar:* Storms at sea destroyed many of the ships of the Spanish Armada after its defeat (1588) and after the Battle of Trafalgar (1805).

line 1672 *sandal-shoon, and scallop-shell:* Emblems of pilgrimage to the Holy Land.

EARLY POEMS

ON LEAVING NEWSTEAD ABBEY

line 1 *Newstead:* Newstead Abbey is Byron's ancestral estate in Nottinghamshire.

line 6 *to Palestine's plain:* That is, to the Crusades.

line 7 *escutcheon:* Shield displaying a coat of arms.

line 11 *Askalon:* Ascalon, a city on the coast of Palestine, taken by the Crusaders in 1153.

lines 13–14 *Cressy ... Edward:* The Battle of Cressy (Crécy) was won by King Edward III and the Black Prince over Philippe VI of France in 1346.

line 17 *On Marston, with Rupert:* The Battle of Marston Moor in 1644 was the first victory in the English Civil War of Parliamentary forces over those loyal to King Charles I. Prince Rupert (1619–1682), nephew of Charles I lead the Royalist troops. Later, Rupert became a privy counselor and admiral under Charles II.

THE FIRST KISS OF LOVE

line 9 *Apollo:* Greek god of music and poetry.

lines 10–11 *the Nine ... adieu to the Muse:* The nine Muses of Greek mythology, when poets evoked for inspiration.

REPLY TO SOME VERSES OF J. M. B. PIGOT, ESQ.

line 1 *Pigot:* John Pigot, a young friend of Byron's at Southwell.

TO THE SIGHING STREPHON

line 39 *the Platonists' school:* Platonic love.

LACHIN Y GAIR:

line 5 *Caledonia:* Scotland.

line 27 *Culloden:* Site of a famous battle in 1746 in which the English forces defeated the Scottish Highlanders under Prince Charles Edward Stuart, ending the Jacobite uprising of 1745.

line 30 *Braemar:* A region of the Highlands.

line 31 *Pibroch:* A piece of music for the bagpipe, usually a dirge.

TO ROMANCE
line 20 *Pylades:* Faithful friend of Orestes, in Greek mythology.

WHEN I ROV'D A YOUNG HIGHLANDER
line 2 *Morven:* A mountain in Aberdeenshire, Scotland.
line 8 *Mary:* Byron's childhood sweetheart, Mary Duff.
line 19 *Dee:* River in Aberdeenshire.
line 34 *Colbleen:* Mountain in Aberdeenshire.

MISCELLANEOUS AND OCCASIONAL POEMS

WELL! THOU ART HAPPY
line 35 *Lethe:* River of forgetfulness in Hades.

STANZAS WRITTEN IN PASSING THE AMBRACIAN GULF
line 2 *Actium:* The Battle of Actium in 31 B.C. ended with Octavian's victory over Mark Antony and Cleopatra. Actium is a promontory at the mouth of the Ambracian Gulf in Greece.
line 11 *Orpheus sang his spouse from Hell:* In Greek mythology, the singing of the heroic musician Orpheus so moved Hades, lord of the underworld, that he agreed to let Orpheus take his dead lover, Eurydice, back to the land of the living.

THE GIRL OF CADIZ
line 42 *Bolero:* National dance of Spain.
line 46 *Hesper:* Hesperus, Venus in its appearance as the evening star.

WRITTEN AFTER SWIMMING FROM SESTOS TO ABYDOS
line 2 *Leander:* In Greek legend, Leander of Abydos fell in love with the virgin priestess, Hero. He swam across the Hellespont strait every night to visit her.

MAID OF ATHENS, ERE WE PART
line 6 Ζωή μον, σᾶς ἀγαπῶ: Byron translates the Greek refrain as, "My life, I love you!"

FAREWELL TO MALTA
line 1 *La Valette:* Valetta; city on the coast of Malta.
line 2 *Sirocco:* An oppressive wind of the northern Mediterranean coast; either dry and dusty or hot and damp.

line 9 *packets:* Small boats that carry mail, passengers, or goods on a regular route.

line 33 *Mrs. Fraser:* Acquaintance of Byron's in Malta. It was at her house that he met Mrs. Constance Spencer Smith.

line 53 *physic:* Medicine.

line 55 *beaver:* Beaver hat.

ONE STRUGGLE MORE, AND I AM FREE

line 29 *Cynthia's noon:* Cynthia is a name for Artemis, Greek goddess associated with the moon. Therefore Cynthia's noon is midnight.

EUTHANASIA

line 17 *Psyche:* The lover of Cupid; also the soul or the mind.

REMEMBER THEE! REMEMBER THEE!

line 2 *Lethe:* River of forgetfulness in Hades.

SONNET, TO GENEVRA

line 12 *The Magdalen of Guido:* The Penitent Magdalene, by the painter Guido Reni (1575–1642).

ODE TO NAPOLEON BUONAPARTE

line 8 *he, miscalled the Morning Star:* Lucifer. Byron is comparing Napoleon's fall to Lucifer's fall from heaven.

line 26 *Pagod:* Idol.

lines 46–53 *He who of old would rend the oak ... prowlers' prey:* Milo of Crotona, a legendary Greek athlete. He attempted to tear apart an oak but caught his hand in the tree and was eaten alive by wolves.

lines 55–63 *The Roman ... abandoned power:* Lucius Cornelius Sulla (138–78 B.C.), Roman general who fought a civil war and became a cruel dictator in 82 B.C. "That hour / Of self-upheld abandoned power" refers to the fact that he willingly gave up his power in 80 B.C.

lines 64–66 *The Spaniard ... for rosaries away:* The Holy Roman Emperor Charles V (1500–1558), who abdicated and entered a monastery.

line 109 *she, proud Austria's mournful flower:* Napoleon's second wife, Marie-Louise, daughter of the Austrian emperor Francis I.

line 118 *thy sullen Isle:* Elba, the island to which Napoleon was exiled in 1814.

line 125 *That Corinth's pedagogue:* Dionysius the Younger (395?–343? B.C.) became tyrant of Syracuse in 367 and was exiled in 343 for his despotic rule.

line 127 *Timour:* Timur, or Tamerlane (1336–1405), Turkish conqueror.

line 131 *he of Babylon:* Nebuchadnezzar, King of Babylonia, who is depicted in the Bible (Daniel 4:33) as going mad and eating grass.

lines 136–39 *the thief of fire from heaven ... his rock:* Prometheus, the Titan of Greek mythology who brought fire from heaven to give to mortals. Zeus punished him by chaining him to a cliff, where a vulture tore out and ate his liver every day.

line 150 *Marengo:* Village in Italy; site of a battle in 1800 that ended with Napoleon's victory over the Austrians.

line 155 *purple:* The color of royalty.

line 168 *Cincinnatus of the West:* Lucius Quinctius Cincinnatus (born c. 519 B.C.) was a Roman who, according to legend, left his farm and became dictator in order to defeat the Aequi and Volscians, and resigned his dictatorship and returned to his farm after he had won. Byron here refers to George Washington.

DARKNESS
line 48 *corse:* Corpse.

CHURCHILL'S GRAVE
line 23 *Newton:* Sir Isaac Newton (1642–1727), English mathematician and scientist.

SONNET TO LAKE LEMAN
line 1 *Rousseau—Voltaire—our Gibbon—and De Staël:* Writers associated with Lake Leman (Lake Geneva) in Switzerland: Jean-Jacques Rousseau (1712–1778), French philosopher and novelist; Voltaire (François-Marie Arouet) (1694–1778), French writer and satirist; Edward Gibbon (1737–1794), author of *The History of the Decline and Fall of the Roman Empire* (1776–1788); Madame Germaine de Staël (1766–1817), French writer.

ON SAM ROGERS
line 2 *Cocker:* Edward Cocker (1631–1675) wrote a famous book on arithmetic (1678).

HEBREW MELODIES

THE HARP THE MONARCH MINSTREL SWEPT
line 1 *Monarch Minstrel:* King David.

ON JORDAN'S BANKS
line 3 *Baal:* The chief deity of Canaan. *Sinai:* Mount Sinai, where Moses was supposed to have received the Ten Commandments.

line 10 *shivered:* Shattered.

JEPHTHA'S DAUGHTER
line 2 *thy Daughter expire:* Jephtha vowed that if he defeated the Ammonites, he would return to his city and sacrifice the first person he saw. When he returned and saw his daughter first, he was forced to sacrifice her.

SONG OF SAUL BEFORE HIS LAST BATTLE
line 4 *Gath:* Ancient city of Palestine.

SAUL
line 1 *Thou whose spell can raise the dead:* This lyric tells the story of how, in the I Samuel 28:8–19 the ghost of Samuel is summoned from the grave by the Witch of Endor. Samuel's ghost prophecies the death of Saul.

VISION OF BELSHAZZAR
line 1 *The King was on his throne:* In the Bible, Belshazzar, the son of Nebuchadnezzar II and last king of Babylon, was warned of his doom by handwriting on the wall that was interpreted by Daniel (Daniel 5).

HEROD'S LAMENT FOR MARIAMNE
line 1 *Mariamne:* King Herod put his wife, Mariamne, to death on suspicion of infidelity. Afterwards he was haunted by her image.

ON THE DAY OF THE DESTRUCTION OF JERUSALEM BY TITUS
line 2 *I beheld thee:* The Roman Emperor Titus Flavius Vespasianus (39–81), who was instrumental in the capture of Jerusalem (70).

THE DESTRUCTION OF SENNACHERIB
line 1 *The Assyrian:* Sennacherib, King of Assyria (704–681 B.C.) who invaded, Judea. In the Bible, his army is destroyed at Tophet in Jerusalem.
line 21 *Ashur:* City in Assyria.
line 22 *Baal:* The chief deity of Canaan.

JEUX D'ESPRIT AND EPHEMERAL VERSES

LINES TO MR. HODGSON
line 16 *Packet:* Small boat that carries mail, passengers, or goods on a regular route.
line 39 *Queen Mab:* The fairies' midwife. In *Romeo and Juliet* (I, iv) Mercutio speaks of her being "In shape no bigger than an agate-stone / On the forefinger of an alderman."

line 49 *Fletcher! Murray! Bob!:* William Fletcher, Joe Murray, and the young Robert Rushton were servants who traveled with Byron.

line 53 *Hobhouse:* John Cam Hobhouse (1786–1869) was Byron's closest friend, with whom he traveled on his grand tour, 1809–1810, 1816–1817.

line 58 *Braganza:* A dynasty of Portuguese rulers.

WINDSOR POETICS

line 3 *Between them stands another sceptred thing:* The much-despised Prince Regent (1762–1830), who, after the death of his father in 1820 became King George IV. He is "Charles to his people" because of his unpopularity (Parliament revolted against and ultimately beheaded Charles I) and "Henry to his wife" because he despised and separated from his wife, Queen Caroline (Henry VIII had six wives, two of whom he executed).

TO THOMAS MOORE

line 2 *bark:* Sailing vessel.

line 3 *before I go, Tom Moore:* Byron began this poem at Dover in April 1816 as he was waiting to leave England forever. Thomas Moore (1779–1852), Irish poet and prose writer, was one of Byron's closest friends.

line 4 *health:* A toast, a polite or complimentary wish for a person's health and happiness.

EPISTLE FROM MR. MURRAY TO DR. POLIDORI

John Murray: Byron's publisher, John Murray II (1778–1843).

line 9 *machinery:* Mechanical devices for producing effects on stage.

line 23 Manuel: A tragedy (1817) by Charles Robert Maturin (1782–1824).

line 25 *Sotheby:* William Sotheby (1757–1833), author of the plays *Orestes* (1802), *Ivan* (1814), and *The Death of Darnley.*

line 31 Ina: A play (1815) by Barbarina Wilmot (1768–1854).

line 35 *it's no more a drama:* Referring to Byron's *Manfred* (1817).

line 36 Kehama: Robert Southey's (1774–1843) long narrative poem *The Curse of Kehama* (1810).

line 45 *My room's so full . . . Gifford:* Murray's drawing-room at 50 Albemarle St., London. William Gifford (1756–1826), poet and editor of the *Quarterly Review,* which John Murray published.

line 46 *Hookham Frere:* John Hookham Frere (1769–1846), author of the poem *The Monks and the Giants* (1817–1818) and one of the founders of the *Quarterly Review.*

line 51 *St. Helena:* The island where Napoleon was living in exile.

line 56 *Crabbes . . . and Wards:* George Crabbe (1754–1832), poet; Thomas Campbell (1777–1844), poet; John Wilson Croker (1780–1857), secretary of the admiralty and contributor to the *Quarterly Review;* John William Ward (1781–1833), member of Parliament.

line 60 *Mr. Hammond to Dog Dent:* George Hammond (1763–1853) was a founder of the *Quarterly Review;* "Dog" Dent was the nickname of John Dent, an MP who helped introduce a dog tax Bill in Parliament.

line 63 *Malcolm … Chantrey:* Sir John Malcolm (1769–1833) was a statesman and historian; Sir Francis Chantrey (1781–1841) was a successful sculptor.

line 66 *De Staël's late dissolution:* Madame Germaine de Staël (1766–1817) had recently died.

line 67 *Her book: Considérations sur les principaux événements de la Révolution française,* published posthumously in 1818.

line 70 *Rocca:* John Rocca (1778–1818), de Staël's second husband.

line 74 *Hum:* Humbug; a lie.

line 75 *the fellows Schlegel:* Friedrich von Schlegel (1772–1829) and his brother, August Wilhelm (1767–1845), writers on German Romanticism. August was a close friend of de Staël.

line 78 *th' extremity of Unction:* Extreme unction, or the anointing of the dying in Catholicism.

line 84 *Coppet:* Location of de Staël's home in Switzerland.

line 88 *O'Neill:* Elizabeth O'Neill (1791–1872), celebrated tragic actress.

EPISTLE TO MR. MURRAY

line 5 *Mr. Hobhouse:* John Cam Hobhouse (1786–1869), Byron's closest friend.

line 13 *"Galley":* Henry Gally Knight (1786–1869), author of *Alashtar* (1817) and *Phrosine* (1817).

line 19 *Sotheby's Tour:* William Sotheby (1757–1833), poet and translator, author of *Farewell to Italy* (1818).

line 27 *Parnassus:* Greek mountain thought by the Romans to be the home of the Muses.

line 30 Tasso's: Torquato Tasso (1544–1595), Italian poet.

line 38 *"Spence" and his gossip:* Joseph Spence (1699–1768), author of *Observations, Anecdotes and Characters of Books and Men, Collected from Conversation,* first published in 1820. The book contained anecdotes about Alexander Pope and other eighteenth-century literary figures.

line 40 *Queen Mary's Epistle-craft: The Life of Mary, Queen of Scots* (1818), by George Chalmers (1742–1825). *new "Fytte" of "Whistlecraft":* A fytte is a division of a song or canto; *The Monks and the Giants* (1818) was a mock-heroic epic poem written by John Hookham Frere (1769–1846) under the pseudonym "Whistlecraft."

line 43 *General Gordon:* Thomas Gordon was a Scotsman who served in the Russian military.

line 57 *the House:* The House of Commons.

line 58 *Canning:* George Canning (1770–1827), politican, wit, and contributor to the *Anti-Jacobin.*

line 59 *Wilmot:* Sir Robert John Wilmot Horton, Byron's cousin.

line 60 *Ward:* John William Ward (1781–1833), member of Parliament.

line 81 *"Tommy" or "Sammy":* Thomas Moore (1779–1852) and Samuel Rogers (1763–1855), whose poetry Byron admired.

To Mr. Murray

line 1 *Strahan, Tonson, Lintot:* William Strahan (1715–1785), publisher of Johnson's *Dictionary* and many other important eighteenth-century works; Jacob Tonson (1655–1736), publisher of Dryden and Pope; Barnaby Bernard Lintot (1675–1736), publisher of Pope and other eighteenth-century authors.

line 3 *Pindus:* Greek mountain range.

line 10 *Quarterly:* The *Quarterly Review,* a journal published by John Murray.

line 15 *Art of Cookery:* Maria Elizabeth Rundell's (1745–1828) *A New System of Domestic Cookery* (1806) was one of John Murray's top-selling books.

line 17 *wist:* Know (archaic).

line 19 Navy List: Annual listing of officers and other information pertaining to the Royal Navy.

Epilogue

line 8 *Peter Bell:* This poem mocks William Wordsworth's (1770–1850) poem *Peter Bell* (1819).

line 19 *Beaumont:* Sir George Howland Beaumont (1753–1827) was a friend and patron of Wordsworth.

line 20 *your place in the Excise:* In 1813, Wordsworth accepted the government post of distributor of stamps for the county of Westmoreland, an appointment that brought him a salary of £400 a year.

My Boy Hobbie O

line 1 *in Hob's pound:* An expression meaning "under difficulties."

line 4 *The House:* The House of Commons.

line 7 *Newgate:* A prison in London.

lines 11–12 *I and Burdett—Gentlemen, / And blackguard Hunt and Cobby O:* Sir Francis Burdett (1770–1844) was a member of Parliament and an advocate of radical causes. Byron considers Burdett and Hobhouse to be gentlemen who should not be politically aligned with Henry "Orator" Hunt, a radical politician (1773–1835), and the journalist William Cobbet (1763–1835), whom Byron sees as demagogic "blackguards."

line 13 *canvass:* Solicit votes.

line 16 *Mobby O:* The mob, the rabble.

line 17 *Whigs:* The generally more liberal party in Parliament, opposed to the conservative Tories. Byron was a Whig.

line 19 *run their rigs:* Engage in their pieces of fun or practical jokes.

line 20 *Walpole:* Sir Robert Walpole (1676–1745), considered the first Prime Minister of England in the modern sense. Walpole was responsible for rampant Parliamentary corruption.

EPIGRAM

line 4 *John Bull:* The personification of the English people.

JOHN KEATS

line 1 *Who killed John Keats?:* These lines refer to the erroneous rumor that Keats sickened and died after reading John Wilson Croker's scathing 1818 review of *Endymion* in the *Quarterly Review.*

line 3 *Tartarly:* Like a Tartar; ferocious.

line 6–8 *Milman ... Southey, or Barrow:* Croker was not known to be the author of the anonymous review when Byron was writing. Byron guesses that the author could have been the clergyman, poet, and historian Henry Hart Milman (1791–1868), the poet Robert Southey (1774–1843), or Sir John Barrow (1764–1848), a contributor to the *Quarterly.*

SATIRES

ENGLISH BARDS AND SCOTCH REVIEWERS

line 1 *FITZGERALD:* William Thomas Fitzgerald (c. 1759–1829), poet.

lines 19–21 *mine own especial pen ... Hamet's:* Referring to the last chapter of *Don Quixote,* in which Cid Hamet Benengeli promises that his pen shall rest.

line 45 *Pegasus:* The winged horse of Greek mythology, traditionally associated with poetic inspiration.

line 55 *LAMB:* George Lamb (1784–1834), contributor to the *Edinburgh Review* and author of the play *Whistle for It.*

line 61 *JEFFREY:* Lord Francis Jeffrey (1773–1850), Scottish critic and editor of the *Edinburgh Review.*

line 65 *hackneyed jokes from MILLER:* Refers to *Joe Miller's Jests* (1739), an enduringly popular collection of low humor by John Mottley (1692–1750).

line 68 *Attic salt:* Classical, elegant, delicate wit.

line 82 *Bœotian:* The Boeotians of Greece were proverbially stupid.

line 94 *POPE and GIFFORD trod before:* Alexander Pope (1688–1744) and William

Gifford (1756–1826), both satirized the writers of their day, Pope in his *The Dunciad* (first published 1728) and Gifford in his *The Baviad* (1794) and *The Maeviad* (1795).

line 100 *Dryden . . . Pye:* John Dryden (1631–1700), poet, dramatist, and critic; the poet laureate and poetaster Henry James Pye (1745–1813).

line 115 CONGREVE . . . OTWAY: William Congreve (1670–1729), poet and dramatist; Thomas Otway (1652–1685), poet and dramatist.

line 127 SOUTHEY'S *Epics:* Robert Southey (1774–1843), poet and man of letters, produced several very long, mediocre epics in a short span of time.

line 128 LITTLE'S *Lyrics . . . hot-pressed twelves:* The poet Thomas Moore (1779–1852) published his *Poetical Works of the Late Thomas Little, Esq.* in 1801. *hot-pressed:* paper that has been smoothed by using a hot-press machine. *twelves:* Duodecimo or "twelvemo" is the size of book pages formed by folding single sheets from a printing press into twelve leaves each; the higher the number the smaller the page size.

lines 129–30 *Thus saith the* Preacher . . . *Is new":* From Ecclesiastes 1:9.

line 132 *Cow-pox . . . Gas:* Cow-pow is a mild, contagious skin disease of cattle, first used as a vaccination against smallpox by Edward Jenner in 1796. *Galvanism:* Applying electricity to the body therapeutically. Experiments were performed on the body of a murderer in 1803. *gas:* Pall Mall in London was lit by gas on January 28, 1807, making it the first street of any city to be illuminated in this way.

line 138 *Baal:* The chief deity of Canaan; i.e., a false god.

line 142 STOTT: Thomas Stott (1755–1829) wrote for the *Morning Post* under the name of "Hafiz."

line 146 *Blank:* Blank verse; unrhymed iambic pentameter.

line 148 *Tales of Terror:* Alluding to the vogue for Gothic novels. Matthew Gregory Lewis (1775–1818) published his *Tales of Terror* in 1799.

line 150 *Dulness:* The Goddess Dulness presides over the degeneration of literature and learning in Pope's *Dunciad.*

line 153 *Lays of Minstrels:* Alluding to Sir Walter Scott's poem *The Lay of the Last Minstrel* (1805), inspired by the Scottish Border legend of Gilpin Horner.

lines 166–67 *Marmion / Now forging scrolls:* Scott's poem *Marmion* (1808), whose main character is a forger.

line 173 MURRAY *with his* MILLER: John Murray and William Miller of London joined with Archibald Constable of Edinburgh to publish *Marmion.*

line 179 *Mammon:* The false god of riches.

line 183 *Apollo:* Greek god of music and poetry.

line 187 MILTON: John Milton (1608–1674), author of *Paradise Lost* (1667).

line 188 *Bays:* Crowns of laurel given as a sign of honor.

line 190 HOMER ... MARO: Homer is traditionally the author of the Greek epics *The Iliad* and *The Odyssey.* Virgil, or Publius Vergilius Maro, (70–19 B.C.), was the Roman poet and author of the *Aeneid.*

line 203 CAMOËNS ... TASSO: Luiz Vaz de Camoëns (1524–1580), Portuguese author of the epic poem *Os Lucíades* (1572); Torquato Tasso (1544–1595), Italian author of the epic poem *Gerusalemme liberta* (1581).

line 205 *Joan of Arc:* Southey's *Joan of Arc* was published in 1796.

line 207 BEDFORD: John of Lancaster, Duke of Bedford (1389–1435).

line 211 *Thalaba:* Another epic by Southey, published in 1801.

line 213 *Domdaniel's:* An undersea abode of evil spirits in *Thalaba.*

line 216 *Tom Thumb:* Hero of French and English fairy tales. Also the name of a farce (1730) by Henry Fielding (1707–1754). The new version of the farce appeared a year later and was entitled *The Tragedy of Tragedies, or, the Life and Death of Tom Thumb the Great.*

line 221 *Madoc:* Another epic poem by Southey, published in 1805.

line 222 *Cacique:* Mexican chief. Part of *Madoc* takes place in Mexico and part in Wales.

line 224 *Mandeville's: The Travels of Sir John Mandeville, Knight,* a popular fourteenth-century book of fabulous travels.

line 231 *Berkeley-Ballads:* Southey's ballad "The Old Woman of Berkeley" (1798) features an old woman being carried off by the Devil.

line 236 *apostate:* A person who forsakes his religion.

line 237 WORDSWORTH ... *lay:* William Wordsworth (1770–1850). *lay:* Song, poem.

lines 239–40 *"to shake off toil ... growing double":* From Wordsworth's poem "The Tables Turned" (1798): "Up! Up! my Friend, and quit your books; / or surely you'll grow double: / Up! Up! my Friend, and clear your looks / Why all this toil and trouble?"

line 248 *"an idiot Boy":* Wordsworth's poem "The Idiot Boy" (1798).

line 255 COLERIDGE: Samuel Taylor Coleridge (1772–1834), poet and critic, associated with Wordsworth and Southey.

line 262 *elegize an ass:* Referring to Coleridge's poem "To a Young Ass" (1794).

line 265 LEWIS: Matthew Gregory "Monk" Lewis (1775–1818), poet, dramatist, and novelist of Gothic horror. His novel *The Monk* (1796) was notorious for scenes of gore and sex.

line 266 *Parnassus:* Greek mountain thought by the Romans to be the home of the Muses.

line 267 *yew:* Tree associated with death.

line 268 *sexton:* Church employee charged with maintaining the grounds and sometimes digging graves.

line 273 *M.P.:* Lewis was a member of Parliament.

line 280 *St. Luke:* Saint known as the "beloved physician."

line 284 *Vesta:* Roman goddess of the hearth.

line 287 *Catullus:* Roman poet known for his erotic lyrics.

lines 297–308 *Hibernian* STRANGFORD . . . *Lusian Bard:* Hibernian: Irish. Percy Clinton, sixth Viscount Strangford (1780–1855), translator of Camoëns (the "Lusian Bard").

line 300 *fustion:* Fustian; turgid language.

line 310 *HAYLEY:* William Hayley (1745–1820), poet and biographer, author of *The Triumphs of Temper* (1781) *and The Triumphs of Music* (1804).

line 319 *Moravians:* Members of a Christian denomination descended from the Bohemiam Brethren, holding that the Bible contains the only rules of faith and practice.

line 321 *GRAHAME:* James Grahame (1765–1811), Scottish poet.

line 324 *Pentateuch:* First five books of the Old Testament.

line 331 *BOWLES:* William Lisle Bowles (1762–1850), poet.

line 369 *each fault, each failing scan:* In 1806, Byron published an edition of Pope's poetry that was highly critical of Pope as an artist.

line 372 *Lord Fanny* . . . *CURLL:* Two figures satirized by Pope in the *Dunciad:* Lord John Hervey (1696–1743), politician and wit, whom Pope mocked as "Lord Fanny" and "Sporus"; Edmund Curll (1675–1747), bookseller and pamphleteer.

lines 377–78 *St. John's soul* ... *MALLET did for hire:* Byron criticizes Henry St. John, Viscount Bolingbroke (1678–1751) for employing the poet David Mallet (Malloch) (1705?–1765) to help him attack Bolingbroke's former friend Pope in print after Pope's death.

line 380 *DENNIS* ... *RALPH:* John Dennis (1657–1734), dramatist and critic satirized by Pope; James Ralph (1695?–1762), American poet and political writer in England, also satirized by Pope.

line 383 *meet:* Proper.

line 387 *COTTLE:* Amos Cottle (1768?–1800), poet, brother of Joseph Cottle (1770–1853), poet and publisher of Wordsworth's and Coleridge's *Lyrical Ballads* (1798). *Bristowa:* Bristol, home of the Cottles.

line 388 *Cambrian:* Welsh.

line 391 *Hippocrene:* Fountain on Mount Helicon in Greece, sacred to the Muses and regarded as a source of poetic inspiration.

line 399 *Phœbus:* Phœbus Apollo, Greek god of music and poetry.

line 400 *trump:* Trumpet.

lines 411–12 *Sisyphus* ... *Rolls the huge rock:* In Greek mythology, Sisyphus was condemned in Hades to eternally roll a rock to the top of a hill.

line 414 *MAURICE:* Thomas Maurice (1754–1824), poet.

line 419 *Alcæus:* (c.620–c.580 B.C.), Greek lyric poet of Lesbos. Byron is referring to the Scottish-born poet and newspaper editor James Montgomery (1771–1854), who lived in Sheffield.

line 427 *the sacred Nine:* The nine Muses of Greek mythology, who inspire poets.

line 433 *harpies:* Monsters from Greek mythology with womens' heads and birds' bodies.

line 437 *Arthur's Seat:* Hill overlooking Edinburgh, Scotland.

line 439 *a judge almost the same:* Byron compares Francis Jeffrey (1773–1850) with the notoriously cruel Judge George Jeffries (1645–1689), the "Hanging Judge."

line 449 *a party tool:* Jeffrey and the *Edinburgh Review* were politically Whiggish.

line 461 *Fife:* Region of Scotland.

line 463 *Mars:* Roman god of war.

line 464 *that eventful day:* Byron tells the story of an abortive duel between Francis Jeffrey and Thomas Moore that took place in 1806. Moore called Jeffrey out over Jeffrey's scathing review of Moore's 1806 *Epistles, Odes, and Other Poems,* but before the duel could begin, the two men were seized by constables. Afterward, reports circulated that one or both of the pistols had not been loaded, which many interpreted to mean that the combat was a sham and both men cowards. When Byron's name appeared on the title page of the second edition of *English Bards,* Moore challenged Byron to a duel. The Byron-Moore duel never occurred, and instead the poets became close friends.

line 467 *Bow-street myrmidons:* That is, London constables. The Myrmidons were the warlike people of ancient Thessaly who took part in the Trojan War.

line 469 *Dunedin's castle:* Edinburgh Castle.

line 472 *TWEED:* Scottish river.

line 475 *The surly Tolbooth:* Edinburgh's prison.

line 483 *Edina:* Edinburgh.

line 485 *Canongate:* District of Edinburgh.

line 490 *Caledonia:* Scotland.

line 495 *Danaë:* In Greek mythology, Zeus appeared to Danaë as a shower of gold.

line 500 *poesy:* Poetry.

line 502 *Albion:* Greek name for England.

line 508 *phalanx:* A tight formation of armed infantry in Greek warfare.

line 509 *The travelled Thane, Athenian Aberdeen:* George Hamilton Gordon, fourth Earl of Aberdeen (1784–1860), politician and writer, a member of the Athenian Society. A thane was a kind of feudal lord.

line 510 *HERBERT shall wield THOR'S hammer:* William Herbert, translator of Icelandic poetry. Thor was the Norse god of thunder.

line 512 *SYDNEY:* Sydney Smith (1771–1845), clergyman, wit, and co-founder of the *Edinburgh Review.*

line 513 *HALLUM:* Henry Hallam (1777–1859), historian.

line 515 *PILLANS:* James Pillans (1778–1864), scholar.

line 516 *Thalia:* The Greek muse of comedy.

line 519 *HOLLAND'S banquets:* Holland House, the home of Henry Richard Vassall Fox, third Baron Holland (1773–1840), was a meeting place for many liberal political and literary figures, including Moore, Sydney Smith, Samuel Rogers, Henry Brougham, and many others. Byron became a frequent guest as well.

lines 522–23 *ere thy next Review / Spread its light wings of Saffron and of Blue:* The cover of the *Edinburgh Review* was colored buff and blue, the colors of the Whig party.

line 524 *BROUGHAM:* Henry Peter Brougham (1778–1868), lawyer and Whig politician; co-founder of *Edinburgh Review.*

line 525 *Bannocks ... Kail:* Bannocks are a kind of flat cake; kail (kale) is cabbage.

line 538 *Pictish:* The Picts were an ancient people of northern Britain, what is now Scotland.

line 542 *HENRY PETTY:* Henry Petty-Fitzmaurice, third Marquess of Lansdowne (1780–1863), politician.

line 547 *Grub-street:* Street in London inhabited in the eighteenth century by impoverished writers and literary hacks. *duns:* Creditors demanding payment.

line 557 *My lady:* Elizabeth Vassall Fox, Lady Holland (1770–1845).

line 562 *a Prince within a barrel pent:* Alluding to *Tekeli,* a play by Theodore Edward Hook (1788–1841).

line 563 *DIBDIN:* Charles Dibdin (1745–1814), dramatist and actor.

line 564 *Rosciomania:* William Henry West Betty (1791–1874), known as the "Young Roscius," was a phenomenally popular child actor.

line 568 *REYNOLDS:* Frederick Reynolds (1764–1841), dramatist.

line 570 *KENNEY:* James Kenney (1780–1849), dramatist, author of *The World.*

line 572 *BEAUMONT'S pilfered Caratach:* Alluding to the actor and theatrical manager Thomas Sheridan's (1719–1788) production of Beaumont and Fletcher's play *Bonduca* (published 1647). Caratach (Caraetacus) was a character in the play.

line 578 *GEORGE COLMAN, CUMBERLAND:* George Colman the Younger (1762–1836), dramatist and manager of the Haymarket Theatre; Richard Cumberland (1732–1811), dramatist.

lines 580–83 *SHERIDAN . . . Pizarros:* Richard Brinsley Sheridan (1751–1816), Irish dramatist, author of the play *Pizarro* (1799), adapted from Kotzebue.

line 587 GARRICK . . . SIDDONS: David Garrick (1717–1779), actor, playwright, and manager of Drury Lane Theatre; Sarah Siddons (1755–1831), popular tragic actress.

line 591 CHERRY, SKEFFINGTON, *and Mother GOOSE:* Andrew Cherry (1762–1812), Irish actor and songwriter; Sir Lumley St. George Skeffington (1771–1850), playwright; Dibdin produced a hugely popular pantomime called *Mother Goose.*

line 592 MASSINGER: Philip Massinger (1583–1640), dramatist.

line 596 LEWIS' *spectres:* Alluding to Mathew Lewis's play *The Castle Spectre* (1796).

line 601 *Greenwood:* The scene-painter for Drury Lane Theatre.

line 602 *"Sleeping Beauties": The Sleeping Beauty* was a play by Skeffington.

line 604 *John Bull:* Personification of the English people.

line 613 NALDI: Giuseppe Naldi (1770–1820), Italian singer.

line 615 CATALANI: Madame Angelica Catalani (1780–1849), Italian singer.

line 618 *Ausonia:* Italy.

lines 622–30 DESHAYES . . . *Gayton . . . Presle . . . Collini:* Dancers at King's Theatre.

line 632 *Suppressors of our Vice:* Referring to the Society for the Suppression of Vice.

line 633 *Saints:* Evangelicals.

line 639 *Greville and Argyle:* Colonel Harry Greville was the manager of the Argyle Institution. These lines accusing him of tolerating gambling at the Argyle nearly led to a duel between Byron and Greville.

line 642 *Petronius:* Roman satirist (c.27–66), author of the *Satyricon* and thought to be a lover of excess and pleasure.

line 644 *Hesperian:* Italian or Spanish.

line 650 *Comus:* Roman god of revelry and mirth.

line 658 *Burletta:* Comic opera or drama containing rhymed lyrics or songs.

line 660 *dow'gers:* Dowagers.

line 661 *loose waltz:* The waltz was considered a scandalous dance because the man held the woman in his arms.

line 671 *swain:* Male lover.

lines 673–75 *calls the rattling main . . . the coming trick:* Byron is describing a dice-game called Hazzard.

lines 678–79 POWELL'S *pistol . . . two* PAGETS *for your wife:* Alluding to a duel fought in 1809 by Sir Arthur Powell, who shot dead Charles John Cary, Viscount Falkland, a friend of Byron's; and the Paget brothers, who eloped with two different married women.

line 686 CLODIUS: Publius Clodius Pulcher (93–52 B.C.), a dissolute Roman politician.

line 699 *Rake:* A dissolute, fashionable man.

lines 710–12 *St. Gile's . . . Tottenham-Road . . . Bond-street or the Square:* London addresses.

line 713 *things of Ton their harmless lays indite:* Write about fashionable life in their harmless poems.

line 717 MILES ANDREWS: Miles Peter Andrews (d. 1814), member of Parliament and author, a hero of Gifford's *Baviad*.

line 723 ROSCOMMON! SHEFFIELD!: Wentworth Dillon, fourth Earl of Roscommon (1633?–1685), poet and translator; John Sheffield, third Earl of Mulgrave (1648–1721), critic and patron of Dryden.

line 726 CARLISLE: Frederick Howard, fifth Earl of Carlisle (1748–1825), dramatist and Byron's guardian. Byron greatly regretted these lines, especially because it seemed as if "paralytic puling" referred to a nervous disorder from which Carlisle suffered.

line 732 *petit-maître:* Fop; effeminate man.

line 738 *calf:* Calfskin leather.

line 739 *Morocco:* Fine leather.

line 745 *"All the Talents":* The "Ministry of All the Talents" was a government administration that lasted from February 1806 to March 1807.

line 747 *Monodies on Fox:* A monody is a poem lamenting a person's death; Charles James Fox (1749–1806) was a powerful leader of the Whig party.

line 748 *Melville's Mantle:* A satire.

line 749 *Lethe:* River of forgetfulness in Hades.

line 756 ROSA: "Rosa Matilda," the pen name of Charlotte Dacre (c.1782–c.1841), poet and novelist.

line 759 CRUSCA'S *bards:* Poets of the the late-eighteenth-century "Della Crusca" school, who wrote highly ornamented and sentimental verse.

line 763 MERRY: Robert Merry (1755–1798), Della Cruscan poet.

line 764 *O. P. Q.:* Poets who wrote for newspapers often signed only their initials.

lines 765–66 *some brisk youth . . . than his awl:* Joseph Blackett, shoemaker and poet.

line 768 *St. Crispin:* Saint Crispin was a shoemaker.

line 774 CAPEL LOFFT: (1751–1824), patron of Robert Bloomfield (1766–1823), a farm laborer and London shoemaker who became a poet.

line 777 BURNS: Robert Burns (1759–1796), Scottish poet who worked as a farmer.

line 778 GIFFORD *was born beneath an adverse star:* Gifford began life as a shoemaker's apprentice.

line 782 *brother Nathan:* Nathaniel Bloomfield, Robert's brother, also a poet patronized by Lofft.

line 795 *Pindaric skill:* The skill to compose Pindaric odes.

line 801 *CAMPBELL:* Thomas Campbell (1777–1844), poet.

line 803 *ROGERS:* Samuel Rogers (1763–1855), poet, author of *The Pleasures of Memory* (1792).

line 810 *COWPER:* William Cowper (1731–1800), poet.

line 818 *SOTHEBY, MACNEIL:* William Sotheby (1757–1833), poet and translator; Hector Macneil, poet (1746–1818).

lines 831–39 *WHITE . . . 'Twas thine own Genius:* Henry Kirke White (1785–1806), poet. Overwork at Cambridge was supposed to have killed him.

line 846 *pinion:* Wing.

line 857 *CRABBE:* George Crabbe (1754–1832), poet.

line 859 *SHEE:* Sir Martin Archer Shee (1769–1850), Irish painter and author of *Rhymes on Art* (1805).

line 872 *Achaian:* Achaean; Greek.

line 877 *WRIGHT:* Waller Rodwell Wright (1755–1826), author of *Horae Ionicae,* a poem on Greece.

line 884 *Aonian:* Pertaining to the Muses.

line 893 *DARWIN:* Erasmus Darwin (1731–1802), poet and botanist; grandfather of Charles Darwin.

line 906 *LAMB and LLOYD:* Charles Lamb (1775–1834), essayist and critic, and Charles Lloyd (1775–1839), poet and novelist. Lamb and Lloyd published a volume of poetry in 1798 called *Blank Verse.*

line 961 *Granta:* The River Cam, flowing by Cambridge.

line 964 *Seaton's prize:* The Seatonian Prize was established in 1750, and was awarded to the Cambridge graduate who produced the best poem on "the perfections or attributes of the supreme being."

line 966 *HOARE . . . HOYLE:* Charles James Hoare (1781–1865) and Charles Hoyle, both clergymen and poets.

line 967 *Not him whose page, if still upheld by whist:* Edmund Hoyle, who wrote *A Short Treatise on the Game of Whist* (1742).

line 973 *CLARKE:* Hewson Clarke, who attacked Byron in the journals *The Scourge* and *The Satirist.*

line 983 *HODGSON:* Francis Hodgson (1781–1852), clergyman and poet. He was a friend of Byron.

line 985 *Isis:* Upper Thames river in the vicinity of Oxford.

line 989 *RICHARDS:* George Richards, clergyman and poet, author of *The Aboriginal Britons.*

line 1000. *Tyre:* The ancient city of Tyre in Phoenecia was known for its splendor.

line 1007 *Cassandra's fate:* In ancient Greek legend, Cassandra could foretell the future but was doomed never to be believed.

line 1015 CANNING: George Canning (1770–1827), politician and contributor to the *Anti-Jacobin*.

line 1016 PORTLAND *fills the place of* PITT: William Henry Cavendish Bentinck, third Duke of Portland (1738–1809), Prime Minister; William Pitt the Younger (1759–1806), Prime Minister before Portland.

line 1019 *Calpe:* Gibraltar.

line 1020 *Stamboul:* Istanbul.

line 1021 *Beauty's native clime:* Georgia.

line 1022 *Kaff:* Mount Caucasus.

line 1026 *Carr:* Sir John Carr (1772–1832), travel writer.

line 1027 ELGIN: Thomas Bruce, seventh Lord Elgin (1766–1841), British Ambassador to the Ottoman Empire, who removed the ancient marble sculptures (thereafter known as the "Elgin Marbles") from the Parthenon and shipped them to England.

line 1029 *Phidian freaks:* Phidias (c. 500–c. 432 B.C.) was a Greek sculptor.

line 1033 *Dardan:* Trojan.

line 1034 GELL: Sir William Gell (1777–1836), archaeologist, author of *Topography of Troy* (1804).

line 1042 *My page, though nameless:* The first edition was published anonymously.

line 1045 MELBOURNE *House:* Home of William Lamb, second Viscount Melbourne (1779–1848), Whig politician.

line 1049 *buckram:* Stiff cotton fabric used for book bindings.

line 1064 *Poetaster:* Bad poet.

line 1067 *incondite:* Crude.

POSTSCRIPT TO THE SECOND EDITION

page 324 *Sir* ANDREW AGUECHEEK: A character in Shakespeare's comedy *Twelfth Night*.

page 324 *Anthropophagus:* Cannibal.

page 324 *Sir Fretful Plagiary:* A character in Richard Brinsley Sheridan's comedy *The Critic* (1779).

page 325 *God wot!:* God knows! (archaic).

page 325 JERNINGHAM: Edward Jerningham (1727–1812).

page 325 *Mæcenas:* Caius Maecenas (c. 70–B.C.), Roman statesman and patron of letters during the reign of the Emperor Augustus.

THE VISION OF JUDGMENT

page 326 Quevedo Redivivus: "Quevedo Living Again." Francisco Gomez de Quevedo y Villegas (1580–1645) was a Spanish essayist and political satirist.

page 326 the Author of "Wat Tyler": Robert Southey (1774–1843), poet and man of letters, who accepted the post of poet laureate in 1813, after Walter Scott had refused it. Byron detested Southey and viewed him as a hypocrite and a political turncoat. Like his friends William Wordsworth and Samuel Taylor Coleridge, Southey abandoned his youthful radicalism and enthusiasm for the French Revolution for political conservatism. In 1794 Southey had written *Wat Tyler,* a politically radical play based on the Peasant's Revolt of 1381, but never published it. In 1817 the play was pirated and published without Southey's consent, embarrassing the conservative laureate. Byron's poem is a parody of Southey's *A Vision of Judgment* (1821), an overblown eulogy of King George III, who died in 1820. In the preface to that poem, Southey excoriated what he called the "Satanic School" of British poetry, chiefly represented by Byron.

page 326 *"A Daniel come to judgment . . . teaching me that word":* From *The Merchant of Venice,* IV, i, 342.

page 327 *Scrub:* Character in *The Beaux' Stratagem* (1707) by George Farquhar (1678–1707), Irish dramatist.

page 327 *William Smith:* A member of Parliament who attacked Southey in Parliament.

page 327 *Martin the regicide:* Southey wrote an "Inscription" for the cell in which Henry Marten the regicide was imprisoned. Martin was one of those who signed the warrant for the execution of Charles I. After the Restoration, Marten was sentenced to life imprisonment in Chepstowe Castle.

page 327 Antijacobin: *The Anti-Jacobin* was a conservative journal that had attacked and satirized Southey and other radical ("Jacobin") poets in 1797–1798.

page 328 *Mr. Landor:* Walter Savage Landor (1775–1864), English poet and and essayist, friend of Southey, author of the epic *Gebir* (1798).

page 329 *Ithyphallics:* Indecent verses.

line 5 *Gallic-era "eighty-eight":* Byron is dating the French Revolution from 1788.

line 17 *Seraphs:* The highest-ranking angels.

line 20 *Recording Angel:* Angel who records good and bad deeds.

line 38 *the crowning carnage, Waterloo:* The Battle of Waterloo (1815), which was the final defeat of Napoleon. In effect, it "crowned" those monarchs of Europe who were thereafter restored to their thrones.

line 48 *he has both Generals in reversion:* Both Napoleon and the Duke of Wellington are destined for hell.

lines 54–55 *"With seven heads and ten horns"* . . . *Like Saint John's foretold beast:* From Revelation 13:1.

lines 57–58 *Freedom's second dawn . . . Died George the Third:* George III died in 1820, a year that saw revolutions in Spain, Portugal, and Greece.

line 64 *One half as mad—and t'other no less blind:* By 1820, the King was mad and blind.

line 85 *balsams:* Preservatives.

line 91 *lapidary scrawl:* Funeral inscription on stone.

line 92 *unless he left a German will:* King George II had hidden the will of his father, George I. The Hanoverian dynasty (to which the Georges belonged) was of German origin.

line 93 *proctor:* In this sense, one who is employed to manage the affairs of another.

line 141 *does he wear his head?:* King Louis XVI was beheaded in 1793.

line 142 *tustle:* An alternate spelling of "tussle."

line 155 *Saint Paul:* He is "cheek by jowl" with Louis because he, too, was beheaded.

line 156 *parvenù:* Person who has recently acquired importance or position.

lines 156–57 *The skin / Of Saint Bartholomew:* Bartholomew was martyred by being skinned alive.

line 207 *Manes:* Spirits of departed ancestors.

line 208 *Tories:* The Tory party was the more generally conservative party in Parliament. Byron was a Whig.

lines 215–16 *when ice-bound, / By Captain Parry's crew:* Admiral Sir William Edward Parry (1790–1855) made several voyages to the Arctic in search of a northwest passage to Asia.

line 224 *Johanna Southcote:* Joanna Southcott (1750–1814), a religious fanatic, attracted a following and she announced that she was about to give birth to the second messiah named Shiloh. Though she was in her sixties she appeared pregnant, probably from edema. She died soon after of a brain tumor.

line 225 *Archangel Michael:* The archangel Michael, chief of the angelic armies.

line 256 *their "Champ Clos" the spheres:* Their tournament field is the stars and planets.

lines 274–75 *thresholds . . . The place where Death's grand cause is argued:* Alluding to the fact that city gateways were often where trials were conducted in eastern countries.

line 305 *Prince of Air:* Satan.

line 321 *quit-rent:* A feudal term for a small payment made to a lord in lieu of services rendered.

line 340 *a minion:* John Stuart, third Earl of Bute (1713–1792), who became Prime Minister (1762–1763) upon George III's accession to the throne.

line 361 *constant consort:* George III was a faithful husband, unlike his son.

line 364 *Apicius' board:* Marcus Gabius Apicius, famed Roman gourmet who is supposed to be the author of a cookbook. *board:* Dinner table.

line 365 *anchorite:* A person who retires to a solitary place for religious reasons.

line 383 *foe to Catholic participation:* George III was an enemy of efforts to give Irish Catholics religious freedom.

line 391 *Guelph:* The Hanoverians were descended from the family of Guelph.

line 393 *Cerberus:* Three-headed dog who guards the entrance to Hades in Greek mythology.

line 415 *Let off the artillery, which Milton mentions:* In the sixth book of *Paradise Lost,* John Milton describes how Satan invented cannons and gunpowder.

line 426 *gilt key:* A golden key was carried by some court officials.

line 444 *Telegraph:* Semaphore, an apparatus for communicating through visual signals, e.g., special flags or changing the position of a light.

line 465 *John Bull:* Personification of the English people.

line 466 *damned away his eyes:* "Damn your eyes" was a traditional curse.

line 467 *Paddy:* An Irishman.

line 471 *Jonathan:* "Brother Jonathan" was a name for the American people.

line 473 *I guess:* Considered at the time to be a particularly American expression.

line 475 *From Otaheite's isle to Salisbury Plain:* Tahiti; Salisbury Plain is in Wiltshire, England.

line 520 *Jack Wilkes:* John Wilkes (1727–1797), radical journalist and member of Parliament. Wilkes opposed George III, was arrested and released by the government, and came to be seen as a hero of the people and champion of liberty.

line 533 *freeholders:* Voters.

line 564 *Grafton:* Augustus Henry Fitzroy, third Duke of Grafton (1735–1811), one of George III's ministers.

line 573 *Charon:* The ferryman of the dead in Greek mythology.

line 580 *Belial:* One of Satan's devils.

line 581 *Fox's lard was basting William Pitt:* Charles James Fox (1749–1806), leader of the Whig party, and William Pitt the Younger (1759–1806), Tory Prime Minister (1783–1801, 1804–1806). Fox and Pitt were longtime political opponents. They died in the same year and were buried beside each other in Westminster Abbey. Byron mentions Fox's "lard" because of his corpulence.

line 584 *'twas one of his own Bills:* The Pitt and Grenville Acts (1795).

line 585 *Junius . . . a shadow:* The pseudonym of a still-unknown author who satirized George III and his allies; his motto was *"Stat Nominus Umbra,"* "A shadow stands for the name."

line 624 *"Iron Mask":* The "Man in the Iron Mask" was a mysterious political prisoner held for over forty years. He died in 1703 in the Bastille.

line 627 *Mrs. Malaprop:* A fatuous misuser of words in Richard Brinsley Sheridan's comedy *The Rivals* (1775).

line 631 *Now Burke, now Tooke:* Edmund Burke (1729–1797), Irish politician, author, orator, and opponent of the French Revolution; John Horne Tooke (1736–1812), radical politician tried for treason by the government but acquitted.

line 632 *certes:* Certainly. *Sir Philip Francis:* (1740–1818), member of Parliament and often suspected of being Junius.

line 647 *Niger's mouth:* Alluding to recent African explorations.

line 679 *Incubus:* Lascivious male demon.

line 685 *Skiddaw:* Mountain in the Lake District in England. Southey was associated with the Lake District, like his fellow Lake Poets, Wordsworth and Coleridge.

line 686 *taper:* Candle.

line 710 *Balaam's:* In the Bible (Numbers 22:28–30), Balaam's ass can speak.

line 719 *hexameter:* Southey's *Vision* was written in hexameters (lines of six feet).

line 721 *spavined:* Broken down, decrepit. *dactyls:* Three-syllable poetic feet with the first syllable stressed and the second two unstressed.

line 728 'Non Di, non homines': From Horace's *Ars Poetica:* "Neither gods nor men can stand bad poets."

line 735 *"What! what!":* An habitual exclamation of George III.

line 736 Pye *come again?:* Poet laureate and poetaster Henry James Pye (1745–1813). Pye was laureate before Southey.

line 739 *Castlereagh:* Robert Stewart, Second Viscount Castlereagh (1769–1822), British statesman and Foreign Secretary, a bête noire of liberals.

line 752 "de se": Suicide.

line 768 *"Rhymes on Blenheim"—"Waterloo.":* Southey's "Battle of Blenheim" (1798) and *The Poet's Pilgrimage to Waterloo* (1816). The latter poem gloated over Napoleon's downfall.

line 769 *Regicide:* Killer of a king.

line 773 *pantisocracy:* In 1795 Southey and Coleridge planned to establish a utopian commune (whose egalitarian precepts they called Pantisocracy) on the banks of the Susquehanna River in America.

line 775 *anti-jacobin:* Opponent of Jacobinism, the radical political principles associated with the French Revolution.

line 785 *Wesley's life:* Southey's biography of John Wesley (1703–1791), the founder of Methodism, was published in 1830.

line 787 *octavo:* Book size created folding the sheets to form eight leaves or sixteen pages; a smallish size book.

line 807 *King Alfonso:* Alfonso X "the Wise" (1221–1284), king of Castile and Léon, was said to have claimed that he could have made a better cosmos than God.

line 816 *"melodious twang":* From a description of an apparition in the antiquarian and author John Aubrey's (1626–1697) *Miscellanies* (1696).

line 828 *Phaeton:* Phaëthon, the son of the Greek sun god Helios, who was killed by Zeus while trying to drive his father's chariot across the sky.

line 840 *Welborn:* A character in Philip Massinger's (1583–1640) play *A New Way to Pay Old Debts* (1625). *precisian:* One who is punctilious in his observance of religious forms.

line 848 *the hundredth psalm:* "Enter into His gates with thanksgiving, and into His courts with praise!"

DON JUAN

DEDICATION

line 1 *BOB SOUTHEY:* Robert Southey (1774–1843), poet and man of letters, accepted the post of poet laureate in 1813, after Walter Scott had refused it. Byron detested Southey and viewed him as a hypocrite and a political turncoat. Like his friends William Wordsworth and Samuel Taylor Coleridge, Southey was known as a Lake Poet because of his association with the Lake District; also like Wordsworth and Coleridge, Southey abandoned his youthful radicalism and enthusiasm for the French Revolution for political conservatism.

line 3 *Tory:* The conservative party in British politics; the Whig party generally favored Parliamentary and philanthropic reforms. Byron was a Whig and a member of the House of Lords.

line 6 *Lakers:* The Lake Poets.

line 9 *Which pye being opened:* George Steevens had used the "old song" to satirize the previous poet laureate and poetaster, Henry James Pye (1745–1813).

line 12 *Regent:* The much-despised Prince Regent, who became King George IV (1762–1830) after the death of his father in 1820.

line 15 *Explaining metaphysics to the nation:* Coleridge introduced German idealist philosophy to England in his 1817 *Biographia Literaria,* which many readers found obscure and convoluted.

line 24 *a-dry, Bob:* "Dry bob" was Regency slang for sex without orgasm.

line 25 *Excursion:* Wordsworth's very long philosophical poem *The Excursion* was published in 1814.

line 26 *quarto:* A large book size, made by folding a sheet of paper into four leaves.

line 30 *when the dog-star rages:* The dog star is Sirius, the brightest star, so called because it is in the constellation Canus Major. In ancient times it was believed that dogs went mad when Sirius rises with the sun, early July through early September, known as the dog days.

line 32 *Tower of Babel:* From Genesis 11:1–9, a tower built in an attempt to reach the heavens. As punishment, the language of its builders was transformed into many mutually incomprehensible tongues.

line 35 *Keswick:* Village in the Lake District where Southey lived.

line 46 *in the Excise:* In 1813 Wordsworth accepted the government post of distributor of stamps for the county of Westmorland, an appointment that brought him a salary of £400 a year.

line 48 *the Immortal Hill:* Parnassus, the Greek mountain thought by the Romans to be the home of the Muses.

line 49 *bays may hide the baldness:* Bays are crowns of laurel given as a sign of honor. Byron alludes to Suetonius's story that Julius Caesar was pleased that his own wreath would hide his baldness.

line 55 *Scott, Rogers, Campbell, Moore, and Crabbe:* All poets whom Byron consistently ranked more highly than Southey, Wordsworth, or Coleridge: Sir Walter Scott (1771–1832); Samuel Rogers (1763–1855); Thomas Campbell (1777–1844); Thomas Moore (1779–1852); George Crabbe (1754–1832).

line 58 *the wingéd steed:* Pegasus, the winged horse of Greek mythology, traditionally associated with poetic inspiration.

line 66 *reversion:* An interest in an estate that reverts to the grantor or his heirs at the end of some period, such as the death of the grantee.

line 70 *Titan:* Helios, the Greek sun god, who rises from the sea in the morning.

lines 74–80 *Milton ... the tyrant-hater he begun:* John Milton (1608–1674), author of *Paradise Lost* (1667), was a Puritan and enemy of King Charles I, and did not "laud" the King's son, Charles II, after his restoration to the throne in 1660. The contrast is with Southey, whose early writings attacked George III but whose later writings lauded him as well as his son George IV.

lines 82–83 *Samuel ... with his prophecies:* In I Samuel 28:8–19, the ghost of Samuel is summoned from the grave by the Witch of Endor. Samuel's ghost prophecies the death of Saul.

line 88 *eunuch Castlereagh:* Robert Stewart, Second Viscount Castlereagh (1769–1822), British statesman and Foreign Secretary, a bête noire of liberals. Byron calls him a "eunuch" (and later, "emasculated") because he was rumored to be a homosexual.

line 90 *Erin's gore:* Castlereagh was secretary to the Lord Lieutenant of Ireland from 1797–1801, and took harsh measures against participants in the United Irish rebellion of 1798. He also helped arrange the Act of Union between Ireland and England, which went into effect on January 1, 1801. Since Castlereagh was Irish, he was regarded by most Irish as a traitor.

line 97 *such set trash of phrase:* Castlereagh was infamous for mixing metaphors and garbling his words.

line 102 *Ixion:* In Greek mythology, King Ixion tried to seduce Hera. Zeus punished him by binding him to an eternally revolving, flaming wheel.

line 109 *Congress:* Alluding to the Congress of Vienna (1814–1815), which reorganized Europe after the Napoleonic Wars and restored monarchies. Castlereagh was a leading figure at the Congress.

line 117 *Eutropius:* A eunuch and consul of the Byzantine Emperor Arcadius at the end of the fourth century. He was hated for his greed and cruelty.

line 136 *ultra-Julian:* Alluding to Flavius Claudius Julianus (c.331–363), a Roman Emperor known as "the Apostate" because he abandoned Christianity for paganism.

CANTO THE FIRST

line 6 *Don Juan:* Byron anglicizes the pronunciation throughout, rhyming "Juan" with such phrases as "new one."

line 7 *pantomime:* In England, a form of theatrical spectacle often based on a fairy tale.

line 8 *sent to the Devil:* The traditional story of Don Juan, the great lover, ended with his descent to Hell.

lines 9–10 *Vernon ... Howe:* Military figures: Edward Vernon (1684–1757), English admiral; William Augustus, Duke of Cumberland (1721–1765); third son of George II, British general (nicknamed "the Butcher" because of his ruthlessness toward the Scottish rebels of 1745); James Wolfe (1727–1759), British army commander, killed capturing Quebec from the French; Edward Hawke, first Baron Hawke of Towton (1705–1781), British admiral whose victory over the French averted an invasion of England during the Seven Years' War; Ferdinand, Duke of Brunswick (1721–1792), Prussian field marshal whose forces fought alongside the British in the Seven Years' War; John Manners, Marquess of Granby (1721–1770), British officer in the Seven Years' War; John Burgoyne (1722–1792), British general and playwright, fought in the Seven Years' War and the American War of Independence; Augustus Keppel, First Viscount Keppel of Elvedon (1725–1786), British admiral and politician; Sir William Howe, fifth Viscount Howe (1729–1814), British general in the American War of Independence.

line 12 *sign-posts … like Wellesley:* A street had recently been named for Arthur Wellesley, first Duke of Wellington (1769–1852), British general, hero of the Napoleonic Wars, and victor over Napoleon at Waterloo.

lines 13–14 *like Banquo's monarchs … "nine farrow":* Alluding to *Macbeth,* in which the Witches conjure up the ghosts of eight kings and then that of Banquo. "Nine farrow" is from Act IV, scene 1: To raise the apparitions that will tell Macbeth his fate, the witch tells him to place in the cauldron "sow's blood, that hath eaten her nine farrow."

line 15 *Dumourier:* Charles-Francois du Périer Dumouriez (1739–1823), French general who deserted to the Austrians.

line 16 *Moniteur and Courier:* French newspapers.

lines 17–21 *Barnave … Moreau:* All men who were involved with the French Revolution and its wars: Antoine Barnave (1761–1793), politician; Jacques-Pierre Brissot (1754–1793), Girondin leader; Marie-Jean-Antoine-Nicolas Caritat, marquis de Condorcet (1743–1794), politician; Honoré-Gabriel Riquetti, comte de Mirabeau (1749–1791), politician; Jérôme Pétion de Villeneuve (1756–1794), politician and associate of Robespierre; Anacharsis Clootz (1755–1794), revolutionary propagandist; Georges Danton (1759–1794), revolutionary; Jean-Paul Marat (1743–1793), revolutionary journalist; Marie-Joseph Gilbert du Motier de Lafayette, (1757–1834), French general and politician; Barthélemy-Catherine Joubert (1769–1799), general; Louis-Lazare Hoche (1768–1797), general; François-Séverin Marceau-Desgraviers (1769–1796), military hero; Jean Lannes (1769–1809), general; Louis-Charles-Antoine Desaix de Veygoux (1768–1800), military hero; Jean-Victor-Marie Moreau (1763–1813), general.

line 25 *Nelson:* Admiral Horatio Nelson (1758–1805), hero of the Battle of Trafalgar.

line 31 *the Prince is all for the land-service:* The Prince Regent tried to join the army.

line 32 *Duncan … Jervis:* Adam Duncan, first Viscount Duncan of Camperdown (1731–1804), admiral; Richard Howe, fourth Viscount and Earl Howe (1726–1799), naval commander, brother of Sir William Howe; John Jervis (1735–1823), Earl of St. Vincent, admiral.

line 33 *Agamemnon:* Leader of the Greek forces in Homer's *Iliad.*

line 41 "in medias res": The Greek poet Horace stated that writers of epics should begin their stories "in the middle of things."

line 66 *Hidalgo:* A man of the lower nobility in Spain.

line 73 *His mother:* Donna Inez is a satirical reflection on Byron's mother and his wife.

line 82 *Calderon... Lopé:* Pedro Calderón de la Barca (1600–1681) and Lope de Vega (1562–1635), Spanish dramatists.

line 85 *Feinagle's:* Gregor von Feinaigle (1765?–1819) lectured on improving the memory.

line 89 *mathematical:* Lady Byron was interested in mathematics; Byron called her the Princess of Parallelograms.

line 91 *Attic:* Classical, elegant, delicately witty.

line 94 *dimity:* a sheer cotton fabric; Lady Byron's favorite dress material.

line 111 *'I am':* Yaweh, that is, God.

line 116 *Romilly:* Sir Samuel Romilly (1757–1818), legal counsel for Lady Byron during the separation. Byron had thought that Romilly would counsel him. Romilly killed himself in 1818. Murray did not publish this stanza in 1819.

line 122 *Miss Edgeworth's novels:* Maria Edgeworth (1767–1849), Irish novelist. Byron is alluding her works' didacticism.

line 123 *Mrs. Trimmer's books on education:* Sarah Trimmer (1741–1810) wrote books on education.

line 124 *"Cœlebs' Wife":* Coelebs in Search of a Wife (1809), a novel by Hannah More (1745–1833), religious writer.

line 127 *"female errors fall":* From Alexander Pope, *The Rape of the Lock,* II, 17: "If to her share some female errors fall, Look on her face, and you'll forget 'em all."

line 134 *Harrison:* John Harrison (1693–1776), expert watchmaker and developer of the marine chronometer which enabled longitude to be found at sea.

line 136 *Macassar:* Popular hair oil, advertised as being "incomparable."

line 165 *"brain them with their lady's fan":* From Shakespeare, *Henry IV* Part 1, II, iii, 25–26: "Zounds, and I were new by this rascal, I could brain him with his lady's fan."

line 167 *falchions:* Swords.

line 237 "malus animus": Malice aforethought.

line 279 *Numa:* Numa Pompilius, legendary King of Rome (eighth to seventh century B.C.) and successor to Romulus. His reign was peaceful.

line 288 *Doctors' Commons:* Buildings of the civil court in London where divorce proceedings took place.

line 289 *intestate:* With no will.

line 290 *chancery suit:* Legal suit in the Chancellor's Court. *messuages:* Houses with adjacent buildings and lands.

line 329 *Ovid's a rake... verses show him:* The Roman poet Ovid wrote passionate love poems; a rake is a dissolute, fashionable man.

line 330 *Anacreon:* Ancient Greek writer of odes (c. 582–485 B.C.) involving wine and sex.

line 331 *Catullus:* Gains Valerius Catulus (c. 84–c. 54 B.C.), Roman poet; here Byron alludes to Catullus's love poems.

lines 332–33 *Sappho's Ode ... Longinus:* Her Ode to Aphrodite, praised by the Greek literary critic Longinus.

lines 335–36 *that horrid one ... Corydon:* "Eclogue II, Alexis," a poem about pederastic love by the Roman poet Virgil.

line 337 *Lucretius' irreligion:* Refers to the Roman poet Lucretius's philosophically materialistic poem *De rerum natura.*

line 339 *Juvenal:* Roman author of harsh satires attacking the vices of the empire.

line 344 *Martial:* Roman writer of epigrams (c. 40–c. 103).

line 353 *"at one fell swoop":* From *Macbeth,* IV, iii, 219.

line 371 *Jerome and Chrysostom:* Celebrated church fathers.

line 375 *Saint Augustine and his fine* Confessions: Saint Augustine's *Confessions* (397) describes his sinful life before his spiritual conversion.

line 420 "Verbum sat": "A word to the wise is sufficient."

line 439 *Her zone to Venus:* The magic belt (zone) of Venus, the goddess of love, made others fall in love with its wearer.

lines 445–46 *When proud Granada fell . . . Boabdil wept:* Boabdil (d. 1527), or Muhammad XI, last Nasrid sultan of Granada, which fell to Spain under Ferdinand and Isabella.

line 494 "mi vien in mente": It comes to me.

line 508 *St. Anthony:* Byron confuses him with St. Francis of Assisi, who was supposed to have thrown himself naked into the snow in order to quell temptation.

line 510 *in mulct:* As a penalty.

line 567 *Armida's fairy art:* In Torquato Tasso's romance *Gerusalemme liberta* (1581), the sorceress Armida enslaves the Christian knight Rinaldo.

line 598 *Tarquin:* Lucius Tarquinius Superbus, traditionally the seventh king of Rome (d. 510 B.C.). He was a despot, and his name "Superbus" means "the proud."

line 684 *Ovid's Miss Medea:* Ovid tells the story of the enchantress Medea in his *Metamorphoses.*

line 701 *The bard I quote:* The lines are from Thomas Campbell's (1777–1844), *Gertrude of Wyoming* (1809).

lines 722–23 *His self-communion ... in its great mood:* A parody of Wordsworthian phrasing.

line 754 *Boscan, or Garcilasso:* Juan Boscán Almegaver (c. 1490–1542), and Garcilaso de la Vega (1503–1536), Spanish poets and friends, whose works appeared together posthumously in 1543.

line 828 *houri:* Beautiful virgin of the Islamic paradise.

line 829 *Anacreon Moore:* Thomas Moore (1779–1852), Byron's close friend and fellow poet, called "Anacreon" because of his translation of the *Odes of Anacreon* (1800).

line 864 *Louis:* Louis d'or, a French gold coin.

lines 921–22 *Plato . . . your confounded fantasies:* Referring to the concept of Platonic (or spiritual, unsexual) love.

line 927 *coxcomb:* A conceited dandy.

line 928 *go-between:* In the sense of an arranger of liaisons.

line 937 *Xerxes offered a reward:* Xerxes I (c. 519–465 B.C.), Persian King. Cicero tells the story to which Byron refers.

line 959 *Aristotle and the Rules:* Referring to Aristotle's *Poetics* and the Aristotelian unities of time, place, and action in dramatic composition derived from Aristotle's work by seventeenth-century neoclassic critics.

line 971 *Adria's:* The Adriatic's.

line 996 *"us youth":* From *Henry IV* Part I, II, 2, 93.

line 999 *Israelites:* That is, Jewish moneylenders.

line 1000 *post-obits:* A post-obit is a bond given to a lender securing a sum for payment of the debt on the death of another person from whom the borrower expects to inherit.

line 1030 *Congreve's rockets:* Sir William Congreve (1772–1828) invented a new kind of explosive shell used in warfare.

line 1031 *the Doctor paid off an old pox:* Edward Jenner (1749–1823) discovered the principle of vaccination, using cowpox to inoculate against smallpox.

line 1034 *Galvanism:* Applying electricity to the body therapeutically. Experiments were performed on the body of a murderer in 1803.

lines 1036–37 *Humane Society's . . . unsuffocated gratis:* Society founded in 1774 which awarded medals to those who rescued or resuscitated drowning persons.

lines 1040–41 *the great. . . . came from America:* Syphilis, supposed to have originated in America.

line 1048 lues: *Lues venerea,* syphilis. *pseudo-syphilis:* Presumably smallpox.

line 1052 *Sir Humphry Davy's lantern:* Davy (1778–1829) invented the miner's safety lamp in 1815.

line 1054 *Tombuctoo:* Timbuktu, in Mali, West Africa. It was visited by European explorers in 1826 and 1828.

line 1110 *levee:* A public court assembly.

line 1177 *Cortejo:* (Spanish) Male companion.

line 1183 *General Count O'Reilly:* Alexander O'Reilly (1725–1794), Irish general in the Spanish army. Julia makes a humorous mistake: O'Reilly's campaign against Algiers in 1775 was a disaster.

line 1270 *Achates:* Faithful companion of Aeneas in Virgil's *Aenead.*

line 1294 *Job's:* In the Book of Job, Job's wife urges her husband to curse God for his afflictions.

line 1328 *Clarence in his Malmsey butt:* In Shakespeare's *Richard III,* the Duke of Clarence is stabbed and drowned in a large barrel of sweet Madeira.

line 1341 *When old King David's blood grew dull in motion:* See I Kings 1:1–3: "Now King David was old and stricken in years; and they covered him with clothes, but he got no heat. Wherefore his servants said unto him, let there be sought for my lord the king a young virgin: and let her stand before the king, and let her cherish him; and let her lie in thy bosom, that my lord the king may get heat. So they sought for a fair damsel throughout all the coasts of Israel and found Abishag a Shunammite, and brought her to the king.

line 1468 *pommelled:* Pummeled.

line 1487 *like Joseph:* In the Biblical story of Joseph and Potiphar's wife (Genesis 40:11–12) after Potiphar's wife asks Joseph to make love with her, "she caught him by his garment, saying, lie with me: and he left his garment in her hand, and fled, and got him out."

line 1508 *to nonsuit:* To deliver a judgment against a plaintiff because he cannot produce enough evidence on his behalf.

line 1511 *Gurney:* William Brodie Gurney (1777–1855), official shorthand writer for Parliament.

line 1582 "Elle vous suit partout": (French) "She follows you everywhere."

line 1594 *Divided in twelve books:* The traditional length of an epic poem.

line 1603 Vade Mecum: "Go with me," i.e., handbook.

line 1611 *ween:* Think (archaic).

line 1638 *Hippocrene:* Fountain on Mount Helicon in Greece, sacred to the Muses and regarded as a source of poetic inspiration. *drouthy:* Droughty, dry.

line 1641 *Mr. Sotheby:* William Sotheby (1757–1833), poet and translator.

line 1643 *"the Blues":* Short for "bluestockings," a pejorative term for literary women.

line 1644 *There's* one, *at least:* Lady Byron.

line 1668 *receive a coral:* A coral is a teething ring.

line 1672 *the British: The British Review:* A conservative literary journal.

lines 1689–90 "Non ego ... Planco": "I would not have borne such insult in the heat of my youth when Plancus was counsel."

line 1693 *Brenta:* River flowing to the Gulf of Venice.

line 1696 *when George the Third was King:* George III was actually king from 1760–1820. However, his son was made regent and de facto sovereign in 1811.

line 1699 *peruke:* Wig.

line 1709 *bag o' the bee:* From "The Triumph," by Ben Jonson (1572–1637): "Have you felt the wool of beaver,/ Or swan's down ever?/ Or have smelt o' the bud o' the brier,/ Or the nard in the fire?/ Or have tasted the bag of the bee?/ O so white, O so soft, O so sweet is she!"

line 1733 *Friar Bacon's Brazen Head:* From Robert Greene's (1560–1592) play, *Friar Bacon and Friar Bungay* (1594).

line 1734 *chymic:* Alchemical.

line 1746 *Cheops:* Greek name for Khufu (c. 2575–c. 2465 B.C.), King of Egypt and builder of the Great Pyramid at Giza.

lines 1769–72 *"Go, little book . . . many days.":* From Southey's poem, *The Lay of the Laureate* (1816).

FRAGMENT

line 8 *hock and soda-water:* A cure for hangovers.

CANTO THE SECOND

line 131 *"Sweets to the sweet":* From *Hamlet,* V, 1, 265.

line 168 *emetic:* A medicine that induces vomiting.

line 172 *quinsy:* An abscess of the tonsils.

line 179 *breathes a vein:* Opens a vein.

line 186 *Leghorn:* English name for Livorno.

line 194 *licentiate:* One who holds a university degree, a scholar.

line 431 *cutter:* Single-masted sailing vessel.

line 448 *aqua-vita:* (water of life); a strong alcoholic drink.

line 596 *Promethean vulture:* The vulture sent daily by Zeus to tear at Prometheus's liver.

lines 658–59 *Ugolino condescends / To eat the head of his arch-enemy:* In Dante's *Inferno,* Cantos 32–33, Count Ugolino is depicted frozen in ice in the ninth circle, gnawing on the head of his mortal enemy, Archbishop Ruggiero. In life, Ruggiero had condemned Ugolino and his two sons and two grandsons to starve to death.

lines 838–40 *have passed the Hellespont . . . and I did:* In Greek legend, Leander of Abydos fell in love with the virgin priestess Hero. He swam across the Hellespont strait every night to visit her. Byron replicated the feat in May 1810, along with a British naval officer named Ekenhead.

line 1000 *piastre:* Unit of currency in Turkey.

line 1002 *Peter the Apostle:* Jesus told Peter to be a "fisher of men" (Matthew 4:19).

line 1010 *Cyclades:* Group of Greek islands in the Aegean Sea.

lines 1031–32 *"to take him in, / A stranger":* The words refer to Jesus in Matthew, 25:43 ("I was a stranger and you took me not in.")

line 1037 *"νους":* Greek for "mind" or "spirit."

line 1057 *pelisse:* A fur cloak.

line 1096 *my grand-dad's "Narrative":* Midshipman John Byron (1723–1786), Byron's grandfather, was shipwrecked on an island off the coast of Chile in 1741, and published a narrative of his experience in 1768. Later he became an admiral and acquired the nickname "Foulweather Jack."

line 1132 *Aurora:* The dawn.

line 1160 *Scio:* Chios, a Greek island.

line 1170 *hectic:* Flush.

lines 1317–18 *Barrow, South, Tillotson ... Blair:* Isaac Barrow (1630–1677), English theologian and mathematician; Robert South (1634–1716), English clergyman; John Tillotson (1630–1694), Archbishop of Canterbury; Hugh Blair (1718–1800), Scottish minister and professor of rhetoric at Edinburgh University.

line 1323 *"dogs, have had my day,":* *Hamlet*, V, 1, 299: "The cat will mew, and dog will have his day."

line 1456 *cast-off dresses:* It was often the privilege of a female servant to receive her mistress's unwanted dresses.

line 1542 *Stygian river:* The river Styx, in the Greek underworld.

line 1608 *Some play the devil, and then write a novel:* Lady Caroline Lamb had an affair with Byron and then wrote a novel *Glenarvon* (1816), featuring thinly disguised versions of herself, Byron, and several other of their acquaintances.

lines 1636–38 *Sappho the sage blue-stocking... overlooks the wave:* Refers to the legend that Sappho leaped to her death from the cliffs of Leucadia because of her unrequited love for Phaon.

line 1642 *jestest with the brows:* Cuckolded men were traditionally said to have grown horns on their heads. The four famous men named in the next line all had wives who were unfaithful (or were rumored or tempted to be).

line 1643 *Pompey:* Gnæus Pompeius Magnus (106–48 B.C.), Roman statesman and general, part of a ruling triumvirate with Julius Cæsar and Marcius Lucinus Crassus. *Belisarius:* (c. 505–565), Byzantine general under Justinian I.

line 1649 *Epicurus:* Although the ancient Greek philosopher Epicurus

(341–270 B.C.) taught that happiness was the highest good, his writings were often misconstrued, and he was thought to have preached hedonism.

line 1650 *Aristippus:* The philosopher Aristippus (c. 435–366 B.C.) taught that sensual gratification was the goal of human life.

line 1656 *Sardanapalus:* Legendary King of Assyria (c. seventh century B.C.) who was supposed to have been a sybarite.

line 1688 beau ideal: Conception of perfect beauty.

line 1713 *lazaret:* Building in which are housed persons with infectious diseases.

CANTO THE THIRD

line 11 *cypress branches:* Associated with mourning.

line 26 *planted:* Abandoned.

line 28 *gallanted:* Wooed; approached by gallants.

line 48 *uxorious:* Foolishly fond of or submissive to a wife.

line 53 *"so nominated in the bond":* The Merchant of Venice, IV, 1, 254.

line 63 *Laura:* The Italian lyric poet Petrarch (1304–1374), addressed many of his poems to his idealized beloved, Laura.

lines 79–80 *Dante's Beatrice ... you conceive:* Byron contrasts Dante's and Milton's idealized female characters with their wives. Dante was traditionally thought to have had an unhappy marriage, and Milton's first wife, Mary Powell, went back to her parents shortly after her marriage and refused to return for a time.

line 436 *Colchian:* In Greek mythology, Jason and the Argonauts sailed to Colchis to retrieve the Golden Fleece.

line 649 *trimmer:* A person who has no firm position, especially in politics. The word comes from the need to trim (adjust) a sail as the wind shifts.

line 655 *meed:* Reward.

line 676 *"Ça ira,":* Song of the French Revolution, literally, "It will succeed."

line 679 *Pindar:* The ancient Greek lyric poet Pindar (c. 522–c.438 B.C.) wrote an ode celebrating the winner of a horse race.

line 686 *Goethe's—(see what says De Staël):* Johann Wolfgang von Goethe (1749–1832), German writer whose works were celebrated by Madame Germaine de Staël (1766–1817), who popularized German literature in her influential book *De l'Allemagne* (1810).

line 687 *"Trecentisti":* Fourteenth-century poets.

line 692 *Delos rose, and Phœbus sprung:* Island birthplace of Phoebus Apollo in Greek mythology, called up out of the waters by Poseidon, the god of the sea.

lines 695–96 *The Scian and Teian muse, / The Hero's harp, the Lover's lute:* Homer, poet of epic heroism, was thought to have been born in Scio, or Chios; Anacreon, lyric poet of love and wine, was born in Teos.

line 700 *"Islands of the Blest":* Blissful abode mentioned by the poet Hesiod in his *Works and Days.*

line 702 *Marathon:* Location of the Battle of Marathon northeast of Athens, where in 490 B.C. the Athenians repelled the first Persian invasion of Greece.

lines 707–12 *A King sate ... where were they?* Xerxes I (c. 519–465 B.C.), Persian king, was said by Aeschylus to have watched the battle of Salamis (480 B.C.) from a high cliff. The Persians were defeated by the Greeks.

line 730 *Thermopylæ:* Famous battle in August, 480 B.C., in which a small number of Greeks heroically held off invading Persians before being overwhelmed.

line 742 *Bacchanal:* Orgy of drunken revelry.

line 743 *Pyrrhic dance:* Ancient war dance.

line 744 *phalanx:* A tight formation of armed infantry in Greek warfare.

line 747 *Cadmus:* Legendary founder of Thebes, who was supposed to have invented the Greek alphabet.

line 749 *Samian:* From the island of Samos.

line 752 *Polycrates:* (died c. 522 B.C.), tyrant of the island of Samos.

line 757 *Miltiades:* The sixth-century B.C. Miltiades the Elder was tyrant of a colony in the Thracian Chersonese.

line 762 *Suli's rock, and Parga's shore:* Suli was the home of the warlike Suliotes; Parga is a coastal town.

line 764 *Doric:* The Dorians founded the militaristic state of Sparta.

line 766 *Heracleidan:* Descendants of the legendary hero Heracles.

line 767 *Franks:* Germanic people who occupied most of Gaul (present-day France).

line 779 *Sunium:* Cape Colonna, Cape Saunion, in east central Greece.

line 787 *Orpheus:* In Greek mythology, a musician whose music was so beautiful it entranced inanimate objects and the dead.

line 813 *Troy ... Hoyle:* Homer made Troy famous in his *Iliad;* Edmund Hoyle made the card game whist famous in his book on the subject (1742).

lines 815–16 *Marlborough's ... Coxe:* William Coxe published his biography of general John Churchill, first Duke of Marlborough (1650–1722), in 1818–1819.

line 821 *Johnson:* Samuel Johnson (1709–1784) wrote an account of Milton's life in his ten-volume *Lives of the Poets* (1779–1781).

line 822 *the Nine:* The nine Muses.

line 825 *certes:* Certainly.

line 826 *Lord Bacon:* Francis Bacon (1561–1626), English philosopher, essayist, and statesman; confessed himself guilty of bribery.

line 827 *Titus' youth, and Cæsar's earliest acts:* The Emperor Titus Flavius Vespasianus (39–81) was supposed to have practiced forgery when young. Julius Caesar was said to have been profligate in his youth.

line 828 *Currie:* James Currie (1756–1845) published his biography of Robert Burns (1759–1796), the Scottish poet, in 1800. Currie emphasized Burns's drinking and carousing.

line 829 *Cromwell's pranks:* Oliver Cromwell (1599–1658), leader of the Puritan forces in the English Civil War, was supposed to have robbed orchards when young.

line 834 *"Pantisocracy":* In 1795 Southey and Coleridge planned to establish a utopian commune (whose egalitarian precepts they called pantisocracy) on the banks of the Susquehanna River in America. The plan was never carried out.

line 835 *unexcised, unhired:* That is, before he was given the government position of Distributor of Stamps.

line 836 *pedlar poems:* Wordsworth's poems, such as *The Excursion* (1814), often featured characters with similarly low or rustic occupations.

line 838 *Morning Post:* Coleridge began writing for this newspaper in 1798.

line 840 *Espoused two partners (milliners of Bath):* Coleridge and Southey married the Fricker sisters, Sarah and Edith respectively, in 1795 while preparing to go to America. They were not actually milliners.

line 842 *Botany Bay:* An English penal colony in Australia.

line 847 *frowzy:* Dirty, ill-smelling, musty.

lines 852–56 *Joanna Southcote's Shiloh ... taken for Divinities:* Joanna Southcott (1750–1814), a religious fanatic, attracted a following when she announced that she was about to give birth to the second messiah named Shiloh. Though she was in her sixties she appeared pregnant, probably Edema. She died soon after of a brain tumor.

line 864 *Ariosto:* Ludovico Ariosto (1474–1533), author of the romance *Orlando Furioso* (1516 and 1532).

line 865 "longueurs": Long and boring passages in literary works.

line 868 *An epic from Bob Southey every spring:* Southey wrote several very long, mediocre epics in a very short span of time.

line 871 Epopée: Epic.

line 873 *We learn from Horace, "Homer sometimes sleeps":* Horace wrote in his *Ars Poetica,* that Homer sleeps, that is, writes poetry below his usual standard.

line 876 "Waggoners": Referring to Wordsworth's *The Waggoner* (1819). The rest of the stanza refers to his poem *Peter Bell* (1819).

line 883 *Charles's Wain:* The Big Dipper.

line 884 *Medea:* Medea is carried in a chariot drawn by dragons in Euripides's play *Medea.*

line 890 *Pope and Dryden, are we come to this?:* Byron generally considered the neoclassical poetry of Pope and Dryden to be superior to all of the poetry of his own age.

line 892 *bathos:* A ludicrous descent from the exalted or lofty to the commonplace.

line 893 *Jack Cades:* Jack Cade (d. 1450) led an unsuccessful rebellion against King Henry VI of England.

line 896 *"Achitophel!":* *Absalom and Achitophel* (1681), a political satire by John Dryden.

line 921 *casuists:* Disingenuous reasoners.

line 933 *last Cæsarian fortress:* The abode of the Roman emperor Flavius Honorius (384–423) in Ravenna.

lines 934–35 *Boccaccio's lore / And Dryden's lay:* Dryden's *Theodore and Honoria* was based on a story from Boccaccio's *Decameron.*

line 937 *cicalas:* Cicadas.

line 941 *The spectre huntsman of Onesti's line:* Referring to Boccaccio's tale in which Nastagio degli Onesti meets a ghost of a woman pursued by the ghost of her knightly lover and two hell hounds.

line 945 *Hesperus:* Venus as the evening star.

line 961 *Nero:* The unstable Emperor Nero Claudius Caesar (37–68), who killed himself after being condemned to death by the Senate.

line 975 *Cantabs:* Cantabrigians, or students of Cambridge. Byron went to Cambridge.

line 984 ΠΟΙΗΤΙΚΗΣ: Aristotle's *Poetics.*

CANTO THE FOURTH

lines 21–22 *"falls into the yellow / Leaf ":* *Macbeth* V, 3, 22–23: "I have lived long enough: my way of life is fall'n into the seas, the yellow leaf ..."

line 29 *Lethe's spring:* Lethe, river of forgetfulness in the underworld of Greek mythology.

line 31 *Thetis baptized her mortal son in Styx:* The Nereid Thetis dipped her infant son Achilles in the river Styx in Hades, to make him invulnerable.

line 89 *"Whom the gods love die young," was said of yore:* By Herodotus, the Greek historian.

line 398 *galliots:* A Small swift galley.

CANTO THE SEVENTH

line 24 *Cervantes:* Miguel de Cervantes Saavedra (1547–1616), author of *Don Quixote* (1605–1615).

lines 25–27 *Swift … Rousseau:* Jonathan Swift (1667–1745), Irish satirist and author of *Gulliver's Travels* (1726); Niccoló Machiavelli (1469–1527), Italian author of *The Prince* (1513); François de la Rochefoucauld (1613–1680), French author of the witty and skeptical *Réflexions ou sentences et maximes morales* (first edition, 1665); François de Salignac de La Mothe-Fénelon (1651–1715), French archbishop and theologian; Martin Luther (1483–1546), German priest and scholar whose writings and actions led to the Protestant Reformation; John Wesley (1703–1791), founder of Methodism; Jean-Jacques Rousseau (1712–1778), French philosopher and novelist.

lines 30–31 *Cato, / Nor even Diogenes:* Marcius Porcius Cato the Younger (95–46 B.C.), Roman Stoic philosopher, and Diogenes (d. circa 320 B.C.), Greek Stoic philosopher.

line 41 *Ecclesiastes:* Ecclesiastes 1:2: "Vanity of vanities, saith the Preacher, vanity of vanities; all is vanity."

line 57 *"Fierce loves and faithless wars":* Byron intentionally misquotes the Introduction to Edmund Spenser's *The Faerie Queen* (1590–1596): "Fierce warres and faitfull loves shall moralize my song."

line 63 *Souvaroff:* Alexsandr Vasilyevitch Suvorov (1729–1800), Russian field marshal. *alderman:* A city official. Aldermen were proverbially well-fed.

CANTO THE NINTH

line 1 *"Villainton":* "Vilain" ("villain") plus "ton" (tone, style).

line 8 *thunder "Nay!":* Punning on the name of the French field marshal Michel Ney (1769–1815), who fought against Wellington at Waterloo. Ney was executed in 1815.

lines 9–10 *Kinnaird quite well / In Marinet's affair:* Lord Charles Kinnaird (1780–1826), the brother of Byron's friend and banker Douglas Kinnaird, warned the British authorities in 1818 about a plot to assassinate Wellington. He was ignored, but after an attempt was made on Wellington, Kinnaird was told to reveal the name of his informant. When Kinnaird did so, the informant, Marinet, was arrested, even though Kinnaird thought he had received assurances that this would not occur. Kinnaird wrote a pamphlet denouncing Wellington over the incident; Wellington attacked Kinnaird's patriotism in return.

line 14 *tabby:* Gossiping elderly lady.

line 19 *repaired Legitimacy's crutch:* Wellington's victory over Napoleon was a blow to liberty in that it helped restore "legitimate" monarchies throughout Europe.

line 25 *"the best of cut-throats":* Macbeth, III, 4, 17.

line 42 *Prince of the Brazils:* King John VI of Portugal (1767–1826), called the "Prince of the Brazils" because he fled to Brazil in 1807 when Napoleon invaded Portugal.

line 51 *Cincinnatus:* Lucius or Titus Quinctius Cincinnatus, a Roman who, according to legend, left his farm and became dictator in order to defeat the Aequi and Volscians, and resigned his dictatorship and returned to his farm after he had won.

line 55 *Sabine farm:* The poet Horace was presented with a farm in the Sabine hills by Maecenas, the Roman statesman and patron of letters.

line 58 *Epaminondas:* The Theban general and politician Epaminondas (c. 410–362 B.C.) defeated Spartan forces at Leuctra in 371 B.C., ending Sparta's military dominance of the Greek states.

lines 62–64 *Pitt too … gratis:* When William Pitt the Elder (1708–1778) became paymaster general in 1746. He countered suspicions of corruption by ostentatiously refusing to accept more than his official salary.

line 129 "Que scaise-je?" *was the motto of Montaigne:* Michel de Montaigne (1533–1592), French essayist. His motto translates as "What do I know?"

line 138 *Pyrrho:* Greek philosopher (c.360–c. 270 B.C.) and father of Skepticism.

line 145 *"But Heaven," as Cassio says, "is above all":* Byron paraphrases the drunken Cassio from *Othello* II, 3: "Well, God's above all."

lines 149–50 *"The sparrow's fall … providence":* Hamlet V, 2, 218–19: "… there is a special providence in the fall of a sparrow." Also see Matthew 10:29 ("Are not two sparrows sold for a farthing? And one of them shall not fall on the ground without your Father.").

line 153 *Theogony:* The origin of the gods.

line 155 *Cosmogony:* A theory of the origin of the cosmos.

line 162 *Melancthon:* Phillip Melancthon (1497–1560), German friend and collaborator of Martin Luther.

line 171 *proem:* Preamble.

line 179 *Peter:* Peter I the Great (1672–1725), czar of Russia.

line 182 *Much flattery—even Voltaire's:* Voltaire corresponded extensively with and flattered Catherine the Great (1729–1796), czarina of Russia.

CANTO THE ELEVENTH

line 1 *Bishop Berkeley said "There was no matter":* George Berkeley (1685–1753), Anglo-Irish clergyman and philosopher. His writings were often misinterpreted as denying the existence of matter.

line 18 *"dainty Ariel":* Referring to the sprite Ariel, servant of the wizard Prospero, in Shakespeare's *The Tempest.*

line 37 *phthisical:* tubercular; wasting away.

line 274 *Russ:* Russian.

line 299 *"Te Deum":* Te Deum laudamus, a medieval hymn of praise.

lines 302–4 *Kiss hands ... worse for wearing:* Byron was appalled that George IV got a lavish welcome from the Irish when he visited them in 1820. The King was not a supporter of Irish causes and was opposed to Catholic Emancipation.

line 309 *"ivresse":* Intoxication.

line 363 *hymeneal:* Of or pertaining to marriage.

line 380 *Ceruse:* White lead pigment used in cosmetics.

lines 427–29 *as in Banquo's glass ... living authors pass:* In *Macbeth* (IV, 1) the Witches conjure up the ghosts of Banquo and a succession of eight dead kings, the last of whom carries a mirror in which Macbeth sees images of Banquo's descendants.

line 432 *every paltry magazine can show it 's:* Literary journals and magazines were fond of writing series of articles on "the greatest living poets."

line 434 *the fisty ring:* The boxing ring.

line 438 *foolscap:* A sheet of paper measuring approximately thirteen by sixteen inches, so named because of the watermark of a fool's cap that was featured on such sheets.

lines 441–48 *But Juan was my Moscow ... for my turnkey Lowe:* This stanza compares Byron's fall in popularity and public esteem to Napoleon's fall from power.

lines 441–42 *But Juan ... seems Cain: Don Juan* was attacked for its alleged impiety and indecency, and Byron's publisher, John Murray, refused to publish any more of the poem after Canto 5 (the radical publisher John Hunt published the rest). Moscow marked the beginning of Napoleon's downfall, when his army entered the city in September 1812, to find it abandoned. The Russian campaign cost Napoleon's army many lives. *Faliero* refers to Byron's play *Marino Faliero, an Historical Tragedy* (1821). The Battle of Leipsic (October 16–19, 1813) was France's worst disaster since the rise of Napoleon. *Mont Saint Jean:* was a ridge where the British resisted a French attack at the end of Waterloo. Byron's play *Cain; a Mystery* (1821) provoked widespread condemnation and outrage.

line 443 La Belle Alliance: Belle-Alliance was a village near Waterloo where Wellington and the Prussian Field Marshal Gebhard Leberecht von Blücher (1742–1819) met after the battle. Byron also refers to the alliance that defeated Napoleon: Britain, Russia, Prussia, and Austria.

line 444 *the Lion:* That is, the literary "lion," the eminent and popular author.

line 448 *turnkey Lowe:* Sir Hudson Lowe (1769–1844), the governor of St. Helena, the island to which Napoleon was exiled. Lowe was much criticized for his slighting treatment of Napoleon.

line 451 *Sion's:* Zion's.

line 452 *With poets almost clergymen, or wholly:* Byron ridicules clergyman-poets such as the sonneteer William Lisle Bowles (1762–1850), as well as the increasing tendency for poets to write on pious themes.

line 454 *the very Reverend Rowley Powley:* The Irish poet, Anglican clergyman, hymn-writer, and novelist George Croly (1780–1860).

line 456 *A modern Ancient Pistol—"by these hilts!":* Pistol was Falstaff's blustering friend in Shakespeare's *Henry IV,* Part II. "By these hilts" was an expression of Falstaff's.

line 460 *Dorus of the Nine:* Dorus is a eunuch in the Roman playwright Terence's *Eunuchus;* the Nine are the Muses.

line 461 *Sporus:* A man who was emasculated by Nero.

line 463 *Cambyses:* Cambyses (a king of Persia) was Croly's nickname. Some of his extravagant poetry featured "roaring Romans."

line 464 *The howling Hebrews of Cybele's priest:* This entire stanza refers to the clergyman, poet, and historian Henry Hart Milman (1791–1868), whose "howling Hebrews" (featured in his 1820 *Fall of Jerusalem*) are unfavorably contrasted with Croly's Romans. The priests of the ancient goddess Cybele were sometimes emasculated.

line 465 *my gentle Euphues:* The English poet Bryan Waller Procter (1787–1874), whose pen name was Barry Cornwall. John Lyly's influential early novel *Euphues* (1579) used a highly elaborate and affected style. The word "euphuism" has come to mean an artificially elegant style of language.

line 471 *deep-mouthed Bœotian "Savage Landor":* Walter Savage Landor (1775–1864), English poet and and essayist, friend of Southey. The Boeotians of Greece were proverbially stupid.

line 473 *John Keats, who was killed off by one critique:* The poet Keats was erroneously rumored to have sickened and died because of John Wilson Croker's scathing review of his poem *Endymion* in 1818.

line 475 *without Greek:* Without being able to read or write Greek; a sneer at Keats's lack of an upper-class classical education.

line 516 *Centaur Nessus garb of mortal clothing:* Heracles was killed by a robe smeared with the poisonous blood of the centaur Nessus.

line 523 *puncheons:* Large casks.

lines 526–27 *"bower"* / *(In Moore's phrase):* Thomas Moore's poetry often featured lovers in "bowers."

CANTO THE TWELFTH

line 430 *Preludios:* (Spanish) preludes.

line 433 *rosin:* A resin applied to the strings of a violin bow.

line 442 *Yclept the Great World:* named high society.

line 460 *"The royal game of Goose":* A board game.

line 469 reticular: Netlike.

line 470 *"Fishers for men," like Sirens:* Jesus told Peter to be a "fisher of men" (Matthew 4:19). In Greek mythology, part-human females whose songs lured sailors to their deaths.

line 474 *trepanned:* Ensnared.

line 476 *stays:* Flat hard strips of material used for stiffening corsets or other articles of clothing; hence, wearing a corset.

line 493 *vitiated:* Debased, weakened, or corrupted.

line 495 *amphibious:* In the sense of not entirely residing either in the water or on the land.

line 496 *neither white nor scarlet:* That is, neither innocent nor a harlot.

line 499 *lee-shore:* That is, caught between the wind and the shore, a dangerous position.

line 502 *Werters:* The hero of Goethe's novel *The Sorrows of Young Werther* (1774) kills himself because of unrequited love. The novel inspired many young men to do likewise.

line 505 *"Ye gods, I grow a talker!":* A misquotation from *The Merchant of Venice* I, 1, 110: "I'll grow a talker."

line 524 *oligarchs of our Gynocracy:* Members of an oligarchy (a political system in which power rests in the hands of a few people or a dominant class or clique). Gynecocracy is rule by women.

line 536 *duns . . . double knockings:* Demands for payment of debts, or those who come to collect such payments. *double knockings:* Loud knocks.

CANTO THE THIRTEENTH

lines 49–50 *Rough Johnson . . . an honest hater:* In James Boswell's *Life of Johnson* (1791), Samuel Johnson says approvingly that Dr. Bathurst was "a very good hater."

line 56 *Goethe's Mephistopheles:* Referring to the Devil in Goethe's drama *Faust* (1808–1832).

lines 68–69 *to fight / His guerdon:* That is, to fight for his fitting reward.

line 74 *caitiff:* Villainous, despicable person. Don Quixote often applies the word to his enemies.

line 89 *"at my old lunes":* Fits of madness (archaic). Byron quotes Shakespeare's *The Merry Wives of Windsor* IV, 2, 19–22.

line 96 *Œdipus, and Life's a Sphinx:* In Greek mythology, Oedipus correctly answered the seemingly unsolvable riddle of the Theban sphinx.

line 269 *Mandarin:* Powerful Chinese official.

line 273 "Nil admirari": Horace wrote that "to wonder at nothing" is the secret of happiness.

line 289 *figure:* Figure of speech; metaphor.

line 309 *Parry's efforts:* Admiral Sir William Edward Parry (1790–1855) made several voyages to the Arctic in search of a northwest passage to Asia.

line 331 *postilion:* Person who rides the near horse of a pair of horses pulling a carriage.

line 333 *post-horses:* Horses kept at inns or post houses for carrying paying riders or the mail.

line 438 *Withal:* With that (archaic).

line 543 *Sir Peter Lely:* (1618–1680), Dutch painter of the English aristocracy.

line 552 *"Star Chamber" than of "Habeas Corpus":* The Star Chamber was an English court abolished in 1641 that tried cases without a jury and meted out harsh punishments. Byron contrasts it with a court that observes the principle of habeas corpus.

line 588 *Dan Phœbus:* Phoebus is Apollo, Greek god of light and music. "Dan" is an old term of honor, equivalent to "sir" or "master."

line 590 *Homer's "Catalogue of ships":* The long list of Greek ships in the *Iliad*.

line 602 *Bacchant coronals:* Crowns or garlands of Bacchus, Roman god of wine.

line 617 villeggiatura: Season in the country.

lines 621–22 *Nimrod's self ... Melton jacket:* In other words, Nimrod, the Biblical "mighty hunter," might leave the Babylonian plains and put on a Melton hunting jacket.

line 626 *the* pas: The right of precedence.

line 639 passée: Passé, no longer fashionable.

line 674 *"Aye, every inch a" duke:* An allusion to "Ay, every inch a king," from *King Lear* IV, 6, 110.

lines 674–75 *twelve peers / Like Charlemagne's:* Charlemagne (742–814) was often depicted in romances as accompanied by twelve paladins.

line 691 soi-disant: so-called; self-proclaimed.

line 750 *Congreve's fool ... Molière's* bête: William Congreve (1670–1729) and Molière (Jean-Baptiste Poquelin) (1622–1673), comic playwrights.

line 789 ragoûts: French stews of meat or fish.

line 793 *the lands which "flowed with milk and honey":* the Promised Land.

line 817 gêné: Constrained.

line 832 *To make each correspondent a new debtor:* Recipients of letters, not their senders, had to pay the postage.

lines 838–39 *Ulysses' whistle ... poor Dolon:* Byron garbles a scene from the *Iliad*, in which Diomedes and Odysseus (Ulysses) kill a Trojan named Dolon after he gives them information. It is not until later that Odysseus whistles to Diomedes as a signal to return to their boats.

lines 846–48 *Izaak Walton ... trout to pull it:* English author (1593–1683), of *The Compleat Angler* (1653), history's most famous book on fishing.

line 850 *conversazione:* Social gathering featuring conversation.

line 853 *glee:* An unaccompanied part song for three or more singers.

line 870 *good thing:* Witticism.

line 875 *As Phidian forms cut out of marble Attic:* Like sculptures made out of Athenian (Attic) marble by Phidias, the Greek sculptor of the fifth century B.C.

lines 876–79 *Squire Westerns ... our Sophias ... like Tom Jones:* Vigorous, goodhearted characters from Henry Fielding's novel *Tom Jones* (1749).

CANTO THE FOURTEENTH

line 6 *Much as old Saturn ate his progeny:* In Greek mythology, Kronos (the Roman Saturn) ate his children as soon as they were born because he was fated to be overthrown by one of them.

line 27 *clay:* That is, flesh.

line 106 *lucubration:* Laborious work, study, or writing.

line 111 *portmanteaus:* It was an old joke that the pages of unsold books and poems ended up being used as linings for trunks.

line 327 tracasserie: (French) Mischief.

line 328 agacerie: (French) Flirtation.

lines 335–36 *a dead set / At:* A determined attempt to attract.

line 497 intrigante: Female intriguer.

line 498 méchante: (French) Mischievous.

line 526 *leading strings:* Strings for leading and supporting a child who is learning to walk.

line 532 bienséance: (French) decorum.

line 537 *the council called "the Privy":* The Privy Council, a body of advisers to the King.

line 539 *some future Livy:* That is, some future historian. Titus Livius (59 B.C.–17 A.D.) was a Roman historian.

line 683 *stone of Sisyphus:* In Greek mythology, Sisyphus was condemned in Hades to eternally roll a rock to the top of a hill.

line 747 *a term:* An end.

line 808 *antipodes:* Geographical locations opposite each other on the globe.

CANTO THE FIFTEENTH

lines 87–88 *Alcibiades . . . living in all climes with ease:* Athenian general and statesman, c.450–404 B.C. Plutarch's *Lives* describes him as easily adapting to different customs.

line 94 *Cupidon:* French for "Cupid."

line 96 *Dandy:* Young men in the high society of early nineteenth-century England who affected an extreme elegance in clothing and manners. The most famous dandy was George Bryan "Beau" Brummell (1778–1840).

line 125 "verbum sat": "A word to the wise is sufficient."

line 128 *Raphael:* Raffaello Sanzio (1483–1520), Italian Renaissance painter.

line 132 *eke:* Also (archaic).

line 137 *Locke:* John Locke (1632–1704), English philosopher.

line 160 Improvvisatore: An Italian performer of extemporaneous rhymes and poems.

lines 161–62 "Omni vult *belle* . . . dic aliquando *male*": An epigram of the Roman writer Martial: "Matho, you want to say everything beautifully— sometimes speak well, sometimes in a middling way, sometimes badly."

line 170 *feeble:* Foible.

lines 214–15 *cutter,* / *Or brigantine, or pink:* Kinds of sailing vessels.

line 216 *non-age:* Nonage, period of youth or immaturity.

line 325 *slight shade of blue:* That is, she was something of a bluestocking.

line 328 *consumptive:* Tubercular.

line 331 *upon a star or a blue string:* In other words, upon a man who wore a star or ribbon as an emblem of honor, such as that of the Order of the Garter (the highest honor of British knighthood).

lines 385–86 *the bust* / *Of Brutus at the pageant of Tiberius:* The Roman Emperor Tiberius did not permit the bust of Brutus to be carried at the funeral of Brutus's sister, because of Brutus's part in Julius Caesar's assassination.

line 446 *Sibyl:* An ancient Greek or Roman prophetess.

line 666 Nem. con.: *"Nemine contradicenti,"* legal term for "unanimously."

line 667 crim. con.: "Criminal conversation," legal euphemism for adultery.

line 675 *Minerva than the Graces:* Minerva is the Roman name for Athena, goddess of wisdom. The graces, Aglaia, Euphrosyne, and Thalia, are the three sister goddesses of beauty and grace in Greek mythology.

line 688 sine quâ: Sine qua non, an indispensible element.

lines 689–90 *the great Lord Coke* / *(See Littleton):* Lord Coke's commentary on Sir Thomas Littleton's *Institutes of the Laws of England* was an important legal text.

line 705 *Apologue:* Moral fable, usually having animals or objects as characters.

line 727 *I wish well to Trojan and to Tyrian:* Paraphrasing Virgil's *Aeneid.* Tyre was an ancient Phoenician city.

line 732 *Eldon on a lunatic commission:* In 1822, John Scott, Lord Eldon (1751–1838) the English lord chancellor, heard the scandalous divorce case of Lord Portsmouth, in which Portsmouth's sanity was called into question. Byron had given the bride away at the wedding.

lines 733–34 *John Bull:* "John Bull" was the personification of the English people.

line 735 *boil like the springs of Hecla:* Hekla is an Icelandic volcano.

Canto the Sixteenth

line 160 *arras:* Wall hanging, curtain, or tapestry.

line 166 *the Sisters weird:* The weird sisters are the three witches in *Macbeth.*

line 238 distrait: (French) Inattentive or preoccupied, especially because of anxiety.

line 490 *A special Titian:* A work by the Italian painter Titian (Tiziano Vecellio, 1488?–1576).

line 503 cápo d'opera: Masterpiece.

line 533 *I had the sad mishap:* In 1809 one of Byron's servants, named Lucy, evidently gave birth to his child.

line 541 *Consistory:* Ecclesiastical council.

line 806 *the sixth year is ending:* Parliaments met for seven years; new elections are about to occur.

line 831 *Cocker's:* Edward Cocker (1631–1675) wrote a famous book on arithmetic.

line 913 Αἴ αἴ τὰν Κυθέρειαν: "Alas for Cytherea." From the ancient Greek poet Bion's *Lament for Adonis.* Cytherea is another name for Aphrodite, Greek goddess of love.

line 915 *Dian:* The moon (Diana was the Roman goddess of the moon).

line 920 Alma Venus Genetrix: "Nurturing mother Venus," quoted from the Roman poet Lucretius's *De Rerum Natura.*

line 931 sans culotte: Without breeches. Also a name for an extreme radical during the time of the French Revolution.

line 966 *tympanum:* Eardrum.

lines 970–71 *"Lasciate ogni speranza, / Voi, ch'entrate!":* "Abandon every hope, you who enter here." The words above the gate of Hell in Dante's *Inferno.*

line 972 rima: *The Divine Comedy* was written in terza rima verse.

line 997 carte *and* tierce: Positions in fencing.

Canto the Seventeenth

line 53 *as some know or knew:* Alluding to a maidservant of Lady Byron's named Mrs. Clermont, whom Byron hated.

line 56 Malgré: In spite of, notwithstanding. *Sir Matthew Hale's great humanity:*

Sir Matthew Hale (1609–1676) was an English jurist who was famed for his impartiality, especially during the English Civil War. However, he was criticized by later writers for his belief in witchcraft and for presiding over the execution of two women accused as witches.

lines 57–60 *Great Galileo . . . embargoed from mere walking:* The astronomer Galileo Galilei (1564–1642) was imprisoned by the Inquisition for having insisted that the earth revolved around the sun.

line 65 *Pythagoras:* Ancient Greek philosopher and mathematician of the sixth century B.C.

line 79 "totus, teres": (Latin) "Whole, smooth."

line 83 "Idem semper": (Latin) "Always the same."

line 86 "Hercules furens": (Latin) "Hercules mad," also the title of a tragedy by the Roman playwright Seneca.

TALES

THE GIAOUR

line 2 *the Athenian's:* Themistocles (c.524–c.460 B.C.), Athenian statesman and naval commander. He helped defend Greece against the Persians.

line 9 *Colonna:* Cape Sunium (Sounion).

line 109 *Thermopylæ:* Famous battle in August, 480 B.C., in which a small number of Greeks heroically held off invading Persians before being overwhelmed.

line 113 *Salamis:* Greek island near which the naval Battle of Salamis was won by the Greeks over the forces of Persia.

line 171 *Mainote:* Mediterranean pirate.

line 172 *caïque:* Long, narrow boat.

line 177 *Port Leone:* Village on the Ionian island of Kalamos.

line 190 *Giaour:* Infidel; pronounced "jowr".

line 199 *Othman's sons:* Turks.

line 212 *ween:* Think (archaic).

line 225 *tophaike:* A Turkish musket.

line 228 *Rhamazani's:* Ramadan, the Muslim holy month of fasting.

line 229 *Bairam:* Turkish "Bayram," Muslim festival following Ramadan.

line 251 *jerreed:* Blunt wooden javelin.

line 282 *Simoom:* A violent, hot wind on the deserts of Arabia and North Africa.

line 339 *Fakir:* a begging dervish.

line 340 *Dervise:* Dervish or Darwish, member of a particular order of Muslim religious ascetics.

line 355 *ataghan:* Yataghan, a Turkish sword or scimitar.

line 358 *salam:* A salaam, an act of deference or obeisance, especially a low bow performed while placing the right palm on the forehead.

line 363 *bark:* Sailing vessel.

line 364 *skiff:* Small boat.

line 389 *insect queen:* Byron refers to a kind of blue-winged butterfly.

line 390 *Kashmeer:* The Vale of Kashmir is a famously scenic valley in India.

line 412 *pinion:* Wing.

line 444 *Serai:* Palace.

line 456 *Georgian:* From Georgia, a country in the Caucasus ruled by Persia and Turkey at various times.

line 465 *Nubians:* Natives of Nubia, a region of Africa.

line 468 *Phingari:* The Moon.

line 479 *jewel of Giamschid:* A legendary ruby.

line 483 *Al-Sirat's arch:* "The path," a bridge over hell.

line 486 *Houris:* Beautiful virgins of the Islamic paradise.

line 491 *Muftis:* Islamic legal authorities.

line 505 *Circassian:* One of a people living in the region of the Caucasus.

line 506 *Franguestan:* A name for Circassia.

line 522 *arquebuss:* Harquebus, a heavy matchlock gun.

line 525 *Arnaut:* Albanian mountaineer.

line 528 *Parne:* Mount Parnassus, in Greece.

line 566 *Liakura:* Another name for Mount Parnassus.

line 568 *Bismillah:* "In the name of God."

line 571 *Chiaus:* Turkish messenger, escort, emissary, or sergeant.

line 589 *van:* Vanguard.

line 602 *carbine:* Lightweight rifle.

line 603 *Amaun:* "Pardon."

line 661 *falchion:* Sword.

line 666 *palampore:* Cotton cloth woven in India.

line 683 *Paynim:* Non-Christian

line 717 *calpac . . . caftan:* Large black cap and long-sleeved, ankle-length garment.

line 729 *Osmanlie:* Osmanli; Ottoman.

line 734 *"Alla Hu!":* "Allah-hu Akbar," "God is great."

line 748 *Monkir:* A spirit who interrogates and punishes the dead.

line 750 *Eblis:* Iblis, the prince of evil spirits.

line 784 *Gouls and Afrits:* Ghul and ifrit, evil jinni (spirits).

line 787 *Caloyer:* Eastern monk.

line 876 *cot:* Cottage.

line 896 *Gorgon:* In Greek mythology, a female monster with snakes for hair and a petrifying gaze.

line 952 *her bosom's stream:* Her blood.

line 1040 *Nazarene:* Here, a Christian.

line 1042 *brands:* Swords.

line 1044 *Galileans:* Christians.

line 1102 *Ætna:* Etna, volcano in Sicily.

line 1169 *brake:* Thickly overgrown area.

line 1267 *orison:* Prayer.

line 1273 *symar:* Simar, a long dress or robe. Byron here means "shroud."

line 1332 *shrived:* Heard confession and gave absolution to.

FROM THE BRIDE OF ABYDOS

line 1 *cypress and myrtle:* The cypress was associated with death; the myrtle, which was sacred to Aphrodite, with love.

line 3 *turtle:* Turtle dove.

line 7 *Zephyr:* The west wind.

line 8 *Gúl:* The rose.

FROM THE CORSAIR

line 1170 *Morea's hills:* The Peloponessus in southern Greece.

line 1175 *Ægina's rock:* The island of Aegina.

line 1176 *the God of gladness:* Apollo, the Greek god of light. Here, the sun.

line 1180 *Salamis:* Greek island near which the Battle of Salamis was won by Greeks over the Persians.

line 1186 *Delphian:* Delphi was the location of the most important shrine and oracle of Apollo.

line 1188 *thy Wisest:* Socrates.

line 1196 *Phœbus:* Apollo.

line 1197 *Cithæron:* Mountain in southeast Greece.

line 1201 *Hymettus:* Limestone mountain, famed for flowers and bees.

line 1210 *Cephisus:* A river god.

line 1214 *Theseus' fane:* In Greek mythology, the hero who defeated the Minotaur. Fane is a temple.

THE PRISONER OF CHILLON

line 35 *a marsh's meteor lamp:* Will-o'-the-wisp.

line 107 *Lake Leman:* Lake Geneva, in Switzerland.

BEPPO

p. 597 (whom I take to be Frere): *The Monks and the Giants* (1817–1818) was a poem written by John Hookham Frere (1769–1846) under the pseudonym Whistlecraft.

line 3 *Shrove Tuesday:* Last day of Shrovetide, a season of merrymaking before Lent.

line 23 *quiz:* Tease.

line 30 *Phlegethon:* The river of fire in Hades.

line 35 *Monmouth-street, or in Rag Fair:* Parts of London famous at the time for selling secondhand clothing.

line 39 *bating Covent Garden:* Excluding. Covent Garden in London was designed in the 1630s as a piazza (residential square) by the architect Inigo Jones.

line 48 *Packet:* Small boat that carries mail, passengers, or goods on a regular route.

line 50 *ragouts:* French stews of meat or fish.

line 60 *the Strand:* Thoroughfare in west-central London.

line 63 *Harvey:* A fish sauce.

lines 85–86 *Venuses of Titian's / (The best's at Florence . . .):* Titian's *Venus of Urbino* (1538), in the Uffizi Gallery in Florence.

line 88 *Giorgione:* Giorgio Barbarelli (c.1478?–1510), Italian painter.

line 91 *That picture:* A painting known as the "Triple Portrait," now attributed to Titian.

line 112 *lost Pleiad:* Merope, one of the Pleiades. Her star was said to be dimmer than the others because she married a mortal and hid her face in shame.

line 117 *Goldoni:* Carlo Goldoni (1707–1793), Italian dramatist.

line 123 *light-heeled Mercuries:* Mercury was the Roman messenger of the gods.

line 129 *Desdemona:* The wife of Shakespeare's Othello, who suffocated her in a jealous rage.

line 130 *fame:* Reputation.

line 136 *"Cavalier Servente":* Male companion of a married woman, a socially accepted lover.

line 139 *sooty:* Black.

line 154 *the Rialto:* The Rialto Bridge spans the Grand Canal in Venice.

line 195 *practique:* A bill of clearance for a ship to leave quarantine.

line 199 *Aleppo:* Syrian city.

line 203 *tanyard:* An area of a tannery set aside for tanning vats.

line 205 *yard:* A long spar to which a sail is attached.

line 224 *Ariadne:* In Greek mythology, the woman who gave Theseus the thread with which he found his way out of the Labyrinth. Afterwards Theseus left her.

line 226 *wearing weeds:* A sign of mourning.

line 246 *buskin:* Laced boot.

line 248 *"seccatura":* (Italian) Boring.

line 257 *Improvisatori:* Italian performers of extemporaneous rhymes and poems.

line 264 *to his very valet seemed a hero:* Alluding to the old saying, "No man is a hero to his valet."

line 293 *from the Po to Teio:* From the Po river in Italy to Teos in Greece.

line 315 *supernumerary:* Extra.

line 320 *tippet:* Woman's shoulder cape made of fur.

line 336 *dray:* Horsecart.

line 337 *becaficas:* Songbirds.

line 357 *Dama:* Equivalent to the English "lady."

line 363 *Raphael:* The Italian painter Raphael (1483–1520) was believed to have died after strenuous lovemaking.

line 366 *the Lyre:* A stringed instrument; here, poetry.

line 368 *Canova:* Antonio Canova (1757–1822), Italian sculptor.

line 370 *Calais:* French coastal town where travelers from England often arrived.

line 371 *lucubrate:* To engage in laborious work, study, or writing.

line 373 *quill:* Pen.

line 374 *Habeas Corpus:* Habeas Corpus was suspended in England in 1817 and restored in 1818.

line 383 *Regent:* The much-despised Prince Regent (1762–1830), who became King George IV after the death of his father in 1820.

line 385 *disbanded seamen:* Unemployed after the Napoleonic Wars.

line 386 *Poor's rate:* Poor rates taxes that funded periodic payments made to the poor in England.

line 391 *our recent glories:* Especially the victory of the allies at Waterloo (1815).

line 392 *Tories:* The Tories were the more generally conservative party in Parliament, and remained in power throughout Byron's life. Byron was a Whig.

line 403 *Parnassus ... inditing:* Greek mountain thought by the Romans to be the home of the Muses. *inditing:* Writing or dictating.

line 408 *Some samples of the* finest Orientalism: Byron is poking fun at the vogue for poetic tales set in the East, several of which he had written himself.

line 412 *Walker's Lexicon:* A rhyming dictionary first published in 1775.

line 448 *"varnished faces.":* masks; from *The Merchant of Venice* II, 5, 33: "Nor thrust your head into the public street to gaze on Christian fools with varnished faces."

lines 455–56 *for fear the Press / Should soil with parts of speech the parts of dress:* In magazines, a sheet was placed between a page with pictures and a page with words in order to keep the ink from transferring onto the picture.

line 461 *Vauxhall:* Vauxhall in London was the location of popular outdoor public gardens where entertainments were frequently offered.

line 481 *Crushed was Napoleon by the northern Thor:* Napoleon's army was destroyed by the harsh weather during his 1812 invasion of Russia.

line 508 *hippish:* Melancholy.

line 528 *like Banquo's kings:* Alluding to *Macbeth*, in which the Witches conjure up the ghosts of Banquo and a succession of dead kings.

line 543 *Wilberforce and Romilly:* William Wilberforce (1759–1833) and Sir Samuel Romilly (1757–1818) were political reformers.

line 555 *philogyny:* Love of or liking for women.

line 560 *"ad libitum":* At one's pleasure.

line 574 *"Blues":* Bluestockings, a pejorative term for literary women.

line 575 Botherby: William Sotheby (1757–1833), poet and translator.

line 581 *Triton:* In Greek mythology a divine son of Poseidon, the sea god.

line 597 *puff:* To praise unduly, as a literary work.

line 598 *the pink:* Very fashionable men.

line 603 *Scott, Rogers, Moore:* Poets whose works Byron admired: Walter Scott (1771–1832); Samuel Rogers (1763–1855); Thomas Moore (1779–1852).

line 605 *the children of the "Mighty Mother's,":* The children of Dulness in Alexander Pope's satire *The Dunciad* (first published 1728).

line 609 *Mussul*women: Muslim women.

line 624 *Nor deal (thank God for that!) in Mathematics:* Lady Byron had been interested in mathematics.

line 639 *old Saturn's reign of sugar-candy:* In Greek and Roman mythology, the reign of Saturn, Jupiter's father, was often referred to as a Golden Age.

line 660 *the season:* The Season was the period of the year in England during which Parliament was in session and all the prominent families converged on London for balls and parties, generally late spring through early August.

line 685 *Bow-street gem'men:* London constables. "Gem'men" is short for "gentlemen."

line 693 *eke:* Also (archaic).

line 711 *hartshorn:* A preparation of ammonia used as smelling salts.

line 712 *cutting stays:* Stays were flat hard strips of material used for stiffening corsets or other articles of clothing. When a woman fainted, her stays were sometimes cut to facilitate breathing.

line 749 *bastinadoes:* Beatings.

line 759 *polacca:* Mediterranean vessel with two or three masts.

DRAMA

MANFRED

ACT I, SCENE I

line 12 *The Tree of Knowledge is not that of Life:* In Eden, Adam and Eve tasted fruit from the Tree of Knowledge, which brought death into the world, instead of from the Tree of Life, whose fruit gave everlasting life.

line 60 *Mont Blanc:* Highest peak in Europe, glacier covered and located in the Alps.

line 90 *bitumen:* Flammable natural substance consisting mainly of hydrocarbons.

line 154 *Promethean:* Referring to Prometheus, the Titan of Greek mythology who brought fire from heaven to give to mortals.

line 237 *brake:* A thickly overgrown area.

SCENE II

line 57 *Chamois:* A kind of small mountain goat antelope.

lines 92–99 *Mountains have fallen ... Mount Rosenberg:* There was a destructive landslide there in 1806.

ACT II, SCENE I

line 40 *William Tell:* Legendary Swiss hero who defied Austrian rule.

SCENE II

line 7 *The Giant steed, to be bestrode by Death:* In Revelation 6:8, Death is one of the Four Horsemen of the Apocalypse and rides a pale horse: "And I looked, and behold a pale horse: and his name that sat upon him was Death."

line 26 *glassed:* Reflected.

line 92 *He:* The philosopher Iamblicus (c.250–c.330) was supposed to have summoned Eros (love) and Anteros (unrequited love or the opposer of love) from a fountain at Gadara.

line 131 *the Furies:* Horrifying female divinities that tormented criminals.

line 142 *Crœsus:* King of Lydia in Asia Minor, known for his enormous wealth.

lines 182–83 *The buried Prophet answered to the Hag / Of Endor:* In I Samuel 28:8–19, the ghost of Samuel is summoned from the grave by the Witch of Endor. Samuel's ghost prophesies the death of Saul.

lines 183–85 *the Spartan monarch ... his destiny:* In Greek legend, the Spartan

King Pausanias accidentally kills the Byzantine maid Cleonice, with whom he was in love. When he calls up her ghost, she tells him to go back to Sparta, where he is killed.

line 188 *Phyxian Jove:* Jupiter, ruler of the Roman gods. *Phigalia:* Ancient city of Greece.

line 189 *Arcadian:* Arcadia was a region of ancient Greece. *Evocators:* Ones who call up spirits.

Scene III

Jungfrau Mountain: A famed Swiss peak.

line 10 *fretwork:* Ornamental work consisting of interlaced parts.

line 14 *Arimanes:* Ahriman, the evil and destructive spirit in the dualistic doctrine of Zoroastrianism.

line 16 *The Captive Usurper:* Napoleon, who escaped from imprisonment on the island of Elba in 1815 and became "Tyrant again," until his defeat at Waterloo.

line 21 *shivered:* Shattered.

line 62 *repairing shattered thrones:* Alluding to the restoration of European monarchies after Waterloo.

Scene IV

line 31 *Magian:* Magi.

line 50 *Avaunt:* Away, hence.

line 82 *One without a tomb:* Byron may be hinting that Astarte killed herself; suicides were traditionally buried at crossroads.

line 100 *hectic:* Flush.

line 117 *baffled:* Thwarted.

Act III, Scene I

line 10 *motliest:* Alluding to motley, the parti-colored dress of a jester.

line 13 *"Kalon":* The morally beautiful.

line 42 *Anchorite:* A person who retires to a solitary place for religious reasons.

line 73 *Would make a hell of Heaven:* Recalling John Milton's *Paradise Lost*, Book I, lines 254–55, where Satan says, "The mind is its own place, and in itself / Can make a Heaven of Hell, a Hell of Heaven."

lines 88–96 *Rome's sixth Emperor ... fidelity:* Suetonius tells this story about the suicide of the Emperor Nero Claudius Caesar (37–68).

line 128 *Simoom:* A violent, hot wind on the deserts of Arabia and North Africa.

SCENE II

lines 5–6 *the giant sons / Of the embrace of Angels:* Alluding to Genesis 6:1–2, which speaks of the "giants" produced by the union of the "sons of God" and the "daughters of men."

line 13 *Chaldean:* Inhabiting Chaldea, an ancient region of southern Mesopotamia.

line 14 *orisons:* Prayers.

SCENE III

line 25 *Beshrew:* Curse.

line 37 *Eigher's pinnacle:* Mountain east of the Jungfrau.

line 47 *The Lady Astarte, his———:* One of Byron's most blatant hints that Astarte could have been Manfred's sister.

SCENE IV

line 15 *the Tiber:* River running through Rome.

line 81 *genius:* Spirit.

INDEX OF TITLES

A NOTE ON THE TYPE

The principal text of this Modern Library edition
was set in a digitized version of Janson, a typeface that
dates from about 1690 and was cut by Nicholas Kis,
a Hungarian working in Amsterdam. The original matrices have
survived and are held by the Stempel foundry in Germany.
Hermann Zapf redesigned some of the weights and sizes for
Stempel, basing his revisions on the original design.

MODERN LIBRARY IS ONLINE AT
WWW.MODERNLIBRARY.COM

MODERN LIBRARY ONLINE IS YOUR GUIDE
TO CLASSIC LITERATURE ON THE WEB

THE MODERN LIBRARY E-NEWSLETTER

Our free e-mail newsletter is sent to subscribers, and features sample chapters, interviews with and essays by our authors, upcoming books, special promotions, announcements, and news.

To subscribe to the Modern Library e-newsletter, send a blank e-mail to: **join-modernlibrary@list.randomhouse.com** or visit **www.modernlibrary.com**

THE MODERN LIBRARY WEBSITE

Check out the Modern Library website at
www.modernlibrary.com for:

- The Modern Library e-newsletter
- A list of our current and upcoming titles and series
- Reading Group Guides and exclusive author spotlights
- Special features with information on the classics and other paperback series
- Excerpts from new releases and other titles
- A list of our e-books and information on where to buy them
- The Modern Library Editorial Board's 100 Best Novels and 100 Best Nonfiction Books of the Twentieth Century written in the English language
- News and announcements

Questions? E-mail us at **modernlibrary@randomhouse.com**.
For questions about examination or desk copies, please visit
the Random House Academic Resources site at
www.randomhouse.com/acmart